CONTINUITY AND CHANGE IN RUSSIAN AND SOVIET THOUGHT

CONTINUITY
AND CHANGE IN
RUSSIAN AND SOVIET
THOUGHT

EDITED
WITH AN INTRODUCTION BY
ERNEST J. SIMMONS

NEW YORK / RUSSELL & RUSSELL

Preface

This volume is the result of an extensive collaborative effort which took the initial form of a Conference held at Arden House, March 26–28, 1954, under the auspices of the Joint Committee on Slavic Studies of the American Council of Learned Societies and the Social Science Research Council. A steering committee of ten of the leading scholars in the field of Russian studies planned the thematic structure of the Conference and selected the participants. Six broad themes ("Realism and Utopia in Russian Economic Thought," "Authoritarianism and Democracy," "Collectivism and Individualism," "Rationality and Nonrationality," "Literature, State, and Society," "Russia and the Community of Nations — Messianic Views and Theory of Action"), representing major focuses in the study of continuity and change in Russian and Soviet thought, were designated. Under each of these themes four or five subtopics were assigned for purposes of research. These papers were intended to effect confrontations of various phases of pre- and post-revolutionary Russian and Soviet thought, confrontations which would in turn point up aspects of either continuity or change. In nearly every case the participants were chosen because they had already done, or were doing, research in the immediate fields of the subtopics.

A period of almost a year was allowed for the research and writing of the papers, which were mimeographed and distributed to all participants and guests well in advance of the Conference. In the meantime, the scholars who had been appointed chairmen of the six sections prepared extensive formal reviews of the papers in their sections. These reviews concentrated on confronting the findings of papers dealing with themes before 1917 with the findings of those treating subject matter in the Soviet period in an effort to bring out the aspects of continuity or change in Russian and Soviet intellectual thought.

At the Conference each participant spoke on the substance of his research, and after the chairman reviewed the papers in his section, a lengthy discussion took place. This discussion was recorded and later distributed to all participants, who made use of it in revising their papers for publication in this book.

As General Chairman of the Conference and editor of the present volume,

I wish to take this occasion to thank Professor Merle Fainsod, former Chairman of the Joint Committee on Slavic Studies, who initiated the Conference, and Professor Cyril E. Black, present Chairman of the Committee, who has given me enthusiastic support in all material matters relating to the Conference. To the members of the Joint Committee on Slavic Studies and to the members of the steering committee who helped to plan the Conference, I am indebted for much, as I am to all who participated in the Conference and assisted in many details connected with the revisions of their papers. Finally, I wish to thank warmly Dr. Mortimer Graves of the American Council of Learned Societies, Dr. Pendleton Herring of the Social Science Research Council, Professor Clyde Kluckhohn of the Harvard Russian Research Center, and Professor Philip E. Mosely of the Columbia Russian Institute for their aid in securing funds that made the Conference and the publication of this book possible. To Mrs. Loreine Kendrick, who assisted me in editorial matters connected with the book, I owe a special debt of gratitude.

Ernest J. Simmons

CONFERENCE AT ARDEN HOUSE

March 26–28, 1954

under the Auspices of the Joint Committee on Slavic
Studies of the American Council of Learned Societies
and the Social Science Research Council

BARGHOORN, FREDERICK C.
Associate Professor of Political Science
Yale University

†BERLIN, ISAIAH
Fellow of All Souls College
Oxford University

BERGAMINI, JOHN D.
Graduate Student, History
Russian Institute
Columbia University

*BERGSON, ABRAM
Professor of Economics
Russian Institute
Columbia University

BYRNES, ROBERT F.
Associate Professor of History
Rutgers University

DOBZHANSKY, THEODOSIUS
Professor of Zoology
Columbia University

*EDGERTON, WILLIAM B.
Assistant Professor of Russian
Pennsylvania State University

ERLICH, ALEXANDER
Research Fellow
Russian Research Center
Harvard University

ERLICH, VICTOR
Assistant Professor, Slavic Languages and Literatures
University of Washington

FAINSOD, MERLE
Professor of Government
Russian Research Center
Harvard University

FLOROVSKY, GEORGES
Dean and Professor of Divinity
St. Vladimir's Theological Seminary

GERSCHENKRON, ALEXANDER
Professor of Economics, and member of the Russian Research Center
Harvard University

†GURIAN, WALDEMAR
Professor of Political Science
University of Notre Dame

HAMMOND, THOMAS T.
Assistant Professor of History
University of Virginia

HANKIN, ROBERT M.
Instructor in Russian, School of General Studies
Columbia University

*HAZARD, JOHN N.
Managing Editor, American Slavic and East European Review
Professor of Public Law
Russian Institute
Columbia University

KARPOVICH, MICHAEL
Chairman, Department of Slavic Languages
Harvard University

KLINE, GEORGE L.
Assistant Professor of Philosophy
Columbia University

KOHN, HANS
Professor of History
City College of New York

MALIA, MARTIN E.
Instructor in History and General Education
Harvard University

MARCUSE, HERBERT
Lecturer, Department of Sociology
Columbia University
Regional Studies Program
Harvard University

MATHEWSON, RUFUS W., JR.
Assistant Professor of Russian Language and Literature
Columbia College

*McNEAL, ROBERT
Instructor, Department of History
Princeton University

McKENZIE, KERMIT E.
Lecturer, Department of History
School of General Studies
Brooklyn College
School of General Studies
Columbia University

*MORGAN, GEORGE A.
Deputy Executive Officer
Operations Coördinating Board
Department of State

MOSELY, PHILIP E.
Professor of International Relations
Director of Russian Institute
Columbia University

* PHILIPOV, ALEXANDER
Former Professor, Universities of Kharkov and Prague

RADKEY, OLIVER H.
Associate Professor of History
University of Texas

*REEVE, FRANKLIN
Lecturer in Russian
Columbia College and School of General Studies

CONTENTS

PART III
COLLECTIVISM AND INDIVIDUALISM

PART IV
RATIONALITY AND NONRATIONALITY

Contents xi

PART V

LITERATURE, STATE, AND SOCIETY

INTRODUCTION

Introduction

ERNEST J. SIMMONS

To its more extreme adherents in the early years, the Bolshevik Revolution seemed to represent a complete repudiation of the past. The old Russia was officially declared to be dead. Maiakovskii symbolized the spirit of the times in his blatant declaration:

> Enough of living by laws
> That Adam and Eve have left.
> Hustle old history's horse
> Left!
> Left!
> Left!

A clean sweep was to be made of history. A new government, a new economic system, new laws, a new culture, a new way of life would replace the old order of things. Aroused from his age-old lethargy by the tremendous release of energy brought about by the Revolution, even peasant Ivan would have to come down from his place on the stove and plunge into an entirely different existence. Human nature itself would change according to Marxian determinants. On the road to Communism a new psychology would transform the behavior pattern of the traditionally passive and fatalistic Russian character into that of the dynamic, optimistic, new Soviet man.

Has "old history's horse" been simply replaced on the road by a shiny six-cylinder auto, Soviet-made, or has the Soviet auto been traveling along a road entirely unknown to Russian history of the past and toward a future destiny never imagined in the Russia of the tsars? Can a revolution, even one dedicated to the establishment of a totally new political, social, and economic system, turn aside the natural path of a country's history, uproot its indigenous customs and habits, and change the character traits of its citizens?

These are questions not easily answered about a revolutionary regime that has existed for only thirty-seven years, and one which has interposed all manner of obstructions to the objective study of scholars. To be sure, Marxian historical materialism would argue — in this case with a little revisionism — that the emergence of the Soviet Union was a natural effect of natural causes in the Russia of the past. In any event, the effect was not achieved by a succession of free choices in the forward march of history, and thus one might posit a certain degree of historical continuity within the orbit of revolutionary change.

One difficulty in appraising the elements of change and continuity in the Soviet Union with reference to the country's past has been the alteration in the Soviet attitude toward the old Russia that had been initially repudiated. Most of the world's revolutions have been concerned primarily with the overthrow of political power; the social and economic structure and sometimes even the political structure of the revolted state have remained unchanged. In the Soviet case what was designed as total revolution now seems, in many respects, to warrant the description of the ancient cliché — the pouring of new wine into old bottles. This has reference not merely to the doctrine of Marx which has ultimately become more a banner than a weapon in the revolutionary battle. In fact, the conservative colors of the old Russian regime have long since begun to show through the fading revolutionary red of Soviet Marxian Communism. Much in the historical past of the tsars is now found glorious, and the internationalism of Communism is not allowed to interfere with the propaganda of nationalistic traditions that are proudly traced back to the time of Ivan the Terrible or even earlier. Even the colonial conquests of the tsars among the minority peoples of Russia are now justified by the Soviets as blessings in disguise, very much to be preferred to the conquests of non-Russian powers. Russian history is being rewritten to prove that many Soviet achievements are simply the fruition of Russian genius of the past. And a compiler of similarities between past and present power structures, governmental operations, and the daily ordering of life, such as spying, censorship, control of education, legal punishments, and official distrust of foreigners, would dizzy the arithmetic of memory with a list as long as it was striking.

As a matter of fact, the early tendency of scholars to search for solutions of the riddle of the Soviet Union in revolutionary change has given way of late to explanations based on various aspects of continuity between the old and the new. However, it would be a mistake to underestimate the tremendous transforming power of the forces let loose by the October Revolution. The conservatism, even reactionarism, that have come with the passage of time have not essentially neutralized or reversed the great changes in Russian life or rule brought about by the Revolution, nor lessened the prevalence of the spirit of Marxian ideology, however much the letter of it may have been revised. Nevertheless, the Revolution itself, the course of Soviet developments since then, and the possible future aspirations of the regime are strikingly illuminated by comparative studies of Russian nineteenth-century political, social, economic, and cultural thought. Thus the continuum of history is established, the present becomes more comprehensible in terms of the past, and the future less of a mystery or a wild prophecy. And equally important — one may observe how an acclaimed Soviet change is often merely an outgrowth or "deviation" from an acquired characteristic from the Russian past.

Thus patterns of economic behavior and thought in nineteenth-century Russia and even certain of the elements of Populism have entered into the stream of Soviet economic development. Such derivations, however, may illuminate but can hardly explain economic theory and practice in the Soviet Union today.

In some respects, to be sure, the rationality of those phases of nineteenth-century Russian economic thought which formed part of the heritage of the early leaders of the Soviet Revolution is in itself a subject worthy of serious study. A comprehensive study in general of rationality and nonrationality in the total development of Russian and Soviet intellectual history is long overdue. For the emphasis upon the scientific nature of Soviet Marxism has perhaps tended to obscure its nonrational elements, a consideration that at once suggests the possibilities of a direct connection between the often intellectually immature prerevolutionary thought and the immaturity of Bolshevik ideology. For example, the rationality of the theory of rule in both the Russian past and present would provide a fruitful theme for investigation.

Though Soviet totalitarianism is often regarded as a continuation of tsarist autocracy, the differences are more fundamental than the similarities. Yet the concept of Soviet power very definitely has its roots in the Russian past. It is not enough, of course, to draw analogies between Stalin and Ivan the Terrible or Peter the Great. One must study the resemblances between the total theory of tsarist autocracy, reflected in the thinking of its most eloquent disciples, such as Pobedonostsev, and the theory of rule expounded in the works of the foremost Soviet Marxian thinkers.

Russian thought, as Berdiaev has pointed out, seemed incapable of developing into abstract philosophy; by its very intensity and concern for practical matters it has tended to take on a totalitarian cast. Or perhaps it would be better to say that the unity of abstract thought and life has been a dominant idea in all Russian thought. In the turbulent stream of Russian and Soviet intellectual history, no two concepts have more frequently bobbed to the surface than collectivism and individualism, and the thinking about them, in both the pre- and post-1917 periods, has revealed a rigidity and undemocratic approach alien to Western formulations of these concepts. Western thought has always emphasized the dignity of the individual and his supreme value in the state. On the other hand, the nineteenth-century Slavophiles — and not only the Slavophiles — defined the individual in terms of the doctrine of *sobornost'* and the institution of the *mir:* a combination of the freedom and unity of the many on the basis of their common love for the same absolute values. The individual personality could never be the source of absolute norms or laws binding upon all men. This initially theological doctrine of *sobornost'*, of the congregation as an organic unity and sole repository of truth, demanding the entire obedience of its members, is clearly reflected in the Soviet notion of collectivity, in which the state is substituted for the congregation. Thus the individual realizes his full personality and achieves freedom through the coercion of the institutionalized collectivity of the Soviet state.

Further than this, the Russian messianism that was part of the Slavophile thinking on *sobornost'* finds its counterpart in the messianic compulsion associated with the Soviet idea of collectivity guided by the higher laws of Communist Party ideology. The fact should not be forgotten, however, that Soviet messianism, with its expansionist policy, rests largely upon a foundation of Marxist-Leninist universalism. On the other hand, as developing Soviet nationalism reverts more and more to the aims and aspirations of old-fashioned Russian imperialism, away from Marxian internationalism, the essential components of prerevolutionary and Soviet Russian messianism seem less and less differentiated.

There is much, too, that is undifferentiated in the cultural patterns of the old and the new Russia. Here again, in dealing with factors of continuity and change, one must never forget the contending forces of conservative or reactionary versus liberal or radical that contributed to the heritage of nineteenth-century Russian thought, a contention not permitted in the prescribed monolithic intellectual unity in the Soviet Union (the struggle of "bourgeois survivals" with Soviet doctrine may well be real, but it is also official propaganda). The censorship of tsarist Russia did not prevent the development of a great and enduring literature; censorship and Party ideological controls in the Soviet Union have resulted in a literature which, with some significant exceptions, amounts to a travesty of the traditional freedom of the creative artist. Where the line of continuity exists is in the Soviet acceptance of the critical theorizing and conception of the hero among the materialist critics of the 1840's and 1860's. Their doctrine of the social significance of literature, of literature as the servant of the state, and of the active, positive hero, selflessly dedicated to the people and to changing society, are notions that have found favor among Soviet official critics. Yet this degree of continuity has not been possible without a good deal of deplorable "rehabilitation" of the ideological positions of the materialist critics.

Another element of cultural continuity may be observed in the widespread Soviet acceptance of the works of nearly all the great Russian writers of the nineteenth century. The fact that these famous novels, plays, and poems, so often written in the libertarian spirit of the great authors of the nineteenth century, are read by millions of Soviet citizens and appear to be preferred by them to the dull productions of contemporary Soviet writers may offer some support for Herzen's conviction that thinking Russians are the most independent men in the world. In fact, in this aspect of continuity one may perceive a hopeful demonstration, as far as that is possible in a police state, of Herzen's belief that the Russian people are revolutionary and democratic by nature and of an essence different from that of the tyrannical state that rules them.

These various problems of continuity and change in Russian and Soviet thought which have been touched upon here, and many others as well, are treated at length and with a wealth of evidence in the many studies of this book. A pattern of thought emerges wherein both variables and constants reveal the startling interrelationships between past and present in the whole course of Russian intellectual history.

PART I
REALISM AND UTOPIA IN RUSSIAN
ECONOMIC THOUGHT

The Problem of Economic Development in Russian Intellectual History of the Nineteenth Century

ALEXANDER GERSCHENKRON

The assigned title of this paper promises much more than can possibly be redeemed by its contents. All that can be done here is to find some significant yardstick and try to apply it to selected portions of the material, in the hope that in this way an interesting problem might be posed for discussion. This, of course, is a highly arbitrary procedure, involving a number of decisions which should be made explicit.

First of all, what is Russian intellectual history? The concept is a vague one, but we are wont thus to translate what, in literal rendition, went in Russia under the alternative names (or misnomers) of "history of Russian intelligentsia" and "history of Russian social thought." Let us accept the term in this sense, but let us also be clear that by so doing we have implicitly decided to deal primarily with those Olympian figures who, in the parlance of the nineteenth century, provided the Russian intellectuals with "nourishment for heart and mind." It is indeed attractive to analyze the caloric content of that diet from a specific economic point of view and to try to see how much light, in addition to heat, was generated in the process. Yet it should be clear that thereby the accent is shifted away from those writers who, for one reason or another, remained excluded from the intelligentsia's pantheon, even though, on substantive grounds, those ordinary mortals may have acquired strong or stronger claims to our attention. Were this an essay on Russian economic development or Russian economic thought during the past century, such a distribution of emphasis would be patently inadequate. It seems justified within the framework of a Conference devoted to Russian intellectual history. Even when so confined, the subject remains much too vast for treatment here. The intelligentsia's Olympus was even more populous than Homer's. How much of our attention can be devoted to its individual denizens must needs depend on their importance for the problem at hand.

The problem at hand! It is to be conceived here as a confrontation between the actual flow of Russian economic history and the direction of
Russia's economic development which our authors considered either desirable,
or likely, or even inevitable. This, no doubt, is a very narrow approach. Still,
an evaluation of the closeness between thought and event, between idea and
reality may contribute in some measure to an appraisal of the degree of
vitality that was encased in Russian intellectual history of the period. We
shall begin, therefore, with a brief and necessarily schematic sketch of Russia's economic development and thereafter turn to a discussion of the relevant
writings.

I

The period of Russian mercantilism, culminating in the policies of Peter
the Great, had marked a period of relatively rapid industrial development.
Viewed for Europe as a whole, it is difficult to conceive of mercantilistic
policies as of an altogether consistent phenomenon. But Russian mercantilism
with its close connection between power policy and economic development,
its clear stress on industrialization and disregard for agriculture, and but a
modicum of interest in consumers' goods industries proper is much more
clearly discernible as a unified system of policy than are its Western counterparts. The reasons for that presumably lay first in the magnitude of the
discrepancy between politics of the government on the one hand and levels
of output and economic skills in the country on the other, and second, in the
absence of both developed vested interests and theoretical thought. In other
words, the backwardness of the country was primarily responsible for the
character of Russian mercantilism. But at the same time it was the backwardness of the country that accounted for still another difference between
Russia and the West. Mercantilist policies in the West were pursued in an
environment in which by and large serfdom had either disappeared or was
in a state of disintegration. In Russia peasant serfdom became an essential
wheel in the mechanism of mercantilist policies. When these policies came
to an end, peasant serfdom lost its connection with economic development
of the country and emerged, more firmly established than ever, as the main
force retarding the economic growth of the country.

The question whether Russia under Catherine the Great was a backward
country has been under discussion for more than four decades, and contemporary Soviet historiography tends to answer the question in the negative. It is less important for the purposes of the presentation that this
view ignores things like the near constancy of the city population over long
decades of the eighteenth century, or the absence in Russia of skills and
standards of commercial honesty comparable to those in the West, or the lack
of wide markets for industrial products which, for instance, led to exports of
a large fraction of the pig iron produced. What does matter is that in the last

quarter of the eighteenth century England experienced a great upsurge in the rate of industrial growth, that postrevolutionary France went through a period of rapid industrial development, even though the speed of that development could not be at all sustained after 1815. At the same time, the territorial spread of serfdom under Catherine, the rapid deterioration of the serfs' juridical position, and the government's withdrawal from mercantilistic policies not only perpetuated serfdom, but also imparted to it an extent and a severity which it had not possessed before. Whatever the actual degree of economic backwardness in Russia in the last decades of the century, dynamically seen, it is in that period that the basis was laid for the growing backwardness of the Russian economy throughout the first half of the nineteenth century.

The rate of growth of Russian industry during that period cannot be ascertained with high statistical accuracy, but there is little doubt that, by and large, it was very low. To be sure, the development was somewhat faster in certain branches of the textile industry, but progress was almost imperceptible in other fields, particularly in the iron industry, the output of which hardly kept up with the increase of the population. As a general proposition the statement may be hazarded that the relative economic backwardness of the country increased not inconsiderably during the first half of the century.

Once a country experiences such a process of increasing lags, it is not unreasonable to expect — in conditions of the past century and within the sphere of European civilization — that at some point the specific mechanism of economic backwardness would come into play, so that, depending on the degree of the country's backwardness, one of the usual patterns of economic development under such conditions will reproduce itself. To repeat what has been said elsewhere,[1] the situation in a backward country may be conceived of as a state of tension between its actualities and its potentialities. For *pari passu*, with the increase in a country's backwardness there is also an increase in potential advantages that can be reaped by a sustained effort to overcome that backwardness. The reason for that essentially lies in the fact that postponed economic development implies the opportunity for borrowing highly developed foreign technology while deriving additional benefits from the process of capital cheapening that has occurred outside its borders. As the tension mounts, it becomes more and more likely that a point will be reached at which the advantages implied in rapid economic development will more than offset those obstacles to economic progress which are inherent in the state of economic backwardness. Clearly, the tension can be artificially increased from two sides, i.e., both by deliberate abolition of such obstacles as can be removed by concerted action and by creating deliberate induce-

[1] Alexander Gerschenkron, "Economic Backwardness in Historical Perspective," in *The Progress of Underdeveloped Areas,* ed. B. Hoselitz (Chicago, 1952).

ments to economic development. The process is to some extent a discontinuous one and this not only because of the suddenness of deliberate actions just referred to, but also because *in conditions of the nineteenth century* the advantages inherent in "bigness" were particularly telling. Thus, economic development either took place as a rapid spurt of industrialization fully utilizing both economies of scale of plants and economies inherent in "balanced growth," i.e., simultaneous development of a considerable number of industrial branches, or else it did not take place at all. It could also be argued that the more delayed was the industrialization process in conditions of secularly growing capital intensity of output the more rapid the spurt of sudden growth which was required in order to break through the trammels of routine and stagnation. In other words, the tension of which we spoke before had under such conditions to become particularly large.

Schematic as has been the foregoing presentation, it seems that it contains a generalized view of important elements of the process in the course of which economic backwardness was overcome in a number of European countries of the nineteenth century (such as France, Germany, and Austria). But the same pattern essentially applies to the economic development of Russia.

The emancipation of the peasantry was no doubt a decisive step in widening the tension and thereby rendering subsequent economic development possible. That it did not lead immediately to a period of rapid industrialization must be explained first in terms of the way in which the abolition of serfdom was carried out. Moreover, in conditions of very considerable backwardness provision of capital by the state was an indispensable part of the industrialization process and accordingly the process could not begin until the beginning of the deliberate industrialization policies by the government in the middle eighties, leading to the magnificent spurt of industrial growth in Russia in the 1890's. In conditions of backwardness far greater than that of countries in Western Europe, supply of capital by dint of investment banking was hardly feasible and the functions performed by the latter came to a considerable extent to be performed in Russia by the state.

These similarities in policies pursued by the respective institutions denote the existence of a common pattern of economic development in conditions of backwardness, while differences in the role of institutional instruments applied denote variations in the degree of relative backwardness. Viewed over a sufficiently long period, the differences tend to disappear as diminishing backwardness makes possible — and did make possible in Russia — gradual transition from the use of government finance to that of investment banking.

The use of either instrument implies temporary reduction in the levels of consumption of the population. The purpose in both cases is to achieve a rate of investment higher than would emerge in the absence of intervention by government or banks. Forced saving (inflation) and taxation perform the same service in achieving a temporary redistribution of income. The Russian experience illustrates the sequence with great clarity. Both the period of the nineties and the period preceding the outbreak of the First World War were periods of high rates of growth, but while the former period was one of considerable pressure upon consumption levels, improvements in standards of living were clearly discernible during the latter period.

To sum up, it may be said that the main drift of Russian economic history reproduced a series of sequences which were familiar from the economic history of the West, and that such deviations from those sequences as could be observed fitted well into a general continental pattern of economic development adjusted to gradations of backwardness. The outstanding feature of the process was the utilization in Russia, as elsewhere, of the advantages which are inherent in delayed economic development.

There is no intention in the foregoing sketch to imply that Russian economic development proceeded *necessarily* in the way it did in faithful obedience to some kind of iron law of evolution. What is implied is that the development as it actually took place seems to conform to a certain pattern and that such conformities and uniformities as can be observed do help us to understand the course of events. In fact, historical understanding essentially consists in the formulation of such patterns. But while the fact that the development followed a certain course does not preclude at all the possibility of alternative routes, it does suggest that the forces which propelled the Russian economy along its actual course must have been strong indeed. It appears justifiable, therefore, to raise the question to what extent an awareness of these forces and, more specifically, of the individual elements which combined to produce the actual pattern of Russian economic development can be discerned in the writings of men who figured so prominently in Russia's intellectual history of the nineteenth century. It is to the discussion of this question that the next section of this paper is devoted.

II

Russian writers were fond of describing Radishchev as the "first Russian *intelligent*." What they had in mind no doubt was his adherence to the two principal articles in the intelligentsia's creed: hatred of slavery and deep concern for the well-being of the peasantry (*narod*). Whatever the strict validity of Radishchev's claim to seniority, a striking change in attitude indeed had taken place over the short period of some seven decades which separate *Puteshestvie* (A Journey) from *Kniga o skudosti i bogatstve* (On Scarcity and Wealth). It is almost difficult to believe that both Pososhkov and Radishchev sprang from the same soil.

Pososhkov's interests turn essentially around one thing — the economic development of the country. His was an altogether dynamic philosophy in

the sense that what concerned him was the *change* in the given data of the
Russian economy. His main attention was devoted to increases in the technical and commercial proficiency of that economy. Introduction of new industries and their placement in economically rational locations; organization
of geological expeditions; reform of Russian handicraft by adapting the
Western craft-guild framework with well-regulated apprenticeship; promotion
of innovations by adaption of patent laws; attraction of foreign skills and
foreign technology; encouragement of thrift; measures to increase the quality
of output and to raise the standards of honesty in commercial dealings;
putting children to work; forced measures to turn the beggar population to
productive employment — all these reflected a mind bent upon rapid changes
in economic structure and willing to consider most social and economic problems from that one point of view.[2] Accordingly, a problem like the judicial
reform was treated largely from the point of view of its effects upon the
taxpaying capacity of the population and its propensity to escape abroad or
into frontier regions. And similarly, peasant serfdom did not interest Pososhkov directly. It is difficult indeed to regard him as opposed to the system
of serfdom. He was much more concerned with legal steps which would
prevent large serf-owners from appropriating the serfs of the poorer gentry.
And beyond that he recognized that the nobility and the gentry and the government competed with each other for the labor or the produce of the serf.
It would indeed strain the imagination to see in Pososhkov's famous phrase:
"The lords are not permanent possessors of the peasants"[3] an attack upon
peasant serfdom. It was rather a threat to replace serfdom to the *pomeshchik*
by serfdom to the state, should the system be used to the detriment of the
government's interest in economic development. And, analogously, his interest in the well-being of the peasants was largely expressible in terms of
the fiscal needs of the government and its desire to increase the productivity
of the economy.[4] It seems to be a fair guess that Pososhkov's statements in
this respect would have turned out even more unambiguous had he not
been writing in the later years of the reign of Peter I, when the disastrous
effects of his policy upon the peasantry had become quite obvious.

How different is Radishchev's case against serfdom. Moral indignation
against ownership of man by man is coupled with deep compassion for the
misery of the peasant. He finds burning words to describe the grain stored
up by the nobility: it has been produced by labor services; it embodies the
sorrow and the despair of the peasantry and carries upon it the curse of
the Almighty.[5] Even more important than what is said by Radishchev is
what he does not mention. Gone is the concern with economic development,

[2] I. I. Pososhkov, *Kniga o skudosti i bogatstve* (Moscow, 1951), pp. 150, 148–149,
146, 142–143, 140, 128, 117–118, 110.
[3] *Ibid.*, pp. 178, 182.
[4] *Ibid.*, pp. 182–183.
[5] A. N. Radishchev, *Polnoe sobranie sochinenii* (St. Petersburg, 1907), I, 159.

the concern with levels of output and economic skills. The people's well-being is no longer a means to an end, it is an end, in fact, a supreme end in itself. "Can the citizens be happy if the granaries are full but the stomachs empty?"[6] At the same time, references to economic progress have been reduced to an occasional phrase concerning "flourishing of trade" and to the brief remark in the "Letter on China Trade" that imports of textiles from China would regrettably reduce Siberian consumption of domestic textiles.[7]

In this sense, Radishchev does appear as an ancestor of several generations of Russian intellectuals. In the field of economic policy, deep interest in the conditions of the peasantry and lack of interest for Russian industrial development seem to be characteristic of a long stretch of Russia's intellectual history. Pososhkov's harshness and his worship of the state had given way to a humanitarian view. That for quite some time the change that had occurred remained almost unrecognized or at least was not conceived as a problem may be explicable by a number of reasons, but perhaps the most important among them was that after the reign of Catherine the Great abolition of serfdom had become in fact a necessary, though perhaps not a sufficient, precondition of economic development. Presumably, Peter the Great had civilized Russia to a point at which a return to his own methods of industrialization no longer was in the stars of practical policies. It required, in our time, a collapse of civilization through an unprecedented war and the establishment of Bolshevik dictatorship to effectuate such a return. In principle, at least, to advocate the emancipation of the peasantry was not to preclude the direction of further economic development. In reality, however, Russian intellectual history in many instances went beyond such a non-committal attitude, and the Decembrists, the "crowd of noblemen" who were expected to become the "liberators of the peasantry," to use Pushkin's words, provide the first case in point.

With Pestel' and N. I. Turgenev, Radishchev's indifference toward industrial development seems to give way to an attitude of opposition to industrial development. This may seem strange, particularly for Turgenev, who is perhaps the most emphatic "Westerner" of the century. "Si l'on se demande dans quel sens le peuple russe est destiné à marcher, je dirai la question est déjà résolue par le fait; il doit marcher vers la civilisation européenne."[8] But did this mean that marching toward European civilization implied industrialization of the country? One might have expected so from a man who was primarily an economist and from a book which was published as late as 1847. But beyond an occasional statement (such as that industry and commerce in Russia failed to show much progress in the last twenty-five years[9]), one would look in vain for any sign of appreciation of industrial

---

[6] *Ibid.*, p. 161.
[7] *Ibid.*, II, 240.
[8] N. I. Turgenev, *La Russie et les Russes* (Paris, 1847), III, 4.
[9] *Ibid.*, p. 20.

progress. It is true that in dealing with the ill effects of serfdom upon the country Turgenev does not forget its retarding impact upon development of industry. He says: "Quant aux fabriques et aux manufactures, l'existence de l'esclavage agit sur elles d'une manière plus facheuse encore que sur l'agriculture; il leur est non moins impossible de prosperer là où le travail n'est pas libre." [10] But the author catches himself in midparagraph for he continues:

> D'ailleurs, lors même que l'esclavage n'existerait plus, la grande étendue des terrains susceptible de défrichement et de culture empêcherait l'industrie manufacturière de prendre une grande extension: car les ouvriers n'iront pas s'enfermer dans les fabriques tant qu'il y aura pour eux d'autres travaux, tant que la terre leur offrira des resources plus faciles.[11]

Should someone feel that the sentence just quoted carries some sense of regret about the fact that availability of free land constitutes an obstacle to industrial development because it limits the labor supply to manufacturing plants, he is quickly disabused. For the very next paragraph reads: "Cependant le gouvernement russe, comme tous les gouvernements, veut à toute force des fabriques et des manufactures, et lui aussi il en encourage l'établissement *aux depens des véritables intérêts de la nation.*" [12]

It is of less interest here that among the many accusations that could have been, and were, leveled against the regime of Nicholas I this particular one was certainly least deserved. What does matter is that in Turgenev's view even the modicum of attention which the government of the period devoted to industry is regarded as being in conflict with the "true interests of the nation."

Pestel's views on the subject are at times less easy to state succinctly, as in some respects they were in a state of flux. In particular, certain discrepancies between his *Russkaia Pravda* (Russian Truth) and the earlier *Prakticheskie nachala ekonomii* (Practical Beginnings of Economies) are fairly obvious. Still, the affinity between the views of Turgenev and Pestel' is undeniable. Like Turgenev, Pestel' accepts the principle of greater efficiency of free labor as against slave labor, even though the actual liberation of serfs, it is said, may best be gradual rather than instantaneous. This position is taken in the *Nachala* and reiterated in *Russkaia Pravda.*[13]

The stress of gradualness should not be taken as denoting a more friendly attitude on Pestel's part toward serfdom as such. Quite the contrary, the passage dealing with the subject of serfdom is almost the only one in *Russkaia Pravda* where the matter-of-fact style of the document is suddenly relinquished and the dry Pestel' almost reaches Radishchev's feverish elo-

---

[10] *Ibid.,* II, 167.

[11] *Ibid.,* pp. 167–168.

[12] *Ibid.,* p. 168.

[13] See Pestel', in *Izbrannye sotsial'no-politicheskie i filosofskie proizvedeniia dekabristov* (Moscow, 1951), II, 16–18, 119–120.

quence. It seems correct to say that the Decembrists were unanimous in this rejection of serfdom on both moral and economic grounds.[14] But what about the stage beyond the abolition? The author of the *Nachala* is still of two minds on the subject.

On the one hand, he produces some statements on development of manufacturing which might be taken as suggesting genuine interest in the subject. In particular, he pleads for the introduction of craft-guilds in order to ensure technical skills and high quality of the product. This paragraph sounds almost like a return to Pososhkov. So does the proposal of market controls by government organs to prevent sales of shoddy goods. And it is at this point that a direct reference is made to the backwardness of the country and the need of educational measures by the government in countries where "factories and mills are in an embryonic state" and the ignorance of the entrepreneurs is great. Just one step seems to separate Pestel' at this point from developing an infant-industry agreement comparable to that of Hamilton and List, and in this way stating at least one aspect of economic development in conditions of economic backwardness. But the step is never taken. In fact, we find in a different passage of the essay (which, incidentally, like *Russkaia Pravda*, remained a fragment) an altogether different attitude. Introduction of machinery is said to be irrational where labor is cheap, so that only rich countries can afford mechanization of production. Pestel' is not quite aware that he uses *two* distinct, though related, arguments — relative scarcity of factors *and* the inability to sustain a high rate of investment — but it is clear that, to his mind, industrial development of Russia is impractical. Indeed, after having referred to difficulties which, according to J. B. Say, were experienced with the introduction of machinery in France, he describes such a policy for Russia as "fantastic." [15] Thereafter, the classical argument of international division of labor is applied and is finally buttressed by the surmise that agrarian countries enjoy greater independence than industrial countries.[16]

Russkaia Pravda reflects this attitude in a rather consistent fashion. The interest in governmental concern for quality of output and development of skills is eliminated and craft-guilds are rejected as useless and inequitable. Alongside private land property, the inalienable right of *every* Russian citizen to land allotment is to be regarded as a fundamental provision of the new order to be established, thus not only incorporating into it a form of the *obshchina,* but also introducing a specific institutional barrier to industrial development by placing a premium upon the flight *from* the city. Finally, Pestel' finds strong words against aristocracy of wealth which is "much more

---

[14] Cf. the summary given by M. V. Dovnar-Zapol'skii, *Idealy Dekabristov* (Moscow, 1907), pp. 156f.

[15] Pestel', ref. 13, pp. 28, 65, 66, 68.

[16] *Ibid.,* pp. 63, 64.

men of pure thought. The gradualness of the abolition of serfdom may have reflected the necessity to secure the support, or at least reduce the opposition, of the nobility to the reforms, but presumably it also reflected the recognition of the fact that a sudden cutting of the Gordian knot in conditions where the gentry economy and the peasant economy were intertwined through labor, capital, and perhaps entrepreneurship would have resulted in an economic crisis, if not catastrophe. With the smashing of the Decembrists' uprising and the establishment of the regime of Nicholas I, Russian intellectuals were freed from paying too close attention to the exigencies of reality. At least for the immediately following decades the change was not favorable for a preoccupation with problems of economic development. Economic treatises began to disappear from the "must" reading lists of Russian intellectuals. If the "younger brother" of the Decembrists, as Kliuchevskii once called Eugene Onegin, still liked to flaunt his knowledge of Adam Smith, the "children of the Decembrists," to use Ogarëv's phrase, primarily had other interests. To be sure, metaphysics and aesthetics, even when not combined with St. Simonism, in many respects were just the mold within which discussion of social problems was cast. But the latter concentrated on fields other than economics, and it was not until Chernyshevskii's time that Hegelian propositions were deliberately used for elucidation — or obfuscation — of problems of economic development. At any rate, it was only in the second half of the forties that such problems were taken up again.

Belinskii, the dominating figure of the period, reflects this change. His Westernism as a rule does not descend into the low plains of economic interests. Belinskii is, of course, quite willing to discuss serfdom from the humanitarian and moral point of view, but its economic implications, let alone the problems of its aftermath, are well outside his purview. For that reason a certain exception to the rule is all the more interesting. The reference is to Belinskii's participation in 1847–48 in the debates between Botkin and Annenkov on the one hand and Herzen on the other. The subject of this discussion was Herzen's *Letters from Avenue Marigny* and specifically the attitude toward the bourgeoisie. The respective positions were succinctly expressed in the two prayers of the antagonists — Herzen: "God save Russia from the bourgeoisie";[22] Botkin: "God give Russia a bourgeoisie."[23] A reflection of Belinskii's attitude is even contained in a published article, the last written — or rather dictated — by him before his death.[24] There Belinskii takes mild exception to Herzen's negative view. But the uncensored letters show how seriously Belinskii — in the last months of his life — struggled with the problem. The letter to Botkin written in December 1847 reflects these struggles. Hesitant to break away altogether from Herzen's

[22] P. V. Annenkov, *P. V. Annenkov i ego druz'ia* (St. Petersburg, 1892), p. 611.
[23] *Ibid.*, p. 551.
[24] V. G. Belinskii, *Sobranie sochinenii v trëkh tomakh* (Moscow, 1948), III, 840.

position, Belinskii seeks to define and redefine the concept of bourgeoisie, distinguishes between rich capitalists and bourgeoisie, explodes in a diatribe against the trader, and still ends on a very different note: "I do not belong to people who take it for an axiom that the bourgeoisie is an evil . . . I shall not agree to that before I have been shown in real life a country which prospers without a middle class; so far all I have seen is that countries without a middle class are doomed to eternal insignificance." [25] But in the letter to Annenkov, written only two months later, an even firmer position is taken:

My never-doubting friend [Herzen] and our Slavophiles have helped me much to shed the mystical faith in the people. Where and when did ever the people liberate itself? Everything is always done by individuals. When in our debates on the bourgeoisie I called you a conservative I was an ass to the second power while you knew what you were talking about. When in the presence of my never-doubting friend I said that Russia needs a new Peter the Great, he attacked my view as a heresy and said that the people itself must do all for itself . . . And now it is clear that the internal process of civil development in Russia will not start before . . . the Russian gentry has been transformed into a bourgeoisie.[26]

In many respects, this is a unique statement. Acceptance of the bourgeoisie with its implied stress on industry; prayer in the same connection for a new Peter the Great which can only mean revival of industrialization policies — these views denote not alone an abandonment of the agrarian position of the Decembrists, but a recognition of special governmental policies in the process of industrialization.

To be sure, this statement also implies complete lack of hope that a Russian bourgeoisie may emerge alongside the gentry rather than from the ranks of that group, a sentiment, incidentally, shared by Botkin.[27] Nor would it be wise to overlook entirely the fervor of the denunciation of the merchant in Belinskii's letter to Botkin — the "base, despicable, vulgar creature who serves Plutus and Plutus alone." [28] But when all is said and done it seems fair to say that the "Furious Vissarion" came closer than anybody else among the great figures in Russian intellectual life of the time to an industrial vision, one might perhaps say a correct prevision, of the country's economic development.

It is tempting to speculate whether Russia's intellectual life was not at the crossroads in these months before the outbreak of the European revolutions. Belinskii's death, the wave of suppression which passed over Russia after the February revolution in Paris, the effect of the course of that revolution upon Herzen himself by greatly reinforcing his still inchoate adverse views on the West — all these factors served to decide the disagreement between Belinskii and Herzen in favor of the latter. The "child of the

[25] V. G. Belinskii, *Izbrannie filosofskie sochineniia* (Moscow, 1948), II, 550.
[26] Annenkov, ref. 22, p. 611.
[27] *Ibid.*, p. 523.
[28] V. G. Belinskii, *Pis'ma* (St. Petersburg, 1914), III, 329.

Decembrists" took up their tradition and transformed it into Populist social-ism. The brief movement of deep doubt in the value of that tradition passed unnoticed. But its existence is important and in any attempt to go beyond the mere report of views held to an interpretation of the reasons for their emergence and persistence, Belinskii's heretical stand should deserve much attention.

Turning to Herzen, it is neither possible nor necessary within the scope of this paper to do more than explore his relation to his predecessors and indicate his general position on the subject of Russian economic development. To say that the struggle against serfdom unites Herzen with Radishchev and Pestel' is of course a flat truism. The problem is what in Herzen's mind was to follow the abolition of serfdom. The espousal of the *obshchina* as the ideal form of organization of agriculture, the view of an economy organized in *obshchiny* freed from the power of the *pomeshchik,* does indeed constitute a vision of Russian economic development, the specific vision of Russian agrarian socialism. But what was new in the vision? Pestel' had in fact, though not in name, incorporated the *obshchina* into the program of his *Russkaia Pravda.* That Herzen's ideas on the subject came from Haxthausen and the Slavophiles while Pestel's work was unknown to him is, of course, true but immaterial from a point of view which is concerned with the basic trends of intellectual development rather than with the question of specific influences, let alone priorities.

What was new in Herzen as compared with Pestel' was something else. The question of Russia's pursuing a road of economic development different from that of the West did not explicitly arise for Pestel'. That Russia will essentially remain an agricultural country was basically the result of general economic laws concerning the international division of labor — valid for both the Orient and the Occident. It is true that Pestel', as we have seen, envisaged special legal measures designed to reinforce and preserve the agrarian character of the Russian economy, but in a sense this was no more than an attempt to buttress the operation of an economic law common to both Russia and the West. By contrast, Herzen's views contain a deliberate rejection of the road traveled by the West. The Russian past was different from that of the West, accordingly also the Russian future need not follow the road traveled by the West. The following sentences present this view in a most concise form. Addressing himself to "the West" Herzen said:

Nothing in Russia . . . bears the stamp of routine, stagnation, and finality which we encounter with nations which, through long labors, have created for themselves forms of life which to some extent correspond to their ideas.

Do not forget that in addition Russia remained ignorant of the three scourges which retarded the development of the West: Catholicism, Roman law, and the rule of the bourgeoisie (*meshchane*). This much simplifies the problem. We shall unite with you in the coming revolution. [But] for that we need not pass through those swamps which you have crossed; we need not exhaust our forces in the twilight of [your] political forms . . . We have no reason to repeat the epic story of your emancipation, in the course of which your road has become so encumbered by the monuments of the past that you hardly are able to take one single step ahead. Your labors and your sufferings are our lessons. History is very unjust. *The latecomers receive instead of gnawed bones the [right of] precedence [at the table] of experience. All development of mankind is nothing else but [an expression of] that chronological ingratitude.*[29]

This is a remarkable passage. There is no need to ask whether Russia of mid-century was an appropriate vantage point from which to accuse Europe of the industrial revolutions of routine and stagnation, nor need one pause to marvel at the hybris which such an accusation reflects. In a sense, not even the rejection of the Western course of development for Russia is so striking; while an innovation in relation to Pestel', it was, at least in principle, none in relation to the earlier Slavophile thought.[30] What is so surprising is the clarity with which Herzen here recognizes the importance of what was to become an essential element of Russian economic development: the advantages of backwardness, which are elevated to the rank of a ubiquitous law, or at least of a ubiquitous phenomenon, of human history. Just one step seems to separate Herzen from asking the question how the industrial development of Russia might differ from that of the West because of her latecomer's position. But the question is never asked; the hatred of the bourgeoisie, the horror of a proletariat (which as often as not is conceived by Herzen as an agricultural labor force[31]), preclude any serious consideration of Russia's industrial possibilities. The vision remains riveted to the *obshchina,* the "advantages of backwardness" are applied not to the mode of industrial development, but to the opportunity to pass from the age of serfdom into the age of socialism, and as a result the preservation of the old rather than the easy introduction of the new comes to be considered the essence of a latecomer's position. When Chernyshevskii adapted Herzen's view and faithfully repeated the operation of holding the key to the understanding of Russia's economic development in his hands only to turn it the wrong way, it required a good deal of strenuous dialectical reasoning to explain that the new and the old were really one and the same thing. But before we look at Chernyshevskii's treatment of the problem, a few preliminary remarks may be in order.

There is little doubt that Herzen's thought after 1848 is representative of much in the views of his former antagonists, the Slavophiles. True, most

[29] A. I. Gertsen, *Polnoe sobranie sochinenii i pisem,* ed. M. K. Lemke (Petrograd [Leningrad], 1919–1925), VIII (1854–1887), 151. My italics.

[30] Herzen's triad in the preceding quotation (Catholicism, Roman law, and the bourgeoisie) is rather curiously paralleled by Ivan Kireevskii's triad (Roman Church, Roman culture, and a State established by violence). Cf. I. V. Kireevskii, *Polnoe sobranie sochinenii v dvukh tomakh,* ed. M. Gershenson (Moscow, 1911), I, 184.

[31] Herzen, ref. 29, VII (1852–1854), 276.

important differences remained with regard to orthodoxy, humility, peasant violence, foreign policies, and so forth; but with regard to the problem at hand the differences are imperceptible. Khomiakov, too, understood the "advantages of backwardness" and, in fact, was willing to apply them to phenomena much more concrete than the advent of agrarian socialism. As early as 1845 he wrote: "With regard to railroads, as in many other things, we are particularly fortunate; we did not have to expend energy on experiments and to strain our imagination; we can and shall reap the fruits of others' labor." [32] And he becomes even more specific: the advantage of easy technological borrowings is complemented by the advantage of not being hampered by the immediately preceding stage of technical development, the network of comfortable roads.[33] And he continues:

We have been imitating Europe for nearly a century and a half, and we shall continue to do so, and for a long time shall utilize European inventions. Possibly, the time might come when we, too, shall serve in many respects as a model for Europe, but it is impossible for her intellectual achievements ever to become completely useless to us.[34]

It is not unlikely that Khomiakov's personal interest in technology explains his views to some extent. After all, he was himself the inventor of a "silent steam engine" which, incidentally, when sent to the World Exhibition in London, is said to have caused the inhabitants of the surrounding district to consider petitioning the government because of its insufferable noise.[35] Probably much more important is Khomiakov's awareness of the military importance of railroads. "When all other countries are crisscrossed by railroads and are able rapidly to concentrate and to shift their armed forces, Russia necessarily must be able to do the same. It is difficult, it is expensive, but, alas, inevitable." [36] The Slavophiles were better equipped than any other group of Russian intelligentsia to appreciate the significance of national power interests and power policies. It is true that their views on Peter the Great did not reveal such an appreciation. But there is always a great difference between appraisal of history and of current problems. And to the extent that power policies in fact cannot be easily disassociated from the cause of Russian economic development in the second half of the nineteenth century, the Slavophiles actually were closer to that development than Herzen. It should not be surprising, therefore, that Khomiakov has much more to say on railroads, a prerequisite of later industrial upsurge, than Herzen or Ogarëv, Herzen's economic expert, who confines himself to a passing and

[32] A. S. Khomiakov, *Polnoe sobranie sochinenii* (Moscow, 1861), I, 420.

[33] *Ibid.*, p. 424.

[34] *Ibid.*

[35] B. S. Zavitnevich, *Aleksei Stepanovich Khomiakov* (Kiev, 1902), I, 243.

[36] Khomiakov, ref. 32, I, 420.

perhaps half-ironical word of approval of governmental programs of railroad building.[37]

For the rest, however, the difference between Khomiakov and Herzen is almost imperceptible, and while Khomiakov does not consider himself a socialist, he is happy to point out the similarities between Russian *arteli* and Fourier's *phalansteres*.[38]

Two honorific titles have been conferred upon Chernyshevskii in Soviet hagiology. He is a "great revolutionary democrat" and, in addition, the "great Russian economist." The second title is both more distinctive and more dubious than the first. It is not clear at all that Chernyshevskii made any independent contribution to economic analysis. But at the same time it is true that by his knowledge of economic literature and by his interest in empirical economic problems he stands out in the line of writers with whom this paper is concerned. There is in particular no doubt that his economic erudition and his comprehension of economic problems is infinitely superior to that of Ogarëv, the man who in the preceding generation devoted most attention to economics. And yet, with regard to the problem of economic development, Chernyshevskii appears to be hardly more than a continuation of Herzen.

Chernyshevskii does not simply ignore industrial developments. He returns many times to the theme of accumulation of capital and of mechanization of productive processes.

> Russia enters upon that stage of economic development in which capital is being applied to economic production.[39]

> We must not conceal from ourselves that Russia, which so far has taken little part in economic development, is being rapidly drawn into it; our economic life, which up till now has remained almost entirely outside the influence of those economic laws which reveal their power only when economic and commercial activities have been enhanced, begins to fall rapidly under the sway of those laws. Possibly we, too, will soon enter the sphere within which the law of competition is fully valid.[40]

In the era of railroads it seemed impossible to ignore the change that was in the making. It is perfectly clear to Chernyshevskii that Russian peasants will be profoundly affected by the growth of the railroad network, the consequent increases in grain prices, and the volume of foreign trade. Factory cloth will enter the huts of the peasants, but:

> Whatever those changes, let us not dare touch on the sacred and saving custom that we have inherited from our past, all the misery of which is redeemed by one

[37] N. P. Ogarëv, in *Izbrannye sotsial'no-politicheskie i filosofskie proizvedeniia* (Moscow, 1952), I, 135.

[38] Zavitnevich, ref. 35, I, 300.

[39] N. G. Chernyshevskii, *Izbrannye ekonomicheskie proizvedeniia* (Moscow, 1948), I, 148.

[40] *Ibid.*, p. 108.

invaluable legacy — let us not dare assault the common use of land — the great bounty on the introduction of which depends now the welfare of land-tilling classes in Western Europe. May their example be a lesson to us.[41]

The *obshchina* must be saved despite the coming great transformation. No one can read Chernyshevskii's statements on the latter without receiving the sense of an impersonal, almost elemental process. How can *obshchina*, the very symbol of everything that is traditional, be preserved when past traditions rapidly give way to innovation? The Hegelian dialectics provide the answer: "In its form, the highest stage of development is similar to the initial stage." [42] A long stream of analogies from geology, zoology, philology, military history, history of economic protectionism, history of fashions, and so on is marshaled to illustrate that "axiom." Languages uninflected in the early stages become inflected, only to drop the inflections later; savages do not protect domestic industries, but after a mercantilistic period of protectionism, the period of free trade returns mankind to the starting point. And if the evolution of the "whole material and moral world is subordinated to that law, is it likely that the area of landownership should remain the lonely exception?" [43] *Obshchina* thus is not an anachronistic survival, it is the inevitable end of development. True, Russia had never known the intermediary stage, which, after all, is an essential link in Hegel's "axiom" or "law." But this is precisely the point. Russia, because of her very backwardness, is able to skip the intermediary stage. A long series of examples is adduced showing on the one hand the gradualness of technological progress and the ability of backward nations to borrow its most recent, most perfect form. After having thus elaborated on Herzen's advantages of backwardness, Chernyshevskii ends by paraphrasing Herzen's words: "History is like a grandmother, it loves the younger grandchildren. To the latecomers (*tarde venientibus*) it gives not the bones (*ossa*) but the marrow of the bones (*medullam ossium*), while Western Europe had hurt her fingers badly in her attempts to break the bones." [44]

Like Herzen, Chernyshevskii stood on the threshold of an understanding of important aspects and, like Herzen, he chose to turn away. To do so was in many respects more difficult for him than it had been for his predecessor. Herzen never concerned himself much with any aspect of technological progress. Chernyshevskii introduced technological change into the very reasoning designed to prove that in Russia advantages of backwardness consisted in the opportunity to preserve the *obshchina*. To overlook the obvious required a considerable effort, and Chernyshevskii carefully avoided use of examples pertaining to modern industrial machinery and preferred to choose

[41] *Ibid.*
[42] *Ibid.*, p. 697.
[43] *Ibid.*, p. 715.
[44] *Ibid.*, p. 727.

his illustrations from instruction of savages in the use of matches and Latin script.

While in the crucial respect Chernyshevskii follows Herzen, the difference between the two writers need not be blurred. *Obshchina* for Chernyshevski is more than a form of land tenure. He likes to think of it as a form of organized production by the associated members.[45] An important consequence is that modern technology then could find its entry into the organized *obshchina,* and Chernyshevskii places much stress on technological progress in agriculture.[46] That presentation of the *obshchina* might militate against introduction of modern technology into agriculture is strongly denied. If agriculture in the past was slow to adopt machinery, the reason does not lie in the *obshchina,* nor with any mental resistance on the part of the peasantry, but in the poverty of the peasant population.[47]

And what about manufacturing? It is astonishing how little the "great Russian economist" has to say on the subject, if we abstract, as we well may, from Vera Pavlovna's dreams, beyond his agreement to the proposition that more important than the growth of factory production is the growth of output of factory wares by the domestic industry, and that concerning the "question of usefulness of direct protection of factories, one should consider not so much the relation of our factories to foreign production of similar goods as their relation to the well-being of people who find work in the factories and still more the effect of factories upon the output of the same products by domestic industries." That the latter deserve to be protected does not raise any question in the author's mind.[48]

The implications of the foregoing are clear. Government policies should discriminate in favor of small-scale domestic production of manufactured goods and against large-scale factory production. After having looked the other way so as not to see the advantages of backwardness in the application of very modern technology, it is only consistent to disregard the importance of large-scale factory production, within which alone, in the conditions of the nineteenth century, these advantages could be efficiently utilized. When, in addition, one might remember that Chernyshevskii was inclined, in his *Annotations to J. S. Mill's Principles,* to view even the Western industrialization and railroadization as a relatively short-lived process, pointing out that newly formed capital will find less and less application in trade and industry and hence will tend to turn to investments in agriculture,[49] and that at the same time large-scale units which are frowned upon in industry are favored in agriculture, the picture is completed. Rus-

---

[45] *Ibid.,* p. 213.
[46] *Ibid.,* pp. 288f.
[47] *Ibid.,* III:2, 418.
[48] *Ibid.,* I, 142.
[49] *Ibid.,* III:1, 301.

sian industrialization, and, by the same token, Russian economic development, remain outside the scope of Chernyshevskii's vision. It is not surprising, therefore, how often our author emphasizes his basic agreement with the
Slavophiles on questions of practical economic policies, even though he refused to side with them on the "more nebulous" problems which separated
them from the Westerners. True, the early incarceration and the subsequent
exile severed Chernyshevskii's immediate contact with Russian economic reality at a fairly early point. Had he remained in the centers of European
Russia throughout the rest of the sixties and the seventies his views might
well have undergone some changes. As it was, the discrepancy between Russian thought and Russian subsequent development perhaps nowhere else
appears as clearly and as strikingly as in the writings of Chernyshevskii.

It would be difficult, indeed, on the basis of what has been said so far,
to visualize Russian intellectual development as guiding and anticipating her
economic evolution. As we move on, however, an unusual and solitary figure
lays claim to our attention. D. I. Pisarev, like Belinskii (and unlike Chernyshevskii), was, despite his interests in science and history, in the main a
literary critic. While in Russia at this time literary criticism necessarily
implied concern with social problems, questions of economic development
as a rule remained outside the purview of the critic. We cannot hope, therefore, to find more in Pisarev than a few disjointed remarks on our problem.
But what we do find is very much worth recording here.

Coming from a line of thought which placed so much emphasis on collectivism in one form and another, and being particularly influenced by Chernyshevskii, Pisarev surprises us by his attitude of strong individualism. At
least, after 1863, Pisarev appears more and more as an advocate of industrial development and a defender of an enlightened capitalism. Following
Russian traditions — or perhaps general traditions of the nineteenth century — these views are presented as emanating from a general law:

There have been many revolutions in the course of history; political institutions, religious institutions disappeared, but the rule of capital over labor emerged
from all these revolutions completely unimpaired. Historical experience and simple
logic alike convince us that strong and intelligent people will always win over
weaklings and dullards . . . Hence to wax indignant over the fact that educated
and well-to-do classes rule over the toiling mass would mean to run against the
indestructible and unshakable wall of a natural law . . . When we encounter an
inevitable fact of this order, what is called for is not indignation, but an action
which would turn this inevitable fact to the benefit of the people. The capitalist
possesses intelligence and wealth. These two qualities assure his rule over labor.
But whether that rule will cause damage to, or confer benefits upon, the people
depends on the circumstances. Give that capitalist some sort of vague education
and he will become a bloodsucker. But if you give him a complete, firm, humanitarian education — the same capitalist will become not indeed a benevolent phi-

lanthropist, but a thinking, calculating leader of people's labor, that is to say, a man a hundred times more useful than any philanthropist.[50]

These words sound indeed like an elaboration of Belinskii's conviction that Russia could not prosper without a bourgeoisie. Pisarev, of course, goes far beyond Belinskii. The interest in specialized disciplines was quite alien to Belinskii: "Do throw away your political economy and statistics; any specialized knowledge lowers and degrades men; thought alone in its general universal sense must be the subject of man's study." [51] For Pisarev, it is the growing body of specialized knowledge that is the earnest of social and economic progress. What is wrong with Tolstoy's Nekhliudov is precisely that he wants to help his peasants without having first acquired a practical profession.[52] Diffusion of such knowledge will solve all problems:

> The time will come — and it is not far off — when all intelligent youth . . . will live a full intellectual life and its outlook will be serious and calculating. Then the young owner of an agricultural estate will organize it in European fashion: then *the young capitalist will establish the factories* which we need, and will organize them in such a way as is required by the interests of both the owner and the workers; and that is all that is needed. A good farm and *a good factory* constitute the best and the only possible school for the people.[53]

Add to the foregoing Pisarev's penetrating idea that introduction of modern methods into agriculture is extremely difficult unless in the atmosphere of a considerable industrial development,[54] and the result is not only a picture of a man for whom industrial development is much more important than agrarian collectivism and social problems in industry, but who also possesses a considerable insight into eminent practical problems of economic development, something that altogether eluded Chernyshevskii.

The preceding quotations from Pisarev's works could be multiplied to show the same trend of thought. It is also true that a considerable number of quotations could be gleaned that would point in a very different direction. In fact, Pisarev's inconsistencies are often staggering. It must suffice here to place on record this second brief departure from the rut of established thought and the willingness on the part of an important representative of Russia's intellectual history to accept industrial development and the philosophy of economic individualism. In fact, Pisarev's acceptance for Russia of the contents of Western economic development goes so far that there is no trace at all of any recognition that in Russia the mechanics of backwardness might have led to not inconsiderable differences in the course

---

[50] D. I. Pisarev, *Sochineniia, Polnoe sobranie v shesti tomakh* (St. Petersburg, 1897), IV, 132.

[51] Belinskii, ref. 28, I, 89.

[52] Pisarev, ref. 50, 237.

[53] *Ibid.,* III, 305. My italics.

[54] D. I. Pisarev, *Izbrannye filosofskie i obshchestvenno-politicheskie stat'i* (Moscow, 1944), pp. 184, 212, 235.

of industrialization. If Pisarev, in addition to his admiration for the figure of Rakhmetov, had taken over from Chernyshevskii the latter's ideas on the advantages of latecoming, the result would have been remarkable indeed.

Yet Pisarev's failure to see an important aspect of Russian economic development hardly deserves any criticism in the light of subsequent intellectual history. As we approach the closing stretches of our review we encounter not a stress on the advantages but the *disadvantages of backwardness*. From the end of the sixties on it becomes almost impossible to ignore the fact of an important industrial development. But the prevailing attitude is to show that in the specific conditions of Russian backwardness the effects of industrialization and its very character must be particularly detrimental and that in such conditions industrial progress cannot proceed very far.

The remainder of this section will be used to illustrate this point briefly. P. L. Lavrov, while stressing the "borrowed" nature of Russian capitalism, claimed that the lateness of capitalist development in Russia implied the importation of a degenerated and debased form of capitalism:

We are passing not only through the transformation of our pre-emancipation economy into a bourgeois economy; that in itself would not be so bad; but together with the whole civilized world we are in the state of transition to the highest, that is to say, to the ugliest form of bourgeois economy. This is the stage at which the capitalists become large financiers; at which little stock-exchange kings become the rulers over the economic life of nations; at which the bourgeoisie develops into a financial aristocracy. This transition causes disastrous developments in the economic life of the masses — [it is] the true reason for the emergence of Western European socialism. But with us matters are much worse than with any other European nation. In the West, a bourgeois economy developed gradually, step by step, paralleling a process of discoveries and inventions. In some measure, the development of the bourgeois economy in the West was beneficial for the whole mass of the population . . . Only by-and-by it became clear that bourgeois economy in its very essence is hostile to [the interests of] the masses. That economy passed through several phases before reaching its present stage at which the inconsistency and irreconcilability of the interests of labor and capital have been revealed in their merciless nakedness . . .

With us the peasants were liberated — and accordingly a bourgeois economy became possible — when in the West it has acquired its latest form. But following the immutable law of competition of the bourgeois economy, the economy of any individual or any nation when drawn into the circle of the capitalist economy must necessarily assume the highest, the most developed, form of that economy. Thus we have passed without any intermediary stages from the economy of serfdom into the economy of stock-exchange kings, concessionaires, shady dealers, and the like. It is easy to understand that this order at once has become diametrically opposed to the interests of the whole population; that it is disadvantageous to our estate owners, our petty bourgeoisie, and the masses of the people. Only a tiny number of crooks and cheats have accumulated fabulous riches on the basis of general impoverishment and bankruptcy.[55]

[55] P. L. Lavrov, *Vperëd*, no. 16 (September 1, 1875/August 20, 1875), pp. 491f.

Thus, because Russia appears late on the industrial scene her industrialization has only negative effects upon the economy of the country.

It would be perhaps more natural to draw for our last illustration on the writings of N. K. Mikhailovskii,[56] who in many respects concludes the long chapter of intellectual history with which we have been concerned here. Nikolai —on, to whose views preference is given here, strictly speaking does not fit into the line of figures we have treated so far. He, like Vorontsov, is essentially an economist rather than a general preceptor of the intelligentsia. But his writings provide an additional and important point of view concerning the specific character of Russian economic development.

What is Nikolai —on's contribution to our problem? Writing in the eighties and early nineties, he, even more than Lavrov, had to take for granted the fact of capitalist penetration into the economy of the country. Like Lavrov, he considered this penetration, the economic history of three decades following 1861, a highly detrimental process. But in analyzing this process he did not confine himself to remarks about the degradation of capitalism, but treated the problem essentially in terms of Marxian contradictions of capitalist development. On the one hand, as output grows the "number of workers engaged in capitalist enterprises is bound to diminish in relation to the value of product,"[57] the share of labor income in total income produced must fall. This is the result, among other things, of increased mechanization of production. On the other hand, capitalist industry destroys the indigenous industrial activities of the peasants. The internal market shrinks. Capitalist production of necessity requires a wide and growing market outside the domestic economy. There is no need, of course, within the scope of this paper to present more than the barest skeleton of this train of thought. In one form or another, the concept of deficiency of effective demand goes through much of modern economic theory from Malthus to Keynes. In the case of Malthus, as was true in the case of Nikolai —on, the discussion bore directly on the problem of industrialization of an agrarian country. What interests us here is the specific application of those ideas to the Russian scene. Nikolai —on believed that in Russia, because of her backwardness and the suddenness of her economic development, the general problem of capitalist development appeared in a much more acute

---

[56] Perhaps a brief reference to Mikhailovskii's review of Dostoyevsky's *Demons* may be in order because it so clearly illustrates the almost unbelievable extent of the Populists' anti-industrialism. Mikhailovskii upbraids Dostoyevsky for fastening his attention upon the insignificant group of criminal fanatics, while Russia is being crisscrossed by railroads, factories and banks are cropping up everywhere, and the real demons, not murderous at all — *mirnye i smirnye* — take possession of the country and destroy all that is worth preserving in Russia (N. K. Mikhailovskii, *Sochineniia* [St. Petersburg, 1888], II, 309–310). Compared with these attitudes, an organization like the Junker-led *Bund der Landwirte* in Germany appears like an association for the promotion of industry.

[57] Nikolai —on (Daniel'son), *Ocherki nashego poreformennogo khoziaistva* (St. Petersburg, 1893), p. 183.

form. Capitalist production in Russia did not increase the value of total output. It merely shifted production from the peasant hut into the factory. The peasant could do nothing save increase the exploitation of the soil; he was unable, in conditions of shrinking income, to improve the techniques of agricultural production, while confronted by American competition which used virgin soil and modern technology.[58] At the same time the growth of the tax burden upon the peasant further reduced the capacity of the internal market. Within the framework of capitalist development industrial exports were indeed the only way out of the impasse into which capitalism had propelled the economy of the country. But precisely at this point the disadvantages of industrialization in conditions of economic backwardness inevitably asserted themselves. Russian industry had been built up behind the shelter of high tariff walls. It was expensive and inefficient. The advanced industrial countries had long established themselves in foreign markets. To compete with such countries Russian industry had neither the requisite knowledge nor the technological equipment.[59] Its industry was, therefore, doomed to collapse. The great famine of 1891 was the catastrophic result of the inept policy of industrialization; it was the price paid for the abandonment of a principle that had been sanctified by long centuries of Russian economic life — the *obshchina*.[60]

Thus, it can be seen that even a generous injection of Marxian theory did not per se necessarily lead to a radical change in the attitude toward the economic development of the country. A different group of people who also drew upon Marxian theories contrived to arrive at very different conclusions. A discussion of that group transcends the scope of this paper, but perhaps it is in order here to venture the surmise that the difference in conclusions followed much less from the theoretical structure used and much more from differences in response to the actual economic change that was taking place in the country. Nikolai —on's book with its extreme pessimistic forecast regarding Russia's industrial development appeared at a moment when the country stood on the threshold of a magnificent industrial upsurge. The very high rate of growth for the remainder of the nineties and the resumption of that growth after the 1905 Revolution effectively disproved the prophecy. It is perhaps not entirely inappropriate to conclude our survey with this glaring discrepancy between prognostication and event.

III

The divorce of the country's intellectual history from its economic history is curious indeed. Of course, its extent varied over the period under review. In a sense, the year 1861 provided an important dividing line. If it

---

[58] *Ibid.*, pp. 129f, 322.
[59] *Ibid.*, p. 213.
[60] *Ibid.*, pp. 331, 375.

is true that the emancipation was a necessary prerequisite to the country's economic development, then the intelligentsia's abhorrence of serfdom entailed at least the acceptance of a long step on the road of industrialization. In addition, there is Belinskii's brief flash of foresight. After 1861, there is indeed a rapidly growing schism between idea and reality which Pisarev tried in vain to bridge. As the industrialization of the country gathered momentum, the process was either overlooked or viewed as transitory, and deplored withal. At the same time, the essential continuity of thought and attitude before and after 1861 cannot be gainsaid. The road of Russian economic development was rarely illuminated by the strong brilliance of prevision and prescience. Nietzsche once remarked that Hesiod's golden age and iron age actually referred to the same period, seen from two different points of view.[61] It is tempting to suggest that what must appear to those interested in literature, sociology, perhaps philosophy, as the golden age of the Russian intelligentsia appears far from brilliant to the economist. The point is not that the prophets of the Russian intelligentsia kept revealing verities that did not materialize. For all we know, their prophecies — or wishes — *might* have materialized and there is no suggestion here that what happened was bound to happen. But they are exposed to a different charge. They proved unable to grasp the nature of the forces that were pushing the country's economy in a direction which was so repulsive to them. Much as they had thought about the peculiarities of Russia's economic evolution, they remained blind to those peculiarities which so greatly increased the chances of successful industrialization. As a result, Russia's economic history appears largely incomprehensible from the point of view of its intellectual history. But it is one thing to ascertain a deep rift between idea and economic reality. It is another to try to find some reasons for its existence.

To some extent the ascendance of socialist ideas and ideals among Russian intellectuals may provide an explanation. Venturi in his monumental work on Russian Populism essentially sees it as a branch of socialist thought. At least from the thirties on, the influence of Western socialist ideas was undeniably strong. Not even Pisarev, not even Botkin completely escaped that spell. Much of nineteenth-century socialism was characterized by two aspects: (1) strong interest in distribution as against production and (2) criticism of the results of capitalist development in the West. To accept industrial development seemed to imply deliberate acceptance of the ills of Western industrialization. Shelgunov, writing in 1861, put this attitude into clear words: "Europe has awakened; she has understood her malady. Russia too has awakened, but has she risen from slumber only in order to walk consciously the road over which Europe has passed unconsciously?"[62] To approve of industrialization then meant to accept deliberately the "cancer of

[61] Friedrich Nietzsche, *Zur Genealogie der Moral, Werke* (Leipzig, 1902), VII, 323.
[62] N. V. Shelgunov, *Sochineniia* (Petersburg, n.d.), I, xxv.

the proletariat," as the phrase ran, to approve the destruction of the *ob-shchina* and the uprooting of a traditional way of life, and the corruption of a value system which apparently contained so many elements of socialist morality, only to see it replaced by the vice and the depravity of a factory town, so vividly and so shockingly described by G. Uspenskii. The cold-blooded concept of economic progress as "service for the future centuries and not as an aid to the lowly and humiliated so scorchingly satirized in one of Konrad Lilienschwager's poems[63] ran counter to all the ingrained ideas of Russian intellectuals. It is therefore not surprising that even a man like Kavelin, who remained free from socialist influences, was genuinely concerned with Russia's industrial development. He thought a good deal about the restrictive elements of communal landownership, but not only shrank away from emancipation of the peasantry "without land," however much such an emancipation might favor industrial progress, not only warned against an "industrial delirium tremens," but also regarded the *obshchina* as the "great reservoir of the people's forces," advocated its retention in a reorganized form, and, while recognizing the "miracles of industrial develop-ment" of which Europe and the United States "are so justly proud," was quick to call attention to "the unfavorable sides of the process," i.e., its so-cial effects.[64] And it is perhaps even less surprising that also Marx, much to the embarrassment of later Russian Marxians, tended on the whole to espouse the basic attitude of Chernyshevskii. Not only did Marx in 1877 explicitly refuse to grant the applicability of his theory of economic develop-ment to Russia beyond the truism that success of industrial development required previous transformation "of a good part of its peasants into prole-tarians"; but, in the drafts of his well-known letter to Vera Zasulich in 1881, he explicitly combines the discussion of the *obshchina* with the problem of advantages of backwardness and envisages a development and trans-formation of the *obshchina* in accordance with "the positive results of the mode of [capitalist] production." It is true that, unlike Chernyshevskii, in speaking of economic development of a backward country, Marx refers to the rapidity with which Russia introduced the modern financial institutions while Chernyshevskii preferred to escape into anthropology in order to make the same point. But this only serves to underscore the remarkable closeness between Marx and Chernyshevskii.[65] While it may make good sense to ex-plain the attitudes taken by the Russian intellectuals by reference to their

[63] "Progress sovsem ne bogadel'nia,
    On sluzhba budushchim vekam,
    Ne ostanovitsia bestsel'no
    On dlia posob'ia bedniakam."
N. Dobroliubov, *Stikhotvoreniia* (Moscow, 1948), p. 138.
    [64] K. D. Kavelin, *Publitsistika,* in *Sobranie sochinenii* (St. Petersburg, 1898), II, 163, 164, 177, 181, 184.
    [65] Karl Marx and Friedrich Engels, *The Russian Menace to Europe,* ed. P. W. Black-stock and B. F. Hoselitz (Glencoe, Ill., 1952), pp. 216–217, 222–223.

socialism and their general humanitarianism, it would hardly be reasonable to suggest that their failure to adopt the specific Marxian socialism prevented them from seeing, let alone foreseeing, the course of the country's industrial development. As the example of Nikolai —on shows and as Marx's scattered thoughts on the subject confirm, any position with regard to Russian industrialization was deducible from Marx's theoretical framework.

But to use socialism as an explanation inevitably raises a further question. Surely, there was no iron law in obedience to which the main current of Russian intellectual thought came to display socialist features. Why was it socialism that Russia borrowed from the West rather than Bentham's utilitarianism? It is again difficult indeed not to associate the peculiar bent of Russian intellectual history with the backwardness of the country, and that in several respects.

First of all, there is something like a counterpart to the play of backwardness in the economic sphere. In a backward country there is a coexistence of abject material poverty with modern humanitarian ideas which to a large extent have developed elsewhere after, and on the basis of, a good deal of economic progress. A comparison between Pososhkov and Herzen may illustrate the point.

This leads directly to the second point. So far it has been possible to maintain the artificial separation of economic backwardness from political backwardness. The relation of the latter to the actual economic development in Russia is a most complex phenomenon and need not concern us here. But the retardation in the development of modern forms of government, that is to say, the preservation of the autocratic regime and the absence of a normal political arena meant that the Russian intellectuals were artificially excluded from active preoccupation with practical problems. Accordingly, they were pushed into abstract thought which, untempered by contact with reality, assumed the form of growing radicalism, and the radicalism in thought in turn led to radicalism in action. In the absence of political oppression it may not have taken Belinskii all his life to arrive at a positive appraisal of the role of the bourgeoisie. Pisarev's "nihilists" were men interested in the study of natural sciences. It was not the fault of the moderate, even though boisterous, Pisarev that Russia's political backwardness deflected the energies of her youth into other channels and that the nihilists, instead of being Benthamite utilitarians in thought and managers of chemical factories or iron and steel mills in practice, actually used their scientific knowledge for the preparation of bombs to be employed in terrorist assaults upon the government.

Thirdly, precisely because of the backwardness of the country, and the resulting absence of a significant gradual change in the value patterns of the population, Western socialism easily coalesced with the system of agrarian value orientations with their emphasis on the value of the plowman's labor and their rejection as sinful of activities which were not directly connected with tilling the soil. Russian socialism of the period deserves its name of *narodnichestvo* because to a considerable extent it adopted the value orientations of the *narod* which placed a considerable opprobrium on trading and industrial pursuits.

And, finally, economic development of backward countries, in the conditions of the nineteenth century with its growing capital intensity of output and its stress on bigness in the sense described in Section I of this paper, also implied the costliness of a big spurt of industrial development in terms of the sacrifices to be imposed upon the population. The transitory detrimental effects of industrialization in Russia were bound to be greater than had been the case in more advanced countries, and a comparison of the change in the levels of consumption in Russia of the 1890's and, say, England of the closing decades of the eighteenth century fully confirms the difference. To accept these sacrifices, however temporary they may be, certainly was difficult, if not impossible, for minds dominated by the feeling of compassion with the misery of the peasant and anxious to improve his position as speedily as possible.

Thus, the strength of socialist doctrine in Russia is at best only a part of the explanation for the inability to accept or even to comprehend the nature of the country's economic evolution.

Perhaps nothing shows this more clearly than the circumstance that if they had wished to do so Russian intellectuals could have extracted a great deal from Western socialism which would have had direct application to the country's industrial progress. Marx is the obvious, but perhaps not the most important, case in point for the period under review. The close relation between St. Simonian tenets and the industrial development in France, Germany, and other Western countries is a matter of historical record. There were indeed men in Russia who were attracted by that aspect of St. Simonian doctrines. One need only mention names like I. Vernadskii, V. Bezobrazov, Tengoborskii, and others. The use of investment banks for purposes of industrial development certainly appealed to their imagination. To some extent, they may even be said to have continued a more indigenous Russian tradition because of similar ideas in Mordvinov's writings. But neither the latter nor the group of men just mentioned properly belong within the scope of what has been treated here as Russian intellectual history. Perhaps Ogarëv alone reveals some traces of St. Simonian influence in this respect, but significantly his interest in credit institutions is confined to the sphere of agriculture rather than industry.[66] In addition, it is not clear that St. Simon and not Proudhon has inspired Ogarëv's ideas in this respect. Thus one could not accuse the Russian intellectuals of wholesale blind acceptance of Western socialism. They took over what fitted into the pattern of their

[66] Ogarëv, ref. 37, I, 740f.

basic predisposition and predilections. The roots of the latter, however, were deeply imbedded in the value systems of the peasantry and the general backwardness of the country.

Some conclusions might perhaps emerge from the preceding survey for the present-day problem of underdeveloped countries. It would seem that the specific *Weltanschauung* of Russian intellectuals with its deep and immediate concern for the welfare of the peasantry and its unwillingness to accept industrialization need not necessarily be confined to Russia of the nineteenth century. We have so far neglected the effects of those attitudes in Russia upon the country's economic development. To some extent such neglect is justified. As we have said before, the Russian autocratic regime effectively excluded most of the intelligentsia from direct participation in political decisions. Their thought could not be translated into action. By the same token, they remained unable to influence, let alone to determine, the nature of the country's economic development. The latter was partly the result of impersonal economic forces, partly an almost accidental by-product of government decisions pursuing other goals, and partly the result of deliberate governmental policies. Even so, the attitudes of the intelligentsia could not fail to have some negative effects. While Chernyshevskii could not affect policies, he could — and did — influence the attitudes of thousands of Russian university students. Their unwillingness to prepare themselves for practical industrial work, their scorn of "careerism," and their preference for pure knowledge untainted by any suggestion of monetary rewards — this "oriental" attitude was no doubt greatly reinforced by the whole tenor of the intelligentsia's general philosophy.[67]

There is no question that to some extent such attitudes served to retard the country's economic development. They belonged to the specific *disadvantages* of backwardness and tended to decrease the "tension" of which we spoke in the first section of this paper.

But the role of the intellectuals in backward countries of today is very different from what it used to be in Russia of the past century. They are no longer doomed to inactivity or confined to passive resistance. They can and they do exert a great deal of direct influence. If it is true that the ideas and attitudes of the Russian intelligentsia which have been described in the preceding pages stem largely from the very backwardness of the country, we may ask whether the same patterns are not likely to reproduce themselves in those countries and to constitute great obstructions in the process of their industrialization. For a number of reasons the advantages of backwardness in conditions of the twentieth century are not as strong as they were during the nineteenth century. It would augur ill for the prospects of industrial

---

[67] It is useful to read in this connection Prince Obolenskii's vivid description of the criteria which he and his generation applied to the choice of profession when entering the universities. (V. Obolenskii, *Ocherki minuvshego* [Belgrade, 1931], pp. 82–83.)

progress of backward countries of our time should it become clear that these *diminished advantages* of backwardness are coupled with *increased disadvantages* of delayed economic development.

In some sense, a belated and precarious reconciliation between intelligentsia and industrial progress was effected in Russia by the Russian Marxism of the eighties and the nineties. There is little doubt that that curious reconciliation itself fits well into the general historical pattern of industrialization in conditions of backwardness. Moreover, it has a natural bearing on the present situation in underdeveloped countries.

Populism and Early Russian Marxism on Ways of Economic Development of Russia (The 1880's and 1890's)

SOLOMON M. SCHWARZ

I. ECONOMIC BACKGROUND

The second half of the nineteenth century was a critical period in the social and economic history of Russia. Her defeat in the Crimean War (1854–1856) foreshadowed the inevitable collapse of the old feudal order. And the emancipation of the serfs, in 1861, was the point of departure for a new process of development, which may be illustrated by a few figures.

Before the emancipation of the serfs, Russia was largely an agricultural country committed to natural farming. There was also a predominance of home production in industry, and the means of transportation were poorly developed in a country that was almost without railroads.

At the beginning of the 1860's, however, rapid development of commercial agriculture set in, industry began to grow and change its character, and the country witnessed a growth of foreign and internal trade, banks, joint-stock companies, etc.

The creation of a railroad network was the basis of this development — especially during the first two decades. By 1861 there were only 1,488 versts[1] — less than 1,000 miles — of railroad in the entire vast expanse of Russia; twenty years later there were 13,926 miles; after twenty more years, in 1901, there were 27,656 miles of railroads in European Russia alone, and 32,404 in both European and Asiatic Russia.[2] These results of a forty-year

---

[1] One verst equals 0.663 mile.

[2] Data about Russia in this section of my paper are taken from P. I. Liashchenko, *Istoriia narodnogo khoziaistva SSSR*, Vol. II (Moscow, 1948). There is an English translation of an earlier edition: *History of the National Economy of Russia to the 1917 Revolution*, by Peter I. Lyashchenko (New York, 1949). Even though the book is marred by official doctrine and scheme of development, it is the best source of information about the economic history of Russia in the last two centuries; in particular, Liashchenko's figures are correct in almost all cases. I have converted all data in the text to units used in the United States. All data for the United States are taken from the *Historical Statistics of the United States, 1789–1945* (Washington, D.C.: Bureau of the Census, 1949).

growth may seem modest by American standards. The growth of the railroad network occurred much earlier and much more quickly in the United States, from 1,098 miles in 1832 to 32,120 miles in 1862, and during the forty years between 1861 and 1901 by 166,000 miles. Railroad construction, however, had a very profound effect upon the Russian economy. The nation freed itself from the strait jacket of a natural economy and began to move into the sphere of a market economy. These developments affected agriculture in particular. It is significant that grain constituted up to 40 per cent and more of the total freight during these first decades.

The transformation of Russian agriculture into a market economy was a painful process. The conditions which emancipation imposed upon the peasantry placed a heavy burden upon the rural population. Insufficient land, heavy redemption payments (for the land), and high taxes made economic progress impossible for large sections of the peasantry — for the majority of the peasants in some provinces — and led quickly to differentiation within the peasantry: a minority of peasants moved upward on the economic scale, while a very considerable majority moved downward.

At the same time, nonpeasant agriculture underwent a profound transformation. Ownership of land by the nobility declined rapidly, and their lands began to pass into the hands of the urban bourgeoisie and the upper layer of the peasantry. By 1877 peasants already owned 7 per cent of all so-called privately owned lands (lands other than peasant allotments and state lands); by 1887 they owned 13.1 per cent of such lands, and by 1905 23.9 per cent.

Under these highly contradictory conditions Russian agriculture had to develop on a commercial basis. The net economic results of this forty-year evolution in agriculture, however, were considerable in spite of the great difficulties. The average yearly grain production, in European Russia, increased from 810,000,000 bushels in 1864–1866 to 1,800,000,000 bushels in 1900–1905. That is to say, the grain production in European Russia increased by 120 per cent while the population increased by 75 per cent. Statistics for all of Russia would show an even more favorable trend.

The increase in the output of noncereal — and much more marketable — agricultural products was even greater: the average annual potato crop increased five and a half times between 1864–1866 and 1900–1905, accompanied by a fifteenfold increase of distillery potato demand: from 113 tons to 1,673 tons. The yearly flax export increased from 75,200 tons in 1857–1861 to 218,100 in 1894–1896. The yearly processing of sugar beets increased from 672,000 tons in the 1860's to 5,740,000 tons in 1896–1898. Other sectors of the economy showed similar movements, all of which indicated rapid unfolding of a market economy.

The development of industry was much more complicated. The first decade after the emancipation of the serfs saw simultaneously the subordination of domestic peasant (*kustar*) industry to market forces and its eventual elimination through the competition of factories, and the displacement of manorial manufacturing either by mechanized factories of a capitalist type, or by decentralized capitalist enterprises relying partly upon homework. This was especially characteristic of the textile industry. This industry underwent a considerable growth during the first half of the nineteenth century, and began to undergo mechanization in the second quarter (first in spinning and cotton printing, and much later in weaving). During the first decade after the emancipation, cotton weaving was organized as a "distributing system": the spinning was done in factories (partly mechanized and partly manual); the yarn was then distributed to peasant weavers (*kustari*), and was returned to the factory for printing. The process by which the capitalist factory displaced the manorial factory (or manufacture), then, temporarily strengthened *kustar* industry. These complicating features of Russian industrial development receded into the background in the 1870's, however; ever stronger subordination of *kustar* production to capitalist relations and rapid displacement of the *kustari* by the factory marked the industrial development.

The over-all results of the forty-year development of Russian industrial capitalism were impressive. Indeed, the textile industry gave up its leading position, even though it had expanded considerably. Iron and steel, coal and oil industries, even a machine-tool industry, grew up alongside textile production.

Development of the iron and steel industries was stimulated by railroad building in particular. Railroads were built exclusively with imported metal in the 1860's; the situation began to change in the 1870's, and the iron and steel industry began to grow rapidly in the 1880's. Iron output was only 321,-000 tons in 1860 (the United States figure for 1840), and 428,000 tons even as late as 1880; it increased to 905,000 tons in 1890, and to 2,900,000 tons (the United States figure for the late 1870's) by 1900. The coal industry also grew rapidly: Russian coal output was a negligible 300,000 tons in 1860 (the United States output of thirty years before). In 1880, 1890, and 1900, however, Russian coal output was, respectively, 3,290,000, 6,027,000, and 16,182,000 tons (the United States output on the eve of the Civil War). There was no oil industry at all in Russia in 1860; at the turn of the century, however, the Russian oil industry produced half the world's oil.

The young Russian capitalism had sunk deep roots by the time the twentieth century opened.

II. POPULISM ON NONCAPITALIST DEVELOPMENT OF RUSSIA

Development of a market economy and crystallization of an industrial capitalist order in Russia was accompanied by destruction of traditional ways of life in the village and by economic degradation of great sections of the peasantry. As in other countries where the transition to capitalism ruined great numbers of small independent producers and created, especially in the early decades, great hardships for industrial workers, the transition to capitalism in Russia led to a characteristic ideological reaction: to attempts to defend the possibility of avoiding capitalist development and of preserving and developing in noncapitalist forms the precapitalist economy. In Russia, this anticapitalist *economic romanticism* expressed itself in so-called Populism (*narodnichestvo*) which dominated Russian progressive thinking for decades and began to decline only in the nineties. Russian Marxism crystallized and grew in its struggle with this economic romanticism.

In this paper I can touch only upon the fundamental features of the Populist view of the possible ways of Russian economic development. This view was based upon the doctrine that the peasant commune (*obshchina*) occupied a special position in Russian life. Populism was formulated very early — before the emancipation. It was Alexander Herzen who laid down the fundamental proposition that Russia could avoid capitalism by relying upon the peasant commune. Herzen had been the most fiery spokesman for "Western" tendencies in Russian literature, but the defeat of the European revolution of 1848, and the victory of political reaction in most European countries, had caused him to pin his hopes on the special features of Russian peasant life. Referring to Haxthausen, a German scholar who had carried out field studies of Russian society and agriculture in 1843–44 and who had published his results in a two-volume work (1847–1850) that "discovered" the peasant commune for Russian as well as Western public opinion, Herzen wrote in 1849:

> According to him [Haxthausen] the peasant commune is "everything" in Russia. It is the key to Russia's past, it is the germ of her future, it is the vital monad of the Russian state. Each peasant commune in Russia is a tiny republic that manages its own affairs, that knows neither private property nor proletariat, that has long since made some of the features of the socialist Utopias established facts. These people cannot live otherwise, and have never lived otherwise.
>
> I agree with Haxthausen fully, but I think, nevertheless, that the peasant commune is not quite "everything" in Russia. Haxthausen has indeed caught the vital principle of the Russian nation, but his natural sympathy for everything patriarchal, and his lack of critical feeling have prevented him from seeing that it is precisely the negative side of peasant communal life that has called forth the St. Petersburg reaction. If complete suppression of personality were not characteristic of the commune, the autocracy, of which Custine speaks with such horror, could not have developed.[3]

This is why Herzen, in spite of the fact that he espoused a Populist position that linked him in some respects to the Slavophiles, continued to

---

[3] A. I. Gertsen, *Sochineniia*, V (Moscow, 1928), 341–342.

stress the significance of Western influence in Russian thought. He returns
to this issue again and again. At the end of the fifties he wrote in his
Memoirs and Thoughts:

Only the great thought of the West, connected with all of its long history, can
fertilize the seed that sleeps in the patriarchal society of the Slavs. *Artel* and
obshchina, division of income and division of the fields, the peasant assembly and
the self-governing local union of villages — all of these are the cornerstones of our
future free-communal life. Of course, these cornerstones are merely stones, and
without Western thought we shall remain with the mere foundations of our future
cathedral.[4]

The Populist tradition had its origin in Herzen. However, it was not
Herzen — whose works, by the way, were not readily available in Russia —
but Nikolai G. Chernyshevskii who was the intellectual leader of the generations that entered the public arena after the emancipation, when the issues
developed by Herzen at the end of the 1840's attracted attention. Chernyshevskii, to be sure, lacked Herzen's brilliant literary style, but he had a
much greater mastery of economics, a powerful analytical mind, a great revolutionary temperament, and, in addition, an extraordinary capacity for work
and literary production. A few years of literary activity (he was only thirty-
four when he was spiritually buried in prison) insured him a position of
profound influence over the new generations of Russian intellectuals for a
quarter of a century.

The remarkable fact, however, is that the Populist movement forgot the
differences on the peasant commune between Herzen and Chernyshevskii —
and there were many important differences — and developed much more
as followers of Herzen than as followers of Chernyshevskii. The present
paper could then perhaps almost bypass Chernyshevskii's views on the
commune, if these views did not constitute a bridge to Marx (not to Russian
Marxism, however) and influence Marx's relation to the differences among
Russian intellectuals.

Two ideas are characteristic of Chernyshevskii's view of the peasant
commune. First, unlike the Slavophiles, Chernyshevskii denied that the
peasant commune is peculiar to Russian or Slavic rural life. He emphasized
constantly that the commune had existed almost everywhere and continued
to exist in Russia only "because of historical circumstances that held
Russian life in a condition close to patriarchal for a long period of time."[5]
There were, indeed, some Populists who agreed with Chernyshevskii on this
point. More important, however, was his second thesis, which separated him
from all other Populists. Chernyshevskii accepted the perspective of "rapid
growth" in Russia of European, i.e., capitalist, forms of large-scale industry

[4] *Ibid.,* XIII (1919), 136.
[5] "Studien Haxthausena," *Sovremennik,* May 1857, in *Izbrannye ekonomicheskie
proizvedeniia* (Moscow, 1948), I, 202.

and rail transportation, and he even foresaw the introduction of large-scale mechanized production in agriculture. He went on to the inference that the peasant commune simply created favorable conditions for such a development in agriculture in noncapitalist forms.[6] He returned to this theme more than once: "Rapid development of mechanical and other means for cultivating and improving the land" will permit the peasant commune to offer the peasantry, "in thirty or twenty-five years, an extraordinary opportunity to form agricultural coöperatives for cultivating the land."[7] Chernyshevskii also applied the idea of producers' coöperatives ("associations") to large-scale industry, and, in accordance with the doctrine popular in European socialist circles at the time, viewed the "associations" as means for the elimination of capitalism. This, however, did not square with the Populist (socialist and nonsocialist) ideas of noncapitalist development for Russia.

It is not surprising, therefore, that doubts were occasionally expressed whether Chernyshevskii was to be considered a Populist. And Plekhanov, after some vacillation, arrived at the conclusion that Chernyshevskii "was never a Populist."[8]

This is largely a question of terminology. There is no doubt that Chernyshevskii, more than anyone else in Russia up to the 1880's, helped spread the idea that the peasant commune would make possible a noncapitalist development of Russian agriculture and would clear the ground for a noncapitalist development of Russian industry. In addition, Chernyshevskii put special emphasis on the thesis that the technological advances that had occurred in Western industry and agriculture could be adopted by a Russia that had taken the road of noncapitalistic development; these advances would facilitate that development.[9]

A considerable body of statistical and other data about Russian agriculture, and the Russian national economy in general, had accumulated by the early 1880's, and the question of a capitalist or noncapitalist development of Russia then assumed another form. Vasilii P. Vorontsov, a prolific writer who gained wide fame under the signature V. V., emerged as the most authoritative Populist spokesman. Already, in his first published book, *The Destinies of Capitalism in Russia* (1882), he unequivocally defended the doctrine that the development of capitalism is "impossible" in Russia: "The characteristics of the present historical situation are such that Russia cannot advance to the higher stages of industrial development along the capitalist route. All measures that would facilitate such an advance can only destroy

[6] *Ibid.*, p. 209.
[7] "Otvet na zamechanie g. Provintsiala," *Sovremennik*, March 1858, in *Izbrannye*, I, 489.
[8] G. V. Plekhanov, *N. G. Chernyshevskii* (St. Petersburg, 1910), p. 309.
[9] Chernyshevskii developed this thesis in great detail in his article "Kritika filosofskikh predubezhdenii protiv obshchinnago vladeniia," *Sovremennik*, December 1858, in *Izbrannye*, I, 689–734.

the people's welfare; they cannot lead to organization of production." [10] Vorontsov vigorously defended the proposition that a noncapitalist development not only in agriculture, but also in industry was possible and necessary in Russia. He expounded this doctrine with extreme clarity — and naïveté — in a book which he published in the mid-1890's:

> The geographic position of Russia is such that our agricultural season lasts between four and eight months, and between four and six months in a large part of the country. Therefore the vast majority of our agricultural working population cannot devote more than between four and six months of the year to work on the land. But in the present state of the Russian economy, and at the level which the economy can attain in the not-too-distant future, the productivity of agricultural labor does not make it possible for the worker on the land, be he hired hand or owner, to make enough, at a half-year's work, to support his family for a whole year, and still supply the state with the means for the satisfaction of its evergrowing requirements. This means that it is necessary for the Russian worker to have an industrial occupation in addition to his vocational occupation. This presupposes a form of industrial organization that satisfies conditions which are natural to our fatherland; this is one of the inevitable controlling factors in economic life! If the conditions that are imposed upon our country by the inflexible laws of nature are such that the Russian tiller of the soil must also be an industrial worker — i.e., if a sharp division between agriculture and industry is impossible — then the great growth of the urban population at the expense of the rural, which distinguishes social conditions in Western Europe, is also impossible.
>
> A form of industrial organization that runs the factory half the year, and permits it to stand idle the other half, does not permit the manufacture of a product at the lowest technologically possible cost. If the organization of production is capitalistic, then, such a product cannot compete in distant markets — especially in world markets — with goods from other lands. Such competition is entirely possible, however, if the organization of production is noncapitalistic, since, if the market price gives the worker an opportunity to obtain the usual, or even a diminished wage, even without any profit for the enterprise, it is a direct gain for him, as he would have to be content with his income from farming if it were not for this industrial work. This defines the second feature which the Russian economy derives from the operation of economic laws: enterprises that do not pursue profits must play an especially important part. These must be publicly owned enterprises (state and zemstvo plants and factories) and coöperatives.[11]

According to Vorontsov, this signifies "the development of independent people's and public (noncapitalist) production on the basis of a union of agricultural and industrial work." [12]

Vorontsov's fundamental argument against the possibility of a capitalistic development in Russia was the extreme narrowness of the country's domestic markets and its inability to secure a significant position in foreign markets that were already controlled by more developed Western nations. This same line of argument lay at the basis of the most important theoretical work of

[10] V. V., *Sud'by kapitalizma v Rossii* (St. Petersburg, 1882), pp. 4–5.
[11] V. V., *Ocherki teoreticheskoi ekonomiki* (St. Petersburg, 1895), pp. 309–310.
[12] *Ibid.*, p. 312.

all Populist literature, Nikolai F. Daniel'son's famous *Essays on Our National Economy after the Emancipation of the Serfs* (St. Petersburg, 1893).[13] Daniel'son, unlike Vorontsov, emphasized the futility, rather than the impossibility, of a capitalist development in Russia. On the basis of a large body of data, Daniel'son traces, in his book, the spread of "artificially superimposed" capitalism in Russian agriculture and industry. "Capitalism takes more in its grasp each day, but at the same time the number of employed workers and their means of livelihood diminish," the domestic market contracts, and "the entire national economy" comes to "bankruptcy." "This is why it is as necessary for us to find a way out of this situation as it was to change the conditions of production after the Crimean War." [14] But which way out? Daniel'son answers:

Our historical past has left us the commune as a heritage which, under the pressure of capitalism and the conditions of production and circulation it has created, and because manufacturing is divorced from agriculture, is unable to supply its members with the means of livelihood. Thus, under existing conditions it is threatened with unavoidable destruction. At the same time, however, the commune is one of the basic material conditions of production, upon which the future structure of the national economy can be built. We do not have to wait until all of the peasants are deprived of their land, and replaced by a capitalist agriculture based upon the application of science to cultivation, as in the West . . . We must graft scientific agriculture and modern large-scale industry onto the commune, and at the same time give the commune a form that will make it an effective tool for the organization of large-scale industry and the transformation of the form of that industry from a capitalist to a public one. There is no other way for the organization of the economy: either growth or deterioration and death.[15]

III. MARX AND ENGELS ON WAYS OF ECONOMIC DEVELOPMENT OF RUSSIA

The Populist view of the possible role of the commune in the economic development of Russia encountered early opposition from the economists, often tied with official and "business circles," who took a positive view of the beginnings of capitalist development in Russia. The influence of this procapitalist temper upon Russian public opinion was very limited, however, and the Populist view was definitely dominant right up to the 1880's, at which time an opposition to this view developed in the "Left" camp of the intellectuals. This was the opposition that advanced the banner of Marxism against Populism.

Marx and Engels had long since learned to read Russian. They followed the Russian economic literature carefully, and maintained personal contact

---

[13] Daniel'son's book appeared in Russian under the pseudonym Nikolai —on, *Ocherki nashego poreformennago obshchestvennago khoziaistva* (St. Petersburg, 1893). The book appeared under his full name in a two-volume German translation (Munich, 1899) and in a French translation (Paris, 1902).

[14] Nikolai —on, *Ocherki*, p. 343.

[15] *Ibid.*, p. 344.

with a number of Russian writers, scholars, and leaders. Their influence was great among Russian intellectuals (this included the country's university professors to a considerable extent). *Capital* had been translated into Russian as early as the end of the 1860's, and was studied diligently. However — astonishing as it may seem — Marx and Engels not only did not further a reorientation of the attitude of Russia's progressive intellectuals toward the commune from the Populist conception to one known later as Marxist, but actually somewhat opposed such reorientation.

Marx's and Engels' view on the question of the Russian peasant commune did not form at once. Both at first exhibited no great interest and, at bottom, showed a negative attitude. In a letter to Marx, dated March 18, 1852, Engels speaks disdainfully of the "old Pan-Slavist dodge, converting the ancient Slavic communal property into communism, and portraying the Russian peasants as born communists." [16] Both remained in this frame of mind for a long time; this is seen in Marx's letters to Engels, dated as late as March 14 and November 7, 1868.[17] This frame of mind changed only at the very end of the 1860's. Marx had begun at that time to study Russian (Engels had begun to study the language as early as 1851), became acquainted with Chernyshevskii's works, and developed a great interest in them.

In a letter dated January 7, 1871, Elizaveta D. Tomanovskaia (a Russian socialist who participated in the Paris Commune subsequently) wrote Marx (whom she had met in London) mentioning that Marx "perceived an alternative view on the destinies of the peasant commune in Russia." [18] No inkling of these "alternative" views can be found in Marx's letters and writings, however. In a letter to Daniel'son, who translated *Capital* into Russian, Marx writes (in December 1872) that he will treat the role of the Russian peasant commune in detail in the second volume of *Capital*.[19] Marx asks Daniel'son, in a letter dated March 22, 1873, about the scholarly polemics in the Russian literature concerning the origins of the commune; Marx's sympathies for the commune are expressed quite clearly in this letter.[20] However, it is only in Engels' article in the *Volksstaat* (April 1875)[21] and in Marx's letter to the editors of *Otechestvennye zapiski* (November 1877)[22] that their views of the question are formulated precisely and deliberately. Engels' article and Marx's letter were reprinted more than once, and played a role in Russian discussions about the com-

---

[16] Karl Marx and Friedrich Engels, *Sochineniia*, XXI (Moscow, 1929), 342.

[17] *Ibid.*, XXIV (Moscow, 1931), 28, 127–128.

[18] *Perepiska K. Marksa i F. Engel'sa s russkimi politicheskimi deiateliami*, 2nd ed. (Moscow, 1951), p. 47.

[19] *Ibid.*, p. 87.

[20] *Ibid.*, p. 93.

[21] *Ibid.*, pp. 195–205.

[22] *Ibid.*, pp. 220–223.

mune. These and subsequent pronouncements by Marx and Engels show, however, that they differed in their views of the possible development of the commune (this, it seems, has never been noted before in the literature). Thus, I shall quit the chronological order and consider Marx's letter and subsequent pronouncements first; I shall consider Engels' afterward.

Marx wrote his letter in connection with a debate that had been going forward in the Russian press between Nikolai K. Mikhailovskii and Iurii G. Zhukovskii. In his letter, Marx considers "the efforts of the Russians to find for their country a way of development different from the way chosen and followed by Western Europe," and emphasizes — without mentioning names — that he "rejects" the views of "the essayist and Pan-Slavist" (his polemical description of Herzen) and "shares" those of "the great Russian scientist and critic" (this manifestly points to Chernyshevskii). Marx did not confine himself to an expression of his solidarity with Chernyshevskii, however, and expressed his view in positive terms:

> In order to form a well-grounded judgment on Russia's economic development, I studied the Russian language, and, over a number of years, I followed official and other publications that dealt with this question. I arrived at the following conclusion: If Russia continues along the road which she has followed since 1861, she will forego the finest opportunity that history has ever placed before a nation, and will undergo all of the fateful misfortunes of capitalist development.

This letter, which gives a positive answer to the question of the commune as a means by which Russia could avoid the line of development "which Western Europe chose and follows," does not indicate, however, how the commune could accomplish this. Marx was still seeking a solution of this problem. In a letter of March 8, 1881 to Vera Zasulich, who wrote to him from Geneva and asked whether the Russian commune was able to "develop in a socialist direction — i.e., gradually to organize the production and distribution of its products on a collectivist basis," or whether Russian socialists and revolutionists must reconcile themselves to the prospects of a Western pattern of capitalist development in Russia,[23] Marx emphasized that the analysis of capitalist development, which he presented in *Capital*, cannot be applied directly to Russia:

> In the process under way in the West [the squeezing-out of the small land-holder], we deal with a transformation of one form of private property into another. In the case of the Russian peasant, however, it would be necessary to transform communal property into private property.
>
> The analysis presented in *Capital*, therefore, gives no special arguments for or against the peasant commune's vitality, but investigations which I have carried out, on the basis of materials taken from primary sources, have convinced me that the commune constitutes the point of support of a social regeneration of Russia. However, before it can begin to act in this way, the poisonous influences that

[23] *Ibid.*, pp. 299–300.

attack it from all sides must be eliminated, and its normal, free development insured.[24]

But how can these "poisonous influences . . . be eliminated," and how is the "normal, free development [of the commune] insured"? This remained unclear. And this was no accident. Marx treated his letter to Zasulich as a very serious matter. Many years later, four drafts (very lengthy in parts) of this letter were found among his papers.[25] These drafts show how much Marx struggled with the problem which Zasulich put to him. In the end, he gave up his attempt to develop his own viewpoint in detail, and limited himself to a short letter to Zasulich. His ideas were developed in much greater detail in the subsequently discovered drafts, however:

> Let us forget, for a moment, the calamities that oppress the Russian commune; let us look only at the commune's possible evolution. It holds a completely unique position, without precedent in history. In all of Europe, only the [Russian] commune constitutes the dominant, organic form of the rural life of a great empire. Communal ownership of the land gives it a natural basis for collective appropriation, and the historical environment — the existence of capitalist production — gives the commune the ready-made material conditions for a coöperative economy organized on a broad basis. The commune, therefore, can utilize all of the capitalist system's positive achievements, without going through the Caudine Forks of capitalism. With the aid of machines, for which the contours of Russian soil are so well suited, the commune can replace small-scale farming by a more complex agriculture. After it is brought into a normal condition, it can become, in its present form, the *direct point of departure* for the economic system toward which modern society strives.[26]

But what is needed if the commune is to be "brought into a normal condition"? Marx gives only a very general answer:

> A Russian revolution is required, if the Russian commune is to be saved . . . If the revolution occurs in time to insure the free development of the commune, the latter can become a force for the regeneration of Russian life, an element of advantage compared with the nations enslaved by the capitalist system.[27]

Then the economic and technological experience accumulated by the West will be utilized for the benefit of the Russian economy:

> If Russia were isolated from the world it would have to work out by its own forces the economic advances which Western Europe has achieved only by passing through a long series of evolutions from the time of its primitive communities

---

[24] *Ibid.*, pp. 300–301.

[25] These drafts were first published, with an introduction by David B. Riazanov (pseud.), in Vol. I of the *Arkhiv K. Marksa i F. Engel'sa* (Moscow, 1924), pp. 265–286, and again in Vol. XXVII (Moscow, 1935), of Marx and Engels, *Sochineniia*, pp. 677–697. A composite letter was put together, from all the drafts, by Paul W. Blackstock and Bert F. Hoselitz in *The Russian Menace to Europe*, by Karl Marx and Friedrich Engels (Glencoe, Ill., 1952), pp. 218–226.

[26] From the third draft, *Arkhiv*, p. 285.

[27] From the first draft, *Arkhiv*, p. 279.

. . . But . . . Russia is the only country in Europe in which communal property on land has been preserved on a vast nation-wide scale, and at the same time Russia is living in a certain historical environment, it is a contemporary of the superior culture of today, it is tied to a world market in which capitalist production prevails.

By appropriating the positive results of this mode of production, it secures the opportunity to develop and improve the still archaic form of its village community, instead of destroying it.[28]

It is quite remarkable that neither in Marx's letter to Zasulich nor in any of the four preliminary drafts is there any trace of the idea that the salvation of the Russian commune is possible only if the Russian revolution is preceded by a European socialist revolution, or if the Russian revolution, which is to save the commune, is answered immediately by revolutions in the West. Indeed, this idea was expressed once over Marx's signature, in the preface to the Russian edition of the *Communist Manifesto:* he and Engels signed this preface on January 21, 1882: [29]

In Russia, alongside a feverishly rapid development of capitalist knavery, and a just emerging bourgeois agriculture, we find more than half the land owned communally by the peasants. The question arises: can the Russian peasant commune — this, to be sure, is a widely decomposed form of primitive communal ownership of the land — evolve directly to a higher form — to communist common property — or does it have to pass through the process of decomposition through which it passes in the historic development of the West?

The only possible answer to this, at the present time, is the following: If the Russian revolution is a signal for proletarian revolution in the West, so that the two can supplement each other, then modern Russian communal ownership can serve as a point of departure for a communist development.

We shall return to this joint statement by Marx and Engels, written just a little more than a year before Marx's death, but we must first consider Engels' article of 1875 which was mentioned above. In this article, Engels takes a rather dark view of the state of the commune in Russia and considers its final decay inevitable, if it is not saved in time by socialist revolution in the West:

Communal property, in Russia, outlived its flowering long ago, and, from all appearances, is on the road to its decomposition. Nevertheless, one cannot deny the existence of the possibility of converting this social form into a higher one . . . But this can happen only if, before the final decay of this communal ownership, there occurs, in Western Europe, a victorious proletarian revolution that will

---

[28] From the second draft, *Arkhiv*, p. 280.

[29] This preface was signed by Marx and Engels, but a letter from Engels to Daniel'son, dated February 20, 1893 (*Perepiska*, p. 174), gave reason for thinking that it was written by Marx alone. Recently, however, a manuscript of this preface has been published, written entirely by Engels, with minor corrections in Marx's hand. See Blackstock and Hoselitz, *Russian Menace*, p. 282. The quotation is from the Russian edition of the *Manifesto* (Moscow, 1938), p. 39.

offer the Russian peasantry the necessary conditions for such a transition — specifically, the material means which the peasantry will need in order to carry through the necessary overthrow in all parts of its system of agriculture.[30]

Engels held fast to the idea that the salvation of the commune, and its transformation into a point of departure for a noncapitalistic development of Russia, is possible only if it accompanies a socialist revolution in the West. It is true that Engels' ideas are somewhat altered in the above-quoted preface to the 1882 Russian edition of the *Communist Manifesto:* it is free of a certain utilitarian line of argument (the "material means" which the socialist West will place at Russia's disposal), and from any indication that the revolution in the West must precede the revolution in Russia. On the contrary, the revolution in Russia must serve as "a signal for proletarian revolution in the West." Engels, actually the author of the preface (see note 29), probably introduced this change in order to mitigate his differences with Marx on this question. But he continued to hold to the point of view he had formulated in 1875. Specifically, in his correspondence with Daniel'son, he returns more than once (at the beginning of the 1890's) to Marx's letter to the editors of *Otechestvennye zapiski*,[31] extending its meaning in the direction of his own (Engels') conception:

There is no doubt but that the commune and to a certain extent the *artel* contain within themselves seeds which, under certain conditions, could develop and save Russia from the tortures of the capitalist system. I endorse completely the letter of our author [i.e., Marx] on Zhukovskii's article. But, in his opinion and mine, the first necessary condition for this is a *shock from without* — a revolution in the economy of Western Europe, and the destruction of the capitalist system in those countries in which it arose. [In Marx's letter, actually, this "condition" does not appear.] Our author, in his preface to the old *Manifesto* with which you are familiar, in January 1882 answered the question whether the Russian commune can serve as a point of departure for a new, higher social development, in the following manner: If the revolution in the economic system in Russia coincides with the revolution in the economic system in the West [this "coincides" was not in the preface of 1882; the Russian revolution was to serve "as a signal for proletarian revolution in the West"] so that the two will supplement each other, modern Russian ownership of the land will be able to become a point of departure for a new social development.[32]

This idea of a "shock from without" was particularly dear to Engels in his thinking about possible ways of Russian development. In 1894, one year before his death, Engels published a small volume of his old *Volksstaat* articles, which had, as its main item, the above-quoted article of 1875, to which, however, Engels wrote a long "Postscript." [33] In this "Postscript,"

[30] *Perepiska,* p. 204.
[31] Engels' letters to Daniel'son, March 15 and June 18, 1892, and February 24 and October 17, 1893 (*Perepiska,* pp. 154, 163, 173–174, and 178).
[32] *Ibid.,* p. 178.
[33] *Ibid.,* pp. 285–297.

on the basis of data on the latest development, Engels formulated anew his views on the commune and its possible role in Russia and developed in detail the idea of the "shock from without":

> The Russian commune has existed for centuries without ever having produced any striving to develop, out of itself, a higher form of social property; just as it was with the German mark, the Celtic clan, the Indian and other communities with primitive-communist orders . . . Thus, if the question can be raised at all whether a different and better fate awaits the Russian commune, it is because the reason for this is not rooted in the commune itself, but solely because it has preserved, in one of the European nations, a certain vital energy until such a time, when, in Western Europe, not only commodity production in general, but even its highest and final form, capitalist production, has fallen into contradiction to the productive forces that it itself has created . . . It follows from this, already, that the initiative in such a transformation of the Russian commune must come not from the commune itself, but exclusively from the industrial proletariat of the West. The victory of the West-European proletariat over the bourgeoisie and, associated with this, the replacement of capitalist production by production that is directed by society — this is the necessary prerequisite condition for raising the Russian commune to such a level of development.[34]

Only "the example and active support of the West," only the example of "how it is done" could open vistas of noncapitalist development before the Russian commune.[35] Engels again refers to Marx's letter of 1877. But,

> in the course of the seventeen years that have elapsed since the time when Marx wrote his letter, both capitalism and the decomposition of the commune have made enormous progress in Russia. How do things stand now, in 1894? . . . In a short time, all of the foundations of the capitalist mode of production have been laid in Russia. But at the same time the axe has been applied to the roots of the Russian peasant commune. Now it is useless to mourn the fact.[36]

When we attempt to characterize Marx's and Engels' view of the commune and the possibility of a noncapitalist development in Russia, and use the terminology that finally crystallized in Russia during the last decade of the century, we cannot avoid the conclusion that Marx took his stand on the Populist conception — basically, on the version which Chernyshevskii had developed. But Engels "accepted," rather than shared, this position. In the "Postscript" of 1894, he attempted to explain retrospectively his — and also Marx's — position:

> The belief in the miraculous power of the peasant commune, from the depths of which there could and would come a social regeneration — a belief from which, as we saw, not even Chernyshevskii was free — served its purpose in raising the spirits and the energies of the heroic Russian fighters. These people, of whom there were only a few hundred, but who, by their selflessness and their courage brought tsarist absolutism to the point where it already had to think about the

[34] *Ibid.*, pp. 288–289.
[35] *Ibid.*, p. 291.
[36] *Ibid.*, pp. 294–295.

possibilities and conditions of capitulation — we will not haul such people into court because they regarded the Russian people as the chosen people of the revolution. But this does not force us to share their illusions. The time of chosen people is forever past.[37]

IV. RUSSIAN MARXISM ON CAPITALIST DEVELOPMENT IN RUSSIA

By the time Engels published his "Postscript," Russian Marxism had long since come forward publicly with a detailed characterization of the economic development of Russia as capitalistic. A wealth of data on the penetration of capitalist relationships, not only into industry, but into agriculture as well; on the involvement of a very large part of the peasantry in commodity production and capitalist exploitation; on the conversion of peasant *kustar* industry into a capitalist form of home industry, etc. were published during the 1870's and 1880's by zemstvo statisticians for the most part sympathetic to Populism. A great literature (chiefly in journals) on the basis of these materials emerged, and in part this literature gave a very realistic description of the formation and strengthening of capitalist relationships in Russia. But, ultimately, this description pointed to a somewhat unexpected conclusion about the possibility and necessity of avoiding a capitalist development and of returning to a strengthening and development of "people's production," that is, fundamentally returning from a commodity to a natural economy.

The opposition to this view, from the comparatively few advocates of capitalism, the advocates of economic liberalism (they were called "Manchesterians" in Russia), and the advocates of government interference and protectionism in economics, did not have any great influence on the broad currents of public opinion, in which more or less diffuse Populist views continued to dominate. Only when the opposition to Populism emerged in the Left camp, not in the name of capitalism and capitalist interests, but in the name of the broad masses of the people and — more remotely — in the name of the abolition of capitalism, did the question of capitalist or noncapitalist ways of development for Russia become (for almost two decades) a central issue.

The pioneer in this new development was the Emancipation of Labor Group, which was formed in Switzerland in 1883 and which consisted of a few former Populists who now entered the struggle against Populist illusions on the basis of the general analysis of capitalism elaborated in Marx's works. In 1884 the Group published its first major work, devoted to the struggle against the Populist conception of the economic development of Russia and to formulation of the Marxist conception of this development. This was George V. Plekhanov's *Nashi raznoglasiia* (Our Differences).

The question whether Russia would move along the road of capitalist

---

[37] *Ibid.*, p. 296.

development was not involved, wrote Plekhanov; Russia already was moving along this road. "At least with respect to industry . . . one should already be man enough to say to oneself, not merely that we shall have capitalism in the near future, but that we have capitalism at the present time." [38] But capitalism had also penetrated very deeply into the agricultural economy and the life of the rural population in general. Plekhanov gives a detailed presentation of facts that testify to the rapidly developing process of disintegration of the commune, to the profound differentiation of the peasantry within the commune, to the subordination of the peasant *kustar* industry to capitalism. Challenging Vorontsov, he shows that the progressing displacement of the natural economy by a commodity economy creates a domestic market for the products of capitalist industry. And the attempts by Russian capitalism to secure for itself a position in foreign markets — and even more, the prospects of securing such a position — are far from hopeless, especially in Asia. But while Marxists espouse this conception, they do not, by any means, become apologists for capitalism, and do not become "knights of primitive accumulation," as the Populists called them in debate.[39] Marxists see their role quite differently, according to Plekhanov. Their problem is to "organize a real rebuff to capitalist exploitation," [40] a rebuff on the basis of capitalism, and in the name of overcoming capitalism in the future. And this rebuff will be all the more successful, and capitalism will be overcome all the earlier, the more rapidly capitalism develops. It is here that we find the winged phrase, repeated more than once during those years by Plekhanov and other Marxists: "We suffer not only from the development of capitalism, but also from the scarcity of that development." This line of argument was realistic and logically flawless, but — for opponents of capitalism — psychologically contradictory. This contradiction was somehow softened by the idea, which was then dominant in European Marxist circles, of the nearness of the downfall of capitalism.

Our capitalism will wither before it can blossom definitely [wrote Plekhanov]. This is guaranteed us by the powerful influence of international relations. But the fact that the cause of capitalism goes forward, nevertheless, to a more or less complete triumph — there is also no doubt of this. Neither groundless denials of existing facts, nor mournful lamentations on the subject of the disintegration of the old, "secular" forms of people's life — nothing will stop the nation that has "stepped in the path of the natural law of its development." [41]

The young Russian Marxists, entering the arena with this line of argument, swam against the current, of course. Naturally, they sought moral support from Engels (Marx was no longer alive). But they did not obtain this support. In the middle of February 1885, Plekhanov sent Engels a

[38] G. V. Plekhanov, *Nashi raznoglasiia* (Moscow, 1948), pp. 252–253.

[39] *Ibid.*, pp. 106–107, 373.

[40] *Ibid.*, pp. 374, 380.

[41] *Ibid.*, p. 380.

copy of the recently published *Our Differences,* and Vera Zasulich wrote to Engels, simultaneously, and asked him to express an opinion about the book, which, she wrote, "will call forth a whole storm against our little Group." [42] Engels answered in a little over two months,[43] but, basically, declined to comment on the book (he had read only some sixty pages): "I am proud," he wrote, "that there exists a party among the Russian youth which, sincerely and without reservation, has acknowledged Marx's great economic and historical theories and which has broken decisively with all of the anarchist and somehow Slavophile traditions of its predecessors. Marx himself would have been proud of this, if he had lived a little longer." But, "I am too little acquainted with the present situation in Russia to have the audacity to be a competent judge of specific questions of the tactics that must be adopted there at this or that moment. Furthermore, the secret inner history of the Russian revolutionary party, especially in recent years, is almost entirely unknown to me. My friends in the People's Will camp never told me about it." By this not unintentional pointing to "my friends in the People's Will camp," and the reduction of the issue to "specific questions of the tactics," Engels discreetly emphasized his unwillingness to be drawn into this debate, in which his sympathies were, to some extent, on the side of the Populists. This impression is strengthened by all of the rest of the letter, where Engels expresses the conviction that the revolution in Russia "can break out any day." "This is one of the exceptional cases in which a handful of people can *make* a revolution — in other words, with one small shock to let the entire system collapse . . ." This old People's Will line of argument, in April of 1885, at the time of the complete collapse of the People's Will movement, could only have a very depressing effect upon the Emancipation of Labor Group. Zasulich never asked Engels about Plekhanov's book again, and Engels never expressed his opinion of it.[44]

The defense of the Marxist conception of the economic development of Russia in the legal Russian press remained impossible for almost another decade. The Populists actually enjoyed a monopoly of the legality in their debate with the Marxists. Only during the summer of 1894 did there appear, legally, the first major work devoted to a critical analysis of the Populist conception and to a defense of the Marxist conception of the ways of the economic development of Russia. This was the *Critical Observations on the Prospects of Russia's Economic Development* by Peter B. Struve.[45]

[42] *Perepiska,* p. 308.

[43] *Ibid.,* pp. 308–311.

[44] It is a curious fact that official Soviet doctrine attempts to establish Engels' complete agreement with Plekhanov's evaluation of Russia's development on the basis of just this letter to Zasulich. Cf. Professor V. M. Shtein, *Ocherki razvitiia obshchestvenno-ekonomicheskoi mysli XIX–XX vekov* (Leningrad, 1948), pp. 239–240.

[45] P. B. Struve, *Kriticheskie zametki k voprosu ob ekonomicheskom razvitii Rossii* (St. Petersburg, 1894). At the same time there appeared illegally, in St. Petersburg, Lenin's first major work, *Chto takoe "druz'ia naroda" i kak oni voiuiut protiv sotsial-*

What distinguished Struve's conception — not so much doctrinally as emotionally — from the defenses of Marxism by his predecessors was his great emphasis on the positive — not only economic, but also cultural — role of capitalism. Here are "some fundamental conclusions" of Struve:

1. The development of an exchange economy, of capitalism in the broad sense of the word, a specific case and consequence of which is the development of large-scale centralized production, or capitalism in the narrow sense of the word, has objectively a tremendous economic and cultural significance.
2. The natural economy is displaced by the exchange economy not only because such a transition is useful for certain classes of society, but directly by virtue of its own economic and cultural failure.

. . . .

10. Commodity production is a mighty cultural factor. Once a country has taken the road of its development, its entire cultural, political, and economic progress depends upon further successes along this road. On the other hand, every step forward in the cultural and political sphere can only contribute to the development and triumph of capitalism.

. . . .

18. The cultural progress of Russia is connected intimately with the social division of labor, i.e., with the development of capitalism.

At the same time, Struve carefully notes that capitalism itself clears the ground for a transition to socialism:

11. Capitalism, having created massive — in other words, socialized — production, cannot compromise with disorderly, puerile, individualistic distribution and consumption. Thus capitalism objectively develops principles that deny its private economy basis.
12. The external circumstances in which modern industry places the working masses develop in them a feeling of activity, a political sense, an ability to act collectively, that prepares them for the role which, by virtue of the objective march of the material process, they are destined to play in the evolution of the capitalist system.[46]

The final paragraphs of the book are a direct challenge to Populism:

Sympathy with the working masses of the people is not a monopoly of the Populists, and we also feel a deep compassion for the destitute martyr-folk. But the picture of its destitution shows its cultural helplessness best of all. On this ground, terrible to say, feudalism is less of a Utopia than the socialization of labor.

Let us admit our lack of culture and undergo the capitalist schooling.[47]

---

demokratov? (*Sochineniia*, 4th ed., I [Moscow, 1941], 111–113), which dealt with very much the same subject. This work, which was not printed but mimeographed, and was issued in a very small edition, did not have any noticeable effect on public opinion in Russia, and was lost and forgotten altogether. It was "discovered" again when Lenin already stood at the head of the Soviet government.

[46] *Kriticheskie zametki,* pp. 282–285.
[47] *Ibid.*, p. 288.

Struve's book raised a storm of indignation in the Populist camp. Daniel'son (Nikolai —on) replied with a long article entitled "Apologetics of the Power of Money, as a Sign of the Times," [48] in which he openly called Struve "an ideologue of plutocracy." [49] Other Populists wrote in the same spirit. But Struve's book also got a critical reception in the Marxist camp.

It was Lenin who reacted critically to Struve's book. His essay "Ekonomicheskoe soderzhanie narodnichestva i kritika ego v knige g. Struve" (The Economic Content of Populism, and Its Criticism in Mr. Struve's Book) was printed — under the name of K. Tulin — in the symposium *Materialy k kharakteristike nashego khoziaistvennago razvitiia* (Materials on the Characteristics of Our Economic Development), together with essays by Struve himself, Plekhanov (under a pseudonym, of course), and others, in the spring of 1895. The fundamental criticism that Lenin levels against the author of the *Critical Observations* is that he pays insufficient attention to the social antagonisms involved in capitalist development. Hence Struve's extreme "objectivism," which cannot satisfy "a materialist" (i.e., a Marxist). In order to understand Lenin's argument correctly, one must take into consideration the somewhat artificial nature of his terminology (perhaps an adaptation to conditions of limited legality). "The fundamental defect of his [Struve's] book" lies in its "objectivism":

The objectivist speaks of the necessity of a given historical process; the materialist states precisely a given socioeconomic formation and the antagonistic relations to which it gives birth. The objectivist, in proving the necessity of a given series of facts, always risks adopting the viewpoint of an apologist for these facts; the materialist discovers the class contradictions, and in this way determines his own viewpoint. The objectivist speaks of irresistible historical tendencies; the materialist speaks of the class that "manages" a given economic order, and creates certain forms of resistance by other classes. Thus, on the one hand, the materialist is more consistent than the objectivist, and pushes his objectivity deeper and more fully. He does not limit himself to indicating the necessity of a process, but he clarifies the specific socioeconomic formation that gives this process its content, and *specifically which class* determines this necessity. [50]

Later, in 1907, when Lenin reissued this essay, he gave it a second, subsidiary title: "Otrazhenie marksizma v burzhuaznoi literature" (Reflections of Marxism in Bourgeois Literature). [51] In this way, Lenin wanted to emphasize his irreconcilable and fundamental hostility to Struve's entire conception. These divergences were not considered so sharp in the middle 1890's, however. These were divergencies between men of the same outlook, not between people fundamentally opposed to each other. And Lenin himself

[48] Nikolai —on, "Apologiia vlasti deneg kak znamenie vremeni," *Russkoe Bogatstvo* (January 1895), pp. 155–185; (February 1895), pp. 1–34.

[49] *Ibid.* (January 1895), p. 157.

[50] Lenin, *Sochineniia*, I, 315–484.

[51] *Ibid.*, p. 380.

read his essay, in manuscript, to Struve at the latter's home[52] — this took several evenings — and Struve (together with Alexander N. Potresov) was responsible for printing the symposium in which Tulin's essay appeared.[53]

From this root, it is true, there began to grow the divergences between "legal Marxism" (led by Struve and Mikhail I. Tugan-Baranovskii) and Marxism in general which were established clearly only at the turn of the century. But these were divergences chiefly over political inferences drawn from the analysis of economic development, and over the philosophical foundations of the Marxist *Weltanschauung*. They hardly touched upon the question of the ways of economic development of Russia. And Marxists of all shades continued to work together in a very friendly fashion until the end of the 1890's. Specifically, the Social Democratic Party, which was founded in 1898 — illegally, of course — entrusted Struve with the writing of the Party platform ("Manifesto"), and Struve, together with Tugan-Baranovskii, edited Marxist journals published for a short time legally (*Novoe Slovo* in 1897, and *Nachalo*, in 1899) to which all of the foremost literary representatives of Russian Marxism contributed in a spirit of solidarity (under various pseudonyms, of course).

The debate with the Populists on the ways of economic development of Russia continued, in the meantime, and revolved mainly around four issues. They are closely interconnected, but they had better be distinguished, for the sake of clarity of presentation. There are first two general questions: (1) Is not Russian capitalism an "artificial" growth on the economic body of the nation, created by mistaken government policy, since the Peasant Reform of 1861? (2) Is it not possible to put Russia back on the road of "people's production"? And there are two specific questions, with one of which we are already familiar: (3) Do Russia's limited domestic market and the inaccessibility of foreign markets constitute an insurmountable obstacle to the development of capitalism in Russia? (4) Is the development of capitalism in Russia accompained by a considerable increase in the number of workers employed in capitalist industry, or is the impoverishment of the peasantry accompanied only by a tremendous (hidden) unemployment? A great deal of light was thrown upon these questions, from the Marxist side, in two books by Plekhanov, *K voprosu o razvitii monisticheskago vzgliada na istoriiu* (On the Question of Developing a Monistic View of History; St. Petersburg, 1895), and *Obosnovanie narodnichestva v trudakh g-na Vorontsova* (The Argumentation of Populism in the Works of Mr. Vorontsov; St. Petersburg, 1896), the first of which appeared under the pseudonym N. Beltov, and the second under the pseudonym A. Volgin, by Tugan-Baranovskii's *Russkaia fabrika v proshlom i nastoiashchem* (Russian

---

[52] Peter B. Struve, "My Contacts and Conflicts with Lenin," *Slavonic and East European Review* (April 1934), p. 591.

[53] Lenin, *Sochineniia*, I, 499, n. 78.

Factory in Past and Present, St. Petersburg, 1898), and by Lenin's *Razvitie kapitalizma v Rossii* (Development of Capitalism in Russia; St. Petersburg, 1899), under the pseudonym of Vladimir Il'in, and by a great number of journal articles. From the Populists, for whom much greater opportunities were open to defend their viewpoint in the periodicals, there came, chiefly, a great number of journal articles, and Vorontsov's above-quoted book, *Ocherki teoreticheskoi ekonomiki* (Essays in Theoretical Economics, 1895).

The discussions of the "artificiality" of Russian capitalism, which occupied a prominent place in the early Populist literature, gradually petered out during the 1890's. The discussion lost the last shadow of pertinence after the publication of Tugan-Baranovskii's *Russian Factory*. With it the question of Russia's ability to return to "people's production" should disappear. But this question had evolved into another, more general question in the meantime — the question of the limits of historical laws, or, to use the language of the debates of the time, the question of the "subjective factor" in history. It is mainly to this question — adapted to the debate over the ways of development of Russia — that Plekhanov's two books were addressed, and the first of these, especially, influenced the spiritual development of an entire generation. During this period, without doubt, the course of the debate was concluded in favor of Marxism. Much later, in different historical circumstances, the question of the role of the "subjective factor" was raised again in Russia and in the West, in another concrete form: as the question of the limits of government interference in the course of economic development — and this, in essence, is our present-day question of the limits of economic planning. However, even in Russia this question arose outside any factual or ideological continuity with the development of Populism. And this was not accidental. The Utopian putting of the question, which was characteristic of Populism in the last quarter of the nineteenth century, could not stand up in the face of the undeniable facts of economic development, and could not influence the further development of Russian economic and sociological thought.

It is Lenin whose interest was mainly concentrated on the question of the market, as a problem of the development of Russian capitalism. In 1893 he began his work on this problem with the report, "Po povodu tak nazyvaemago voprosa o rynkakh" (On the So-Called Question of Markets).[54] This very question is the fundamental pivot of Lenin's *Development of Capitalism in Russia*, his most valuable scientific work. Lenin emphasized the significance of the problem of the market in the very title of his book, to which, in addition to the main title, *The Development of Capitalism in Russia*, he gave the subtitle, *The Process of Formation of a Domestic Market for Large-Scale Industry*. That the development of a domestic market is paramount for the development of capitalism in Russia, and that the foreign

[54] Lenin, *Sochineniia*, I, 59–108.

market can play only a secondary role in this development, was established firmly in Marxist literature from the appearance of Struve's *Critical Observations*.[55] After the publication of Lenin's book, the question of the market, as a problem of the development of capitalism, was basically solved for Russian economic science.

Only the exceptionally chaotic state of Russian industrial statistics can explain the fact that the growth of the number of workers employed in Russian industry could be disputed even in the second half of the 1890's. The thesis that the number of workers in Russian capitalist industry was not growing was first put forward by Vorontsov in his *Destinies of Capitalism in Russia* (1882),[56] and was strongly held as part of Populism's ideological inventory afterward. Even so well-grounded, deep-thinking, and careful an economist as Daniel'son accepted this thesis and wrote Engels repeatedly that "the number of factory workers [in Russia] is not increasing," [57] even that "the number of workers employed in modern [Russian] industry is decreasing steadily." [58] Daniel'son repeated the same assertion, even more emphatically, in the *Essays*.[59]

Plekhanov, in *Our Differences* (1884), had already attacked this view energetically with factual data,[60] and it was subjected to criticism, from the Marxist side, more than once after that. But nothing helped. When, in January 1898, Tugan-Baranovskii presented his paper, "Statistical Results of the Industrial Development of Russia," before the Imperial Free Economic Society, this paper called forth a controversy that occupied three evenings,[61] and the central issue about which the controversy revolved unexpectedly turned out to be the growth of the industrial proletariat; and almost all of the disputants — some in softened form — defended Vorontsov's old thesis. These were the last peals of the old thunder. The appearance a few months later of Tugan-Baranovskii's *Russian Factory*, the publication of the results of the population census of 1897, and — perhaps the most important — the increasingly obvious economic upswing in the 1890's and the early years

[55] Struve, *Kriticheskie zametki*, p. 284; Struve's fourteenth "fundamental conclusion" is: "The greater the territory and population of a given country, the less the country's need for foreign markets for its capitalistic development."

[56] V. V. (Vorontsov), *Sud'by kapitalizma*, pp. 26–31.

[57] Letter of December 18, 1889, *Perepiska*, p. 141.

[58] Letter of March 12, 1892, *Perepiska*, p. 157.

[59] *Ocherki*, pp. 334–335: "The expansion of capitalist production which, in our country, is based exclusively upon the demands of the domestic market, finds itself entirely dependent upon the purchasing power of the pauperizing sections of the population — pauperizing because capital has taken away their nonagricultural occupations, capitalized them, and, as a consequence of the increased productivity of labor, the amount of labor — the number of workers necessary for the manufacture of products that satisfy society's demands — unavoidably undergoes a sharp decrease."

[60] *Nashi raznoglasiia*, pp. 224ff.

[61] This paper, together with a stenographic report of the debates, was published by the Imperial Free Economic Society, in a separate volume, *Statisticheskie itogi promyshlennago razvitiia Rossii*, St. Petersburg, 1898.

of the new century, forced even the skeptics to quiet down gradually. The question of capitalist or noncapitalist development for Russia seemed to have been settled conclusively as the new century began.

This, it is true, did not mark the end of the disputes between Marxists and Populists. The disputes continued, but the issues changed, became more complex, and the boundaries between the Populist and the Marxist conceptions of the development of Russia became blurred in many areas. And when, after the Revolution of 1917, the question of a noncapitalist development for Russia again came to the fore, it was debated without any connection with the old disp te between Populists and Marxists, and the grouping of the disputants was entirely different. But an analysis of all this is beyond the scope of the present paper.

Chernov and Agrarian Socialism Before 1918

OLIVER H. RADKEY

Agrarian socialism in Russia went under the name of Populism. It is customary to distinguish between legal Populism, a milk-and-water philosophy seeking to propagate its ideas within the framework of the existing system, and revolutionary Populism, which stressed the deed as well as the word and was as hostile to the political as the social order. It is with this second or activist branch of the movement that the present study is concerned. There were two phases of revolutionary Populism, so different from each other that one observer would deny the name to the second phase, contending that it was rather the counterpart of revisionism in the West operating under an established trade name in Russia.[1] The first phase opened in the 1870's with the "into the people" movement and closed in frustration a few years later with the debacle that befell the *Narodnaia Volia*. For a generation the current, a mere trickle, disappeared underground, where it absorbed a new mineral content and, fed by the subterranean waters that were gradually dissolving the old Russian order, flowed to the surface once more in a stream of considerable size. The second phase began about 1900 with the formation of the Socialist Revolutionary Party (PSR). By 1906 the crystallization of its program had produced a double schism, the People's Socialists (*Narodnye Sotsialisty*) branching off on the Right and the Union of SR Maximalists on the Left, but since neither of these side currents ever attained much volume, to all practical intents and purposes agrarian socialism, Populism, and Social Revolutionism are after 1900 synonymous terms. The essential unity of Populism lasted until the war gave rise to another and more formidable schism, the Left Socialist Revolutionaries carrying away so much strength into their new party at the end of 1917 that the Bolsheviks were able to pick off the enemy in detail and lay hands on the class it had tried to defend.

Much has been written about the theory of Populism, more than is necessary, in the opinion of this investigator, for Populism was always more a state of mind than a systematic body of thought. The older Populism arose out of the ferment of the Alexandrian reforms, at a time when the ideals of

[1] N. Sukhanov (N. N. Gimmer), *Marksizm i Narodnichestvo* (n.p., n.d.; about 1915).

the French Revolution were growing cold in the West and socialism had come into vogue. The intellectuals who bore its standard were hospitable to the boldest conclusions of contemporary thought; they did not wish to be caught lagging behind the West, and so could only be socialists, and they saw, or wished to see, only the negative aspects of nineteenth-century capitalism. But in becoming socialists, these intellectuals were not content simply to import their ideology. Desiring both to spare their people the evils of the industrial revolution and to make a contribution of their own to the world movement for the emancipation of labor, they cast about for some other approach to socialism than through the portals of capitalist development. The agrarian problem in Russia and certain ideas of the Slavophiles came to their aid by holding out the promise of a peasant revolution with a socialist outcome. Agrarian upheavals in other lands, notably in France, had led to the establishment of an individualist order based on private appropriation, in which a large number of small owners imparted stability to a society that was not free of greed and exploitation — a solution that in no way satisfied the Populists, since it was not perfect and did not accord with their collectivist bias. And so they rejected out of hand, in the name of the Russian peasantry, an issue to the revolution which would have been only natural in view of its basically agrarian character, and which that peasantry itself, for all of its darkness and lack of cohesion, had nevertheless managed to achieve by 1929 despite the exertions of all brands of collectivists, both those who thought of themselves as its champions and those who viewed it with ill-concealed hostility.

How to harness the elemental discontent of the peasantry to the needs of an ultramodern revolution, how to draw a collectivist order out of the fires of an agrarian upheaval, was the problem that captivated the minds of the Populists. They thought they saw the solution in the existence of communal tenure in Great Russia. Much has been made of their indebtedness to the Slavophiles in this and other respects, but while it is true that Right-Wing Populism never did shake off the incubus of Slavophilism, the history of revolutionary Populism is one of progressive emancipation from Slavophile dogma. In the beginning, however, all Populists were undoubtedly influenced by this school of thought, even though from the same vantage ground of communal tenure they had marched off in an opposite direction, toward a revolutionary instead of a patriarchal social order. Like the Slavophiles, the early Populists imputed the most extravagant virtues to the *obshchina,* seeing in it a school for the inculcation of socialist beliefs; less fantastic but still high-flown was the idea of N. K. Mikhailovskii — borrowed, apparently, from Herzen — that this institution contained the embryo of a new concept of law in which toil and not ownership would be the source of rights.[2] The effort to derive an advanced collectivist society

[2] See V. M. Chernov, *Zemlia i pravo; sbornik statei* (Petrograd, 1919), pp. 44–45.

from the primitive collectivism of the past, restricting intervening forms of social development to as narrow a scope as possible or eliminating them entirely, is a distinctive feature of Populism.

In its earlier phase, however, Populism never descended from the clouds. It had no program, agrarian or otherwise, but only some articles of faith and an inspiration. The views of the revolutionary Populists on the peasantry, or rather on the feasibility of work among the peasantry, oscillated as violently as their attitude toward the state, the fatuous optimism of the first years giving way to the handwashing mood of the *Narodnaia Volia,* just as an effort to ignore the regime had yielded to exclusive preoccupation with its overthrow. Even a generation later, in the heart of the agrarian country, neo-Populists in Saratov were neglecting the peasantry to concentrate on a handful of urban workers, heedless of the slow ferment which was transforming the rural toilers into a revolutionary force as a result of worsening economic conditions and the growth of a literate stratum.[3] At the outset of its career the Socialist Revolutionary Party officially designated as the objects of its attention the industrial workers and the intellectuals, particularly the student youth, leaving to some better day the cultivation of the rural masses.[4] Thus the older Populism did not mark the advent of agrarian socialism in Russia except, perhaps, in the inspirational sense, nor was Chernyshevskii its founder; even the neo-Populists who called themselves Socialist Revolutionaries started out with their back to the village.

Matters had to await the peasant disorders on the left-bank Ukraine in the spring of 1902 and the eclectic genius of V. M. Chernov before the doctrine of agrarian socialism could be evolved. The riots in Poltava and Kharkov Provinces, answered at the other end of the black-earth belt by an even more serious movement in the district of Saratov,[5] convinced the SR's that they had been on the wrong track in deferring work in the village until after the attainment of political freedom, and led to a rededication of effort and a shift of emphasis from the town to the village, where it ever afterwards remained.[6] In the next few years the program of land socialization was worked out, it is generally assumed by Chernov, though Sukhanov

[3] A. A. Argunov, "Iz proshlago partii sotsialistov-revoliutsionerov," *Byloe,* no. 10/22 (October 1907), pp. 103–104; S. N. Sletov, *K istorii vozniknoveniia Partii Sotsialistov-Revoliutsionerov* (Petrograd, 1917), pp. 56–59, where the influence of a literate stratum is brought out.

[4] "Neotlozhnaia zadacha," *Revoliutsionnaia Rossiia,* no. 3 (January 1902), pp. 8–9; "Nasha programma," *Vestnik Russkoi Revoliutsii,* no. 1 (1902), pp. 8–9.

[5] See V. Gorn, "Krest'ianskoe dvizhenie do 1905 g.," *Obshchestvennoe dvizhenie v Rossii v nachale XX-go veka* (St. Petersburg, 1909–1914), I, 245–250.

[6] The entire issue of the central organ after the riots was devoted to the peasant movement (*Revoliutsionnaia Rossiia,* no. 8 [June 25, 1902]). A Marxist source reports that of fifty-seven titles published by the PSR in 1902 only one dealt with the problems of the urban proletariat. See P. P. Maslov, "Narodnicheskiia partii," *Obshchestvennoe dvizhenie v Rossii,* III, 98–99.

says Vikhliaev,[7] and was officially adopted by the PSR in 1906 at its first or Imatra congress. The program and the activity that accompanied it made neo-Populism the chief force in rural Russia and gave it in 1917 an advantage over its rivals which the war soon destroyed.

Victor Mikhailovich Chernov (1873–1952) was born into a family of peasant antecedents which moved during his early childhood from Samara to Saratov province. His grandfather had been emancipated from serfdom; his father rose through the state service to personal ennoblement. The river and the "boundless plain" on the eastern side of the black-earth zone were the elements in his childhood environment[8] which linked his fortunes forever with those of rural Russia and made certain that his socialism and the socialism of Karl Marx would never be the same. Coming from a region which had been since the seventeenth century a center of peasant disaffection, the youthful thinker could not have escaped the impact of the agrarian problem even had he been so minded. From the older Populism Chernov inherited the conviction that the Russian peasant could be claimed for collectivism, and from contemporary socialist thought in the West, particularly of the revisionist variety, he derived the elements of a new theoretical setting into which this jewel could be fitted without doing violence to the scientific approach or being at war with the whole trend of economic development. From the older Populism, also, Chernov took over the unwillingness to subordinate ethical to material values and the insistence upon the free development of human personality as a goal of socialism, no less than the improvement of the material lot of the toilers. It was a formidable task that Chernov set himself, for not only did he have to justify the inclusion of the Russian peasantry in the world socialist movement, but he had to reconcile socialism with liberty, the collective good with the free individual. Whether or not we agree with Sukhanov that he expended great energy and vast art in an impossible undertaking,[9] it is necessary to recognize his creativeness as well as his talent for synthesis. Wide and extensive though his borrowings were, there was yet a certain logic and symmetry in the structure he reared, and to deny him originality would be like denying the distinctiveness of Saracenic architecture merely because it is a blend of older forms.

In constructing the edifice of agrarian socialism Chernov was at all times independent of his sources. The older Populism, Western revisionism, and Marx himself were the quarries he worked most diligently, but if he drew freely from each he also discarded freely. He divested the village community (*obshchina*) of the mystical halo with which the elder generation of Populists had so fatuously surrounded it, and instead of active emanations in the

  [7] *Zapiski o revoliutsii* (Berlin, Petersburg, and Moscow, 1922) — hereafter cited as *Zapiski* — VII, 255; Chernov, *Zemlia i pravo*, p. 236.
  [8] See the first chapter of his recent memoirs, *Pered burei* (New York, 1953).
  [9] *Zapiski*, III, 141–144.

direction of socialism ascribed to it merely an important equalizing tendency and the negative significance of having served as a block to the development of a property consciousness.[10] Here he undoubtedly was on solid ground, having laid his finger on the circumstance which, more than any other with the exception of war, made possible the establishment and continuance of a socialist regime in Russia. Chernov acknowledged himself to be a follower of Marx in political economy but wanted a whole series of corrections in Marxian sociology.[11] His attitude was neatly summed up in a statement at his party's first congress: "Marx," he said, "is our great common teacher in the realm of economics, but we do not feel constrained to make of him an idol." [12]

Grumbling on the Right fringe of the party to the effect that Chernov paid too much deference to the founder of scientific socialism and had incorporated too many of his teachings in the SR program was wholly unjustified. As a socialist, Chernov naturally was influenced by Marx, unlike these critics — the future People's Socialists — who were getting ready to abandon socialism except in name and who more appropriately would have been styled nationalists than Populists. But the socialism that Chernov was formulating was not Marxian socialism, nor was it even revised Marxian socialism, despite all the affinities that Sukhanov might point to in urging a fusion of the Social Democrats with the Socialist Revolutionaries.[13] The experience of 1917 would demonstrate that the existence of two separate movements in Russia instead of two factions of the same movement as in other countries was dictated, not by differences in theory long since obscured in practice, but by something far more real and tangible — by a preference, in the last analysis, for a different segment of the population.

For in his work of rejuvenating Populism, which at the same time was a work of Europeanizing it,[14] Chernov had confirmed the old predilection for the peasantry which the disorders of 1902 had revived by giving this school of thought for the first time an agrarian program as the heart of its prescription for the ills of Russian society. Henceforth neo-Populism or

[10] See various articles in the original *Revoliutsionnaia Rossiia,* especially "Russkaia krest'ianskaia obshchina i blizhaishiia zadachi revoliutsii," no. 53 (September 30, 1904); see also Chernov's *Zapiski sotsialista-revoliutsionera* (Berlin, St. Petersburg, and Moscow, 1922), I, 164, 176. Above all, see his *Zemlia i pravo,* pp. 208–210, 226–230, 233–236.

[11] *Zapiski sotsialista-revoliutsionera,* I, 105.

[12] *Protokoly pervago s"ezda Partii Sotsialistov-Revoliutsionerov* (n.p., 1906), p. 136. On distinction between neo-Populism and Western revisionism, see *Zemlia i pravo,* pp. 231–233.

[13] This was the burden both of his pamphlet, *Marksizm i Narodnichestvo,* and of his more ambitious brochure, *Nashi napravleniia: Marksizm i "narodnichestvo"* (Petrograd, 1916).

[14] See B. I. Nikolaevskii's introduction to Chernov's memoirs, *Pered burei,* pp. 9–12; see also Chernov's article, "Proekt novoi partiinoi programmy," *Revoliutsionnaia Rossiia,* nos. 33–34 (January–February 1924), pp. 12–14. On distinction between old and new Populism, see especially his *Zemlia i pravo,* pp. 204–210.

Social Revolutionism was as irrevocably committed to the peasantry as social democracy to the proletariat, though each offered some bait to the class favored by the other. In this respect the SR's were more sincere than the SD's, for only the extreme Right Wing of the PSR ever betrayed any hostility to the working class, whereas the whole mass of Social Democrats regarded the peasantry as petty bourgeois and so on the wrong side of the class demarcation line, whatever they might do to cover this up and however willing the Bolshevik faction might be to use the peasantry, or elements of it, for purposes of a proletarian-dominated revolution. Chernov's movement, in fact, must be characterized as peasant-centered rather than as peasant, partly because the bulk of the membership — certainly of the articulate membership — was always intellectual, and partly because the SR's were never willing to define themselves as narrowly a peasant's party but always claimed to be champions of the toilers in general.[15]

Older Populists had not concerned themselves with the class struggle; Chernov accepted the principle but so altered the line-up as to make the Marxists' hair stand on end: instead of the banner of socialism being borne by the worker who neither owned the means of production nor sold the products of his labor, but only the labor itself, Chernov would entrust it to the "toiler" who might work independently with his own means and dispose of what he produced so long as he did not hire someone else in the process. In the eyes of the neo-Populists personal toil was ennobling, in whatever guise it was carried on, by the worker in the factory, or by the peasant on his own plot with his own implements, or by the intellectual at his desk; the evil lay in having an excess of the means of production, especially of land, which denied to others a status of equality and forced them into a relationship of dependence (and so of exploitation). The whole enterprise of Chernov in the realm of class theory may be defined as an exercise to justify the inclusion of the "toiling peasantry" on the right side of the class struggle, just as the whole essence of the controversy between the SR's and the SD's was to be found in the attitude toward this type of peasant — "toiling" in the terminology of the SR's, "middle" in that of the Bolsheviks — the peasant who worked his own plot without recourse to hired labor.

Although they adjusted their program to the persistence of the small producer in agriculture, in their hearts the Social Democrats never surrendered the hope of promoting the class struggle in the village by building up the landless proletariat and the capitalistic peasants at the expense of this middle category. The Socialist Revolutionaries proposed to do precisely the opposite: they meant to shut the class war out of the village by eliminating the kulaks and the hired hands, leaving the middle peasants as the sole

---

[15] On this point see Sukhanov, *Marksizm i Narodnichestvo*, p. 30; see also below, pp. 74–75.

representatives of a homogeneous class. For all of the loose organization, lax discipline, nebulous ideology, and wide diffusion of opinion which are usually and justly attributed to the Populists, on this point they were single-minded. The only chip from the monolith would be the tenderness betrayed by some of the Right-Wing SR's for the kulaks in 1917. Otherwise all shades of opinion were as one in respect to their class position, and when the movement broke up at the end of 1917 on the shoals of the war question, the fire-eating Left SR's were just as much, or even more, the champions of the middle peasantry as the regular SR's with whom they were now at war.

To preserve or secure the unity of the peasantry in order to render it proof against the class struggle was one broad and basic objective of the program for socialization of the land. The other was to prevent the peasantry from acquiring a taste for private property. Through the magic charm of socialization the two evils of the class war and the Roman law would be exorcised or kept from the village. It has generally been assumed that Chernov conceived the idea of socialization — the first congress paid tribute to him for "having borne on his shoulders for five years the whole burden of the theoretical formulation of our program" [16] — and nothing he himself says discourages the assumption, but Sukhanov in his memoirs makes the bald statement that Vikhliaev was the author,[17] and Sukhanov's connection with the question is such that his testimony cannot be lightly dismissed. Panteleimon Alekseevich Vikhliaev was perhaps the most eminent SR specialist in agrarian problems, and it is quite likely that he and Chernov worked out the program together, just as they collaborated in 1917 when Chernov was Minister of Agriculture in the Provisional Government and Vikhliaev was Deputy Minister. Opinion will differ as to whether socialization of the land could have served as a basis for the reconstruction of Russian society or whether it was a myth that would have been dispelled at the first touch of reality,[18] but none can deny that it was the heart of neo-Populism and the talisman of its success.

Perhaps the best way of explaining socialization is to say that it proposed to make land as nearly like air as possible. No one was to buy or sell it, or to rent or lease it; no one was to own it — it was to "belong to all the people." This terminology (*obshchenarodnoe dostoianie*) is typically Chernovian and, taken in the light of his prideful defense at the congress, is incontrovertible evidence of at least his coauthorship of the plan. Land could be used, on a basis of equality, by all who wished to cultivate it with their own labor, and only so long as they worked it themselves. To create the general land fund, private property in land was to be expropriated with-

---

[16] *Protokoly pervago s"ezda P.S.-R.*, p. 294.

[17] *Zapiski*, VII, 255.

[18] See Lenin, "Sravnenie stolypinskoi i narodnicheskoi agrarnoi programmy," *Sochineniia*, 2nd ed., XVI, 10–14. Lenin saw negative value in the plan but said the equalization feature would not hold for a year.

out compensation, and into the fund would also go the allotment lands, state properties, and everything else. Unfortunately for those who conceived this idyllic scheme, however, a host of problems arose out of the circumstance that in some respects land did not resemble air. It was more limited in quantity, more varied in quality, its properties were more easily exhaustible, and, being more tangible, it had served as an object of private or group appropriation, which created, even in Russia, a many-sided vested interest problem.

Who or what would own the land, a host of critics asked, inside as well as outside of Chernov's own camp? All efforts to fix legal ownership, however, encountered the steady resistance of the party leader, who chided his questioners with being imprisoned within the concepts of the Roman law instead of listening to the conscience of their own people, which would have told them that land was not a fit object for private rights, but a natural good that ought to be equally accessible to all who wished to fructify it with their labor. Chernov had taken over from Mikhailovskii and developed further the idea that the Roman law represented the highest stage of development of an inferior system of law enshrining the principle of private rights, whereas the Russian folk conscience contained in crude form the elements of a superior system of law addressed to the common good.[19] Socialists ought to make their own law and not try to fit their reforms into the framework of the Roman law, impregnated as this was with the individualist spirit. They should turn to account the priceless boon at hand and break ground in the legal as well as the economic field, at the same time doing all in their power to insure that the Roman law, a recent importation from above which had not sunk into the consciousness of the Russian people, should "wither and die on our soil without ever having come to bloom." [20] Chernov's haste to stifle the Roman law betrays his fear that in sustained competition with the "toilers' sense of right" the principle of individual ownership might win the upper hand. In his flight from Western legal concepts he would not even use the word "property" (*sobstvennost'*), styling the land the "belonging" (*dostoianie*) of all the people — an action that some of his comrades considered extreme.

Having ruled out individual ownership of the land, Chernov and his associates opened wide the gates to individual cultivation. This was by all odds their chief concession to economic reality and also to the inarticulate will of the peasantry. They emphasized that socialization would not involve any change in the way farming was carried on — no collectivization of the productive process, in other words. Socialization was not socialism. They had taken over with gusto the revisionist view that in agriculture the small producer would hold his own, escaping the fate under capitalism of his

---

[19] *Zemlia i pravo*, passim.
[20] *Protokoly pervago s"ezda P.S.-R.*, p. 221.

counterpart in industry, and they did not consider the question of the manner of cultivation — whether individual or collective — to be of primary importance as long as use of the land was equalized.[21]

We consider it as both inevitable and fully compatible with socialist principles to extend the holdings (on a basis of use, not of ownership) of those peasants who cannot be engaged in large-scale, socially organized farming, for want of the material prerequisites for such enterprise, and who will prefer a small-scale, individualistic economy. It will be our task gradually to draw them into socialism through the intrinsic attractiveness of a collectivist society.[22]

Inevitable it certainly was, but whether compatible with socialist principles is another matter. Chernov went out of his way to reassure the public that nothing in the program would restrict the individual's right to work his share of socialized land.[23] The SR's were prepared to see farming continue on a predominantly individualist basis for some time to come, perhaps for a number of decades, until the growth of voluntary coöperation had demonstrated the superiority of collective effort and induced the peasant to abandon cultivation in isolation from his fellows. Coöperation would be the decisive factor in overcoming the fragmentation of agricultural production, in causing the myriads of small producers, protected by socialization against the property contagion, to coalesce in larger social units.[24] Coercion was ruled out. Anything on the order of what the Stalinist regime did after 1928 was wholly foreign to the spirit and doctrine of neo-Populism.

In general, the agrarian socialists took the line that their program could be adapted to existing conditions with a minimum of inconvenience to the toilers themselves, whether they practiced communal tenure, or household tenure, or held in private right. The bad people with more land than they personally could work alone would suffer. Socialization of the land would dissolve all forms of property[25] — communal, household, and individual — but the toilers would go on using it much as before, the main difference being that they would have more of it. The fate of the Great Russian peasant commune (*obshchina*) under the reform was never clarified. Apparently some of its partisans hoped that it could be held together and converted into the new and higher type practicing collective cultivation[26] (kolkhoz in Soviet terminology) — these people were as extravagant in their hopes as the original Populists. On one occasion in 1917 Chernov said that the commune would become a land society to which land would be assigned as a

---

[21] E. A. Morokhovets, *Agrarnye programmy rossiiskikh politicheskikh partii v 1917 godu* (Leningrad, 1929), pp. 78–79.

[22] "Sotsialdemokraty i sotsialisty-revoliutsionery," *Revoliutsionnaia Rossiia*, no. 16 (January 15, 1903), p. 4.

[23] *Zemlia i pravo*, pp. 235–236; *Agrarnyi vopros i sovremennyi moment* (Moscow, 1917), p. 20.

[24] See, for example, Sukhanov, *Marksizm i Narodnichestvo*, pp. 14–15.

[25] Chernov, *Zemlia i pravo*, p. 236.

[26] *Protokoly pervago s"ezda P.S.-R.*, pp. 119–120.

whole, but he did not say how it would be cultivated.[27] The agrarian socialists never were fond of laying down specifications for their reform. They
kept it vague — and popular.

Both the propensity for avoiding detailed specifications and the desire
to make socialization as painless as possible — for the toilers — are seen in
the way the agrarian socialists dealt with the problem of equalization, one of
the two main features of their reform. Here they realized they would be in
deep water, and their solution was to skirt the edge of the pond without
getting their feet wet. Neither the Socialist Revolutionaries nor any of their
offshoots, in so far as these retained the principle, ever said officially how use
of the land was to be equalized over the vast extent of this great country,
with its unevenness of population, climatic differences, marketing considerations and soil variations, although they were warned at their very first congress that rivers of blood might flow from the failure to come to grips with
the problem.[28] They accorded the orator an ovation — and did nothing more.
But there exists on paper, in the words of their most authoritative specialist,[29] an intimation of what would have been done had they been so unfortunate as to have to move from the realm of speculation into that of achievement.

The principle that each citizen engaged in farming should take equally
from what belonged to all underlay the fixing of a general standard for all
of Russia: the gross income from agriculture would be divided by the
number of people living from agriculture, and the result would be the return
from the land each person was entitled to receive. It would devolve upon
the local organs of self-government, under the supervision of the central
authority, to determine on the basis of local conditions, according to local
standards of cultivation, how much land was needed to yield this amount.
Where present holdings fell short of the needed quantity, they were to be
brought up to it by award from confiscated property; where they exceeded
it, but not the point beyond which hired labor would be required, they were
to be left undisturbed, but the advantage of this surplus land was to be
taxed away. Only where a peasant had so much land that he could not farm
it himself with the help of his family would he have any taken away. "The
toiling peasantry, tilling the soil with its own hands, will in any event keep
its lands." [30] Kulaks would be eliminated, hired hands likewise, and left
would be toiling peasants with the average allotment and toiling peasants
with somewhat more than the average, but unable to benefit from it. Through
the pressure and proceeds of taxation areas with surplus land would be kept
open to newcomers and areas of congestion relieved. So did Vikhliaev pro-

[27] *Agrarnyi vopros i sovremennyi moment,* p. 20. A good surmise is that he did not
say because he did not know.
[28] *Protokoly pervago s"ezda P.S.-R.,* pp. 184–186, 205–212.
[29] P. A. Vikhliaev, *Kak uravniat' pol'zovanie zemlëi* (Petrograd, 1917).
[30] *Ibid.,* p. 16.

pose to ease the impact of socialization upon the toiling peasantry and armor-plate it against the class-war designs of the Social Democrats.

One other feature of socialization requires brief comment: the administration of the land fund. In their zeal for individual freedom — except in the economic sphere — the SR's had always favored maximum decentralization. Applying this principle to the land reform, they assigned the chief role in management to the local organs of self-government, which were closest to the land and could be expected to make the most intelligent decisions. But they also wanted to equalize the use of land and, optimistic as they were in their views of human nature, they were not so simple as to think that they could dispense with all regulation from above. Yet, once again, they failed to follow through by defining the competence of the local and national authorities. In 1917, with the submission of the program to the Constituent Assembly supposedly only a few months away, and ten years after its formal adoption by the party, Chernov thought to enlighten an audience with this sort of nonsense: "Besides these immediate organs of administration of the land fund, there are also higher organs, which merely supervise the activity of the former and take note of local differences." [31] Vikhliaev, being an economist, did somewhat better: he felt that the state must pass on the estimates of land productivity submitted by local bodies and apportion the equalization tax.[32]

Ardent as the Socialist Revolutionaries were for the socialization of land, they were in no hurry to socialize industry; in fact, they considered this to be impossible at the existing stage of economic development. The two measures were analogous only in sound, for socialization of land would not touch production[33] or distribution, whereas socialization of industry would involve fundamental changes in both. Property relationships, said Chernov, were subject to swift alteration by revolutionary action, but productive relationships yielded only very slowly to long-sustained, creative effort. Because of their fetish of collectivism the SR's dared not push their argument to the point where they would have had to acknowledge that agricultural production was individualist in essence, the peasant being a producing unit to himself, as the workingman was not. The fact that industrial production involved two classes instead of one, however, did not escape them, and they failed to see how the workingman at his present level of achievement could supplant the entrepreneur without a breakdown in the process. Socialization of industry was equivalent to collectivization of agriculture; socialization of the land, merely to municipalization of the sites of factories and other buildings. Chernov and his associates could maintain that they were holding the balance even between the urban and the rural

---

[31] *Agrarnyi vopros i sovremennyi moment*, p. 17.
[32] *Kak uravniat' pol'zovanie zemlëi*, pp. 9–12.
[33] In 1917 they were less sure of this. See below, p. 74.

toilers in refusing to take over industry because they were displaying equal caution in respect to introducing socialism into the village. Nevertheless, the fact remains that neo-Populism had nothing to offer the worker comparable to the landowners' property it promised to bestow on the peasant, and hence could never have in the town the appeal it had in the village. And this arose as much from innate preference as from economic logic. A very clear example of the desire to serve first the peasantry is seen in Chernov's conduct in 1917, when he tried to drive a wedge between landowners and industrialists and form an alliance with the latter in order to clear the tracks for agrarian reform. That his maneuver ended in dismal failure probably surprised no one but himself.[34]

A minority element in the PSR, unable to reconcile itself to a program that seemed to it to be revolutionary on the agrarian side and reformist on the industrial, seceded in 1906 to form the Union of SR Maximalists, an ultraradical group in the twilight zone between Populism and anarchism. The Maximalists demanded the socialization of everything, industry as well as land, upon the outbreak of revolution, and for an interesting reason: the workers had better take the factories, they reasoned, when the peasants took the land, for later on the peasants might not regard so indulgently an assault upon property rights.[35] Here was a clear intimation on the part of the most radical element in the neo-Populist camp that the vaunted "conscience of toil" might not withstand the enticements of personal ownership, once the peasants had the *pomeshchiki*'s land.

The inclusion of land socialization in the minimum program and the relegation of the socialization of industry to the maximum program indicates that the agrarian socialists conceived of the approaching revolution neither in terms of an enthronement of the bourgeoisie nor in terms of a victory for socialism. The revolution would be of the intermediate type, and the fertile brain of V. M. Chernov combined with the flexibility of the Russian language to find an expression for it that is foreign to the genius of English: it would be *narodno-trudovaia*. A Soviet source comments on the lack of unanimity among the Populists as to the effect of land socialization upon the bourgeois order, some holding that it was not basically incompatible, and others that it would undermine that order.[36] As a matter of fact, they wanted it both ways, believing that the program could be fitted into the framework of capitalism while protecting the largest element in the population against the capitalist (or private property) viewpoint until society was ready for further advances toward the collectivist goal. Chernov always insisted that

[34] For Chernov's views on the socialization of industry, see especially *Protokoly pervago s"ezda P.S.-R.*, pp. 148–158; "Programmnye voprosy: Sotsializatsiia zemli i programma-minimum," *Revoliutsionnaia Rossiia*, no. 42 (March 1, 1904), pp. 3–7.

[35] B. I. Gorev, "Apoliticheskiia i antiparlamentskiia gruppy," *Obshchestvennoe dvizhenie v Rossii*, III, 521–523.

[36] Morokhovets, *Agrarnye programmy rossiiskikh politicheskikh partii*, p. 80, n. 3.

socialization of the land would constitute the first great breach in the wall of property rights, after which others would follow with greater ease until the wall crumbled and fell into ruins.[37]

The edifice of agrarian socialism sustained two shocks of earthquake proportions, the first in connection with Stolypin's agrarian reform, the second in 1917. Stolypin's assault upon the *obshchina*, his sink-or-swim program for the peasantry, raising the specter of a numerous class of small property holders who would be proof against socialism, so disheartened the Populists that many were reduced to a state of funk. This was particularly true of those who, unlike Chernov, had never really made the shift from the older to the newer form of Populism and who had continued under the spell of the old illusions. For these people the end of the world had come. Some clutched at a straw such as the idea that the communal spirit might survive the institution that bred it; others drew near to the Social Democrats, writing off the peasants as a loss; others turned up their toes and made ready to die. Agrarian socialism might have died with them had it not been for Chernov. Maneuvering desperately and with great skill, he managed to salvage socialization of the land and, with it, the party program from the threatened collapse of the commune. In the first place, he drew a much sharper distinction than ever before between the old Populism, with its adulation of traditional forms, and the new, with its realism and broadened point of view. In the second place, he abandoned the *obshchina* as the basis for social ownership but praised it for having nurtured the principle of equal use of the land which the party had abstracted, cleansed, and caused to overflow the bounds of the commune; then he reintroduced social ownership as the only means of securing that principle. In the third place, he was able to show by what might be called the Ukrainian argument that the appeal of the agrarian program was much broader than the extent of communal tenure, and hence was in no sense dependent on its continued existence, having met with an enthusiastic response in the Ukraine and other parts of the empire where that type of tenure did not prevail. And, finally, he blew a blast on the trumpet and said Stolypin would never expropriate the landowners and so could never appease the peasants. Thus did Chernov rally his dispirited followers and save agrarian socialism from extinction.[38]

It is a remarkable circumstance that the revolution of 1917 should have contributed nothing to the fund of agrarian socialism except a record of lost

---

[37] *Ibid.*, pp. 74–75, 93–95; succinct statement of Chernov's concept in his *Rozhdenie revoliutsionnoi Rossii (fevral'skaia revoliutsiia)* (Paris, Prague, and New York, 1934), pp. 237–240.

[38] "Sotsializatsiia zemli, kak takticheskaia problema," *Zemlia i pravo*, pp. 199–240. Chernov claimed to have evidence that the Little Russian toilers were prepared to forego private ownership in order to enjoy equality in the use of the land after dispossession of the *pans*. They are quoted as saying that land tenure should be "obcheska, iak u katsapov."

opportunities. One would have expected its adherents to get busy and cloak their formulas in earthly form, preparing for land socialization through the Constituent Assembly. They did nothing of the kind. They were so hopelessly divided by the war and so taken up with the tactical questions of the hour that even the agrarian problem was slighted at their conferences and the program remained exactly as it had been, without revision or elaboration. Chernov's tenure in the Ministry of Agriculture was barren of achievement, aside from measures to suspend the Stolypin reform[39] — having denied that the *obshchina* was essential to the party program, Chernov hastened to its rescue at the first opportunity — and to protect the land fund against panicky transactions. But he failed to secure it against depredations of the peasants by getting through a law that would satisfy them until the Constituent Assembly. Administratively he was crippled by the dearth of experienced party men and was forced into dependence on bureaucrats who may have adopted a socialist coloration but who had no sympathy with what he was trying to do.[40]

The paralysis that extended to every sphere of party activity in 1917 was due in the last analysis to the state of mind of the Populist intellectuals, for whom the achievement of political freedom was the supreme good, leaving them with little desire for a social revolution, even under favorable conditions, and with no desire at all in the setting of 1917. Imperial Germany had succeeded the domestic social order at the head of their list of enemies, and men who had built an entire political movement around the idea that Russian problems must be solved independently of Western forms now stood revealed as partisans of the Western powers — quite blind partisans, in many instances. To preserve the "union of all vital forces" — i.e., the class truce — they deferred all revolutionary demands to the Constituent Assembly, and then permitted the Constitutional Democrats to defer the Constituent Assembly. These intellectuals were even prepared to emasculate the agrarian program, throwing overboard such mainstays as expropriation without compensation, total expropriation, equalization, and the abolition of hired labor, but here the peasants balked and forced them to toe the line.[41] The intellectual core of agrarian socialism had come, in effect, to share the Menshevik concept of the revolution. The large element that wanted to make revolution instead of playing at it found this attitude intolerable and looked increasingly to Bolshevism, which had long since cast off any moderate restraint and so was able to preëmpt the leadership of the extremist cause. The two wings of Russian social democracy acted as powerful magnets, rending the larger and softer body of Populism with their irresistible pull. The

[39] See his remarks at the northern regional congress of the PSR in the Petrograd *Zemlia i Volia*, no. 49 (May 24, 1917).

[40] V. Kerzhentsev, "Eserovskoe povetrie," *Novaia Zhizn'*, no. 61 (June 29, 1917).

[41] See N. Oganovskii, *Dnevnik chlena Uchreditel'nago Sobraniia* (Petrograd, 1918); Morokhovets, *Agrarnye programmy rossiiskikh politicheskikh partii*, pp. 104–105.

center under V. M. Chernov, striving desperately to preserve the unity of the movement, achieved some Pyrrhic paper victories at party congresses, but was powerless to subdue the warring extremities and itself fell under the magnetic pull. In the end, agrarian socialism lost its unity and underwent destruction, having recapitulated in itself all the weaknesses of the class it represented, along with some others that only intellectuals could contribute. Some of its adherents freely acknowledged the default on social reform, the failure to provide clear answers to the questions of the day, the absence of concrete proposals, and, in short, the unreadiness of the party for the role destiny had called it to play.[42] The agrarian socialists could not speak out clearly, however, when they had ceased to be of one mind.

The promise of equalized, individual holdings for all who wished to farm brought the SR's great popularity and gave them the peasant suffrage, so that in the Constituent Assembly they achieved, with their national offshoots, an absolute majority. Circumstances converted this victory into ashes even as it was being registered, but as far as the Russian people were concerned, they had their mandate to proceed with socialization of the land. Assuming that they had been able to do so, would they have succeeded in placing Russian agriculture on a new and satisfactory basis or would their program have been exposed as a myth, imposing in its popular appeal but impossible of execution?

To answer this question the services of both a prophet and an economist would be necessary, if, indeed, they could reach a definitive conclusion from the bare outline, which was all the SR's ever supplied. But one does not have to be either a prophet or an economist to say that the administrative difficulties of putting this program into effect would have been enormous. From the administrative standpoint the two basic principles of socialization and equalization were contradictory. The term "socialization" had been deliberately preferred to "nationalization" in order to emphasize that the administrative center of gravity would reside in the localities.[43] But how was use of the land to be equalized without strong and frequent intervention from a supervisory authority? Vikhliaev admitted that the local organs would tend to underestimate the yield per unit of land in order to raise the local quota, but observed that this tendency would cancel itself out.[44] It would — if they all lied absolutely; restrained lying on the part of some would penalize their communities. He would give the central authority power to confirm estimates, but how conflicts were to be ironed out was one of those details of the program never sketched in by its authors. The anarchic seizures of 1917 would have greatly complicated the task of equalization,

---

[42] *Kratkii otchët o rabotakh chetvërtago s"ezda P.S.-R. (26 noiabria — 5 dekabria 1917 goda)* (Petrograd, 1918), pp. 44–45, 50, 78.

[43] *Protokoly pervago s"ezda P.S.-R.,* pp. 219–228; Chernov, *Zemlia i pravo,* pp. 131–137.

[44] *Kak uravniat' pol'zovanie zemlëi,* pp. 9–12.

for the peasants had divided estates while preserving their own inequalities, thus depriving Vikhliaev's scheme of much of its flexibility and increasing the numbers, and so the power of resistance, of those whose surplus land would subject them to taxation. At the last moment the realization dawned on some of the SR's that in socializing the land they might have to bring production as well as property under their guns because of the question of disposing of livestock and farming equipment on confiscated estates;[45] and Vikhliaev held that the use of machinery should be placed on a coöperative basis.[46]

Socialization also raised grave problems in relation to the improvement of land and methods of cultivation. In his attempt to reconcile it with the task of increasing agricultural productivity Vikhliaev is wholly unconvincing.[47] He unctuously states that whole communities would be brought to better methods of farming instead of individual families, as under Stolypin's law. But the yield per unit of land was to be computed on the basis of the prevailing methods of cultivation in each locality instead of by some national standard.[48] Now if all communities all over Russia advanced their standards more or less evenly there would be no difficulty, or if scattered individual cultivators improved their farming they might not suffer at the next redistribution, though if they left the land there would apparently be no compensation for what they had put into it. But if the members of a local community generally went over to better farming, then they would eventually be penalized in favor of a laggard community by having less land assigned to them as a result of computing the yield per unit of land on the basis of the customary local methods of cultivation in determining the amount needed to give the peasant, wherever he might be, his equal share of the national income from agriculture. It is difficult to see how socialization could have operated otherwise than as a brake upon progress.

Not the least of its disadvantages would have been its effect on the birth rate. Whereas under the existing system the individual got more land by having more money, under socialization he would get more by having more children.[49] This tying of the greed for more land to procreation could not have failed to raise still further a birth rate which had already led to very serious problems of congestion in some of the most fertile parts of Russia. Chernov ridiculed the fear that there would not be enough land to go around in a country with an "almost limitless expanse of *chernozëm*," [50] while Vikhliaev was already writing of the need for irrigating deserts, drain-

[45] *Protokoly pervago s"ezda partii levykh sotsialistov-revoliutsionerov (internatsional-istov)* (n.p., 1918), p. 73.
[46] *Kak uravniat' pol'zovanie zemlëi*, pp. 29–31.
[47] *Ibid.*, pp. 26–31.
[48] *Ibid.*, pp. 7, 11.
[49] *Ibid.*, p. 24. This is stated specifically.
[50] *Agrarnyi vopros i sovremennyi moment*, p. 18.

ing swamps, and clearing forest lands[51] as though nature had not limited, even in Russia, the amount of arable land. Like so many socialists, neither seems to have been aware of the duplicity involved in promising a great improvement in the standard of living while pursuing a population policy that maintained a constant pressure upon advancing means of subsistence.

In the soul of agrarian socialism there was always a certain dualism. There was the desire to please and lead the peasantry, and there was the fetish of collectivism. If the two had ever come into conflict, the result might have been a branching of the movement. And they quite likely would have come into conflict, once the revolutionary ardor of the rural toilers had been slaked by the disappearance of the estates. Indeed, the conflict duly appeared in the emigration, though there it was nothing more than the stirring of dry bones. Men like Rudnev, the ex-mayor of Moscow, and Maslov, of the *Krest'ianskaia Rossiia*, advocated a frankly peasant party pointed against the working class. Quite obviously, these men would have accepted the conversion of individual holdings into privately owned plots had the peasants so desired. Chernov, on the other hand, upheld the collectivist principle and the character of the movement as representative of all groups of toilers.[52] Had Russian society after 1917 undergone a normal evolution, many of the agrarian socialists might well have accepted for Russia the issue of the French Revolution — that is, they would have seen nothing amiss in the situation that prevailed in 1928 and would have been willing to proceed further toward a society of small peasant proprietors in which the predominance of the middle peasant over the kulak would have satisfied whatever zeal for equalization they still might have retained.

In a double sense agrarian socialism marked a sharp break with Russian tradition. It was opposed to the concentration of governmental authority and sought to shift the center of gravity from the metropolis to the localities, from Petersburg and Moscow to the villages of the black-earth zone. The term "socialization" had been deliberately preferred to "nationalization" of the land fund with this purpose in mind. Too much should not be made of the aversion to centralization, however, for the principle of equalizing the use of the land worked in the opposite direction by placing a premium upon a strong supervisory authority, and the centrifugal tendencies of the national minorities offended the latent nationalism of neo-Populist intellectuals. They might have reversed themselves on this point had they continued in power.

But agrarian socialism would not have wavered in its second departure from Russian tradition. It would have tried to give the peasant a status dif-

---

[51] *Kak uravniat' pol'zovanie zemlëi*, p. 29.
[52] For these polemics see especially his article "Stikhiia revoliutsii i politicheskie trezvenniki," *Revoliutsionnaia Rossiia*, no. 12–13 (September–October 1921), pp. 4–6. He spoke highly of the proletariat on this occasion.

ferent from that best described by Frederick the Great as the "beast of burden of human society" — a status that the Russian peasant has had at least since the sixteenth century and still retains. The harshness of his lot has never varied, and this iron law the agrarian socialists would have tried to break. Not even their own belief in collectivism would necessarily have stood in the way. It might have been that in the long run — the very long run — their faith in coöperation would have come to their rescue. But well before then it is likely that agrarian socialism would have been dissolved into its component elements — devotion to the cause of the peasantry and devotion to socialism — and that the agrarian socialists would have had to choose between them and declare their political coloration, whether red or green. Quite likely they would have chosen the green and thus would have stood revealed as what Lenin always said they were — revolutionary democrats.

Stalin's Views on Soviet Economic Development

ALEXANDER ERLICH

I

On s'engage, et puis on voit: this phrase borrowed from Napoleon was used by Lenin more than once to describe the position of his party after November 1917.[1] With regard to the issues of economic policy the interval between getting involved and seeing, or even looking, was rather protracted. During the first few years the pressure of external events was so overwhelming as to leave virtually no room for choice. The spontaneous seizures of factories by the workers in early 1918 and the exigencies of the Civil War forced upon the reluctant Lenin and his collaborators the policy of "War Communism." With similar inevitability the swelling tide of popular unrest climaxed by the Kronstadt revolt and by the peasant uprisings of Central Russia imposed the retreat toward the NEP. And in both cases there was always the great expectation that the European revolution would link up before long with its Russian bridgehead and assist the Soviet republic with equipment, industrial consumers' goods, and organizing ability. In 1924 the situation was entirely different. Chances of a quick rescue from the West, which had already been declining at the time of the transition to the NEP, had now passed. The discontent of the peasants, moreover, was no longer restrained by the fear of the "White" counterrevolution: they had just forced the regime off the "War Communist" path, and they were grimly awaiting the results of this victory. Under such circumstances the policy could no longer consist of spasmodic responses to catastrophes and of fervent hopes for the future. Only positive action directed toward improvement in the wretched living standards of the population could stabilize the regime; only forceful economic development aimed at enlargement of the productive capacity of the country could provide a durable basis for such action and make the Soviet Union a viable state. But how could this be done, how could these two objectives be reconciled in conditions of a backward, war-

[1] The author acknowledges gratefully the support of the Russian Research Center of Harvard University in the preparation of this study. He is also indebted to Professor Alexander Gerschenkron and Dr. Joseph S. Berliner for valuable suggestions.

ravaged country in the thick of a great egalitarian upheaval? This was a question to which the "old books" provided no answer.[2]

Bukharin, who was at that time the leading economic theorist of the Party, felt that the solution was clearly at hand. It was contained, according to him, in continuing the NEP as conceived by Lenin and as elaborated on in his famous *O prodnaloge*. The vicious circle of idle industrial capacity in the cities and the supply strikes in the villages was to be broken by lifting restrictive measures which had hitherto inhibited the peasant's willingness to produce a surplus above his bare needs or at any rate to part with it. Transformation of the wholesale requisitioning into a limited "tax in kind"; opening the channels of trade through which the nontaxable part of peasant surplus could be profitably sold; denationalization and encouragement of small-scale industry which would not need, because of the nature of its plant, any protracted reconditioning in order to start producing goods demanded by the peasants — these were the key devices which were expected to unfreeze the productive energies of agriculture and make increased supplies of foodstuffs and raw materials flow into the nearly empty pipelines of the urban economy. The part of this flow which would reach the large-scale industrial sector would set some of its idle wheels turning and make possible a counterflow of manufactured products to the goods-starved village, thus providing the latter with an additional incentive to increase its marketings. A genuine process of cumulative growth would be set in motion hereby. The logic of the reasoning seemed compelling, and even more impressive was the

[2] It goes without saying that the men who faced this question approached it with some definite, preconceived ideas. All of them were emphatic in recognizing the need for rapid economic development and in taking the latter to be synonymous with industrialization; in this respect they were faithfully following the line of Russian Marxism of the prerevolutionary era. They sharply deviated from the traditional approach by accepting Lenin's view that a proletarian party which succeeded in rising to political power in a backward country had a clear duty not to leave the task of industrialization to the bourgeoisie but to put itself in charge after dislodging the propertied classes from their positions of control. But this amendment, which came in response to the massive *faits accomplis* of the first revolutionary years, could not by itself make the original doctrine grind out solutions which would provide a clear-cut directive for action. The Marxian theory, to be sure, helped to bring sharply into focus some phenomena and relationships which were of relevance for the impending decisions, like advantages of large-scale production, capital-consuming and labor-displacing effects of technological progress, importance of the relative size of investment and consumers'-goods industries. It was equally categorical in assigning to the transformation of property relationships the key role in the process of social change. But it provided no criterion for optimal solutions within each of these areas, or more particularly, for appropriate speed at which the transition from the existing state of affairs to a more satisfactory one should take place. Moreover, even determined efforts toward establishing such optimum conditions would not change the situation to any substantial extent. They could, at best, lead to a more clear-cut formulation of existing alternatives and, consequently, to elimination of some minor errors and inconsistencies from the judgments: but this would not eliminate the need for choosing nor reduce the formidable risks and uncertainties attendant upon the final decision and due to the nature of the problems involved.

impact of facts: between 1920 and 1924 the output of large-scale industry increased more than threefold.

Could this upward trend be relied upon to start off a process of long-range expansion and set the pattern for it? Lenin was never explicit about it: but his strong emphasis on the need of attracting foreign investment seemed to indicate some doubts whether the policy of "developing trade at all costs" would be sufficient to do the job. Bukharin, writing three years later, betrayed no such qualms. He enthusiastically proceeded to sharpen up Lenin's analysis by praising the high allocative efficiency of the market mechanism, denouncing the tendencies toward "monopolistic parasitism" in the nationalized industry, and sounding solemn warnings against "applied Tuganism" (*prikladnaia Tugan-Baranovshchina*), which postulated the possibility of expansion of productive capacity without proportionate increase in effective demand on the part of the final consumer. This disproportion, in his view, had been ultimately responsible for the downfall of tsarism as well as for the Soviet "scissor crisis" of 1923. In order to prevent this from happening again, a consistent policy of "small profit margins and large turnover" was called for. Nor was this all: Bukharin outlined an elaborate system of institutional arrangements serving the same purpose. Marketing and credit coöperation in agriculture were, in his opinion, the most desirable devices for enlarging the peasant demand for industrial goods. But he had some words of appreciation also for the village kulak whose relentless drive to raise his output and to expand his demand made him, like Goethe's Mephisto, *ein Teil von jener Kraft, die stets das Boese will und stets das Gute schafft.* In the long run, this stratum was expected to be gradually squeezed out under the joint pressure of the proletarian state and the growing coöperative movement among the peasants.

It was the last-mentioned aspect of Bukharin's conception that evoked particularly violent attacks. The conciliatory attitude toward the village rich could not but arouse most deeply the Left Wing of the Party, which had considered the compromise with the individualist peasantry a bitter, if temporarily unavoidable, sacrifice and which was pushing toward resumption of the offensive against propertied classes both on the domestic and on the international scene. But spokesmen of this group, with Preobrazhenskii as its leading economist, did not leave things at that; they penetrated to the core of Bukharin's reasoning and denounced his extrapolation of past experience into the future as a typical "psychology of the restoration period." They were explicit, if rather brief, in dealing with long-range issues like modernization of industry, opening up areas with untapped natural resources, absorption of agricultural surplus population, the importance of what we would call today "social overheads" like transportation and the power system (as well as of industrial development in general) for the efficiency of peasant farming, and, last but not least, the requirements of national defense. They were equally specific in emphasizing some of the basic characteristics of modern productive technology which made its adoption a costly proposition. But the crux of their argument lay in pointing to definite short-term features of the situation of the Soviet economy which made it imperative to move toward these long-range objectives at a high speed in spite of the high cost involved. According to Preobrazhenskii and his friends, people who rejoiced in record-breaking rates of increase in industrial growth up to 1925 lived in a fool's paradise. The expansion at small cost was easy as long as the large reserves of unutilized capacity existed; but with every leap forward in industrial output the time at which future increases would require investment in additional productive facilities was drawing closer. To wait with such investment until that stage, however, would be dangerous. The replacement of a large part of equipment actually in service had been due, but not carried out, in the period of Civil War and in the early years of the NEP. Yet while such a life-extension was possible for a while, each passing year would increase the probability of breakdown of overaged equipment; and this would imply a shrinkage in the capital stock of the economy unless the replacement activities were drastically stepped up. Another powerful source of increased pressure for expansion of capacity lay in the redistribution of income along egalitarian lines which was brought about by the Revolution and which expressed itself in a steep increase in the share of consumption in income. At the same time the large-scale import of capital which had played an important role in the economic development of prerevolutionary Russia was now reduced to a trickle.

But the very circumstances which called for rapid expansion created a grave danger for the stability of the economy. The limitations of resources permitted the required increase in investment to develop only by keeping down the levels of current consumption, while the low real income and the egalitarian mode of its distribution made it more than unlikely that this restriction in consumers' spending would take place voluntarily. Such a situation, if left uncontrolled, would mean a "goods famine," more specifically, a shortage of industrial consumers' goods; and since the Russian peasant then enjoyed, in Preobrazhenskii's words, "a much greater freedom [than before the Revolution] in the choice of the time and of the terms at which to dispose of his own surpluses because of the decrease in 'forced sales,' "[3] he would be likely to respond to an unfavorable turn in the terms of trade by cutting down his marketable surplus and thus administering a crippling blow to the industrial economy. The way out of this deadlock was to be sought in compulsory saving, with monopoly of foreign trade and price manipulation

---

[3] "Ekonomicheskie zametki," *Pravda*, December 15, 1925. The notion of "forced sales" referred to the part of the produce sold by the peasant in order to meet such obligations as taxes or (in prerevolutionary Russia) payments to the landlords.

at home as its main tools; the first would secure high priority for capital goods in Russian imports, the second was expected to contain the pressure of consumers' demand at home against the existing industrial capacity by keeping the prices of industrial commodities higher than they would be under conditions of a free unrestricted market. As a result, the capital stock of the society would be permitted to increase up to a level at which the demand for high current output of consumers' goods and requirements of further expansion of productive capacity could be met simultaneously and not to the exclusion of each other. In the planning of this initial increase, moreover, particular care had to be exercised to keep its inflationary potentialities to a minimum: the largest volume of capital outlays would fall into the initial year of the Plan, when large reserves of the old capacity could provide a cushion for the unstabilizing effect of newly started construction projects, and then gradually taper off in the following years during which these reserves would approach exhaustion.

This last-mentioned point caused little interest at the time of its enunciation; it was, incidentally, brought up not in the actual debate but in a rather technical proposal of a committee of experts known by its initials as *OSVOK*.[4] But the proposals for compulsory saving (bracketed by Preobrazhenskii under the anxiety-provoking name of "primitive socialist accumulation") did call forth an immediate reaction; indeed, they proved an ideal target for attack. The representatives of the Bukharin group were quick to point out that a policy recommended by the Leftists would in its immediate effects greatly increase the tensions which its long-range consequences were expected to alleviate. The policy of monopolistic price manipulation would make the peasants worse off; they would be certain to resist this deterioration by using all the devices Preobrazhenskii and his friends had so eloquently described; and the possibility of steering through the economic and political trouble caused by such a policy toward the time at which the new investment would smooth the waves by starting to deliver the goods could be asserted merely as an act of faith.[5]

II

The assertion that Stalin's interventions in the debate of 1924–1927 did not break the impasse would be an understatement. Indeed, his pronouncements on controversial issues of economic policy in these years exhibit

---

[4] Abbreviation for *Osoboe soveshchanie po vosstanovleniiu osnovnogo kapitala promyshlennosti SSSR*.

[5] For a more detailed account of the controversy, see Maurice Dobb, *Soviet Economic Development Since 1917* (New York, 1948), ch. viii; my "Preobrazhenskii and the Economics of Soviet Industrialization," *Quarterly Journal of Economics*, LXIV (February 1950), 57–88; and my "The Soviet Industrialization Controversy" (unpublished Ph.D. dissertation on deposit at the New School for Social Research, New York, and the Russian Research Center, Harvard University, 1953).

such a definite tendency against sin and in favor of eating one's cake and having it too that it appears at first almost hopeless to distill out of them a clear view not only of the nature of the problems, but also of the attitude of the man. But after a closer examination of the record, there can be no doubt that Stalin's statement at the Fourteenth Party Congress: "We are, and we shall be, for Bukharin," [6] provides a substantially correct description of his position at that time. True, in certain respects he sounded a somewhat different note. He showed a strong inclination to indulge, on every propitious occasion, in exalting the glories of the coming industrialization; moreover, the aspect of the future developments which received the fondest attention on his part was the possibility of making Russia a self-contained unit, economically independent of the outside world — "a country which can produce by its own efforts the necessary equipment." [7] He started to emphasize the need for intensive reconstruction of Soviet industry earlier than Bukharin did; and in the same speech in which he dramatically refused to give "Bukharin's blood" to the opposition, he did not hesitate to disassociate himself from the "get rich" slogan.[8] But neither these nor similar instances could alter the fact that on issues which were relevant for actual policy the agreement was practically complete. When Stalin was applauding the removal of "administrative obstacles preventing the rise in the peasant welfare" as "an operation [which] undoubtedly facilitates any accumulation, private capitalist as well as socialist," [9] or when he denounced on an earlier occasion any attempt to fan the class struggle in the village as "empty chatter," while praising peasant coöperation as a road toward socialist transformation of agriculture,[10] he was talking like a Bukharinite pure and simple; his wailings about "get rich" sounded, in view of this, very much like the famous admonition given to Eduard Bernstein, the father of German "revisionism," by one of his senior friends: "Such things should be done but not said." The identity of position on the larger issue of relationships between industry and agriculture was equally evident. Although Stalin did not invoke the ghost of Tugan-Baranovskii (he was at that time somewhat chary of incursions into the field of theory), he believed firmly that "our industry, which provides the foundation of socialism and of our power, is based on the internal, on the peasant market." [11]

[6] *XIV s"ezd vsesoiuznoi kommunisticheskoi partii* (b). *Stenograficheskii otchët* (Moscow-Leningrad, 1926), p. 494. In Volume VII of Stalin's collected works containing the text of this speech the words "and we shall be" are omitted.

[7] I. V. Stalin, *Sochineniia* (Moscow, 1947), VII, 355.

[8] *Ibid.*, p. 382.

[9] *Ibid.*, p. 153.

[10] *Ibid.*, pp. 123, 125.

[11] *Ibid.*, p. 29. How seriously Stalin took this idea can be seen from the fact that in the immediately following sentence he expressed grave concern about the situation in which Russia would find itself after her industry had "outgrown" the internal market and had to compete for the foreign markets with the advanced capitalist countries.

The last point, to be sure, did not jibe very well with his other declared objectives: if industry had to be oriented primarily toward the satisfaction of peasant needs, it would be impossible to spare an adequate amount of resources for a large-scale effort toward reconstruction of industry, particularly if this should be done with a view to future self-sufficiency in the sphere of capital-goods production. But to proclaim long-term goals was one thing, and to rush toward them at a high speed was another. Stalin in these days showed no inclination toward the latter. In the same speech in which he extolled the virtues of economic independence, he readily admitted that large-scale imports of foreign machinery were, at least for the time being, indispensable for the development of the Soviet economy; and in his polemics against Trotsky at a somewhat later date, he went to considerable lengths in order to emphasize that the Soviet Union would not endanger her economic sovereignty by trading extensively with the capitalist world — first of all because the dependence involved would be a two-way affair and, secondly, because nationalization of large-scale industry and banking as well as state monopoly of foreign trade would provide powerful safeguards against any attempt at foreign encroachments.[12] His attitude toward the problem of the rate of industrial development was characterized by similar circumspection. At one point he would attempt to sidetrack the issue by injecting a larger one and by insisting that a reconstruction of fixed capital in industry would not solve the problem of building socialism in Russia as long as agriculture had not been transformed along collectivist lines.[13] On another occasion, he praised glowingly the rapid increase in output of the Soviet metal industry as proof that "the proletariat . . . can construct with its own efforts a new industry and a new society," [14] without mentioning the obvious fact that this increase had been so rapid precisely because it had been based on increased utilization of the old industrial capacity and *not* on the creation of the new. But when he actually came to grips with the problem in his report to the Fourteenth Congress, he left no doubts as to his real attitude:

[12] "Our country depends on other countries just as other countries depend on our national economy; but this does not mean yet that our country has lost, or is going to lose, its sovereignty [*samostoiatel'nost'*], . . . that it will become a little screw [sic] of the international capitalist economy" (*ibid.*, IX, 132–133). Contrary to what may be the first impression, this passage is not incompatible either with the above-quoted statements or with Stalin's well-known pronouncements of later years. It does, however, provide an additional indication that Stalin's real long-term goal was superiority and not insularity. Such a policy, and more particularly the high rate of economic growth implied in it, did in fact make it rational to develop the domestic capital goods industry on a substantial scale since the demand for the services of this industry was known to be large and sustained and a sizable initial stock was already in existence; but it would also call for making extensive use of the advantages of international division of labor. Still, in the middle twenties, all this sounded rather academic because, as will be shown presently, the decision in favor of the high rate of growth had not yet been made.

[13] *Ibid.*, VII, 200.

[14] *Ibid.*, p. 131.

In order to switch from maximal utilization of everything we had in industry to the policy of constructing a new industry on a new technological basis, on the basis of the construction of new plants, large capital outlays are needed. But since we are suffering from a considerable capital shortage, the further development of our industry will proceed, in all probability, not at such a fast rate as it has until now. The situation with regard to agriculture is different. It cannot be said that all the potentialities of agriculture are already exhausted. Agriculture, in distinction from industry, can move for some time at a fast rate also on its present technological basis. Even the simple rise in cultural level of the peasant, even such a simple thing as cleaning the seeds could raise the gross output of agriculture by 10 to 15 per cent . . . That's why the further development of agriculture does not yet face the technological obstacles our industry has to face . . .[15]

Stalin could not be more frank in formulating the basic problem which was, as we have seen, at the core of the whole discussion: the very same factors — limited productive capacity and low levels of income — that called for expansion in Soviet industry were putting obstacles in its way. In the paragraph quoted the emphasis was clearly on the obstacles. Still, when the arch-moderate Shanin applauded heartily, he must have done so with a twinkle in his eye: in fact the Fourteenth Party Congress did signalize the transition from "filling-in" to reconstruction — but reconstruction on a limited scale and in a cautious mood. Although the volume of capital outlays increased substantially in the years 1926 and 1927, the Leftists led by Preobrazhenskii and Trotsky immediately opened fire. The new investment program, they claimed, was neither here nor there; it was too limited to secure an increase in capacity large enough to stabilize the situation in a not too distant future, too ambitious not to cause inflationary disturbances now in view of the absence of drastic taxation measures.

In the face of these attacks, and of actual difficulties which did not fail to materialize, something more than a sober and judicious description of the two horns of the dilemma was called for. A characteristic division of labor developed at this point. Bukharin and Rykov, who were the guiding spirits of the new line, were wrestling with large, clear-cut issues — the relation between heavy and light industry, the limits for investment in time-consuming projects, the possibility of absorbing the surplus labor in production lines with low capital requirements — in a desperate search for solutions which would make the adopted policy work. Stalin followed a different procedure. He visibly tried to avoid sharply delineated problems; instead, he let his argument seesaw from bold statements of principles to sobering but comfortably loose observations on present-day realities, and he switched from obtuse mystique to gruff common sense. Rapid industrialization? Yes, indeed! More than that: it should be kept in mind that "not every development of industry constitutes industrialization" and that "the focal point of industrialization, its basis, consists of development of heavy industry (fuel, metals,

---

[15] *Ibid.,* pp. 315–316.

etc.) and of eventual development of production of the means of production, development of domestic machine-building." [16] But right on the heels of such proclamations there would come a caustic remark about those who "sometimes forget that it is impossible to make plans either for industry as a whole or for some 'large and all-embracing' enterprise without a certain minimum of means, without a certain minimum of reserves," [17] and a warning that "an industry which breaks itself away from the national economy as a whole and loses its connection with it cannot be the guiding force of the national economy." [18] Could the Soviet economy in its present shape afford a rate of economic development which would exceed that of the capitalist countries? Of course! The capitalist countries had based their expansion on exploitation of colonies, military conquest, or foreign loans. But the Soviet Union expropriated the capitalists and the landlords, nationalized strategic areas of the economy, and repudiated the tsarist foreign debts. This circumstance enabled her to provide a sufficient volume of accumulation without having recourse to any of these devices.[19] Furthermore, it permitted this accumulation to unfold alongside of "a steady improvement in the material conditions of the working masses, including the bulk of the peasantry . . . as contrasted with the capitalist methods of industrialization based on the growing misery of millions of working people." [20] No specific reasons for any of these assertions were given. However, the most elaborate of such attempts at solution by definition concluded by admitting that the socialist principles along which the Soviet economy was organized offered merely a *possibility* of achieving the appropriate level of accumulation, but no more than that; and the concrete proposals for policy which followed were in their sum total excruciatingly modest not only in comparison with the grandiloquent claims that preceded them but also, and more significantly, with regard to the size of the investment programs they were supposed to sustain.[21]

All this looked very much like trying to buy a second-hand Ford for the price of a discarded piece of junk while pretending that a brand-new Packard was being obtained. True, there was another line of defense: to

[16] *Ibid.*, VIII, 120.

[17] *Ibid.*, p. 131.

[18] *Ibid.*, p. 132.

[19] *Ibid.*, pp. 122–125.

[20] *Ibid.*, p. 287.

[21] They include (1) improved incentives for peasant saving; (2) reduction in retail prices of industrial goods; (3) orderly amortization policies; (4) building up export reserves; (5) creation of budgetary surplus (*ibid.*, pp. 126–129). In other contexts elimination of waste and inefficiency in economic and political administration receives the top billing (*ibid.*, IX, 196 and joint declaration by Stalin, Rykov, and Kuibyshev in *Pravda*, August 17, 1926). Some of these measures, while pointing in the right direction, could hardly be expected to have much effect in the immediate future, and others involved putting the cart before the horse, e.g., price reductions not preceded by substantial expansion in productive capacity.

play down the importance of recurrent spells of "goods famine" and to present them as transient phenomena. Although Stalin tried this device occasionally, it was obviously a tenuous argument to use, particularly since the assertion that "quick development of our industry is the surest way to eliminate the goods famine" [22] sounded too much like conceding a point to the Left opposition. It was therefore only logical for him to shift the battleground to the territory of the adversaries, to concentrate on the crucial weak spot in their position and to pound relentlessly upon it:

The oppositionist bloc assumed a conflict between industry and agriculture and is headed toward breaking industry away from agriculture. It does not realize and it does not admit that it is impossible to develop industry while neglecting the interests of agriculture and hurting these interests in a rude fashion. It does not understand that if industry is the guiding force of the national economy, the agricultural economy represents in turn the basis on which our industry is able to develop . . .

. . . The Party cannot and will not tolerate [a situation in which] the opposition continues to undermine the basis of the alliance of workers and peasants by spreading the idea of an increase in wholesale prices and in the burden of taxation upon the peasantry, by attempting to "construe" the relationships between proletariat and peasantry not as relationships of economic *coöperation* but as relationships of exploitation of the peasantry by the proletarian state. The Party cannot and will not tolerate this.[23]

At the Fifteenth Party Congress, which carried out this solemn vow by expelling the Left-wingers, Stalin was surveying the field once more. He displayed again the full array of the familiar arguments: praise for the growth of the Soviet industrial output at a rate which, while declining continuously since 1924–1925, was still showing "a record percentage which no large capitalist country in the world has ever shown";[24] reaffirmation of faith in the superiority which the Soviet system possessed with regard to capitalism in its ability to accumulate and which should make it possible to increase the industrial output by roughly 75 per cent during the coming five years in spite of the exhaustion of the capacity reserves; strong emphasis on the possibility of developing "in an atmosphere of constant *rapprochement* between city and village, between proletariat and peasantry," [25] as one of the greatest advantages of Soviet industry. His backhanded remarks about what he termed the "shadowy aspects" of the Soviet economy ("elements" of goods famine, lack of reserves, etc.) contained no specific proposals for remedy but carried a clear implication that if people on the spot would apply themselves to their tasks with more energy, all would be well. There was, however, no complacency in his remarks on agriculture, and here indeed something new was added: in view of the slowness of agricultural develop-

[22] Stalin, *Sochineniia,* IX, 120.
[23] *Ibid.,* pp. 288, 352–353.
[24] *Ibid.,* X, 300.
[25] *Ibid.,* pp. 301–302.

ment, Stalin declared, the task of the Party would now consist in bringing about "a gradual transition of pulverized peasant farms to the level of combined large-scale holdings, to the social collective cultivation of land on the basis of the intensification and mechanization of agriculture." [26] He was careful not to give any hint as to the anticipated speed of this movement, and, in an enunciation antedating by a few weeks his report to the Fifteenth Congress, he was explicit in emphasizing that it would take a long time to collectivize the bulk of the peasantry because such an undertaking would require "huge finances" which the Soviet state did not yet have.[27] Still, his statement was surprising: but events which were even then fast advancing were to provide *ex post* a clue to it.

III

The beginning of 1928 saw large consignments of the Leftist "super-industrializers" move toward places of exile in Siberia and Central Asia. But at the same time their dire predictions were coming true. For the first time since the "scissors crisis" of 1923 the peasant bolted the regime. By January 1928 the amount of collected grain fell by roughly one-third as compared with the same period of the preceding year. During the following few months it rose again only to drop in the spring; and the emergency methods by which the temporary increase was enforced stirred up once more the feelings of bitterness and resistance which had been dormant in the villages during the seven years of the NEP. The crisis of the system was there — the first crisis Stalin had to cope with as the undisputed leader of the Party and of the state. During the eighteen months that followed, Stalin was no longer arguing, as before, against opponents who had been isolated and outmaneuvered before they began to fight; he was reappraising a policy which had promoted his rise to power and which seemed now to explode in his face. It is therefore not surprising that his pronouncements of that period differ significantly from those of the earlier years. They certainly contain their due share of crudeness, obfuscation, and outright distortion; but at the same time they show flashes of astonishing frankness and incisiveness clearly due to realization that everything was at stake and that the time of muddling through was over.

The prime task consisted, understandably enough, in providing the explanation of the agricultural debacle. One can clearly distinguish several parallel lines of attack in Stalin's statements on the subject. The first of them was already indicated in his report to the Fifteenth Congress when he mentioned the low productivity of small-scale peasant agriculture and its low marketable surplus as a serious obstacle for the rapid industrial development of the country. This proposition was in itself neither new nor con-

[26] *Ibid.*, p. 309.
[27] *Ibid.*, p. 225.

troversial, provided that the "obstacle" was taken to be a retarding factor rather than an insuperable barrier. It was a breath-taking jump to conclusions, however, when Stalin went on to claim that "there is no other way out" except for collectivization. In the audience to which he was addressing himself there were, to be sure, no doubts as to the superiority of the large-size units in agricultural economy. But it was generally understood that there was still a wide range of opportunities for increases in the productivity of peasant farming which would not call for large-scale mechanized equipment and for drastic expansion in the size of the productive unit; and it was agreed that the extensive application of the latter category of improvements should be postponed, in view of the high capital requirements involved, until after the capital-goods industry had been sufficiently expanded. Consequently, while the idea of collectivization of agriculture as a long-range objective held a place of honor in the Party program of 1919 and was repeatedly invoked after that, particularly in the pronouncements of the Left, no one had thus far suggested putting it into effect on a large scale within the next few years in order to solve difficulties facing the Soviet economy at the end of the "restoration period." In fact, Stalin himself seemed to take quite an edge off his argument and to hark back to his earlier views when he admitted the existence of considerable reserves for improvement within the framework of the small-scale economy,[28] and as late as April 1929 he still kept insisting that "the individual farming of poor and middle peasants plays and will play the predominant role in supplying industry with food and raw material in the immediate future." [29] But, and most important, the whole point seemed to have no direct bearing on the concrete issue under consideration. By the end of 1927 and at the beginning of 1928 the Russian peasants had not less but more grain at their disposal than in the preceding years; still, they were willing to sell less of it than in the years of bad harvest. The reference to the low productivity of small-scale farming, even if reduced to sensible proportions, was definitely too "long run" to provide an explanation for this phenomenon.

The second line of argument was succinctly summed up in the phrase "as long as the kulak exists, the sabotage of grain collections will exist too." [30] This point, made in Stalin's speech in January 1928 and repeated by him with increasing vehemence ever after, was certainly straightforward enough; still it raised more questions than it answered. The fact of formidable kulak

---

[28] "There is every indication that we could increase the yield of the peasant farms by 15–20 per cent within a few years. We have now in use about 5 million hoes. The substitution of ploughs for them could alone result in a most substantial increase in the output of grain in the country, not to speak of supplying the peasant farms with a certain minimum of fertilizer, improved seeds, small machinery and the like" (*ibid.,* XI, 92).

[29] *Ibid.,* XII, 59.

[30] *Ibid.,* XI, 4–5.

resistance did not fit very well, to begin with, into the rosy picture of the Soviet village Stalin had been unfolding before his listeners only slightly more than a year earlier when he proudly referred to the steadily increasing proportion of middle peasants in the agricultural population and asserted, with a long quotation from Lenin on hand to bear him out, that nobody but panic-stricken people could see a danger in the growth of "small private capital" in the villages because this growth "is being compensated and over-compensated by such decisive facts as the development of our industry, which strengthens the positions of the proletariat and of the socialist forms of the economy." [31] True, in this case also there were, at first, important qualifications which softened the impact of the shock: stern warning against any talk about "dekulakization" as "counterrevolutionary chatter," condemnation of the excessive zeal in applying reprisals, and announcement of moderate increases in prices of agricultural products.[32] But after all this had been said and done, it was still to be explained why the kulak was so successful in his criminal endeavor — more particularly, why he was able, as Stalin reluctantly acknowledged, to carry along with him the "middle peasants" who were supplying the bulk of the marketable surplus at that time.[33]

Stalin had a clear answer to this as well as to all other questions the previous explanations had left unanswered; between the "low-productivity" argument and the cloak-and-dagger theory of the kulaks' plot he had a third line of reasoning which hit the nail straight on the head. It was less publicized than the former two and for good reasons: it amounted to a clear and unqualified admission of a complete impasse. Stalin no longer tried to play down the impact of the goods famine; he stressed instead that the shortage of industrial goods on the peasant market, aggravated by an increase in peasant earnings in the preceding period, had hit not merely the kulaks but the peasants as a whole and had made them strike back by cutting the grain deliveries.[34] He spelled out more fully than ever before the connection between the goods famine and the discontinuous increase in the volume of investment:

Industrial reconstruction means the transfer of resources from the field of production of articles of consumption to the field of production of means of production . . . But what does it mean? It means that money is being invested in the construction of new enterprises, that the number of new towns and new consumers is increasing while, on the other hand, the new enterprises will begin to turn out additional masses of commodities only in three or four years' time. It is obvious that this does not help to overcome the goods famine.[35]

[31] *Ibid.*, VIII, 291–292.
[32] *Ibid.*, XI, 15, 124–125.
[33] *Ibid.*, p. 12.
[34] *Ibid.*, p. 14.
[35] *Ibid.*, p. 267.

He rounded out the picture when he dropped his usual double talk and shocked his colleagues of the Central Committee by revealing his views on the true sources of accumulation in the Soviet economy:

> The peasantry pays to the state not only the normal taxes, direct and indirect, but it *overpays*, first of all, on the relatively high prices of industrial goods, and is being more or less *underpaid* on the relatively low prices of agricultural products . . . This is something like a "tribute" [*nechto vrode "dani"*], something like a supertax we are temporarily compelled to impose in order to maintain and to develop further the present tempo of development of industry, to secure the industry for the whole country, to raise the well-being of the village still further, and to abolish entirely this supertax, these "scissors" between the city and the village.[36]

All this sounded very much like a somewhat awkward rephrasing of Preobrazhenskii's "law of primitive socialist accumulation." The crucial task at that time of the day, however, was not to restate an old diagnosis but to construe a "tribute"-collecting device that would work: and this was exactly what Stalin did. The collective farm, in which decisions about size and disposal of the marketable surplus were made not by individual farmers but by management carrying out the orders of the state, was to serve as a high-powered tool for enforcing the necessary rate of saving in the most literal sense of the standard Marxian definition: it could make the peasants "sell without purchasing" to a much greater extent than they would have done if left to themselves. Here was the decisive point. Still, Stalin was undoubtedly right in not being too ostentatious about it and in holding on firmly to the two other arguments referred to above in spite of their inadequacy. To proclaim in so many words that collectivization was needed in order to squeeze out the peasants in a most effective way would clearly be a poor tactic; it was much smarter to present the collective farm as an indispensable vehicle for modernizing Soviet agriculture and for drastically increasing its productivity. In view of everything Stalin had to say about the impact of the "goods famine" on the peasantry as a whole and about the inevitability of the "supertax," the diatribes against kulak sabotage could not be taken very seriously. They could, nevertheless, be of appreciable help in whipping up emotions against an alternative solution which was advanced at that time by Stalin's former comrades-in-arms. The representatives of the Bukharin-Rykov group did not propose to revise the investment plans below the fairly impressive levels set by the Party leadership at the end of 1927. They believed, however, that in order to carry out these plans it was not necessary to abandon support for individual peasant farming and to renounce the policy of no interference with the growth of large-scale kulak farms while curbing the nonproductive and exploitative activities of their

[36] *Ibid.*, p. 159 (italics in original). It may be worth noting that this speech, which led to the final break between Stalin and the Bukharin-Rykov group, was not published until 1949.

owners. On the contrary, although by that time the controversy had already been quite muffled, and it was difficult to ascertain what exactly the leaders of the Right Wing were prepared to do, the general tenor of their pronouncements, as well as occasional statements of second-string representatives and "fellow travelers" of this group, indicated a willingness to go to greater lengths than ever before toward placating the peasants in general and the kulaks in particular, in order to provide them with incentives for increasing the marketable surplus and the volume of voluntary saving in an effort to contain the mounting inflationary pressures.

Stalin never earnestly tried to assail the economic logic of this position. He never attempted to prove that it was impossible for socialized industry and kulak farming to operate smoothly within one economic system, although he made a few obiter dicta to that effect. Neither did he care to show (which would be a more serious point) that an investment policy, sustained to a considerable extent by the peasants' free decision to restrict their consumption, would tend to be rather narrow in scope and susceptible to rude shocks as a result of such uncontrollable events as drought or changes in international terms of trade. Instead, he asked: "What is meant by not hindering kulak farming? It means setting the kulak free. And what is meant by setting the kulak free? It means giving him power." [37] Taken literally, this seemed to be one of the dubious syllogisms Stalin was notoriously fond of whenever a weak case was to be defended. It is quite conceivable, however, that in this particular instance he believed every word he said; and, what is vastly more important, there can be no doubt that the consistent application of the Rightist recipe would be fraught with gravest political dangers. The efforts to enlist voluntary support of the peasantry for the industrialization developing at considerable speed would require a veritable tightrope performance on the part of the Soviet rulers. In order to maintain the precarious balance and to steer clear of trouble at every sharper turning of the road, the regime would have to combine compulsory control measures with additional concessions; and since there was little room for compromise in the economic sphere, it could become well-nigh indispensable to explore a new line of approach and to attempt to earn the good will of the upper strata of the peasantry by opening up for them avenues of political influence even if confined, at first, to the level of local government. There was nothing either in the logic of things or, for that matter, in the tenets of the accepted doctrine to warrant the conclusion that such a situation, if permitted to endure, would inevitably result in "giving power to the kulaks" and in restoring capitalism. But it is quite probable that under the impact of initial concessions and of further maneuvering the system of authoritarian dictatorship would have become increasingly permeated by elements of political pluralism and of quasi-democratic give-and-take. The vacillating and

[37] *Ibid.*, p. 275.

conciliatory attitude which, judging by Stalin's own testimony,[38] was shown by the lower echelons of the Party hierarchy and governmental apparatus, during the critical months of 1928, underlined the gravity of the situation. The choice was clear: either a deep retreat and the gradual erosion of the dictatorial system or an all-out attack aimed at total destruction of the adversary's capability to resist.

Stalin's pronouncements since early 1928 showed beyond possibility of doubt that he had decided in favor of the second alternative. The transition from theory to action, however, was all but a masterminded advance toward a well-defined goal. Stalin evidently planned at first to move in the agricultural field by stages; his repeated declarations about the predominant role of individual farming for many years to come, as well as his condemnations of "dekulakization" and readiness to meet the restive peasantry part of the way by granting price increases, can be taken as a clear indication of this. And the impression of caution and groping for solution is still further reinforced when the position on issues of agricultural policy is viewed in a broader context. There was, undoubtedly, a perceptible change of emphasis in Stalin's declarations on questions of industrialization policy after January 1928. He no longer spoke about Soviet industry as "the most large scale and most concentrated in the world," as he had at the Fifteenth Party Congress.[39] Instead, he denounced its "terrible backwardness" and sounded a call for catching up with the West as a condition for survival: the old aim of "economic independence" was now transformed into "superiority" and further dramatized by the stress upon the element of tempo at which the catching up was to take place. And while all this talk was still couched in most general terms, the language of the drafts of the First Five-Year Plan, which were at that time being prepared by the official governmental agencies and which reflected in their successive versions the changes of the official policy, was much more outspoken: during the whole period between the Fifteenth Party Congress and adoption of the final draft of the First Five-Year Plan in the spring of 1929 there was a clear upward trend in all the crucial indicators of the "tempo" — rate of growth in industrial output, volume of investment and its increase over time, share of heavy industry in the total capital outlays. But at the same time there was strong evidence that the momentous implications of the new policy were not yet fully grasped. Stalin was, no doubt, most persistent in stressing that industry and agriculture were interdependent, the first constituting a "leading link," and the second being a "basis." Still, whenever he went beyond these generalities, he pointed out that industry would have to expand and to reëquip itself in order to start reëquipping agriculture; in fact this was, in his view, one of the strongest forces pushing for speedy industrialization.[40] The implication was clear: the

[38] *Ibid.*, pp. 3–4, 235.
[39] *Ibid.*, X, 301.
[40] *Ibid.*, XI, 252–253.

bulk of the reorganization of agriculture was to take place *after* the completion of a cycle of intensive industrial expansion and not *simultaneously* with it. Moreover, although Stalin kept extolling the superiority of *"smytchka through metal"* over *"smytchka through textile,"* he could not refrain from remarking wistfully that it would be very fine indeed "to shower the village with all kinds of goods in order to extract from the village the maximum amount of agricultural products" and from leaving at least a strong implication that the attainment of such a happy state of affairs was one of the major objectives of the industrialization drive.[41] Stalin was merely hinting at these diverse points, but they were spelled out fully in the targets of the First Five-Year Plan: more than doubling of the fixed capital of the whole nonagricultural sector over the quinquennium, increase in output of industrial consumers' goods by 40 per cent, and no more than an 18 per cent share of the collective farms in the marketable output of agriculture.

No doubt, if the planned sizes of the first two items of the blueprint had been mutually consistent, the comparatively moderate targets for the third would be appropriate. But they were not; moreover, in view of Stalin's own statements about the causes of the "goods famine," the high target for consumers' goods could be to him only a pious wish, if not plain eyewash. As a result, there was an awkward dilemma. From the standpoint of reducing the pressures on the facilities of the capital goods industry, a postponement of full-dress collectivization seemed wise. But the function of collective farms consisted, first and foremost, in providing the technique for imposing the required volume of compulsory saving, and since the astronomic rate of planned expansion in fixed capital would inevitably entail, at the very least in the first years of the Plan, a drastic cut in consumption levels, such a technique was desperately needed from the very beginning of the process. How could the conflict be resolved? The answer was not slow in coming. Before the Plan was two months old the moderate targets in the agricultural field mentioned above went overboard, because Stalin had reversed himself; in response to the repeated and more dismal failure of the grain collections, all-out collectivization was sweeping the country.

Up to this point the whole development looked like some sort of cumulative process gone mad. To begin with, there was a "goods famine" generated by expanding industry and throwing agriculture into a crisis, with an incipient collectivization drive as a result. Then, there was the perspective of an extremely rapid transformation of agriculture imparting additional impetus to plans of industrial expansion and pushing them to lengths which would disbalance agriculture more than ever and, finally, the sudden burst of all-out collectivization spread disruption in the social fabric of the countryside and left in its wake the wholesale slaughter of livestock by rebellious peasants. But after reaching what seemed to be the stage of explosion, the

[41] *Ibid.,* p. 40.

fluctuations began to subside as the new device went to work. Collective farming pulled the Plan over the hump because it did what an agriculture based on individual ownership would never have done, even if confronted with an equally formidable display of terror and repression: amidst mass starvation, in the face of contracting agricultural output and an appalling shortage in industrial consumers' goods, the new set-up secured an iron ration of food sufficient to keep alive the workers of rapidly growing industry, and provided an export surplus big enough to finance record-breaking importations of foreign machinery. The feat was achieved to a large extent on the basis of old, decrepit equipment; the capital-goods industry was permitted to make huge forward strides in its own expansion before being called upon to supply the collective farms with technology which would correspond to their size. The moral of the story was clear: if a half-completed structure of collective farming and a capital-goods industry still in the throes of acute growing pains succeeded in making possible economic expansion at an unparalleled rate, there was every reason to maintain this pattern of development after these two key elements had been firmly established and to continue using up at a high rate the opportunities for investment in enlarged productive potential and increased power, with the satisfaction of consumers' needs firmly relegated to the rear.

Such was, in fact, the conclusion Stalin had drawn. But while the practical consequences of this decision were momentous, little would be gained by discussing his running comments on them in any detail. There is no doubt that after 1929 Stalin was more assertive than ever before in proclaiming his long-range goals and in exhorting to further efforts. All his earlier pronouncements on the need of catching up with the West look pallid in comparison with his famous "we-do-not-want-to-be-beaten" speech.[42] Although the successes of the five-year plans failed to improve the quality of their architect's theorizing, it was only natural that in the process of directing Soviet industrialization he sharpened some of his earlier notions of its distinctive features and made a few new observations: his remarks on short-term profit considerations as an inadequate guide for developing new areas of economy, and on Russia's advantage in not being weighted down in her attempts to adapt new technology by the massive stock of old-type equipment already in existence are cases in point.[43] And he displayed to the full his uncanny ability to change tactics and recast arguments in the face of unexpected difficulties.[44] For all these new touches and variations, however,

---

[42] *Ibid.*, XIII, 29–42, esp. 38–40.

[43] *Ibid.*, pp. 192–93 and *Voprosy leninizma,* 11th ed. (Moscow, 1947), p. 575.

[44] His "Golovokruzhenie ot uspekhov" (Stalin, *Sochineniia,* XII, 191–199), which put a temporary halt to the forced collectivization, is, to be sure, the best-known example of this. It may be worth while, however, to quote a similar instance from a different area. In 1930, with reports from industrial battlefields claiming big victories, Stalin allowed himself another brief spell of "dizziness with success": he called for raising the 1933 target

there was no longer any real change either in the structure of the system or in the views of its builder. He summed up his ideas once more shortly after the war when he contrasted the "capitalist" pattern of industrialization, putting the development of consumers'-goods output first, and the "socialist" pattern starting with the expansion of heavy industries.[45] And he restated the same position in a more generalized way a few years later when he answered one of his last self-addressed questions: "What does it mean to give up the preponderance of the production of the means of production [over production of consumers' goods]? This means to destroy the possibility of the uninterrupted growth of the national economy." [46] Bukharin would have called it *prikladnaia Tugan-Baranovshchina*. Indeed, this it was: "applied Tuganism" harnessed to the service of a totalitarian state.

---

for steel from 10 to 15–17 million tons and used abusive language against the "Trotskyite theory of the leveling-off curve of growth" (*ibid.*, pp. 331, 349–352). In 1933, however, when the actual level of steel output fell far short of the initial target and the rate of over-all industrial expansion slumped heavily, he did not hesitate to move more than halfway toward this much-detested theory: he argued then that the rate of growth in output had shown a decline as a result of the transition from the "period of restoration" to the "period of reconstruction," and went on to say that there was nothing sinister about it (*ibid.*, 183–185). But in the following years the rate of increase went up again, if not quite to the level of the preceding period, and the unholy distinction between "restoration" and "reconstruction" disappeared from Stalin's vocabulary.

[45] Speech to the voters of the Stalin electoral district of Moscow, *Pravda*, February 10, 1946.

[46] I. Stalin, *Ekonomicheskie problemy sotsializma v SSSR* (Moscow, 1952), p. 24. It goes without saying that this is much too strong a condition. An "uninterrupted growth of the national economy" is secured whenever the volume of investment exceeds the amount needed to maintain the capital equipment at a level sufficient to keep the income per head of growing population constant. This requirement might indeed involve a "preponderance [for example, more rapid tempo of growth] of the production of the means of production" if at least one of the following assumptions could be taken to hold: (1) abnormally high rate of wear and tear due either to low durability of the average piece of machinery or to the unusually large share of old-vintage equipment in the existing capital stock; (2) necessity to provide productive facilities for a discontinuously large increase in the total labor force in order to offset the pressure of increasing population on the income-per-capita levels; (3) the capital-goods industry exposed to these pressures being adapted in its capacity to a very limited volume of net capital construction over and above the "normal" replacement levels. It would certainly be bold to argue that any of these assumptions actually prevailed in the Soviet economy of 1952. But it would be even more drastic to assume that when Stalin said "uninterrupted growth" he meant precisely this, and nothing else.

Part I

Review

ALEXANDER GERSCHENKRON

It is not the purpose of these remarks to sum up the preceding papers. This is hardly necessary. Each of the papers stands on its own feet. Still less is it intended to take issue with one or another point in the papers. If nothing else, my double role as participant and chairman would effectively bar me from following that course. The purpose rather is to point to certain general problems which are evoked by the foregoing story of ideas on economic development in Russia's intellectual history from Radishchev to Stalin, and to discuss them briefly.

The problems I have in mind refer (1) to the question of continuity and discontinuity in that intellectual history, more specifically to the question whether the changes that could be observed in the closing decades of the nineteenth century, and perhaps even in 1917, were really as far-reaching as one is tempted to assume; (2) to an evaluation of the broad significance of the official ideology in Soviet Russia in its relation to the country's economic development; and (3) to the general role of ideology in an economic development that proceeds in conditions of considerable backwardness.

As Mr. Schwarz has said in his paper, the Russian Marxians of the 1890's achieved an indubitable victory in their disputes with the Populists. In some sense, this is an unexceptional statement. It was certainly a victory within the ideological context of the time. The swing in public opinion was unambiguous indeed. But, viewing that victory half a century or more after the event one cannot but wonder at its belatedness. It took the magnificent development of the nineties to open the skulls of the intelligentsia to the comprehension of a process that had been going on for almost four decades. Johann Nestroy's immortal "Ah, der Leim!" is indeed apposite here.

Nor was the victory won, strictly speaking, by Marxian theory. As I have tried to show in my paper, Marxian theory lent itself just as well to a rejection as to an acceptance of Russian industrialization. Nikolai —on operated exclusively with weapons fetched from Karl Marx's intellectual armory and Marx did not upbraid him for shooting at the wrong bird. Quite the contrary is true. We may leave open the question how much Marx's own thoughts on the subject were influenced by the false hope of an impending seizure of power by Populist revolutionaries or by his strong German nationalism. What matters here is that the Populists were confounded neither by Marx's economics in the strict sense of the word nor by his materialistic conception of history, but by hard pressure of irrefutable economic facts. That people who were willing to look at those facts a little earlier than their adversaries preferred to appeal to different aspects of Marxian theory and to call themselves Marxians or "Russian students of Marx" should not disguise what actually occurred.

Mr. Schwarz's paper aptly points up the importance of published statistics in the conversion process. And equally significant in this respect is what Mr. Radkey has stressed: namely, how easily and how readily Chernov accepted Marxian concepts in their revisionist form for the purpose of constructing his brand of agrarian socialism. Max Weber's famous and oft-repeated phrase — which he borrowed from Henry Adams — about Marxism not being a hansom the Marxians can jump off any time that a discussion of Marxism itself is at stake inevitably comes to mind here. That Russian Marxism of the nineties was also a "reflection" can be safely asserted, except that what was reflected was not class interests but emotional preferences and predilections of intellectuals as adjusted to a "given" character of economic development in the country.

To have convinced fellow humans on the basis of more than three decades of accumulated experience that barking at the moon did not alter her course was hardly an impressive achievement. By the same token, one need not be overmuch impressed with the specific brand of verbal or conceptual magic used to make the facts palatable. But in addition, it should also be considered that the victory that had been won remained singularly incomplete. And that seems to be so for a variety of reasons.

In many respects, Stalin, the last link in the series of figures discussed in these papers, constitutes a return to Pososhkov. It is the tragedy of today's Russia that patterns of economic behavior and trains of thought that should have remained confined to long-bygone ages have been revitalized and reproduced in contemporary Soviet reality. But at the same time, there is little doubt that a good many specific elements of Russian Populism were taken over by the Bolshevik wing of Russian Marxism and celebrated their reincarnation in Lenin's and Stalin's thought and action.

The reference here is not only to peasant discontent with which the revolutionary hopes of most, though not all, Populists had been connected and which Lenin used so deliberately in designing the strategy of the revolution. Lenin did steal the Populist thunder and the Bolsheviks were brought to power on the crest of a peasant rebellion reaching out for the long-craved-for land of the gentry. But another fact may be equally important. The unwillingness of the Populists to accept the economic development in the country in conjunction with autocratic oppression provided the background for a radicalism in thought which kept wavering uneasily between anarchism on the one hand and the apotheosis of the omnipotent Jacobinic state on the other. In practice, it provided the background for the disastrous "race against time" and it created a moral climate that displayed a most complex bundle of contradictory features: the spirit of self-sacrifice, heroism, love of the people, conjoined with the idea that means justified the ends and that any method, from forged imperial manifestoes to murderous conspiracy, was justified in the struggle against the absolute evil of absolutism. That these latter aspects of Populism were carried over and absorbed within the fold of Bolshevist thought and practice is undeniable. These considerations, it may be argued, are essentially political in nature, a ground an economist perhaps cannot venture upon with impunity. His only justification in doing so is that the connection between those political aspects and an either profoundly pessimistic or highly Utopian view of the Populists on the subject of economic development is fairly obvious.

There is, however, another aspect of the basic continuity in Russian thought that is more important from our point of view and bears more directly on our subject. Why was the vehicle of Marxism chosen in order to teach the Russian public opinion a simple lesson in empirical facts? Again Mr. Schwarz rightly remarks that as long as "Manchester Liberals" or "List Protectionists" preached the same simple truth, their sermons fell on deaf ears. It was different in the case of Marxism.

Mr. Radkey refers briefly to the problem and states that "the intellectuals desired to be in fashion and so could only be socialists." There is something to that explanation. Since the days of the Russian Voltairians the desire to take over "the last word of Western thought" certainly was widespread in Russia and we have many testimonies, including that of Professor Trubetskoi, that Russian university students of the period did consider Marx "the last word of Western social science." Still, this view does not seem to be the whole story. It tends to neglect the whole flow of preceding intellectual history. I do not disagree at all with Mr. Radkey when he points at the inchoate and inarticulate character of nineteenth-century Populist socialism. But such as it was, its strength and its influence in forming opinions and conditioning emotions were undeniable. It seems at least plausible to assume that an inevitable shift in public opinion assumed the form of Marxism *because* Populism had been its predecessor. The violence of the literary clashes should not conceal from us the important fact of continuity in Russian intellectual development. Marxism, in preaching acquiescence in industrialization, also showed that the socialist goal need not be relinquished along with the abandonment of the *obshchina*.

But perhaps we may go even a step further and relate the victorious emergence of Russian Marxism to the specific stage of the country's economic development. Just because in viewing the historical processes of industrialization our eyes so often remain riveted to the case of England, there is a tendency to assume that nineteenth-century industrial development was essentially associated with the ideology of economic liberalism. This, however, is far from being the general case. It is, on the contrary, possible to hazard the opinion that the specific ideologies which accompany the process of industrialization tend to vary in accordance with the degree of backwardness in which a given country finds itself on the eve of its great upsurge in economic growth.

I have referred in my paper to the role of the St. Simonian doctrines in connection with the fine spurt of industrial development which France experienced after the advent to power of Napoleon III. The paradox of a vigorous capitalist development sustained by a group of great entrepreneurs who professed to be fervent adherents of a socialist creed must remain baffling unless we assume that in a backward country a very strong ideological medicine is needed to overcome the barriers of stagnation and routine and to elicit popular support for a policy which as a rule involves some temporary material sacrifices for large groups of the population and necessarily entails losses in terms of traditional values and beliefs. In the case of Germany, which was still more backward than France, St. Simonian doctrines were effectively supplemented, if not supplanted, by placing nationalist ideology in the service of the industrialization process.

That in Russia, which in turn was ever so much more backward than Germany, the same function was performed by the still more virulent doctrines of Marxism seems to fit well into a general European pattern. It is perhaps this connection rather than the long socialist tradition which helps to explain the attraction which Marxian doctrines exercised in the 1890's upon men who, like Struve (and in some sense even Miliukov), neither by temperament nor by general philosophy were predisposed to accept such doctrines. To present the costly and (for those idyllic days) in so many ways ruthless process of industrialization not as a deliberate decision but as a product of iron laws of economic development obviously tended to appease the disturbed conscience of the intelligentsia, a group traditionally ridden by guilt complexes of all kinds. They all were "guilty without guilt" — *bez viny vinovatye*, as the Russian phrase goes. For all those successors of the repentant nobleman of the nineteenth century, for the repentant merchant, the repentant factory owner, and particularly the repentant intellectual, for all those guilty innocents, abroad in the stream of industrialization, Marxism provided a welcome relief. And it also appeared most convenient to those who were primarily interested in civilizing the country through the processes of industrialization as well as to those who desired industrialization for nationalistic reasons.

In the first section of my paper I referred to the fact that as economic backwardness was being diminished in Russia by the process of industrialization, the temporary reductions in the standard of living gave way to its improvement, and the use of government finance in industrialization tended to be replaced by the use of investment banking. In the period preceding the outbreak of World War I the results of the great upswing of the nineties began to tell and Russia was clearly moving to a new stage in her economic development. It is perhaps not too hazardous to suggest that these gradations of backwardness in the economic and institutional spheres were, to some extent, paralleled by similar processes in the sphere of ideology.

The appearance of the *Vekhi* symposium with its broad attack upon the intelligentsia's traditional creeds is usually attributed to the general climate of reaction which followed in the wake of the defeat of the 1905 Revolution. It is true that the strictures of the symposium were not directed against Marxism alone; nor could it be said that revision of attitudes toward industrialization was the *primary* concern of the seven contributors. Still it seems reasonable to suggest that *Vekhi* reflected a fundamental fact: the sway of Marxism over the minds of the intelligentsia had been weakened as a result of the progressing industrialization of the country. Mr. Radkey suggests that Stolypin's reform imparted a severe blow to Russian agrarian socialism. If the course of the reform had not been interrupted the blow might well have been a final one. The prospects of Marxian socialism were much less dim because the continued growth of the industrial labor force was bound to strengthen the Social Democratic Party and trade unions. But this process was perfectly compatible with a decline in the appeal of orthodox Marxian ideas to the intelligentsia, even though the rate of that decline was not hastened by the unyielding policies of the autocracy. Thus from two sides the foundations were being laid for the development of a nonsocialist, bourgeois ideology in Russia. For the understanding of the significance of the intellectual movements that have been discussed here these processes deserve to be mentioned even though they were, of course, halted and reversed by the outbreak of war and revolution.

Thus, for a number of reasons the victory of Marxism in prerevolutionary Russia was neither as complete nor as final as is often believed. But what about the reversal just mentioned? Did not the Bolshevik Revolution constitute the second and this time both complete and final victory of Marxism in Russia? This is claimed by the *communis opinio* and corroborated by the appearances. It seems to me that Mr. Erlich's paper performs a valuable service in showing, at least indirectly, that the extent of that victory may be easily exaggerated. To say this is not to deny, of course, the obvious fact that Marxism in Soviet Russia has been elevated — or lowered — to the position of absolute monopoly. But even in this respect a somewhat more penetrating view would easily disclose that much of what sails in Soviet

Russia under the name of the established doctrine has in reality little, or nothing, to do with Marxism, however generously we may conceive the term. That the Soviet government can derive considerable political advantages from evoking the image of an unchanged system of basic beliefs is clear. It should be equally clear that to accept that deliberately misleading image would mean barring ourselves from perceiving important processes of change in Soviet ideology and from understanding the relation of that ideology to political and economic decisions which in the course of nearly four decades have hewed and shaped the economy of the country.

Few would disagree that among those decisions the decision taken in the second half of the twenties to embark upon the road of rapid industrialization and collectivization of agriculture occupies the central place. In a general sense, that decision seemed to be broadly consonant with the general tenor of accepted Marxian doctrines. But as soon as we are tempted to attribute the great change that concluded the NEP period to the influence of Marxism, we are inevitably baffled by a number of facts that do not fit well into such an interpretation. The debates of the twenties in Soviet Russia with regard to the basic policies to be pursued were obviously not debates between Marxians and non-Marxians. They were conducted by people who from early youth had been bred and steeped in the tenets of Marxism. To suggest that Stalin was a better Marxian than, say, Bukharin or Preobrazhenskii makes good sense within the context of a Soviet purge trial, but is meaningless without it. What Mr. Erlich has described so well in his paper is the great break in Stalin's thinking on the subject of industrialization and attitude toward the peasants.

After having asserted the need to preserve the *smychka,* after having maintained that the rate of growth in agriculture would exceed that of industry, after having dragged out of the historical cupboard the Populist skeleton of internal market, and after having accused his opponents of nursing the plans to exploit the peasantry, Stalin embarked upon a policy which was contradictorily opposed to his previous views. What had caused Stalin to change his mind? Surely not a belated remembrance of the Marxian preference for large-scale units in agriculture? Mr. Erlich rightly mentions the significance of the disastrously declining volume of grain deliveries to the cities. It is not unlikely that toward the end of the NEP period, as the prewar capacity of Russian industry was being attained and considerable inflationary pressures developed, the Russian economy was headed toward an impasse and that the traditional measures of higher prices or higher taxes were politically intolerable and could not be used to break the deadlock. The bold idea of a large investment effort compressed within the period of a few years in order to break the deadlock from the commodity side — because it could not be broken from the money side — seems to have been the original purpose of the First Five-Year Plan. Collectivization was to remain within moderate limits and its purpose — not unlike that of Stoly-pin — was to buttress up the industrial program by creating for the regime some *points d'appui* in the villages. When the bitter resistance of the peasantry to collectivization threatened to develop into a full-fledged civil war, the nature of collectivization policy was changed. From an infiltrating operation it evolved into a frontal attack upon the peasantry. And once the great gamble was won, once Russia's great opportunity to rid herself of the dictatorship was lost and the peasantry was well encased in the strait jackets of the *kolkhozy,* once the produce of the land could be appropriated by the government however small the *quid pro quo* in terms of industrial products, the need for a limited industrialization program designed to reëstablish the monetary equilibrium in the country was removed. Industrialization could and did become an end in itself, or rather a means for further strengthening of the internal and external power of the Soviet government.

There is a certain tendency nowadays to view Soviet intellectual history from a static point of view. Such a view, probably inadequate at all times, is particularly unsatisfactory when applied to a period of very rapid social change. That an ideology is likely to undergo considerable changes as the social movement with which it is associated passes from a purely intellectual into an organizational and then into a "power" stage has been impressively shown by R. Mayreder. In this particular case, the changes have been momentous indeed. Basic tenets of Marxian ideology suffered a radical revision. One may refer alone to such pillars of the Marxian edifice as the view on the role of great men in history, the principle of internationalism, the marcescence of the state, and the idea of egalitarianism, and consider in that light the shameless idolization of Stalin, the excesses of Soviet Russian chauvinism, the hyptertrophy of the Soviet state, and the deliberate policy of a far-reaching income differentiation. To be sure, all these have been incorporated by the Soviets into a body of ideology that still goes under the name of Marxism. A totalitarian dictatorship which monopolizes the instruments of communication need not fear the charge of inconsistency when it tries to create the false impression of ideological constancy. Stalin's clumsy, but persistent, attempts in his *Economic Problems of Socialism* to preserve the Marxian concept of economic law in conditions which are patently unsuitable for the concept provide a vivid illustration of the importance which the regime attributes to ideological stability. But all this should not prevent scholarly opinion from recognizing that the name of Soviet ideology has long become *Schall und Rauch,* even though — to continue Goethe's line — what is thus shrouded in fog has nothing to do with heavenly fire. In this sense it can be said that also the October Revolution did not carry with it a complete and final victory of Marxism. Quite the contrary, it is tempting to suggest that in a very real sense the advent of the Bolsheviks to power spelled the end of Marxian ideology in Russia.

Thus one cannot help observing the subsidiary character of the generally recognized and much advertised ideologies in their relation to economic development in Russia. The problem, of course, is not one of metaphysical choice between "idealistic" or "materialistic" factors. Also Stalin's *libido dominandi* had an ideology and a value system of its own. Without it, his reaction to the situation as it developed in the second half of the 1920's may well have been very different. What is so surprising, rather, is how little the different ideas which have dominated the visible flow of Russian intellectual history for the last hundred and fifty years can be said to have exercised a determining influence upon the sequence of economic events and the course of economic change in the country. Those who disagree with this view might wish to point to the persistent clamor — from Radishchev to 1861 — for the liberation of the peasantry. In some measure, the point would be well taken. But its validity does not extend beyond the significance which, among a large variety of competing factors, can be imputed to the attitudes of the intelligentsia as one of the forces that prompted the act of emancipation. And one must beware of overrating that significance.

Perhaps a few words on the general significance of the Russian intellectual experience may be added in conclusion. In the last section of my paper I stressed the connection between anti-industrial ideologies (anti-industrial socialism in particular) and the general conditions of economic backwardness and expressed the view that while in Russia the retarding effect of such ideologies upon industrial development remained moderate on the whole, it is likely to be much stronger in the underdeveloped countries of our day. We can now go one step beyond what was said in the paper. If what has been argued in the present review is at all correct and the intelligentsia's approval of industrialization assumed the form of Marxism because of the preceding intellectual history and the specific economic backwardness of the country, then it is perhaps plausible to expect that also industrialization of backward countries of our day may similarly proceed under the auspices of a rather radical ideology. In a broad sense, this would be only a repetition of what occurred in European countries of the nineteenth century.

And yet the situation is a rather different one in important respects. As intimated before, the connection between such a radical ideology and industrialization tended to characterize just the first phase of the rapid spurt of modern economic development. St. Simonism was a powerful force in France of the fifties; it was dead and buried in France a quarter of a century later. The influence of Marxism was on the decline in Russia after the Revolution of 1905 and in addition Marxian ideology itself was in a state of transformation through infusion of Revisionist elements. There is little doubt that those changes were the effect of the very success of industrialization. Can we assume that in backward countries, too, the specific connection between industrialization and Marxian ideology will remain a temporary one?

Can we take for granted that previous patterns will faithfully reproduce themselves in contemporary conditions in backward countries? Again we must point to the differences between the twentieth and the nineteenth centuries. On the one hand, it is often claimed that the pressure for rapid increases in the levels of consumption is particularly strong in underdeveloped countries and some observers (Ragnar Nurkse, for instance) speak of the "demonstration effect," that is, of the keen desire of underdeveloped countries to adopt quickly the full consumption pattern of the advanced countries. Considering that any sustained industrialization effort will presumably require a temporary *decline* in consumption levels, the discrepancy between wish and reality is likely to become as large as it will be painful. This consequence must be particularly strong in those underdeveloped countries where the pressure of overpopulation is very considerable. As an incidental by-product of this discrepancy a good deal of credence will be lent to the theory of increasing misery and the temporary decline in consumer's welfare will be taken as flowing irresistibly from an inevitable law of capitalist industrialization, thus reinforcing the belief in the validity of Marxian theories.

On the other hand, as has been indicated before, the intelligentsia in those countries are in a position of doing things rather than philosophizing about them. While in Russia the influence of Marxism may at length have caused young men to study engineering rather than philosophy or philology, in a modern underdeveloped country ideologies of the type discussed in these papers may at least for some time become main determinants of action and, specifically, the influence of Marxism may be directly translated into practical policies of the government. Moreover, it is likely to be an altogether different brand of Marxism, strongly influenced and distorted by ideological importations from Soviet Russia. Russian Marxism began to evolve very early in a revisionist direction. What happened in Russia under the impact of the First World War may be regarded as a tragic accident brought about by extraneous circumstances. But developments in present-day backward countries may follow the Russian path as a result of a much more continuous play of internal forces.

The situation no doubt is complex and shot through with irrational elements. Increase in the levels of consumption of the people seems to be the primary concern. Slow industrialization or its absence is decried because standards of living are not raised quickly enough. But also very rapid industrialization leading to a passing reduction in standards of living is likely to arouse formidable opposition and to result in considerable radicalization of both the intelligentsia and the population. And, illogically, the establishment of a dictatorship upon the Soviet pattern, which would keep down the levels of consumption permanently, may begin to loom as a natural solution to minds who fail to realize that both their genuine compassion for popular misery and the ideology of Marxism would be among the first victims of such a dictatorship.

Thus no easy inferences can be drawn from the Russian experience for the present conditions in underdeveloped countries. Lessons from history are precarious at all times, and perhaps never more so than in this case. But to say this does not mean that the Russian experience is not suggestive of possibilities that may be worth considering.

If it be true that both rapid industrialization and its absence are pregnant with grave perils, the question should at least be raised whether or not a period of rapid industrialization, sufficiently long to turn upward the curve of per capita consumption, may be expected to break the fatal link between industrialization and radical ideology. If it is likely at all to "normalize" the situation in terms of the historical experience of West European industrialization and to eliminate the danger of totalitarian dictatorships, then the essential problem would seem to minimize the burdens which a high rate of investment must impose upon the shoulders of the populations concerned by generous injections of capital from advanced countries. To follow such a course no doubt involves great and real risks, and a historian should not be surprised at all if hardened statesmen refuse to act on the basis of uncertain historical analogies. It is not suggested that they should. But perhaps they may be reminded of a much broader and much more valid lesson of human history. In a situation where both action and inaction appear to threaten disaster, the statesman's choice should lie among different forms of action.

PART II

AUTHORITARIANISM AND DEMOCRACY

Pobedonostsev on the Instruments

of Russian Government

ROBERT F. BYRNES

Konstantin Petrovich Pobedonostsev, who was the Over Procurator of the Holy Synod or the lay administrative head of the Russian Orthodox Church from April 1880 through October 1905, is known to history as the "evil genius" or the "Grand Inquisitor" of the reigns of Alexander III and Nicholas II, when he was considered the intellectual and political leader of the reactionary forces in Russia. This essay will not attempt to discuss Pobedonostsev's career as a reactionary statesman, or to determine to what degree his reputation is deserved, but it will seek to analyze his political philosophy, with emphasis upon his views concerning the instruments by which Russia was governed and should be governed.[1]

Pobedonostsev was born in Moscow in 1827 and died in St. Petersburg in 1907. His life thus approximately spanned the eighty years separating the Decembrist Revolution and the Revolution of 1905. He entered service in the bureaucracy in 1846, beginning as a law clerk in the Eighth Department of the Senate. He rose steadily, becoming a Senator in 1868 and a member of the Governing Council in 1872. He was a prolific author, editor, and translator throughout his entire career. There are probably more data available in the West concerning Pobedonostsev's activities and opinions than concerning those of any other nineteenth-century Russian statesman because of the quantity of his published works, the governmental and other records which have been published, the care with which he collected letters and other source material (much of which he published late in his life, and some of which was published after 1917), and the large number of his Russian and foreign acquaintances who wrote memoirs containing information concerning him.

A thorough examination of this immense mass of data reveals that

[1] This essay is a product of a Senior Fellowship of the Russian Institute of Columbia University awarded the author for two years of training in the Russian area and for research upon a forthcoming book: "Pobedonostsev: An Analysis of His Political and Social Philosophy."

Pobedonostsev's philosophy remained remarkably constant throughout his long life. Indeed, he reprinted, without change, in the 1890's or in the first decade of the twentieth century several books which he had written or translated originally in the 1860's.[2] There were, of course, exceptions, and there were minor variations in his views from time to time, as new issues arose. However, the variations and new concepts were almost invariably developments of Pobedonostsev's established concepts. Thus, when he advocated the parish school system in the 1880's and 1890's, he was in fact just developing into practical and concrete form ideas he had expressed twenty years earlier concerning education by the church.[3] Even his most daring essay, his bitter indictment of Panin's administration of the Ministry of Justice, which was published in London in Herzen's *Golosa iz Rossii* (Voices of Russia), was a faithful representation of views he held throughout his life concerning sound administrative principles. Pobedonostsev's statements in the Governing Council in 1905 and 1906 are very similar to those made in the Panin article, which was written in 1858.[4]

Pobedonostsev had firm ideas concerning the issues most fundamental to any political philosophy. To begin with, he was convinced that by nature men were evil and unequal. He repeated frequently that "every man is a lie" and that "every word said by man is an idle word of self-delusion." He shared the views of Hobbes, though he had never read Hobbes. He shared too the view expressed by Dostoyevsky's Grand Inquisitor that man is "weak, vicious, worthless, and rebellious." He told an English journalist that neither the spiritual instincts nor the moral restraints of the Russian people were adequate to subdue "the ferocious passions that lie dormant in their breasts"

---

[2] Konstantin P. Pobedonostsev, tr., *Kristianskiia nachala semeinoi zhizni* (Moscow 1861; 2nd ed. Moscow, 1901); Pobedonostsev, tr., *Fomy Kempiiskago o Podrazhanii Khristu* (St. Petersburg, 1869; 6th ed. St. Petersburg, 1896); *Prazdniki Gospodni* (St. Petersburg, 1894), a series of intensely personal religious meditations which Pobedonostsev wrote between 1856 and 1864. *Starye listia*, a poem he translated in *Russkaia beseda*, II (1859), Part I, 7–8, reappeared in *Moskovskii sbornik* (5th ed., Moscow, 1901), p. 223.

[3] Pobedonostsev, *Pis'ma Pobedonostseva k Aleksandru III* (Moscow, 1925–1926), II, 27–28, 271. Pobedonostsev, *K. P. Pobedonostsev i ego korrespondenty. Pis'ma i zapiski. Novum Regnum* (Moscow, 1923), II, 452, 1048. Pobedonostsev, *Kurs grazhdanskago prava* (2nd ed., St. Petersburg, 1868–1896), II, 155, 169. Pobedonostsev, *Pis'ma o puteshestvii po Rossii ot S. Peterburga do Kryma* (Moscow, 1863), pp. 519–520. Pobedonostsev, tr., "O khristianskom brake," *Pravoslavnoe obozrenie*, IV (1861), 307–334. Pobedonostsev, *Vsepoddanneishii otchët ober-prokurora Sviateishago Sinoda za 1883 g.* (St. Petersburg, 1885), pp. 55–70.

[4] Pobedonostsev, "Graf V. N. Panin," *Golosa iz Rossii*, Book VII (1859), pp. 1–142. Vladimir Kokovtsov, *Out of My Past* (Stanford, 1935), p. 104. Vasilii Gurko, *Features and Figures of the Past* (London, 1939), pp. 303–304. *Istoricheskaia perepiska o sud'bakh Pravoslavnoi Tserkvi* (Moscow, 1912), pp. 32–48. M. Klevenskii, "Gertsen-izdatel' i ego sotrudniki," *Literaturnoe nasledstvo*, nos. 41 and 42 (1941), p. 605. A. G. Dementev, *Ocherki po istorii russkoi zhurnalistiki, 1840–1850 gg.* (Moscow, 1951), p. 423. The Panin article, of course, was anonymous, but it is clear from A. A. Polovtsev, "Dnevnik," *Krasnyi arkhiv*, III (1923), 79, that Pobedonostsev was its author.

without the aid of physical sanctions. He believed that the Slavs were by nature sluggish and lazy and that they required firm leadership. He was convinced that the Russian man was inferior to all others, and he once described Russia beyond the imperial palaces as "an icy desert and an abode of the Bad Man." [5]

Pobedonostsev's ruthless attack upon rationalism or "the fanaticism of formal logic" was a corollary of his views concerning the nature of man. He derided those who believed in the perfectibility of man. He severely condemned those who assumed that man could reason or that reason could be an effective tool for any but a tiny minority, whom he called "the aristocracy of intellect." He believed that the search for truth makes the average man a dangerous "rational fanatic" and threatens the unity and very existence of society. "True, sound intelligence is not logical but intuitive, because the aim of intelligence consists not in finding or showing reasons but in believing and trusting." The great, essential and living truths are above the mind, and the great mass of men can receive ideas only through feeling.

Speculative, abstract thought in particular drew Pobedonostsev's wrath, and he declared that abstract principles were "destructive, suicidal, and sinful." He saw man, except for the minority, as an object of soft wax molded and formed by three forces utterly beyond his control: the unconscious, land, and history. Probably no statesman or politician in modern times, even Hitler, has so directly attacked rationalism and openly glorified the unconscious as Pobedonostsev did. Noting that "the healthy do not think about health," he urged that society be allowed by man to operate as an organ of the body does, "simply and unconsciously."

Pobedonostsev believed that, except for the minority, man's knowledge should be restricted to the sacred books and the "correct version" of his national history. He would have accepted the apothegm of Barrès that the necessary foundation of a state is a cemetery, for he saw the "congenial seed" of a state in "the unconscious sphere of feeling, accumulated hereditarily from our ancestors." Since the capabilities of all but the minority are so limited, man must realize simply that his roots are in the past and that he derives from his ancestors. More he cannot understand.[6]

Pobedonostsev's views on government reflect not only his concept of the nature of man, but also his ideas concerning the nature and character of

[5] Pobedonostsev, "Gosudar Imperator Aleksandr Aleksandrovich," *Russkii arkhiv*, I (1906), 619–621. Sergei Petrovskii, ed., "Perepiska K. P. Pobedonostseva s Nikanorom episkopom Ufimskim," *Russkii arkhiv*, II (1915), 369–370. Pobedonostsev, "Russia and Popular Education," *North American Review*, CLXXIII (1901), 349–351. Grand Prince Alexander Mikhailovich, *Vospominaniia* (Paris, 1933), p. 189. Maurice Bompard, *Mon Ambassade en Russie, 1903–1908* (Paris, 1937), pp. 257–258. Fëdor Dostoyevsky, *The Brothers Karamazov* (New York: Modern Library, 1929), p. 300.

[6] Pobedonostsev, *Moskovskii sbornik*, 3rd ed., pp. 33–34, 73–76, 186–194, 267–276; 5th ed., pp. 151–156, 327–331. Pobedonostsev, "Le-Ple," *Russkoe obozrenie*, XXIII, (1893), 14–15.

societies and of the differences between societies. Pobedonostsev equated society and religion, and he would have accepted Professor Toynbee's thesis that the great religions have created the different characteristics which make one "civilization" distinct from another. The role of the church in each society (Pobedonostsev considered Russia both a state and a society) was to create a "community of believers" and to answer "the deep-rooted human need for unity of belief."

From his belief that the character of a state or society was shaped by its "national faith" or by its church, Pobedonostsev drew the logical conclusion that no healthy state or society could have more than one creed. The Roman Empire collapsed because it tolerated many beliefs, which meant it had no faith or principle. Indeed, any state which tolerates more than one creed will be torn apart by conflict. Accordingly, Pobedonostsev believed that the states of continental Europe were doomed to civil war and destruction. He predicted that freedom of religion would ultimately disappear in the United States, because otherwise the Catholic Church would grow so strong as to threaten the very existence of Protestantism, which was the historical American creed.[7]

Pobedonostsev believed too that each society or state possessed distinctive political and social beliefs and institutions which helped to shape its character. Each nation's development represented an organic process based on immutable laws. Each state was thus a prisoner of its past, and Pobedonostsev believed that historical research was beginning to reveal why the various states had different institutions and philosophies. Thus, he explained that some states, such as Russia, had centralized, authoritarian governments because in their distant past the emphasis had been upon communal life and upon firm control over the family by the father or by the patriarch; consequently, each person remained dependent, political power was respected and became more highly concentrated, and strong central government developed. On the other hand, "the Anglo-Saxon and Scandinavian states" had decentralized, democratic governments because in their distant past the emphasis had been upon individualism, and the father did not acquire absolute power in the family; consequently, democratic local government developed, and central authority remained comparatively weak.

Pobedonostsev, of course, was severely critical of parliamentary democracy, and he believed that representative institutions in the states of continental Europe were fatally stricken. However, he was convinced that constitutional and democratic government would continue to flourish in those states in which it developed from historical roots. Thus, all systems were

---

[7] Pobedonostsev, *Istoriia Pravoslavnoi Tserkvi do nachala razdeleniia tserkvei* (2nd ed., St. Petersburg, 1895), pp. 1–9. Pobedonostsev, "O reformakh v grazhdanskom sudoproizvodstve," *Russkii vestnik*, XXI (1859), 541–542. Pobedonostsev, *Moskovskii sbornik*, 3rd ed., pp. 1–24, 199–227.

consecrated by history. The principal problem, from his point of view, rose when a continental European state, such as France or Russia, sought to graft an alien institution upon its old foundations. This he considered fatal, particularly in those states where there were several national groups.[8]

Pobedonostsev believed that each faith is intolerant and uncompromising and that it was both impossible and dangerous for one state or society to attempt to borrow ideas and institutions from another or to impose its customs and beliefs upon another. The idea of an active Orthodox mission or a Pan-Slav mission was, therefore, foreign to his philosophy. He believed Russia should concentrate upon attaining unity and increasing its national strength. He wrote nothing concerning the "third Rome" (the belief that Moscow was to succeed Rome and Constantinople as the capital of the universal empire), or concerning Russia's "sacred mission" of carrying civilization to the rest of the world.

While Pobedonostsev believed that other states and other religions as well would continue to thrive, at the same time he made clear that they should have no influence within Russia. In other words, he accepted "peaceful coexistence" and believed that the world should consist of a group of independent states which meet "only at the top," as they had during the greatest periods of absolute monarchy in Western Europe.

Pobedonostsev considered stability the supreme virtue of a political or social organism. His political philosophy glorified static relationships, with old institutions, traditions, and customs embodying the sacred ideas. Change was necessary, even in the most shielded and isolated society, but it would be minor, gradual, and elemental. If one compares Pobedonostsev's aims with those expressed in the preamble of the American Constitution, it becomes apparent that he sought two of the goals sought by the American leaders, unity and tranquillity. For the founders of the United States, however, unity and tranquillity were not to the same degree ends as they were for Pobedonostsev. They were also means to the attainment of three other goals, justice, the general welfare, and the blessings of liberty. Of these, Pobedonostsev says nothing.[9]

For Pobedonostsev, government was maintained by three kinds of instruments: those which coerced or repressed, those which educated, and those which offered and provided rewards and incentives. He considered the co-

---

[8] Pobedonostsev, *Istoricheskiia issledovaniia i stati* (St. Petersburg, 1876), pp. 273–285. Pobedonostsev, *Moskovskii sbornik*, 3rd ed., pp. 45–47, 208–216; 4th ed., pp. 50–55; 5th ed., pp. 54–57. Pobedonostsev, *Novum regnum*, II, 833–834. Pobedonostsev, "O reformakh," *Russkii vestnik*, XXI, 541–542; Pobedonostsev, "Russia," *North American Review*, CLXXIII, 349–354. E. J. Dillon, *The Eclipse of Russia* (London, 1918), p. 83. Andrew White, "A Statesman of Russia: Constantine Pobedonostzeff," *Century Magazine*, LVI (1898), 114–116.

[9] Pobedonostsev, *Moskovskii sbornik*, 3rd ed., pp. 71–76, 140–156, 186–194; 5th ed., pp. 327–331.

ercive and repressive instruments the most vital, but he devoted more attention to the instruments for indoctrination. He ignored incentives, except for
the ruling elite.

Pobedonostsev thought first of the state, as naturally as an American
thinks first of the individual. He agreed with Rousseau that "the union of
its members" makes the state one and that this union derives from the obligations which bind the members. However, he was not clear concerning the
source of the binding obligations. Fundamentally, he asserted that the state
was an expression of truth and represented the national will. The state's
power was based "solely on the unity of consciousness between the people
[*narod*] and the state, and on the national faith." He advised the tsar
always to speak of "the people" of Russia, never of "the peoples," and he
believed there was a mystical connection existing between the *narod* and the
state.[10]

The autocracy was the foundation upon which Pobedonostsev's political
philosophy was erected. He bitterly opposed constitutional and democratic
government for Russia, particularly because it restricted the powers of the
ruler and divided political power in such a way as to make government
impossible. He was opposed even to advisory councils, such as the *Zemski
Sobor*. Parliamentary government surrendered control in the state to parties,
which meant that the true rulers were party organizers, vote manipulators,
and eloquent demagogues, all interested in personal profit and none interested
in the welfare of the state. Democratic government, in other words, "satisfied the personal ambition, vanity, and self-interest of its members," and
prevented men of genuine ability from governing.[11]

Pobedonostsev believed that power should be tightly concentrated and
that there could be no institution or individual whose powers did not derive
from the power of the state, which was absolute. Even though he first became
prominent as a scholar of Russian civil law, he denounced the rule of law
for distributing power and allowing conflict within the state. He even defended Russia's passport system in his *Course on Civil Law* on the ground

---

[10] Pobedonostsev, "Gosudar," *Russkii arkhiv*, I, 619–624. Pobedonostsev, *Pis'ma*, I,
170–171; II, 3–4, 46–47, 145, 204–206. Pobedonostsev, *Novum Regnum*, II, 832–835,
1004–1008. Pobedonostsev, *Moskovskii sbornik*, 3rd ed., pp. 31–33, 250–266.

[11] Pobedonostsev, *Moskovskii sbornik*, 3rd ed., pp. 25–52, 100–105. A. Presniakov, ed.,
"Moskovskii adres Aleksandru II v 1870 g. Iz perepiski K. P. Pobedonostseva," *Krasnyi
arkhiv*, XXXI (1928), 151–154. Pobedonostsev, *Pis'ma*, I, 379–381, 426. Pobedonostsev,
Novum Regnum, I, 247, 261–263. Iuri V. Gotie, "Bor'ba pravitel'stvennykh gruppirovok
i manifest 29 aprelia 1881 g.," *Istoricheskie zapiski*, II (1938), 259. Gotie, "K. P.
Pobedonostsev i naslednik Aleksandr Aleksandrovich, 1865–1881," *Publichnaia biblioteka
SSSR imeni V. I. Lenina. Sbornik*, II (1929), 133. P. A. Valuev, *Dnevnik, 1887–1894*
(Petrograd, 1919), pp. 199–200. Evgenii Feoktistov, *Vospominaniia* (Leningrad, 1929),
pp. 206–212; "Perepiska Vitte i Pobedonostseva, 1895–1905," *Krasnyi arkhiv*, XXX
(1928), 102–105.

that the passport identified the bearer as a citizen of Russia and provided him the autocracy's protection against local government.[12]

Pobedonostsev's emphasis upon absolutism was constant, but it was strengthened by his experience with the Pan-Slav movement in 1876 and 1877. The drive to free the Balkan Slavs had inflamed even Pobedonostsev temporarily, but he soon realized that the government would have to control all such popular movements or face the danger that they might turn against the state in distrust and then in enmity. As a consequence, after 1877 he was particularly insistent upon autocratic government, the "binding" of Russian society, and international peace.[13]

The uses of absolute government for Pobedonostsev are quite clear. It was, first of all, to distinguish between good and evil, light and dark. It was to provide "rational direction," by means of "calm, humane, indulgent, and arbitrary administration." It was, of course, to ensure stability. Above all, by using force and by ensuring equality for all, it was to prevent the rise of nationalisms in the multinational Russian empire.

Pobedonostsev would have agreed with Ammianus Marcellinus that "life is never sweeter than under a pious king." His ideal monarch was Louis IX, King of France in the second half of the thirteenth century, when everyone in each of the "estates" knew his place, social peace prevailed, the church and the state ruled in harmony, and the king, a saint, sat under a tree and decided those few disagreements which arose within the society.[14]

However, his opinion of most Russian rulers was not favorable, and the autocrat in his view was most important as a symbol. He had a high regard for Peter the Great, because Peter saw the needs of his age clearly, used the established institutions when possible to increase the state's power and authority, and revised the established institutions when necessary. He praised Alexander III for knowing Russian history and traditions and for reflecting "the nature of his land and of his people." [15] However, he was sharply critical of Alexander I, who knew neither Russia nor the Russian people and who sought to introduce dangerous foreign ideas. He condemned Nicholas I for using only lackeys in his administration, for isolating his court from

---

[12] Pobedonostsev, *Moskovskii sbornik*, 3rd ed., pp. 87–91, 252–253. Pobedonostsev, *Pis'ma*, I, 53. Pobedonostsev, *Kurs*, 1st ed., III, 392–394.

[13] I. S. Aksakov, "Pis'ma I. S. Aksakova k K. P. Pobedonostsevu, 1876–1885," *Russkii arkhiv*, III (1907), 168–169. Pobedonostsev, *Pis'ma*, I, 48–53, 67–79, 89–95, 107–120. Pobedonostsev, *Novum Regnum*, II, 1016–1018. Sergei Skazkin, *Konets Avstro-Russko-Germanskago Soiuza* (Moscow, 1928), pp. 177–178.

[14] Pobedonostsev, *Proshchanie Moskvi s tsarem svoim* (Moscow, 1894). Pobedonostsev, "Le-Ple," *Russkoe obozrenie*, XXIII (1893), 27. Pobedonostsev, *Moskovskii sbornik*, 3rd ed., pp. 1–2, 46–48, 87–88, 121–122, 247–256; 4th ed., pp. 258–259. Pobedonostsev, *Pis'ma*, I, 170–171; II, 3–4, 41–42, 144–145, 205–207. Pobedonostsev, *Novum Regnum*, I, 51–54; II, 1004–1005.

[15] Pobedonostsev, *Istoricheskiia issledovaniia*, pp. 14–15, 47–55, 116–185, especially 116–118, 156–159. Pobedonostsev, "Gosudar," *Russkii arkhiv*, I, 619–624.

the *narod,* and for placing his personal interests above those of the country. He was particularly critical of Alexander II, whom he called "a pitiful and unfortunate man" guilty of wasting and dishonoring the power given him.[16]

Pobedonostsev's autocrat had several functions, the most important of which was setting a high standard for all government officials by working hard, by surrounding himself with serious and able men, and by living a sober Christian life. The autocrat was to represent the *narod's* interests, and by his travels and his presence at ceremonies he was to strengthen the love of the *narod* for the state.[17] In addition, he was to select tough, able, and energetic executive aids and to accept their advice in directing the state. These executive agents for Pobedonostsev were the principal instruments of rule, and efficient operation of the entire system depended upon them. Essentially, he sought to modernize the autocracy. His advice to Alexander III was, "cherchez des capables," and his letters to the tsar constantly reiterated that a few able men in responsible positions could resolve Russia's principal problems.[18]

These executives were first of all to be men of courage, willing to accept responsibility and to speak frankly to the tsar. They were to be hard-working, practical, efficient; they were to have organizing ability; they were to operate in a system which had clear lines of authority and responsibility. In other words, they were to possess the qualities which Pobedonostsev believed the Russian bureaucracy lacked, for he had great contempt for the craven and irresponsible "typical bureaucrat," who, he believed, delighted in eliminating efficiency and personality from government.[19]

In their advice to the Russian ruler, these aids were to consider "history, tradition, the actual position of the state, and the needs of national life." However, they were to ignore and smash Russia's laws and institutions whenever they believed this was required in the state's interests. Pobedonostsev justified violent and arbitrary governmental action and angrily denounced the moralistic interpretation of history and of politics. He emphasized that "the rulers of the world" have always acted forcefully, and

---

[16] Pobedonostsev, "Panin," *Golosa iz Rossii,* Book VII, 3–10, 37–39. Gotie, "K. P. Pobedonostsev," *Publichnaia biblioteka SSSR,* II, 116–125.

[17] Pobedonostsev, "Privetstvie starago vospitatelia velikomu kniaziu," *Starina i novizma,* XII (1907), 1–9. Pobedonostsev, *Vseposddanneishii otchёt za 1883 g.,* pp. 1–3. Pobedonostsev, *Pis'ma,* I, 248–250; II, 3–5, 32–34. Pobedonostsev, *Pis'ma o puteshestvii,* pp. 85–86. Pobedonostsev, *Novum Regnum,* II, 1004–1005.

[18] Pobedonostsev, tr., *Osnovnaia konstitutsiia chelovecheskago roda* (St. Petersburg, 1897), p. 221. Pobedonostsev, *Pis'ma,* I, 73–76, 111, 170–171, 193–196, 206–209, 215, 250–252, 270, 338–339, 346–347; II, 46–47, 197–202, 215–219. Pobedonostsev, *Novum Regnum,* I, 52–66, 232–235. Gotie, "K. P. Pobedonostsev," *Publichnaia biblioteka SSSR,* II, 126.

[19] Vladimir Markov, *K istorii raskola-staroobriadchestva. Perepiska Prof. N. I. Subbotina* (Moscow, 1915), p. 645. Pobedonostsev, *Moskovskii sbornik,* 3rd ed., pp. 228–234, 259. Pobedonostsev, "Panin," *Golosa iz Rossii,* Book VII, 5–7, 15–31, 76–92, 112–124. Pobedonostsev, *Pis'ma,* I, 259–260, 346–347; II, 53.

he believed that superior men should be beyond criticism in life as well as in history. Thus, although he had been trained as a jurist and a scholar and as a young man had hoped to become the Russian Savigny, as a statesman he was intellectually dishonest. For example, he deliberately distorted the meaning of some of the books and articles he translated.[20]

It is clear that Pobedonostsev had little interest in the landed nobility and that he preferred representatives of the middle classes for these executive positions. Indeed, he stated in the fifth edition of his *Moscow Collection* in 1901 that the landed nobility as a class had ceased to have power and influence in Russia.[21] He constantly praised the middle-class virtues, and he placed particularly high value upon self-made men. He apparently never visited a landed estate, except for brief visits to his father-in-law's Smolensk property when he and his wife were enroute to Salzburg for vacation.[22] His three-volume *Course on Civil Law* is a mine of information concerning Russian property law and the various kinds of landholding before 1861, but even the final edition in 1896 shows that Pobedonostsev failed to analyze developments on the land after the emancipation of the serfs. Indeed, his very significant 1889 essay, which advocated that "family plots" be "indivisible and inviolable," reveals that he was totally ignorant concerning developments in Russian landownership after 1861.[23]

It is obvious that Pobedonostsev was more interested in the policy-making instruments of government than in the administrative instruments. As a consequence, while he constantly interfered with the operations of the administrative departments, especially the various censorship offices, he did not devote much thought to the ordinary operations of government and he never mentioned the army or the police. According to him, the principal governmental instruments of the autocrat and his executive associates were law and the judicial system, the censor, the intellectuals, the printing press, and the Orthodox Church. The final instrument, and one of the most important, was the family.

[20] Egor Peretts, *Dnevnik, 1880–1883* (Moscow, 1927), pp. 31–38. "Kniazia tserkvi. Iz dnevnika A. N. Lvova," *Krasnyi arkhiv*, XXXIX (1930), 124. Pobedonostsev, *Moskovskii sbornik*, 3rd ed., pp. 242–266. Pobedonostsev, *Pis'ma*, I, 338–339. Pobedonostsev, *Novum Regnum*, I, 232–235; II, 865–867. Pobedonostsev, *Istoricheskiia issledovaniia*, pp 116–125, 175–180.

[21] For an indication of Pobedonostsev's lack of interest in the landed nobility, see the accounts of his three trips through European Russia with the heir to the throne in the 1860's: Pobedonostsev, *Pis'ma o puteshestvii*, especially pp. 249–251, 348–349; A. A. Shevelev, "Puteshestviia po Rossii," *Russkoe obozrenie*, XLVI (1897), 52–92; XLVII (1898), 821–832; Pobedonostsev, *Pis'ma*, II, 46–47.

[22] Pobedonostsev, *Moskovskii sbornik*, 5th ed., p. 31.

[23] Even the editor of *Russkii vestnik* confessed that he was confused by Pobedonostsev's references in this article in his journal. It is noteworthy that the data on which Pobedonostsev's 1889 suggestions were based were taken from recent American, English, Irish, French, German, and Austrian land history and law, not from Russian experience since 1861. Pobedonostsev, "Semeinye uchastki," *Russkii vestnik*, CCIV (1889), 56–72, especially 71–72. Pobedonostsev, *Kurs*, 4th ed., I, 494, 532, 570, 730–745.

Pobedonostsev had a thorough appreciation of law and the judicial system as instruments for the state. When he was a young man, he had hoped to publish a history of Russian judicial procedure since the middle of the seventeenth century. He spent the two decades after 1846 accumulating and analyzing the materials for his study of serfdom and for his essays on the history of Russian judicial procedure, which lifted him into prominence in the years just before serfdom was abolished. His three-volume *Course on Civil Law* was a significant contribution to Russian historical scholarship. His master's thesis and many of his articles ridiculed the overcentralized, complicated, ritualistic, and corrupt judicial system, and he was an important member of the committee which drafted the judicial reform of 1864.[24]

Even during the years when Pobedonostsev supported judicial reform, he asserted that law and the judicial system should be servants of the state. For example, he insisted that the state should have the deciding voice in determining whether an issue involving the state should go before the courts, and he consistently opposed permanent tenure for judges.[25] He considered law a superlative conservative force. Thus, he used it to prevent civil marriage and divorce.[26] He recognized its contribution to uniformity throughout the empire. He valued it as a defense for private property and for traditional property relationships.[27] Above all, he advocated the use of Russian law "to safeguard the dominant religion" and to deny rights and privileges to non-Orthodox religious groups and to national minorities, especially the Poles and the Jews.[28]

Just as Pobedonostsev's heavy reliance upon law and the judicial system reflects his early interest in legal scholarship, so also his ideas concerning both censorship and propaganda reflect his career as an intellectual. He grew up in a family of intellectuals and in a close university circle, and he came as a boy to know and to respect scholars and writers, such as the

[24] *Arkhiv istoricheskikh i prakticheskikh svedenii otnosiaschikhsiia do Rossii*, I (1858), iii–vii. Pobedonostsev, *Vechnaia pamiat'* (Moscow, 1896), pp. 36–62. Pobedonostsev, *Novum Regnum*, I, 68–69. Pobedonostsev, "Statistiki angliiskykh grazhdanskykh sudov za 1858 god," *Iuridicheskii vestnik*, V (1860–1861), 46–54. Pobedonostsev, "Iuridicheskiia zametki i voprosy," *Zhurnal Ministerstva Iustitsii*, XXIII (1866), 33–34. Pobedonostsev, *Istoricheskiia issledovaniia*, pp. 236–325. A. F. Koni, *Na zhiznennom puti* (Moscow, 1914–1929), III, 191–192. Grigorii A. Dzhanshiev, *Epokha velikikh reform* (8th ed., Moscow, 1900), pp. 365–367, 552.

[25] *Istoriia pravitel'stvuiushchago senata za dvesti let, 1711–1911 g.* (St. Petersburg, 1911), IV, 472; *Sudebnye ustavy 20 noiabria 1864 goda, s izlozheniem rassuzhdenii na koikh oni osnovany* (St. Petersburg, 1867), I, 118–119; *Sudebnoe preobrazovanie v 1863 i 1864 g.* (St. Petersburg, n.d.), Part III, sec. i, Part I, pp. 151–163. Pobedonostsev, *Novum Regnum*, II, 508–514.

[26] Pobedonostsev, *Kurs*, 2nd ed., I, 1; 2nd ed., II, 60, 69, 96.

[27] Pobedonostsev, *Kurs*, 3rd ed., I, 125–143, 661–663; 1st ed., II, 428–433; 2nd ed., II, 47–60. Pobedonostsev, "Veshchnyi kredit," *Russkii vestnik*, XXXIII (1861), 440–441. I. Orshanskii, "Kurs grazhdanskago prava," *Zhurnal grazhdanskago i ugolovnago prava*, Book II (1876), pp. 267–271.

[28] Pobedonostsev, *Kurs*, 3rd ed., I, 707, 712–713; *Kurs*, 4th ed., I, 33–34; 494, 599, 612–613. Pobedonostsev, "O Reformakh," *Russkii vestnik*, XXI, 544–555.

Aksakovs, Lazhechnikov, the historical novelist, and Pogodin, the celebrated historian. He was brought up to assume that study, writing, and publishing were important achievements to which an educated man naturally devoted his life. Everyone who became acquainted with him, from his closest colleagues to foreign visitors such as Senator Beveridge, was astonished at his capacity and love for intellectual work and at the depth and range of his knowledge.[29]

Pobedonostsev believed that the great dangers to Russia derived from intellectuals and the ideas they produced and carried. He considered freedom of the press a Western device for inundating Russia with lies. He hoped to isolate Russian intellectuals from the West. Consequently, the censor was an important instrument. He reorganized and invigorated the Holy Synod's censorship, he intervened to nominate and to remove individuals from the various censorship offices under the Ministry of Interior, and he maintained close scrutiny of Russian intellectual life to guarantee that control remained thorough and effective.[30] He paid especial attention to Russian newspapers, and he bombarded the censors with evidence of slackness and with fervent exhortations. Whenever he visited a library or a bookstore, he examined the shelves for forbidden books. He persuaded the censors to close heretical or dangerous plays, and he watched shop windows as well as art galleries to prevent the display of posters, paintings, or statues which might harm the state or the church. Above all, he sought to restrict and to destroy the influence of men such as Count Leo Tolstoy, whose doctrines he considered a direct challenge to the security of the state.[31]

Pobedonostsev believed that repression could halt or control hostile or harmful ideas, but that indoctrination of the proper views was vital to ensure triumph.[32] The principal burden for indoctrination he placed upon the

[29] Peter V. Pobedonostsev, "Liubov k otechestvu," *Trudy Obshchestva Liubitelei Rossiiskoi Slovesnosti pri Imperatorskom Moskovskom Universitete*, XV (1819), 5–13. Peter V. Pobedonostsev, *Slovo o sushchestvennykh obiazannostiakh vitii i o sposobakh k priobreteniiu uspekhov v krasnorechii* (Moscow, 1831), pp. 27–33. Konstantin P. Pobedonostsev, ed., "Pis'ma I. I. Lazhechnikova k S. P. i K. P. Pobedonostsym," *Russkoe obozrenie*, XXXII (1895), 881–886. Alexander N. Pypin, *Belinskii* (St. Petersburg, 1908), pp. 167–168. Claude G. Bowers, *Beveridge and the Progressive Era* (Cambridge, Mass., 1932), pp. 147–148. Hermann Dalton, *Lebenserinnerungen* (Berlin, 1906–1908), III, 98–99. Louise Creighton, *Life and Letters of Mandell Creighton* (London, 1904), II, 150–155.

[30] "Pis'ma K. P. Pobedonostseva k E. M. Feoktistovu," *Literaturnoe nasledstvo*, XXII–XXIV (1935), 502–554. Anatolii Egorov, "Stranitsii iz godov moei zhizni," *Russkaia starina*, CIL (1912), 139–143. Feoktistov, *Vospominaniia*, preface, p. xiii.

[31] Pobedonostsev, *Moskovskii sbornik*, 3rd ed., pp. 54–74. Pobedonostsev, *Pis'ma*, I, 249–250, 255–258, 302–303; II, 251–254. Pobedonostsev, *Novum Regnum*, I, 69–70, 86–89, 94, 171, 323–324; II, 498–499, 505–507, 643–650, 687, 934, 963. Petrovskii, "Perepiska," *Russkii arkhiv*, II, 254–256. Feoktistov, *Vospominaniia*, pp. 242–243; Markov, *K istorii raskola-staroobriadchestva*, pp. 210–216. Savva, Archbishop of Tver, *Khronika moei zhizni* (Sergiev Posad, 1897–1911), VIII, 716–717. Ernest J. Simmons, *Dostoevski. The Making of a Novelist* (New York, 1940), pp. 335–338, 420, 448–450, 572, 608.

[32] "Pis'ma Pobedonostseva k Feoktistovu," *Literaturnoe nasledstvo*, XXII–XXIV, 540.

Orthodox Church and its schools. However, he was aware that artists and other intellectuals were significant and that incentives and rewards would assist in winning their support. Therefore, he urged government encouragement and aid for papers and journals which were sympathetic to government policies. He obtained awards and promotions for scholars and publicists whose works supported his views. Finally, he provided grants and honors for "truly Russian" composers and musicians, such as Tchaikovsky and Anton Rubinstein.[33]

Pobedonostsev was not an original thinker, but fundamentally a propagandist. He was particularly interested in promoting the publication of literature which advocated his goals or which criticized his opponents. He devoted especial attention to the Holy Synod Press, and he made it one of the largest and most efficient in Russia. He used this press mainly to print and to distribute enormous quantities of literature for the Orthodox Church and its parish schools. However, he also used it to publish historical works which represented his point of view, or which he believed would stimulate an interest in and love for the history of Russia. For example, it was the Holy Synod Press which first published Kliuchevskii's famous *Course in Russian History*.[34]

For Pobedonostsev, the Orthodox Church was the state's principal servant and weapon. The Church was to act as a cement for society. No state could have more than one religion, regardless of the number of races it contained, for other beliefs and churches would be "agents of disintegration." "He who deserts the Orthodox belief ceases to be Russian, not only in his thoughts and acts but also in his way of living and in his dress." [35]

The unity which the Church provided Pobedonostsev called the "community of believers." He asserted that "the Church and the Church alone has allowed us to remain Russians and to unite our scattered strength." Thus, when many of his contemporaries in Western Europe were developing systems labeled "integral nationalism," Pobedonostsev sought an "integral Christianism." He considered that this system above all ensured equality: the Orthodox Church more than any other was "a house where all are equal." [36]

---

[33] Pobedonostsev, *Pis'ma*, I, 342–344, 403–404. Pobedonostsev, *Novum Regnum*, II, 557–558. "Pis'ma Pobedonostseva k Feoktistovu," *Literaturnoe nasledstvo*, XXII–XXIV, 550.

[34] Sinodal'naia tipografiia, Moscow, *Katalog knig, prodaiushchikhsia v sinodal'nykh knizhnykh lavkakh* (Moscow, 1896). Vasilii O. Kliuchevskii, *Kurs russkoi istorii* (1st ed., Moscow, 1904–1910). Pobedonostsev, *Pis'ma*, II, 64–65. "Pis'ma K. P. Pobedonostseva k S. D. Voitu," *Russkii arkhiv*, Book I (1917), p. 77.

[35] General Hans von Schweinitz, *Denkwürdigkeiten* (Berlin, 1927), II, 384. Pobedonostsev, *Kurs*, 4th ed., II, 180–181; Creighton, *Life and Letters*, II, 160–161.

[36] Pobedonostsev, *Moskovskii sbornik*, 3rd ed., pp. 3–9, 12–15, 20–23, 154–156, 216–221. Pobedonostsev, *Pis'ma*, II, 79–82, 102–104, 108–110, 191–192, 259–260, 308–309. Pobedonostsev, *Novum Regnum*, II, 332–334, 876–877, 921, 961–969; Schweinitz, *Denkwürdigkeiten*, II, 243–244, 275, 302, 388, 395–396.

The Church was to accomplish its mission by providing and supporting the traditions, the loved ceremonies and spectacles, and the revered beliefs. It was to preach submission to authority and to invest the important acts of life with a sacred aura. It was, above all, to control education, particularly in the primary grades. Pobedonostsev had firm and clear ideas on education, and he was a staunch advocate of a national parish school system. These schools emphasized the "four R's," reading, writing, arithmetic, and religion, and they placed a great stress upon singing. Pobedonostsev believed that schools must fit the people, and he sought to provide children "the basic elements of intellectual and moral culture." He asserted too that primary school education should not be a step toward higher education for most children, but should concentrate upon inculcating sound habits and feelings and upon leaving the children "in that place and in that milieu in which they belong." Pobedonostsev, of course, attacked rationalism and "the logical man"; it was natural, therefore, for him to advocate trade schools as well as the parish school system. He had a deep scorn for most university professors and wanted to restrict advanced education. It is worthy of note that most of the friends about whom he wrote essays late in life were well-educated people who devoted their lives to primary schools in the countryside.[37]

The Church was also to help eliminate the religious and national minorities. Pobedonostsev boasted of freedom of belief in Russia, but he considered all non-Orthodox religious groups "enemies of the state because the laws of the Orthodox Church are the laws of the state." He characterized the Old Believers as "dark, ignorant, stagnant in thought, and distinguished by deceit, slyness, meanness, and frivolity." He charged the German Lutherans in the Baltic provinces with seeking to destroy the Orthodox Church and the Russian state.[38]

Pobedonostsev had a particular interest in gaining for Orthodoxy the Russian border territories and those areas of Central Asia and Siberia not yet fully under Russian political and cultural control. He hoped to seal these areas off from outside influence and to acquire that community in Orthodoxy which he considered fundamental. Thus, he sought to restrict all religions but Orthodoxy, to promote Orthodoxy and Russian culture, and to crush all minority nationalist feeling. He used his influence upon the tsar to maintain firm, nationalistic administrators in those areas, he built schools and churches, and he persuaded the tsar to send icons, grant money to schools,

---

[37] Pobedonostsev, *Vechnaia pamiat'*, pp. 9–20, 56–62, 74–100. Pobedonostsev, *Uchenie i uchitel'* (Moscow, 1900–1904), *passim*. Pobedonostsev, *Moskovskii sbornik*, 3rd ed., pp. 31–52, 84–86, 142–146. "Kievskii Sobor 1884 goda," *Russkii arkhiv*, III (1908), 88–89. Boris Veselovskii, *Istoriia Zemstva za sorok let* (St. Petersburg, 1909–1911), II, 296–297. Petrovskii, "Perepiska," *Russkii arkhiv*, I (1915), 463; II (1915), 370, 468–469. N. Nikol'skii, "K. P. Pobedonostsev," *Tserkovnyi vestnik*, XXXIII (1907), 382.

[38] Pobedonostsev, *Vsepoddanneishii otchët ober-prokurora za 1888–1889* (St. Petersburg, 1891), pp. 72, 79–123, 464–467. "Pis'ma Pobedonostseva k S. D. Voitu," *Russkii arkhiv*, II (1905), 360, 525–535.

and in other ways demonstrate his interest. While he was frank and even eager in the use of "firm power" to crush the "mad dream" of national independence held by some minorities, he hoped above all to convert them to Orthodoxy. In 1889, for example, he had two Orthodox Baltic Germans placed on the Governing Council, citing their loyalty to the state as proof of the success his mission was enjoying.[39]

Pobedonostsev's ideas concerning the Church's role in "extending and fortifying the empire" are demonstrated clearly by his own writings and by those of one of his closest friends, Nikolai Il'minskii, who was the founder of the Kazan Teachers' Seminary for Non-Russians and who also was a member of the Holy Synod's Educational Council. Il'minskii persuaded Pobedonostsev that Mohammedanism represented a serious threat to Russia and that a religious and cultural counterattack alone could save the Volga area and Central Asia from the Tartars and Mohammedanism. Il'minskii saw that "the primary education of non-Russians in their own language is the most certain means of persuading them to adopt the Russian language and Russian culture." He encouraged the cultural diversity of the national groups along the Volga and in Central Asia, and he sought to make their cultures "national in form, but Orthodox in content." He began with a school for baptized Tartars, and trained a native Orthodox priesthood for each national group. Soon he had more than one hundred schools for non-Russians in the Kazan area alone. These schools trained thousands of teachers and missionaries to carry Orthodoxy and Russian culture to the various national minorities. Il'minskii, with Pobedonostsev's support, also established a translating commission, which translated and published hundreds of thousands of copies of Orthodox texts in the various minority languages.[40]

There were two religious and racial minority groups whom Pobedonostsev believed it was impossible to convert or to assimilate in entirety. The Jews should be erased from Russian public life; one third would be converted, one third would "wander away" across the frontier, and one third would die out. While this was being accomplished, their influence was to be restricted in every way possible. Pobedonostsev, therefore, supported the government's anti-Semitic campaign during the reign of Alexander III, although he sought to curb the popular movement against the Jews.

The Polish enclave was an object of Pobedonostsev's bitter hatred also,

[39] Pobedonostsev, *Pis'ma*, II, 51–59, 78–83, 102–104, 108–110, 115–117, 119–121, 137–138, 257–260. Pobedonostsev, *Novum Regnum*, II, 922–923, 980, 993–994. Pobedonostsev, *Vechnaia pamiat'*, pp. 74–86. White, "Statesman of Russia," *Century Magazine*, LVI, 116. Schweinitz, *Denkwürdigkeiten*, II, 388, 395–396.

[40] Nikolai Il'minskii, *Pis'ma Nikolaia Ivanovicha Il'minskago k Ober-Prokuroru Sviateishchago Sinoda Konstantinu Petrovichu Pobedonostsevu* (Kazan, 1895), pp. 6–10, 73–78, 112–124, 177–180, 374–382. E. N. Medynskii, *Istoriia russkoi pedagogiki do velikoi oktiabrskoi sotsialisticheskoi revoliutsii* (Moscow, 1938), pp. 350–359. Petrovskii, "Perepiska," *Russkii arkhiv*, II, 510–512.

for he believed "the existence of a Polish state means slavery and oppression for all of the Russian people." He asserted that he did not know "a single Catholic who is not hostile to us and who does not dream of seizing our western provinces." The Polish problem was, of course, indissolubly linked with that of relations with the West. Pobedonostsev sought to incorporate Poland into the empire so that this problem would become only a domestic issue. He helped delay the long negotiations from 1878 through 1883 with the papacy, and during the late 1890's he fought resolutely against allowing a papal nuncio to reside in St. Petersburg. He declared to the tsar in 1899 that the Polish-Lithuanian issue was "a matter of life or death" for Russia. Since he believed religion could not be separated from nationality, accept-ance of a nuncio would only give the Poles, the Catholics, "the Latins," a nest of intrigue inside Russia.[41]

For Pobedonostsev, the primary instrument for controlling and educating man was the family, "the foundation of the state" and "the eternal element of prosperous societies." He was extremely well informed concerning Euro-pean and American scholarship on the history of the family in all societies, and his most important translations were those of the studies of the family made by Heinrich Thiersch and Frederic Le Play.[42]

Pobedonostsev described the family as "the spiritual and cultural nursery for citizens," and he assigned it the functions of maintaining tradition, en-suring social stability, harnessing and controlling man's most fundamental instincts, and providing for the orderly perpetuation of the human race. The parental power, "the only power established by God in the Decalogue, is the highest power." The function of the parents, especially the father, was to repress the child's evil instincts, to instill a knowledge of and respect for the Decalogue, and to provide the proper moral and physical education so that the child would become a patriotic, dutiful, and hard-working adult.[43]

In summary, a brief analysis of Pobedonostsev's political philosophy and a quick survey of his state's armory of instruments reveal several striking characteristics. To begin with, his ideas concerning the nature of man were fundamental to his entire philosophy and "justified" the arbitrary and au-thoritarian government he advocated. In addition, his belief that the charac-ter of the state was shaped by its national religious faith and its traditional

[41] Adrien Boudou, *Le Saint-Siège et la Russie* (Paris, 1922–1925), II, 541–544. Pobedonostsev, *Pis'ma*, I, 209; II, 26–27, 65–68, 197–202, 323–325; Pobedonostsev, *Novum Regnum*, II, 569–570, 896. "Pis'ma K. P. Pobedonostseva k Grafu N. P. Igna-tievu," *Byloe*, XXVII–XXVIII (1924), 58–59, 72–80. P. Tverskoi, "Iz delovoi perepiski s K. P. Pobedonostsevym," *Vestnik Evropy*, XII (1907), 665–666. Koni, *Na zhiznennom puti*, I, 570–573.

[42] Hermann Dalton, *Lebenserinnerungen* (Berlin, 1906–1908), I, 326–331. Pobedo-nostsev, *Kurs*, 3rd ed., I, 504–507, 523–547; 2nd ed., II, 445–656; 2nd ed., III (*Uka-zatel' i Prilozhenie*), 109–110.

[43] Pobedonostsev, tr., *Osnovnaia Konstitutsiia*, preface, pp. xlii, 1–6, 82–87. Pobedo-nostsev, *Pis'ma*, II, 147–148. Pobedonostsev, *Kurs*, 4th ed., I, 730–745; II, 93.

political and social institutions provided a base from which he could oppose "alien" ideas and institutions.

Nevertheless, Pobedonostsev's system was not so secure as it appeared. Perhaps this can be shown most clearly by neglecting for the moment the obvious weapons in the state's hands and by identifying some of the principal instruments or elements Pobedonostsev ignored or slighted. First of all, neither the army nor the police play an important role. In addition, Pobedonostsev did not appreciate the significance of a political façade, and there is a striking absence of color and trappings. However, it is in his treatment of the established nineteenth-century political trinity, the throne, the altar, and the aristocracy, that the most serious lacunae appear. For Pobedonostsev, of course, the main bulwark of the state was the Church. The other two members of the trinity, though, were very shaky indeed. Pobedonostsev was a fervent supporter of autocracy, but his advocacy was based neither on functional nor on religious grounds, and his arguments were generally vague. His autocrat was in effect a figurehead. Finally, he sought to replace the aristocracy or the nobility with a group of middle-class executive managers and efficiency experts.

Two Types of Russian Liberalism:
Maklakov and Miliukov

MICHAEL KARPOVICH

The weakness of prerevolutionary Russian liberalism has become a common-place in historical literature. Too often, it has been asserted as something self-evident, and thus not in need of further investigation. This attitude has been based largely on an a priori reasoning, the weakness of Russian liberalism being deduced from the weakness of the middle class in Russia. The latter, in turn, has been rather assumed than investigated. Moreover, another broad assumption has been involved — that of an organic connection between liberalism and middle classes, as if it were natural and almost inevitable for a middle class to favor a middle-of-the-road policy. Coupled with this, there has been a fairly common tendency to identify the middle class with the business community, the bourgeoisie in the Marxian sense of the term.

The validity of neither of these basic assumptions can be taken for granted. The designation of a social group as a middle class merely indicates its central position in a given society, and consequently the nature of the middle class can vary from one country to another, in accordance with the country's social structure. Thus it might be argued, as it has been argued in the case of the Polish *szlachta,* that the bulk of the Russian gentry was a middle class as distinguished from the landed aristocracy. Much more important, however, is the other point — the one referring to the relationship between the middle class and liberalism. We know from historical experience that under certain conditions middle-class groups might support extremist political movements, as in the cases of Italian Fascism and German Nazism, for instance, or that at least they might retreat from their liberal positions as they did in France under the Third Empire and again in Bismarck's Germany. On the other hand, the history of European liberalism cannot be reduced to that of the "businessman's creed," as Laski attempted to do. This was only one of its component parts, and de Ruggiero convincingly demonstrated the primary importance of other elements that went into its make-up — such as religious dissent and the defense of "ancient liberties" by the privileged estates of feudal origin.[1]

It is neither necessary nor possible for me to discuss these general questions in the present paper.[2] The purpose of the foregoing remarks was to point out the complexity of the problem and the need for its further investigation. The history of Russian liberalism has been sadly neglected. To many, the a priori assumption of its weakness seems to have been fully justified by the course of events in Russia since the Revolution. Why should one pay much attention to a political trend which could not achieve any lasting results and which suffered such a crushing defeat? The answer to this question is twofold. In the first place, the historical process does not know any "ultimate" results — any "final" defeats or victories. And secondly, the importance of historical phenomena should be assessed as of the time when they occurred, and not only in the light of the historian's *post factum* wisdom. Certainly, *vae victis* is not a principle for historians to follow!

As elsewhere, liberalism in Russia was not a homogeneous movement. It proceeded from different social groups, and various motives induced people to join it. This lack of homogeneity was clearly reflected in the make-up of the Constitutional Democratic Party founded in October of 1905. It has been repeatedly pointed out that it came into being as the result of the merging of two forces: the zemstvo liberals, on the one hand, and the liberal-minded part of the professional class, on the other. Strictly speaking, this is an oversimplification. There were other elements in the party which by their social provenience did not belong to either of the two groups, and inside each of the latter there could be found a considerable variety of political attitudes and aspirations. By and large, however, one can accept the accuracy of this summary characterization of the two main components of the Cadet Party, and it is in the light of this division that I am going to discuss the two types of Russian liberalism as exemplified by Maklakov and Miliukov respectively.

Vasilii Alekseevich Maklakov, born in 1869, was exactly ten years younger than Pavel Nikolaevich Miliukov. If I begin my discussion with Maklakov it is because he represents some of the prevailing trends of the zemstvo liberalism which historically preceded that of the professional class.[3]

[1] Harold J. Laski, *The Rise of Liberalism: The Philosophy of a Business Civilization* (New York, 1936); Guido de Ruggiero, *The History of European Liberalism* (New York–London, 1927).

[2] I attempted a more general discussion of liberalism in prerevolutionary Russia in my Ilchester lecture delivered at Oxford University in May 1952. Its text is scheduled to be published in the *Oxford Slavonic Papers*.

[3] V. A. Maklakov has reviewed his political life and commented upon it in the following writings: "Iz proshlogo," *Sovremennye zapiski*, Vols. XXXIII, XL–XLIV, XLVI–XLVIII, L–LI, LIII–LIV, LVI, LVIII, LX (Paris, 1926–1936); *Vlast' i obshchestvennost' na zakate staroi Rossii*, Vols. I–III (Paris, 1936), a revised and enlarged version of the preceding work; *Pervaia Duma* (Paris, 1939); *Vtoraia Duma* (Paris, 1947); *Iz vospominanii* (New York, 1954).

Not that he was a zemstvo worker himself, but it so happened that his political education was greatly influenced by the zemstvo liberal tradition. In his reminiscences, he speaks of his father and those around him as being imbued with the spirit of the Great Reforms of the 1860's, strongly favoring their continuation and extension, but remaining rather indifferent to politics. He also pictures them as being resolutely opposed to the terroristic activity of the *Narodnaia Volia*. Both in the secondary school and in the university, he found the Russian youth of the time on the whole sharing the attitude of their elders. According to his observations, even the student disturbances of 1887 and 1890, during the years when he himself was a student at the University of Moscow, as yet were devoid of "politics." The great majority of the students were motivated by the concern for academic freedom and their own corporate rights as well as by a feeling of "student solidarity," and they resented the attempts of some of their more radical colleagues to inject into the movement general political slogans. When in 1890 the Moscow students organized a memorial service for Chernyshevskii (d. 1889), this again was an expression of their sympathy for a man who suffered for his convictions rather than a political manifestation. In his last volume of memoirs, speaking of himself as he was at the age of twenty, Maklakov says that all his sympathies were "with those representatives [of the period] of Great Reforms who wanted to continue to improve the [Russian] state on the bases of legality, freedom, and justice, taking for their starting point that which already existed in reality . . ."[4]

Characteristically, a trip to France that he made in 1889 served for him as a "lesson in conservatism." What impressed him was the picture of a country where "rights of the state could be reconciled with the rights of man" and where even the opposition "showed a concern for what had been created by history." The centenary of the French Revolution made him read the recent literature on the subject, and from this reading he derived a "new, historical understanding" of the Revolution — as opposed, one must assume, to the romantic and idealizing interpretation of it that was current among the Russian radicals of the time. It is not without significance that of all the revolutionary leaders Mirabeau became his favorite hero.

While in Paris, Maklakov got in touch with some leaders of the French student organizations, of a professional rather than a political nature. Their existence and the character of their work largely inspired young Maklakov in that active part which, upon his return to Russia, he took in the attempts to develop nonpolitical student organizations at the University of Moscow (mutual-aid societies and the like), within the rather narrow limits of the then existing legal possibilities. Thus he was one of the early leaders of what later became known as "academism" (a term which acquired a derogatory meaning for the opponents of this tendency from among the radical students) — in a sense, a student counterpart of that "economism" among the

----

[4] *Iz vospominanii*, p. 87.

workers which was supported by some of the early Social Democrats and served as a target for Lenin's violent diatribes. For Maklakov, however, it was a step in the development of his liberalism, not in opposition to, but in harmony with the general program of "improving the Russian state" by starting from "that which already existed in reality."

During these years, Maklakov was greatly influenced by his association with the so-called Lubenkov circle, one of the traditional Russian discussion groups, in this case gathered around an eminent Moscow jurist and consisting of various public leaders mostly from among the zemstvo workers.[5] A decade later, Maklakov became a recording secretary of a similar discussion group known as *Beseda* (here best translated as "Symposium") and headed by D. N. Shipov, subsequently one of the founders of the Octobrist Party. Together with some more politically minded zemstvo constitutionalists, the *Beseda* included also, besides Shipov, such other representatives of the "purer" zemstvo tradition as N. A. Khomiakov and M. A. Stakhovich. Both Lubenkov and Shipov had definite Slavophile leanings. While not accepting the original Slavophile doctrine in its entirety, and certainly not sharing its almost anarchical aberrations as exemplified, for instance, by Konstantin Aksakov's political theory, they still showed a strong affinity with Slavophilism in their somewhat diluted antistatist attitude, their emphasis on "public work" as distinguished from, if not opposed to, political activity, their relative indifference to forms of government and strictly defined constitutional formulas, as well as in their traditionalism. There can be no doubt that the influence of these men left its traces on Maklakov's brand of liberalism.

There was one point, however, where Maklakov substantially differed from the Slavophiles, and the difference can be defined by calling him a Slavophile who had learned the necessity of legal guarantees for the preservation of human rights and freedom. After several years of intense preoccupation with historical studies which led Maklakov to think of an academic career, he decided to shift to jurisprudence and to become a lawyer. The final choice was made not on the basis of either intellectual interests or practical considerations, but in response to the call of civic duty. This is what Maklakov himself has to say on the subject: "My brief life experience had shown me . . . that the main evil of Russian life was the triumph of arbitrariness that went unpunished, the helplessness of the individual in the face of administrative discretion, the lack of legal bases for his self-defense . . . The defense of the individual against lawlessness, in other words, the defense of the law itself — this was the substance of the Bar's public service."[6] This defense of the individual, however, was not to be waged in

[5] For details on the Lubenkov circle, see Maklakov's *Vlast' i obshchestvennost' na zakate staroi Rossii.*

[6] *Iz vospominanii*, p. 220.

a spirit of aggressive partisanship, and the lawyer's task was to seek for a synthesis between the rights of the state, on the one hand, and those of the individual, on the other. Here, in a nucleus, is that philosophy of compromise which became characteristic of Maklakov the politician.

The role played by Maklakov's legal career in the development of his liberal views has more than a mere biographical interest. It has a broader significance in so far as it points toward another important element in the make-up of Russian liberalism — the Russian counterpart of the German *Rechtsstaat* idea which while not necessarily connected with political liberalism eventually led many of its exponents to strive for the abolition of autocracy and the establishment of a constitutional regime.

Unfortunately, in the case of Miliukov, we are not in a position to trace the formation of his political views as fully as it can be done for Maklakov. Miliukov's personal memoirs as yet have not been published, and the manuscript so far has remained inaccessible to scholars. Several chapters of Miliukov's political reminiscences, published in an *émigré* Russian periodical in Paris, in 1938–39, cover a rather limited period (1904–1906) and are not as self-revealing as Maklakov's much more personal writings. The same is true of Miliukov's other political works.[7] Nor is there any adequate biography of Miliukov available. All one can do under the circumstances is to indicate those points in which Miliukov's political upbringing seems to have differed from that of Maklakov. We knew from Miliukov himself that in his youth he was strongly influenced by both Spencer and Comte, and that as a university student he was seriously interested in Marx's writings. As the same intellectual fare was typical of the radical youth of the period, one might assume in Miliukov a somewhat greater affinity with their *Weltanschauung* than one could expect in the case of Maklakov with his mildly Slavophile leanings. While being associated with the moderate wing of the student movement, Miliukov watched with sympathy the *Narodnaia Volia's* assault upon autocracy, seeing in their terroristic activities "one of the means of political struggle." [8] This is significantly different from that attitude of unreserved condemnation of political terror which, according to Maklakov's reminiscences, prevailed in his milieu a decade later. If the

[7] See in particular the following: *Russia and Its Crisis* (Chicago, 1905); *God bor'by: publitsisticheskaia khronika, 1905–06* (St. Petersburg, 1907); *Vtoraia Duma: publitsisticheskaia khronika, 1907* (St. Petersburg, 1908); *Tri popytki (k istorii russkogo lzhe-konstitutsionalizma)* (Paris, 1921); "Sud nad kadetskim liberalizmom," *Sovremennye zapiski,* Vol. XLI (Paris, 1930) and "Liberalizm, radikalizm i revoliutsiia," *ibid.,* Vol. LVII (1935) — these two articles were written as a reply to Maklakov's "Iz proshlogo"; "Rokovye gody (iz vospominanii)," *Russkie zapiski,* Vols. IV–XXI (Paris, 1938–39). I understand that Miliukov's personal memoirs mentioned in the text will be published by the Chekhov Publishing House.

[8] See on this point the biographical sketch by S. A. Smirnov (undoubtedly authorized by Miliukov himself) in *P. N. Miliukov: Sbornik materialov po chestvovaniiu ego semidesiatiletiia, 1859–1929* (Paris, 1929).

latter reflected the views of the moderate zemstvo majority, Miliukov's position agreed with that of the somewhat more radical minority among the early zemstvo liberals. One of them, I. I. Petrunkevich, who even attempted to form a kind of working alliance with the revolutionaries,[9] later became Miliukov's chief political mentor.

In the volume of essays dedicated to Miliukov on the occasion of his seventieth anniversary,[10] S. A. Smirnov dates Miliukov's "actively political attitude" from the famine year of 1891, while V. A. Obolenskii asserts that he already was a "convinced liberal and democrat" at the time of his graduation from the university. The fact remains, however, that in Miliukov the politician matured much more slowly than the scholar. For a number of years after graduation, he was almost completely absorbed in historical research and teaching. Within the period 1892–1903 appeared all of his most important scholarly works, beginning with the *National Economy of Russia and the Reforms of Peter the Great* and ending with the third volume of *Outlines of Russian Culture*. Miliukov's intensive scholarly activity went on even after his academic career had been brusquely terminated by his dismissal from the University of Moscow on rather flimsy charges of a political nature. One is tempted to say that Miliukov became an active politician almost in spite of himself.

Miliukov's real political activity began in the first years of the century, simultaneously with the general revival of the opposition sentiment in the country, and more particularly in connection with the formation of the Union of Liberation. From the outset, he took an active part in the Liberation movement, in contrast to Maklakov, who, according to his own admission, remained on the periphery until the establishment of the constitutional regime. The difference, of course, was not accidental. Miliukov joined the movement with an intention of forcing its zemstvo elements to adopt a more radical attitude and to ally themselves more closely with the professional intellectuals on the Left. To Maklakov, such a development was a source of serious doubts and misgivings. In retrospect, he sees the initial strength of the Liberation movement in the fact that it was primarily a zemstvo movement, organically connected with the "era of Great Reforms" and nurtured in the tradition of public work performed within the framework of local self-government institutions. It was losing rather than gaining strength in

[9] On this point see Petrunkevich's memoirs, published as Vol. XXI of the *Arkhiv russkoi revoliutsii* (Berlin, 1922–1937). It should be made clear that Petrunkevich did not approve of the terror, but considered it unavoidable under the political conditions of the time. The purpose of his negotiations with the revolutionaries, which took place in Kiev, in 1878, was to persuade them to suspend their teroristic activities, while the liberals were organizing peaceful pressure on the government. The implication, however, was that in case of the failure of this effort a resumption of terror would be justifiable. In a way, this approach foreshadowed the position taken by the Cadet Party in 1906–1907.

[10] See note 8.

allying itself with other public elements which were devoid of practical political experience. These new allies differed from the majority of the zemstvo men not only in their final aims, but, which was more important, also in the choice of means for the achievement of the immediate objectives. Under their influence, "the Liberation movement became too indifferent to that dividing line which should have separated the evolution of the state from the evils of a revolution." [11]

Maklakov has been accused by some of his critics of evaluating past events from the vantage ground of wisdom acquired in the course of subsequent historical experience. But while to some extent this is true, there is enough evidence to permit us to believe that in a large measure his present judgment reflects the attitude he had at the time when the events he is evaluating were taking place. This attitude explains his relative aloofness from the Liberation movement. It explains also the casual way in which he joined the Cadet Party and accepted election to its central committee. He freely admits that he was not a very good Cadet, and it is on the record that on several important occasions he found himself in disagreement with the majority of the Party members and with its leaders. In its turn, the Party, while glad to make use of Maklakov's remarkable oratorical gift as well as of his legal erudition and ability, did not look upon him as a dependable Party regular.

It would be impossible, within the scope of this paper, to follow the Miliukov–Maklakov controversy through all the stages of its development. Nor is it necessary for my present purpose. What is of importance is the fundamental cleavage between these two outstanding representatives of Russian liberalism, the difference in the main premises and the general spirit of their political actions. In this case, as in that of many other Russian political trends, the Revolution of 1905 played the part of a catalyst. In Maklakov, it strengthened his fear of all and every revolution, his conviction that revolutionary methods were not only undesirable but in the long run futile. He counted on the evolutionary process in the course of which the regime was bound to change "under the pressure of life itself." In his opinion, it was preferable to try to contribute to the regime's peaceful evolution and not to aim at its complete overthrow. The "historical state power" had one decisive advantage on its side: the people were in the habit of obeying it. It was precisely this inertia of obedience that would be destroyed by a revolution, and with it would go that legal continuity which was so important for the normal growth of a nation. The results could be foreseen on the basis of historical experience: the new government issuing from the revolution either would be so weak that it could not maintain itself in power or else it would be forced to become a ruthless dictatorship.

[11] *Iz vospominanii*, pp. 297–300.

Maklakov had no illusions as to the nature of the Russian regime of the period. But he still thought that it would be amenable to the pressure of organized public opinion had the liberals used every opportunity to reach an agreement with it, on a program of gradually introduced reforms. In this lay the historical task of Russian liberalism. Maklakov felt that the liberals were missing their chance of contributing to Russia's peaceful evolution by assuming an uncompromisingly hostile attitude toward the regime and thus allying themselves with the destructive revolutionary forces in the country. This appeal to the Acheron (the symbol of the "lower world" in Greek and Latin poetry) was bound to end in the liberals' undoing: their cause would be lost whether revolution won the victory or suffered defeat.[12]

In the eyes of Maklakov the failure of the Russian liberals to approach their political task in a proper spirit became obvious after the proclamation of the constitutional regime. The October Manifesto of 1905 opened a real opportunity for the peaceful solution of Russia's problems, and it was up to the Cadet Party to lead the way in this undertaking. But for this a kind of psychological demobilization was necessary. Unfortunately, the Party could not get rid of its "wartime psychology," and instead of seeking a lasting peace with the government, which could be based on a compromise only, insisted on continuing to wage the struggle until the "final victory." In this connection, Maklakov cites an extemporaneous speech made by Miliukov in Moscow, upon the receipt of the news of the Manifesto's publication, in which he said "that nothing was changed, and the war still was going on." [13]

It is on the basis of these general premises that Maklakov has severely criticized the Cadet policies of the years 1905–1907. The main points of his indictment can be summarized as follows:

The maximalism of the Party's programmatic demands, such as, in particular, the convocation of a Constituent Assembly which could not be realized unless there was a complete capitulation on the part of the imperial government;

The Party's uncompromising attitude toward both Witte and Stolypin who, according to Maklakov, could and should be used as allies rather than abused as enemies;

The peremptory way in which the Cadet leaders rejected the idea of Cadet participation in the government advanced both by Witte and Stolypin;

The Party's tendency to use the Duma as a tribune for antigovernmental agitation rather than for constructive legislative activity;

Its dogmatic insistence on the immediate revision of the Fundamental

---

[12] All of the foregoing is based on Maklakov's "retrospective" writings. I believe, however, that on the whole they reflect his former attitude correctly.

[13] Commenting upon this statement in his "Rokovye gody," *Russkie zapiski*, Vol. XIV, Miliukov admits that the "sense of his words" has been reported by Maklakov correctly. To this he adds that he was expressing not only his own, but also the "general" feeling.

Laws, aiming at a universal franchise, reduced powers of the upper chamber, and ministerial responsibility — matters which, in Maklakov's opinion, could be settled gradually as the constitutional regime grew stronger and took firmer roots in the Russian soil;

And finally the issuance of the Vyborg Manifesto — essentially a revolutionary measure in so far as the dissolution of the Duma and the appointment of new elections were in accordance with the constitution.

Maklakov admits that the other Cadet leaders neither wanted a revolution nor acquiesced in its eventual triumph. But he feels that, unlike himself, they were not afraid of it — some because they did not believe in the possibility of its victory, others because they thought that it could be stopped in its initial stages. Meanwhile, "as the threat of the revolution might have forced the government to make [further] concessions, they continued to play this card, not realizing that they were playing with fire." [14]

Once more it should be mentioned that, because of the nature of the material available, Miliukov's views cannot be presented in the same systematic fashion in which I have tried to summarize Maklakov's "political philosophy." The two volumes in which Miliukov has collected his articles and papers, written in 1905–06, contain precisely what their subtitle indicates — a running comment of a publicist on current political events, and his later writings (those of the *émigré* period) likewise do not offer any exposition of the author's liberal creed. Even the two articles written in response to Maklakov's criticism of Cadet policies[15] have the nature of *ad hoc* contributions, and they merely touch upon the divergent premises underlying the controversy.

Miliukov begins his defense of the Cadet Party by a characteristically empirical reference to the actual conditions in which the Party had to formulate its program and to make its tactical decisions. The Party, he reminds Maklakov, was not living "on abstractions and armchair (*kabinetnye*) deliberations." Its position was shifting now to the right and now to the left, "together with the life of the Russian society." Elsewhere[16] he refers to the psychology of the time — that surge of emotion which was caused by the events of 1905, and from which the rank and file of the Party did not remain immune. He points out that the Party leaders, while trying to maintain the central position, were forced to make occasional concessions to the more impatient spirit of many of their followers. He insists, however, that the Cadet program, while "radical," was not Utopian. What Miliukov means by "radical" becomes clear from his reference to "neoliberalism" as a kindred movement in Western Europe. Back in October 1905, in his opening address at the first ("constituent") convention of the Constitutional Demo-

---

[14] *Iz vospominanii,* p. 351.
[15] See note 7.
[16] In his "Rokovye gody" (see note 13).

cratic Party, he made the same comparison in slightly different terms: ". . . our Party stands closest to those groups among the Western intellectuals who are known under the name of 'social reformers' . . . our program is undoubtedly the most Leftist of all those advanced by similar political groups in Western Europe." [17]

In a different context, Miliukov accuses Maklakov of stressing the tactics at the expense of the program, attaching more importance to the means than to the aims. He argues that under certain conditions even a liberal might become a revolutionary, and that thus one cannot equate liberalism with a strictly legal way of political action. It is equally erroneous to confuse a defense of the rule of law with that of a given positive law, as Maklakov's reasoning tends to do. Nor should one ascribe such a decisive role to the preservation of legal continuity in the transition from one political order to the other.

If, in these last arguments, Miliukov opposes to Maklakov's traditionalism his own historical relativism, in another case, when dealing with a proper approach to political problems, he blames his opponent for an excessively relativist point of view. Miliukov sees the chief defect of Maklakov the politician in his attempt to transfer into the sphere of politics the psychology and methods of a lawyer. The latter inevitably acquires a professional habit of "seeing a share of truth on the opposite side, and a share of error on his own." A politician cannot allow himself the luxury of such an indifferent and "objective" [18] attitude toward "the contents of truth." [19] Here Miliukov is striking at the very heart of Maklakov's "philosophy of compromise."

Apart from this theoretical disagreement, a radically different interpretation of political events was involved in the controversy. Miliukov did not share in the least Maklakov's optimistic appraisal of Russia's chances of peaceful evolution after the proclamation of the constitutional regime. I have cited above Miliukov's admission that at the time of the publication of the October Manifesto he did not see in it any real change that would induce him to stop fighting the government. Twenty-five years later Miliukov still asserted the correctness of his original diagnosis. Referring to Nicholas II's statement that after the revision of the Fundamental Laws "autocracy remained the same as of old," he declared the Tsar to be closer to the truth than Maklakov, "even from the formal point of view." He also stoutly

---

[17] *Konstitutsionno-demokraticheskaia partiia: s"ezd 12–18 oktiabria 1905 g.* (St. Petersburg, 1905), p. 7. Elsewhere in the same address Miliukov speaks of "social reform" as the main aim which "the Russian liberation movement wants to achieve by the way of political reform," and he mentions the Party's "implacable opposition" to the Manchester brand of liberalism. Certainly, not all of the members of the Cadet Party shared this attitude either at that time or later. But the division in the Cadet Party along this line is a separate subject, which lies beyond the scope of the present paper.

[18] The ironical quotation marks are Miliukov's.

[19] Obviously, a pragmatic political "truth" is meant in this context.

maintained that the Cadet leaders had been right in repelling the overtures of both Witte and Stolypin, as in neither case had there been any evidence of sincerity. By joining the government on conditions that were proposed to them, Party representatives would have walked into a trap: while being unable to exercise a decisive influence on governmental policies they would have compromised themselves in the eyes of the people.[20]

How these considerations affected the tactical line which was followed by Miliukov in 1905–06 can be seen from the various statements made by him at that time in his capacity as party leader. Thus in his opening address at the first Party convention[21] he expressed himself as follows: ". . . in fighting for our aim we cannot count on any agreements and compromises [with the government], and we should raise high the banner already unfurled by the Russian liberation movement as a whole, striving for the convocation of a Constituent Assembly . . ." This was said a few days before the publication of the October Manifesto. But in its closing session, which took place on the morrow of this event, the convention adopted a resolution (undoubtedly edited by Miliukov) in which it reiterated that "in so far as the state Duma cannot be recognized as an adequate [organ of] popular representation, the aim of the Constitutional Democratic Party remains the same as before — namely, [the convocation of] the Constituent Assembly." As to the Duma, "it can serve for the Party only as one of the means towards realization of the above-mentioned aim, while a permanent and close contact should be maintained with the general course of the liberation movement outside the Duma."

The last sentence obviously implied a coördination of the Cadet Party's efforts with the activities of the parties of the Left. This subject was discussed by Miliukov at the convention in the following terms:

> Between us and our allies, not adversaries, from the Left (this is how I prefer to call them) there also exists a certain dividing line, but it is of an altogether different nature from the one that we have drawn to the right of us. Together with them we stand on the same Left wing of the Russian political movement. We do not join them in their demands for a democratic republic and nationalization of means of production. To some of us these demands are generally unacceptable while others consider them as being outside [the realm of] practical politics. But so long as, in spite of different motives, it remains possible for us to march together to a common goal, both party groups will act as a single unit.[22]

In the course of time, the difference between Miliukov and Maklakov lost a good deal of its sharpness as far as *tactical* problems were concerned. Events themselves took care of that. By the fall of 1907, the revolutionary energy was totally spent, and there were no visible prospects of its resur-

---

[20] This problem is discussed by Miliukov in *Tri popytki* (see note 7).

[21] See note 17.

[22] This and the preceding quotations are from *Konstitutsionno-demokraticheskaia partiia* (see note 17).

gence. The government had recovered its control over the country, and there was a conservative majority in the Duma. The Cadets had to adjust themselves to the new situation. "To preserve the Duma" now became the official slogan. This meant to make the best of the existing circumstances, and to take part in the legislative activity, modest as its scope might be. In this way, the Cadet Party, still led by Miliukov, was moving to the right, in Maklakov's direction. But there was also a reverse process, this time affecting the moderates of the Maklakov type and even those to the right of him. As yet it has not been studied by historians, but it surely can be traced as a slowly but steadily developing trend in the life of the last two Dumas. As the Duma was growing more sure of itself, even its conservative majority was becoming less and less inclined to acquiesce in the arbitrariness of the administration or to overlook its inefficiency. By the end of the period, the opposition spirit in the Duma was by no means limited to the Cadets and those to the left of them. Thus was prepared the ground for the formation of the Progressive Bloc in 1915 and through it for the first Provisional Government.

All this, however, does not deprive the controversy as it developed in 1905–06 of its considerable historical interest. It was then, in a period of crisis, that the two different concepts of an appropriate liberal policy found its fullest and most articulate expression. Essentially, the Russian liberals faced the same problem with which the Social Democrats were struggling at the same time: What was the nature of the transformation Russia was undergoing, and what were its possible limits? Closely linked with this problem was another question: What were the forces in the country that would be able to bring this transformation to a successful conclusion? Maklakov saw the historical need of the hour in the continuation and completion of the Great Reforms of the 1860's, in the establishment in Russia of a political order based on the rule of law and self-government, and he believed that it could and should be effected in an evolutionary way, without the destruction of the existing political and social structure. In his eyes, even a thorough democratization of the latter was not immediately feasible and could be left to the future. For the time being, lasting reforms could be achieved only under the direction of those elements in the country which were prepared for the task by their previous practical experience in the field of public or governmental work. This was why the liberals had to ally themselves with those groups to the right of them which recognized the necessity of reforms, and why they had to seek an agreement with the government whenever an opportunity presented itself. Maklakov minimized the danger of reaction for which he saw no solid base in the prevailing trends of national life. To him, the main danger was on the left and not on the right. It was the danger of uncontrollable and chaotic revolutionary outbreaks, spurred, even if not provoked, by demagogic policies and appeals.

Miliukov expected from the Russian crisis much more far-reaching results than those envisaged by Maklakov. In his concept, the introduction in Russia of a full-fledged parliamentary regime was an immediate necessity and not a program for a more or less remote future. Unlike Maklakov, he considered the country ripe for popular sovereignty, and he felt that it was the duty of the liberals to wage a battle for this aim so long as there was a chance of its attainment. A much more politically minded person than his opponent, he also wanted the constitutional guarantees to be fully spelled out at once. The extreme importance that he attached to institutional arrangements, which to his critics was a sign of his doctrinaire spirit, in reality proceeded from his firm belief in the logic of political institutions.[23] He did not neglect the social aspects of the Russian problem either, and he emphasized the immediate necessity of a radical agrarian reform as vigorously as he fought for political democracy. I know that the Cadet agrarian project, of which Miliukov was one of the sponsors, appeared rather modest as reflected in the peculiarly slanted looking glass of the Russian political life of the time. The fact remains that it proposed compulsory alienation of private property on such a scale as would be deemed revolutionary in any one of the contemporary Western societies.[24] Miliukov knew, of course, that his political and social program could neither win any support among the Russian moderates nor serve as a basis for an agreement with the government. Thus, in pursuing his aims, he was forced to look for allies among the Left-Wing opposition parties, much as he disliked some of their objectives and methods. If Maklakov minimized the danger of reaction, Miliukov at that time apparently minimized the danger of revolution. To him, the real enemies were on the right and not on the left.

It is not the purpose of this paper to pass judgment on the respective merits of the two political approaches I have tried to outline on the preceding pages. What I want to point out is that both stood in a direct and close relationship with the realities of prerevolutionary Russian life and both had their roots in the native tradition.

Maklakov could cite as his predecessors those public leaders and en-

[23] Miliukov's advice to Witte to follow "the Bulgarian or the Belgian model" in preparing a constitution for Russia has been often cited as an example of his political "formalism." In "Liberalizm, radikalizm i revoliutsiia" (see note 7) he points out that in his conversation with Witte he opposed the two constitutions he mentioned to those of Prussia and Japan, from which the governmental experts were inclined to borrow, and then he adds that "apparently there exists an *ABC* of constitutional law which remains the same wherever political freedom and constitutional government are being established in earnest, and not as a sham."

[24] It is significant that Maklakov took no part in the elaboration or defense of the Cadet agrarian project. What he was preoccupied with was the problem of bringing the *legal and civic status* of the Russian peasants in line with that of the rest of the population. He was the Party's chief expert in that field and one of the prime movers behind the Duma's corresponding legislative projects.

lightened bureaucrats who throughout the nineteenth century, from Speranskii on, were concerned with the problem of introducing legality into the
Russian government, the mid-century defenders of individual and civil
liberty, the architects of the Great Reforms, and the moderate zemstvo
liberals. Miliukov's political genealogy would include the Decembrists,
Herzen in some of his phases, the more radical zemstvo constitutionalists of
the Petrunkevich type, and those of the late nineteenth-century revolutionaries who were prepared to subordinate all other aims to the more immediate
task of obtaining a constitutional regime for Russia.

Neither Miliukov nor Maklakov were any more "uprooted" than was
the whole liberal movement in Russia, the two different aspects of which
they exemplified. Too much has been made of the alleged absence of a social
base for a liberal party in Russia. Strictly speaking, none of the Russian
political parties had a stable and properly organized social base. If the
revolutionary parties benefited from a mushroom growth in a period of
national excitement, as happened both to Social Democrats and Socialist
Revolutionaries in 1905, the moment the revolutionary wave receded the
suddenly acquired social base began to disintegrate, and before long party
organizations were reduced to their former, more than modest, proportions.
After all, the liberals too had their periods of widespread popularity, first in
1904, and then again in 1906.

It might be argued that the *potential* social base of revolutionary parties
was larger than that of the Constitutional Democrats. This is undoubtedly
true — if one assumes the inevitability of revolutionary upheavals in imperial Russia. But from this it does not follow that the liberals had no
potential base at all. Miliukov and Maklakov agree in their testimony that
the Cadet Party was meeting with a mass response among the lower middle
class of the cities, and that its ties with this milieu were growing. As the
size of this group certainly was not smaller than that of the industrial working class, for instance, it cannot be dismissed as a *quantité négligeable.*
Apparently, some of these Cadet constituencies survived even the revolutionary turmoil of 1917 as otherwise it would be difficult to account for the
two million votes received by the Cadet Party in the election to the Constituent Assembly. Professor Oliver H. Radkey, in his excellent study of the
election,[25] speaks of this result as a "washout" for the Cadets. I am inclined
to think that on the contrary, with practically all odds against them, the
Cadets did surprisingly well.

At any rate, no conclusion can be made on the basis of the Cadet Party's
defeat in the revolution as to the actual or potential strength of liberalism
in prerevolutionary Russia. The Russian liberals shared the historical fate
of all moderate groups caught in a revolution. There is no need of looking

[25] *The Election to the Russian Constituent Assembly of 1917* (Cambridge, Mass.,
1950).

for some specific reasons peculiar to Russia for an explanation of this phenomenon. It is one of the concrete examples of that political polarization which we have observed of late in several Western countries, all of them with a much more numerous middle class and a far stronger liberal tradition than Russia ever possessed, and as yet not in throes of a revolution. Obviously, the assessment of the historical importance of Russian liberalism must be made on different grounds.

Leninist Authoritarianism Before the Revolution

THOMAS T. HAMMOND

One of the basic assumptions of what we call Western democracy is contained in the phrase: "The people know best." People like Jefferson labored in the belief that the wishes of the people, as expressed through democratic political procedures, are the best guide to the general welfare; that if you give the people freedom to choose on the broad issues of social development, they will choose the right thing; and that the free competition of conflicting ideas will bring about the development and triumph of the best ideas.

Dictatorships, including the Soviet one, tend to operate on the opposite assumption, that the people have to be told what to do, for otherwise they will do the wrong thing. Not only must they be told what to do, but if necessary they must be forced to do it against their will. The spontaneous initiative of the masses must be kept within carefully prescribed limits, for the natural inclinations of the people cannot be trusted.

Marx professed great faith in the ability of the proletarian masses to overthrow capitalism and construct a new and juster order of society. Yet Marxism as transformed into Leninism contains a strange mixture of faith and lack of faith in the proletariat, with now one and now another tendency predominating. Usually Lenin maintained that the workers, while having great revolutionary potentialities, would not fight for revolution unless they were carefully controlled by an elite of professional revolutionaries. Although at times he professed allegiance to Marx's doctrine that the objective conditions of capitalist society would lead inevitably to revolution, at other times he asserted the contrary view that the revolution would not take place unless intellectuals assumed the leadership of the proletariat and imposed their will upon history.

This is Lenin's famous theory of the "Vanguard," of the revolutionary elite organized in the Party, who would guide the proletariat along the right path. This authoritarian trend in Lenin's thought is perhaps best known in connection with the controversy which took place between the Bolsheviks and the Mensheviks over the requirements for admission into the Russian Social Democratic Labor Party. It can be seen still earlier in Lenin's fight with the "Economist" faction, and in the whole development of his attitude toward the Russian trade-union movement before the Revolution. The attitudes expressed by Lenin in these days provide a good preview of the authoritarianism which was to carry over into the postrevolutionary period and impose its mark on so many areas of Soviet society. An examination of these Leninist attitudes should also show that although Soviet authoritarianism attained its most extreme form under Stalin, the foundation for it had been laid much earlier by Lenin.

While tracing on the following pages the history of Lenin's attitude toward trade unions, the following aspects of his thought should be borne in mind: (1) *Fear of spontaneity* — his distrust of the spontaneous tendencies of the proletariat and doubt that the proletariat would automatically bring about revolution; (2) *Vanguardism* — his conviction that, for this reason, the workers must be led and objective revolutionary developments pushed by a Vanguard of politically conscious leaders; (3) *Eliteism* — the idea that this Vanguard should consist of a small, carefully selected Party of only the most conscious professional revolutionaries; (4) *Party monopoly* — Lenin's insistence that no organizations be permitted to compete with the Party, and that all organizations such as trade unions be brought under the control of the Party.

1. *The "Economists" and Spontaneity.* In the late 1890's Lenin became involved in a polemical dispute with a group of Social Democrats known as the "Economists," the name deriving from the fact that they wished to place more emphasis on the economic struggle against the employers than on the political struggle against the government. The "Economists" also argued that Party members should not attempt to impose their ideas on the revolutionary movement, but should observe the spontaneous activities of the workers and learn from them. Characteristic of the "Economists" was the following statement:

> The revolutionary Social Democrat is confronted only with the task of accelerating objective developments by his conscious work; it is not his task to obviate them or substitute his own subjective plans for this development. *Iskra* knows all this in theory. But the enormous importance which Marxism quite justly attaches to conscious revolutionary work causes it in practice, owing to its doctrinaire view of tactics, *to belittle the significance of the objective or the spontaneous elements of development*.[1]

Whereas the "Economists" accorded little importance to ideology and the role of the intellectuals, Lenin discounted the reliability of the spontaneous tendencies of the proletariat:

> Subservience to the spontaneity of the labor movement [he said], the belittling of the role of "the conscious element," the role of Social Democracy, *means* . . .

[1] B. Krichevskii, "Printsipy, taktika, i bor'ba," *Rabochee delo,* no. 10 (1901), p. 18. For a view similar to Krichevskii's see: "R.M.," "Nasha deistvitel'nost'," *Otdel'noe prilozhenie k "Rabochei mysli"* (September 1899), pp. 3–16. *Iskra* was the famous revolutionary newspaper.

whether one likes it or not, strengthening of the influence of bourgeois ideology among the workers.[2]

The workers, if left free to choose, said Lenin, would never develop real Social Democratic consciousness:

[This consciousness] could be brought to them only from without. The history of all countries shows that the working class, exclusively by its own effort, is able to develop only trade-union consciousness.[3]

The natural inclination of the workers, says Lenin, would be to fight for piecemeal reforms, through such organizations as trade unions, and to neglect the most important activity of all — the fight for revolution. Whereas the "Economists" and other "Reformists" claimed that progress could be made through peaceful reform, Lenin insisted that "only the revolutionary struggle of the masses is able to achieve any serious improvement in the life of the workers."[4] For that reason, he said, it was necessary to subordinate "the struggle for reforms . . . to the revolutionary struggle for liberty and socialism."[5] And to ensure this the leadership of professional revolutionaries was essential.

The workers, said Lenin, would tend not toward revolution but toward bourgeois "Reformism":

The *spontaneous* development of the labor movement leads to its becoming subordinated to bourgeois ideology . . . for the spontaneous labor movement is trade unionism . . . and trade unionism means the ideological enslavement of the workers to the bourgeoisie. Hence our task, the task of Social Democracy, is *to combat spontaneity, to divert* the labor movement from its spontaneous, trade unionist striving to go under the wing of the bourgeoisie, and to bring it under the wing of revolutionary Social Democracy.[6]

These statements by Lenin caused considerable controversy. Several Social Democrats — and not only "Economists" — wrote articles attacking Lenin's views as being un-Marxian. George Plekhanov stated the issue as follows:

The debated question is precisely this: Does there exist an economic necessity which calls forth in the proletariat a "demand for socialism," makes it "instinctively socialist," and drives it — even when left to "its own resources" — along the road to socialist revolution, notwithstanding the stubborn and continual efforts of the bourgeoisie to subject it to their own ideological influence? Lenin denies this, in the face of the clearly expressed opinions of all the theorists of scientific

---

[2] "Chto delat'?" *Sochineniia,* IV, 390 (February 1902). All references to Lenin's *Sochineniia* refer to the 3rd Russian edition (30 vols., Moscow, 1932–1937) unless otherwise indicated. After each article by Lenin the approximate date when it was written is indicated in parentheses.

[3] *Ibid.,* p. 384.

[4] "Uroki revoliutsii," *ibid.,* XIV, 369–370 (October 1910).

[5] "Chto delat'?" *ibid.,* IV, 409 (February 1902).

[6] *Ibid.,* p. 392.

socialism. And in that consists his great mistake, his theoretical fall into sin . . . In the view of Lenin we see not Marxism but . . . a new edition of the theory of the hero and the crowd . . . Since he declares himself to be the only active element in history, he considers the masses as only . . . strong but obedient tools.[7]

This aspect of the dispute was a foretaste of a basic difference in viewpoint that was to break out time and again during the whole history of the RSDLP. It was the difference in attitude on the role of *leadership* in the revolutionary movement, on the question of whether revolutionary developments unfold naturally, mechanically, at their own immutable pace, or whether revolutionaries could impose their will on the course of history, speed up events, and perhaps even skip some of the stages through which society normally developed. Surprisingly enough, Lenin later reversed himself and expressed great faith in the spontaneous tendencies of the Russian proletariat. But, as will be seen, this faith did not last long; he soon returned to what was essentially the attitude expressed in the quotations above.

2. *Vanguardism, Eliteism, and "Front" Organizations.* Lenin's distrust of the spontaneous tendencies of the proletariat was the foundation stone upon which his theory of Vanguardism was built. If the workers could not be depended upon to move spontaneously in the direction of socialist revolution, then obviously someone would have to lead them there. This role he assigned to the Marxist intellectual. The politically conscious ideologist, he said,

marches *ahead* of the spontaneous movement, points out the road, and is able ahead of all others to solve all the theoretical, political, tactical and organizational questions which the "material elements" of the movement spontaneously encounter . . . To say . . . that ideologists (i.e., conscious leaders) cannot divert from its path the movement created by the interaction of environment and [material] elements is to ignore the elementary truth that consciousness *participates* in this interaction.[8]

In his controversy with the "Economists" Lenin gave a concrete example of what he considered to be the desirable relationship between the Party leaders and the working masses — in this case represented by the trade unions. It was a mistake, he said, to think of merging the trade unions with the Party; the Vanguard must be kept separate from the masses:

The workers' organizations must in the first place be trade organizations; secondly, they must be as wide as possible; and thirdly, they must be as public as possible . . . On the other hand, the organizations of revolutionaries must be comprised first and foremost of people whose profession is revolution.[9]

[7] "Rabochii klass i sotsial'demokraticheskaia intelligentsiia," *Iskra,* no. 71 (August 1, 1904). Italics have been omitted. For similar criticisms of Lenin's view see: A. Martynov, *Dve diktatury* (Geneva, 1905); Iiuli Martov, "Tak li my gotovimsia?" *Iskra,* no. 62 (March 15, 1904); Plekhanov, "Chego ne delat'," *Iskra,* no. 52 (November 7, 1903), and "Nechto ob ekonomizme i ob ekonomistakh," *Iskra,* no. 53 (November 25, 1903).

[8] "Beseda s zashchitnikami ekonomizma," *Sochineniia,* IV, 341 (December 1901).

[9] "Chto delat'?" *ibid.,* IV, 447 (February 1902).

There would be a division of function between the Party and the trade
unions, with a corresponding distinction in the organization of the two
bodies. The trade unions would be *mass* bodies, with admission open to
every worker who saw the need for some kind of labor organization, whereas
the Party would include only an elite of professional revolutionaries. The
direction of the trade unions, moreover, would be in the hands of secret
cells of Party members:

> A small, compact core, consisting of reliable, experienced and hardened
> workers . . . can, with the wide support of the masses . . . perform *all* the
> functions of a trade union organization, and perform them, moreover, in the
> manner Social Democracy desires . . .
>
> . . . If we begin with the solid foundation of a strong organization of revolu-
> tionaries, we can guarantee the stability of the movement as a whole, and carry
> out the aims of both Social Democracy and trade unionism.[10]

Lenin desired the formation not only of trade unions but also of other
mass organizations, all of them controlled by the Party, and through which
Party influence would be greatly extended:

> The centralization of the more secret functions in an organization of revolu-
> tionaries will not diminish, but rather increase, the extent and the quality of the
> activity of a large number of other organizations which are intended for wide
> membership and which, therefore, may be as loose and public as possible; for
> example, trade unions, workers' circles for self-education and the reading of illegal
> literature, and socialist and democratic circles for *all* other sections of the popula-
> tion, etc., etc. We must have *as large a number as possible* of such organizations
> having the widest possible variety of functions.[11]

Here half a century ago was formulated the concept of the "front"
organization which has been so cleverly utilized by Communist parties in
subsequent years. The pattern is the same: a mass organization, bearing no
Party label, is created for some objective supported by many non-Communists, but it is dominated by the Party and used for Party ends. Such
"front" organizations were advocated by Lenin because, in contrast to
Blanqui, he realized that by itself the revolutionary elite could not carry
out the revolution; the support of the masses was essential.[12] Through the
use of such "fronts" as trade unions, Lenin could mobilize many people
other than Party members, and the impact of the Party would be multiplied
accordingly.

Lenin's idea of the "front" organization was in a way his answer for
those Social Democrats (the Mensheviks) who attacked his concept of

---

[10] *Ibid.,* pp. 452–453.

[11] *Ibid.,* p. 458.

[12] "Blanquism expects to deliver mankind from wage slavery, not through the class
struggle of the proletariat, but through a conspiracy of a small minority of intellectuals."
"K itogam s"ezda," *ibid.,* IX, 237 (May 1906).

restricted Party membership, to those who, in fact, accused him of Blanquism and insisted that Party membership should be expanded. By forming mass "front" organizations, Lenin argued, it would be possible to get the support of large numbers of people, without having to admit them to membership in the Party.

3. *The Revolution of 1905 Changes Lenin's Attitude.* The dispute with the "Economists" and the split with the Mensheviks took place during the early stages of the Russian Marxist movement, when the RSDLP was able to maintain only a tenacious existence as a few scattered circles of intellectuals, when trade unions were illegal, and the longed-for revolution seemed far away. Then in 1905 the revolutionary movement broke out with unexpected fury, trade unions spread in spite of the police, and Russia was swept by a wave of strikes unprecedented in history.

Heretofore Lenin had expressed little faith in the revolutionary nature of the Russian workers, but now they demonstrated abilities far beyond his expectations, thus forcing him to revise his views on the subject of spontaneity. He now made several statements quite different from what he had been saying in 1902. He declared, for example, that "the working class is instinctively, *spontaneously Social Democratic.*" [13]

At about the same time he said: "The special condition of the proletariat in capitalist society leads to a *striving* of the workers *for socialism;* a union of them with the socialist party bursts forth with spontaneous force in the very early stages of the movement." [14]

How to explain the difference between the statements of 1902 and those of 1905? It may be simply that the revolutionary behavior of the Russian workers during 1905 convinced Lenin that they could be trusted more than he had thought. But this does not mean that he considered it possible to do away with the Party Vanguard. While admitting that "the working class is instinctively, spontaneously Social Democratic," he further pointed out that more than ten years of work by the Party had "done a great deal to transform this spontaneity into class consciousness." [15] What he seems to mean is that the condition of the workers under capitalism made them *ripe* for socialism, but it remained for the Party leaders to reap the harvest. Or, to change the metaphor, the spontaneous labor movement naturally led the workers onto the road toward socialism, but the Party had to guide them along the twists and turns of the road.

Support for this interpretation may be found in another quotation from 1905:

Thousands of circles are now springing up everywhere . . . The Social Democrats must strive to establish and maintain direct contact with the greatest possible

---

[13] "O reorganizatsii partii," *ibid.*, VIII, 375 (November 1905). Italics added.

[14] "Sotsialisticheskaia partiia i bezpartiinaia revoliutsionnost'," *ibid.*, VIII, 413 (November 1905). Italics added.

[15] "O reorganizatsii partii," *ibid.*, VIII, 375 (November 1905).

number of these circles, to assist them, to enlighten them . . . The revolutionary sentiment alone . . . is sufficient — *if Social Democrats go to them and energetically present our views* — to transform these circles, under pressure of events, at first into democratic assistants of the Social Democratic Labor Party, and then into staunch members of it.[16]

If these statements by Lenin are not flat contradictions of his earlier preachings on the spontaneity of the workers, at the very least they represent a decided shift of emphasis. Whereas previously he had expressed pessimism because of his conviction that the workers would tend to go in the wrong direction, now he was expressing optimism over the fact that the workers, because of the revolution and also because of the influence of the Vanguard, were heading in the right direction.

The year 1905 also brought about a change in Lenin's attitude toward membership in the Party. As he acquired greater faith in the spontaneous tendencies of the workers toward revolution, he became more willing to admit them in large numbers into the Party. The man who previously had insisted upon rigid rules for admission now demanded (in February 1905) that membership in the Party be greatly increased:

A revolutionary epoch is to Social Democracy what wartime is to an army. We must extend the ranks of our army, transfer it from peace to war strength, mobilize the reservists, call up all those on furlough, organize new auxiliary corps, units, and services. We must not forget that in war it is inevitable and necessary to fill the ranks with less trained recruits, very often to put plain soldiers in the place of officers, and to speed up and simplify the promotion of soldiers to the rank of officers.

Speaking without metaphor: We must greatly increase the membership of all Party and kindred organizations in order to be able to keep in step with the stream of popular revolutionary energy that has increased a hundredfold.[17]

This certainly sounds different from the Lenin of 1902 or 1903. In those days Lenin had been much concerned lest anyone be admitted to the Party who was not a professional revolutionary. Yet in 1905 he discounted this danger:

It might be thought dangerous for a large number of non-Social Democrats to join the Party suddenly. [It might be thought that] if this occurred the Party would become dissolved among the masses, it would cease to be a class-conscious vanguard of the class, and its role would be reduced to that of a tail. That would be a very deplorable thing indeed . . .

Comrades, let us not exaggerate this danger . . . At the present time, when the heroic proletariat has proved by deeds its readiness and ability to fight unitedly and consistently for clearly understood aims, to fight in a purely Social Democratic spirit — at such a moment it would be simply ridiculous to doubt whether the workers who are members of our Party and those who will join it tomorrow . . . will be Social Democrats in ninety-nine cases out of a hundred.[18]

[16] "Novye zadachi i novye sily," *ibid.,* VII, 150 (February 1905). Italics added.
[17] *Ibid.,* pp. 148–149.
[18] "O reorganizatsii partii," *ibid.,* VIII, 374–375 (November 1905).

Lenin even went so far as to recommend that the expansion in the Party be quite large. Workers, he said, should be incorporated "into the ranks of the Party organizations by the hundreds and thousands." [19]

These ideas about greatly enlarging the Party did not last long with Lenin. Within a few months, as will be seen below, he was again denouncing those who favored permitting large masses of workers to become members of the Party.

4. *Lenin Reverts to his Former Views.* The Revolution continued at a rather high level throughout 1905 and 1906, but by 1907 it had definitely declined. For a few months during the Revolution the government had been so paralyzed that the Social Democratic Party had been able to carry on most of its activities in the open, but as the tsar's government regained control of the situation, the Party found its operations more and more restricted by the police.

Some Party members argued that since open activity (such as trade-union work) was becoming increasingly difficult, it should be abandoned and all effort should be concentrated on the underground organization and activities of the Party. A group of Mensheviks whom Lenin labeled "Liquidators" (he claimed that they wished to "liquidate" the Party), took the opposite view that the underground Party organization was less of a help than a hindrance. To burden the trade unions with Party matters, they said, led to their dissolution by the police and thus weakened the labor movement. It would be far better, so they argued, to forget about the old methods of underground conspiracy and to concentrate on the fullest possible utilization of legal trade unions, the increased liberty of the press, and any other possibilities presented by the somewhat liberalized regime. Paul Axelrod advanced the idea of a labor congress, the purpose of which was to unite several political parties, trade unions, and other mass organizations into a legal working-class party.[20] Lenin denounced this idea as an attempt "to weaken the Party organization" and to transform "Social Democracy into a non-Party political organization of the proletariat." [21]

Instead of advocating a labor congress, the "Liquidators" sometimes argued that the Party should greatly expand its membership and should operate in a strictly legal manner. Lenin ridiculed them on both points:

People of the narrow, petty-bourgeois type are tired of revolution. Better the small, dull, miserable but peaceful legality than the stormy change from revolutionary tempest to counterrevolutionary fury. Within the revolutionary Party this striving expresses itself in the desire to reorganize the Party. Thus the basic idea of the Party becomes the narrow view that "the Party must be a *mass* Party." [22]

[19] *Ibid.,* p. 375.
[20] Pavel B. Aksel'rod, *Narodnaia duma i rabochii s"ezd* (Geneva, 1905).
[21] "Proekty rezoliutsii k piatomu s"ezdu R.S.-D.R.P.," *Sochineniia,* X, 389 (March 1907).
[22] "Obyvatel'shchina v revoliutsionnoi srede," *ibid.,* X, 103 (October 1906).

The man who in November 1905 had suggested the admission into the Party of "hundreds and thousands" of workers, eleven months later denounced those "Liquidators" who said that "the Party must be a mass Party." As the revolutionary fervor of the workers declined and the power of the tsarist government reasserted itself, Lenin reverted to his former conception of an illegal underground Party consisting of a small, select group of professional revolutionaries.

For Lenin the organization of primary importance was the illegal apparatus of the Party, and trade unions were to be used for its purposes even if they suffered in the process. Whereas the "Liquidators," he said, were inclined to have the mass organizations control the Party, Lenin intended that the mass societies operate as "fronts" for the Party.

At the Party Conference in December 1908 Lenin proposed a resolution embodying this point of view:

> For work among the masses . . . the center of gravity must be transformed to the creation and strengthening of the illegal Party organization . . . Only under the steady influence of this organization can there be successfully carried out work among the masses . . . [and the] utilization of legal and semilegal organizations.[23]

5. *"Neutrality": The Relation between the Party and the Trade Unions.* That Lenin likewise reverted to his old fears regarding the spontaneous tendencies of the workers is shown by his repeated insistence that the trade unions be kept under the strict control of the Party lest they head in the wrong direction. This view also led to a big controversy in Russian socialism, a controversy about union neutrality, i.e., the question of the proper relationship between the unions and the Party. Here again can be found authoritarian elements in Lenin's thought.

In this dispute three main questions were intertwined: (1) *Ideology* — should the Party attempt to have the unions adopt the Social Democratic ideology, or should the unions be neutral toward political parties? (2) *Organizational connections* — should there be formal organizational connections between the Party and the trade unions, or is it sufficient merely to have Party members work as individuals inside the trade unions? (3) *Independence and equality* — should the unions be controlled by the Party and be used for Party ends, or should they run their affairs as independent equals?

It has already been noted that at the time of the dispute with the "Economists" Lenin favored "front" unions which were externally neutral toward the Party, but which in reality were secretly directed by a core of professional Party revolutionaries, i.e., the Party Vanguard controlling the union masses. During the following years Lenin continued to demand that the unions adopt the Social Democratic ideology and have close relations with the Party. Once he spoke of "strengthening the connection" between

[23] "Direktivy dlia komissii po organizatsionnomu voprosu," *ibid.*, XIV, 9 (December 1908).

the two types of bodies and of "saturating the trade unions with Social Democratic flavor." [24] The Party, he said, must by all measures strive to achieve the "leading role" in the unions, and should "under certain conditions" arrange for the unions to "affiliate directly to the Party." [25]

As Lenin fought for closer connections between the trade unions and the Party, he came into conflict with some of the Mensheviks who believed that too much Party interference would hinder the development of the union movement, and were afraid that the Bolsheviks would frighten away many non-Social Democratic workers. This dispute reached its climax in July 1907, at the Second Conference of the RSDLP, with Lenin and other Social Democrats arguing over proposed resolutions on neutrality. Lenin's draft demanded that Social Democrats "bring into being organizational connections of the trade unions" with the Party, that Social Democrats not follow a "neutral" policy in the trade unions, but that they "persistently further the recognition by the trade unions of the ideological leadership of Social Democracy." [26]

Fears regarding the effect of close connections between the Party and the unions were expressed in the resolution proposed by V. G. Grinevich, an active trade unionist:

> The establishment of formal organizational connections (meaning the unions' incorporation into the Party or the recognition of its ideological leadership) is inadmissible in those cases where it: (a) leads to a division of the trade union organizations, (b) narrows the circle of their members or of their influence, or (c) hinders the unity of the unions with the same kind of unions in other cities, or fusion with related unions in larger organizational units.[27]

Another resolution was presented in opposition to Lenin by Theodore Dan. He likewise sounded a note of caution against the subordination of the trade unions to the Party:

> The demand for the recognition by the trade unions of the Social Democratic program and the subordination of them to the Party organizations not only cannot contribute to the strengthening of the connection between the economic and political movements of the proletariat, but is capable, on the contrary, of sowing seeds of discord between the trade unions and the Party, leading to disunity in the trade-union movement and tearing away the Party from the working masses organized in trade unions.[28]

[24] "Pis'mo S. I. Gusevu," *ibid.*, VIII, 286 (September 1905). See also: "O reorganizatsii partii," *ibid.*, VIII, 377–378 (November 1905).

[25] "Takticheskaia platforma k ob"edinitel'nomu s"ezdu," *ibid.*, IX, 48 (March 1906).

[26] "Tret'ia konferentsiia R.S.-D.R.P. ('Vtoraia obshcherossiiskaia')," *Sochineniia*, 4th ed., XIII, 46 (July 1907).

[27] "Vtoraia obshcherossiiskaia konferentsiia," *Sochineniia*, XII, 440–441. For a discussion of these resolutions see: Solomon Schwarz, *Lenine et le mouvement syndical* (Paris, 1935), pp. 59–60, and Isaac Deutscher, *Soviet Trade Unions* (London and New York, 1950), pp. 10–11. Deutscher mistakenly says that these events took place at the London Congress in May 1907.

[28] "Vtoraia obshcherossiiskaia konferentsiia," *Sochineniia*, XII, 442.

This was the same difference in point of view which so often divided Bolsheviks and Mensheviks. The Mensheviks, having greater faith in the spontaneous tendencies of the proletariat, were generally interested in making the labor movement as broad as possible, even at the price of some weakening of Party domination. Lenin, generally having little faith in the natural inclinations of the workers, insisted upon rigid control by the Party elite, even at the price of some narrowing of the labor movement. He demanded, therefore, not only that the unions adopt the ideology of the Party, but that they establish close organizational connections with the Party.[29]

On several occasions Lenin asserted that the best way to establish organizational connections between the Party and the unions was through forming *Party cells* in the unions. He first mentioned this idea in a general way in 1902, and he revived and elaborated it during the period of reaction following the Revolution of 1905:

All our Party recognizes now . . . that the Party nature of the trade unions must be attained exclusively by the work of Social Democrats within the unions, and that Social Democrats must form solid cells in the unions.[30]

Some years later he discussed the same idea in greater detail:

Social Democrats must attract in all workers' societies the broadest possible circles of workers, inviting into membership all workers without distinction according to Party views. But the Social Democrats must within these societies organize *Party groups* and through long, systematic work within all these societies establish the very closest relations between them and the Social Democratic Party.

In all the work of the trade unions . . . while defending . . . the subordination of the minority to the majority, *the Party line must be followed,* and one must strive for the election to all responsible posts of Party adherents.[31]

Having Party cells in the unions was the ideal solution for the kind of trade union–Party relationship Lenin desired. Through cells the Party could control the unions effectively, yet this domination could, if necessary, be kept secret from the police and from the workers, thus making possible wider union membership.

Some Russian socialists were afraid of having close organizational connections between the trade unions and the Party because they felt that this might cause the unions to lose their independence. They believed that the trade unions were just as important as the Party and thought that Party dictation would be both undemocratic in principle and harmful in practice. Peter Struve, for example, insisted that the unions had "a self-sufficient sig-

---

[29] A contrary position was taken by Plekhanov in *VIIe Congrès Socialiste International tenu à Stuttgart du 16 au 24 août 1907* (Bruxelles, 1908), p. 209. See also the resolution on neutrality adopted by the Congress, *ibid.,* pp. 424–425.

[30] "Neitral'nost' professional'nykh soiuzov," *Sochineniia,* XII, 138 (February 1908).

[31] "Rezoliutsii letnego 1913 goda soveshchaniia Ts.K.R.S.-D.R.P. s partiinymi rabotnikami," *ibid.,* XVII, 10–11 (summer 1913). Italics added.

nificance." [32] Victor Chernov, the Socialist Revolutionary leader, declared at the Eighth International Socialist Congress:

> Trade-union action, coöperative action, and political action are means and not the end . . . Each form . . . has need of independence and autonomy . . . Coördination must be free, spontaneous, and not forced from without; it must have for its basis the principle of equality of rights.[33]

On another occasion Chernov dwelt on the dangers to the trade-union movement of domination by a political party:

> Party tutelage can be extremely inconvenient and harmful for the trade-union movement. This is especially true in those cases when the party looks on the trade union as a simple tool for recruitment and agitation . . . and when, as a consequence of this, the development of the trade-union movement itself does not have independent interest and significance for it.[34]

Lenin's point of view was of course just the opposite. Trade unions, he said, were needed to provide mass support for the revolutionary movement, and in that sense they were as important as the Party. But they were important only in so far as they played a role in the revolutionary movement to overthrow capitalism, and for them to play that role correctly they would have to be under the constant control of the Bolshevik Party, the monopolistic guardian of correct revolutionary tactics.

The trade-union movement according to Lenin should act as an "auxiliary" to the Party.[35] It should serve "as a base for the organization of the workers in a revolutionary party." [36] Those who looked upon trade unions as having independent importance, he declared, were following a bourgeois rather than a socialist policy. "If you regard the economic struggle as something self-sufficient," he said, "then in it there is nothing socialist." [37]

In directing the revolutionary drama, Lenin assigned the leading role exclusively to the Party. The trade-union movement would be permitted to act in the supporting cast; in fact, it was even essential to the success of the show. As long as the trade-union movement took its cue from the star and remained in the background, it was welcome on the stage of history. But once it began to overplay its part, to distract attention from the Party, or to act independently, the director felt called upon to reprimand it and put it back in its proper subordinate place.

---

[32] "Nasushchnaia zadacha vremeni," *Osvobozhdenie,* no. 63 (January 7, 1905).
[33] "Speech of 30 August, 1910," *Huitième Congrès Socialiste International tenu à Copenhague du 28 août au 3 septembre 1910. Compte Rendu Analytique* (Brussels, 1911), p. 115.
[34] "Professional'noe dvizhenie i marksistkaia ortodoksiia," *Sbornik statei,* no. 1 (1907).
[35] "Chto delat'?" *Sochineniia,* IV, 450 (February 1902).
[36] "Po povodu 'Profession de foi,'" *ibid.,* XXX, 6 (end of 1899).
[37] *Ibid.*

6. *After the Revolution.* The fact that in the days before the Bolshevik Revolution Lenin wanted to have the trade unions dominated by the Party would not be of great importance if it were not that these authoritarian ideas were carried over into the Soviet scheme of things. The same system of mass trade unions controlled by a Party Vanguard was frankly described by Lenin in December 1920:

> The trade unions establish connections between the vanguard and the masses . . . Thus we get, as it were, a system of cogwheels . . . The dictatorship of the proletariat cannot be effected by organizations that embrace the whole of the proletariat. It is impossible to effect the dictatorship without having a number of "transmission belts" from the vanguard to the masses of the advanced class, and from the latter to the masses of the toilers . . . the peasants.[38]

The Party would control the trade unions, which would control the proletariat, which in turn would control the rest of the population, principally the peasants.

Another related technique which Soviet society inherited from prerevolutionary Leninism was the device of the "front" organization — the method of having Party-dominated organizations pretend to be non-Party. In his famous book, *"Left-Wing" Communism, an Infantile Sickness,* Lenin explained how his concept of "front" trade unions was put into effect after the Bolshevik Revolution:

> In its work the Party relies directly on the *trade unions* . . . which, formally, are *non-Party.* Actually, all the controlling bodies of the overwhelming majority of the unions . . . consist of Communists and carry out all the instructions of the Party. Thus . . . we have a formally non-Communist, flexible, relatively wide, and very powerful proletarian apparatus, by means of which the Party is closely linked up with the *class* and with the *masses,* and by means of which, under the leadership of the Party, the *dictatorship of the class* is effected.[39]

Thus the principles which Lenin preached in the prerevolutionary years found their fulfillment in the Soviet state. Since the spontaneous inclinations of the masses could not be trusted, they would have to be guided by a Vanguard, organized in the revolutionary Party. This Party would consist of the elite, of those whose political consciousness was sufficiently developed for them to understand Marxism correctly. Trade unions and other organizations would not be permitted to compete with the Party; it would have monopolistic rights to political leadership. The majority of the proletariat, excluded from the Party, would be controlled in part through "front" organizations, the largest and most important of which would be the trade unions. Thus authoritarianism in prerevolutionary Leninism naturally and perhaps inevitably gave birth to Soviet authoritarianism.

[38] "O professional'nykh soiuzakh, o tekushchem momente i ob oshibkakh tov. Trotskogo," *ibid.,* XXVI, 64–65 (December 1920).
[39] "Detskaia bolezn' 'levizny' v kommunizme," *ibid.,* XXV, 192 (April 1920).

Stalin and the Theory of Totalitarianism

ADAM ULAM

Few among the great historical figures have had the good fortune of Stalin. If the USSR continues on its course of internal and external expansion, Stalin's role as a great architect of history will be made secure. Should the system collapse, historians (with the exception of a few carping moralists) will find a lesson in the inability of the successors to continue the work of the great man. It will even be difficult to reconstruct the history of the crucial years, for so much of it has been distorted beyond the hope of reconstruction by the official myth-building and by the destruction of records and of men, and, one is tempted to add, of events.

A man's historical role cannot be measured only according to his good or bad historical fortune. It is his theory or philosophy of government which helps to establish his historical stature. Stalin was not a political theorist in the proper sense of the word. His theoretical writings consist of heavy, unoriginal, and often tautological arguments designed to deal with the political problems of the moment. His Marxist enemies may forgive him at times his totalitarian ways, but they are much harder put to forgive what they term his vulgarization of Marxism, his lack of the subtlety and erudition which allegedly shine from the pages of Lenin and Trotsky.[1] But it is clear that from the work, writings, and speeches of the greatest practitioner of totalitarian government there does emanate a theory of totalitarianism. It is not an elegant or original theory but a most perceptive one in its critique of the weakness of its opponents: liberalism, and what there is of liberalism in the orthodox social democratic doctrine.

I

Stalinism is a clear antithesis of liberalism. The world of liberalism, the world of a middle-class, intellectually inclined Englishman of the nineteenth century who read Hume and Bentham, was a world of concrete and tangible objects. This frame of mind did not tolerate myths, deities, or even historical forces superior to human volition. Liberalism looked sharply at man's external behavior and refused to look further. Marx and Freud were entirely absent from the *outlook* of liberalism, even though they were more than anticipated by some of its theorists. The view of human nature propounded by liberalism was then, by our current lights, unrealistic. Yet, where this unrealistic view is not held by a large number of people free institutions cannot flourish.

Marxism has made the world of liberalism appear unreal. For Marx and Engels, the "competition" and "interests" of liberalism were but surface manifestations of deeper historical forces. Poverty, economic slavery, and political oppression were not just social evils to be overcome by material progress, education, and legislation but the unavoidable symptoms of a decay· ing economic system. What remained of liberalism in Marx and Engels was the rationalistic setting of the new doctrine and its final vision of a world where after the catastrophes and revolutions human freedom would be established.

Marxism is both deterministic and revolutionary. The combination was not incongruous in view of the social and economic condition of Europe when Marx and Engels were formulating their theories. It did become bothersome to the faithful toward the end of the nineteenth century. The worker's lot was visibly improving, while capitalism was expanding and consolidating its position. The bourgeois state was beginning to behave in a manner not entirely consistent with its characterization as "the executive committee of the exploiting class." The new situation called for attempts to reinterpret Marxism and it was one of them which laid the foundations of Bolshevism.

Today the issues which stimulated the Revisionists and the Economists in their quarrels with Lenin remain of academic interest, but Lenin's *What Is To Be Done* is still the most complete expression of the mood which was to crystallize into Bolshevism and Stalinism. Lenin wanted Marxism to be preserved in its entirety as a *doctrine,* but in effect this doctrine was to be interpreted, shifted around, and changed as it fitted the needs of revolution. But Lenin does not advocate the rule of political expediency. On the contrary, *What Is To Be Done* advocates taking the most difficult road, but the one Lenin feels *Marx must have meant* even though he did not phrase it exactly in Lenin's words.

The shift from Marx's way of thinking is quite obvious. No idea is more violently attacked by Lenin than the idea of the *spontaneous* growth of political consciousness among the workers. Political notions and concepts must come to them from without, and not from the circumstances of their economic life and struggle. The notion of the Party as a rigidly centralized and controlled body is generated not only by the need to infuse the worker with incontrovertible revolutionary ideas, but also by the general setting and traditions of the Russian revolutionary movement. But what emerges from the very violence of Lenin's language is his genuine totalitarian impulse which already finds itself awkwardly combined with social democratic and liberal phraseology. One has to give a push to man, ideas, and events in order to set them on the road to revolution. The definitions of propaganda and agitation are spelled out and through them shines unmistakably the elitist quality of Lenin's thinking. The Party which he is about to build is likened to an army sending its detachments in every direction.

Lenin, as early as 1902, was particularly attracted by the sociological part of Marxism. The worker provides the most suitable human material for revolution because the habits and circumstances of factory work endow him with an instinct for organization and discipline. Bourgeois society creates continually vast areas of ignorance and discontent. It is up to the revolutionary party to transform the apathetic and misdirected discontent of the masses into active and organized revolutionary aspirations. Marxism becomes an analysis of the sociological weaknesses of the bourgeois system. Years later Lenin took a liberal critique of imperialism by J. A. Hobson and transformed it into a Marxist analysis of the weaknesses of the bourgeois system on the international plane. Internally and externally capitalism is creating the forces of self-destruction, not only because of its economic development, though that is the master cause, but most immediately through the social and cultural tendencies it generates.[1] Joined with Lenin's theoretical habits was his temper of impatience and intolerance which he bequeathed to his party. The Bolshevik Party as it existed prior to April 1917 was a social democratic party in name and in its self-estimation. But it was already grounded in the habits of conspiracy and intolerance. It was, in a sense, Lenin's party, dominated by Lenin organizationally and incomparably more so intellectually. The Bolsheviks were hopelessly unsuited to compete for power under peaceful and democratic conditions. They were well prepared to fight for power in the circumstances of social and economic anarchy and political vacuum.

II

Much is made by some writers of Stalin's alleged obscurity and intellectual mediocrity when compared with other leaders of the Revolution. Such judgments are usually colored by the conviction that many of the old Bolsheviks were endowed with almost superhuman intellectual and oratorical gifts, while Stalin had nothing but his passion for administrative details and work. There were in the early days of the Soviet regime Communist leaders like Trotsky and Zinov'ev who possessed the agitator's gift — the gift of inflammatory revolutionary rhetoric. Others, like Bukharin, had a highly developed technique of Marxist scholasticism — the ability to juggle quotations from Marx and Engels and to apply them to any and every concrete situation and problem. It is somewhat naïve, and to the persons involved it proved to have been disastrous, to confuse those abilities with intellectual

[1] The same type of analysis emerges clearly from Trotsky's *History of the Russian Revolution*.

preëminence or political influence. Stalin's own appearances at the Party congresses and conferences prior to the crystallization of his personal dictatorship denote him as a very effective political speaker. The speeches were clear and precise, not without eloquence and a sense of humor, and they did not reveal, as did those of Trotsky and Bukharin, personal vanity and intellectual arrogance of the speaker.

Stalin's role in the early postrevolution days and his rise to power have been attributed to his exceptional administrative ability. The main outlines of his political intrigues, of his skillful use of the Party apparatus and the control organs of the Party and the state have all been well discussed. What has not emerged clearly is the reason why the Communist Party, so full of strong and discordant leaders, submitted fairly easily to the iron hand of Stalin and his apparatus. Where was the original political force which propelled Stalin into such a commanding administrative position?

The answer must be found, first, in the character and historical tendency of the Bolshevik Party even before Lenin's death. It is sometimes asserted that while the Bolsheviks instituted a merciless dictatorship they themselves enjoyed, as long as Lenin was alive and well, a kind of intra-Party democracy. The truth is that after its October victory the Communist Party began to grope its way toward totalitarianism. Lenin's methods in dealing with his intra-Party opponents were different from those of Stalin, but his toleration of opposition was not much greater than that of his successor. To be sure, the veterans of Bolshevism were not as yet publicly humiliated and then imprisoned for disagreeing with Lenin. But they were likely to be censured and transferred to obscure provincial or diplomatic positions. Had a more efficient Party machinery been at Lenin's disposal the penalties would have been much more drastic.

It is difficult, in the last analysis, to have any kind of democracy without democratically inclined people, and the leaders of the Bolsheviks without an exception had long before left behind their last lingering democratic ideas. Even while fighting for his political life Zinov'ev was to denounce as an "outrageous libel" the accusation that he wanted to substitute a democratic republic for the dictatorship of the proletariat.[2] While declaiming against the dictatorship of the Secretary-General, Kamenev, on another occasion, could submit nothing better as his recipe for governing the Party than an omnipotent Politburo, i.e., dictatorship by a committee.[3] And as an example of the democratic feeling on the part of another group of leaders, one may quote Rykov's words at the Fifteenth Party Congress, where he declared his full solidarity with those who were imprisoning Party members for their anti-

---

[2] *XV Konferentsiia vsesoiuznoi kommunisticheskoi partii, stenograficheskii otchët* (Moscow, 1927), p. 562.

[3] *XIV S"ezd vsesoiuznoi kommunisticheskoi partii (b), stenograficheskii otchët* (Moscow-Leningrad, 1926), p. 274.

Party (read anti-Stalin) activities.[4] The quotations are drawn from the post-Lenin period, yet they reflect not unfairly the temper of those who had been Lenin's chief lieutenants.

If the Party was already in Lenin's lifetime developing toward a totalitarian pattern, then the only problem was what character and philosophy this totalitarianism was to take. During the crucial years of his struggle for power Stalin represented himself, and perhaps not entirely hypocritically, as a simple follower of Lenin and a "common man" of Communism leading the Party masses in their sorrowful fight against the sinning "leaders." The pose reflected Stalin's understanding of the dynamics of the Party. For the Party was being officered to an increasing extent, especially at its local level, by young and rather unsophisticated people who had joined it during the war or during or shortly after the Revolution. Such people were different in their habits and thinking from the older type of the revolutionary worker. They were already acquiring the habits and the mentality of a bureaucracy. For them the figure of Lenin dimmed that of any other Communist thinker or leader, and any attack, real or purported, upon the principles of Leninism was a threat to their very existence. It is among this demi-intelligentsia of the Bolshevik Party that Stalinism found its first political base, and the type itself was to become the Stalinist model to be imposed upon the whole of Soviet society.

The struggle for the succession to Lenin took place at several levels. There was still the level of theory where Stalin had to assume the unwelcome role of a theorist to establish his claim to the only correct interpretation of Marxism-Leninism; there was the level of politics, manipulation, and alliances in the central organs of the Party; and there was the field work among the lower Party echelons. Every aspect of the struggle was handled with meticulous care, providing an accurate forecast of totalitarian society where absolute political power is supplemented by, but is *not* a substitute for, the doctrinal infallibility of the leader. It is instructive to review some incidents of the struggle. They provide a necessary insight into the technique of totalitarianism.

The initial fight was against Trotsky. The intensity of the feeling aroused by Stalin against Trotsky and the continuous abuse heaped upon him down to and after his assassination is a bit surprising in view of the fact that Trotsky had, very early in the game, been outmaneuvered and that he never enjoyed great popularity among the Party cadres. The choice of the first enemy was dictated not only by political expediency, but also by a correct differentiation between political popularity and political importance. Feared and disliked by the Party leaders, without great following in the Party bureaucracy, Trotsky had still enjoyed a unique position in

[4] *XV S"ezd vsesoiuznoi kommunisticheskoi partii, stenograficheskii otchët* (Moscow-Leningrad, 1928), p. 256.

Lenin's entourage. All the others shone with Lenin's reflected glory, while Trotsky's stature was independent and almost as great. He embodied the revolutionary energy and romance of the October Revolution, and it is significant that his main support was found in the Comintern and among the Communist youth.

Stalin's fight against Trotsky was underlined by the difference between two political temperaments both equally totalitarian. One sees problems in their intellectual guise and prepares to attack through oratory and intellectual arguments. The other one sees political problems as being grounded in habits and organization. Theory and intellectual conviction are necessary but they come after the main battle has been fought and won. In his political thinking Stalin showed himself to be more militarily minded than the creator of the Red Army. Trotsky counterposed his "world revolution" to Stalin's "socialism in one country" as an intellectual argument designed to give a sense of direction to the Communist regime. Stalin reinterpreted it as a concrete political program and as such it appeared visionary and ridiculous. What does Trotsky want? asked Stalin in effect at the Fifteenth Party Conference. And with his now firmly ingrained habit of answering his own questions he gave these answers: Trotsky wants the Soviet regime to postpone the building of socialism until revolution sweeps the West. He wants the young and weakened Soviet state to risk its existence in a foolhardy war upon all the capitalist powers.[5] In addition, added Stalin piously, the opposition wants us to alienate the peasant by exploiting him under the cover of a war against the kulak. The opposition, which then consisted of Kamenev and Zinov'ev in addition to Trotsky, was completely dumbfounded. Beaten before organizationally, they now found themselves in an ideological and political morass from which they could not extricate themselves. Such theoretical attempts as Trotsky's statement that one can build socialism in one country but not finish building it while capitalism survived elsewhere would have been regarded at one time as a fine example of Marxist sophistication and subtlety. The assembled Party functionaries now heard them with grim incomprehension. It was as if Lenin, after proclaiming "all power to the soviets," were immediately denounced as a counterrevolutionary and defeatist, for the soviets were not at the time controlled by the Bolsheviks!

Trotsky's defense had some of the old brilliance with which he could sway even a hostile audience. In 1925 it was still thought important to have some of the classic Marxist oratory thrown back at the opposition, and Bukharin was delegated to match Trotsky and Kamenev in the art of quoting Marx and Engels. Bukharin spoke in most vituperative tones, drawing Stalin's ungrudging admiration: "Well, Bukharin, well. He does not speak, he cuts with a knife." [6] But what was the wave of the future was more suc-

---

[5] *XV Konferentsiia*, pp. 437, 456.
[6] *Ibid.*, p. 601.

cinctly expressed by Stalin when he ventured to say that were Engels alive at the moment he would undoubtedly exclaim: "May the devil take the old formulas; long live the victorious revolution in the USSR!"[7] He was never again to be as blunt in his appraisal of the role of theory as in the moment of his triumph over the despised theoreticians and intellectuals of the Party.

The Fourteenth Congress and the Fifteenth Conference provided the most dramatic moments of the struggle against the Left opposition, though the real struggle had taken place before and behind the scenes. Kamenev and Zinov'ev, in terminating their alliance with Stalin and in trying to combat his political ascendancy, fell into an ideological trap similar to the one provided by Stalin's "socialism in one country." They attacked the policy of concessions to the peasant, seeing in it a challenge to the socialist character of the revolution. Again Stalin could appear as an advocate of revolutionary "normalcy" and common sense. His new allies, Bukharin, Rykov, and Tomskii, really believed in the policy of concessions and in very gradual and cautious industrialization. He himself took probably a pragmatic point of view: the policy of a full-scale attack upon the peasant ("kulak" is used almost constantly as a euphemism for all peasants) was not indicated at the time (1924–1926) and anyway a decisive social struggle could not be waged before the Party had been firmly united in his hands. But to the mass of the Party Stalin defended the policy of concessions and moderation as an ideological principle. The majority of the Party functionaries, some of whom were of peasant origin, could not but respond favorably to the policy of moderation and to the call to eschew violent experiments and repression. It is only after the opposition had been chastised that Stalin was willing to reveal some of his inner thoughts on the subject. The Bolsheviks have not one but three plans for dealing with the peasant problem. Which one they will apply depends on the concrete revolutionary circumstances of the moment.[8] Kamenev and Zinov'ev let themselves be maneuvered into a rigid and untenable ideological position.

At the Fourteenth Party Congress Stalin had to withstand a full-scale assault upon his position. His handling of the Party, his attitude on foreign affairs, and his economic policy all come under the determined fire of a minority of the Congress. Kamenev and Zinov'ev, as yet estranged from Trotsky, were leading the solid bloc of Leningrad delegates. Stalin's position was secured by his alliance with the leaders of the future Right opposition. Yet in spite of his overwhelming numerical superiority the dictator took the most meticulous care to meet and refute every accusation. In his introduction he mentioned with approval the Soviet leaders' alleged habit of reporting to foreign workers' delegations and denounced indignantly the mutter-

---

[7] *Ibid.*, p. 721.
[8] *XV Konferentsiia*, p. 749.

ings (which if heard at all came from his faction) that foreign Communists are a lot of bother and expense.[9] Here, some delegates must have reflected with emotion, was the man accused of being unmindful of the needs of the world Communist movement. Modestly refusing to indulge in personalities, Stalin revealed his willingness to step down as Secretary General when the Party leaders wanted to transform the Secretariat into a political organ.[10] His indignation was aroused by the Kamenev-Zinov'ev attempt to demolish Bukharin: "We will not give you his blood," [11] — the blood of the leading theorist of the Party.

It fell to Stalin's henchmen to denounce and ridicule the opposition. But the opposition itself was tied up in its own contradictions and confusions. To replace Stalin's dictatorship Kamenev could only propose dictatorship by a committee — the Politburo. Yet, it was pointed out, the leaders of the opposition were in fact in the commanding state and Party position with Kamenev, e.g., presiding over the Politburo, and Sokol'nikov over the Commissariat of Finance.[12] It was not Stalin's fault if the administrative ineptitude of the oppositionists was so great that all practical policies had to be formulated by Stalin!

The opposition was caught in a dilemma of its own making. If the "interests of the proletariat," i.e., the Party, were superior to democracy, how could they object to being treated undemocratically by the majority of the Party? The time to protest was in 1912 or in October 1917, but while assailing Stalin's undemocratic chicaneries and manipulations Kamenev and Zinov'ev were fervently apologizing for their democratic scruples before the October coup. The opposition made the point that its numerical weakness at the Congress reflected the faulty social composition of the Party. Were the Party more proletarian it would, like the workers of Leningrad, follow Zinov'ev. But the strength of the opposition in Leningrad reflected not only the agitational skill of Zinov'ev, but the same type of machine politics which Stalin was employing more successfully and on a larger scale.

It was in the course of his struggle against Trotsky and the Leningrad opposition that Stalin used the psychological devices that became later on his standard techniques of propaganda. Marxist politicians, and among them par excellence the Bolsheviks, have often appealed to something very deep in human nature by their ability to see "hidden significance" in perfectly obvious and self-explanatory events and statements. The Mensheviks and the Social Revolutionaries in fighting the Bolsheviks were not "really" objecting to the Communists dictatorial ways. They were "really" supporting the capitalists and landowners in their counterrevolutionary schemes. In pre-

[9] *XIV S"ezd*, pp. 20–21.
[10] *Ibid.*, p. 506.
[11] *Ibid.*, p. 504.
[12] *Ibid.*, p. 397.

senting the peasant policy of Stalin and Bukharin as antisocialist, Zinov'ev gave the hypothetical case of a Menshevik who wanted to return to Russia supposedly to pursue his antirevolutionary designs. Were he allowed to return would he openly embrace the kulak's cause? "No, he would accuse us of underestimating the middle peasant." [13]

Conscious of the strange fascination for the semieducated mind of "inside stories" and "plots," Stalin already in 1924–1925 shifted his attack to the general character of the opposition. Was the opposition really what it purported to be, a group within the Party fighting for its point of view, or was it something else?

The question was asked more and more insistently and it was not without its point to the people who had spent the days before the Revolution in an atmosphere of suspicion, always on the lookout for an *agent provocateur*. The preliminary admission demanded from the opposition, after their defeat and as a price of their remaining in the Party, was that they should acknowledge their ideology to have been not Bolshevik but social democratic and antirevolutionary. The way of dealing with the opposition — any opposition — was to be indicated by Stalin at the Sixteenth Congress when speaking this time of the Right opposition: "What does the Congress want from the former leaders of the opposition? Recantation; self-flagellation? Of course not. Never will our Party . . . demand from its members something humiliating." [14] The Congress wanted *just* three things: an admission that the "line" of the opposition led to capitalism; a resolute fight against their own views; and that they should fight against the opposition, i.e., recant and denounce themselves. Repeated several times throughout the speech is the phrase: "If you don't press these people you don't get anything." [15]

Another example of the recourse to the reservoir of deep-rooted prejudice and hysteria was undercover anti-Semitism, which was used freely in the struggle against Trotsky, Kamenev, Zinov'ev and their followers, many of them also Jewish. Ostensibly the dictator and his Party struggled against anti-Semitism as an ignominy and barbarism. Some of Stalin's most effective hatchetmen, like Kaganovich and Yaroslavskii, were Jewish. But no weapon was scorned if the task was urgent. While denying the anti-Semitic charge thrown against Stalin's faction, Yaroslavskii quoted in effect several instances of anti-Semitic slander indulged in by local Party organizations and directed against Trotsky.[16] The appeal to popular passions and prejudices for the resolution of a Party conflict would have been unthinkable in Lenin's time. Its use by Stalin marks an important advance in the totalitarian technique. The ideas and formulas of Lenin, still coldly intellectual in their

---

[13] *XIV S"ezd*, p. 110.

[14] *XVI S"ezd, vsesoiuznoi kommunisticheskoi partii, stenograficheskii otchët* (2nd ed., Moscow-Leningrad, 1931), p. 291.

[15] *Ibid.*, p. 292.

[16] *XV S"ezd*, p. 358.

phrasing, are now beginning to be buttressed by frankly irrationalist techniques.

After 1925 the leadership still remained collegiate in its appearance. The new "troika," like the Three Musketeers, consisted really of four people. Rykov, Tomskii, and Bukharin were more firmly entrenched in the Party than had been Stalin's former coadjutors. They enjoyed genuine popularity and, Tomskii, at least, had the organizational backing of the trade unions. At one point, in the period 1925–1927, Stalin himself appeared to be a captive of Bukharin's evolutionary economic policy. Stalin's crushing victory at the Fourteenth Congress was secured with the help of the future "Right" opposition. It was Uglanov who steered the Moscow delegation away from its projected alliance with Leningrad and averted the danger of the two capitals combining in revolt against the regime — a specter too reminiscent of 1917.

The Right's acceptance of Stalin's dictatorship was conditioned upon the character of his policies and his behavior within the Party. His dictatorship appeared to be preferable to that of Trotsky or of the Zinov'ev-Kamenev bloc. In retrospect it is easy to blame the Right for its blindness and to forget that they would not have fared better, at least initially, in the event of Trotsky's or Zinov'ev's victory. Their error lay in allowing Stalin to subvert the Party's machinery and to set the precedent for the ejection and humiliation of the Bolshevik oligarchy.

The whole complex of causes, political, social, and economic, which led to the real Russian revolution — the collectivization and industrialization of the late twenties — remains still to be fully investigated and understood. The defeat of the Right opposition and the final clamping of totalitarian shackles upon the whole society could not have taken place without the feeling of dynamism and mission aroused among the rank and file of the Communist Party. It showed once again how a totalitarian movement needs a concrete and visible enemy as well as a constructive task in order to display its full character and energy. The campaign was against the kulaks — actually against the mass of the peasants. Behind the "kulak" Stalin's propaganda arrayed a suitable representation of the regime's enemies, real and imaginary, including Trotsky. The campaign for industrialization also had to have its proper demonology. Wreckers and disloyal engineers were uncovered to spur the faithful to ever greater watchfulness and production. Left behind like the Chekhovian figures of daydreaming and indecision, to whom Stalin compared them contemptuously at the Sixteenth Congress, were the leaders of the Right opposition. They themselves had to go through the routine they had helped to impose upon Kamenev and Zinov'ev and their followers: vilification, public recantation, and demotion.

A story of collectivization in a Cossack village, Sholokhov's *Podniataia tselina,* pictures vividly the stereotypes the regime was trying to impose upon the population. The story opens and ends with a counterrevolutionary plot —

no matter how great the successes, the class enemy is always somewhere around. The official myth does not completely erase the reality: the over-zealous and brutal Party functionary whose eyes are "opened" by Stalin's "Dizzy with Success," the frankly lying agitator, and the anguish of the mass of the peasants are portrayed with full realism. The aims and methods of the struggle do not stop at industrialization and collectivization. What is at stake is the creation of a new type of Soviet personality.

III

At the Sixteenth Party Congress in June 1930 Stalin was hailed as the leader, and he fully accepted the role he had modestly repudiated at the Fourteenth Congress. The victory within the Party was complete; there were no oppositions to be conquered. The struggle was now for the totalitarian transformation of society.

The speeches of the leader now assumed the character usually associated with Stalin's oratory: they are didactic, increasingly and unbearably repeti-tious. They are speeches of a pedantic schoolmaster to a crowd of semicivi-lized pupils. There is no longer the problem of convincing anybody; there remains only the problem of instilling the right ideas and motivations, first in the bureaucracy, then in the population as a whole.

The teacher also assumes the role of the theorist. He is no longer the bold pragmatist who could exclaim: "To the devil with the old formulas." The more the reality of everyday life in the Soviet Union departs from Marxism the more important it is to show every departure to be in accord-ance with the spirit and the letter of Marx and Lenin. At the Seventeenth Party Congress he elucidates his slogan that the collectivized peasant should become prosperous. Is it the same thing as saying that the peasant should become rich, the slogan that Bukharin and other counterrevolutionaries ad-vocated during the NEP? Of course not! Stalin goes into a long, semi-semantic and semidialectical effusion designed to show that being "rich" is antirevolutionary, while being "prosperous" is in strict accordance with Marxism. Has Marxism anything to do with the tendency toward equality? Does it advocate equalization of wages under socialism? Of course not! Marxism is an enemy of "uravnilovka." Let us not burden socialism with some petty-bourgeois notions of equality.[17]

The regime eschews easy pragmatism as a substitute for ideology. Every departure from Marxism has to be done in the name of Marxism, and not as a step justified by temporary expediency. The leaders realize, probably con-sciously, that the people will endure a great deal in the name of an ideology but that they will balk at purposeless suffering. Occasionally while building a stratified caste society the regime will initiate a discussion of the final stage of Communism.

[17] Stalin, *Sochineniia* (Moscow, 1951), XIII, 355.

It is important to analyze the regime's attitude toward the ideology. Totalitarianism cannot be complete without an ideological basis. Fascism and National Socialism, the latter having some ideological pretensions but never taken very seriously by its proponents, foundered upon military adventurism. They both reached the point where the series of military conquests became the only way of perpetuating the regime. Stalin saw more clearly that an elitist society and dictatorship require an ideology if corruption and privilege, and sheer human restlessness under the denial of all freedoms, are to be held in check. Every dictator wants (but seldom obtains) a government of laws and not of men — except in so far as he himself is concerned. Stalin wanted every Soviet citizen to be ideologically motivated, with the proviso that he himself formulate and interpret the ideology.

Terror and ideology became indissolubly linked in the Soviet system. In his famous letter to *Proletarskaia revoliutsiia* in 1931, Stalin attacked all the historians of Bolshevism, including his most slavish apologist Yaroslavskii, for their failure to present Trotskyism in its proper light.[18] Some Bolsheviks evidently still thought of Trotskyism as having been a deviation *within* the Bolshevik Party. How could they fail to realize that the slightest tinge of liberalism in dealing with that treasonous and counterrevolutionary grouping was in itself anti-Soviet? Stalin's raving tones in the letter, the ostensible cause of which was some unsensational historical observations of an obscure Soviet publicist, presage the great purge of the thirties. Mr. Deutscher saw in the Moscow trials a result of Stalin's apprehension about the coming war and of his fear lest the former oppositionists turn against him during an invasion and defeat. We do not know the chain of courses which unleashed the terror of the middle and late thirties. It is, however, at least probable that the trials were staged to serve as the final revision of the Party history. Otherwise the old Bolshevik could have been liquidated quietly, the fate which befell Rudzutak, Kosior, and others most closely associated with Stalin in his struggle for power. The new state with its new constitution — "the most democratic constitution in the world" — had no further use for the ghosts of the past. The departing opposition could perform one last service: they straightened out the Party's history and provided a suitable explanation for the sufferings and shortcomings of the first five-year plans.

The only opposition Stalin was encountering by the late thirties was from the social forces the regime itself was creating. The peasant had been defeated but the defeat was not complete. The kolkhoz enslaved the peasant but its very concept underwent a significant modification from the original formulation. In his speech to the agricultural shock workers of February 1933 Stalin, with the jovial vulgarity he assumed on such occasions, reassured the delegates, promised a cow to every peasant woman, and criti-

[18] *Ibid.*, pp. 84–102.

cized the local officials for their highhanded ways.[19] The peasant with his instinct for private property and his small individual plot has remained on the agenda of Communism.

Elsewhere the regime discovered that the price for a highly industrialized society was the creation of a privileged class of directors, technicians, and shock workers. The same phenomenon then spread to the state and military bureaucracy. Perceptive sociologists have noted how, with industrialization and the new class society, the Soviet Union began to acquire official mores, ethics, and aesthetics that were sometimes more reminiscent of Victorian England than of post-October Russia.

The war gave a startling demonstration of how the new social atmosphere encroached upon the old ideological impulses. Already in the early thirties Stalin had chastised some of the Soviet historians and writers for their, until then official, negative attitude toward Russia's past. Now the appeal to patriotism and especially Russian patriotism all but extinguished the ideological motive. Stalin at the end of the war, in his famous toast to the Russian people, spoke with genuine gratitude of the willingness of the people to support the government. He was not, it seems, among the least surprised.

But the war with its victories and territorial expansion, and the postwar era with its prodigious economic recovery and growth, did not diminish the gravity of the main dilemma confronting the regime. The great purge had destroyed the remnants of the Bolshevik Party of the Lenin era. The purge had to be arrested lest it destroy the Soviet state. Zhdanov's report at the Eighteenth Congress in 1939 abounded in incidents illustrating the utter demoralization of the Party through the hysteria and endless denunciations of the purge. The Communists swelled their ranks during the war but now a Party card became simply a badge of success and privilege in any field of activity. No Party congress or conference took place between 1939 and 1952. The Central Committee seems to have atrophied. The Politburo became identical in its composition with the very top of the state hierarchy. The logic of events pushed the Party and its ideological meaning into the background and was transforming the Soviet Union into a purely bureaucratic dictatorship.

To Stalin, and probably to the more thoughtful members of his entourage, the situation must have appeared menacing. Their view of totalitarianism has always implied that there must be in society no class or group capable of developing a viewpoint or an *esprit de corps* of its own. Various groups and classes might be accorded concessions and privileges but never security. The regime had in the past chastised every social class and every element of the state machinery — peasants, workers, the army hierarchy, and the secret police. Yet through its very policies it had created a new middle

[19] *Ibid.*, p. 259

class of bureaucrats and technicians. They were no longer, as in the earlier period of the revolution, merely "specialists" tolerated by the Party. They were now within the Party and comprised much of its hierarchy. They were not unlikely to develop, like the other middle classes before them, a thirst for intellectual independence and legal security. It is possible to see in the series of legislative measures dealing with the most outward characteristics of the Soviet Union a policy of appeasement of the new class. The reëmergence of elaborate uniforms, titles, and decorations, the abolition of the title of commissar, and, finally, the elimination of "Bolshevik" from the title of the ruling Party, are some of the concessions, whether conscious or not, to the new spirit. They tend to enforce the impression that the old revolutionary romanticism and the old quarrels and purges are a thing of the past.

But just as insistently the regime has refused to abandon the really important elements of its totalitarian creed. The campaign against cosmopolitanism, for all its nationalistic undertones, was designed to destroy any possibility of an independently thinking and writing intelligentsia. While still clearing away some obsolete relics of Marxism, as in the field of linguistics, the regime was also trying to revive revolutionary dynamics and to attack the *status quo* in agriculture.

There is no reliable evidence as to the significance of the disturbances which affected the Soviet regime before and after Stalin's death and as to the meaning of the "doctors' plot." Stalin's personal dictatorship must have assumed a different character after the war, when in view of his advanced age he no longer could have exercised simultaneous and detailed control of the most important departments of the state and the Party. But it is probable that the Nineteenth Party Congress reflected the conviction of the regime that the process of bureaucratic consolidation had gone far enough and that Soviet society must be given another reorientation if bureaucratic ossification were to be avoided.

Stalin's *Economic Problems of Socialism,* his "ideological" testament as it turned out to be, reflected the same motif: the need of totalitarianism to persuade its elite that there is "something else" in the art of government in addition to the performance of concrete political and economic tasks — and in addition to the enjoyment of privileges. The attempt is pathetic in its theoretical incoherence combined with its pleading insistence that there must be some laws to guide the state and society.[20] It is at once a theoretical defense of the status society arrived at in the USSR and a plea not to be fully satisfied with it. The article states its political aim when it pictures the new cadres joining the Party as being brought up in the spirit of uncritical pragmatism: "What to do with these comrades? How to educate them in the spirit of Marxism-Leninism?"[21] This question Stalin fails to answer, for

[20] I. Stalin, *Ekonomicheskie problemy sotsializma v SSSR* (Moscow, 1952).
[21] *Ibid.,* p. 10.

his real aim is not to formulate a doctrine or to reinterpret one but to endow the new ruling class with a frame of mind which was peculiar to himself and to his generation.

It is too early to draw any lesson from Stalin's experiments in social and psychological engineering. It must be suspected that the concept of human nature toward which totalitarianism strives is as much if not more of a myth as the early liberal ideas: the apolitical man who responds obediently to artificially stimulated hysteria and indoctrination and who seeks only economic and status security and rewards has not been perfected in the Soviet Union. Some writers have seen in Stalin, to quote a famous parody on historical writing, "a bad man but a good thing," a tyrant who created the necessary material prerequisites for a future democracy. Such judgments are based on some very shallow historical comparisons. The Bolsheviks took over not a barbarous country but a rapidly industrializing and developing society. Stalin, while not entirely successful in his totalitarian aims, destroyed completely and beyond the possibility of an early restoration what there was in the way of humane and democratic forces both in Russian Marxism and in Russian society.

Part II

Review

MERLE FAINSOD

The search for patterns of change and continuity in Russian and Soviet political thought has its own special pitfalls. It is always tempting to fasten on the victorious creed of the moment and to view it as the inexorable expression of deep-seated national needs and aspirations. Yet the march of events plays tricks on the best of us, and the dominant intellectual fashions of one generation or century become the castoffs of the next. For the Communist the only Russian intellectual history which matters is that which can be fitted into the role of a prologue to the triumph of Bolshevism. Yet even the Communist finds himself compelled to reinterpret the past, to reclaim what he has discarded, and to discard what he has reclaimed, as changing circumstances present new problems and new challenges.

The theme of the preceding papers is "Authoritarianism and Democracy." Perhaps in view of the character of the papers, it might better be reworded into "Autocracy, Totalitarianism, and Liberal Constitutionalism." The choice of the topics has a rhythm all its own. We are almost invited to see Russian political history in terms of the merging of autocracy into a triumphant totalitarianism, while liberal constitutionalism plays a recessive and fading role. Viewed from the vantage point of Arden House in the year 1954, such a formula may not be without its justification, but it is worth reminding ourselves that the Russia of the post-totalitarian era, if such there should be, may well regard its heritage differently. We are the unavoidable victims of our time span, and it behooves us to be modest in rendering judgments which future events may belie.

My unhappiness at this confrontation goes even deeper. The participants in this symposium have contributed a series of scholarly and illuminating essays on the subjects which they have chosen to discuss, but in their collective wisdom they have avoided the issues of continuity and change like the plague, and they have left me to rush in where prudent men fear to tread. I think I can understand their hesitation. How, for example, does one relate Pobedonostsev to Stalin? What values did they share, and wherein were they different? Is it of major significance that they both appeared to have a low view of human nature, that they both believed in firm leadership, that they both sought to impose unity of belief on their subjects, that they both condemned parliamentary governments, that they both put primary reliance on coercion and repression, that they both recognized the efficacy of indoctrination, and that they both stressed the key importance of a ruling administrative elite? Or should major emphasis be put on their differences — the relatively static, tradition-bound, and national frame of Pobedonostsev's authoritarianism as compared with the dynamic, totalitarian, and messianic goals of Stalin's Communism? To put these questions is to suggest that resemblances do not always imply continuities, and that profound changes may be initiated under the cover of systems of rule which appear superficially similar.

It is hardly necessary to say that prerevolutionary Russia was a storehouse of the most diverse political notions, and that Russian intellectual history can almost be written as a series of raids on the Western larder and of the reactions and repulsions which inadequate mastication sometimes produced. Yet, despite the richness of the banquet which spreads before us, there is virtue in beginning with Pobedonostsev, for there is probably no one who better symbolizes the intransigence of the autocracy in its twilight period of rule. If there is any single fault line which created an almost unbridgeable chasm between "the ruling spheres" and the bulk of Russian public opinion, it derives from the theory of autocracy to which Pobedonostsev adhered.

It has often been observed that in an authoritarian political system the opposition tends to ape the pattern of the regime which it opposes. Intransigence generates intransigence, and autocratic methods of rule breed their authoritarian counterparts. Applied to prerevolutionary Russia, this formulation captures part of the truth, but it does not represent all of the truth. The history of Russian liberalism from Radishchev to Miliukov and Maklakov is a reminder that there was always an articulate body of opinion which recognized that the alternative to autocratic government was not another form of authoritarianism, but a constitutional regime. However falteringly, the zemstvo and the judicial reforms and the activity of the four dumas testify to the impress which this group was beginning to make. Frustrated though their constitutional impulse may have been by the polarization of political force which an uncompromising autocracy and revolutionary extremism imposed, they were nevertheless gaining strength in the closing years of the empire, and it is not completely futile to suggest that they might have continued to broaden their influence, had the pressures for modernization been allowed to run their course uninterrupted by war and revolution.

Yet it also is true that even this citadel of moderation found itself compelled to behave immoderately by the conditions of combat which tsarism imposed. The aspirations of the zemstvo liberals for a constitution were dismissed by Nicholas II and Pobedonostsev as "senseless dreams." Constitutional agitation had to be carried on by conspiratorial means. The distrust which Pobedonostsev demonstrated toward the liberals was reciprocated by the liberals themselves. In the words of the "Open Letter" which some of them addressed to the Tsar in reply to his speech of January 17/29, 1895:

You challenged the Zemstvos, and with them Russian Society, and nothing remains for them now but to choose between progress and faithfulness to autocracy. Your speech has provoked a feeling of offense and depression; but the living social forces will soon recover from that feeling. Some of them will pass to a peaceful but systematic and conscious struggle for such scope of action as is necessary for them. Some others will be made more determined to fight the detestable regime by any means. You first began the struggle; and the struggle will come.[1]

Thus an increasingly maximalist and revolutionary temper began to characterize this most moderate of liberal circles. Even former conservatives like Chicherin began to challenge Prince Meshcherskii's dictum that "Russia will not be Russia without autocracy." In Chicherin's view, "a regime of legality" had become "the most urgent need of Russian society," and though he paid tribute to the historical services of autocracy, he made clear his own conviction that the time had come to transform the autocracy into a limited monarchy bound by constitutional restraints.[2]

Within the bosom of liberalism, as Professor Karpovich has indicated, two currents of opinion struggled for ascendancy. One, the more conservative, associated with Maklakov, clung to the hope that a decisive break with the autocracy could be avoided and that somehow the tsarist regime could be persuaded to make use of the talents and experience of the liberals in modernizing itself along Western constitutional lines. The other view, which Miliukov voiced, put little trust in the willingness of the regime to make any concessions except under the most extreme pressure. It was convinced that the regime would cast aside the liberals when it felt strong enough to dispense with their services, and it insisted that coöperation be withheld until firm constitutional guarantees could be erected.

This difference in outlook between the two wings of Russian liberalism was strikingly manifest in the maneuvers which followed the vote of censure on the Goremykin government in the First Duma. For Miliukov the only acceptable way of resolving the crisis was the formation of a Cadet ministry fully empowered to carry out its program of democratic reforms. Maklakov, on the other hand, was disposed to accept Stolypin's suggestion of a ministry of "moderates" recruited from both the Duma and the bureaucracy. By

---

[1] Paul Milyoukov, *Russia and Its Crisis* (Chicago, 1906), p. 328.
[2] *Ibid.*, pp. 329–332.

sharing in authority, Maklakov hoped to temper the influence of the Tsar's more reactionary advisers. The proposal for a "mixed cabinet" seemed to him to hold out the possibility of bridging the gulf between the regime and public opinion. It was a step toward responsible government which might prepare the way for small, steady, but constructive reforms.

After the dissolution of the First Duma, differences in outlook again revealed themselves. Under Miliukov's leadership the Cadet deputies joined in the Vyborg appeal requesting all Russian subjects to withhold taxes, to refuse to report for military service, and to withdraw deposits from savings banks until the lawful Duma was restored. Maklakov doubted the wisdom of the Vyborg appeal; in his view civil disobedience could only serve to strengthen the forces of extremism and foreclose the moderate constitutional solution which he sought to attain.

Like Professor Karpovich, I have no desire at this late date to debate the respective merits of Miliukov and Maklakov, but what does bear stressing is the extent to which influential segments of that most Western of all Russian political parties, the Cadets, found themselves forced to conclude that the unyielding quality of tsardom made revolution the only feasible path to constitutional reform.

But revolutions operate under laws of their own, and he who helps open the floodgates does not necessarily control the course of the turbulent stream. This was Maklakov's great insight, and it made him reluctant to sanction the maximal demands which some of his Cadet colleagues were all too ready to embrace. Revolution is an art in which revolutionaries excel; whatever may have been the Cadet virtues, the management of revolutions was not their forte.

This brings me to Lenin and the essays by Dr. Hammond and Professor Ulam. My basic theme here is at least as old as Drahomanov. "Every political configuration, once formed, seeks to consolidate itself." [3] Every revolutionary movement leaves its organizational imprint on any regime which it creates. If we are looking for continuities in Russian and Soviet political thought, this seems to me to be an area in which they can readily be discerned. Both Hammond and Ulam tell us, and I readily agree, that although Soviet totalitarianism attained its most extreme form under Stalin, the foundations for it were laid much earlier by Lenin.

Dr. Hammond has traced these foundations in the great struggle between the advocates of consciousness and spontaneity in the late 1890's, in the emergence of Lenin's theory of the "vanguard," the disciplined Party elite which purports to guide the proletariat on the road to socialist revolution and utilizes mass organizations such as the trade unions as "fronts" through

[3] Mykhaylo Drahomanov, "The Centralization of the Revolutionary Struggle in Russia," *Annals of the Ukrainian Academy of Arts and Sciences in the U.S.*, II (Spring 1952), no. 1 (3), 187.

which the Party projects its influence and in which it insists on a monopoly of control.

Dr. Hammond points out in his paper that the Revolution of 1905 marked an important, if temporary, shift of emphasis in Lenin's thinking about the Party and the state. Under the influence of the revolutionary upsurge, Lenin's faith in the spontaneous "striving of the workers for socialism" seemed to mount and he declared himself in favor of mass admissions into the Party. But, in my view, Dr. Hammond properly stresses that even in this phase of Lenin's development, he never abandoned his insistence on the necessity of a Party vanguard, and indeed as the revolution ebbed and police repression mounted, his faith in a conspiratorial revolutionary elite was constantly reiterated.

I linger on this point because it seems to me that the legend of Lenin as a democrat at heart largely derives from a misreading of some of his pronouncements of the 1905 period. It is, of course, true that in his polemic against Trotsky's theory of permanent revolution he stated: "Whoever wants to approach socialism by any other path than that of political democracy will inevitably arrive at absurd and reactionary conclusions both economic and political." [4] But this was merely his way of saying that Russia was not yet ripe for a socialist revolution, that an immediate effort to establish a minority dictatorship of the proletariat à la Trotsky and Parvus was doomed to defeat, and that it was first necessary to form an alliance with the peasantry before the proletarian seizure of power could be ventured. The bourgeois-democratic revolution was never a final end for Lenin; at best it was a stage which had to be traversed on the road to proletarian dictatorship, and indeed, as the events of 1917 were to disclose, it finally became a stage to be skipped as Lenin overcame his so-called democratic scruples in his eagerness to take power. Lenin's real feelings about democracy emerge with unmistakable clarity in his reply to criticism of the dissolution of the Constituent Assembly in January 1918:

> Every attempt, direct or indirect, to consider the question of the Constituent Assembly from a formal, legal aspect, within the framework of ordinary bourgeois democracy ignoring the class struggle and civil war, would be a betrayal of the cause of the proletariat and the adoption of the bourgeois standpoint.[5]

And again:

> Every time I speak on this subject of proletarian government some one . . . shouts "dictator." . . . You cannot expect . . . that socialism will be delivered on a silver platter . . . Not a single question pertaining to the class struggle has ever been settled except by violence. Violence when committed by the toiling and

[4] Lenin, "Dve taktiki sotsial-demokratii v demokraticheskoi revoliutsii," *Sochineniia*, 4th ed., VIII, 14.

[5] Quoted in Merle Fainsod, *How Russia Is Ruled* (Cambridge, Mass., 1953), p. 125.

exploited masses against the exploiters is the kind of violence of which we approve.[6]

I do not regard these statements as a "betrayal" of Lenin's so-called democratic aspirations. Rather, they seem to me to constitute the logical fulfillment of an authoritarian faith to which he was basically committed.

I turn now to Professor Ulam's paper on "Stalin and the Theory of Totalitarianism." Professor Ulam sees in Lenin a "genuine totalitarian impulse which already finds itself awkwardly combined with social democratic and liberal phraseology." He sees the Communist Party under Lenin's leadership groping "its way toward totalitarianism," and though he concedes that Lenin's methods in dealing with his intra-Party opponents were milder than Stalin's, he suggests that if "a more efficient Party machinery had been at Lenin's disposal the penalties would have been much more drastic." [7] While I find myself in general sympathy with the direction of Professor Ulam's argument, respect for the historical record makes it essential to stress the differences, as well as the similarities between Lenin and Stalin. As I have put it in another place:

> As long as Lenin remained active, his influence was clearly exerted in the strengthening of Party discipline and consolidation of the hold of the central machine on the Party. The Party faction was anathema to him, and in the Resolution on Party Unity, which he drafted for the Tenth Congress, he did everything in his power to destroy the embryonic development of a two- or multi-faction system within the framework of the single-party dictatorship . . . At the same time, his intolerance of opposition in principle was tempered by a practical realization that differences of view within the Party were unavoidable and that the function of a Party leader was to persuade first and to invoke sanctions only as a last resort. Thus he cajoled, argued, and even pleaded with his Party opponents before he confronted the necessity of declaring open war on them. Despite violent threats and tirades, the most drastic penalty which he imposed on dissenters was expulsion from the Party, and even this penalty was rarely utilized against Party members of any prominence who had rendered distinguished service in the past. If on occasion Lenin seemed to equate dissent with treason, he still shrank from drawing the practical consequences, at least so far as intra-party struggles were concerned.[8]

Professor Ulam is of course correct in his contention that Lenin was responsible for the germinating conception on the basis of which all intra-Party opposition came to be extinguished. It also seems to me that he has described some of the attributes of Stalin's totalitarian formula with great skill and perception. There is one point in his analysis which I should like to single out for more extended comment.

"Totalitarianism," he suggests, "cannot be complete without an ideologi-

---

[6] *Ibid.*
[7] Above, p. 158.
[8] Fainsod, *How Russia is Ruled*, pp. 137–138.

cal basis." And he attributes to Stalin a realization that every important decision, no matter how pragmatic its basis, must be justified in ideological terms if more than passive acquiescence in state purposes is to be enforced. As he puts it:

> Every departure from Marxism has to be done in the name of Marxism . . . The leaders realize, probably consciously, that the people will endure a great deal in the name of an ideology, but that they will balk at purposeless suffering. . . . An elitist society and dictatorship require an ideology if corruption and privilege, and sheer human restlessness under the denial of all freedoms, are to be held in check.[9]

Now I have no objections to any of these formulations in the abstract, but I wish that Professor Ulam had been somewhat more explicit in identifying the content of Stalinist ideology, in tracing its changes and continuities, and in relating its various facets and shifting emphases to the social and economic transformations of the Stalinist era. Stalinist ideology is many things — it is history rewritten, it is Soviet patriotism, it is a defense of a status society, it is a promise of world victory, and on occasion even a vision of the Heavenly City of the Classless Society. Each has its uses and its diverse appeals. And they do not necessarily operate with the same effect or in the same direction. Thus Stalinism as a defense of a status society has an obvious appeal to the new elite which Stalin created; it does not carry the same conviction to the millions of Soviet subjects who are outside the charmed circle. The vision of the final stage of Communism may excite the enthusiasm of the young zealot; it is hardly likely to stir the imagination of an older generation which has endured endless hardships and has seen the Utopia which has been dangled before it continuously postponed. Soviet patriotism may tap the deepest wellsprings of national pride, but if it is given too exclusive a Great Russian content, it risks alienating the lesser breeds for whom it does not adequately provide.

What I am trying to suggest is that the manipulation of these ideological themes is a delicate art, and that unless it is performed with the greatest skill, the product may well be an erosion rather than a consolidation of faith. Indeed, the increasing disposition of Stalin over the years to rely on bureaucratic and repressive controls and to utilize incentives to reinforce indoctrination points to his own lack of confidence in Marxist-Leninist ideology as a cementing force in Soviet society. Many observers have noted a decline in ideological *élan* as a characteristic of the evolution of Soviet society, and Stalin in his last testament, *Economic Problems of Socialism in the USSR,* came close to admitting it when he referred to the "new and young forces who . . . do not possess an adequate Marxist education, are unfamiliar with many truths that are well known to us, and are therefore

[*] Above, pp. 167–168.

compelled to grope in the darkness." [10] Professor Ulam has shrewdly observed that this last "ideological" testament of Stalin "is at once a theoretical defense of the status society arrived at in the USSR and a plea not to be fully satisfied with it." [11] The picture of the road to Communism is perhaps the most explicit which Stalin ever painted, but it is accompanied by a reminder that it is a long, hard road which can be paved only by the most intense efforts. There is, as Professor Ulam has pointed out, an element of the pathetic in the last effort of Stalin to recharge the Party with ideological zeal. And there is food for ironical reflection in the fact that, when his heirs faced the problem of consolidating their own power, they did not turn to Stalin's *Economic Problems* for ideological inspiration, but took the more pragmatic path of reviving production incentives and strengthening the position of the new bureaucratic elite.

Yet whatever significance one attributes to the changes of the last year, there is no evidence of any disposition on the part of Stalin's successors to dismantle the totalitarian apparatus which he perfected. This legacy of Stalin lives on, and while it has its roots in the Russian past, it seems to me important to emphasize that it is different in many respects from the tsarist autocracy with which it is often compared.

The tsarist regime was authoritarian, but it was not totalitarian. There was after all an opposition press, and opposition parties operated in relative freedom in the Duma. Judges and juries functioned with some independence, and from time to time rendered judgments which sharply challenged the wishes of the tsar's ministers. Entry and exit from the Russian empire were fairly easy for both Russians and foreigners, and travel comparatively uninhibited. The tsarist regime had its political police and its exile system, but the political exiles never numbered more than 50,000 at one time, and all of us who have read the memoirs of revolutionaries are familiar with the relative ease with which many of them escaped and the comparative freedom in which they were left to pursue their occupations, their literary labors, and even their revolutionary activities.

I have no desire to conclude this critique with an apologia for tsardom. The responsibility which it bears before history for nurturing the seeds of totalitarianism is too great to impel me to gloss over its defects. But in a symposium devoted to Pobedonostsev, to Miliukov and Maklakov, to Lenin, and to Stalin, it is important to stress that there is a deep gulf dividing authoritarianism and totalitarianism, and if we treat the two as identical political formations, we end by revealing our inability to distinguish between continuity and change.

[10] Joseph Stalin, *Economic Problems of Socialism in the USSR* (New York, 1952), p. 12.
[11] Above, p. 170.

PART III
COLLECTIVISM AND INDIVIDUALISM

Khomiakov on *Sobornost'*

NICHOLAS V. RIASANOVSKY

I

Although the concept of *sobornost'* was of fundamental importance for the entire thought of Aleksei Stepanovich Khomiakov, his voluminous writings contain only one explicit definition and discussion of that term. This is found in his "Letter to the Editor of *L'Union Chrétienne* Concerning the Meaning of the Words: 'Catholic' and '*sobornyi*,' with Special Reference to the Speech of the Jesuit Father Gagarin," a brief theological treatise published in 1860.[1]

Gagarin accused the Orthodox Church in Slavic lands of deleting the word "Catholic" from the Creed and of replacing it with the adjective "*sobornyi*," corresponding to "synodal," "a vague and obscure term utterly incapable of rendering the idea of the universality"[2] of the Church. Khomiakov meets the charge by arguing that "*sobornyi*" is precisely the right translation for "Catholic," that, in fact, it gives a new insight into the true meaning of the Greek word itself. St. Cyril and St. Methodius, he claims, selected this translation advisedly and for an excellent reason, even though they had several Slavic words meaning "universal" at their disposal:

> They stopped on the word *sobornyi*. *Sobor* expresses the idea of a gathering not only in the sense of an actual, visible union of many in a given place, but

---

[1] The "Letter," first published in the *Union Chrétienne* in the original French, appeared in a Russian translation in the second, the theological, volume of Khomiakov's collected works. I am using the fifth edition of the volume: A. S. Khomiakov, *Polnoe sobranie sochinenii* (Moscow, 1907), II, 305–314. Henceforward I shall refer to this book as Khomiakov, II.

Actually, Khomiakov employed the terms "sobornyi" or "sobornost'" on remarkably few occasions. In addition to the major discussion already mentioned, one may cite examples, *ibid.*, pp. 5, 12, 25, 70–71. In the first three cases the adjectival form of the word is included as a part of the set description of the Church taken from the Creed. The last instance is more interesting: the usage is more individual, and the key term is the noun "sobornost'." "Sobor" is, of course, used often throughout Khomiakov's writings to denote a church council. Because Khomiakov discussed the term "sobornyi" only once, and that in the year of his death, one is tempted to suggest that he had not realized its full potential value for his own theological doctrines until he began to compose his rebuttal of Gagarin's speech, and that he would have employed it much more frequently had he lived longer.

[2] *Ibid.*, p. 305.

also in the more general sense of the continual possibility of such a union, in other words: it expresses the idea of *unity in multiplicity*. Therefore, it is obvious that the word *katholikos,* as understood by the two great servants of the Word of God sent by Greece to the Slavs, was derived not from *kata* and *hola,* but from *kata* and *holon;* for *kata* often has the same meaning as our preposition "according to," for instance: *kata Matthaion, kata Markon,* "according to Matthew," "according to Mark." The Catholic Church is the Church *according to all,* or according to the *unity of all, kath' holon tōn pisteuontōn,* the Church according to free unanimity, according to complete unanimity, the Church in which all the peoples have disappeared and in which there are no Greeks, no barbarians, no difference of status, no slaveowners, and no slaves; that Church about which the Old Testament prophesied and which was realized in the New Testament — in one word, the Church as it was defined by St. Paul.[3]

It was this Church "according to all," "according to the unity of all" in love and freedom that Khomiakov preached all his life. "The Church is one. Her unity follows of necessity from the unity of God; for the Church is not a multitude of persons in their separate individuality, but a unity of the grace of God, living in a multitude of rational creatures, submitting themselves willingly to grace."[4] And again: "The Church is a revelation of the Holy Spirit, granted to the mutual love of Christians, that love, which leads them up to the Father through His incarnated Word, Our Lord Jesus Christ."[5]

Man could fully realize himself only in the Church:

A man, however, does not find in the Church something foreign to himself. He finds himself in it, himself not in the impotence of spiritual solitude, but in the might of his spiritual, sincere union with his brothers, with his Savior. He finds himself in it in his perfection, or rather he finds in it that which is perfect in himself, the Divine inspiration which constantly evaporates in the crude impurity of every separate, individual existence. This purification comes about through the invincible power of the mutual love in Jesus Christ of the Christians, for this love is the Holy Spirit.[6]

No external, legal expression of these bonds of love which formed the essence of the Church was necessary or possible: "We confess the one and free Church. It remains one, although it has no official representative of its unity, and it remains free, although its freedom is not expressed by a division of its members."[7] The Church meant life, and truth, and freedom, and love, but not authority:

[3] *Ibid.,* pp. 312–313. Italics in the original. I am indebted to Professor J. F. Gilliam of the Departments of History and of Classics of the State University of Iowa for his advice on Khomiakov's use of Greek in the latter's discussion of *sobornost'.* Printer's errors in the Greek have been corrected.

[4] A. S. Khomiakov, *The Church Is One* (London, 1948), p. 14. Published for the Fellowship of St. Alban and St. Sergius.

[5] Khomiakov, II, 220.

[6] *Ibid.,* p. 112.

[7] *Ibid.*

No! The Church is not authority, just as God is not authority, just as Christ is not authority; because authority is something external to us. Not authority, I say, but truth, and at the same time the life of a Christian, his inner life; for God, Christ, the Church live in him a life which is more real than the heart which beats in his breast, or the blood which flows in his veins; but they live in him only inasmuch as he himself lives an ecumenical life of love and unity, that is, the life of the Church.[8]

Khomiakov emphasized that every single member of the Church formed an organic part of it. No man or group of men stood at its head; the Orthodox Church knew no pope in any form, but only Jesus Christ. There was no excessive differentiation between the clergy and the laity, no assertion that the hierarchy had the exclusive right of teaching, while the masses were entitled only to the passive reactions of listening and following. Khomiakov was overjoyed by the Encyclical of the Eastern Patriarchs in 1848 which was directed against the growing papal claims in the domain of the Christian dogma, and which proclaimed that both the immutability of the dogma and the purity of the rite were entrusted not to the hierarchy alone, but also to the entire people of the Church who were the Body of Christ. Similarly, in the organization of the Russian church itself, Khomiakov favored all democratic popular elements, and was invariably opposed to centralization, regimentation, and bureaucracy, in fact, to the whole system represented by the Holy Synod and its management of the Russian church.

The concept of *sobornost'*, of the organic unity of all in love and freedom as the essence of the Church, determined Khomiakov's entire analysis and appreciation of Orthodoxy. It also served him as his main weapon against the rival creeds of Roman Catholicism and of Protestantism.[9] Indeed, the very Letter about the term *sobornyi* was written as a counterattack against the Jesuit Gagarin, and, once Khomiakov had formulated his definition of the key word, he proceeded, on the same page, to assail his Western opponents with it:

Papists, you who claim the apostles to the Slavs as your own, repudiate them as fast as you can! You who broke the harmony of thought and the unity by changing the Creed without participation or counsel of your eastern brothers, how are you going to cope with the definition of the Church bequeathed to us by Cyril and by Methodius? . . . The Apostolic Church of the ninth century is neither the Church *kath' hekaston* (according to the understanding of each) as the Protestants have it, nor the Church *kata ton episkopon tēs Rōmēs* (according to the understanding of the bishop of Rome) as is the case with the Latins; it is the Church *kath' holon* (according to the understanding of all in their unity), the Church as it existed prior to the Western split and as it still remains among those

[8] *Ibid.*, II, 53.

[9] Most of Khomiakov's theological writings were polemical in nature. The attitude of opposition and struggle was extremely common not only in the case of Khomiakov, but among the Slavophiles in general. I used it as the basic approach to the movement in my book on *Russia and the West in the Teaching of the Slavophiles* (Cambridge, Mass., 1952).

whom God preserved from the split: for, I repeat, this split is a heresy against the dogma of the unity of the Church.[10]

Just as *sobornost'*, "this one word" which contains "an entire confession of faith," [11] sums up admirably Khomiakov's writings about Orthodoxy in the course of some fifteen years, so the attack quoted above presents in a capsule form Khomiakov's tireless polemical activity against the Western creeds over the same period of time. For Khomiakov was overwhelmed, virtually obsessed with the idea that the one great turning point in the history of Christianity was the break between the Western and the Eastern churches, and that the reason for this break was the Western repudiation of what he came to designate as *sobornost'*. This motif is the most common of all in Khomiakov's writings, and its most striking instance deserves to be quoted in spite of the length and the cumbersomeness of the passage. It deals with the addition of *filioque* to the Creed in the West and the resulting split of the Western and the Eastern churches, and it represents a unique combination of basic Slavophile theology and the psychology, the ethos, the spirit, so to speak, of the movement.

Now let us betake ourselves to the last years of the eighth or the beginning of the ninth century, and let us imagine a wanderer who had come from the East to one of the cities in Italy or in France. Pervaded by the feeling of ancient unity, and quite confident that he is in the midst of brethren, he enters a church to sanctify the last day of the week. Full of love, he concentrates on pious thoughts, follows the service, and listens to the wonderful prayers which had gladdened his heart from early childhood. Words reach him: Let us kiss one another, that we may with one mind confess the Father, the Son, and the Holy Ghost. He is listening carefully. Now the Creed of the Christian and Catholic Church is proclaimed, the Creed which every Christian must serve with his entire life, and for which, on occasion, he must sacrifice his life. He is listening carefully. But this Creed is corrupted, it is some new, unknown creed! Is he awake, or is he in the power of an oppressive dream? He does not believe his ears, begins to doubt his senses. He wants to find out, asks explanation. An idea occurs to him: he may have walked into a gathering of dissenters cast away by the local church . . . Alas, this is not the case! He heard the voice of the local church itself. An entire patriarchate, an entire vast world fell away from unity . . . The shattered wanderer complains; he is comforted. — "We but added the smallest thing," they tell him, just as the Latins keep repeating it to us today — "If it is so insignificant, then why add it?" — "Oh, this is perfectly abstract matter." — "How do you know that you have understood it?" — "Well, this is our local tradition." — "But how could it find a place in the universal Creed, in spite of an explicit rule of an Ecumenical Council prohibiting any change in the Creed?" — "Well, this is a tradition of the universal Church, the meaning of which we expressed following our local opinion." — "But we do not know of any such tradition; and in any case, how could a local opinion find a place in the universal Creed? The comprehension of divine truths, is it not given to the entire Church in its totality? Or did we for some reason deserve to be excommunicated from the Church? You

[10] Khomiakov, II, 313.
[11] *Ibid.*

not only did not think of turning to us for advice, but you did not even take the trouble of sending us notice. Or is it that we have fallen so low? However, no more than a century ago, the East produced the greatest Christian poet and, perhaps, the most glorious Christian theologian, John of Damascus. And now too there are among us confessors and martyrs for the faith, learned philosophers full of Christian wisdom, ascetics whose entire life is a continuous prayer. Why then did you cast us away?" But whatever the poor wanderer could say, the work had been done: the schism had occurred. *By its very action (that is, by the arbitrary change of the Creed) the Roman world made an implicit assertion that in its eyes the entire East was not more than a world of helots in matters of faith and doctrine. Life in the Church ended for an entire half of the Church.*[12]

Once the proud peoples of the West had willfully and insolently rejected their Eastern brothers, once they had sinned against the sacred principle of *sobornost'*, the die was cast and the history of the West was determined for all ages. The Roman Catholics, after they separated themselves from the Church, that is, from the only free and true unity of all believers, had to find another basis for cohesion. They discovered it in the artificial, outward union of a strongly centralized, authoritarian system headed by the new and unique official, the pope. This external order and conformity of the Roman Catholic world, imposing as it admittedly was, could, however, merely hide but never remove the essence of the Roman Catholic heresy which lay precisely in the arbitrary disregard of the community of all believers in favor of a local opinion. Therefore, Roman Catholicism naturally gave rise to Protestantism. The Protestants came merely as a logical extension of the original Roman Catholic revolt against the Church: whereas Rome asserted the sufficiency of the opinion and of the judgment of the Western patriarchate apart from the totality of all Christians, they claimed the same sufficiency for the individual conscience. Both denominations argued by means of clever syllogisms; both substituted private, rational judgment for *sobornost'*, the true community of life, love, faith, and understanding to be found only in the Church.

But this private, rational opinion, divorced from the living unity and wisdom of the Church, would not stop with Luther. Indeed, the decomposition of Protestantism was swift, sure, and frightful. "In its final result Protestantism must pass into a purely philosophic analysis with all its consequences." [13] "Kant was a direct and a necessary continuer of Luther." [14] He, in turn, had able followers in Hegel, Schelling, and other German idealistic philosophers, but it was quite beyond the capacity of those well-meaning gentlemen to retrieve the lost truth of *sobornost'*. They could only stretch the fundamental rationalism and falsehood of Western thought to its logical *reductio ad absurdum* in their several systems. With the failure of philosophy, nothing was left to the West, but complete negation and chaos. The wanderer

---

[12] *Ibid.*, pp. 48–49. Italics in the original.
[13] A. S. Khomiakov, *Polnoe sobranie sochinenii* (3rd ed., Moscow, 1906), VII, 213.
[14] A. S. Khomiakov, *Polnoe sobranie sochinenii* (4th ed., Moscow, 1911), I, 298.

had good reasons to be shattered by the change in the Creed he unexpectedly heard in a Western church!

Khomiakov's view of the Church, his concept of *sobornost'*, was the main meaning and message of his religious teaching. It became a battle cry of his followers, both the immediate disciples and the more distant admirers.[15] Berdiaev, for instance, wrote with power and passion:

At the basis of his theological thought Khomiakov put the idea of freedom — of *sobornost'*, the organic union of freedom and love, community. He had a feeling for spiritual freedom; all his thinking was permeated by it; he had a genius's intuition for *sobornost'* which he perceived was not in the historical reality of the Orthodox Church, but behind it. *Sobornost'* belongs to the image of the Church which is comprehensible to the mind, and in relation to the Church of experience it is an obligation to be discharged.[16]

It is this constructive aspect of Khomiakov's teaching, his appreciation of the Church and his insight into its nature, that has exercised a lasting influence on Orthodox religious thought. But the destructive side of the doctrine, its sweeping denunciation of Roman Catholicism and of Protestantism, was also well remembered. In fact, Khomiakov's most faithful disciple, Samarin, cited it as the reason why his master should be given the hallowed designation of a doctor of the Church.

In the days of old those who had rendered a service to the Orthodox world, such as Khomiakov rendered — those to whom it had been given to obtain a definitive triumph for Orthodoxy over this or that fallacy, by means of a logical explication of one aspect or another of the teaching of the Church — were called doctors of the Church.[17]

Samarin went on to declare in ringing language:

When we call him by this name we know very well that some will take our words as impertinent challenge, and others as the blind partiality of the student for his teacher; the former will become indignant, the latter will laugh at us. All this we know beforehand; but we know also that future generations will be amazed, not that in 1867 someone decided to print and sign this with his name, but that

[15] In order to appreciate Khomiakov's religious doctrines one should read the entire eight volumes of his works, although only the second is devoted to theology in the strict sense of the term. Similarly, as should become increasingly clear in the course of this paper, an appraisal of Khomiakov as a religious thinker is bound to be intrinsically connected with a more general evaluation of his position in modern intellectual history. Therefore, virtually everything written on Khomiakov is of relevance to the subject of this study. A fine bibliography of this enormous material is provided in A. Gratieux, *A. Khomiakov et le mouvement Slavophile*, Vol. I (*Les hommes*), Vol. II (*Les doctrines*) (Paris, 1939), I, xiii–xxxii. Zavitnevich's list is very detailed, but out of date: V. Z. Zavitnevich, *Aleksei Stepanovich Khomiakov*, 2 vols. (Kiev, 1902). See also the annotated bibliography in my *Russia and the West*, pp. 219–234.

[16] N. A. Berdyaev, *The Russian Idea* (London, 1947), pp. 162–163.

[17] Iu. F. Samarin's long essay on Khomiakov as theologian was published as the "Introduction" to the second volume of Khomiakov's works; the exact reference is to p. xxxvi.

there was a time when such an act could have demanded even the very smallest resolution.[18]

The verdict of later generations, however, has not been as clear-cut as Samarin predicted. While appreciation and praise have been lavished on Khomiakov, he has also often been the subject of curt dismissals and even denunciations. The positivists, the materialists, the Marxists made no sense at all of _sobornost'_ and condemned it together with the rest of Khomiakov's ideology as fantasy, ignorance, and superstition.[19] But many religious writers too were not at all willing to follow Khomiakov. Some of them objected especially to the very point Samarin praised most, namely, Khomiakov's unmeasured arraignment of Western Christian denominations. Others went to the crux of the matter and challenged his concept of _sobornost'_ itself.

Father Paul Florenskii, for instance, came to the conclusion that Khomiakov's religion was immanent and humanitarian, not transcendent and Christian. His Church, with its denial of authority and its apparent self-sufficiency, was an attempt to substitute human communion and human altruism for divine foundation and divine mystery. Small wonder that Khomiakov attacked the Roman Catholics more than the Protestants and that he especially disliked such concepts as transubstantiation and such feelings as the fear of God.[20] Others who did not join in Florenskii's wholesale denunciation agreed with him that Khomiakov's discussion of the Church was at best incomplete, being very weak in its treatment of the hierarchy and of authority in general.

In fact, just as _sobornost'_, his concept of the Church, with its many implications, formed the key preoccupation of Khomiakov, so it became his chief legacy to Orthodox theology, and it still remains a vital and controversial issue in that theology.

II

The concept of _sobornost'_ belonged properly to the domain of theology, but Khomiakov's use of his favorite idea was by no means limited to that realm. We saw how Khomiakov employed _sobornost'_ to criticize Roman Catholicism and Protestantism and how in the process of this criticism he drew a complete and necessary outline of Western history. Khomiakov also used _sobornost'_ or concepts closely related to _sobornost'_ to explain world

[18] _Ibid._

[19] Some of them, it is true, found certain interesting exceptions in Khomiakov's ideology and even praised parts of it, but this is not the place to discuss that subject.

[20] P. A. Florenskii, _Okolo Khomiakova_ (Moscow, 1916). Also in _Bogoslovskii vestnik,_ nos. 7 and 8 (1916).

Berdiaev's counterassault on Florenskii was just as violent as Florenskii's assault on Khomiakov. Berdiaev concluded that Florenskii's "secret" was the same as that of Dostoyevsky's Grand Inquisitor: "We are not with Thee, but with _him._" N. A. Berdiaev, "Khomiakov i sviashch. P. A. Florenskii," in _Russkaia mysl'_, February 1917, pp. 72–81, especially p. 81. Italics in the original.

history, to assail everything he disliked in life, to promote all the institutions and all the doctrines he championed, in short, for every purpose. In the process the Church was at least partially replaced by such alien entities as the Iranian principle, Slavdom, Russia, or the peasant commune.

Khomiakov was convinced that he had discovered the essence of human history: "Freedom and necessity compose the secret fundamental principles around which are concentrated, in various ways, all thoughts of man."[21] Khomiakov called the first principle the Iranian and the second the Kushite, for he believed that its original home had been in Ethiopia, and the Bible referred to Ethiopia as "the land of Kush." The proponents of the two principles formed two hostile camps, based on spiritual affinity rather than on blood ties or political allegiance, and were engaged in a constant and manifold struggle for the world, not only in Europe, Africa, and Asia, but also in the Americas, and even in Australia and in Polynesia.

The Iranian principle expressed itself in the belief in creation and in spiritual religion, in the alphabet, literature, and song. The Bible belonged to it, and Christianity was its logical culmination. Typically Iranian details included the legend of the great flood and enmity against the serpent. The link which united the Iranians was their faith, but they also belonged to the same white race which alone preserved the tradition of true spirituality.

The Kushites were mute men who believed in necessity, and directed their efforts toward enormous constructions, such as the pyramids of Egypt or the temples of Southern India. They were engaged in hewing out of stone rather than talking; they wrote little, and they wrote only in hieroglyphics. They worshiped the serpent. The Kushites were slaves of nature, whether in the form of stone or in the sensuous form of a serpent. They developed phallic religions; often they gave themselves up to complete sensuality, as, for instance, in Indian Shivaism. Sometimes, however, Kushitism evolved in what appeared to be the opposite direction. Thus Buddhism denied the world and all its attractions. In reality, Shivaism and Buddhism represented the two sides of the same medal: both were based on the same principle, on the recognition of necessity, be it in a sensuous abandon or in nirvana. Kushite elements penetrated into the Iranian tradition itself. They always revealed themselves in formalism, legalism, and necessity, as opposed to free creativity and life. Through the Kushite Roman state they entered the Roman Church, and from Roman Catholicism they were taken up by Protestantism.

In fact, although the Iranian could defeat the Kushite in battle, in one important respect he was much more vulnerable than his opponent. Kushitism could not be corrupted any more than the material necessity, the facts themselves, could be. But the free spirit of Iranianism demanded the great-

---

[21] A. S. Khomiakov, *Polnoe sobranie sochinenii* (4th ed., Moscow, 1904), V, 217. Khomiakov's world history is a huge compilation of notes, arguments, hypotheses, and examples, which was published in three parts, after his death, to constitute the fifth, sixth, and seventh volumes of his works. It is a first draft at best.

est effort, and the highest purity; it was constantly in danger of contamination, and the slightest taint was noxious. History provided numerous examples of this degeneration of Iranian elements and their subsequent revival to meet once more the challenge of Kushitism, which remained always massive and solid, in spite, or rather because, of the fact that it was essentially dead.

"The Iranian principle" was not the same as *sobornost'*. In particular, the former concept did not explicitly include in its definition the idea of an organic community which was fundamental to the latter. But there were also basic similarities between the two: both represented freedom, creativity, and life, as opposed to necessity, mechanical routine, and death. Both were true; in fact, they were truth itself in our world.[22] And, of course, Khomiakov tried to bring the Iranian principle and Orthodoxy together in his interpretation of human history. Their relation, however, remained an ambivalent one: whereas on the one hand the Church came as the real fulfillment of Iranianism, as the one truth, life, and light, it was, on the other hand, merely an instance in the eternal struggle of this Iranianism against its Kushite opponent. Other instances included not only the Hebrew religion of the Old Testament, but also Brahmanism, and many other creeds as well. Furthermore, because of this association with "the Iranian principle," Orthodoxy, as expounded by Khomiakov, came to be linked with a weird and frightful variety of national, racial, linguistic, and virtually all other prejudices. It should be added that Khomiakov had a high regard for his history of the world as the correct statement of his religious as well as his other views, and that this high regard was shared by his fellow Slavophiles.

Of the bearers of the Iranian principle, the Slavs were the most promising. Khomiakov's world history assigned an overwhelmingly important role to Slavdom, and many of his other writings, including much of his poetry, dealt with the same themes of Slavic greatness and Slavic mission. The Slavs had contributed the most important elements of European civilization, for which biased historians failed to give them credit. They built towns, introduced commerce and navigation, and developed arts and crafts. They were the most highly spiritual, the most artistic, the most talented people on the face of the earth. Keeping the concept of *sobornost'* in mind, it is especially interesting to note that Khomiakov emphasized the peace-loving, fraternal, and communal qualities of the Slavs. Indeed, he presented them, by contrast with the Germanic conquerors and exploiters, as the epitome of a peaceful agricultural society based on the peasant commune. It was this brotherly living in love and concord that made the Slavs especially receptive to the Christian message, and promised them a unique Christian role in

---

[22] It would be very interesting to trace the genesis of "the Iranian principle" and of *sobornost'* in Khomiakov's thought. That is hardly possible, however, because there are very few writings of Khomiakov that can be ascribed safely to the 1830's, and in the 1840's both concepts are already present. It is my guess that "the Iranian principle" preceded *sobornost'*.

history. Again, as in the case of "the Iranian principle," it is fair to ask Khomiakov where Christianity begins and Slavdom ends, and what is the relation between the two?

The Russians were the greatest Slavic nation. They possessed an abundance of vital, organic energy, revealed in their unsurpassed language, in their glorious institutions, in the entire life of the people. They had the blessed Slavic qualities of humility, brotherhood, and love. Moreover, they were successful in preserving their country and their way of life, while other Slavs were either conquered by the Moslem Turks, or, a much worse fate, seduced by the Catholic West. To Khomiakov, as well as to the other Slavophiles, Russia prior to the reforms of Peter the Great was that land of spontaneity, freedom, and brotherly love which was their hope and their vision. It is this vision that inspired their unmeasured praise and their ardent defense of the Moscow state, society, and culture. The historian S. M. Solov'ëv and some other critics pointed out at the time that the Slavophile view of the Russian past had very little connection with any historical reality. And, indeed, it had come from quite other realms.

Peter the Great introduced the Kushite principles of rationalism, legalism, and formalism into Russia, destroying the spontaneous relations and the organic harmony of the nation. But although "the St. Petersburg period of Russian history" was a most harsh and cruel burden for the Russian people, Khomiakov was convinced that it marked merely a passing phase. Russia was bound to return to her true principles. Beyond that, it was her mission to carry her message of salvation to the dying West where Kushite rationalism had run its full course and had left only a waste behind it. The Russian message was, of course, the Christian message, the Orthodox message — brotherhood, and love, and *sobornost'*. These saving principles were the essence not only of the Church, but also of Russia (and Slavdom) although certainly not of any other society.[23] Russia was not simply "the most Christian nation"; sometimes, in Khomiakov's scheme of things, it is actually difficult to distinguish between its ideal image and Orthodox Christianity.

Of all the "true Russian and Slavic" institutions, the Slavophiles loved the peasant commune the most. Khomiakov championed it on many occasions and in different ways, but his greatest emphasis was on the "moral link" it established among the people, on its "moral," "ennobling" qualities. The best elucidation of these moral qualities was made not by Khomiakov himself, but by his very close associate and fellow Slavophile Konstantin Aksakov:

A commune is a union of the people who have renounced their egoism, their individuality, and who express their common accord; this is an act of love, a

[23] Not of Byzantium: Khomiakov explained that while Byzantium had the true religion its political, social, and cultural foundations dated back to the pagan days of the Roman empire and had never become really Christian.

noble Christian act, which expresses itself more or less clearly in its various other manifestations. A commune thus represents a moral choir, and just as in a choir a voice is not lost, but follows the general pattern and is heard in the harmony of all voices, so in the commune the individual is not lost, but renounces his exclusiveness in favor of the general accord — and there arises the noble phenomenon of harmonious, joint existence of rational beings (consciousnesses); there arises a brotherhood, a commune — a triumph of human spirit.[24]

Berdiaev remarked most appropriately: "The Slavophiles were under the influence of their *narodnik* illusions. To them the commune was not a fact of history, but something imposing which stands outside the realm of history; it is the 'other world' so to speak within this world." [25] And, again, we are back to Khomiakov's concept of *sobornost'*.

While assorted nationalists, chauvinists, and Pan-Slavs were only too willing to accept at its face value this extreme Slavophile praise of Slavdom, of Russia, of the peasant commune, and of other mundane objects besides, the more discriminating and especially the more religious admirers of the movement were properly embarrassed and disturbed by the remarkable identification of the Church with things of this world practiced by Khomiakov and his friends. They tried to explain away whole sides of the Slavophile doctrine, and they apologized for what they could not explain away.

For instance, F. Smirnov attempted to demonstrate in *The Orthodox Review* why Khomiakov's juxtaposition of religion and of nationality would not lead to error: he argued that the Slavophiles were justified in linking inextricably Roman Catholicism with the Romance element and Protestantism with the Germanic because these connections were of the very essence of the two "false creeds which had fallen away from ecumenical Christianity"; Orthodoxy, on the other hand, was, to the Slavophiles, universal truth and as such by no means limited to Slavdom.[26] Berdiaev combined his extremely high evaluation of Khomiakov with the apologetic admission that Khomiakov's ideology retained to the last much "national-Russian paganism," that in fact Khomiakov had confused "the pagan city with the millennial kingdom of Christ." [27]

Some religious critics were not nearly as tolerant as Berdiaev. The most famous as well as one of the most devastating attacks of all was delivered by the philosopher Vladimir Solov'ev who had himself at one time been strongly influenced by Khomiakov and by the Slavophile thought in general. Solov'ev turned against his former guides because he became convinced that

[24] K. S. Aksakov, *Sochineniia istoricheskie* (Moscow, 1861), pp. 291–292. This book constitutes the first volume of Konstantin Aksakov's collected works.

[25] Berdyaev, *The Russian Idea,* p. 50.

[26] F. Smirnov, "Vopros o protestanstve v vozzreniiakh Khomiakova," *Pravoslavnoe obozrenie,* March 1884, pp. 533–552, especially p. 547.

[27] N. A. Berdiaev, *A. S. Khomiakov* (Moscow, 1912), p. 15 *et passim*. In addition to Berdiaev's monograph on Khomiakov, see his views on the subject expressed later in *The Russian Idea.*

they had identified the Orthodox Church with the Russian people. In spite of their professions to the contrary, Orthodoxy was for them merely "an attribute of the Russian people; it is the true religion, in the last analysis, only because it is the religion of the Russian people." [28] Therefore, Solov'ëv concluded, chauvinism was the logical outcome of Slavophilism, and all the extreme Russian nationalists its legitimate progeny.

Father G. V. Florovskii offered a more balanced and penetrating judgment:

> The sphere of society and the sphere of the Church are, with all their resemblance, two incommensurate orders of things. In the Slavophile ideology this incommensurability was not fully recognized and accepted. This lack of differentiation injured not so much the theology of the Slavophiles, not so much their teaching about the Church itself, as it injured their philosophy of history, more exactly, their philosophy of society.[29]

III

The origin of Khomiakov's concept of *sobornost'* is a most difficult problem. Much of the difficulty lies in the fact that that concept has at least two distinct sets of affiliations and antecedents. On the one hand there is the teaching of the Orthodox Church; on the other, European romanticism.

Khomiakov was very well versed in the literature of the Orthodox Church. He learned Greek, Latin, and even Hebrew, as well as several Western European languages, in addition to Russian and Church Slavonic, and he used all this impressive scholarly equipment to study the Bible and the Doctors of the Church, to follow and criticize research and writing in the field of religion in several European countries, to compose his own

---

[28] V. S. Solov'ëv, *Sobranie sochinenii,* ed. E. L. Radlov (St. Petersburg, 1901), V, 185. Solov'ëv's writings against the Slavophiles were collected in the fifth volume of his works.

[29] G. V. Florovskii, *Puti russkogo bogosloviia* (Paris, 1937), p. 251. Indeed, Khomiakov's theological treatises are free from national or racial bias and are generally unexceptionable from the religious point of view. Even when he discusses the Church in his historical, literary, or journalistic works, or simply in private correspondence, his treatment of it is virtually impeccable. It is when he turns to other topics, to "the sphere of society," that the highly questionable concepts of Iranianism, of the Slavic character and the Russian mission, of the peasant commune, and of the popular assembly of the Russian land appear in profusion together with their attendant prejudices. In those passages in which Khomiakov discusses both the Church and his other favorite ideas interesting contrasts and contradictions result.

To cite just one such instance, a reference may be made to Khomiakov's analysis of religion and race in his outline of world history. Khomiakov follows Christian tradition in declaring: "The dissemination of opinion or of faith is not limited by the natural division into tribes . . . Faith and enlightenment belong equally to every thinking being, whether his skin is as black as coal or as poetically white as snow, and whether his hair is the curly felt of the African or the chestnut ornament of an English head." But, as we learn on the same page: "A certain nobility and purity from time immemorial distinguish the white tribe in Asia and in Europe." "In that tribe, and only in that tribe, were preserved the living tradition and the clear teaching of Iranian spirituality." Khomiakov, *Polnoe sobranie sochinenii,* 4th ed., V, 358–359.

theological treatises in French, to carry on a long and fascinating correspondence with the Oxford don, William Palmer, in English and to translate several of St. Paul's epistles into the Russian language. The discussion of *sobornyi*, which was written in French, in answer to a Russian Jesuit, and which derived its main argument from a comparative reading of the Greek and the Church Slavonic texts of the Creed, symbolized well much of Khomiakov's activity in the field of theology and religion. Some of this widely scattered effort was bound to be that of a dilettante, and the amateurishness of Khomiakov's scholarship became especially apparent when he took on such opponents as C. K. Bunsen. But the total impression produced by Khomiakov as student of religion and theologian is not only that of energy and enthusiasm, but also that of ability, originality, and learning.

In particular, Khomiakov knew his Bible, both the Old and the New Testament, very well. This is demonstrated not only by his polemical writings directed at the German higher critics, or by his translation of Pauline epistles, but also by the content, tone, and sometimes even style of his own theological treatises. Khomiakov also studied the Doctors of the Church, although we do not know the extent of this study. It should be emphasized that he willingly and gladly accepted the sacred writings of the Orthodox Church as his guide; in fact, these were the only writings he so accepted. And, of course, Khomiakov lived all his life as a member of the Orthodox Church. Therefore, it is appropriate to seek the origin of Khomiakov's concept of *sobornost'*, of this freedom in unity and truth in common love, in the fundamental tradition of the Orthodox Church and particularly in the words of St. Paul, to whom Khomiakov refers directly in his one definition and discussion of *sobornyi*.

But this is only one half of the story. The other is the fact that Khomiakov was a romantic intellectual, part and parcel of the romantic movement which swept Europe during the first decades of the nineteenth century.[30] Khomiakov's history, his philosophy, his poetry, and his fiction were all thoroughly romantic, and this is notably true of such concepts of his as the Iranian principle, the Slavic character, or the Russian mission. And these concepts were very closely connected with *sobornost'*. Furthermore, the idea of *sobornost'* itself was not foreign to the nineteenth century. Similar concepts could be found in such religious romanticists as F. Baader; more than that, they could be derived from the basic doctrines and aspirations of the entire romantic movement. Thus Khomiakov could have obtained his organic view of the Church from St. Paul and from various patristic sources, but the concept of organism and organic unity was also one of the most common, and most influential, fundamental ideas of European romanticism. Similarly, Khomiakov's attack on rationalism and his search for complete knowledge

[30] I analyzed the romantic nature of Slavophilism at length in my above-mentioned book.

and truth in *sobornost'* had countless counterparts in the assaults and the seekings of other romantic intellectuals, all of whom had rebelled against the Age of Reason. Again, the achievement of freedom in unity, another main aspect of *sobornost'*, was also another key theme of romanticism, and its treatment by various romantic thinkers closely paralleled Khomiakov's insistence on the inner belonging to and acceptance of the community as the way to eliminate all outer authority.

It seems that Khomiakov's romantic views had been formed before he turned to a thorough study of Orthodoxy. And when his theological treatises began to appear, many of those trained in Russian theological seminaries and academies, including at least one of Khomiakov's translators, found it difficult to understand these writings, let alone accept them. Indeed, the novelty of Khomiakov's approach to Orthodox theology is one of the very few things on which the admirers and the opponents of Khomiakov have been in agreement. Nor is the romantic influence in Khomiakov necessarily to be condemned as some religious critics have assumed. There is no a priori reason why romanticism could not serve Orthodox theology just as other philosophic doctrines served it in the past. Finally, it is necessary to note that romanticism itself cannot be properly understood without its Christian background.

Khomiakov's concept of *sobornost'* can be legitimately considered in two contexts: in the framework of the Orthodox theological tradition and in the framework of the European romantic movement. But his identification, juxtaposition, and confusion of the Church with things of this world has only one explanation — the romantic. For romanticism, in its rebellion against rationalism and skepticism, proceeded to create strange gods. In truth, the mighty idols of today, the idols of nation, and race, and class, all owe much to the romanticists. The latter did their work well: even now it takes an effort to realize that once upon a time, for instance in the Gospels, all these things were not believed.

Khomiakov was really a tragic figure. He remained throughout his life a devoted member of the Orthodox communion, and he became a brilliant theologian. He championed the One Holy Catholic and Apostolic Church, and he stigmatized the idolatries of the age. Yet, through the force of time and circumstance, he too became a prophet of the Iranian principle, of the superiority of the Slavs, of the Russian mission, and of other forms of darkness as well. There is a heart-rending contrast between his glorious vision of the Church and the militancy, passion, and evil of his national and his racial appeal. This duality was the tragedy of Khomiakov — and, perhaps, it is also the tragedy of the entire modern world.

Herzen and the Peasant Commune

MARTIN E. MALIA

Alexander Herzen has gone down in Russian history as the founding prophet of revolutionary Populism and the author of the theory that the repartitional commune could serve as the basis for the creation of socialism in Russia. Certainly the "discovery" of the commune for socialism is no small part of Herzen's significance. Yet it would be an error to reduce his socialism to this article of faith alone, and still further from the truth to construe his idealization of the commune as an indication of a "collectivist" bent of mind, fundamentally antagonistic to any form of "individualism." Paradoxically, Herzen eulogized the collectivism of the commune because he was first and last an intransigent libertarian and an uncompromising individualist. For Herzen, the commune was the ideal image of an anarchist Utopia.

Herzen's initial reaction to the commune was a negative one, because, significantly enough, at first glance it seemed to offer no possibility for the development of personal freedom. His attention was first called to the "socialist" character of the *obshchina* by the Slavophiles as early as 1843. His reaction to this claim was a categorical rejection:

> Our Slavophiles discourse on the communal principle, on the fact that we do not have a proletariat, on the division of lands [in the commune]; all these things are excellent seed-buds, but in part they are based on a primitive level of historical development; in the same way the right of private property among the Bedouins does not possess the egotistical European character; but they [the Slavophiles] forget that on the other hand there is a total impossibility of respect for one's self, they forget the stupid endurance of all sorts of oppression — in a word, they forget the impossibility of life under such conditions. Is it to be wondered at that our peasant has not developed the right of property in the sense of personal possession, when his strip of land is not his strip of land, when even his wife, daughter, and son are not his? What property can a slave have? He is worse than a proletarian. He is a *res*, a tool for the cultivation of the fields. His master may not kill him just as under Peter, in certain places, he could not cut down an oak; give him [the peasant] the right of trial by due process of law, and only then will he become a human being. Twelve million people *hors la loi. Carmen horrendum*.[1]

[1] A. I. Gertsen, *Dnevnik* for June 26, 1943, in *Polnoe sobranie sochinenii i pisem,* ed. M. K. Lemke, 22 vols. (Petrograd, 1919–1925), III, 177. This is the authoritative edition of Herzen's works and is hereafter cited as *Sochineniia,* the title of the work being given where this is deemed necessary.

For Herzen in 1843 the commune was not socialist since it failed to protect the sacred rights of the individual against the combined power of the state and the *pomeshchiki* (landowners). In the face of this fundamental defect, the supposedly "socialist" property arrangements of the commune sank into insignificance. For socialism to Herzen was much more than a set of administrative devices to secure the equal distribution of wealth; it was the exaltation of each man individually and of all men collectively as free and autonomous human beings.

Still the Slavophiles had planted a potent seed in Herzen's mind which the events of 1848 were to bring to fruition. Even before he left Russia, there were moments when he allowed himself to succumb, partially at least, to the seduction of the Slavophiles' suggestion:

> But do we have the right to say that the coming epoch, on whose banner is written, not the individual, but the commune (*obshchina*), not liberty, but fraternity, not abstract equality, but the organic division of labor, does not belong to Europe? In this is the whole question. Will the Slavs, fertilized by Europe, realize its ideal and unite decrepit Europe to their life, or will Europe unite us to her rejuvenated life? The Slavophiles decide such questions simply, as if the matter had been long since settled. There are signs [of a settlement] but we are far from a complete decision.[2]

The question, then, Europe or Russia, was at least an open one for Herzen. But on the whole before 1848 it seemed more logical to look for the answer in the revolutionary and already half-emancipated West than in enserfed Russia. With the failure of the West in 1848 to complete emancipation this no longer seemed so logical, and the old suggestion of the Slavophiles suddenly appeared more plausible.

It was in 1849 in an essay entitled "La Russie: à G.H.," usually referred to as the "Letter to Herwegh," that Herzen for the first time spelled out in full the conclusions he drew from the experience of 1848. In the course of the next four years he repeated his views in four other essays: "Du développement des idées révolutionnaires en Russie" and "The Russian People and Socialism: A Letter to Jules Michelet," both of which appeared, in French, in 1851,[3] followed in 1853 by "Baptized Property" (published by the Free Russian Press in Russian) and in 1854 by "The Old World and Russia. Letters to the Editor of *The English Republic*, W. Linton," in English.[4]

The form of Herzen's argument in all of these essays is the same: that of a contrast between Russia and the West. The "failure" of the Revolution

---

[2] *Dnevnik* for February 21, 1844, *ibid.*, p. 321.

[3] "Du développement des idées révolutionnaires en Russie," *ibid.*, VI, 197–297. "Russkii narod i sotsializm. Pis'mo k Zh. Mishle," given in Russian text only, *ibid.*, VI, 433–462.

[4] "Kreshchenaia sobstvennost'," *ibid.*, VII, 263–288, almost literally reproduced in English under the title "Russian Serfdom," for *The Leader* in the same year; "The Old World and Russia," *ibid.*, VIII, 339–360.

of 1848 had demonstrated that the West was "old," "decrepit," and incapable of further progress. The essence of Europe's "failure" was her inability to free herself from authoritarian ideas and institutions inherited from the past. Europe's successive revolutions, both ideological and political, had simply substituted one principle of authority for another — the deist for the theist, the republican for the monarchical — but transcendent moral values and the transcendent state still remained, and man was neither spiritually nor socially liberated.[5] The final and socialist revolution would, on the other hand, destroy *all* principles of authority, indeed the very principle itself of any authority external to the completely autonomous individual, coöperating freely and fraternally with other autonomous individuals. Europe was "old" because even the most radically minded members of European society were in the last analysis unable to cast aside the religious principle of authority, either in their thinking or in their politics. The sacred power of the sovereign state, with its courts, its police, and its armies, the Roman notion of inviolable property, the established churches, a transcendentally based code of morality, the sacred character of the family, in short, the whole "feudal, Catholic, Roman" tradition of Europe, all this was too highly and intricately developed for Europe ever to find the energy to shake herself free. Since 1789, in spite of three attempts at a revolutionary break with the past, in essence nothing had changed; or rather, things had changed for the worse, for with each unsuccessful attempt, and with each wave of reaction, Europe only dug herself in deeper. The need for radical change became more urgent, while at the same time "the life force ebbed away," dissipated in futile convulsions, such as that of 1848.

Put more simply, too many groups had a vested interest in preserving the structure of European society basically as it stood, and these groups were too strong for that society to be swept away completely. The Revolution of 1848 had "failed" because Europe was in the last analysis conservative, and Europe was conservative because most Europeans felt they had something worth conserving. Only an unorganized minority — the urban proletariat — acting out of desperation rather than knowledge, had a real interest in radical change; and this minority was strong enough only to frighten the rest of society into suicidal reaction, but not strong enough to destroy the old world.

But if the West was "old" Russia was "young." By Russia's "youth" Herzen meant several things at once. First of all he meant something quite metaphysical; the analogy with the life cycle of an organism was intended seriously. Russia was "young" because, historically speaking, she had experienced less and created less than Europe. But basically Herzen meant that Russia, unlike Europe, was not conservative, since so few groups in Russian society had a vested interest in the preservation of the *status quo*.

[5] *Ibid.,* VI, 434–435, and VIII, 29–38.

Almost the entire population was fundamentally and irreconcilably discontented with things as they were. The educated minority chafed under the lack of freedom imposed by the autocracy, as the revolt of the Decembrists showed. Above all, the peasantry was radically opposed to the whole existing social structure. An entire population had nothing to lose but its chains, unlike Europe where too numerous and too powerful segments of society had a great deal to lose besides their chains, and hence wore them all the more lightly.

Russia is in a completely different position [from Europe]. The walls of its prison are of wood; raised by brute force alone, they will give way at the first blow. A part of the people [the Westernized gentry], denying its entire past with Peter the Great, has shown what power of negation it possesses; the other part [the peasantry], remaining estranged from the present state structure, has submitted, but it has not accepted the new regime [the autocracy], which has the look of a temporary bivouac. People obey because they are afraid, but they do not believe.[6]

Unlike Europe, Russia presents a true "revolutionary situation" because no one, other than the autocracy and the insignificant minority that profits from autocracy, has a vested interest in the preservation of the existing state of affairs. Again unlike Europe, none of the institutions or values created by Russia's past is dear to any but the same minority. "We are free from the past because our past is empty, poor, and narrow. It is impossible to love such things as Moscovite tsarism or the Empire of Petersburg."[7] Europeanized minority and peasant majority alike rejected both Russia's past and its present totally and uncompromisingly. They were held in subjection by brute force alone, by a state power external and alien to them, and not by the self-imposed "moral servitude" to the past characteristic of Europe. "We are independent [of the past] because we have nothing, because there is nothing for us to be attached to; bitterness and resentment are in every memory."[8] Russians were anarchists and revolutionaries by nature and by history, and this for Herzen was the essence of their youthfulness.

Behind this perceptive analysis of the basic instability of the nineteenth-century autocracy lay a more dubious theory of Russian history. Its purpose was twofold: to justify the idea of Russia's youthfulness in the face of the long historical existence of the Russian state; and to vindicate the essentially revolutionary and democratic nature of the Russian people in the face of their centuries-long submission to tyranny and autocracy. The solution to both problems lay in proclaiming the Russian state to be of another essence than the Russian people, and in rejecting the autocracy as not really Rus-

[6] *Ibid.*, VI, 279.
[7] *Ibid.*, p. 280.
[8] *Ibid.*, VI, 456, and VIII, 25.

sian at all. By establishing a convenient distinction between the "true" Russia of the people and the "false" Russia of the state, Herzen abolished with one stroke both Russia's past history and the undemocratic aspects of that history. Reassured by this neat trick of metaphysical legerdemain, he was able to substitute his wishes for reality and to write in all tranquillity that:

The true history of Russia dates only from 1812; before that there had only been the introduction. The vital forces of the Russian people have never been effectively absorbed by their development, as have those of the Germano-Latin peoples." [9]

By eliminating the disagreeable aspects of the past as in a sense an illusion, the way was prepared for seeing only what he wanted to see.

The vision ran as follows. Originally, before the appearance of the state, the Slavs had lived a life of primitive democracy and socialism in the peasant commune, a type of free association which of all forms of social organization was most natural to the Slavic character.

In all the world there is perhaps no situation more compatible with the *Slavic character* than [that which existed] in the Ukraine from Kievan times to the period of Peter I.

Here was a Cossack and agricultural republic, ruled with military discipline, but on the basis of democratic communism, without any centralization, without any state power, subject only to ancient custom, submitting neither to the tsar of Moscow nor the king of Poland. There was no aristocracy; each individual who was of age was an active citizen; all offices, from sergeant to hetman, were elective . . . In the Ukraine, in Montenegro, and even in the case of the Serbs, the Illyrians, and the Dalmatians, everywhere the Slavic genius manifested its nature and aspirations but did not develop a strong political form. [10]

The state, when it appeared, was an alien force, imposed by harsh necessity, but not arising spontaneously out of the Russian character. The pressure of other peoples, the Mongols first, then later the "de-Slavicized" Poles and the Swedes, made necessary the creation of a strong centralized state in order to insure national survival. [11] Otherwise the Russians would have known the fate of the Balkan Slavs at the hands of the Turks, or the Czechs at the hands of the Austrian Germans — loss of independence and of national character. Later the mission of the state became to bring enlightenment, progress, and the influence of the West to Russia. [12] With this act Russia became a part of the main stream of human development. Still, in spite of these services, the state always remained an alien force in Russia, unlike the West, where the deified Roman state was a natural phenomenon. The "true" life of the nation withdrew into the still surviving peasant commune,

[9] *Ibid.,* VI, 209.
[10] *Ibid.,* VIII, 32.
[11] *Ibid.,* pp. 32–33.
[12] *Ibid.,* p. 33.

crushed under the weight of an imported Byzantine autocracy and a German bureaucracy, yet tenacious and vigorous:[13]

> The Slavic peoples, properly, like neither the state nor centralization. They prefer to live in scattered communes, as far removed as possible from all interference on the part of the government. They hate military organization, they hate the police. A federation would be the most authentically national form of organization for the Slavic peoples. The Petersburg period was a terrible ordeal, a painful education in state life. Forcibly it performed a useful function for Russia, uniting her scattered parts and welding them into a whole, but it must pass.[14]

But this alien state had never tapped the vital life forces of the people, those forces hidden in the democratic commune, where they had lain unused since the dawn of time. In fact one could say that the real history of the Russian people had not yet begun.

The "true" beginning of Russian history was heralded by signs that the age of the Russian state was drawing to a close. Since the time of Catherine the state had no longer served any historically useful purpose, neither one of national self-preservation, nor one of enlightenment. "The state, having separated itself from the people in the name of civilization, did not delay in renouncing enlightenment in the name of autocracy."[15] But this meant that the historical mission of the state had ended, and that it had become a parasite, a dead weight around the neck of the Russian people:

> It [the autocracy] renounced civilization as soon as through its aspirations began to appear the tricolored sign of liberalism; it tried to return to its national roots, to the people. But this was impossible. The people and the state no longer had anything in common: the former had become alienated from the latter, and the state seemed to see in the depth of the masses a new specter, a still more terrible specter — the *red* cock [symbol of peasant revolt].[16]

And from this time, state power and its preservation became an end in itself. But "autocracy for autocracy's sake in the end becomes impossible. It is too absurd, too sterile."[17] Repression at home and reactionary intervention abroad represented the only possible future for such a regime, until the day the red cock of *pugachëvshchina* would finally destroy it. "For such a regime nothing else remains to do but to conduct foreign war," and to become the gendarme of international reaction.[18] And this was the essence of Nicholas I's government, which Herzen hoped would be the end of the "old world" for Russia:

> The Winter Palace, like the summit of a mountain toward the end of autumn, is being covered more and more with snow and ice. The life-giving sap, artificially

[13] *Ibid.*, VI, 297.
[14] *Ibid.*, VIII, 45.
[15] *Ibid.*, VI, 448.
[16] *Ibid.*
[17] *Ibid.*
[18] *Ibid.*, VIII, 34.

raised to the governmental heights, is little by little freezing into immobility; there remains only force and the hardness of the cliff, still holding back the pressure of the revolutionary waves.[19]

The peasant masses were rumbling with discontent, and sooner or later the autocracy would have to face the alternative of liberation or revolt. But Nicholas hesitated, knowing that emancipation meant the beginning of the end of the entire "old world." "He has understood that emancipation of the peasants is linked with emancipation of the land, and that emancipation of the land in its turn is the beginning of a social revolution, the proclamation of agrarian communism." [20]

By "agrarian communism" Herzen did not mean simply the primitive communism and democracy of the Slavic peoples before the appearance of the state, the "Cossack republic" of the pre-Petrine Ukraine. The already existent "communism" and "democracy" of the commune would be only a beginning, the culmination of which would be the rationalist and libertarian Utopia, which Herzen called socialism:

The commune saved the Russian people from Mongolian barbarism and from imperial civilization, from the gentry with its European veneer and from the German bureaucracy. Communal organization, although strongly shaken, withstood the interference of the state; it survived fortunately *until the development of socialism in Europe.*" [21]

For the commune represented everything that Europe was not, and was vainly striving to become. First of all, by its very nature it was incompatible with the Roman and Western notion of the state. "Centralization is contrary to the Slavic spirit; federalism is far more natural to its character." [22] Hatred of the state, distrust of all political authority coming from above and claiming to transcend the free association of individuals in the commune, had been made second nature for the Russian because of his long and bitter experience with state power as it had existed in Russia. The Russian would never deify state power as did the European; politically speaking he was a natural-born anarchist. The proof of this was in the whole of Russian history; in the innumerable peasant revolts, from Bolotnikov to Pugachëv, and in the Cossack republics of the past;[23] in the uncompromising hostility of the Old Believers to the state and the established church;[24] in the people's ingrained distrust of all complicated, formalized administration by bureaucracy in the German manner: "the Russian people even today does not like paper dealings between equals; close the deal with a hearty handshake and a swig of

[19] *Ibid.,* VI, 448–449.
[20] *Ibid.,* p. 449.
[21] *Ibid.,* p. 447.
[22] *Ibid.,* p. 440.
[23] *Ibid.,* VII, 278.
[24] *Ibid.,* VI, 446.

vodka, and that's an end to it." [25] If state power and a complicated administrative machinery as such were incompatible with true freedom — and Herzen was convinced they were — then Russia presented far more favorable conditions for a truly libertarian revolution than did Europe.

The same contrast could be seen in the Russian's attitude to the traditional Western means for maintaining public order — the law, the courts, and the police. The European made a fetish of these things; the Russian had nothing but hatred for them, submitting only under the compulsion of force. The Russian's instinctive reaction to the law and the courts was not respect, but evasion and noncoöperation. "The sentence of a court does not blacken a man in the eyes of the Russian people: exiles and convicts are called by him the *unfortunate*." [26] A giant conspiracy of an entire people existed against the official law and the agents of its enforcement. On the other hand, the people settled such legal problems as the state left in their hands through the commune peacefully and justly by the free coöperation of equals. Judges, like all officials of the commune, were freely elected; there was no distinct judicial class any more than there was a distinct bureaucratic class in the submerged world of the commune.[27] All its affairs were administered and its members judged by their freely elected equals, as in the old days before the coming of the state. The use of force or any formal constraint by the commune on its members was unknown. Likewise deceit was nonexistent in personal dealings between peasants: "between them reigns almost unlimited confidence; they know no formal contracts or written understandings." [28] Moreover, the peasant mentality was deeply democratic and egalitarian, formed as it was by this state of affairs. "The Russian peasant knows no morality which does not arise instinctively and naturally from his communism; and this morality is deeply rooted in the character of the people." [29] Here indeed — or so at least it might seem with the application of a little good will — was the socialist ideal of equality through fraternal coöperation already present in embryonic form.

The same was true with respect to the question of property. The European made an idol of the right to private property. The Russian peasant knew neither the institution nor the idea. His understanding of property was profoundly "communist." [30] The *pomeshchik's* property right to the land had never been recognized by the peasant. Land belonged to the community, and each member had an equal right to its use, but never to absolute ownership of it in the Roman and Western sense. And, of course, the irrefutable

---

[25] *Ibid.*, VII, 269.
[26] *Ibid.*, VI, 445.
[27] *Ibid.*, VIII, 51.
[28] *Ibid.*, VI, 445.
[29] *Ibid.*, p. 446.
[30] See "Annexe" to "Du développement des idées révolutionnaires en Russie," *ibid.*, VI, 293–297, for the fullest exposition of Herzen's ideas on this subject.

proof of this was the practice of periodic redivision of the land among the members of the commune. In so far as they were left to their own devices, the peasants treated property in the same democratic manner in which they administered justice and decided questions of communal government — by election and on a basis of the complete equality of all members of the *obshchina*. With property, as with questions relating to the public order, all was harmony and coöperation in the commune; nowhere was there coercion or constraint.

Now the periodic redistribution of land is obviously what made possible Herzen's belief in the socialist future of the commune; without this it would be impossible to associate the commune with Western socialism. Yet it is significant that in the finished theory this trait bulks no larger than communal self-government, administration of justice by elected officials, and the psychological characteristics of the peasants — distrust of the state, of bureaucracy, and in general of all authority. He writes of all these things with equal enthusiasm and often at greater length than of the periodic redistribution of land. And with respect to the latter he seems to be as much impressed by the fraternal harmony with which it is carried out as by the principle of collective ownership on which it is based:

[The peasant] has preserved only his insignificant, modest commune; i.e., the possession in common of the land, the *equality* of all members of the commune without exception, the *fraternal* division of the fields according to the number of workers, and the *autonomous direction* by the commune of its affairs.[31]

The grass-roots democracy of the commune is emphasized fully as much as its "communism." And again:

The problems of marking off the boundaries of fields are necessarily very complicated in the constant divisions of land according to the number of households; nevertheless the process is carried out without complaints or lawsuits . . . Minor disagreements are submitted for judgment to the elders or to the assembly of the commune, and their decisions are accepted unconditionally by all. The same is true in the artels.[32]

What is essential in the commune is not so much the collective ownership of land as the absence of constraint and of authority imposed from above. But this is quite consistent with Herzen's conception of socialism as the religion of the unconditional liberation of the individual. He was first drawn to the commune by the obvious parallel it presented with the various collectivist devices recommended by Western socialism. Yet in the last analysis he idealized the commune not so much for this as for the more general trait of the voluntary association of equals he saw in all aspects of the commune: in administration, in justice, and in a generally antiauthoritarian mentality, as much as in matters of property.

[31] *Sochineniia,* VII, 279. Italics mine.
[32] *Ibid.,* VI, 446.

That this was the essence of the commune's socialism for Herzen is shown by the reservations he entertained concerning it. He had to admit that a collectivist form of social organization by its very nature was somewhat detrimental to the development of the individual, who was "swallowed up" by the commune.[33] The commune as it stood was far from adequate; it would become truly socialist only when some means was found for combining it with freedom for the individual in the Western sense. "To keep the commune and give freedom to the individual, to spread that self-government now existing in the villages and the districts to the cities and to the whole country, while at the same time preserving national unity — in this consists the question of the future of Russia." [34]

Herzen knew from history that a peasant commune by itself did not lead to socialism. All peoples possessed the commune in their "youth." Western Europe had once possessed it, but had lost it in the development that led through feudalism and Roman notions of private property to a one-sided and "antisocial individualism." [35] The Asiatic peoples, too, had once possessed the commune, but it had led to nothing because they had been unwilling to renounce a narrow self-sufficiency and enter into the main stream of history as represented by Europe.[36] Russia, unlike Europe, was "young" in that she still possessed the commune; moreover, unlike Asia, she had shown a remarkable capacity to renounce her own narrow past, as the "antinational" revolution of Peter and the Westernization of the educated classes clearly showed. Russia, then, found herself in an extraordinarily favored historical position. "Fortunately, we arrive with our commune in an age when anticommunal [individualistic] civilization has run up against the absolute impossibility of resolving, on the basis of its principles, the contradiction between individual right and social right." [37]

In less Hegelian language, the coming era of socialism would result from the fusion of the democratic equality of the Russian commune with the Western principle of the dignity of the individual. Young Russia, awakened at last to a truly historical existence by the "West, which alone could still illumine the abyss of Russian life," carrying on where the European creative effort left off, would lead mankind on to a "future henceforth common to Orient and Occident." [38] Far from turning its back on the West, or withdrawing into its own purely Slavic past, as reactionaries such as the Slavophiles desired, salvation for Russia lay in assimilating the heritage left by the West — scientific enlightenment and a heightened sense of the worth of

[33] *Ibid.*, VIII, 49.
[34] *Ibid.*
[35] *Ibid.*, VI, 296.
[36] *Ibid.*, VIII, 47.
[37] *Ibid.*, VI, 296.
[38] *Ibid.*, p. 282.

the individual — and in developing the primitive peasant commune to accommodate these principles.

To do this it was not necessary for Russia to retrace the historical evolution of the West. Russia could simply appropriate for her own uses the historical conquests of the West — enlightenment and individualism. "Russia has gone through her revolutionary embryogeny in 'the European class' . . . The Russian people does not need to begin from the beginning this heavy labor." [39] Indeed, to retrace the bourgeois development of the West would be fatal to the one advantage Russia's "youth" conferred on her — the commune — and was therefore something to be avoided at all costs. In particular, the bourgeois notion of private property would destroy the "communism" of the *obshchina,* and turn the peasantry into the same defenseless rural proletariat that existed in the West. When the historical form of the future was socialism, repetition of the Western development would be historical suicide for Russia:

> The Russian people has suffered everything, but has retained the commune; the commune will save the Russian people; to destroy it would be to hand the people over, tied hand and foot, to the *pomeshchik* and the police. And to touch the commune at a time when Europe is bemoaning the parceling out of her countryside and is striving with all her strength toward some sort of communal social order! [40]

For Herzen the Russians were by nature an agricultural people, and presumably would always remain so.[41] He never seems to have envisioned the possibility of an urban, industrial development for Russia. So when he proclaimed that it would be unnecessary for Russia to retrace the European development, he was not thinking of bourgeois industry but of bourgeois legal forms — private property and Roman law. In particular, he was arguing against emancipation of the peasantry without the land and against destruction of the commune: [42]

> Imagine the European agricultural situation with Petersburg autocracy, with our bureaucrats, with our rural police. Imagine twenty million proletarians seeking work on the gentry's lands, in a country where there is no legality, where all government is venal and aristocratic, where the individual is nothing and influence is all.[43]

When Herzen said that Russia need not repeat the European historical development he meant, as always, at the same time something quite metaphysical and something quite concrete, in this case, no individual emancipation without land. To adopt a European solution to the peasant problem

[39] *Ibid.,* VIII, 46.
[40] *Ibid.,* VII, 277.
[41] *Ibid.,* p. 267.
[42] *Ibid.,* pp. 276–280.
[43] *Ibid.,* p. 276.

would be to forfeit Russia's historical chances for a socialist future; still worse, it would be inhuman for the present.

And, how, in Herzen's view, was the principle of individuality to be united with that of the commune? Through the intermediary of those members of the Westernized minority who, like the Decembrists and the radicals of his own generation, were in revolt against the existing order. Like the peasantry, this group was "young" and "free of the past" in that its only inheritance was slavery and degradation. Unlike the European intellectual, the educated Russian could afford to be ruthlessly revolutionary; already a gagged slave, what could he lose, since he had nothing, not even the "half-freedoms" of the West:

> Thrown into an oppressive world, armed with a clear view and an incorruptible logic, the Russian quickly frees himself from the faith and the ways of his fathers.
> The thinking Russian is the most independent man in the world. What can stop him? Respect for the past? But what is the starting point of modern Russian history if not a negation of nationality and tradition? [Peter.]
> Or perhaps, the tradition of the Petersburg period? This tradition, this "fifth act of a bloody drama transpiring in a brothel," binds us to nothing; on the contrary, it unbinds us definitively.
> On the other hand, the past of the Western peoples serves as a lesson for us and nothing more. In no way do we consider ourselves the executors of their historical testament.[44]

The Russian could be absolutely logical in his criticism of inherited ideas and institutions, since the Russia of Nicholas I was so obviously absurd, oppressive, and inhuman that no enlightened, civilized person could feel any attachment to it, or want to preserve any part of it. Nor was the Europeanized Russian moderated in his revolt by his European education. It did not mean the same thing to him, an outsider, as it did to a European. On the European his civilization conferred tangible, if imperfect, benefits; it meant parliaments, free speech, partial enlightenment, and a decent life, at least for some. On the Russian, contact with European civilization conferred no tangible benefits; it simply furnished a corrosive comparison that enflamed his hatred and fanned his revolt, leading him to demand revolution where the European was content with reform. A European education, far from inspiring in the Russian any sentimental loyalty to a past which was not his, made him equally discontent with the barbarism of Russia and the pusillanimity of Europe. In short, it made him the ideal revolutionary, unafraid to follow ideas through to their logical conclusion:

> We share your [Europe's] doubts, but your faith does not warm us. We share your hate, but we do not understand your attachment to what your ancestors have bequeathed to you; we are too oppressed, too unhappy to be content with half-

44 *Ibid.*, VI, 455–456.

freedom. You are bound by scruples, you are held back by *arrière-pensées*. We have no *arrière-pensées*, no scruples. We lack only strength.[45]

There could be no clearer statement, or no better explanation, of the traditional maximalism of the Russian radical than this.

The presence of this deeply revolutionary class in Russia was almost as much the source of Herzen's hope for the future as was the commune. To be sure, the commune was the more important of the two, and Herzen always deferentially ceded the first place to the peasant. "We Russians who have passed through Western civilization, we are no more than a means, a leaven, no more than intermediaries between the Russian people and revolutionary Europe. The man of the future in Russia is the *peasant*, just as in France he is the *worker*." [46] Still, the revolutionary gentry was as essential as the peasantry. Without it the commune could not become truly socialist. Indeed, Herzen speaks almost as much of the intellectuals as he does of the peasant. The bulk of "Du développement des idées révolutionnaires en Russie" is devoted to the awakening of the radical gentry. Half of the "Letter to Michelet" is concerned with the same. The peasantry alone, without the "leaven" of the radical gentry, could never advance beyond a primitive stage of development, just as the "communism" of the *obshchina*, without personal freedom and the full development of the individual, would never give socialism. Europe and Russia, collectivism and individualism, peasantry and radical gentry were equally necessary for the creation of the "new world" of socialism.

This, then, was the context of revolutionary hopes in which Herzen situated his belief in the peasant commune. These hopes were not tied exclusively, or even primarily, to the collectivist property arrangements prevailing in the *obshchina*. They arose much more from the structure of Russian society as a whole. For Herzen the coming revolution had to be maximalist, or it would not be a real revolution at all. And Russian society presented a unique set of conditions for the realization of this revolution. No appreciable group in Russia was tied either by interest or by sentiment to existing institutions or values; an alien state, standing for nothing more positive than blind preservation of the *status quo*, was holding in subjection, by brute force alone, both peasant mass and educated minority, whose every instinct demanded a revolutionary reversal of the *status quo*:

Too many chains lay upon us for us voluntarily to lay on more. In this respect we are on a footing of complete equality with our peasants. We submit to brute force. We are slaves because we do not have the possibility of freeing ourselves, but we accept nothing from our enemies.

Russia will never be Protestant.

Russia will never be *juste-milieu*.

[45] *Ibid.*, p. 456.
[46] *Ibid.*, p. 450.

Russia will never make a revolution with the aim of getting rid of Tsar Nicholas and of replacing him with tsar-representatives, tsar-judges, tsar-policemen.[47]

The essence of Herzen's theory is that *Russia could never be moderate in her rejection of authority imposed from without*. His attitude toward the commune fits in quite logically with this view. For the commune represents this radical negation of external authority in three essential respects: negation of the Roman idea of the state as something that transcends the sum of the individuals that compose it; negation of the Roman idea of law as something that exists over and above the freely expressed will of the members of the community; negation of the sacred right of private property as something that transcends the humane purposes for which material wealth ought to exist. The commune was socialist and revolutionary because it was the living negation of all authority not based on voluntary association. As such Herzen's idealization of it was perfectly in harmony with his fundamentally individualistic and libertarian cast of thought.

The question remains of how deeply and exclusively Herzen's socialism was committed to the commune, even after 1848. In actual fact his theory admitted of several significant reservations. First of all, the socialist development of the commune was by no means expected to work itself out automatically. "I do not believe that this [development] is *necessary*, but that it is *possible*. Nothing is ineluctably necessary." [48] The future would depend on the energy of the enlightened elements of Russian society, for example in preventing emancipation without land. It would also depend on what would happen in Europe:

It does not follow that we should believe blindly in the future. Every seed has a right to development, but not every one develops. The future of Russia depends not on her alone. It is linked with the future of Europe. Who can predict the fate of the Slavic world if reaction and absolutism should definitively conquer the revolution in Europe." [49]

Moreover, Herzen's optimism regarding the commune depended to a large degree on the circumstances and the moment of writing. For example, the "Letter to Michelet" had been provoked by some deprecatory remarks Michelet made about Russians in an article on the Polish revolutionary hero, Kosciuszko. Herzen began his reply with a categorical assertion of faith in the commune. In the course of composition, however, the second installment of Michelet's article appeared, in which he took a more friendly attitude toward Russians. Immediately Herzen's tone became less confidently optimistic.

[47] *Ibid.*, p. 457.
[48] *Ibid.*, VIII, 38.
[49] *Ibid.*, VI, 457.

For us the hour of action has not yet struck; in justice France may still be proud of her forward position. Until 1852 [the date set for the election of Louis Napoleon's successor] to her belongs an onerous right. Europe without doubt will reach the grave or a new life before us. The hour of action for us perhaps is still far off.[50]

We should not be deceived by the rhetoric and the apocalyptic imagery. The socialist future of the commune was a hope and not a certainty for Herzen. In spite of habitual recourse to the notion of natural "laws" in history governing the growth and decay of nations, and of flaming invocations of the inexorability of change, Herzen never maintained that his theory was "scientific" or that the evolution he envisaged was inevitable in any sense. This perhaps was inconsistent, but then the logic of Herzen's life lay not so much in his ideas as in his monolithic devotion to liberty. In reality his historicism was a very vague and flexible thing, capable of accommodating almost unlimited quantities of free will. In the last analysis his belief in the commune is presented only as plausible, no more; it is an expression of desire much more than of certitude.

Nor was Herzen really proclaiming Russian superiority over the West, as any real Slavophile must. In spite of a certain hyperbole he was no more certain that Europe was "dying" than he was that the commune would necessarily develop along socialist lines. What his glorification of the commune really proclaimed was Russia's equality with the West, and in order to make his point he often overstated it. In less polemical moods, however, he knew how to moderate his claims, as in the passage last quoted, or in the following:

Europe . . . has not resolved the antinomy between the individual and the state, but she has set herself the task of resolving it. Russia too has not found the solution. Before this question begins *our equality*.[51]

Or again, in still more revealing terms:

It is painful and ugly to live in Russia, this is true; and it was all the more painful for us in that we thought that in other countries it was easy and agreeable to live.

Now we know that even there it is painful, because there too that question around which the whole energy of mankind now centers has not been solved — the question of the relationship of the individual to society and of society to the individual. Two extreme, one-sided developments have led to two absurdities: to the Englishman, proud of his rights and independent, whose independence is founded on a form of polite cannibalism, and to the poor Russian peasant, impersonally swallowed up in the village commune, given over into serfdom without rights and, in virtue of this, become the "victuals" of the landowner.

How are these two developments to be reconciled, how is the contradiction between them to be resolved? How is the independence of the Englishman to be

[50] *Ibid.*, p. 458.
[51] *Ibid.*, p. 450.

kept without the cannibalism, how is the individuality of the [Russian] peasant to be developed without the loss of the principle of the commune? Precisely in this [dilemma] lies the whole agonizing problem of our century, precisely in this consists the whole [problem] of socialism.[52]

Here Herzen is saying "we *too* have something to offer," much more than "we *alone* have anything to offer," and this is the import of all his thinking on the commune.

But this brings us to the question of Herzen's underlying motives in idealizing the commune. As the passage last quoted suggests, hurt national pride was certainly one of them. Nothing irked Herzen more than the combination of arrogance and ignorance with which Western Europeans dismissed Russia as a morass of reaction and barbarism, unrelieved by even the glimmerings of enlightenment or the stirrings of protest. As the critic Mikhail Gershenzon has pointed out, one of Herzen's motives in calling attention to the commune was to prove this blithe assumption false by showing that Russia was just as socialist and revolutionary as Europe, indeed perhaps even more so, and hence deserving of respect and consideration by the European Left as a fellow sufferer, instead of contempt and scorn as the enemy of all progressive mankind.[53] In the passage last quoted England and Russia are put on an equal footing; both are "backward" and both are "progressive," but each in different respects, and in the last analysis there was little to choose between the two. The Russian needed to feel no inferiority toward the West, just as the airs of superiority of the European were unjustified and uncalled for. Russians at least realized their inadequacies; they were humble and willing to learn from the West. Europeans might well imitate this humility and recognize that they had something to learn from Russia, in particular that the commune might very conceivably prove to be the salvation of both in the terrible revolutionary crisis they had got themselves into together. It is significant that four out of the five essays Herzen wrote on the commune were first published in Western languages — three in French and one in English — that the fifth was almost immediately translated into English, and that all but one were intended primarily to convince a Western public. In particular the "Letter to Michelet" was called forth by what Herzen felt to be an insult to the revolutionary honor of Russia. In attempting to defend this honor before a skeptical and prejudiced West, Herzen often claimed more for Russia than he really intended, and made his hopes for the commune sound more unequivocal than they were in reality.

But national pride, in order to be hurt, had first to exist; if Herzen was a socialist, he was also — and just as deeply — a Russian patriot, and it was his patriotism which in the last analysis determined his belief in the com-

---

[52] *Ibid.*, VII, 279–280.
[53] See M. Gershenzon, "Gertsen i zapad," in *Obrazy proshlogo* (Moscow, 1912).

mune. But here a word of caution is in order. Herzen was not an exclusive nationalist, still less an aggressive one. His friendly attitude toward the Poles, all his life long, and in particular during the revolt of 1863, is in itself sufficient proof of this.[54] He was a nationalist after the manner of Mazzini rather than of Treitzschke. He believed in the natural right of every national group to political and cultural autonomy and in the fraternal coöperation of peoples, just as he held the autonomy of the individual sacred. Under no circumstances could he condone the oppression of one people by another, even if the oppressor were Russia, as in the case of Poland. Yet within this context he was deeply patriotic, and although his whole life was devoted to the liberation of man in general he was quite naturally concerned in the first instance with the liberation of Russia. But to fight for the liberation of Russia it was first necessary to believe that liberation was possible. Hence the violence with which he reacted against all Western suggestions to the contrary, as in the case of the "Letter to Michelet." Hence the readiness with which he seized on whatever encouraging elements existed in the Russian situation — the commune and the awakening of the radical intelligentsia — inflating and exaggerating their "socialist" significance in order the better to flatter his hopes. This was no doubt wishful thinking; but what could be more natural in someone who was at the same time a socialist and a Russian patriot? And it was all the more natural in that there seemed nowhere else to turn, since as of 1848 Europe had sadly disappointed those hopes for a liberation common to all mankind once so trustingly confided in her.

Yet it must be pointed out that this sort of wishful thinking was by no means peculiar to Herzen, or even to Russians. It was the stock in trade of radicals of the day all over Europe. In fact, Herzen's belief in the commune is but one of many examples of a phenomenon common to all currents of social reform in his day and in ours — the fixation of Utopian hopes on some seemingly promising institution, on some plausible device, which if properly used would automatically realize the aspirations associated with it. Like radicals of his day all over Europe, Herzen basically believed in three things: the people, the nation, and liberty — but most of all liberty, indeed liberty to the point of anarchy. A first fixation — the old capital of revolution, Paris — satisfied only the last of these beliefs, but let the other two go begging — obviously an unsatisfactory situation. After 1848 it satisfied

[54] Herzen's attitude on the Polish question is, I think, sufficient refutation of those writers who see in his "Slavophilism" the expression of an aggressive nationalism. See, for example, Jan Kucharzewski, *The Origins of Modern Russia* (New York, 1948), ch. iv, and Alexander von Schelting, *Russland und Europa im russischen geschichtsdenken* (Bern, 1948). For a reply to von Schelting, in particular with respect to his opinions on Herzen, see B. I. Elkin, "The Conflict between East and West: a Philosophical and Historical Approach," *The Slavonic and East European Review*, XXVII, no. 69 (May 1949), 579–592.

none of them. But this cleared the way for a far more satisfactory fixation, which satisfied all three simultaneously — the Russian peasant commune. Herzen seized on it with a mixture of enthusiasm and desperation which silenced all objections. The result was a theory of socialism peculiarly Russian. But the hopes it embodied and the process of fixation of these hopes were general to the age.

To take just one contemporary example, John Stuart Mill's infatuation with Coöperation in the latter part of his life is as instructive as any. Like Herzen, Mill believed in the people and in liberty, perhaps not to the point of anarchy, but very near to it. Nationalism, whether political or cultural, was not a sensitive point with him, since as an Englishman living in a century dominated by English values he only felt comfortably, if unaggressively, superior to other nations. Unlike Herzen, he was no radical and no revolutionary, nor was he given to immoderate use of rhetoric; but then as an Englishman he was not faced by an arbitrary and autocratic power which made moderate opposition and a calm tone of voice an unlikely attitude. Yet this difference, capital though it is, should not obscure the equally important fact that the two shared a common devotion to libertarian democracy. And, after 1848, Mill reached, in more moderate and tentative form, conclusions Herzen had arrived at earlier: that true freedom could not be achieved without some form of collective ownership and enjoyment of wealth. Since he was a constitutionalist and a moderate he rejected revolution as a means to achieve this end. Since he was of an empirical bent of mind he was not attracted by imaginary fantasies such as the Fourierist phalanstery; he wanted something real and existing. Since he lived in an industrial and commercial society he looked around for a device which would provide for the fraternal coöperation of equals in that kind of society. He found the device which met these three qualifications in the nascent Coöperative movement, and his attitude toward it was in all essential respects the same as Herzen's toward the commune, and not one whit less Utopian. In 1852 Mill wrote:

> The form of association, however, which if mankind continue to improve, must be expected in the end to predominate, is not that which can exist between a capitalist as chief, and work-people without a voice in the management, but the *association of the laborers themselves on terms of equality, collectively owning* the capital with which they carry on their operations, and working under *managers elected and removable by themselves.*[55]

In 1862 he expatiated:

> It is hardly possible to take any but a hopeful view of the prospects of mankind, when, in two leading countries of the world [France and England], the *obscure depths of society contain simple working men* whose integrity, good sense,

[55] J. S. Mill, *Principles of Political Economy*, ed. W. J. Ashley (London, New York, Toronto, 1929), pp. 772–773. Italics mine.

self-command and *honorable confidence in one another* have enabled them to carry these noble experiments to a triumphant issue.[56]

And three years later he added:

It is scarcely possible to rate too highly this material benefit, which yet is as nothing compared to the *moral revolution in society* that would accompany it: . . . the *transformation of human life,* from a conflict of classes struggling for opposite interests, to a *friendly rivalry* in the pursuit of a good common to all; a new sense of *security and independence* in the laboring class; and the conversion of each human being's daily occupation into a *school of the social sympathies* and the practical intelligence.[57]

In all essential respects Mill's vision of a grass-roots socialist democracy is the same as Herzen's; only the device for bringing it about is different. Mill, as an Englishman and a moderate, fixed his hopes on Coöperation; Herzen, as a revolutionary and a Russian, fixed his on the *obshchina;* but the ends that both devices were expected to serve were identical, as was the process of fixation itself.

But there are kinds and degrees of fixation, and practical consequences vary radically according to both. Neither Herzen nor Mill committed themselves completely or irrevocably to their respective Utopian devices. For both, the means advocated remained less important than the ends it was hoped they would serve. Another of Herzen's contemporaries, Marx, represents a very different case. For Marx the end was the same as for Herzen, or for Mill, or for men of good will in general among their generation: the liberation of man. But the means upon which Marx's hopes fixed — the class struggle in an industrial society — were of a very different kind, and the degree of fixation much greater than in the case of Herzen. Herzen's commune, like Mill's Coöperation, was a weak reed, and he knew it. It did not necessarily and of itself lead to socialism; it had to be pushed. It had no historical dynamism of its own (although socialism as a general idea did); the dynamism which would bring socialism out of the commune had to be supplied from without by the intelligence, the effort, the devotion — in short, the free will — of individuals. Socialism was a creation of man rather than a product of nature. But Marx needed to rely on nothing so aleatory or capricious as the desires, the hopes, or the mere will of man, for he had fixed on an infinitely more real and potent revolutionary force than Herzen's commune. Industrialization and the power of technology were unmistakably transforming the world. The class tensions this process created had proved in numerous real insurrections that they were cracking the existing structure of society. These were hard, "scientific" facts, and no mere Utopian wishes. The vessel of Marx's hopes was self-moving; it contained in itself its own historical dynamism; industrialization led necessarily and

[56] *Ibid.,* pp. 788–789.
[57] *Ibid.,* pp. 789–790.

inevitably to socialism. No amount of effort, no act of the will could change things *fundamentally* one way or the other; and to think so was sentimental, "idealistic," and "Utopian." That this is the basic implication of Marx, can, I think, be maintained in spite of the ambiguous reservation he included in his system to the effect that the "inevitable" is brought about only through human agents, that socialism will not just arrive of itself, and that effort and will, after all, are required. Marx, to a degree, attempts to have things both ways; but basically he has things the way of determinism, and the general tone of his thought is one of scorn for the wrong-headed, naïve desires and aspirations of mere individuals, an attitude which begins to tread seriously on the toes of any meaningful idea of liberty, and an attitude which is utterly foreign to Herzen.

Now there is no denying that Marx had seized on a real force making for revolutionary and, in a sense, unavoidable change, whereas Herzen had hit upon an institution without a future, socialist or otherwise. But that the force was real does not mean that the changes it was operating were necessarily those that Marx thought. And his particular form of utopianism was to have failed to distinguish between the force, which was real, and his vision, which was not, and thereby to have treated as a positive science what was in fact an eschatology. The confusion is perhaps understandable in view of the impressive nature of the historical force involved, but the consequences were none the less an essentially authoritarian, rather than a libertarian, version of socialism. Marx made that total, irrevocable, and intolerant commitment to his particular scheme which Herzen never made. There was no socialism but historical materialism, and Marx was its prophet. Such a position is at the same time dogmatic and authoritarian, since the fixation on which it is based has come to be synonymous with absolute truth itself.

But Herzen's fixation was most decidedly not of this sort. Where Marx felt he could be certain, Herzen was only hopeful. His psychological commitment to the commune was not absolute; it was always relative to the libertarian ends he hoped the commune would serve, and never did advocacy of this particular means imply possession of absolute truth. In this Herzen is much nearer to Mill than to Marx: liberal as opposed to authoritarian and dogmatic, if not as opposed to revolutionary and maximalist. The only absolute commitment in Herzen's socialism was to liberty, to a ceaseless war against all authority not freely consented to by the individual. And it is significant that the authoritarians of the Russian Revolution when it finally came were the spiritual heirs of Marx. That all of his heirs were not in this camp, as the example of the Mensheviks shows, indicates that Marxism does not lead to this alone; it is sufficiently complex — or sufficiently ambiguous — to lend itself to more than one construction. But the fact remains that one of the most obvious and easy of these constructions is authoritarian. On the other hand, that none of Herzen's heirs was in this camp attests with equal significance that his tradition does not lend itself to an authoritarian construction at all. Both wings of the Socialist Revolutionaries, the Right sooner, and the Left later, refused to accept coercion by a minority, no matter how pure its intentions, as a substitute for the free consent of the majority and the creation of socialism from below by the masses. The villain of the piece, if villain there must be, was not Herzen, or people who thought like him, the Lavrovs, the Mikhailovskiis, the Chernovs, or even the Spiridonovas. All collectivist theories are not necessarily authoritarian; and we should not let the letter of Herzen's socialism deceive us as to its spirit. Although the former may have been collectivist, this in itself tells us relatively little; what is important is that the latter was profoundly and uncompromisingly individualistic, open, and liberal.

Stalin and the Collective Farm

JOHN D. BERGAMINI

"Stalin, the Greatest Reformer of Agriculture of All Times and All Nations"
— so runs a title in a Cominform periodical of four years ago. We may take
issue only in part with this particular example of Soviet idolatry: we may
disagree with the epithet "reformer" and we may balk at "great man"
interpretations of history, as did Stalin himself on occasion. Yet, we cannot
ignore one basic proposition, the probability that the late Russian dictator
presided over greater changes in the fate of a greater number of farmers
than did any other individual.

Stalin was not the discoverer of the collective farm, but he was the chief
theoretician as well as chief administrator of mass collectivization in Russia
and presumably was a major consultant in the export of the radically new
agricultural institutions to the peasant millions of Eastern Europe and
China. On this much all scholars will agree. Also significant but hardly ad-
missible by Soviet historians is the likelihood that the collective farm system
is intimately tied to Stalin's subjectively motivated conquest, consolidation,
and maintenance of power.

A study of Stalin's *Collected Works*[1] reveals much of his scheme of the
transition from individualism to collectivism in the countryside. There are
definite limitations, of course, to the simple organization and reporting of
Stalin's views, the approach used here because of demands of time and
space. Ideally, the writings of Stalin should be analyzed with greater consideration given to contemporary events, to his actions and influence in
policy-making, and to the views of his opponents.

These are some of the pertinent questions: Stalin's general approach to
the peasant problem, his analysis of the need for the collective farm, his

[1] Actually four titles by Stalin are used for this study. His writings from 1901 to
1934 are contained in the *Sochineniia,* Vols. I–XIII (Moscow, 1946–1952). Some of the
same writings and later materials are found in English translation by the Foreign
Languages Publishing House: *Problems of Leninism* (Moscow, 1940), hereafter cited as
*Leninism; History of the Communist Party of the Soviet Union (Bolsheviks): Short
Course* (Moscow, 1939) — hereafter, *History;* and *Economic Problems of Socialism in
the USSR* (Moscow, 1952) — hereafter, *Economic Problems.*

view of the prerequisites of mass collectivization, his appraisal of the results, his concept of the future collective farm, and his thought on the applicability of his program in other countries. While dealing with these specific points, there will be opportunity to touch upon the broader problems of foresight, consistency, clarity, and realism in Stalin's thinking and to assess the matter of dogma or expediency in his action.

I. THE PEASANT PROBLEM

The repeated statements by Stalin that the peasant problem is not the fundamental problem of Leninism add up to the conviction that the goals for future society are non-peasant, even anti-peasant goals. To base one's social schemes on the wants, the needs, the potentialities of the majority of the population in Russia made one a "simple peasant philosopher" and not a scientific Marxist.[2] This was the mistake of the Socialist Revolutionary Party, which failed to realize, wrote Stalin in 1905, "that the city appears as the leader of the countryside, and, accordingly, that any socialist deed should begin with the city."[3] Stalin's contention that the blueprinting of the "good society" should and would be done by the proletarian minority, or by its minority of Bolshevik spokesmen, arose from the notion that the proletariat is the advanced social force which fulfills the economic law of the necessity of harmonizing production forces and production relations. The goals were objectively founded, he modestly explained, and were not "the whim of economic adventurers."[4]

The nature of these city-orientated goals is familiar enough, even if such terms as "socialism" and "communism" want precision. One formulation by Stalin will serve to stress the key problems:

> To create the economic base of socialism means to merge farming with socialist industry in one integral economy, to subordinate farming to the direction of socialist industry, to set up relations between city and country on the basis of exchange of products of farming and industry, to create in the long-run such conditions of production and distribution as will lead directly and immediately to the elimination of classes.[5]

The goal of industrialization mentioned above has special bearing on the peasant problem. When Stalin asserted "we must transform our country from an agrarian country into an industrial country and the faster the better,"[6] he was thinking of more than general welfare, defense, and future abundance. To Stalin industrialization also involved power, power to control the peasants. "Each new factory, each new mill is a fortress in the hands

---

[2] *Leninism*, p. 121.
[3] *Sochineniia*, I, 219.
[4] *Economic Problems*, pp. 10–11, 94.
[5] *Sochineniia*, IX, 22–23.
[6] *Ibid.*, VIII, 123.

of the proletariat, securing for it the direction of the masses of peasantry." [7]
Or consider the goal of products-exchange, that is, allocation of goods between industry and agriculture by some central agency without reference to
trading in money. Incidentally, this is not a new aim that Stalin sprung in
October 1952.[8] As far back as 1906 Stalin was looking toward the elimination
of commodity-turnover between city and countryside.[9] Exchange of products,
the mark of the future, is the ultimate defeat of individualistic peasant
usages.

Let us review briefly Stalin's analysis of the nature of the Russian peasantry after 1917, specifically his view of its positive and negative reaction
on the goals already set. The key thing for Soviet policy and for the intra-
Party struggle after 1923 was Stalin's particular allocation of the peasants
into rich, poor, and middle strata.

On top of the heap of the twenty-five million peasant proprietors were
the kulaks, the wealthiest strata who, according to Stalin, were the exploiting
"bloodsuckers" of the rest and, through grain speculation the would-be
"stranglers" of the city workers.[10] As a supporter of capitalism "the kulak is
the enemy of the Soviet government," Stalin stated, "and there is not and
cannot be peace between him and us." [11] One particular evil was that the
"cleaner quarters and better food" offered by kulaks demoralized Bolshevik
agents.[12]

At the other extreme were the poor peasants, exploited semiproletarians
with meager land and inventory, constituting 30 per cent of all by Stalin's
usual estimates. When Stalin averred that "as long as there are poor peasants
we should have an alliance with them," [13] he was assuming that this social
stratum was almost solidly and continually available to the cause of collectivism. It should be noted here that Stalin did not find a completely landless
rural proletariat, nor should the poor peasant millions be confused with
actual Party members in rural districts, who in 1925 numbered only .0037
per cent of the adult rural population.[14]

The vast majority of Russian farmers, in Stalin's estimate, were middle
peasants, petty proprietors just removed from subsistence farming. Stalin
characterized the middle peasant as possessing "two souls," one as a kulak-
emulating seller of grain and the other as a nonexploiting, exploited toiler.[15]
Accordingly, the middle peasant stratum stood "at the crossroads between
capitalism and socialism." [16] One of Trotsky's "metaphysical" mistakes,

[7] *Ibid.*, IX, 156–157.
[8] See below, note 128 and related text.
[9] *Sochineniia*, I, 219.
[10] *Leninism*, p. 289.
[11] *Ibid.*, p. 335.
[12] *Sochineniia*, XI, 4.
[13] *Ibid.*, VII, 331.
[14] *Ibid.*, p. 337.
[15] *Leninism*, p. 263.
[16] *Ibid.*, p. 165.

observed Stalin, was to see the middle peasants as an eternal "given," whereas, actually, under external pressures they vacillated between the kulaks and the proletarian government.[17] The individualistic or "capitalist" soul of the middle peasants had been nurtured in part by the Bolsheviks themselves, by the act of allowing them to expropriate and divide large holdings in 1917, a paradoxical policy endorsed by Stalin as early as 1905.[18] At the same time, however, the fact that the peasants "received" the land from the proletariat and the fact that all the land was nationalized, given for use but not as private property, favored the collectivistic outlook of the peasant masses, according to Stalin.[19] Without the private property "fanaticism" of European farmers and "schooled in three revolutions" in coöperation with the proletariat, the Russian middle peasants had a soul amenable to proletarian-directed socialism.[20] In sum, Stalin saw grounds for collaboration as well as the traditional conflict between city and countryside.

The relative weights of the different strata were hotly disputed within the Party. Stalin insisted that the middle peasants were the majority and were increasing and that the polar differentiation in progress before 1917 could not be repeated in Soviet conditions.[21] Trotsky, so Stalin said, saw only poor peasants and kulaks, while Bukharin's error was to find only middle peasants: the "Left" overestimated and the "Right" underestimated the "kulak danger."[22]

The dynamic aspect of Stalin's analysis must be noted. In his view, the class struggle in the countryside, in part an intraclass struggle, became even more acute after the Revolution; it was the "decisive force" of progress ahead or reaction.[23] When Stalin proclaimed, for example, that "the poor and middle peasants must be mobilized against the kulaks," he saw at once an objective struggle and its susceptibility to outside influence.[24]

---

[17] *Sochineniia*, VIII, 345, 347.

[18] *Ibid.*, I, 224.

[19] *Ibid.*, XI, 150.

[20] *Leninism*, pp. 45–47. Stalin did not follow Russian revolutionary tradition and tie the collectivistic soul of the peasant to the village commune, the age-old institution of political-economic self-government. For example, Herzen in the 1850's based his hopes for avoiding capitalism in Russia on the commune-bred collectivism of the peasants allied with the liberalism of the Westernized intelligentsia. The semi-Marxist Lavrov in the 1870's had the same scheme but allowed that the peasantry, having become proletarianized, might have to produce their own intelligentsia and their own collectivist society in coöperation with the city workers.

These programs were drastically changed by the Bolsheviks. Stalin apparently inherited Lenin's conviction that the commune had essentially dissolved by 1900 in the face of urban and rural capitalism; the institution is ignored in his writings. Yet, he found a collectivistic outlook among the masses of the peasantry, who, although not proletarianized, were thoroughly involved in the class struggle within and without the village against "capitalist" forces.

[21] *Sochineniia*, X, 316.

[22] *Leninism*, pp. 234, 261.

[23] *Sochineniia*, XI, 168–171.

[24] *Leninism*, p. 289.

From his examination of the internal condition of Russia and with an eye to the failure of revolution abroad, Stalin became convinced that the proletariat *must have* and *could have* an alliance with the peasantry that would satisfy both the short-run interests of the countryside and the long-term aims of the city. Here, Stalin said, arose his main dispute with Trotsky and the Left.

The peasant problem, according to Stalin, was precisely "the problem of the ally of the proletariat," the problem of "utilizing" and "transforming" the rural masses. Although derivative to the question of proletarian power, the peasant problem was "one of the most vital problems of Leninism." [25] Over and over again, Stalin threw at his opponents Lenin's slogan that "ten-twenty years of correct relations with the peasantry and victory is assured on a world scale." [26]

Trotsky and the Left were variously accused of underestimating the role of the peasantry in 1917[27] and of defying them afterwards with schemes for the "exploitation" of the countryside through discriminatory taxes and prices.[28] Acute disharmony between industry and agriculture would be disastrous, said Stalin. Rather, "the fate of Soviet power" depended on a political "alliance" of the proletariat with the peasantry and on a related economic union, or *smychka,* revolving around a tolerable urban-rural price ratio.[29]

Further, Stalin insisted, such an alliance and *smychka* could be fully and durably realized. He asserted in this regard:

> The fundamental sin of Trotskyism is that it does not believe in the strength and ability of the proletariat of the USSR to lead . . . the basic masses of the peasantry . . . in the struggle for the victory of socialist construction in our country.[30]

Trotsky was accused of considering the conflict between the proletarian minority and peasant majority so bitter that the problem could be solved only on an international scale.[31] It was futile to dream of allies abroad, Stalin countered, when "the peasantry is the single ally who may *now* render our revolution direct aid," even if in the long run a less reliable ally than the others.[32] Without controverting the cause of world revolution, Stalin held to the feasibility of "socialism in one country," based on the preponderance of collectivistic over individualistic factors in the Russian countryside when combined with the city. The October Revolution, in Stalin's view, had been

---

[25] *Ibid.,* pp. 39–40.
[26] E.g., *Sochineniia,* IX, 39.
[27] *Leninism,* p. 25.
[28] *Sochineniia,* IX, 47.
[29] *Ibid.,* VI, 240 and IX, 159.
[30] *Ibid.,* X, 73.
[31] *Ibid.,* VIII, 347.
[32] *Ibid.,* VII, 21.

won by following Engels' formula of combining a "proletarian revolution" with a "peasant war";[33] now Stalin proposed to carry Lenin's achievement further with the same team of proletariat and peasantry.

Utilization of the peasantry as an ally meant an "indivisible" triple task: complete reliance upon the poor peasants, active union with the middle peasants, and unrelaxed struggle against the kulaks.[34] The task dictated various policies at different times, concessions as well as pressure. The whole New Economic Policy (NEP) after 1921 was regarded as a bow to peasant individualism,[35] and Stalin supported further retreats in 1925 which permitted the leasing of land and hiring of labor and thus benefited the kulaks.[36] All the while the alliance enabled the proletariat to hold and amass political and economic power.[37]

The final point in Stalin's approach to the peasant problem was his insistence that the proletariat must actively *direct* its peasant junior partner toward socialism. The degree, the ruthlessness, and the means of this direction are the questions where Stalin most often found himself in conflict with Bukharin and the Right, and, probably, with himself.

In 1925 we see Stalin advising rural teachers to propagate the idea that "the direction of the peasantry by the proletariat is necessary for the dictatorship of the proletariat, which secures the independence of the country and progress toward socialism." [38] Later, when challenged to correlate the seemingly contradictory slogans "proletarian dictatorship" and "worker-peasant alliance," Stalin denied trying to fool the masses and asserted that there was no inconsistency between the hard and fast concept of the "rule of one class" and the proletariat's chosen policy of alliance with the nonproletarian strata in the countryside.[39]

Basically, the direction of the alliance was antipeasant. In Stalin's words, "the alliance of the workers and peasants is necessary to us not for the maintenance of the peasantry as a class, but for its reformation and alteration." [40] The alliance must be "based upon a struggle against the capitalist elements of the peasantry," [41] whatever temporary concessions were allowed.

In the middle 1920's Stalin appeared to confine proletarian direction of the peasants to keeping and developing the "commanding heights" in industry and trade and to promoting the gradual development of marketing and credit coöperatives in agriculture. He contented himself with the prospect

[33] *Ibid.,* V, 344–345.
[34] *Leninism,* pp. 219–222.
[35] *Sochineniia,* V, 91.
[36] *Ibid.,* X, 196–197.
[37] *Leninism,* p. 167.
[38] *Sochineniia,* VII, 3.
[39] *Ibid.,* IX, 179.
[40] *Ibid.,* p. 183.
[41] *Leninism,* p. 261.

that naturally "the rural districts . . . follow the lead of the towns both in material and cultural matters." The "non-socialistic" peasantry was to be "drawn into" socialist construction by force of economic aid and example.[42] The common interest of the two allies in socialism was held to be overriding.[43]

In January 1928, however, Stalin was barking a new note: "Lenin says that as long as individual peasant business predominates in the countryside, breeding capitalists and capitalism, there will exist the danger of the restoration of capitalism."[44] Proletarian "commanding heights" were no longer enough. In fact, paradoxically, the more socialist industry developed in technique and scale and the further apart it grew from agriculture, all the more unavoidable became the collapse of the national economy and the restoration of capitalism.[45] Stalin now declared that the countryside would not follow the city to socialism "spontaneously."[46] The solution he proposed was more immediate and ruthless direction by the proletariat, direction in the form of instigating mass collectivization and class war against the kulaks, policies which he had skirted earlier. To the delight of the defeated Left, Bukharin and the Right were now denounced for holding the idea that the kulaks would eventually "grow into" socialism,[47] that the "parallel lines" of capitalism and socialism would meet.[48] Rather, Stalin announced, the towns must "reorganize the rural districts on a new socialist basis."[49]

There is considerable foresight and consistency in Stalin's view of the peasant problem, although the charges of "opportunism" by critics on both Right and Left have some justification. What Stalin lacked in pragmatic proofs of his theories, he compensated for with intuition or dogmatism. Throughout his writings is the traditional Marxist insistence on the existence of class struggle within and without the village. From this he derived his particular ideas on how the peasants could be manipulated to serve nonpeasant ends, his theory of the necessity and possibility of a peasant-proletarian alliance. Stalin's threefold division of the peasantry and his analysis of the "two souls" of the middle peasants were persistent themes, but vague and flexible ones. Accordingly, he was forced eventually to make a drastic revision of his notions on the balance of proletarian direction and peasant spontaneity necessary to achieve socialism.

[42] *Ibid.*, pp. 165–167.
[43] *Sochineniia*, VII, 177.
[44] *Ibid.*, IX, 6.
[45] *Ibid.*, p. 254.
[46] *Leninism*, pp. 232–233.
[47] *Ibid.*, p. 254.
[48] *Ibid.*, p. 308.
[49] *Ibid.*, p. 311.

II. THE NEED FOR THE COLLECTIVE FARM

When we consider Stalin's thoughts on the need for collectivization, we encounter the vital question of dogma versus expediency in policy-making. His writings indicate that while Stalin was aware from the start of the Marxist-Leninist vision of socialized agriculture he consistently underplayed it until faced with a crisis.

The aim of socialized production in farming is first touched upon in one of Stalin's articles of 1907.[50] The term "collective farm" first occurs in his *Collected Works* in 1919, ironically, in an order for investigation of compulsory collectives as a cause of local unrest.[51] Before the later 1920's, however, Stalin wrote very sparingly about the collective farm, restricting himself to generalities about "gradually introducing in agriculture the principles of collectivism, first, in the sphere of marketing and, later, in the sphere of the production of agricultural products." [52] At the Fourteenth Congress in 1925 Stalin found occasion to denounce schemes for a "second revolution" in the countryside and declared that peasant farming could move ahead "for a certain time with a rapid tempo and with its present technical base." [53]

A change in his attitude became evident in late 1927 when Stalin told foreign interviewers that Russia was on the "threshold" of voluntary, "not quick" collectivization.[54] At the Fifteenth Congress in December, Stalin announced a new policy of establishing collectives to "supplement" peasant agriculture.[55] In the heat of the "grain crisis" in January 1928, when the kulaks allegedly withheld provisions, Stalin began to look beyond partial collectivization for a "durable" food supply to be secured for growing industry,[56] and he pouted suddenly in April that "we have hideously few collective farms." [57] But he still maintained, in October, that it would take "years and years" to transform Russia from a small-peasant country.[58] As late as April 1929 he declared that individual farming "will continue to play a predominant role." [59] In the next few months came the abrupt revelation that 1929 was "the year of great change" and that "the bulk of the peasantry" had been turned toward collectives.[60] Stalin found it necessary in December to state that the Engels tradition of gradualism was "excessive circumspection" which could not apply to Russia where the peasants had no

[50] *Sochineniia*, I, 334.
[51] *Ibid.*, IV, 256–257.
[52] *Leninism*, p. 48.
[53] *Sochineniia*, VII, 315, 373.
[54] *Ibid.*, X, 221–226.
[55] *Ibid.*, pp. 305–309.
[56] *Ibid.*, XI, 5.
[57] *Ibid.*, p. 42.
[58] *Leninism*, p. 233.
[59] *Ibid.*, p. 271.
[60] *Ibid.*, p. 298.

"slavish attachment" to private property.[61] The chronicle may appropriately end with Stalin's famous article in March 1930, "Dizzy from Success," where he mingled boasts with complaints concerning the achievement of 50 per cent collectivization of the total peasant farms, more than twice the Five-Year Plan estimates for 1932.[62]

From this brief review it appears that mass collectivization was essentially a product of the events of 1928, the grain shortage in particular and the pressures of industrialization on the economy in general. It has been argued that conditions "forced Stalin's hand" unexpectedly and completely apart from ideological considerations. What should be kept in mind, however, is that the only cards dealt to Stalin to meet situations were Marxist solutions. Stalin led off with industrialization and, confronted thereupon with difficulties, played the card labeled "collectivization." Here is an inseparable mixture of dogma and expediency.[63]

The collective farm as an institution arises directly out of Stalin's analysis of proletarian goals and peasant materials. The collective farm was designed as simply a means, a compromise, an expression both of what should be and what could be. In point of time, the collective farm was a new stage of the peasant-proletarian alliance of the NEP, a step beyond the old smychka, a turn from the restoration to the reconstruction of agriculture. In form, the collective farm was just one, the most important one, of various rural institutions designed to build "socialism in one country" and to promote the transition to complete collectivism (for example, state farms, rural soviets, coöperative stores, Communist youth organizations).

Stalin's most frequent characterization of purpose was that the collective farm was needed to secure for agriculture a technical base comparable to that of industry and thus to allow agriculture to grow as fast as industry. The offensive in industry was launched at the Fourteenth Party Congress in 1925, and the lag in agriculture became the preoccupation of the Fifteenth Congress in 1927. Industrialization was an unalterable given for Stalin: it would be a "reactionary, antiproletarian Utopia" to seek economic proportionality through cutting down the tempi of industrialization to suit agriculture.[64] Moreover, Stalin meant concentration on heavy industry: he rejected a policy of favoring light, consumer industry so as to stimulate the farmers through the market.[65] The agricultural sector would always lag behind, Stalin conceded, but "excessive backwardness" was a newly made

[61] Ibid., p. 314.

[62] Ibid., p. 332–333.

[63] The turn toward collectivization that Stalin made in the late 1920's may be compared to Herzen's awakening to the peasant commune after 1848 or to Chernov's focus on the peasantry as a revolutionary force after 1902.

[64] Sochineniia, X, 304–305.

[65] Leninism, p. 213.

problem and could not be tolerated.[66] The only solution he found was the industrialization of agriculture itself in the form of collective farms.[67]

The collective farm, representing the pooling of the labor, land, and possessions of small peasants, was held to offer great technological opportunities because of its size:

> The strength of large-scale farming, irrespective of whether it is landlord, kulak, or collective farming, lies in the fact that large farms are able to employ machinery, scientific knowledge, fertilizers, to increase the productivity of labor, and thereby to produce the maximum quantity of grain for the market. On the other hand, the weakness of small peasant farming lies in the fact that it lacks, or almost lacks, these opportunities.[68]

From this statement it follows that Stalin considered any kind of big mechanized farm, even capitalistic enterprises, superior to small holdings. The choice of the collective farm, of course, was influenced by additional factors.

One of the significant problems of scale is farm marketing. Stalin cried in 1928 that "we may not put our industry in dependence on kulak caprices" [69] and pointed to the fact that the few existing collective farms were handing over a high percentage of their production for consumption by the multiplying factory workers and for export.[70] Why was collective farm production more marketable than that of other type enterprises? Was it more efficient, in Stalin's view, or was it simply less "capricious," more easily controlled? Stalin seemed to count on both things.

That large-scale enterprise *per se* is more productive is a Marxist dogma which Stalin never questioned publicly. Stalin cited figures which showed that even the simple pooling of the peasants' labor and primitive tools allowed the profitable cultivation of waste and virgin land; with tractors and complex machines put on collective fields productivity would make tremendous strides.[71] This is not the place to argue whether the long-term, aggregate performance of collective farms justified Stalin's enthusiasm for scale. It is worthwhile, however, to note that Stalin found it necessary at times to play down the efficiency criterion. He observed once that the question whether collective farms "pay" or not should not be approached from the "huckster's point of view." [72] Even more remarkable are his boasts of the "success" of 100,000–200,000 acre "grain factories," a size possible only in Soviet conditions where he said it was permitted to forego maximum profits, to forego minimum profits, to forego any profits.[73]

[66] *Sochineniia*, XI, 258.
[67] *Leninism*, pp. 409–410.
[68] *Leninism*, p. 207.
[69] *Sochineniia*, XI, 55.
[70] *Leninism*, p. 211.
[71] *Ibid.*, p. 315.
[72] *Ibid.*, p. 283.
[73] *Ibid.*, p. 434.

What is important is that Stalin found the collective farm also a more amenable source of grain supplies than small farms. He lectured Bukharin that "we cannot be indifferent" as to whether grain is bought from the kulaks or from collective farms or (Malenkov take note) from abroad.[74] Stalin began talking about "introducing the planning principle in agriculture" in terms of prices and production,[75] planning to which collective farms obviously lent themselves. Early in 1928 Stalin brought up the matter of imposing economic penalties on collective farms that failed to deliver their quotas.[76] He openly stated that industrialization was to be financed by means of the "scissors," by a policy of making farmers pay high prices for industrial wares and accept low prices for their grain.[77] Collective farms facilitated extorting this "supertax" from the peasants. The collectives were "economic base points" for "securing the directing role of the working class" with special reference to marketings.[78]

The need for the collective farm was not exhausted by the economic considerations of mechanization and planning. Stalin also envisaged the collective farm as "the principal base for remolding the peasant, for reworking his psychology in the spirit of proletarian socialism." [79] More than just a means of getting increased bread supplies, the collective farm produced a "revolution in the peasants' heads." [80]

The negative side of this political-social motivation for collectivization is revealed in Stalin's fear that "until the small peasant farms are united in large collective farms the danger of the restoration of capitalism would be the most real of all possible dangers." [81] Peasant individualism was a threat, especially since the kulaks were pictured as plotting to turn it against Soviet power. Aims and means are clear in the dictum that "the basic means of liquidation of the kulaks as a class is the method of mass collectivization." [82]

The newly discovered political crisis with the kulaks gives the collective farm the aspect of being an immediate means of keeping the regime in control wholly aside from its aspect of securing the gradual remolding of peasant psychology. This same mixture of dogma and expediency is revealed in the economic side of Stalin's thinking on the need for collectivization discussed earlier.

[74] *Ibid.*, p. 283.
[75] *Sochineniia*, X, 223–224.
[76] *Leninism*, p. 211.
[77] *Sochineniia*, XI, 159–160.
[78] *Ibid.*, pp. 193–195.
[79] *Ibid.*, XII, 165.
[80] *Ibid.*, XI, 268–269.
[81] *Leninism*, p. 460.
[82] *Sochineniia*, XII, 187.

III. THE PREREQUISITES OF THE COLLECTIVE FARM

Stalin once likened the establishment of collective farms to a military offensive. Favorable conditions had to be created, the moment carefully chosen, positions consolidated, and forces regrouped.[83] How far did this general reveal his strategy in his writings before and after the campaign?

It has already been noted that Stalin did not earnestly propagandize the cause of mass collectivization until the late 1920's. In reply to charges that this "Leftism" in peasant policy was abrupt and capricious, Stalin claimed that the Party leadership had been acutely aware of the need for collectives ever since 1917 but that a slogan could not be made out of need until the right conditions were "created and organized." [84] The preconditions of 1929 that Stalin mentioned at various times may be grouped under the headings Party-governmental organization, tractors, finances, and mass support. Here arises the vital question of foresight or hindsight. Is it true or not that Stalin early advocated measures to bring about the overthrow of individual peasant farming even if concealing their explicit aim? Insofar as Stalin made preparations, that is, "created and organized" the "right conditions," the case is strengthened that ideological conviction rather than expediency governed the decision to start the general collective farm drive.

The necessity for organized governmental and Party forces to push the peasants into collectives was not spelled out by Stalin, but he mentioned it in various ways. For example, he implies a great deal when he termed indoctrination of the mass of Party members concerning the need for collective farms as the first prerequisite of the movement.[85] The lag of socialism in the countryside in 1927 he blamed on an "unbold approach" to the matter,[86] just as in March 1930 he attributed excessive speed to compulsory methods and "Communist vanity." [87] An example of the variety of political pressures were the "worker brigades" sent to rural areas, which Stalin praised as "the best possible propagandists." [88] Finally, there is his revealing formula of 1938 that the new revolution in agriculture was "accomplished from above, on the initiative of the state," as well as supported from below.[89] These citations from Stalin essentially exhaust what he has written directly on the subject of the immediate political preparation for collectivization. In view of the scope of compulsion actually applied in 1929, it is evident that Stalin was hardly candid with others before or after the event, and it is conceivable that he was less than candid with himself until rather late.

[83] *Leninism*, pp. 348–349.
[84] *Ibid.*, pp. 272–273.
[85] *Ibid.*, p. 284.
[86] *Sochineniia*, X, 307.
[87] *Leninism*, p. 346.
[88] *Ibid.*, p. 301.
[89] *History*, p. 305.

Here it is also worthwhile to take note of Stalin's political actions in the 1920's and their effect on the collectivization drive. The matter is complicated, and it is easier to raise questions than attempt answers. On the one hand, the brutal conquest of supreme power within the Party by Stalin at the expense of all other considerations may well be held an actual and necessary prerequisite to the later pursuit by the Party of a brutal policy toward the peasants. On the other hand, Stalin's purges of his opponents and their followers, particularly in the case of the kulak-hating Trotskyites, may have substantially weakened Party strength in the countryside when it should have been brought to peak effectiveness.

Aside from political pressure, according to Stalin, the government should and did set up economic prerequisites for collectives. The need for an "industrial base" for the collective farm movement was stressed by Stalin in 1928 when he called for a "metal" smychka, the dispatch of producers' goods to agriculture, as a step beyond the "textile" smychka involving the supply of consumers' goods to the peasants.[90] Take Stalin's celebrated exhortation to the Stalingrad tractor factory workers that "the 50,000 tractors which you should give the countryside are 50,000 shells exploding the old bourgeois world and laying the way for the new socialist mode of life in the countryside."[91] By Stalin's reasoning, the peasants "could not but clutch at this assistance"; any dissatisfaction with the collectives would center on lack of enough tractors.[92] Just how many machines had to be available before mass collectivization should and would start is a painful question Stalin never discussed in his writings.

Financial aid from the state was another precondition. According to Stalin, "the funds necessary for the subjugation of farming to the state or collective principle" were needed in the "millions" and appeared only in 1927 and afterward at an increasing rate.[93] Government credits, tax alleviation, and other privileges for newly established collective farms were extended as a kind of economic pressure.[94] The subtlety of the workings of the peasant-proletarian alliance is revealed here: the peasants are subjected to a "supertax" and then bribed with the money to join collectives.

What did Stalin reckon upon, finally, when he said a "mass movement" of peasants was necessary for setting up collectives? What did he see as the psychological basis of the "movement" of late 1929, when he reported that peasants were joining up no longer just individually but in "whole villages, whole districts, even whole areas."[95]

We have already noted Stalin's view of the relative responses of different

[90] Sochineniia, XI, 161–164.
[91] Ibid., XII, 234.
[92] Leninism, pp. 301–302.
[93] Sochineniia, X, 307.
[94] Leninism, p. 353.
[95] Ibid., p. 303.

strata of peasants to socialist progress. Simply "lack of inventory" in the case of the poor peasantry was a "special condition" favorable to their co-operating in large-scale enterprises.[96] To forget about the middle peasants would be a mistake, Stalin warned in 1928, for they too could be "given the perspective" that the collective farm was the best and fastest way of im-proving their welfare.[97] "Classes and the class struggle" must be kept in mind if one was neither to "lag behind" nor "rush ahead of" the peasants in the matter of collectivization.[98]

One concrete means of preparing "mass response" in favor of producers' coöperatives was getting peasants into the less advanced forms of coöpera-tion, the marketing, credit, supply, and machine coöperatives. "The wide-spread development of coöperative organizations in the rural districts paved the way for a change in the attitude of the peasant in favor of the collective farms."[99] Here again Stalin tells us that the collective farm was a logical culmination in a master plan. Only in this instance, however, is the evidence conclusive that Stalin was early laying the groundwork for 1929: through-out the NEP period Stalin propagandized the lower forms of farm coöpera-tion as stepping stones to the higher.

Another factor in "convincing" the peasants was the existence of a few "well-organized" collective and state farms. These overcame the instinctive "hostile" and "contemptuous" attitude of the individual proprietor toward large-scale businesses by force of example and by technical aid, Stalin re-ported.[100] Thus, partial collectivization, if economically successful, was con-sidered a preliminary to a mass movement.

While Stalin upheld throughout the 1920's the principle of voluntariness and mass persuasion as the basis for collectivization, extensive instructions on what this meant appeared only after the deed in the spring of 1930. He then lectured that "Leninism teaches that every attempt to impose collective farming by force . . . can only produce negative results, can only repel the peasants . . ."[101] Coercion, "cavalry raids," "paper" collective farms filled with "dead souls," collective farms "by decree" were excesses already com-mitted which Stalin termed "impermissible and disastrous" for relations with the middle peasants.[102] Such "Left" distortions would lead to "Right" re-sults, to the restoration of kulaks and capitalism.[103] Stalin halted the offen-sive in favor of a "regrouping," and peasants were allowed to leave collec-tives. Stalin reaffirmed his vague but persistent belief in a social basis for

---

[96] *Sochineniia*, VII, 82.
[97] *Ibid.*, XI, 41.
[98] *Leninism*, p. 338.
[99] *Ibid.*, pp. 210–211.
[100] *Ibid.*, p. 274.
[101] *Ibid.*, p. 341.
[102] *Ibid.*, p. 340.
[103] *Ibid.*, p. 350.

collectivization when he said "we shall certainly convince tomorrow" the peasants who left.[104]

The kulaks were involved, of course, in the mass psychology of collectivization. The existence of these allegedly capitalist elements was a cause for the collective farm, an obstacle to it, and, in a sense a prerequisite for it. The grain crisis of 1928, according to Stalin, was the "first serious" bid by the kulaks against Soviet power,[105] to which the Party replied by "kindling" class war and by fostering partial collectivization. The antikulak campaign, an artificial effort seeking support in objective social antagonisms, served to put the rest of the peasants more fully under the influence of the Party and, Stalin claimed, thereby facilitated mass collectivization.[106] Moreover, the supply of grain forthcoming from the few collectives of 1928 helped to end government dependence on kulak production, Stalin said, and allowed the new revolution.[107]

No peace was possible with the kulak, in Stalin's view, for "he is the sworn enemy of the collective farm movement." [108] Desperate resistance by the kulaks could not be avoided by Stalin's government, he explained, because there are "no cases in history where dying classes have voluntarily departed from the scene." [109] The kulaks were pictured to the end as the provokers, not the provoked.

As for the peasant masses, Stalin believed that they would "depart" from their old way of life if their partially collectivistic instincts were subjected to the right degree of political and economic pressure. The basic ingredients of Stalin's recipe for mass collectivization are revealed in his writings, but some of the secret touches used are only alluded to, and quantities are hardly given at all. Much of the recipe is an afterthought, particularly in the matter of political compulsion versus local spontaneity.

IV. THE RESULTS OF COLLECTIVIZATION

Stalin's second thoughts on the collective farm generally validate his previous theories. If it had been otherwise, collective farms, as well as the need to study them, might no longer exist.

Probably a case could be made that Stalin conceived the "second revolution" in agriculture a much easier task than it proved to be, although one might also argue that he took a calculated but unexpressed risk. In 1934 Stalin complained of "enormous difficulties," [110] and Churchill heard him

---

[104] *Ibid.*, p. 351.
[105] *Sochineniia*, XI, 363.
[106] *Leninism*, p. 335.
[107] *Ibid.*, pp. 323–325.
[108] *Ibid.*, p. 326.
[109] *Ibid.*, p. 259.
[110] *Ibid.*, p. 495.

confide that the struggle with the peasants was a greater undertaking than the battle of Stalingrad.[111]

One of Stalin's most important discoveries after 1929 was that large-scale, mechanized collectives *per se* did not solve the Party's immediate problems in the countryside. He found that the collective farm was only a form, a "weapon" which might be used either for or against Soviet power.[112] Giving content to the form became as important as creating it. The problem of "individualistic and kulak survivals" in the collectivized peasantry was noted by Stalin already in late 1929, but he held further mechanization to be the easy means of removing them.[113] By 1933 Stalin was seriously alarmed at anti-Soviet "wreckers," everyone from "White Guards" to Mensheviks, who had found that the collective farms gave greater organizational opportunities than existed before.[114] The conclusion drawn was that "the collective farm system does not diminish but increases the cares and responsibility of the Party and government in regard to the development of agriculture."[115] Politically, the call was for "Bolshevik" collective farms: a collective could not be neutral, just "pro" or "anti."[116] Economically, it was up to Communist officials to "make collective farms prosperous," since the ex-peasants had thrown off managerial responsibilities.[117]

Accordingly, increased outside control was one aspect of giving content to the form of collective farm. Perhaps the most striking new control method was setting up a network of institutions parallel to the collective farms, the machine and tractor stations (MTS). These were state enterprises acting not only as suppliers of tractor work, but also as production planners, with noneconomic functions emphasized in their special political departments.[118]

Another discovery Stalin made was that the degree of collectivization within the unit was vital. Stalin maintained that he had always opposed the "commune" type of collective, where all property and even consumption were socialized, and had wisely favored the "artel" type, where petty plots of land, simple tools, and a limited number of livestock were left unpooled as the collective farmers' private property.[119] Contradictorily, however, Stalin told the deadly serious joke that the government had entered and lost a struggle with the collective farm women "over a cow";[120] that is, a modi-

---

[111] David Mitrany, *Marx Against the Peasant, a Study in Social Dogmatism* (Chapel Hill, 1951), p. 257, n. 55.
[112] *Leninism,* pp. 448–450.
[113] *Ibid.,* p. 350.
[114] *Ibid.,* p. 449.
[115] *Ibid.,* p. 447.
[116] *Ibid.,* p. 452.
[117] *Ibid.,* p. 463.
[118] *Ibid.,* p. 454.
[119] *Ibid.,* pp. 336, 518–519.
[120] *Ibid.,* p. 466.

cum of private enterprise had been demanded and won. A related partial retreat to individualism was the allowance of a "free" collective farm market in addition to compulsory deliveries to the government.[121]

Only after major readjustments had been made could Stalin decide that the collective farm was a success in political-social terms. "Our Soviet peasantry has definitely and unalterably come under the red banner of Socialism," Stalin told the applauding Seventeenth Congress.[122] Eliminated with the kulaks was the last hope of restoring capitalism. Collective farms could now be lenient about letting in former enemies.[123] At the Eighteenth Congress in 1939 Stalin boasted that there was no class hostility in the Soviet Union, that the peasants had risen from allies to friends of the proletariat.[124]

In terms of food supplies, Stalin publicly found the achievements satisfactory. If productivity lagged behind plans, there were always the huge marketings to point to. "Nobody can deny the colossal development of the productive forces of our agriculture in the past twenty to twenty-five years," [125] Stalin concluded before he died and before Khrushchëv began the denials.

In terms of peasant welfare, Stalin's second thought was that the collectives had transformed the poor into middle peasants.[126] As before, the categories lacked precise statistical foundation. Collective farms were getting clubs, radios, and movies, and the peasants were no longer oppressed by kulaks and police officers.[127]

Finally, Stalin reconcluded that the collective farm was a useful educational lever driving the peasants toward further collectivism. The audit justified the original theories and actions, if one reads Stalin, but we must remember that his plans had to be greatly amplified and amended.

V. THE FUTURE OF THE COLLECTIVE FARM

Stalin's projection of the collective farm deserves exhaustive treatment separately. Consideration here will be confined to two of the important features: communalization of all property within the future farm unit, and the complete integration of this unit in a national collectivism.

The Stalinist artel, "the only proper form of the collective farm movement under present conditions," combined internally two sets of interests: the social sector centering around the collectivized large fields and livestock farms, and the private sector based on the household and garden activities of the collective farmers. In the institution of the future, the commune, the private interests are to be eliminated, as a result of a "profusion" of collec-

[121] *Ibid.*, p. 444.
[122] *Ibid.*, p. 500.
[123] *Ibid.*, p. 467.
[124] *Ibid.*, p. 645.
[125] *Economic Problems*, p. 69.
[126] *Leninism*, p. 462.
[127] *Ibid.*, p. 507.

tively produced goods. The collective farmer will no longer have need of a cow, and he will be content to eat in a community dining room. The transition to the commune must proceed gradually, not artificially, and on the basis of persuasion, the same preconditions Stalin applied in word to the establishment of the artel.[128]

Another "backward" feature of the artel is that it combines state (public) property and private community property. The problem here is that the present collective has some autonomy in the disposal of its output, despite compulsory deliveries to the state. "Commodity-turnover" with prices and markets is the only system collective farmers will now "accept," according to Stalin. Although used by the state to its advantage and thus precluded from breeding capitalism, commodity-turnover represents an obstacle to the realization of Communism and specifically to the "full coverage of agriculture by state planning." The task, in Stalin's view, is gradually to turn all collective farm property into public property and to replace commodity-turnover by "products-exchange." These features of the future commune do not mean that the artel is expropriated and made into a state farm, according to Stalin. State farms are impossible without a state, and the existing state is to be eliminated in favor of a "social-economic agency" regulating exchange of products between factories and farms without reference to money.[129] Whatever else this means, it is clear that the future collective farm is to be part of an overriding national collectivism, conceived by the Party and removed incredibly far from peasant traditions. The realism or utopianism of Stalin's project depends, of course, on the success of the earlier vision.

VI. THE INTERNATIONAL SIGNIFICANCE OF THE COLLECTIVE FARM

Stalin seemed confident that his whole theory of the collective farm could be exported. What he calls the "Leninist path" for agriculture has not only "justified itself" in Russia but is "the only possible and expedient path in the case of all capitalist countries with a more or less numerous class of small and medium proprietors."[130] Colonies do not fit this category, and England is specifically excluded.

A damaging contradiction in Stalin's thinking arises at this point. Stalin always maintained that the Communist solution for agriculture would sooner or later be chosen by workers and peasants because there was only one alternative and that intolerable, namely, the "capitalist" solution. In traditional Marxist parlance the "capitalist" path for farming meant the expropriation of all land by a few and the proletarization of the mass of peasants. But just before his death we find Stalin saying that only England has had this experience of concentration of farm ownership. Accordingly, Stalin's "capitalist" solution is largely an unreality for the world, and, insofar as this solution is a premise, the "Communist" conclusion may be exceptional.

[128] *Ibid.*, pp. 518–520.
[129] *Economic Problems*, pp. 17–20, 32, 74–75, 101–104.
[130] *Ibid.*, p. 17.

Some countries, Stalin conceded, would have difficulties in copying the Russian example. Far back in 1921 he observed that "the weakness of proletarian revolution" in Europe was that the proletariat there lacked connections and support in the countryside, since the liberation of the European peasants had obligated them not to the proletariat but to the bourgeoisie.[131] Later, Stalin advised the Comintern to play down immediate nationalization of the land in its peasant program, having in mind the property fanaticism of the European peasants.[132] Also, there is some indication that Stalin learned enough from Russian experience to caution postwar Communist regimes against reckless extremes of mass collectivization.[133] The appearance of collective farms in Eastern Europe and China, however, suggests that Stalin did not see any persistent obstacles to the fulfillment of his ideas.

What Stalin taught the world was this. Once power has been seized and the socialist goals set by the proletarian minority, the only solution for a single country is to manipulate the peasant masses with both carrot and knout into accepting the goals. This task can be accomplished if the class divisions and partially collectivistic instincts of the peasants are played upon and if the proletariat (or its Party) exercises firm direction. A key way station in the process is the collective farm, serving to adjust agriculture to the needs of industrialization and to reëducate the peasantry. Mass collectivization is an offensive requiring organized political pressure, a supply of tractors, financial reserves, and the persuasion of the peasants by socialist examples. After its initiation, the collective farm must be closely controlled, and it is vital to achieve the right balance of private and social interests within. Eventually, the original collective farm can be transformed into a commune embodying complete internal collectivism and integration in a planned economy.

It would be erroneous to conclude from the above summary of Stalin's writings that he had this whole blueprint for the peasantry in mind from the outset: the events of 1929 were too chaotic and the groping for the right form of collectivization afterward too obvious. Yet, it would be equally wrong to view collectivization as a suddenly decreed tactic based entirely on force, without regard to its roots in Marxist dogma and without regard to the preparations underlying it. Stalin's achievements in the countryside, whether good or bad, suggest impressive acumen at cajoling and threatening, duping and pressuring the peasantry further into the throes of proletarian-directed collectivism. To halt the spread of Communism in peasant countries may well require primarily a sounder agrarian theory, a better judgment of objective rural conditions and forces, and a firmer political line for the village than Stalin has willed his successors.

[131] *Sochineniia*, V, 86–87.
[132] *Ibid.*, XI, 149–150.
[133] Mitrany, ref. 111, pp. 185–186

Vyshinsky's Concept of Collectivity

JULIAN TOWSTER

. . . the Russian idea is the idea of community and the brotherhood of men and peoples.

> Nicholas Berdyaev
> *The Russian Idea*

The spirit of the people could very easily pass from one integrated faith to another integrated faith, from one orthodoxy to another orthodoxy, which embraced the whole of life.

> Nicholas Berdyaev
> *The Origin of Russian Communism*

In the light of the over-all pursuit of our studies, two observations must be made at the outset: that Vyshinsky's concept of collectivity is in all essentials the accepted Soviet concept of collectivity, and that its nature can be properly assessed only against the background of the modern Western and the pre-Soviet Russian concepts of collectivity.

One could hardly expect Andrei Vyshinsky to be recognized in the Soviet Union as the architect of an original concept of collectivity. For, somewhat akin to the medieval idea of law, the Soviet view of theory is that it is something to be discovered rather than made. And only Lenin and Stalin — and now perhaps Stalin's most intimate lieutenants — are deemed to have sufficiently mastered the dialectic and gained the "historical insight" for such creative discovery. The very logic of Soviet totalitarianism precludes any toleration of individual theories and unique points of view, varying from the higher law of the Party and the pronouncements of its acclaimed leaders. Only in the sense that Vyshinsky's treatment of the subject is distinguished by an emphasis from the viewpoint of the lawyer and legal scholar may one speak of Vyshinsky's concept of collectivity. But here too one must remember that in keeping with the monolithic unitarianism demanded by the Party, the precept has long since been established that, like a living organism, the Party appropriates the accomplishments of its members, just as the object held by the hand is possessed by the person and not by the hand which holds it.[1] Hence Vyshinsky's discourses invariably invoke the authority of

[1] See J. Stalin, *Political Report of the Central Committee to the Fifteenth Congress of the C.P.S.U.(b)*, December 3, 1927 (Moscow, 1950), p. 136.

Marxism-Leninism-Stalinism and his interpretations have become part and parcel of the body of accepted Soviet theory.

It would be incorrect, however, to view the Soviet concept of collectivity, as articulated by Vyshinsky, solely in terms of Marxist lineage. A proper elucidation of this ideological construct and its genesis calls for at least a cursory examination and comparison of the nineteenth-century Russian tradition and the recent Western heritage in the understanding of collectivity.

I. THE WESTERN CONCEPT OF COLLECTIVITY

The Western concept of collectivity in the modern era may in part be traced back to a reaction against the eighteenth-century enlightenment.[2] This so-called Age of Reason rested upon certain historical and cultural developments: the disintegration of Roman Catholicism as a universal Western European religion, the emergence of modern scientific thought, the industrial revolutions of the seventeenth and eighteenth centuries, and the rise of the bourgeoisie — claiming a place in the sun. The intellectual climate of the time was dominated by individualism, deism, and faith in reason and progress. Political democracy was erected on the doctrine of natural right and later buttressed by *laissez faire,* utilitarianism, and the idea of the natural harmony of interests.

Perhaps it was not by chance that *fraternité* became a neglected member of the idealized triad of the French Revolution. Fraternity was to be a function of individualism. The harmony of the whole was to be achieved through the self-seeking interests of each. The medieval bond of community had been torn asunder. Society became merely the sum of all individuals, and the individual emerged as a free floating atom, devoid of a definite status. Once a meaningful participant in the work of society, he had become a helpless cog in a vast production machine.

Of the voices raised in protest against the changed state of affairs, that of Karl Marx was only one among many.[3] In Britain, Conservatives such as Shaftesbury, Southey, Matthew Arnold and Carlyle were declaiming the lack

[2] For a brief and coherent summary of the Western tradition of collectivity, see Robert A. Nisbet, *The Quest for Community: A Study in the Ethics of Order and Freedom* (New York, 1953).

[3] Although with the venom and vehemence which seemed to be basic ingredients of his writings, his denunciation was one of the bitterest. In 1848 he wrote: "The bourgeoisie, wherever it has got the upper hand, has put an end to all feudal, patriarchal, idyllic relations. It has pitilessly torn asunder the motley feudal ties that bound man to his 'natural superiors,' and has left no other bond between man and man than naked self-interest, than callous 'cash payment.' It has drowned the most heavenly ecstasies of religious fervour, of chivalrous enthusiasm, of philistine sentimentalism, in the icy water of egotistical calculation. It has resolved personal worth into exchange value — in one word, for exploitation, veiled by religious and political illusions, it had substituted naked, shameless, direct, brutal exploitation." Marx and Engels, *Manifesto of the Communist Party* (New York, 1948), p. 11.

of a deeply rooted formula as a guide to life for the industrial masses of nineteenth-century England. The Liberals, John Stuart Mill, Martin Kingsley, and T. H. Green, all sensed the loss of community and criticized the social injustices of urban life. The fact that the traditional pride in craftsmanship had been replaced by the specialization of the industrial armies of the mill towns, was felt particularly keenly by Carlyle, who wrote before Marx.[4] To all of these thinkers it appeared that the idea of mutual helpfulness had been destroyed, that the age was witness to the isolation of the human atoms, the lack of fellowship, the feeling of not belonging, the futile sense of purposelessness. The social fabric had been seriously weakened, and traditional values and ways of behavior had been undermined. Man was left without an anchor to afford some protection in his insecure and unstable life.

However diverse their individual outlooks, these thinkers all sought an answer in a concept of collectivity. Marx, Green, and Carlyle equally espoused a return to community and an emphasis on coöperation and mutual aid, rather than competition and a struggle for survival. And in Britain at least their efforts were perhaps not without results. A. V. Dicey describes what he terms a spirit of collectivism permeating public opinion and parliamentary government from 1865 on. By 1900, he contended, the doctrines of *laissez faire* and individualism were already dead in Britain.[5] Similar observations could be made with regard to most of the other Western European countries.

The succeeding decades saw the growth of a collectivist approach in the West, and the progressive disappearance of all rigid distinctions between the conservation of traditions and amelioration of the condition of the masses. But essentially collectivity in the Western tradition has meant only an awareness that man is a social animal and that the state as a collective institution, controlled by the people, may contribute substantially to making man's lot on earth a happier one. The tenor of this approach lies in its rational-empirical nature. The West's concept of collectivity has been secularized, rationalized, stripped of all mystical qualities, and guided by a conviction that the individual must not be swallowed up by a general will or world consciousness. The empirical gauge of the scientific method has become the model of Western thinking, whether one views democracy with Dewey and Russell as

[4] See his *Past and Present* (London, 1912, originally published in 1843), pp. 131–217. Compare the following passage (p. 141) with that of Marx and Engels, ref. 3. "True, it must be owned, we for the present, with our Mammon-Gospel, have come to strange conclusions. We call it a Society; and go about professing openly the totalest separation, isolation. Our life is not a mutual helpfulness; but rather, cloaked under due laws-of-war, named 'fair competition' and so forth, it is a mutual hostility. We have profoundly forgotten everywhere that *cash-payment* is not the sole relation of human beings; we think, nothing doubting, that *it* absolves and liquidates all engagements of man."

[5] *Lectures on the Relation Between Law and Public Opinion in England During the Nineteenth Century* (London, 1920), the first edition of which was published in 1905.

a great social laboratory or accepts Popper's advocacy of piecemeal social engineering.[6] In this concept the state serves as a potent practical means for realizing the needs of the collectivity, but it is a limited and circumscribed entity nonetheless. The fundamental premise of the Western idea is that the possibilities of the state are finite, and that the worth of man — the dignity of the individual — remains at all times the supreme value.

II. THE PRE-SOVIET RUSSIAN CONCEPT OF COLLECTIVITY

The Russian tradition of collectivity is of a radically different texture than that of the West. An index of this difference is to be found in the basic traits of Russian thought in the nineteenth century, which can be characterized as religiosity, historicism, and instrumentalism.[7]

A religious philosophy (energized in part by German idealism, particularly Schelling and Hegel), was Russia's unique contribution to the world of learning. Chaadaev, Belinskii, Herzen, Bakunin, and Solov'ëv were all deeply concerned with religion and their thinking on religious problems was overlaid with mysticism. As Zenkovsky puts it: ". . . Russian thought remained at all times connected with *its own* religious elementality, its own religious soil; this was, and is, the chief root of its specific quality, but also of various complications in the development of Russian philosophic thought." [8]

Closely related to this religiosity is a historicism of a messianic character. Russian thought was ever concerned with the meaning of history, its ultimate end, the nature of man, and his role and fate in history. The Russian thinkers produced great theodicies of history charged with moralisms and permeated with the conviction that moral purpose was the dynamo of the social scene. In Berdyaev's phrase: "Russian thought was by its very intensity too totalitarian; it was incapable of remaining abstract philosophy; it wanted to be at the same time religious and social, and there was a strong ethical feeling in it." [9] Ever a "people of the end," as Berdyaev aptly describes them, the Russians strained to catch a glimpse of a millennium, which they believed was bound to come. Time and time again they affirmed an apocalyptic belief in the salvation of the community.

As for the instrumentalism in Russian thought, it was expressed in the

---

[6] For a short summary — with useful bibliographical references — of the concept of collectivity in the social sciences, see Earl Latham, "The Group Basis of Politics: Notes for a Theory," *American Political Science Review* (June 1952), pp. 376–398.

[7] This section is largely based on the following works: Nicholas Berdyaev, *The Russian Idea* (New York, 1948); Richard Hare, *Pioneers of Russian Social Thought* (London, 1951); N. O. Lossky, *History of Russian Philosophy* (New York, 1951); Sir John Maynard, *Russia in Flux*, ed. S. Haden Guest (New York, 1948); V. V. Zenkovsky, *A History of Russian Philosophy*, trans. George L. Kline, 2 vols. (New York, 1953) — hereafter cited as *History*.

[8] Zenkovsky, *History*, I, 2.

[9] Berdyaev, *Russian Idea*, pp. 156–157.

conscious linking of theory and practice. The mind was not encompassed as a *tabula rasa*, passively receiving the imprint of sense data. Knowledge was deemed to become possible only through man's actual relationship to the world, only through his activity in it. This idea of unity of abstract thought and life, with its pronounced moral *Unterschlag*, became one of the most important postulates in Russia's intellectual heritage.[10]

The profile of the Russian concept of collectivity becomes more clearly etched against the background of an indigenous idea, *sobornost'*, and an indigenous institution, the *mir*. Among the most important religious philosophers who nourished the idea of *sobornost'* was the Hegelian and Slavophile A. S. Khomiakov. In the succinct characterization of Professor Lossky: "The most valuable and fruitful of Khomiakov's ideas is his conception of *sobornost'*. *Sobornost'* means the combination of freedom and unity of many persons on the basis of their common love for the same absolute values."[11] Khomiakov visualized the Church as an all-embracing organic unity through which the individuality of its members could be fully realized. Freedom, truth, and love can only lie within the collectivity. Hate, ignorance, and destruction are found outside of it, in the realm of necessity.

A similar concept of freedom was held by Pëtr Chaadaev. Freedom, said he, depends upon our subjection to a higher principle, God. According to this Hegelian, if we do not subordinate our reason to a world consciousness, we slip into the trap of individualism, which he regarded as a perversion of true freedom. The philosophy of the individual contained in the doctrine of *sobornost'* was perhaps best stated by Iu. F. Samarin — a follower of Khomiakov — in the following words: ". . . only an artificial association can be based upon an individual person who makes himself the absolute measure of all things; no absolute norm, no law binding upon all men, can be logically deduced from the concept of individual personality, nor will history offer such a law."[12] Standing alone the individual is lost. His personal talents can only flower through the congregation. This loving congregation, of which he is a full participant, is the measure of all truth. Hence, once strayed from the fold, an individual can return to it only through complete renunciation and penitence.

The doctrine of *sobornost'* had a tremendous influence on most subsequent Russian thought, culminating perhaps in the writings of Vladimir Solov'ëv, considered by many to be Russia's greatest philosopher. For Solov'ëv, who was greatly influenced by Spinoza and Hegel, mankind was a real, collective organism. His pantheistic ideal of Godmanhood — the unity

---

[10] Zenkovsky, *History*, I, 5–7. For the present-day Soviet application of such a doctrine, see the statement on the unity of theory and practice in *History of the Communist Party of the Soviet Union (Bolsheviks): Short Course* (New York, 1939), pp. 355–359.

[11] Lossky, *History of Russian Philosophy*, p. 41.

[12] Zenkovsky, *History*, I, 231.

of godman as epitomized in Christ — was a universalized doctrine of *sobornost'* in which the transcendental essence of each individual is an aspect of the total organism.

Lastly, it should be pointed out that to many Russian thinkers the *mir* became the embodiment of the doctrine of *sobornost'*. K. S. Aksakov, another Hegelian and an important Slavophile publicist, discovered in the *mir* the social whole, to which the individual must be subordinated. "In the Russian *obshchina* the individual person is not suppressed, but merely deprived of his tumultuousness, exclusiveness, and egoism — only the egoistical aspect of personality is swallowed up in the *obshchina* — but the individual person is free in it, as in a chorus." [13] Aksakov saw the *mir* as society in minuscule which, as compared with the enslaving institution of the state, will liberate man. Herzen too shared the Slavophiles' veneration of the *mir*, believing that it would provide the foundation of a Russian collectivistic society, which might blaze a path for the rest of Europe to follow.[14] Likewise Chernyshevskii, who had no great faith in the Russian peasant, at the same time valued the *mir* for its collectivistic aspects. Similar views were held by other prominent Russian thinkers. There is little doubt that this traditional Russian institution became symbolized as the principle of collectivity in practice.

It will be seen, thus, that in its estimates and prescriptions concerning the respective roles and fates of individual and community, the pre-Soviet Russian concept of collectivity stands in substantial contrast to the Western outlook. The eschatological overtones and concept of individual submission to the corporate whole are unmistakable. There would seem to be, therefore, some plausibility in the argument that it provided a not wholly unfavorable milieu for the Soviet counterpart which emerged subsequently, that all that appeared to be necessary to bridge the gap between the two concepts of collectivity was to substitute the state for the congregation as the visible embodiment of community. In any case, whether consciously or otherwise, this is precisely what the ideologues and rationalizers of the present regime proceeded to do.

III. VYSHINSKY'S CONCEPTION OF COLLECTIVITY IN SOVIET SOCIETY

Unquestionably the outstanding Soviet rationalizer since the mid-thirties, put to the service of manipulating political symbols to sustain the Soviet

[13] *Ibid.*, pp. 235–236.

[14] It may be interesting to note that in 1870, the year of Herzen's passing, Marx referred to his hope of a future agrarian socialism based on the *mir* as "the imaginative lies of Citizen Herzen." Within the following decade both Marx and Engels changed their minds and took a far more favorable view of the *mir*. After Marx's death in 1883, Engels lost all interest in the *mir*, as did in fact Marx himself just before his death. See Marx and Engels, *Selected Correspondence, 1846–1895* (London, 1943), pp. 253, 284; *Selected Works* (Moscow, 1950), I, 23–24, II, 49; and David Mitrany, *Marx Against the Peasant* (London, 1951), p. 49.

regime, has been Andrei Vyshinsky, earlier Procurator General of the U.S.S.R. and now Deputy Minister of Foreign Affairs. Vyshinsky visualized his primary task as a dual one: (1) to undermine the thesis of the withering away of the state in the Soviet Union and to eradicate all vestiges of legal nihilism, and (2) to foster a positive sentiment for the state and its appurtenances as the living expression of community. The effort took the form of cultivating a set of rationalizations which may be classified under three main categories: the view of the Soviet state as the institutionalized collectivity, the idea of realization of individuality through this collectivity, and the concept of freedom through coercion.

A. The View of the Soviet State as the Institutionalized Collectivity

It may be recalled that Vyshinsky rode into prominence in the thirties on the basis of violent attacks on Stuchka, Pashukanis, Krylenko, Reisner, and other leading jurists, whom he accused as "wreckers" undermining the Soviet regime by distorting the Marxist teaching concerning the transition period, underestimating the nature and role of state and law in the U.S.S.R., and positing the thesis of their early demise. Quoting or paraphrasing Lenin and Stalin, Vyshinsky argued that "Marxism-Leninism makes no schematic outline of the withering away of the state," emphasizing instead the gradual, elemental, protracted nature of the withering process and underscoring its inevitable connection with such preconditions as the highest development of the economy, culture, and productivity and the radical transformation of human psychology. Only "under complete communism," when all citizens will have learned to administer social production and habitually to observe the basic rules of society, does the state's withering away become possible. But even then, he contended:

> The triumph of communism in the USSR cannot *per se* decide the question of relegating the state to a museum of antiquities. With a definite international situation — particularly, with the conditions of capitalist encirclement still preserved — the USSR will not be able, and will not have any right, to renounce such force as the socialist or communist state . . . In these conditions there can be no talk of any "withering away" of the state under victorious communism.

Hence Vyshinsky concluded with Stalin's dictum that the withering away of the state will come not through the weakening but the "maximum intensification" of state power, and he called for "reinforcing the socialist state and law by every means." [15]

From the standpoint of forging an identification between people and state such a call threatened to remain barren unless the citizenry could be shown that somehow the institution of the state in the U.S.S.R. was not the sheer instrument of repression which it was represented to be elsewhere. This

---

[15] Andrei Y. Vyshinsky, gen. ed., *The Law of the Soviet State*, trans. Hugh W. Babb (New York, 1948), ch. i, sec. ii, esp. pp. 53–62.

Vyshinsky proceeded to do in an avalanche of writings designed to prove that the Soviet state was a true people's state, a genuine collectivity.

His lengthy, intricate, and verbose expositiia can be summarized as follows.[16] While the "bourgeois" proposition that the state is a neutral institution standing above classes and law an expression of social solidarity is a myth, the Soviet state has become the supreme embodiment of such solidarity. It is "the most democratic form of authority in the world" and the actual realization of popular sovereignity.[17] The Soviet state is a new state, having smashed and replaced the old state machinery, retaining only some of its functions — such as banking and postal operations — in altered form.[18] This new state is needed by the proletariat during the period of transition to communism to crush the former exploiting groups and forge a bond between the proletarian and non-proletarian strata of the populace. As the political form of the proletarian dictatorship, it combines compulsion with training in discipline. But it is not fenced off from the people. Lenin scorned the idea that only the higher classes are capable of ruling and, although he valued the knowledge of the intelligentsia, he preferred the practical knack for organization of the workers and peasants and foresaw the rapid mastery of the art of government by the people. Accordingly, from its very inception the new state was designed "to attract the masses in every way to the management of state matters," to convert them from an object into the subject of government.[19]

The mechanism for this attraction comprises the soviets and mass organizations and activities. Intimate ties merging the millions of the masses with the governmental machinery are woven by such activities as the election and recall of deputies to the soviets, standing committees, deputy groups, street and bloc committees; mass meetings, consultations and delegate assemblies; criticism and self-criticism, the registering of complaints and suggestions; factory patronage over institutions, the employment of activist groups and other devices of mass observation or participation. And it is from these ties that the Soviet state draws its power and strength.[20]

The soviets themselves, which unlike the older parliaments are both

[16] While this summary is based upon an exhaustive examination of Vyshinsky's writings, primary reference for documentary purposes will be made here to *The Law of the Soviet State* — hereafter cited as *Law* — and *Voprosy teorii gosudarstva i prava* (Moscow, 1949) — hereafter cited as *Voprosy teorii* — comprising eleven papers and articles written between April 1938 and May 1948.

[17] Vyshinsky, *Law*, pp. 12, 23, 161, 165, 168.

[18] Vyshinsky, "Problema gosudarstvennogo upravleniia v trudakh V. I. Lenina" [1940], *Voprosy teorii*, pp. 195–196; *The Teachings of Lenin and Stalin on Proletarian Revolution and the State* (London, 1948), pp. 102–103, 112 — hereafter cited as *Teachings*.

[19] Vyshinsky, *Law*, pp. 40–43, 173; *Teachings*, p. 61; *Voprosy teorii*, pp. 196–198.

[20] Vyshinsky, *Law*, pp. 41–43, 174–176, 368, 468–469, 485–488; "Voprosy gosudarstva i prava v trudakh tovarishcha Stalina" [1939], *Voprosy teorii*, pp. 218, 221; *Sovetskoe gosudarstvo v otechestvennoi voine* (Moscow, 1944), p. 25.

representative and working organs, are huge mass institutions in which participation by peasants and intellectuals, no less than workers, has grown immensely. Consequently, the new Constitution properly renamed them "Soviets of Toilers' Deputies" because of their special character "as an *all-encompassing* mass organization, embracing all toilers." [21] Under this Constitution, introducing universal, secret, direct, and equal suffrage, elections to the soviets "are the broadest form" of drawing the masses into administration, since no limitations are placed upon the right to elect and be elected, and even "the initial disfranchisement of the bourgeoisie was only a temporary measure." [22] Likewise the system of justice, with people's assessors participating in court decisions and groups of volunteer collaborators and correspondents assisting the procurators, is designed to attract the people into state administration and makes the Soviet court "the only genuine people's court in the world." [23] The civil service, the territorial distribution of functions — the entire system of public administration is built to preserve the voice and protect the interests of the people. "There is no bureaucracy in the U.S.S.R." Soviet officials are not isolated caste-like from the populace, but are servants of society. And, while there is a high degree of centralization in administration, it is not a bureaucratic but a "democratic centralism." The state allows the separate localities initiative in ways and means of realizing general goals, striving at the same time "to unify these parts by a common conscious will, by common interests and tasks." [24]

All this adds up to a picture of "authentic democracy" and is proof that Lenin was right in criticizing theories concerning the general incompatibility and mutual exclusiveness of dictatorship and democracy. The Soviet dictatorship is guided by the Communist Party, which places its candidates in the responsible state posts, supplies directing decisions on all important matters, and verifies the work of the governmental organs. But this unique directing role does not alter the mass character of the dictatorship since, as Stalin explained, the Party operates through such "levers" and "transmission belts" as the trade unions, the soviets, coöperatives, and Youth League. The Party teaches the toilers methods of state work, and even the non-Party members of the soviets "are also convinced in practice of the correctness of the Party directions." [25]

As for the question of how the erstwhile dictatorship of one class — the proletariat — can be squared with the claim that Soviet authority embodies

[21] Vyshinsky, *Law*, pp. 166–168.

[22] *Ibid.*, pp. 665–666.

[23] *Ibid.*, p. 506; *Revoliutsionnaia zakonnost' na sovremennom etape* (Moscow, 1933), p. 76 — hereafter cited as *Revoliutsionnaia zakonnost'*; "Sovetskii sud i sovetskaia demokratiia," *Bolshevik*, no. 10 (1936), pp. 22–35; Speech at Second Session of Supreme Soviet, *Sovetskoe gosudarstvo*, no. 5 (1938), p. 42. This publication, later renamed *Sovetskoe gosudarstvo i pravo*, will be hereafter cited respectively as *S. g.* and *S. g. i p.*

[24] Vyshinsky, *Law*, pp. 230, 366–368, 370.

[25] *Ibid.*, pp. 160–161; *Teachings*, pp. 51–86.

the will of the entire people, Vyshinsky offers a tortuous explanation of a transmutation and fusion of wills by dialectical processes. Again dismissing as false assertions of a "general will" or "popular will" elsewhere, on the ground that such a phenomenon is impossible where antagonistic classes are in existence, he maintains that a general will *has* emerged in the U.S.S.R. It was part of Lenin's doctrine that where political power is held by a class whose interests coincide with those of the majority, government actually accords with the will of the majority. Prior to the Revolution, Lenin urged the incorporation of the majority of the Russian petty bourgeoisie into the revolutionary proletariat. The Bolsheviks, says Vyshinsky, sought and attained such incorporation on the eve of October, by winning over the majority of the toiling peasantry. The proletariat guided the peasantry and by word and deed helped to temper its will and associated it in fundamental matters. "As a result, the will of the worker class and of the peasantry basically coincided, blending into a general will of the overwhelming majority of toilers . . . Of course, this was a complex and dialectic process." Subsequently, with the victory of socialism and complete liquidation of exploiting classes in Soviet society, this will became "the will of the entire Soviet people." [26] And Soviet law is now the expression of the collective will of the whole people.[27] Ethnically too the friendship and equality of the Soviet nationalities makes for a singular unity of will. In sum, the Soviet state "is the first state in history where there is a genuine brotherhood of men collaborating in fraternal unity." [28] It is a true collectivity.

B. The Idea of Realization of Individuality through the Collectivity

In erecting this imaginary edifice of collectivity in Soviet society, Vyshinsky had recourse primarily to the pronouncements of Lenin and Stalin, as the architects of the new regime. In his attempt to project the emerging role of the individual in this collectivity Marx's philosophic constructs regarding the individual in the old society appeared to offer more useful background.

Marx and Engels believed that essentially human nature was subject to change through mutual interaction with its environment, that circumstances make men just as much as men make circumstances. "But the human essence," wrote Marx, "is no abstraction inherent in each single individual. In its reality, it is the ensemble of the social relations." [29] Labor, which is

---

[26] Vyshinsky, *Law*, pp. 168–172.

[27] "The will of the working class of the U.S.S.R. fuses with the will of the entire people. This provides the basis for speaking of our Soviet socialist law as the expression of the will of the entire people." Vyshinsky, "Osnovnye zadachi nauki sovetskogo sotsialisticheskogo prava" [1938], *Voprosy teorii*, p. 87. See also "Protsessual'noe pravo v sotsialisticheskom gosudarstve rabochikh i krest'ian," *S. g.*, no. 6 (1938), pp. 28–29, and compare *Law*, p. 50.

[28] Vyshinsky, "Lenin i Stalin — Osnovopolozhniki i stroiteli sovetskogo gosudarstva," *Pod znamenem marksizma*, no. 8–9 (1942), p. 15.

[29] "Theses on Feuerbach," no. 6, *Selected Works*, II, 366.

essential to human existence, is social in character, since man works in coöperation with other men. Man himself is a social animal "but an animal which can develop into an individual only in society."[30] Of all animals, man alone is capable of creating his own conditions and, within the limits of the economic framework of society, of making his own history. Man is by nature purposeful and creative. But his creativity has been debauched by the modern economic order and class warfare. Man has become isolated from the community, from life itself. The division between town and countryside has resulted in the mental atrophy of the peasant and physical aberration of the proletarian. The fissures of society have brought about the fragmentation of the individual: "In the division of labor man is also divided." True creativity can return to him only with the disappearance of classes under socialism, and the emergence of an integrated society.[31]

This thesis served as a springboard for Vyshinsky's dissertation on the new dispensation for the individual in the U.S.S.R. His argument comprises three principal postulates: that the establishment of socialism has opened the floodgates of opportunity for the citizenry; that the interests of personality and society are entirely identical; and that individual creativity finds its expression through the collectivity in the Soviet Union.

Quoting chapter and verse from Marx regarding the corrupting influence of private property on human virtues and feelings, Vyshinsky contends that the attainment of a socialist economy registered by Article 4 of the Constitution has eliminated the exploitation of man by man in the U.S.S.R. and released the means for the full flowering of the personality.[32] The hypothesis maintained by bourgeois social scientists that the individual and society are constantly and irrevocably antithetical has no application in the U.S.S.R. "Only in exploiter societies is such antithesis inherent: to socialism it is foreign."[33] The attempt of earlier Soviet jurists to emphasize the dependent and subordinate nature of the individual's rights and interests in the U.S.S.R. were crude distortions, since there is no contradiction between general interests and individual interests in the Soviet state.[34] As Stalin told H. G. Wells:

There neither is nor should be an irreconcilable contrast between the individual and the collective, between the interests of the individual personality and those of

---

[30] Marx, *A Contribution to the Critique of Political Economy*, trans. from 2nd German edition by N. I. Stoke (Chicago, 1904), p. 268.

[31] Friedrich Engels, *Herr Eugen Dühring's Revolution in Science* (Anti-Dühring), trans. Emile Burns, ed. C. P. Dutt (New York, 1939), p. 318; Karl Marx and Friedrich Engels, *The German Ideology*, Parts I and III, ed. R. Pascal (New York, 1939), p. 44.

[32] Vyshinsky, "20 let proletarskoi diktatury i Stalinskaia konstitutsiia," *S. g.*, no. 6 (1937), pp. 40–41; *Law*, p. 77.

[33] Vyshinsky, *Law*, p. 539.

[34] *Ibid.*, pp. 76, 629–630, 665; *Voprosy teorii*, pp. 26–28. *Rech' tovarishcha Stalina 4 maia i zadachi organov iustitsii* (Moscow, 1935), p. 11. Vyshinsky leveled his main criticisms against Kobalevskii, Evtikhiev, and Krylenko.

the collective. There should be none forasmuch as collectivism — socialism — does not deny individual interests; it amalgamates them with the interests of the collective.[35]

The idea that socialism must mean a leveling of individual wants and personal tastes is sheer fiction. The Soviet Constitution is graphic proof that the social and economic equality inaugurated by socialism "creates such conditions for all-sided development of all the capacities and creative forces of the individual that man's complete freedom and happiness are assured for the first time in history." [36]

C. The Concept of Freedom through Coercion

The missing link in this conception of Soviet man's new-born freedom cradled in a synthesis of society, state, and personality was some elucidation of the whys and wherefores of the violence and compulsion facing the citizen at every turn. The pattern of explanation chosen by Vyshinsky draws a sign of equation between state constraint and legitimate limits of liberty, posits law as the great molder of the collectivity, elevates work and discipline to a position of paramount importance in the system of rights and duties, and evolves a concept of the "rule of law" fundamentally reserving freedom of action for the Soviet rulers.

Taking up the relationship between the state, law, and freedom, Vyshinsky deprecates all theories which posit the rights of the personality as a limitation upon the state and divine the essence of civil rights as freedom from the state. Every land and epoch has known limitations on man's freedom. Law limits the will of the individual, and "unlimited freedom of the will of man cannot exist and never has existed anywhere." [37] Those who assert that freedom for all becomes possible only with the disappearance of governmental power are nurturing a baseless concept of the "autocracy of personality" and denying the possibility of coexistence of law and freedom. "Between 'freedom for all' and the dictatorship of the proletariat there is no contradiction." [38] Under this dictatorship law constitutes a method of control on the part of society over the measure of toil and consumption. For, law is ever tied to economic relations, the totality of which Hegel had called "civil society." Insofar as there is still inequality in Soviet society in the distribution of the social product, with citizens being remunerated according to their work rather than needs, Soviet law is still unequal law.[39]

[35] Vyshinsky, *Law*, p. 540.
[36] *Ibid.*, p. 539.
[37] Vyshinsky, *Voice of the USSR* (London, 1946), pp. 18–19; *Law*, p. 563, n. 22.
[38] Vyshinsky "Dvadtsat' let sovetskogo gosudarstva," *S. g.*, no. 5 (1937), p. 17. Vyshinsky attacked particularly A. G. Goikhbarg, who wrote in 1919: "With the complete consolidation of collectivism all civil and general laws will disappear. The harmonious existence of people cannot be built on social compulsion, social necessities, or in other words rights, but on complete social freedom." See Vyshinky, "Polozhenie na pravovom fronte," *S. g.*, no. 3–4 (1937), pp. 30–31.
[39] *Voprosy teorii*, pp. 232–233.

The dictatorship likewise preserves the function of violence. Lenin and Stalin "completely refuted" the assertion that violence is incompatible with democracy. "Proletarian revolutionary violence" is democratic in essence and form, because it is directed to the defense of the interests of the majority of toilers and is realized with their active participation. Democracy is a form of political organization of the state, and as such "unachievable without violence." So long as democracy is present, violence in some form will also be present. What distinguishes Soviet democracy is that it is a means toward the ultimate elimination of violence, toward "building society without classes, without a state, and consequently without violence." [40]

In this progressing reorganization of society Soviet law plays a tremendous role as molder of the collectivity. The dictatorship operates not only by force but by means of persuasion, seeking to eliminate "the survivals of capitalism" from the consciousness of men, which — as Lenin predicted — persist long after the proletarian seizure of power. In the process of reëducation and inculcation of new attitudes and traditions, law serves to foster a legal consciousness among the citizenry, thus contributing to the progressive formation of a habit of observance of community standards without constraint.[41] Thus, in both its compulsive and educative aspects, law is an active instrument in the struggle for communism in the U.S.S.R.

To balance the admission of the role of force, Vyshinsky makes much of the rights of the Soviet citizens inscribed in the Constitution. What is more significant, however, is that he not only underscores the equal importance of duties, but places an extraordinary emphasis on work as a duty and the primacy of discipline in all spheres of Soviet life. His arguments in this sphere are designed to show that the Soviet Union is moving toward realization of Marx's concept of work as discipline and at the same time emancipator of man — the means to his freedom and the vehicle to his resurrection as a complete, balanced, harmonious individual. And the *raison d'état* behind this claim is to justify in the citizen's mind the state's perpetual demands for his obedience, loyalty, and sacrificial devotion to duty.

"The right to work," says Vyshinsky, "is the foundation whereon the Soviet citizen's rights and freedoms rest." [42] At the same time, the Constitution makes it a duty and matter of honor for every able-bodied citizen, in accordance with the principle: "He who does not work, neither shall he eat" (Article 12). The Soviet order encourages socially beneficial labor through such practices as socialist competition, shock-working, a system of professional schooling, and training to raise qualifications. All of these open up vistas of developing the citizen's creative capacities, and comprise the conditions essential "for turning labor completely into a natural need of man-

[40] Vyshinsky, *Law*, pp. 161–163.
[41] *Ibid.*, p. 52; *Teachings*, pp. 59, 108.
[42] Vyshinsky, *Law*, p. 563.

kind in the higher phase of communism."[43] But telling progress toward that phase hangs first of all on discipline. The proletariat itself must go through a school of education in discipline: ". . . the problem of discipline is the fundamental problem of socialist organization, socialist society, and socialist work."[44] The toilers must follow in the footsteps of the record-breaking Stakhanovites, who are prime examples in the present of disciplined workers possessed of new attitudes toward work and social duty. Their achievements are not a matter of overexertion, but of a cultural approach to work. For, as Molotov pointed out, reckoning the minutes and seconds of one's work establishes order in the work process and gets things completed without idling and wasting of time. Stakhanovism provides the means for overcoming the contradictions between mental and physical toil, the vast development of production, and the attainment of material abundance: it is one of the main paths for the transition to communism.[45]

This all-pervading conception of work and discipline as the twin keys to the Communist millennium, provides the standing justification for the invasion of the citizen's freedoms in the name of the new "freedom." Its significance is enhanced by Vyshinsky's fundamental thesis concerning the nature and scope of revolutionary legality in Soviet society.

The designation "revolutionary legality" (like "revolutionary expediency" and similar terms) owes its inception to a duality of attitude concerning the realm of law in the Soviet state. On the one hand there was the demand for recognition and strict observance of law, on the other the reservation that extra-legal, administrative action was permissible to meet the needs of revolutionary expediency.[46] The vagueness of the concept gave rise to contradictory interpretations, and in the early twenties voices were raised to emphasize the "legality" part of the formula for governors and governed alike. Bukharin, for instance, declared in 1923: "Revolutionary legality means an end to any arbitrary administration, including the revolutionary."[47] With the forced pace of industrialization and collectivization, however, the emphasis shifted to expediency; and Vyshinsky emerged as the champion of unrestricted power for the regime in the pursuit of its revolutionary course. Taking violent issue with Bukharin's contention, he declared: "In a proletarian state, every measure — regardless of whether it is 'legal' or 'extraordinary' — has as its source the dictatorship of the proletariat. Were it otherwise, revolutionary legality would become its own contradiction — a fetter upon the proletarian revolution." The proletarian dictatorship is itself "the highest law," defining the concrete content of all and every law. It

---

[43] *Ibid.*, p. 207.

[44] Vyshinsky, *Revoliutsionnaia zakonnost'*, p. 81; *Teachings*, p. 60.

[45] Vyshinsky, "Glava sovetskogo pravitel'stva," *S. g. i p.*, no. 2 (1940), pp. 12–13; "Lenin i Stalin o gosudarstve i prave," *S. g. i p.*, no. 1 (1939), pp. 59–60.

[46] See Vladimir Gsovski, *Soviet Civil Law* (Ann Arbor, 1948), I, 154ff.

[47] Vyshinsky, *Revoliutsionnaia zakonnost'*, pp. 50–51.

is what Lenin called it: "a power not limited by any laws, not restrained by any absolute rules, resting directly on force." [48] The dictatorship employs both laws and extraordinary administrative measures. Law is *one* of its means of struggle, a method of the dictatorship. Consequently, judges and jurists must always look at a law from the standpoint of whether or not it answers the needs of the revolution, rather than stress the wording or legal formula of the law. "The formal law is subordinate to the law of the Revolution," Vyshinsky concluded. "There might be collisions and discrepancies between the formal commands of laws and those of the proletarian revolution . . . The collision must be solved only by subordination of the formal commands of law to those of Party policy." [49]

There was one danger lurking in the above formulation. Since policy is all too frequently a fluctuating quantity, were the tie between law and policy taken too literally, law would lose the character of a firm guide for the citizen's conduct. Its utility as an instrument of the regime would actually diminish. The problem became particularly acute by the mid-thirties when the exactions of the economic program made discipline the watchword of daily life. Taking his cue from Stalin's call in 1936 for "stability of laws," Vyshinsky unleashed a vigorous program in Soviet jurisprudence and legal practice to emphasize strict legality. Now denouncing theories reducing law to policy on the ground that they raise doubts with the citizens regarding the defense of their interests, he loudly called for the firm observance of the laws: "Why is stability of statutes essential: Because it reinforces the stability of the state order and of the state discipline . . . The law not merely gives rights, it imposes obligations." [50]

By thus redressing the balance of emphases, Vyshinsky became the leading traditionalizer and conventionalizer of Soviet legal science. The modified approach leaves executive irresponsibility untouched. For the citizens it means strict obedience to law as the first rule of conduct. For the rulers it means fundamental freedom of action and the primacy of politics. Claiming legitimacy by reference to a higher law of dictatorship leading the citizens on a road to ultimate statelessness, it is a concept of freedom through coercion.

In sum, by a series of ideational and semantic equations, identifying the interests of the citizens with those of society, and of society with the state, equating democracy with dictatorship, and freedom with state compulsion, Vyshinsky has arrived at a totalitarian concept of the collectivity in the U.S.S.R. which promises to keep the individual submerged for a long time to come in Soviet society.

---

[48] Vyshinsky, *Revoliutsionnaia zakonnost'*, pp. 51, 52, 55.

[49] Vyshinsky, *Sudoustroistvo v SSSR* (Moscow, 1936), p. 24.

[50] Vyshinsky, *Law*, p. 51.

IV. THE SIGNIFICANCE OF VYSHINSKY'S THEORIES

The above rationalizations of the Party line represent an attempt by an important spokesman of the Party leaders to spin a web of legitimacy about the *Machtpolitik* of the Kremlin. It is not within the province of this paper to essay a refutation of the maze of myths and apologia interlacing Vyshinsky's exposition. The mocking realities of Soviet life have provided a sufficient answer to the principal theses of his exegesis. What lies within our purview is at least a cursory attempt at a genetic assessment of the place of his theories in the realm of ideas.

There seems to be an obvious affinity between certain elements in the Russian intellectual heritage and various constituents of the Marxist-Soviet world view expounded by Vyshinsky. Certainly the older idea of collectivity, with its conception of the Congregation as an organic unity and sole seat of truth and freedom which requires the service and absolute obedience of its members and through which alone the brethren attain their salvation, finds its counterparts in the Soviet conception. In Vyshinsky's theory too the new collectivity — the Soviet polity — is conceived as a monolithic unity, guided by the higher laws of the Party's ideology, and demanding the disciplined conformance of the citizens in the name of their own self-realization through service to a supreme common cause in the present and emerging future. And the strands of instrumentalism, religiosity, and messianism (as expressed in the thesis of a beautiful, classless, and ultimately stateless order) are as strong in the Soviet concept as in the older Russian tradition. That tradition appears to have exercised a definite, if perhaps unconscious and unheralded, influence upon Soviet thinking, including that of Vyshinsky.

Apparently another strong influence upon him were the writings of Hegel. A striking parallelism exists between the thought of the two, and the analogy becomes even more significant in the light of the known influence of Hegel upon nineteenth-century Russian thought.[51] Like Vyshinsky, an articulate rationalizer of the values of an autocratic state, Hegel sought to entrench the position of law as a tool of the state. His castigation of the legal nihilists of his day are reminiscent of Vyshinsky's vitriolic polemics against the early Soviet jurists.[52] If for Hegel the Prussian state was "the Divine Idea as it exists on Earth,"[53] for Vyshinsky the Soviet state is the apotheosis of the

---

[51] By far the best single work on the subject is D. I. Chizhevskii, *Gegel' v Rossii* (Paris: Dom Knigi, 1939).

[52] See, for example, his criticism of von Haller in *Hegel's Philosophy of Right*, trans. with notes by T. M. Knox (Oxford, 1942), p. 158.

Herbert Marcuse might well have spoken of Vyshinsky when he wrote: "For Hegel the rule of law 'was to be the lever' of the transformation from an anarchic social order to a society based on reason and regulated through an all-powerful state" (*Reason and Revolution: Hegel and the Rise of Social Theory* [London, 1941], pp. 181–182).

[53] Hegel, *Philosophy of History*, trans. J. Sibree (New York, 1912), p. 87. For valuable surveys of Hegel's thought see, in addition to Marcuse's work, M. B. Foster, *The*

Marxist idea in the current epoch. For both, the law of the state is the expression of the true will of the citizenry, and is identical with their interests — the state becomes the embodiment of reason, morality, and freedom.

Hegel views the state as the "actualization of freedom," and law as the expression of this "content of objective freedom." [54] Since the individual is only the particular manifestation of the state, which corporealizes the universal, the ends of the state are not different from the specific ends of the individual. If a clash takes place between the two, the individual must alter his ends, for — by Hegel's very definition — they cannot have been in his true interests. In the Hegelian purview, the individual has become a means to the end of the state, freedom is submission to the state, and justice what the high priests of the state say it is.[55] These conceptions are remarkably reminiscent of Vyshinsky's justifications of the Party summit as an infallible elite, whose interpretations of the Communist creed and guidance of the Soviet ship of state are in the nature of a higher law.

Thus, for both Vyshinsky and Hegel, freedom is achieved when man's subjective will yields to and is molded by law. Both emphasize the importance of man's duty to the state as the prime way in which his objective or true freedom may be realized. Duty limits man's subjective will and liberates his objective will. By policing himself — by fulfilling his duty — the citizen becomes integrated into the whole, the true community or *Allgemeinheit*. He becomes a purposeful, conscious participant in the collectivity. As Hegel put it in a passage which may have inspired the many similar statements in Vyshinsky's writings:

> The conjunction of duty and right has a twofold aspect: what the state demands from us as duty is *eo ipso* our right as individuals, since the state is nothing but the articulation of the concept of freedom. The determinations of the individual will are given an objective embodiment through the state and thereby they attain their truth and their actualization for the first time. The state is the one and only prerequisite of the attainment of particular ends and welfare.[56]

Thus, in the labyrinthine concept of collectivity of Hegel and Vyshinsky, the distinction between freedom and necessity has been obliterated. The individual is ground under the wheel of "objective freedom" and the state emerges as a towering authoritarian institution.

To summarize, Vyshinsky's concept of collectivity has been an effort to conserve the institutions of the regime, to legitimize the status quo, and to

---

Political Philosophies of Plato and Hegel (Oxford, 1935) ; W. T. Stace, *The Philosophy of Hegel: A Systematic Exposition* (London, 1924). For Hegel's influence on Marx, see Sidney Hook, *From Hegel to Marx* (New York, 1936), pp. 15–76 and Karl Popper, *The Open Society and Its Enemies* (Princeton, 1950), pp. 661–662, n. 2.

[54] *Philosophy of Right*, p. 279, and *Philosophy of Mind,* as quoted in Marcuse, *Reason and Revolution*, p. 218.

[55] See particularly the statement on freedom in his *Philosophy of History*, pp. 91–92.

[56] Hegel, *Philosophy of Right,* p. 280.

traditionalize values and beliefs deemed fundamental by the Party leadership. In the making of this concept the Russian tradition of collectivity and adaptation of Marxism have played a distinct role. For the West, collectivity has come to mean sufficient public intervention to secure the citizen's welfare without negating his freedom. For the East, collectivity has ushered in a tyranny in the name of the general will, the collective consciousness — predicated on a dialectical mystique. The West has stripped Marxism of its Hegelian mysticism. The East has taken Marx as a prophet and made his ideas the servants of a religious fanaticism. As one of its important proselytizers, Vyshinsky appears to have wedded the Hegelian inspired concept of collectivity, grown on his native soil, with the Hegelian constituents of the imported doctrine of Marxism. This metaphysical symbiosis has absorbed the individual and obliterated any distinction between might and right. Its implications for the future of man and the world are at the very heart of the current struggle for the minds of men.

The Hero and Society: The Literary Definitions
(1855–1865, 1934–1939)

RUFUS W. MATHEWSON, JR.

Vladimir, upon seeing his church completed, entered it and prayed to God, saying "Lord God! . . . Make these new people, whose heart thou hast turned unto wisdom, to know thee as the true God."

> *The Primary Chronicle*

Monks are not a special sort of men but only what men ought to be.

> Father Zosima in
> *The Brothers Karamazov*

There are only three like you in the town at the moment, but in future generations there will be more — ever more and more — and a time will come when everything will change to your way and people will live like you, then you too will grow old and people will be born who will live better than you.

> Vershinin in
> *The Three Sisters*

In answer to the *narodnik's* assertion that the masses are nothing but a mob, and that it is heroes who make history and convert the mob into a people, the Marxists affirmed that it was not heroes that make history but history that makes heroes, and that, consequently, it is not heroes who create a people but the people who create heroes and move history onward. Heroes, outstanding individuals, may play an important part in the life of society only in so far as they are capable of correctly understanding the conditions of development of society and the ways of changing them for the better. Heroes, outstanding individuals, may become ridiculous and useless failures if they do not correctly understand the conditions of development of society in the conceited belief that they are the "makers" of history.

> *History of the C.P.S.U. (B.)*

I

A kind of spiritual history which is unique to Russia may be read in the succession of emblematic men who dominate so much of her literature from the baptism of Vladimir to the beatification of Stalin.[1] Cast in roles both

[1] Vladimir and Stalin stand in a similar relation to the company of heroes who perform great patriotic deeds in their names. Neither is, or can be, a positive literary hero himself.

subversive and conformist, supplying inspiration, instruction, or consolation, they make up an extravagant gallery of human types: tsar-despots, both benevolent and terrible; martyred saints, bandit revolutionaries, *bogatyri, raisonneurs;* and now commissars, factory managers, bureaucrats, and bee-keepers. But in few cases or to only a minor degree do these images represent living men or observed behavior. They are rather models for men, and their adventures tend to illustrate a design for life as it should be, or as it should have been, or as it should be thought to be. With this reservation in mind we are able to "read" these men as emblems of the extra-literary purposes which shape their characters and direct their destinies, even as they fail as figures of genuine literary or human interest.

When the Russians overcame the literary lag in the nineteenth century and became full-fledged contributors to the European literary community, the preoccupation with the persuasive function of the literary hero underwent important changes. He was relieved to a large degree of his role as a controlled spokesman for nonliterary ideas, for example, 'and he was permitted to exhibit personal weakness and to fail in his public commitments. But it did not end. The "superfluous man" was ironically intended as a hero of his time. And the "new man," thought up by the radical democrats between 1855 and 1865 to replace him in life and literature, represented a return to the explicitly virtuous, emblematic men of earlier forms. This latter type was to find it very difficult to enact his earnest, uplifting message in the broad reaches of the realistic novel, a form notably hostile to the tendentious representation of virtue. Yet even though he disclosed fatal (and sometimes tragic) weaknesses in the glare of Turgenev's and Dostoyevsky's insight, he found permanent sources of vitality in the needs of the sequence of revolutionary movements, which have prolonged his life down to the Soviet present.

The striking resemblances between the "nonsuperfluous" new man of the radicals and Stalin's new Soviet man suggest a direct transmission of ideas across the turbulent years separating their respective formulations.[2] We must be content simply to note the similarities between them, and pass over the question of the channels of transmission, only naming the two permanent preoccupations of the Russian intellect that seem to be most closely bound up with the matter of the positive political hero: first, the utilitarian aesthetic developed by Chernyshevskii, now echoed everywhere by Soviet critics; and second, the body of moral ideas which may be said to constitute a Russian revolutionary ethos.

The nearly universal concern in intellectual circles between 1855 and

[2] In an earlier paper, "The Soviet Hero and the Literary Heritage," *American Slavic and East European Review* (Winter, 1953), pp. 506–523, I have been concerned with some of the indications that these early Russian radicals were the first formulators of the theories of Socialist Realism, and that they have become, together with Lenin, of course, the foremost authorities on Soviet literary matters, replacing Marx, Engels, and Plekhanov.

1865 with the self-assured young atheists of the new generation suggests that an identifiable new type had indeed appeared on the Russian scene. We shall not here attempt to confirm or deny this, nor to say that Chernyshevskii's or Turgenev's is the more accurate description. Our interest in him is in his less tangible but more enduring existence as the pilot-model for a kind of moral personality that is at the center of the Soviet cult of heroism.

The origins of these Soviet ideas are most clearly exposed in the decade surrounding the emancipation of the serfs. In the complicated intellectual debates that flared up at that time a great deal of attention was devoted to the moral nature and the social utility of the new candidate for heroism. We find here two contrasting views of a personified political morality which has proved to be more durable than the changing doctrines it has been called upon to support. This complex of ideas was examined more closely by both its critics and its advocates than at any time since. If we are justified in thinking that the Soviet cult of the hero began in the nineteenth century, the searching critique of the new man by the nonradical writers of the mid-century should apply as aptly to its present manifestations as it did to the hopeful and unreal portrait drawn by the radical democrats.

The new man was felt to be necessary before anyone claimed to have seen him in Russian life. Belinskii, who initiated the major trends of radical democratic thought, provided him with an essential ingredient of any optimistic revolutionary philosophy: a theory of progress — borrowed, of course, from Hegel — which he conceived as a dialectical movement issuing from the universal struggle of moral ideas — healthy *vs.* unhealthy, altruistic *vs.* egotistic — which would result finally in a state of national "self-awareness" and the victory of the ascendant phase of the dialectic. Though "negative" phenomena crowded in on Belinskii and his contemporaries, there were signs that the war in the universe would soon go well for the partisans of the upward, positive trend. These signs of change, Belinskii felt, were to be most clearly observed in men's moral personalities:

> It is a fact beyond a shadow of doubt that the number of people who are endeavoring to realize their moral convictions in deeds to the detriment of their private interests and at the risk of their social position has been growing perceptibly with us . . .[3]

In Belinskii's view, the process of social change happened first *inside* men,[4] who then became active fighters for progress in the world of ideas

---

[3] V. G. Belinsky, *Selected Philosophical Works,* ed. M. Yovchuk (Moscow, 1948), p. 338.

[4] Belinskii wrote: ". . . the source of all progress and advance lies in human nature . . ." (*Ibid.,* p. 375). The human intellect, not the objective world of social forces, was the primary battleground of the contending forces in the universe. Though this seems to contradict Marxian materialism, Soviet ideologists have simply transferred the locus of the struggle without questioning Belinskii's (or Marx's or Lenin's) assurances as to its happy outcome. Belinskii's particular contribution to Soviet critics has been his insistence that imaginative literature reflect this general view of history.

and institutions outside themselves. A major responsibility of those already liberated was to liberate others, and it was not long before writers were enlisted in this effort. In 1856 Chernyshevskii issued an impatient call for a "successor" to the earlier archetype, widely known by this time as the "superfluous man." New conditions had made the older type obsolete, Chernyshevskii felt, and he issued a general description of the new type for the benefit of writers who would search him out, presumably, and build their novels around him:

We are still waiting for this successor, who, having accustomed himself to the truth from childhood, regards it not with tremulous ecstasy but with joyous love; we are awaiting such a man and his speech, a very cheerful . . . calm . . . decisive speech, in which would sound not theory's timidity before life, but proof that reason can achieve mastery over life and that man can harmonize his life with his convictions.[5]

In this first a priori prescription are listed not only some of his principal character traits, but also as we shall see below, the key elements in his adjustment to the world. In the definition of the terms "reason," "convictions," "mastery," and "life" are contained the permanent dimensions of the moral universe this archetypical individual was to inhabit.

In the sketch we are about to make of his personality, it is important to understand the ambivalent relation he bore to his unhappy predecessor. In one sense the new man was a progressive mutation beyond the older type, incorporating his best features and adding new ones which corrected basic deficiencies in the latter's make-up. But with the added qualities, notably his capacity to act in the face of overwhelmingly hostile circumstance, he became in the eyes of the radical critics the opposite of his idle, frustrated, self-centered, self-pitying predecessors. It is true, the radical description of the early types seems hasty, careless of distinctions, and is admittedly based on a single outward consequence of their quite disparate inner natures, namely, their inability to act effectively in a social milieu. It has been argued that men as different as Pechorin, Rudin, and Oblomov simply do not belong within the confines of a single generalization. But there are still grounds for grouping them together under the broader heading, "alienated men." Their apartness, whether chosen or enforced, their state of paralysis, whatever combination of inhibition and prohibition has brought it about, and their final condition of aloneness, deprivation or defeat, are all functions of their human incompleteness, and of their disengagement from life. The radicals, in contrast, sought a formula for the full realization of the self, a kind of integration which would engage the whole of man's generous natural endowment of human qualities in the performance of specific public tasks.

[5] N. G. Chernyshevskii, *Estetika i literaturnaia kritika*, ed. B. I. Bursov (Moscow-Leningrad, 1951), p. 409. The article in question, "The Poetry of Ogarëv," appeared three years before Dobroliubov's "What Is Oblomovism?"

Some of the most detailed models for the new harmonious man are to be found in Dobroliubov's critical articles between 1859 and his death in 1861. The deepest source of the new man's assurance is in his understanding of his situation in a dialectically unfolding universe. In language which recalls Engels' famous definition of freedom as "the recognition of necessity," Dobroliubov wrote:

> Recognizing the immutable laws of historical development, the men of the present generation do not place unreal hopes upon themselves, do not think they can alter history at their own will, do not think they are immune to the influence of circumstance . . . But at the same time they do not in the least sink into apathy and indifference, for they are also aware of their own worth. They look upon themselves as one of the wheels of a machine, as one of the circumstances which govern the course of world events. As all world circumstances are interconnected and to some extent subordinated to each other, they too are subordinated to necessity, to the force of things; but beyond this subordination they do not bow to any idols whatsoever, they uphold the independence and sovereignty of all their actions against all . . . claims.[6]

In this formula for individual release through knowledge from the blind rigors of a determined universe, direct connection is established between awareness of the world and the kind of independent, defiant, self-contained personality which can operate most successfully in it. The ingredients of heroism, it is suggested here, are implicit in the very nature of the historical process.

The knowledge that liberates the new man is of two kinds. First he must have a full, rational understanding of the irrational and unjust environment that surrounds him. Social consciousness, according to Dobroliubov, grew in men's minds in the following sequence: from awareness of the unjust fact, to the formulation of a general idea about it, thence to the generation first of an intellectual intention, and then of an emotional "striving" to change or abolish it. But this was not enough. The best and bravest members of the superfluous generation had reached this point and then had been halted by the hitherto insuperable obstacles between the striving and the deliberate, socially useful *act* which alone could bring the formula to completion. The cerebration could be considered completed, and the superabundant flow of good intentions, long dammed up by the barriers to action, had stagnated and only added to the noisome atmosphere. The superfluous man deserved credit for keeping alive the spirit of dissent during the darkest hours of the Nicholas era, but now, when the arenas for action were rapidly widening, the mere proclamation of noble intentions was seen as a contemptible act of vanity.

The missing ingredient which would close the circuit and propel men of good will into fruitful activity was a matter not of intellection but of moral

[6] As quoted in M. Yovchuk's introductory article in N. A. Dobrolyubov, *Selected Philosophical Essays* (Moscow, 1948), p. xxiv.

character. To achieve this a second kind of knowledge was necessary: each individual had to become aware of the "natural" endowment of energy and virtue within himself. Through constant and close communion with this fund of innate qualities he would become increasingly conscious of the discrepancies between the instinctive demands of his sense of his human dignity, which he shared with all men, and their daily violation by the tyrannous and unhealthy environment. With this awakened sensitivity he could no longer remain submissive to injustice or prejudice: "it is impossible to live any longer with tyranny's violent and deadening principles." [7]

The virtues that proceed out of the sense of one's "inalienable right to life, happiness, and love" are precisely those that overcome ennui, inertia, and the faint heart. "One must have the mind of a genius," Dobroliubov conceded, but one must possess as well "the pure heart of an infant and a will of titanic power" to dare to enter upon the only kind of activity which proposes itself to the new man, "real and effective struggle against the environment." [8]

Dobroliubov found a nearly perfect illustration of his heroic blueprint in the Bulgarian revolutionary, Insarov, hero of Turgenev's *On the Eve*. He was more than a catalogue of the requisite virtues; he had achieved the harmonious welding of "convictions" with personal emotions that Chernyshevskii had called for in 1856. And in this integration, Dobroliubov felt that he had discovered a formula which was an infallible corrective for the fractured personality of the alienated man. In the unity of his private and public emotions and in his total dedication to the liberation of his country, Insarov displayed an integration of mind, body, conscience, and heart that guaranteed mastery over life. This individual had no loose ends, was susceptible to no casually arising claims:

> Insarov's love for the freedom of his country lies not alone in his mind, nor in his heart nor his imagination: it permeates his whole being, and whatever else penetrates his being is transformed by the power of this feeling, submits to it and merges with it.[9]

Guided "by its nature, its whole being," this monolithic individual had achieved a focus for his energies which brooked no hesitation, faltered before no obstacles. This kind of character "is concentrated and resolute, undeviatingly loyal to the sense of natural truth, imbued with faith in new ideals and is self-sacrificing in the sense that it prefers death to life under a system which it detests." [10] At a time when discussion of revolutionary strategy and tactics was largely academic, the moral code of the new hero contained the

[7] *Ibid.*, p. 626.
[8] *Ibid.*, p. 287.
[9] *Ibid.*, p. 412.
[10] *Ibid.*, p. 597.

program for action as well as the guarantee of its success. As the instrument which first freed itself from the disfiguring environment, and then conducted the assault against it, the new hero *was* the revolution.

But Dobroliubov could find no more than scattered hints in either life or literature that the "new strong Russian character" had made his appearance on the scene. Neither fictional Bulgarians nor the traditionally more forceful heroines of several works (notably Goncharov's *Oblomov,* Turgenev's *On the Eve,* and Ostrovskii's *Storm*) were entirely adequate images of the new man as Dobroliubov and his colleagues conceived him. The public was calling for him, conditions were ripe to sustain him, and the sufferings of the people made his tangible presence obligatory. But none of these pressures was sufficient to force him into being.

Chernyshevskii continued the search and produced the first, and, as it turned out, the only official, full-length "portrait" of the hero the radicals sought, in his novel, *What's to Be Done?* subtitled *From Stories About the New Man.*[11] True to his prescription for the new man's harmonious fusion of "conviction" with "life," he has rooted every motive of his characters in a creed and has made their every action illustrate a phase of his program for the good life. An ethical theory underlies the entire work and guides the behavior of the principals at every step in this bizarre story of a model marriage between two representatives of the new people, a subsequent triangle involving a third new man, and a miraculously rational resolution. The source of control over their own emotions is the moral formula, "enlightened self-interest," borrowed without alteration from the French rationalists, which is repeatedly commended to the reader's attention for his instruction and benefit. These marriages are made complete — we might almost say that in that arid atmosphere they are consummated — in a program of shared activity in the service of others, as scientists, doctors, educators, directors of coöperatives. At the basis of these doctrinal tags which direct their lives and which their lives, in turn, illustrate, is the public emotion "Love of Mankind." No action of the characters occurs — or can conceivably occur, without their forfeiting their standing as new men — which violates this all-embracing, if highly abstract, commitment.

One character stands apart from all the others, a truly uncommon man among uncommon men. Though he plays a minor role in the central intrigue — intervening at only one crucial point to set everything right with his superior wisdom — the entire novel, in a sense, is his vehicle. He is Rakhmetov, the "rigorist," and, though Chernyshevskii can never say so, a dedicated

---

[11] N. G. Chernyshevskii, *Chto delat'?* (Moscow, 1947). The novel was written in the Peter and Paul Fortress, and first appeared in 1863. I have used a recent Soviet edition, which contains an interesting postscript by N. Vodovozov on the novel's reception by later revolutionaries.

professional revolutionary.[12] Having made this choice of career consciously and deliberately, he embarks on a fantastic training program designed to broaden his mind, toughen his body, and harden his will. His regime of gymnastics, hard physical labor, raw beefsteak diet, voracious though selective reading, and sexual continence reaches heights of absurdity when he arises one morning soaked in blood from head to foot after a night spent on a bed of nails. Once trained, every resource of his heart and mind is subjected to a self-defined concept of duty. He is impersonal, abrupt, and businesslike in all his relations with others. Though he is once tempted by a beautiful widow, he is "not free" to love or to marry. In all his character traits he is a nearly perfect model of the ideal Bolshevik.[13] He has not the apparatus of the Party to discipline and direct his energies and Chernyshevskii cannot tell us much about his specific political activity. But in his *mystique* of dedication and above all, in his reliance on a will of steel, Rakhmetov prefigures the personal, moral code of the "leather men in leather jackets." He is, like them, a member of a tiny elite which, despite its size, aspires to change the world. "They are few in number," Chernyshevskii wrote, "but through them the life of all mankind expands." [14] He is "marked" for leadership, but not in the Nietzschean sense, by birth or by intrinsically superior qualities. He is a self-made superman who has shaped himself into a revolutionary instrument out of the natural resources that are given to all men. Men like him are, at the height of their powers, "the flower of the best people, the movers of movers, they are the salt of the salt of the earth." [15]

The new man enters his state of grace not by study alone (Dobroliubov has already suggested that too much intellection might blur the need to act), nor by responding consciously or unconsciously to his experience as a member of an economic class (none of them is from the lower orders). The beginning of awareness comes through a simple revelation, by opening one's eyes and stepping from the cellars of prejudice and regressive values into the sunlight of "natural truth." This illumination, which is most often

[12] A comment by the Bulgarian Communist, Georgi Dimitrov, is very much in point here: "I must say that . . . there was no literary work which influenced me so strongly in my revolutionary education as Chernyshevskii's novel. For months I literally lived with Chernyshevskii's heroes. Rakhmetov was my particular favorite. I set myself the goal of being as firm, as self-possessed, to temper my will . . . in my struggle with difficulties . . . to subordinate my personal life to the interests of the great cause of the working class — in a word to be like this irreproachable hero . . ." (quoted by Vodovozov in the postscript to Chernyshevskii, *Chto delat'?*, p. 470). A similar comment by George Plekhanov (*ibid.*, p. 464) and another in the *Literaturnaia Entsiklopediia* (VIII, 190–191) indicate the novel's great influence on Soviet thinking and suggest some of the channels by which the idea of the new man was transmitted to them.

[13] Chernyshevskii, *Chto delat'?*, p. 278.

[14] *Ibid.*

[15] *Ibid.*, p. 92.

achieved with the help of an earlier convert, is then followed by a deliberate decision to act forever after in the light of its dictates:

> . . . consciously and firmly he decided to renounce all the advantages and honors which he might have demanded of life in order to work for the benefit of others, finding his own greatest interests in the pleasure from that kind of work.[16]

The life that follows is rigorous, dedicated, and self-disciplined, we are told, but surprsingly lacking in inner struggle, or doubt. When the new man has reached his full stature, he is a model of modest, virtuous behavior. He has overcome "inertia," "ennui," "exaltation," "romanticism," "whimsicality," the vices of his superfluous predecessors, and has learned "tact, coolness, activity . . . the realization of common sense in action." He is "bold," "resolute," and of "irreproachable honesty." [17]

Because he knows that his role is exemplary and that his function is to give attractive publicity to all his convictions and to every statute of his personal code, as well, his most private act has a public aspect. He emerges finally as the monolithic man Dobroliubov had sought — self-assured, incorruptible, serenely optimistic, and apparently unable to hesitate, stumble, or fail. He is the wholly political man, too, and I think it is clear that the fusion of emotion with convictions really involves a total surrender of his personal claims on life in the name of the public cause. His "mastery of life" gives him the freedom and the courage to act in its name, but deprives him of many other kinds of freedom, most notably, since all the big questions have been answered and those that remain are only "tactical," of the freedom to make complex moral choices. The present world is intolerable and the ordinary human questions must be set aside until it is done away with. That this act of renunciation involved genuine sacrifice was not publicly admitted by the radicals, but it was poignantly if obliquely acknowledged by Chernyshevskii in a letter to Nekrasov:

> . . . I myself know by experience that convictions do not constitute everything in life — the demands of the heart exist, and in the life of the heart there is genuine joy and genuine sorrow for all of us. This I know by experience, I know it better than others. Convictions occupy our mird only when the heart rests from its joy or sorrow. I will even say that for me personally my private affairs are more significant than any world problem — men do not drown themselves, or shoot themselves or become drunkards because of world problems — I have experienced this and I know that the poetry of the heart has the same rights as the poetry of thought — for me, personally, the first is more attractive than the second . . . I have allowed myself this frankness not only to tell you that I look on poetry by no means exclusively from the political point of view. On the contrary, only

---

[16] *Ibid.*
[17] *Ibid.*, p. 190.

by force does politics dig its way into my heart, which does not by any means live by it, or at least, would not like to live by it.[18]

The last wistful qualification suggests the final outcome of the tension between heart and mind in his own case. The heart's temptations are valid and compelling. Even when the balance is irrevocably tipped in favor of the mind, when all emotion is diverted into political channels as it was in Rakhmetov's career, the decision to do so involves genuine sacrifice and a sense of damaging loss.

One more important dimension of the new man's moral world needs to be sketched in: his relations with the masses of the people. The ultimate sanction for his rejection of the tsarist *status quo* is the suffering caused by the regime of tyranny and exploitation. The foremost victims, of course, are the peasants and it is in their name, finally, that he acts. What are his relations with the mass; in what sense, if at all, is he their representative? Belinskii's use of the concept of *narodnost'*, the untranslatable term used by so many factions in the nineteenth century to anchor their theories in the aspirations of the peasant mass, gives a partial answer. He included the whole people as integral parts of the nation, hence as participants in the great forward movement toward national self-awareness. The educated man, as Belinskii conceived him, who is in the forefront of this struggle, is a leader in the vast upsurge toward enlightenment, is, in a Soviet commentator's phrase, the "crest of the wave." [19]

As this image suggests, the link was to be an organic one, and the identification of interests complete. It is not clear how the new man receives his mandate or by what process, exactly, he functions as the representative of the masses. It is difficult to avoid the impression that he is self-appointed and that he represents them entirely on the basis of his own estimate of their needs. His constituents are a source of energy and strength; their plight documents his critique of the social order; and their unarticulated needs are the basis of his program for the future. But neither the channels of communications nor the pattern of mutual responsibility between them are clearly set forth.

Belinskii has posed a question here that is to assume increasing importance in the decades to follow; that of the relationship in the revolutionary movement between the leader and the led.[20] In positing the identity of in-

---

[18] N. G. Chernyshevskii, *Polnoe sobranie sochinenii* (Moscow, 1949), XIV, 320. The letter was written on November 5, 1856, at the very beginning of the hectic decade.

[19] A. Lavretskii, *Belinskii, Chernyshevskii, Dobroliubov v bor'be za realizm* (Moscow, 1941), p. 65.

[20] A Soviet comment on Belinskii is of interest: "He found a profound and in general correct solution for the problem for the role of the individual and of the masses of the people in history . . . The masses could be raised to the level of . . . historical activity by the progressive, educated people in society who must be guided by the requirements of society, by the spirit of the times, by the interests of the people" (M. Yovchuk, "A Great Russian Thinker," introduction to Belinskii, ref. 3, p. xl).

terests, and the sharing of energies and skills between the directing minority and the directed mass, he has prefigured, albeit indistinctly, the general formula evolved by the Bolsheviks for the problem. The ultimate sanction for the Communist's behavior, when he acts as leader or as disciplinarian of the masses, rests on his assurance that he represents their best interests, acts always in their behalf, and forfeits his right to membership in the vanguard movement — becomes "an enemy of the people" — if he transgresses this mandate.

Dobroliubov felt that the new man had much to learn from the natural virtues of the peasant masses. But as he went to the people to school himself in their virtues, he was not to forget his main responsibility toward them: to instruct them in correct principles, to focus their anger, and to direct their terrible strength.[21] The certainty that he was the authorized custodian of the people's grievances added the final element to the radical formula for the new man's reintegration with life.

II

The radicals' point of departure was the disastrous state of alienation which had crippled their liberal predecessors. This condition is complexly — even mysteriously — brought about, as the literature so often tells us, but the younger generation felt that they had, with their design for a new personality, found a foolproof antidote to it. The three points where the new man thought he had made himself most secure were: first, his liberation from all the values and institutions of the *status quo;* second, his complete faith in human reason and the principles it made known to him; and finally, his assurance that he was the personal instrument of the historical process. Thus armed, the new men proposed to complete the hazardous journey on which the liberals had become lost midway: from integration with the *status quo,* thence to a state of estrangement from it through the action of education and of the moral sensibility, and finally to a renewed state of integration, through a philosophy of action, with a rational future world of which they were the first heralds. They were convinced that they had found the path to a state of personal engagement which could sustain them in their struggle with the tsarist system, because they believed in the justice of their assault and in the inevitability of its ultimate issue. But if we view it critically we note that it rested on an "adjustment" that was composed in large part of hostility to existing institutions, and in equally large part of commitment to a world that had not yet come into being. Described so, its precariousness becomes obvious. The critique leveled at this state of mind by the liberals and others who were antagonized by the radicals' raucous criticism of their motives, their values, and their art, suggests that the antiradicals were quick to sense its vulnerability.

[21] See Dobroliubov's article "Features For the Characterization of the Russian Common People," ref. 6, especially pp. 525–542.

The burden of their charge was that, behind his rationalizations (and, to a degree, because of them), the new man was inadequate as a person: deficient in intellect and deformed in both a moral and a psychological sense. Herzen's attack on him was very much *ad hominem* and unconcerned with hypothetical moral dilemmas.[22] His own generation, he felt, had been grievously slandered by the men of the sixties. Herzen was prepared to admit that in spite of their gallant resistance to tyranny, his own contemporaries had become pathological types by the end of their ordeal, prematurely burned out, disillusioned, and "sick in body and soul."[23] But for all their sins and shortcomings they were guiltless of the insulting charges directed at them by the "sullen" new men who were, if anything, sicker than their forbears. Herzen characterized the new types in vividly uncomplimentary terms. They were, he said, gravely deficient in sensibility. They were able, for example, to surmount the defeat of the revolutions of 1848 without pausing to weep a single tear for its fallen heroes. There is a sinister "lightness" to all their emotional responses which, combined with the immoral pleasure they find in negation and the "terrible ruthlessness" of their personal code, makes for a most unappetizing kind of person. They display a monk's hatred for human frailty; they have the speech, the manners, and the sudden explosive rages of bureaucrats; and, they are, Herzen insists, hypochondriacs to a man. At bottom he detects the starved egos of ambitious and unsuccessful mediocrities: on their faces are the marks of a "gnawing, short-tempered and curdled self-love."[24] Although they too were victims of traditionless Russian barbarism and their intentions were no less exalted than their predecessors', their essential *rudeness* made it impossible to admire them, or to share their convictions or their hopes. They were inadequate as people, hence unworthy of the principles they professed.

Turgenev's indictment is far gentler than Herzen's but more searching. Bazarov's disintegration has many aspects, but all the major ones seem to proceed, ironically, from the qualities of mind and of personality in which the young radicals had placed the greatest reliance. Bazarov's self-assurance, through which he expresses his admirable courage and energy, is at the same time a crippling malformation of character. When it has effectively cut him off from love, family, and friends in the series of personal encounters that make up the substance of *Fathers and Sons*, it flares up briefly into a Nietzschean image of himself, superior to all men and utterly alone because of it. To the extent that faith in doctrine contributes to his egocentricity, it too is shown to be an obstacle to the fulfillment of his emotional needs, existing in a state of fatal tension with them. Yet, since the qualities which lead to his downfall are the ones he needs most in order to establish himself

[22] See A. I. Gertsen, "The Superfluous Man and the Men With a Grudge," *Polnoe sobranie sochinenii i pisem*, ed. M. K. Lemke (Petrograd, 1919–1925), X, 413–442.

[23] *Ibid.*, p. 417.

[24] *Ibid.*, pp. 418–419.

and his values in the face of a world that "refuses" him, his outcome is inescapably tragic. In a famous description of Bazarov, Turgenev makes it clear that commitment to the future was the real cause of his tragedy:

> I dreamed of a dark, wild, large figure, half growing out of the soil, strong, malicious, honorable — and doomed all the same to perish because he stands on the threshold of the future . . .[25]

The source of the radicals' optimism became in Turgenev's eyes, since he did not share their faith in the rapid, upward evolution of things, the very source of Bazarov's undoing. The doctrinal motives which sustain his aspirations become devalued and evaporate in the face of his present personal needs. Thus stripped of his ideals he is confronted with the last responsibility of all great men, of "dying with dignity." [26]

The advocate of social change could be presented as well in "a comic envelope." But the source of his comedy, as it was in Bazarov's tragedy, is in his shortcomings. Turgenev's image of Don Quixote, though it enraged the radicals, is one of the most sympathetic efforts to come to terms with their champion. Turgenev's description of Quixote's relation to his ideal is very nearly a paraphrase of the radical formula:

> Faith, above all, faith in something eternal, immovable, in truth, in a word, in a truth which is outside the individual man, to which it is not easy to give oneself, which demands sacrifices and service . . . Don Quixote is penetrated with devotion to the ideal, for which he is prepared to subject himself to every possible deprivation, to sacrifice his life; he values his life only to the extent that it will serve as a means for the realization of the ideal, for the establishment of truth and justice on earth.[27]

But, though he is the "most moral being" on earth, he must pay a stiff price for his single-mindedness:

> A constant striving toward one and the same goal lends a certain monotony to his ideas, a onesidedness to his mind; he knows little, but he need not know much: he knows what his cause is, why he lives on earth, and this is the principal knowledge. Don Quixote can seem at one moment a complete maniac, because the most indubitable materiality disappears before his eyes, melts like wax in the flame of his enthusiasm (he really sees live Moors in wooden dolls, knights in sheep) — at another moment, limited because he does not know how to sympathize easily or to enjoy himself . . .[28]

His self-assurance is costly, leading to delusions on one hand, and to emotional sterility on the other. In another essential article of the radical's creed, his commitment to the future, Quixote falls constantly into the ridiculous: only the "fates" will decide whether the chamberpot on Don

[25] Letter to K. K. Sluchevskii, dated April 14, 1862, in N. Turgenev, *Sobranie sochinenii* (Moscow, 1949), XI, 215.

[26] Letter to A. A. Fet, dated September 4, 1862, *ibid.*, p. 219.

[27] *Ibid.*, XI, 6.

[28] *Ibid.*, p. 7.

Quixote's head will turn out later to be what he knew it to be all the time, a gleaming helmet.

Dostoyevsky completed the nonbelievers' portrait of the new man. A disfiguring self-assurance lay behind the reasoned rebellion of his proud intellectuals, which might lead to crime, revolution, blasphemy, or treason. "The new man may well become the man-god," Ivan Karamazov's devil says to him.[29] And in that awful eminence he will find himself, as Raskolnikov did, cut off from love, God, and mankind. There in his solitude, or as a member of a tiny, guilt-ridden elite, he will relieve the mass of men of the burden of free choice and of knowledge of the truth, and will govern them in their best interests. Ivan Karamazov's terrible despair is the price one must pay even for thinking one's way into that fearsome position.

We have come a long way from Chernyshevskii's call for a "successor" to the superfluous man. Though the power of poetry has heightened and intensified the image of the new man, his central moral diagram has remained fundamentally unchanged. And the writers claimed to have discovered weaknesses in it that led as surely to alienation as Pechorin's search for self-immolation or Rudin's fatal eloquence. The new man paid a terrible price for his political efficacy in the loss of awareness and in the blighting of his emotions, and ran the risk of finding himself always a stranger in the present, an exile among his fellow men.

III

It is difficult at first to imagine that a single emblematic image of human conduct, so markedly a product of one historical moment, could preserve its currency across a century of change and through an event as apocalyptic as the October Revolution. The new Soviet hero may be accounted for quite satisfactorily by the conditions he lives under and by the needs he has been evoked to meet. But the resemblances to his Russian ancestors are too striking to dismiss as accidental.

The properties of literature — the medium in which he has been preserved — tend to support the hypothesis: literary archetypes are rare coinages indeed, with a tendency to last until they exhaust their relevances to life (or beyond that, as stereotypes).[30] The radicals' effort to install their image of the new man at the center of the Russian realistic tradition failed, and is therefore premature as a literary experiment. But the new man had a continuous existence in the intellectual climate of successive radical gen-

---

[29] Fyodor Dostoevsky, *The Brothers Karamazov* (New York: Modern Library, 1950), p. 688.

[30] Consider the life span of the surprisingly durable superfluous man. Professor Harry Levin's illuminating essay on the hero-types in French literature, "From Priam to Birotteau," *Yale French Studies*, III, no. 6 (1950), has encouraged me in the assumption that literary types are much longer-lived than the successive ideologies they may be called upon to serve.

erations. He was preserved in a romantic mutation in the *narodniki's* "little band of heroes," and as the Old Bolsheviks first went forth to battle, Lebedev-Polianskii tells us, they carried the heroic image of Belinskii, himself, in their hearts: "The youth gave each other the works of Belinskii when, inspired by a great love for the people, by the idea of struggle, they went out, in Chekhov's words, 'into the unknown distance.' "[31]

And as for Lenin? It seems certain that the keys to many problems in the continuity of ideas will be found in the isolation of the native strand in Lenin's thought. Suffice it to say here that he admired Chernyshevskii greatly and voiced characteristic praise of his novel: ". . . it breathes the spirit of class struggle."[32] And it seems reasonable to suppose that whatever ingredients of the Russian revolutionary ethos are embedded in his prescriptions for the organization and function of the Communist Party, they contain the germ plasm of the new man.

The situation of the hero had changed, of course, after the October Revolution. Above all, he had given up the role of a rebellious nonconformist and become a defender of the revolutionary *status quo*. But this apparent reversal was less abrupt and far-reaching than it seems. For it must be remembered that in both capacities he was equally enthralled by the general ethical imperative derived by both Belinskii and Marx from Hegelianism: So act that thy act forwards the historical process. It must be acknowledged that Marxism laid new metaphysical foundations for the revolutionary imperative, but without changing its inner nature or lessening the claims it made on its adherents. The self-defined duty of Chernyshevskii's heroes may seem to bear little resemblance, at first glance, to the institutionalized duty represented by the Communist Party with its hierarchy, rules, protocol, and means of coercion. But, once the ritual act of subordination to either concept of duty has been made, the kind of willing and self-sacrificing compliance it calls for is essentially the same.

The biggest divergence between the two is to be found in the changes introduced by the successful revolution in the parental relations between the leader and the led. The new man of the mid-nineteenth century was never called upon to exercise his parental role. He could always envisage it in its most benevolent guise as the respectful, solicitous guardian and teacher of the people. But the nursery was empty; there were no children to dispute his word or to upset his flattering view of himself. The Soviet Communist, on the other hand, found himself in charge of a vast and unruly brood, many of whom felt they had the most solemn grounds to dispute the legitimacy of their parentage. To the role of the solicitous instructor —

---

[31] P. I. Lebedev-Polianskii, *V. G. Belinskii, literaturno-kriticheskaia deiatel'nost'* (Moscow-Leningrad, 1945), p. 301.

[32] V. I. Lenin, *Sochineniia,* eds. N. I. Bukharin, V. M. Molotov, M. A. Savel'ev (Moscow-Leningrad, 1929), XVII, 342.

Lenin's "patiently to explain" — was added the quickly apparent need to pry, to goad, to deceive, and to punish.

Thus when the Leningrad worker Davidov, hero of Sholokhov's *Virgin Soil Upturned,* enters the sluggish, suspicious village he is to organize into a collective farm, he directs his attention first to the people he must manipulate. The human problem is complex:

> He had been by no means a naïve town dweller before he went to work in the country, but he had not realized all the complexities of the class struggle, its tangled knots and frequently secret courses, until he arrived in Gremyachy. He could not understand the stubborn reluctance of the majority of the middling peasants to join the collective farm despite the tremendous advantages of collective agriculture. He could not find the right key to an understanding of many of the people and their inter-relationships . . . All the inhabitants of Gremyachy passed before Davidov's mental vision. And there was much in them that was incomprehensible to him, that was hidden behind a kind of impalpable curtain. The village was like a new type of complicated motor, and Davidov studied it intently and tensely, trying to understand its mechanism, to see clearly every detail, to note every interruption in the daily, incessant throbbing of this involved machine.[33]

His job is to persuade the reluctant Cossacks (by any means that promise success) to act against tradition, belief, and instinct, in the name of a drastic redefinition of their own and the nation's interest which he has brought with him from distant Moscow. Acting out of his core of Communist virtue, he improvises the local virtues and techniques appropriate to his task. But it is the core itself that concerns us here, the combination of personal qualities and abstract ideas which enable this severely functional hero (who is a figure of myth at the same time) to gain mastery over any situation life and the Party place before him.

The doctrinal component of his concept of duty, apart from the general fund of Marxist-Leninist ideas, is embodied in the directive on collectivization which he carries in his pocket. He quarrels with the district leaders on the correct interpretation to be put upon it, but he never questions it. It provides the rational framework for every decision he makes, sometimes affecting the most minute details. When the doctrine has led Davidov's villagers to the point of mutiny, his situation is miraculously resolved by the arrival of Stalin's new policy statement, "Dizzy with Success," ordering among other things the decollectivization of chickens. Davidov is saved in the nick of time from the defeat of his plans, or from the unthinkable alternative of having to abandon handed-down orders. The entire grotesque episode suggests that Davidov is the instrument of an all-seeing, infallible power, and that his faith in doctrine will never betray him.

But Davidov is not merely the blind executor of policies drawn up by

[33] Mikhail Sholokhov, *Virgin Soil Upturned* (London, 1948), pp. 136–137. The novel was first published in 1932 and served as a primary exhibit of the new literature of "positive heroes" all through the thirties to the present.

others, nor simply a technician or administrator. He is a leader, imposed from without on the men he is to lead, and in the resourceful and flexible application of the policy to the local scene, he is forced to act decisively in a number of painful and difficult human situations. In these decisions there is revealed in Davidov that perfect, monolithic fusion of conviction with emotion the nineteenth-century radicals had sought in their champion. In significant contrast to Davidov, both his local Communist assistants come unstuck at the very point where the two elements are joined. Nagulnov, the overzealous "Leftist," is carried away by the frenzied emotions which the Civil War had generated in him, and makes impulsive, half-cracked decisions which threaten the success of the entire program. Such unlimited display of emotion is viewed as a kind of self-indulgence, and neither his years of loyalty to the cause nor the evident sincerity of his intentions are permitted to interfere with the punishment that is visited upon him. Davidov's rigid control over himself makes this kind of irresponsible outburst impossible in his case. But the furious emotion is there, nevertheless, as an apparently inexhaustible fund of hatred for the old regime, the dismantling of which he conceives as his world-historical mission. When Razmiotnov, his other assistant, announces that he refuses to go on dispossessing kulaks and their families because it is no part of his work to wage war on children, Davidov erupts in a fury. "Did they ever weep over the orphans of those they killed?" he shouts at Razmiotnov and recounts the bitter suffering the old society inflicted on him when he was a child.[34] The emotion is there but it has been harnessed and put at the service of doctrine. In this case, when duty demands inhuman acts, Davidov's experience, generalized into the sufferings of his class, enables him to administer the awful individual injustices implicit in the concept of "class justice," without apparent damage to his own conscience.

The same subordination of personal emotion to the public interest, as he conceives it, determines his behavior in the novel's crisis. At its height, Davidov is attacked by furious women and beaten through the streets of the village while the men plunder the grain from the collective seed fund. One woman beats him with her fists in tearful, impotent rage, not because he is wicked, but because he is so inevitably and unshakably correct. His personal reputation survives unblemished. When order has been restored, Davidov's speech is a model of Communist leadership. He instantly overlooks his personal humiliation, but exploits the Cossacks' guilt by indicating that the only expiation open to them is wholesale support of the collective farm. An act of Communist forgiveness, like any other act, serves as a goad toward the desired social resolution.

Finally the questions arise: what are the rewards and what are the costs implicit in Davidov's design for living? We cannot expect to find the

[34] *Ibid.*, p. 84.

broad-ranging answers provided by the open discussion of the matter in the nineteenth century. But enough hints are to be found that tend to suggest, albeit in very sketchy form, that the negative features of the new man — the aridity, the one-sidedness, the blunted moral sensibility — have been duplicated in his Soviet counterpart. The calculus of his personal happiness, and the means he seeks to justify his life to himself must be set in this context of damage and deprivation.

The rewards are few enough. The uncertain pleasure of serving as history's dedicated instrument finds its chief expression in an occasional vision of the future. In one of his rare moments of introspection, Davidov discloses how bare and prosaic, yet how intensely felt that vision is. A talk with a child has prompted him to speculate about what is to come:

We'll build a good life for them. Fact! . . . In twenty years time he'll [the little boy] probably be plowing up this very earth with an electric plow . . . Machinery will do all the heavy work for man. The people of those days will have forgotten the smell of sweat, I suppose. I'd like to live till then, by all the devils. If only to see what it was like . . . You'll die . . . brother Davidov, as sure as you're alive! Instead of descendants you'll leave behind the Gremyachy collective farm. The farm will become a commune, and then you'll see, they'll call it by name of the Putilov locksmith, Semion Davidov . . .[35]

Davidov lives in great solitude. It is not the terrible metaphysical aloneness that Dostoyevsky has inflicted on his rebels, but it is nonetheless complete and unrelieved. The image of the woman beating him reminds us as much of his isolation as of his rectitude. He is unmarried. His shirt is dirty — so dirty that, as Razmiotnov points out, "you couldn't cut through that shirt with a sword."[36] But Davidov needs no help in this matter: an ex-sailor, he has learned to wash and mend his own clothes. His most outspoken display of personal emotion, which follows the receipt of a modest gift-box from his former comrades in the Putilov Works, merely accents the austerity of his private life.[37] That the Soviet Communist's life is very often loveless is a cliché of pre-World War II literature. Sholokhov has given the cliché a special emphasis by exposing Davidov to the strategies of a beautiful temptress, the wife of a Party colleague. Davidov is, indeed, tempted; he asks himself, "Am I a monk, or what?"[38] But, as always, public concerns govern his response. "Though he was attracted to Lukeria, he had feared that his association with her would undermine his authority."[39] His final grudging acceptance of her favors gives rise not to a feeling of release but to new anxieties. Nor does it promise any kind of communion

---

[35] *Ibid.*, pp. 345–346.
[36] *Ibid.*, p. 162.
[37] *Ibid.*, p. 161. Davidov's comment: "A touching fact."
[38] *Ibid.*, p. 476.
[39] *Ibid.*, pp. 479–480.

with the people he has manipulated, by involving him in the emotional substance of their everyday lives.

The costs of his rigidly exemplary life are not counted out in full. There is no suggestion, for example, that his burden of duty is in any way increased by a further burden of guilt arising from injuries he has inflicted on others in the name of that duty. We are left with the impression that his conscience is entirely contained within the concept of Party obligations. But it takes only a small adjustment of the lense to see Davidov as his enemies might have done: ruthless, fanatical, and remote, insulated against all the ordinary human weaknesses, yet protected against a true knowledge of his condition by the narrowness of his vision.

Pavel Korchagin, the hero of Ostrovskii's *The Making of a Hero,* carries the notion of the moral monolith to the limits of plausibility, or perhaps beyond, to the point of absurdity. To the extent that the novel is autobiographical, the author has sacrificed the essential remove from his protagonist that enabled Sholokhov to exercise a measure of control over his Davidov, to trace the outline, at least, of his fallible underside, and to suggest that there are values in life not easily given up. For Korchagin the universe is completely demarcated into blacks and whites, according to his simplicistic political morality. The lips of the bourgeois girl twitch for cocaine; the Communists' eyes are clear and steady.

From the moment Korchagin joins the Komsomol, his only guiding principle is to serve: service is happiness; happiness, service. Since there are no other large choices, since there can be no question of moral fallibility, the only genuine tests he can undergo involve his capacity to endure physical suffering. In addition to the routine wear and tear of war, famine, cold, and hunger, Korchagin's body endures a beating in prison, a hip wound, a head wound, a spinal wound, a smashed knee, typhus, pneumonia, and rheumatic fever. When the cumulative effect of these afflictions result in paralysis and blindness, his "tempered" Bolshevik will responds to this ultimate challenge: he learns to become a writer and continues his life of service to the cause.

Korchagin's personal moral code is indistinguishable from the Party program. The habits of service and leadership in its name, we are led to believe, have become basic *character traits.* From this total absorption in Party work he derives whatever spiritual nourishment his intense and dehydrated nature requires. Thus powered, his actions are always successful (though, it should be pointed out, the successes are never magically easy), whether he is tracking down a murderer on the frontier or discouraging kissing games among the Komsomol. From his central fund of belief he, like Davidov, develops problem-solving virtues as required by the situation. He is endowed variously with technical skill, civic initiative, administrative subtlety, and military resourcefulness. As a leader he displays a range of qualities appropriate to the many roles he plays: patience, tact, indignation, courage, or, if the presence of the class enemy is sensed, intolerance and ruthlessness. We must recall that we are always viewing Korchagin from within, as he justifies his own behavior to himself. No attention is paid, therefore, to the likelihood that the people he manipulates or clashes with might regard him as a prig, a busybody, or a fanatic.[40] Since he is not seen at all from an outside vantage, we are only able to guess at the degree or the costs of his alienation from the rank-and-file members of the various communities he inhabits, or from the normal human experiences he has voluntarily foregone. We note, with a few exceptions, not the absence so much as the unimportance of friendship, love, or family ties. His personal attachments, such as they are, have an invariable political cast: they are with members of his own elite, or they are initiated, sustained, or ended on political grounds. In Korchagin's case, the question of rewards and costs must be changed to: What are the costs of *non*participation? As it happens, they are very nearly fatal. His deepest spiritual crisis is brought on by a doctor's decision that his multiple injuries have ended his usefulness to the Party. If he cannot serve it, life is without meaning and he has no alternative but to succumb to his wounds. But by overcoming the handicaps he wins through to a new kind of service, hence to a renewal of his life.

In this extraordinarily naïve and incomplete human image the myth of the monolithic, functional, political man as it was first set forth in the nineteenth century has reached some kind of apotheosis. His author would have us believe that he has made the move from life as it is with its challenges, temptations, and ambiguities to a fabricated, self-contained universe of ideology, and irremovably anchored himself in it. Doctrine has replaced life.[41] His activist political faith "permeates" his entire being as it does with Insarov and, like him, if he is denied participation in his cause, he will die. In the same way, Rakhmetov's bed of nails accurately forecasts Korchagin's terrible physical battering. The costs and the scars discovered by the nineteenth-century writers are present, as we have seen, though in the novels we have examined, they are only sketchily explored or unintentionally dis-

---

[40] An episode is revealing: "There was not much to learn, but these things were noted: Razvalikhin drinking and gathering all the rotters around him and keeping the better comrades out of things. Paul reported all this to the Bureau. The other comrades . . . were all for reprimanding Razvalikhin severely, when Paul surprised them by saying: 'I am for expelling him without the right to apply for membership again.' Everybody thought this much too severe, but Paul said again: 'This scoundrel must be expelled . . .' " (Nicholas Ostrovski, *The Making of a Hero* [New York, 1937], pp. 377–378).

[41] Consider this passage: "He was in a constant hurry to *live;* not only in a hurry himself, but anxious to urge others on too . . . Often a light could be seen in his window late into the night, and people there gathered round a table — reading and studying. In two years they had worked through the third volume of *Capital,* and had gained an understanding of the delicate mechanics of capitalist exploitation." (*Ibid.,* p. 377.)

closed. A more literate novelist like Leonov has shown a much greater awareness of the inopportuneness of the revolutionary. In his concept of the Bolshevik as an imperfect interim being, "the man-mountain from the summit of which we see the future," [42] who nevertheless dies with the bitter knowledge that he will never see it himself, he has ventured toward the vision and honesty of tragedy. But he has not reached it (by his own design, I think) and the note of affirmation, muted though it is, commends the example of his hero's life directly to the reader. In this respect he has remained true to the myth of the positive hero as we have seen it in two of the most typical products of Socialist Realism, and as it has been repeated with minor variations a thousand times over in Soviet writing since 1932.

I have assumed that in imaginative literature the myth of the political man would be found in its most concentrated form. Actually its reëmergence in the 1930's did not occur only in the normal, undirected evolution of literary forms. Great — and, it should be noted, directed — changes were under way in philosophy, psychology, literary theory, educational theory, and many other fields at this time which would benefit from the concept of a conscious, disciplined, energetic, history-compliant individual. The single most important element in this vast intellectual upheaval has been the effort to extend the Leninist ethic of partisanship, developed first for the needs of an embattled revolutionary elite, to the entire Soviet population. If the new man had not existed it would have been necessary to invent him.

After 1932, and the First Writers' Conference in 1934, writers were enjoined to make the pursuit and capture of the new Soviet hero the first order of business. We cannot say how much they are indebted to the past, since it is beyond our scope here to trace in detail the transmission of the earlier myth. Let us be content with the resemblances already noted. In one basic dimension, the two images are most impressively similar: the relation of the individual to his community. In one case the formula for this relationship was entirely hypothetical; in the other, presumably, it has been subject to empirical test on a vast scale. But as statements of the desired, not of the actual, the human situation of each new man reveals identical outlines. Each is representative of the community he inhabits in a nonelective sense, yet administers his mandate in the name of a central authority — whether in the form of abstract doctrine or of the coercive apparatus of the Party. And because of this superior allegiance, because of the distance it opens between himself and the group whose best interests he claims to represent, and because of the manipulative controls he must exercise over it, he lives in damaging isolation from his constituents, an isolation which the austerity of his own code only tends to reinforce.

Is this harshly parental and unequal relationship envisaged as eternal? History will give the actual answer, of course, but on the level of theory we

[42] Leonid Leonov, *Road to the Ocean* (New York, 1944), p. 453.

should note that the framers of the old and the new versions of this code envisioned its end, and presumably with that, the end of the necessary estrangement it gave rise to. In a word, the children were to grow up in the parents' image. Few could belong to Rakhmetov's elite, but on a lower level, the number of new men was expected to increase by arithmetic progression, through the power of example, until they encompassed the entire population.[43] The recent extension of the Leninist ethic to all levels of the population through every channel of expression seems to contemplate the same eventual reunion of the leaders and the led. The life of the interim man has been long — it is a century since he was first conceived, a third of a century since he inherited the Russian earth — but, in theory at least, it is not intended to last forever. And if it ends, one wonders, will anyone remember how to live, as Marx hoped man would, as "a total man" in his full "human reality," "seeing, hearing, smelling, tasting, feeling, thinking, contemplating, willing, acting, loving?" [44] Or will the alienation of the incomplete, inopportune socialist man have become universalized?

[43] See Chernyshevskii, *Chto delat'?*, pp. 12, 55–56, 191.
[44] Karl Marx and Frederick Engels, *Literature and Art: Selections from their Writings* (New York, 1947), p. 61.

Part III

Review

MICHAEL KARPOVICH

If one looks for a common denominator in the preceding five papers, it can be found in the fact that all of them deal with theories or schemes whose implied or avowed purpose is to achieve a synthesis between the individual and the collectivity.

Thus Khomiakov defines *sobornost'* as "unity in multiplicity" and asserts that man "finds himself in the Church," and that only there can he fully realize himself.

In Herzen's case, the eagerly anticipated era of socialism was to result "from the fusion of the democratic equality of the Russian commune with the Western principle of the dignity of the individual" (the wording is Mr. Malia's).

The "idea of realization of individuality through . . . [the] collectivity" is indicated by Mr. Towster as being one of the main categories of Vyshinsky's concept of collectivity.

A similar synthesis is implied in the "enlightened self-interest" of the "new man" of the 1860's whose counterpart Mr. Mathewson has found in the Bolshevik hero of the Soviet literature of the 1930's.

On a somewhat different level, we find a combination of collectivist and individualist elements in the organization of Stalin's collective farms discussed in Mr. Bergamini's paper.

While the common denominator can thus be stated very briefly, to list the differences would take a little more time. Khomiakov's *sobornost'*, applied primarily to the Church, is a free "union in love" or a "union in Christ." The concept implies a rejection of external authority, absence of an excessive differentiation between the clergy and the laity, and the denial of the hierarchy's monopoly in the interpretation of the dogma. When applied to society in general, *sobornost'* means the reign of spontaneity and free creative activity as opposed to centralization and regimentation.

Mr. Malia believes that Herzen's guiding ideal was the unconditional freedom of the individual personality from all external constraint and from all authority which did not arise from the voluntary association of the individuals. To Herzen, the essential thing in the commune was precisely "the absence of constraint and of authority imposed from above."

Contrasted with this attitude, is Stalin's approach to the problem of the collectivization of agriculture, among the purposes of which Mr. Bergamini lists the establishment of a more powerful control over the peasants and the use of the peasant material for the proletarian goal. Mr. Bergamini does not find in the scheme, as finally developed, any idea of a spontaneous predisposition on the part of the peasants to join the collectives. It was because of the lack of such spontaneous predisposition that it became necessary for the government and the Party "to push the peasants into the collectives." As to the partial "retreat to individualism" it was a concession forced upon Stalin by the peasant opposition.

Mr. Towster sees in Vyshinsky "a Soviet rationalizer . . . put to the service of manipulating political symbols to sustain the Soviet regime." The purpose of Vyshinsky's concept of collectivity is to elucidate "the whys and wherefores of the violence and compulsion facing the [Soviet] citizen at every turn," "to justify in the citizen's mind the state's perpetual demands for his obedience," in short, "to spin a web of legitimacy about the *Machtpolitik* of the Kremlin." Finally, Mr. Mathewson, comparing the "new man" of the mid-nineteenth century with the "new man" of the Soviet period, speaks of the reversal of roles from that of a "rebellious nonconformist" to that of a "defender of the revolutionary *status quo.*"

The balance of the similarities and differences as outlined above raises some questions which I would like to see elucidated. How much relative weight should be given to similarities and differences respectively in our discussion of continuity and change as between the prerevolutionary and postrevolutionary Russian thought?

With reference to the specific problem under discussion, can one establish continuity merely on the basis of a very general similarity of the final aim — that of reconciling collectivism and individualism in some kind of a synthesis?

To make the meaning of my doubt clear, I shall start with one case in which I feel that the continuity has been established. I have in mind Mr. Mathewson's comparison between the image of the "new man" as construed by the mid-nineteenth-century Russian radicals, on the one hand, and the officially approved image of the "new man" as we find it in the Soviet literature, on the other. Here, in spite of some important differences created by the change in political and social conditions, I agree with Mr. Mathewson that the resemblances "are so striking that they suggest the direct transmission of ideas across the turbulent decades which separate their respective formulations."

It is easy to see why in this case a continuity can be established. There are two reasons. First, there is not only a general similarity but also a very specific affinity between the two types of the "new man" — an affinity of ideological and psychological nature as exemplified by utilitarian ethics and aesthetics and the concept of revolutionary elitism. In the second place, one can point out a definite human milieu within the confines of which the continuity was preserved — from the 1860's to the 1930's. This was the milieu of the Russian revolutionary underground, or more exactly, some corners of it. In other words, the continuity is not between prerevolutionary and postrevolutionary Russian thought in general, but between one specific trend of prerevolutionary thought and the ideas of Soviet leaders who had been brought up in that tradition. In some cases, beginning with that of Lenin himself, this can even be supported by available biographical evidence.

The question I would like to raise is whether there is a similar situation when dealing either with Khomiakov's *sobornost'* or with Herzen's brand of individualist collectivism. To begin with, each of these concepts seems to be based on premises which are not only different, but actually antagonistic to the underlying premises of the Soviet concept of collectivity. In the second place, the transmission belt seems to be lacking. No doubt, Khomiakov and the Slavophiles in general exercised considerable influence on some trends of Russian religious and philosophical thought. But I wonder whether in the last prerevolutionary decades one can find many instances of Slavophile influence in Russian political and social thought. And in those rare cases when one can find it, it would be in such quarters that were not frequented by Lenin and his associates. In a somewhat different sense and in a different degree, it could be applied to Herzen also. I have in mind his collectivism in particular. Herzen was greatly admired, and by a miscellaneous assortment of people, as a personality, a writer, a *libre penseur*, a champion of human freedom; but I do not see much evidence of the continued influence of his socialist ideas — even as far back as the 1870's.

I would like to point out still another problem: to what extent are the ideas treated in the present discussion unique to Russia or even particularly characteristic of Russia?

In the introductory parts of his paper (sections I–II), Mr. Towster stresses the indigenous nature of the Russian concept of collectivity and the "stark contrast" it forms to the Western outlook. Mr. Riasanovsky, on the contrary, emphasizes the similarity of Khomiakov's ideas (*sobornost'* not excluded) to those of Western romanticism. Mr. Malia sees in Herzen's socialism one of the extreme forms of general European utopianism of the time, and he also finds a close parallel to Herzen's attitude toward the commune in J. S. Mill's ideas on the role and significance of the coöperative movement. Mr. Mathewson, while treating the transition from the "alienated man" to the "new man" within the Russian context, points out, however, that the basic idea of the "enlightened self-interest" was borrowed by Chernyshevskii, "without alteration," from the French rationalists. Mr. Bergamini does not raise the issue in his paper. But the only ideological element he refers to when discussing Stalin's collectivization policy is the Marxist dogma. No mention is made of any prerevolutionary Russian tradition.

With reference to Mr. Mathewson's paper, it could be added that an elitist idea very close to that of the Russian radicals can be found in the writings of some representatives of the French Enlightenment, and that subsequently it was taken over and developed by some French revolutionaries, beginning with the Jacobins and ending with Blanqui. The "alienated man," likewise, was not unknown to Western European literature of the first half of the nineteenth century. In both cases, a direct influence on Russian thought and literature can be established.

It seems to me also that some of the "typical Russian traits" that are mentioned by Mr. Towster can be found in the Western world as well. The concept of "individual submission to the corporate whole" is not outside the Western tradition, and "popular sovereignty" and "general will" were interpreted in such a fashion not in Russia alone. One certainly can find this tendency in Rousseau, and throughout the nineteenth century the submission of the individual to the "corporate whole" was repeatedly warned against as a present danger by such writers as Benjamin Constant, de Tocqueville, J. S. Mill, Taine, and Jakob Burkhardt.

Again, if one accepts the broad definition of "religiosity" as used by Mr. Towster, then, as the late Simon Frank pointed out, Rousseau, Feuerbach, Marx, and Nietzsche should be recognized as being "not less but rather more intensely religious thinkers than Belinskii, Herzen, and Chernyshevskii." Nor should it be forgotten that the Church as an "all-embracing organic unity" and the "embodiment of truth" is a concept common to both Western and Eastern Christianity.

Finally, "instrumentalism," defined by Mr. Towster as "conscious linking of theory and practice," makes one think of, among others, such representatives of Western thought as Kirkegaard, the American pragmatists, and the modern existentialists.

PART IV
RATIONALITY AND NONRATIONALITY

Reason and Faith in the Philosophy of Solov'ëv

GEORGES FLOROVSKY

I

To vindicate the faith of our fathers, by raising it to a new level of intelligent understanding; to show that this faith, when disentangled from the bonds of provincial isolationism and national self-love, does coincide with the eternal and universal truth . . .

Thus Solov'ëv describes the aim and purpose of his famous book, *The History and the Future of Theocracy*.[1] The same description can be extended to his philosophical endeavor taken as a whole. It was indeed an essentially *synthetic* endeavor. Solov'ëv's hope was precisely to sketch that "Great Synthesis," in which, as he believed, all human aspirations will be accomplished and satisfied, all partial findings and achievements of man in history will be integrated and reconciled, and perennial strife and conflict of human convictions will be brought to a final and ultimate peace. This ultimate pacification of history was inevitable, it was coming. Eternal Destiny could not miss its immanent goal. There was some absolute or "divine" necessity in the play of the historical dialectics. The purpose of Reality could not be frustrated. Still, active and devout participation of men in this generation and the next was indispensable since the purpose had to be accomplished in freedom. This mysterious interconnection of an ultimate "necessity" (and of the assurance implied) and of "freedom," was the main metaphysical problem with which Solov'ëv wrestled throughout the whole of his philosophical career. Or, rather, this was his basic assumption, or perhaps his "original intuition." The course of cosmic destiny had been inwardly oriented toward a preordained goal, and this goal was nothing other than "freedom." Solov'ëv's search for truth was inspired and guided by two main convictions. In the first place, he did not believe that contradictions in human life and history were final or insoluble. In particular, he did not believe that "faith" and "reason" were intrinsically incompatible, nor could he agree with Auguste Comte that "religion" had been superseded by "metaphysics" in the course

---

[1] *Sobranie sochinenii Vladimir Sergeevicha Solov'ëva*, eds. S. M. Solov'ëv and E. L. Radlov (2nd ed., St. Petersburg, 1911–1914), IV, 243. All subsequent references are to this edition, hereafter cited as *Sochineniia*. Translations of quotations are my own.

of the intellectual evolution of mankind. For Solov'ëv, "Religion," "Metaphysics," and "Science," are in no sense just "stages," but rather permanent categories of human existence, and none could be eliminated, if man was expected to continue in his essential humanity. Of course, Solov'ëv was fully aware of that sharp conflict between faith and reason which had been especially accentuated in modern times. But, in his interpretation, this very conflict was precisely a necessary step in the development toward a free integration. The final synthesis had to be preceded by an antithesis, in which both components of the prospective synthesis had to be given free sway. Thus, disruption and alienation, and all antagonisms and divergencies, belong organically to the dialectics of integration. The "negative" development of the modern West, which radically broke away from the Church, and from the faith itself, especially since the Age of Enlightenment, was for Solov'ëv just a sign and token, a prophesy and a promise, of the impending return to God:

> It represents the complete and logical falling away of the human, natural forces from the divine principle, their exclusive self-assertion, an attempt to base the edifice of universal culture on themselves alone. Through the inconsistency and doomed failure of this attempt comes forth self-denial, and it leads to the free reunion with the divine principle . . . When Western humanity will be convinced by the very facts, by historic reality itself, that self-assertion of the will, in whatever manner it may be manifested, is the source of evil and suffering, then pessimism, the turn toward self-renunciation, will pass from theory into life, and Western humanity will be ready to accept the religious principle, the positive revelation of true religion.[2]

The pattern of Solov'ëv's thinking was intrinsically "historical." All problems had to be regarded in the perspective of the total development. This brings him back to the concept of "succession," but not in the sense of the positivist "law" of the three stages. The basic scheme is still triadic. But the first article of the scheme is outside history, or, as it were, "before" history, before the process. It is precisely the "eternal" or ideal world — in a sense, a "pre-existing" world — in relation to the world of our experience. In this world reign harmony and concord. But this harmony is simply given, and in this sense there is no "freedom." The process begins when all manifold members of the primordial cosmos start asserting themselves. It breaks the peace and concord. The world is, as it were, fragmentized. All tendencies are progressively dissociated. The world of history is essentially a broken world, a world dominated by partiality, and ruled by "detached principles."[3] It is a chaotic world, a world of strife and struggle and, consequently, of pain and suffering. Everything goes astray, because everything asserts itself,

---

[2] *Chteniia o Bogochelovechestve* (1881–1883), *ibid.*, III, 13–14.
[3] This is the accurate rendering of Solov'ëv's phrase "otvlechënnye nachala," and not "abstract principles," because in English the word "abstract" is much narrower than the corresponding Russian word.

apart from and in opposition to any other thing. But no new "thing" emerges. All elements are still the same, and only *order* has been broken. And yet, this process of disruption and dislocation has ultimately a positive significance and meaning. It is, as it were, a training in freedom. Selfish assertion of divers elements or members of the whole drives all of them into a helpless impasse out of which they can escape only by free acceptance of the initial "order," that is, precisely by a reversal of self-determination, in the spirit of common recognition, and in relation to the Supreme Principle which is the only true center around which all derived realities can be properly "ordered." This reversal of the will only corresponds to the real nature of the universe and of each of its members. And yet it must be exercised freely, in other words, by members of the whole themselves. It is in this way that we can tentatively summarize the main thoughts of Solov'ëv, as he formulated them in his early works, such as *The Crisis of Western Philosophy* (1874), *The Philosophical Principles of Integral Knowledge* (1877), and, especially, *The Critique of Detached Principles* (1880) and *Lectures Concerning Godmanhood* (1877–1881).[4] The same basic conception is maintained in the French book of Solov'ëv, *La Russie et l'Eglise Universelle* — some minor changes are of no importance for our present purpose. Solov'ëv's argument may be dismissed as abstruse or fantastic. But it is only in the light of his basic metaphysical presuppositions that we can assess what Solov'ëv had to say on the relation between faith and reason in a more practical and prosaic way. His conviction that "faith" and "reason" should ultimately agree on all points was rooted in his metaphysical conception. In a sense, they are

---

[4] The *Chteniia* (Lectures) were given at St. Petersburg in 1878. It is important to bear in mind that in the printed text (as it appeared originally in *Pravoslavnoe obozrenie*, and then was reproduced in the *Sochineniia*) the last lectures are given in a *revised version*, which differs very considerably from that actually delivered by Solov'ëv orally. This has not been noticed by the editors or any other student of Solov'ëv. The result is that we miss the *plan* of the lectures: the real climax of Solov'ëv's argument is missing in the printed text, and consequently we do not see the point to which the argument was leading. Fortunately, we have the original program of the *Lectures*, as advertised in advance. It has been published in the same periodical in which the *Lectures* themselves first appeared (*Pravoslavnoe obozrenie*, February 1878, pp. 343–345). The program of the last two lectures (XI and XII) was as follows: XI — The Church as a Divine-human organism or the Body of Christ. The Church, visible and invisible. The growth of man "into the fullness of the stature of Christ." XII — The Second Coming of Christ and the Resurrection of the dead (the redemption or restitution of the world of nature). The Kingdom of the Holy Spirit and the full revelation of the Godmanhood. Obviously it was a more logical conclusion of the *Lectures* than what we find in the printed text. The combined eleventh and twelfth lectures in the printed text were written by Solov'ëv in 1881 and have nothing in common with the actual lectures. S. Solov'ëv's letters to the editor of *Pravoslavnoe obozrenie*, Fr. Peter Preobrazhenskii, in *Pis'ma*, IV (Petersburg 1923), 233. The original lectures had an emphatically "eschatological" or "apocalyptic" turn, including the theme of the "apocatastasis ton panton" and universal salvation. See the letters of N. N. Strakhov (who attended the last lecture) to Leo Tolstoy, April 9, 1878, in *Tolstovskii Muzei*, II, 160–161, and Solov'ëv's letter to Olga Novikov, in *Pis'ma*, IV, 183.

bound to diverge, when practiced as "detached principles." But, on the other hand, they must "coincide," when brought together, in a wider and "synthetic" perspective, in the context of the "integral knowledge." It is precisely the integration that works miracles and quenches all strife. Fragmentation of the universe does not create anything new, although it may produce illusions and fictions, which of course will disappear when the synthesis had been achieved. And, secondly, for Solov'ëv, "reason," strictly speaking, has no content, by and in itself. "Reason" is a *formal principle;* it has no independent access to reality. It is, as it were, *essentially abstract,* i.e., precisely *"detached* from reality," i.e., from the being. It is imprisoned in itself. It cannot ascertain reality, and in this sense it is blind. It cannot ascertain existence, unless it is made available to it by other means. On the contrary, "faith" is precisely an insight into existence. It touches reality, even if it cannot, by itself, give an account of what it possesses. At this point, Solov'ëv walks in the steps of the late Schelling, with his strict distinction between a "negative" philosophy, purely rational, and a "positive," of which the first is inescapably "formal," and the latter supplies an existential content out of the religious experience. One may again compare Solov'ëv's contention with what Bergson had to say on the relationship betwen *instinct* and *intellect.* Bergson opposes "the *material* knowledge of instinct" to "the *formal* knowledge of intelligence," and concludes: *"there are things which intelligence alone is able to seek, but which, by itself, it will never find; these things instinct alone could find, but it will never seek them."* [5] It is along a similar line that Solov'ëv develops his argument. "Faith" alone is an existential or "substantial" principle; it establishes link and contact with true reality. And yet it needs a "rational" elaboration, otherwise its experience remains, as it were, not organized. "Faith" has an obvious existential priority; it gives the true assurance of existence, but it is the "reason" alone which can give a coherent account of the apprehended reality. Our comparison with Bergson is legitimate, because Solov'ëv uses the concept of "faith" in a very wide sense, in which it denotes almost the same basic "insight" into existence as the "intuition" of Bergson. In fact, for Solov'ëv, faith is an integral element of any act of knowledge. "Faith," (intellectual) "imagination," and "realization" (in sensual images) are for him "fundamental elements of any objective knowledge." [6] There is no sharp division between "religious" and "secular" knowledge. Knowledge is inescapably "religious" because it fulfills its function only if it succeeds in relating every particular or partial information to the absolute center of reality. In other

---

[5] Henri Bergson, *Creative Evolution,* authorized trans. by Arthur Mitchell (New York, 1944), pp. 166–167.

[6] *Kritika otvlechënnykh nachal* (1877–1880), *Sochineniia,* II, 324ff. Cf. the discussion of this conception by Evgenii Trubetskoi, *Mirosozertsanie Vl. S. Solov'ëva,* 2 vols. (Moscow, 1913), I, 237ff. Trubetskoi seems to be right in his objections to V. Ern (see Ern's article in *O Vladimir Solov'ëve: Sbornik pervyi* [Moscow, 1911], pp. 129ff).

words, for Solov'ëv, there is no separate or distinct "religious" sphere which could be contrasted with something else. The "religious" sphere should be, as it intrinsically is, all-inclusive. Otherwise it would be a pseudoreligion, another specimen of "detached principles." Or, in other words again, religion, by its very essence, is omnicompetent — truly "universal." It is to be the center of the prospective synthesis. Indeed, by its very nature, religion is "synthetic." It is precisely "synthesis." To attempt synthesis on any other basis would inevitably imply violence, or would presuppose the unlawful claim for an absolute or unconditional authority on behalf of this or that particular and partial element of the universe. Consequently, a synthesis attempted on such a basis in no case can be "free," as it will of necessity subordinate the rest of the principles or elements to what, actually, is no more than one of many factors of the being and cannot, in virtue of its inherent limitation, sustain claims for a rightful supremacy. This kind of "synthesis" would mean just bondage and domination of the "detached principles":

Religion is reunion of men and of the world with the absolute and integral principle. This principle, as integral and all-inclusive, does not exclude anything, and therefore the true union with it, the true religion, cannot exclude, or suppress, or forcibly subdue to itself, any element whatever, any living power, either in man or in his universe. Reunion, or religion, consists in the bringing of all elements of human existence, of all particular principles and powers of humanity, into rightful relation with the absolute central principle, and, through it and in it, into right and harmonious relationship to each other. As the absolute principle, by its very nature, does not allow for any exclusiveness or compulsion, this reunion of particular aspects of life and of individual forces with the integral principle and with each other must be absolutely free. All these principles and forces, each in its own limits, in the limits of its purpose and idea, have equal rights for existence and development. As they are united into one common and unconditional whole, to which they are related as its different but equally indispensable elements, they represent among themselves a total solidarity or brotherhood. Thus, from this point of view, the principle of religion appears to be the only real manifestation of freedom, equality, and brotherhood. I said that, according to the meaning of the religious idea, reunion of separate beings and of particular principles and forces with the absolute principle must be free. This means that these separate beings and particular principles should of themselves or by their own will come to reunion, should renounce their own exclusiveness, their own self-assertion or egoism.[7]

Religion alone can give cohesion or unity to human life. The main grief of Solov'ëv was that, in modern times, religion, at least in the West, retired into seclusion and even renounced its synthetic role and function:

Contemporary religion is a very pitiful thing. Strictly speaking, today there is no religion, in the sense of a ruling principle, of a center of spiritual gravitation. Instead, there is the so-called "religiosity," just as a personal mood, or a

[7] *Sochineniia*, III, 12–13.

personal taste: some people have this taste, others have not, just as some people like music and others do not.[8]

Religion survived in the homes and in the temples. But there is little religion in the actual life of men; there is no *social religion*. But the ultimate aim and purpose of the true religion is in that it succeeds in reuniting and reconciling all human activities into *one common and universal action*. Otherwise even the common and universal faith would risk remaining just an abstract formula and a dead dogma. Faith without works is dead.[9] Solov'ëv began his philosophical preaching in the firm conviction that "philosophy, in the sense of an abstract and exclusively theoretical knowledge, had completed its course of development and passed away, never to return." [10] Even in the past, the true justification of philosophy was in its "historic deeds." It had emancipated the personality of man from external oppression and supplied him with inner content.[11] But the present needs of humanity surpass the resources of pure philosophy. Religion alone can accomplish the urgent task of social reintegration, by which alone the "integral life" of mankind can be inaugurated.

II

It is not difficult to detect Solov'ëv's sources, and it has been done fairly well by various students of his thought.[12] His close dependence upon German idealistic philosophy and German mysticism is obvious. The impact of the Slavophile tradition on the formation of his thought has been firmly established. Other minor links have also been detected. What is much more important, however, is to recover that concrete and existential setting in which Solov'ëv's thought grew and blossomed. One may describe his philosophy as a "romantic philosophy." But "romanticism" is an ambiguous term, and there is a tendency to use it in a narrow sense. In fact, the early French socialism and even the positivism of Auguste Comte were also typically "romantic." Their impact on Solov'ëv's development has not yet been sufficiently appreciated. It is still unusual to treat the French "Utopian" socialists as "philosophers." Their philosophical impact, however, was very considerable (it is enough to mention Charles Renouvier). There are good reasons to believe that Solov'ëv's early interest in socialism had left much more profound traces in his later system than is usually admitted. The "socialism" of his youth, attested by Lopatin, was more than an irrelevant episode in his life and in the story of his mind. It is hardly an accident that he begins *Lectures Concerning Godmanhood* with a lengthy section on

[8] *Ibid.*, p. 4.
[9] *Tri rechi v pamyat' Dostoevskago* (1881–1883), *ibid.*, III, 202–203.
[10] "Krizis zapadnoi filosofii" (1874), *ibid.*, I, 27.
[11] "Istoricheskiia dela filosofii" (1880), *ibid.*, II, 411–412.
[12] The best analysis is by D. Strémooukhoff, *Vladimir Soloviev et son oeuvre messianique* (Paris, 1935).

socialism, and precisely on the "truth of socialism," which he regards as a "necessary" last step in Western development, and which he is not prepared to eliminate from his ultimate synthesis.[13] Again, in his brief survey of the *Historic Deeds of Philosophy* (1880), he alludes to Charles Fourier (without naming him) and his attempt at a *"rehabilitation de la chair"* — his philosophy, he adds, had served the Christian truth, without knowing it.[14] One should not forget also that some of the best friends of Solov'ev, in his formative years — Dostoyevsky and Nikolai Fëdorov — were strongly influenced, in one sense or in another, by Fourier. Again it was hardly an accident that Dostoyevsky, in his "Pushkin Speech," should introduce Orthodoxy precisely as "our Russian socialism." The point was obviously that Christianity alone could solve the problem raised by "socialism," but the problem itself was accepted and in this way the partial "truth of socialism" recognized. For Solov'ev, Dostoyevsky was the great prophet of the coming "universal and social" religion of the future.[15]

Solov'ev's early "socialism" was not just a "typical nihilism of the sixties," as Lopatin suggested.[16] He was deeply impressed by that unexpected outburst of a socialist "lay-religion" in the early seventies, which the late Professor George Fedotoff aptly described as an exodus, "if not into the Thebaid, at least into the Montanist Phrygia." [17] To this "movement" (*khozhdenie v narod*) Solov'ev openly refers in one of his early letters to Selevina (written precisely at the time when Solov'ev was working on his "Crisis").[18] During his stay at London (in 1875) Solov'ev was very much interested in the socialist communities in North America, perhaps in connection with the Russian "Utopian" settlements there (the dates approximately coincide), namely of William Frey and Nikolai Chaikovskii. Both of them were building at that time a "new religion." It was a "religion of humanity," and had little to do with the historic Christianity. Yet it is very curious to observe that one of the members of this peculiar group, A. K. Malikov, developed a theory of "Godmanhood" and even founded a sect of the *Bogo-cheloveki*, the ideology of which could be traced back to Pierre Leroux and probably to other French "Utopians." Now, Malikov was well acquainted with Solov'ev. He attended his lectures in 1878, and corresponded with Solov'ev for a period of time (these letters seem to be lost). Later Malikov

---

[13] *Sochineniia*, III, 5ff.

[14] *Ibid.*, II, 411.

[15] See his *Tri rechi, ibid.*, III, 197ff.

[16] L. M. Lopatin, "Filosofskoe mirosozertsanie V. S. Solov'ëva (1900)," in his *Filosofskiia kharakteristiki i rechi* (Moscow, 1911); cf. S. M. Lukianov, *O Vl. S. Solov'ëve v ego molodye gody; materialy k biografii* (Petrograd, 1916-), I.

[17] E. Bogdanov (G. P. Fedotov), "Tragediia intelligentsii," *Versty*, no. 2 (Paris, 1927), pp. 171f. Cf. also Nadejda Gorodetzky, *The Humiliated Christ in Modern Russian Thought* (London, 1938), pp. 86f., and my *Puti russkago bogosloviia* (Paris, 1937), pp. 294ff.

[18] *Pis'ma* (St. Petersburg, 1911), III, 97-98.

returned to the Church.[19] It was not just a curious accident, there was a true parallelism in patterns. The Russian movement of the seventies, this religious "Populism," as well as the original French Utopianism (of Saint Simon or Fourier), was in the search for "faith" and was very critical of "reason." The motives were precisely the same in all cases: "reason" was "critical" and only "faith" was "organic," and therefore constructive; it was impossible to build the "new society" *except on some "faith,"* and therefore a *new religion* had to be created which would at least take into account the recent findings of "empirical science." No society could be built except on "enthusiasm," which only can give cohesion to community and overrule individual egoisms. This conviction was the link between Solov'ëv and ("Utopian") "socialism" of various descriptions.

This identity of the pattern, between Solov'ëv and the "radicals," has been recognized by some students of Solov'ëv, who regretted that he combined his progressive social vision with the obsolete and archaic Christianity of the dogmatic Church.[20] It is of great importance that we should not overlook the striking similarity of approach to the problem of "synthesis" in Solov'ëv and the French socialists, including Auguste Comte. It is the same antithesis of a disrupted state of humanity at the present and the coming reintegration by love and insight. It may be objected that this is just a romantic commonplace, which would be certainly true. And in no case do we insist that Solov'ëv was influenced only by the French trend of thought, or that he had no other sources of inspiration. Obviously, he could have learned a lot in Baader, although up to now the question is still open, as no one has attempted to study the relationship between these two social thinkers in any detail. For the moment we are concerned with a particular instance, the relationship between "faith" and "reason" in the perspective of the prospective synthesis. It is significant, in any case, that in his later years Solov'ëv himself should turn to Auguste Comte and greet him as an unconscious forerunner of his own conception.[21] Of course this does not prove that Solov'ëv knew Comte well in his earlier years. On the contrary, Solov'ëv says that he came to know and appreciate Comte only when he was writing his article (1898), and we may conjecture that he turned to Comte under the influence of Nikolai Fëdorov. Yet, even in his earliest year,

[19] See David Hecht, *Russian Radicals Look to America, 1825–1894* (Cambridge, Mass., 1947), p. 196; the treatment is not complete, especially on Malikov. For additional bibliography see my *Puti*, p. 552. It was A. Prugavin who mentions the correspondence between Malikov and Solov'ëv: "Lev Tolstoi i bogocheloveki," in *Russkoe bogatstvo*, August 1911, pp. 147–165. That Malikov attended Solov'ëv's "lectures" we know from Strakhov. (See the letter to Tolstoy, quoted earlier.)

[20] S. A. Gizetti, "O mirosozertsanii Vlad. Solov'ëva," *Zavety*, February 1914, pp. 1–21; cf. the same author's "Pëtr L. Lavrov i Vladimir Solov'ëv," *Sbornik v pamiat' Lavrova* (Petrograd, 1923), pp. 385–403.

[21] "Ideia chelovechestva u Ogiusta Konta" (1898), *Sochineniia*, VIII, 240ff.

Solov'ëv polemized with Comte (in a special appendix to the "Crisis") and should have read at that time at least his famous *Cours de la philosophie positive,* in which already the main lines of the later system were briefly sketched. And he could not have failed to observe Comte's appraisal of the Middle Ages, as a period of order, contrasted with the modern disorder: there was a "spiritual power" in the medieval order, for which, since the Reformation, an "intellectual anarchy" has been substituted. This was the heritage of Saint Simon; this was the basic idea of Saint Simon's *Nouveau Christianisme.* That is to say, "Reason" could not serve as a basis for social reconstruction, being, as it actually is, just a critical or negative principle. It is sympathy, or affection, that is the source of social cohesion. There was a curious affinity in spirit between this "Utopian socialism" and the "theocratical school" of the French "traditionalists," such as Lamennais or Ballanche, and one can even detect some unexpected parallels between Joseph de Maistre and Comte, as different and antagonistic to each other as they obviously were. "Faith" had different content in these two cases, but its function was identical in both systems. There was the same radical dismissal of "Reason," as a revolutionary and anarchical principle. It can be said that, in a sense, this "Utopian socialism" was a kind of "Catholicism without "Christianity," but still some sort of "faith" was indispensable.

It has already been pointed out (for example, by L. M. Lopatin) that Solov'ëv's belief in the coming consummation of the historical process had been the same all his life, although the concrete forms in which he visualized the ultimate end varied.[22] One should add that, to a very large extent, the structure of the vision also remained the same and this identity of structure gives the impression of continuity in the development. In fact, there were radical changes, from a vague conception of a *free theocracy* in Solov'ëv's youth to the "Romanizing" conception of his mature years. At all times he would persistently plead for "faith" and "freedom," but his historical terms of reference considerably change. The theocratic conception of his "Romanizing" years has not been properly studied up to now. No serious consideration has been given to the enigmatic role which the "empire" had to play in the establishment of the ultimate social and universal order. He was pleading in fact not only for a universal spiritual authority of the Roman Pope, but for a universal temporal authority of an emperor. The immediate historical context of this Utopian dream can be easily assessed,[23] but it does not explain it in full. Strangely enough, the theme of the "empire" Solov'ëv inherited from the Slavophile tradition, from Tiutchev first

[22] L. M. Lopatin, "Pamiati Vl. S. Solov'ëva," *Voprosy filosofii i psikhologii* (1915), V (105), 633ff.

[23] Strémooukhov's analysis should now be supplemented by the important information of Eduard Winter, in his recent book *Russland und die slawischen Völker in der Diplomatie des Vatikans, 1878–1903* (Berlin, 1950), p. 186.

of all,[24] to whom probably V. Lamanskii should be added.[25] But he mentions also the name of Dante,[26] and we know that in the early eighties he was studying some Italian sources.[27] Now, Dante's *De Monarchia* could have supplied him not only with impressive suggestions on the basic question of "theocracy," but also with manifold hints on the subject of "faith" and philosophy. In any case, it had to introduce him into another religio-philosophical tradition, substantially different from that of German idealism.[28] What is of real interest is that Solov'ëv, while occupied chiefly with the problem of the "spiritual authority," [29] was nevertheless resolutely committed to the cause of spiritual freedom. In fact, in his interpretation, it was precisely "authority" of the divine truth, mediated through the hierarchical stewardship of the Church, that could secure true freedom. Freedom indeed is possible only through obedience (to the truth), by "faith." [30] On the other hand, the orthodoxy of beliefs is justified only by the integrity of life. The main emphasis of Solov'ëv was always on the organic synthesis of the divine and the human, and consequently of "faith" and "reason," and both components were equally indispensable. Their divorce or distortion would lead to a double heresy, in theory and in life. In theory it would result (as it had in fact variously resulted) in the conceptions of an "inhuman God" or of a godless and self-sufficient humanity. In life it would inaugurate a regime of compulsion. Freedom can be secured only by the Truth (which is divine, because absolute by definition, as obviously a relative truth is not Truth), but this truth must be accepted, freely, that is, by conviction, by man's reason and will.

III

Following E. N. Trubetskoi, we may speak of a "collapse" or crisis of theocracy in the thought of Solov'ëv in the early nineties.[31] Nevertheless, this period of disappointment and hesitation was a period of reconstruction also.[32] Not only was Solov'ëv still concerned with the same problem, but his approach remained basically the same. Perhaps one should mention at this

[24] Cf. my articles: "Tiutchev i Vladimir Solov'ëv," *Put'*, no. 41 (November-December 1933) and "The Historical Premonitions of Tjutchev," *The Slavonic Review*, III, no. 8 (December 1924).
[25] Cf. Lamanskii's interesting remarks on the idea of the "empire" in his "Ob istoricheskom, izuchenii greko-slavianskago mira v Evrope," in *Zaria*, 1870, and in separate edition, St. Petersburg, 1871, and especially in his "Vidnye deiateli zapadno-slavianskoi obrazovannosti . . . ," in *Slavianskii sbornik*, I (1875), 422ff.
[26] *Pis'ma*, IV, 27.
[27] *Ibid.*, p. 85.
[28] I am preparing a detailed essay on this topic.
[29] Cf. his article, "O dukhovnoi vlasti v Rossii (1881)," *Sochineniia*, III, 227–242.
[30] See especially his "Velikii spor' i khristianskaia politika. 1883," *ibid.*, IV, 1–114.
[31] See Trubetskoi's *Mirosozertsanie*, especially Vol. II.
[32] Cf. the remarks of Strémooukhov, *Vladimir Soloviev*, pp. 215ff., and Ludolf Müller, *Solovyew und der Protestantismus* (Freiburg, 1951), pp. 6off.

point the increasing influence of Nikolai Fëdorov, which is strongly felt, not only in the article on the "Meaning of Love" (1892–1894), but especially in the last systematic book of Solov'ëv, *The Justification of the Good* (1894–1899), and which probably induced Solov'ëv to restudy Comte.[33] It must not be overlooked, however, that on the question of "faith" and "reason" Solov'ëv and Fëdorov radically disagreed. Fëdorov was a consequent rationalist, in spite of his insistence on sympathy and brotherhood, and an avowed antagonist of everything mystical. But Solov'ëv never wavered from his conviction that "reason" was no more than a formal principle, and "faith" had existential priority. In the present context it would suffice to refer to an important letter of Solov'ëv to Eugene Tavernier, a French friend of his, in which he restates briefly his conception of history (1896). The scheme is still the same: a universal proclamation of the Gospel, that is, of the Divine Truth, and the expected response on man's side. Now, Solov'ëv anticipates that only an "insignificant minority" of the true believers will accept the Truth, the majority siding with the antichrist. Yet, after a violent but brief struggle, it is precisely the minority that will win. The practical task, within the limits of history, is still to present the Truth in such a way that everybody would be confronted with a clear choice. This implies not only the propagation of knowledge, but, above all, formal training, in order to remove all intellectual errors which may make the *understanding* of the Truth difficult or even impossible. The Divine Truth must be restated in definitive and unconditional terms, and the problem for man must be thereby to seek a simple decision, either absolutely moral, or absolutely immoral. Thus it is of decisive importance that "a general instauration of the Christian philosophy" should take place, otherwise the proclamation of the Gospel cannot be effective. All efforts to establish "theocracy," in its power and external grandeur, should be abandoned. And yet the final victory will not come just by the way of pure miracle; this would have rendered the whole of history superfluous. Its meaning is in the human collaboration in the cause of God and Christ. The problem of rallying human forces around a spiritual center remains, but now Solov'ëv expects but a rally of a faithful remnant, of the persevering minority. Of course, this is just a brief sketch, but Solov'ëv's point is made quite clearly.[34]

It may be objected that Solov'ëv now renounces any hope of the historical triumph. On the other hand, it is by no means certain that even in his most "Utopian" period he expected the ultimate victory to come smoothly: in his reply to Leont'ev (1883) he openly stated that "the universal harmony, or the Church triumphant, will be brought about not by peaceful progress, but in the pangs and travail of the new birth, as it is described in

[33] I plan to return to this question in a special essay; cf. my *Puti*, pp. 462ff. and — on Fëdorov — pp. 322–330.

[34] *Pis'ma*, IV, 196–198.

the Book of Revelation." [35] And probably in this manner his actual *Lectures Concerning Godmanhood* were concluded, when he delivered them at St. Petersburg.[36] In his last years, however, Solov'ëv seems to have gone one step further. In his remarkable "Story of the Antichrist" he discriminates between the two kinds of "universal synthesis" and gives a tentative scheme of the wrong "synthesis," which will be attempted by the antichrist. We may observe that now the main tension is not just between a state of "disintegration" and the scheme of an all-healing "integration," but ultimately between the two *"syntheses."* Of course, even in his early years Solov'ëv was fully conscious of the existence of false "syntheses," but his main emphasis was then on the lack of cohesion. Now he is afraid, as it were, of "synthetic deceits," not only of synthetic "illusions." And what he imputes now to the antichrist has a striking resemblance to certain dreams of his own early years. Solov'ëv anticipates that in the "last times" there will be but a tiny band of believers, that is, of those who would still "believe in things spiritual." And then he introduces an important personality: a remarkable man, almost a superman, at once a great thinker, writer, and social worker. He did *believe* in God, in Good also, but he *loved* only himself, preferring himself, in the depth of his soul, even to God. He had no fundamental enmity toward Jesus, but he regarded himself as somebody greater. His title for greatness was that he could overcome all boundaries and splits. "Christ brought a sword: I shall bring peace." His conception was developed in a remarkable book, *The Open Way to Universal Peace and Prosperity.* As Solov'ëv puts it, "it was something all-embracing and calculated to reconcile all disputes." It was, in a sense, a project of an all-inclusive "Great Synthesis."

In it was united a noble reverence for ancient traditions and symbols, with a broad and daring radicalism in socio-political claims and requests; a boundless freedom of thought with the deepest understanding of all mysticism; unconditional individualism with an ardent zeal for the common good; the most exalted idealism in guiding principles with the complete concreteness and vitality of practical solutions. And all of it was united and connected with such genius and skill that it was easy for every one-sided thinker or worker to see and to accept the whole, even from his particular point of view, without sacrificing anything for the truth itself, or rising above his own self for the sake of it, or giving up his own one-sidedness, or in any way correcting his mistaken views and aspirations, or trying to complete their insufficiency . . . No one made any objections to the book, for it seemed to everyone a revelation of the all-embracing truth. It did such complete justice to the past, it interpreted so dispassionately every aspect of the present, it brought the future so concretely and tangibly within reach . . .

There was but one omission in the book: Christ was not mentioned there at all. But even certain Christians were prepared to reconcile themselves with

---

[35] *Sochineniia,* III, 223.
[36] See ref. 4 above.

the omission since "the whole book was permeated by the truly Christian spirit of active love and all-embracing benevolence." The author of the book finally became "Roman emperor," and under his rule all social and political problems were solved. Even Christians, on the whole, received these peaceful reforms with sympathy and enthusiasm. Ultimately, an ecumenical council was convened in order to solve the religious problem. And then the deceit was detected. In all this magnificent "synthesis" there was no room for Christ Himself, in Whom all the fullness of the Godhead dwells bodily. And it was precisely what the antichrist would not include in his all-embracing peace. Of course, the "Story of Antichrist" is just a parable or a fiction, or rather a "legend" (like the "Legend of the Great Inquisitor," with which, by the way, it has various links), and one cannot expect here any philosophical precision. And yet Solov'ëv's contention is perfectly clear. No "synthesis" is possible unless it is built on the belief in the "Historic Christ," the God Incarnate and made Man, Crucified, and Risen. Any other synthesis is a lie, even if it succeeds in including all "Christian" ideas and values.

Of course, *The Open Way* of the antichrist is a travesty of Solov'ëv's early plans. *The Open Way* is explicitly based on a luciferian self-love. And Solov'ëv's plans were always definitely *theocentric*. Yet, even in his *Lectures Concerning Godmanhood* the Historic Christ was more a manifestation of a general idea than a true Person. As Solov'ëv himself puts it, "the originality of Christianity is not in its general views, but in positive facts — not in the speculative content of its idea, but in the personal incarnation of that idea." [37] It is true, Solov'ëv emphasizes here *personal* incarnation, but still the stress is rather on the (eternal) *Idea*, which, as he points out himself, is essentially the same in Philo or Plotinus, in Origen or Gregory of Nazianzus. As much as Solov'ëv did say about Christ in his various writings, he never was in the center of his speculations. Now, in his last "Story" he radically changes the approach. And in this new perspective the whole problem of "faith" and "reason" had to assume a radically new content. But Solov'ëv did not live long enough even to start this revision. In a sense, his "Story" was his "Retractationes." The "Story" ends in a double synthesis, a false peace of the antichrist and a true "reunion of churches," and the latter is based on a common confession of Jesus Christ Who came in the flesh (I John 4.2–3). The test is here historical, and not philosophical. And what is required now is not just a renunciation of one's self, but a positive commitment to the Living Person.[38]

[37] *Sochineniia*, III, 82–83.

[38] "The Story of the Antichrist," incorporated in *Tri Razgovory*, was written in 1899; *Sochineniia*, X, 81–221. An interesting analysis of the "Story" is given by Fritz Lieb, "Der Geist der Zeit, als Antichrist," in *Orient und Occident*, May 16, 1934, pp. 7–22; included, in a revised form, in his *Russland unterwegs* (Bern, 1945), pp. 117–144. The interpretation given in the text was developed in my unpublished course on the "Philosophy of Solovyov," delivered at the Russian Institute at Prague in 1922–1923; cf. my *Puti*, p. 466.

Solov'ëv began his philosophical pilgrimage in an age when both religion and metaphysics seemed to have been finally discredited. But he did not feel himself to be just an apologist of obsolete and "lost causes." On the contrary, he had a firm conviction that the tide would change. His ultimate reason for this expectation was his vision of the "Total Unity" of the Being (*Vseedinstvo*). It was at once an insight (or a mystical experience) and a conviction, which could be logically argued. He was strongly inspired by the recent attempt to vindicate the metaphysical truth of Christianity, that is, the metaphysical validity of its essential doctrines, which had been made in Germany, for example, by Schelling and Baader. These doctrines, at least in their philosophical reinterpretation, provided him with a comprehensive view of human destiny and could serve at the same time as a basis for ethical practice much better than any other system. He simply could not see any valid objection against the truth of Christianity, in which for him the best traditions of the previous human history had been summarized. As far as he could see, "reason" spoke in history rather for "faith" than against it. One had to "believe" because it was only through "faith" that one could "understand." *Credo ut intelligam.* On the other hand, one gets the impression that it was precisely the "intelligence" that supplied him with the ultimate assurance or security. It was not just "Hegelian," but simply "romantic" (because Hegel was one of the "romanticists" in what he had to say against the others) that Solov'ëv regarded "alienation" as an inevitable and necessary stage in the normal growth of belief. There was no immediate evidence or assurance in the act of "faith" as such. It had to go through an intellectual trial and testing. At the same time, he would not admit the existence of any genuine break or discord in the Being, as everything had been eternally chained together in absolute Wisdom. Solov'ëv's preaching was powerful and convincing. He succeeded in reintroducing the religious theme in the universe of discourse of many in his, and in the next, generation. He rekindled also religious "emotion'" in many souls. He founded if not a school, in the strict sense of the word, at least a tradition. And above all he succeeded in exonerating religion (Christianity, first of all) from the charge of political or social reactionarism. In himself he exemplified the freedom of belief. Criticism does not belong to the scope of this paper. It would be incomplete, however, if we failed to mention that Solov'ëv can be criticized not only from the point of view of conservative dogmaticism in religion, but also in the name of the "living religion," and, of course, from the point of view which would not provide any room for religion in the search for objective truth. One may object to Solov'ëv, to the excess of "reason" in his "theosophical" speculations, the excess which in the last resort endangers precisely that freedom of conviction which he professed to cherish and to defend. One may also object that his "universe of discourse" had been strangely narrow. There was a peculiar selectiveness in his erudition. It is strange indeed that his mystical perspective was limited by Jacob Boehme and others of the same type, and he never displayed any interest in the major traditions of Christian mysticism. All this is said here not in order to judge Solov'ëv, but simply to suggest that, for serious reasons, one should not expect that the future search for "Christian synthesis" would follow in his steps. There are grave reasons to expect that, already in our days, the main emphasis will be not on "recapitulation," but rather on "discrimination," as had been suggested by Solov'ëv himself in his last legacy. The test is not in "synthetic consistency," but in loyalty to the Incarnate Lord.[39]

[39] Some recent writers paid me undeserved honor by quoting my very old bibliographical article, buried in a provincial periodical, to allege my authority for the full conformity of Solov'ëv with "the genuine spirit of the Eastern Orthodoxy"; see K. Mochul'skii, *Vladimir Solov'ëv. Zhizn' i uchenie* (2nd ed., Paris, 1951), p. 119, and Peter P. Zouboff, *Godmanhood as the Main Idea of the Philosophy of Vladimir Solovyov* (Poughkeepsie, 1944), p. 43. The latter author adds, in a footnote, that this estimate of mine "has been disputed by at least one contemporary Church authority." He could have added that it had been strongly repudiated by me, as one could have learned, e.g., from my later (and also bibliographical) article, "Molodost' Vladimira Solov'ëva," in *Put'*, no. 9 (January 1928). How could it escape the attention of readers that the article they quoted had been written when the writer was still in his teens and therefore should not be imputed to him thirty-five years later? I use this opportunity for a formal "retraction" of my fully incompetent "estimate" of my undergraduate youth.

Partiinost' and Knowledge

WALDEMAR GURIAN*

I

The *Communist Manifesto* of Marx-Engels (1848) states that the bourgeois is unable to know truth and reality, for the bourgeois transforms "into eternal laws of nature and reason the social forms springing from the present mode of production and form of property." He regards his transitory world erroneously as *the* world, for he is not able to realize its provisional, temporary character — since he does not know the laws and forces of history and development which will replace the present forms of society, political institutions, social customs, human relations, and ideas by new ones. The bourgeois does not know the present because he has no understanding of the future. He does not grasp the present moment of history, because he does not know the laws and forces determining the whole of history. But truth cannot be grasped by stating isolated facts and observations, it can only be seen when we know the whole system, of which the individual facts and events are only parts and in connection with which they receive their meaning and significance. But the knowledge of the whole includes the knowledge of the laws and forces shaping and determining its development. And, according to Marx, the economic-social changes basically determine all other changes — consciousness is determined by the social-economic basis. Thus, in Marxism, the forms of knowledge and institutions are seen as dependent upon the social character of the group in which they originate. Lenin, also, repeating Marx, emphasized this in one of his earliest writings. (His discussion of the views of the *narodniki* in 1895). But this view does not signify a kind of sociological relativism and agnosticism, which discerns no objective difference between various worlds, systems of knowledge, and institutions.

History is the realization of justice, or the complete unmutilated human nature, the fulfillment of a truly human and reasonable reality. The bourgeois world is a particular world corresponding to particular interests. The bourgeois consciousness is therefore a wrong consciousness — which takes

* This paper, because of Professor Gurian's death, did not receive his final revision.

parts for the whole, superficial appearances for the full reality, the transitional for the eternal. Different from this bourgeois limitation, the proletarian consciousness is based upon the perfect economic social order which is free from the fetters of private ownership of the means of production and corresponds to the disappearance of all class differences; therefore it is, according to Marxist creed as expressed in the *Communist Manifesto,* related to full truth and reality. For the proletariat is the class destined to abolish the division of human society into classes and to replace incomplete and mutilated human beings, under the direction and domination of particular interests, by the truly human, complete man. The victory of the proletariat will replace the incomplete and distorted reality of the bourgeois consciousness by a true consciousness determined by a complete reality. The practice of the fight of the proletariat creates the true theory — and the theory of the proletariat and its struggle help to develop the right practice. For, as Marx has proclaimed, theory is not designed to develop a pure abstract knowledge, to look contemplatively upon the world, but it is destined to change it. Therefore the proletarian knowledge is not only a passive and observing one, regarding likewise from outside and from above the flux of the events, but a shaping and transforming force. Theory and practice form a unity — whereas this unity does not exist for the bourgeois mind. The bourgeois theory does not correspond to the practice, is only a means to cover up its imperfections and errors, to express general ideas without relation to concrete situations.

II

But where is the proletarian consciousness located which is able to understand the future and is not imprisoned in the transitory conditions of the present world? The Communists present and express this consciousness. As the Manifesto puts it: "The Communists are the most advanced and resolute section of the working class parties of each country."

We have sketched the basic claim of orthodox Marxism that there is a proletarian-communist knowledge which is the knowledge giving truth and corresponding to full reality. The bourgeois knowledge is, on the contrary, full of errors and falsification. These errors and falsifications are not only the result of conscious attitudes, accepted by individuals who are eager to serve their egoistic interests. The bourgeois ideology is the expression of the limitation of the bourgeois by his social position — he is incapable of seeing through it, of springing above his own shadow. His claim to objectivity is simply a cover-up for his extreme subjectivism, for his being imprisoned in his social situation. His claim to objectivity is therefore only a pretense — a method to make his particular interests and his world appear as *the* human interests and *the* eternal world.

This scheme is the basis of Bolshevik thinking on knowledge and science.

It is well revealed in the Bolshevik demand, formulated first by Lenin, that all true knowledge ought to be determined by *partiinost'*, that is, knowledge is to be in accord with the Party, indeed, knowledge is to be determined by accepting the authority of the Party, of course, the Communist Party.

A first basic statement of this Bolshevik attitude is to be found in Lenin's philosophical study of 1908, *Materialism and Empiriocriticism*. It would be wrong to regard this work today as outdated because it fights an attempt to combine Marxian demands with a bourgeois positivistic philosophy, abandoning its materialistic basis. This basis is, as Marx himself emphasized in the preface to the second edition of *Das Kapital*, inseparably linked with Hegel — by "turning right side up again" the idealistic Hegelian dialectic. Lenin fought the various attempts of his contemporaries, such as Bogdanov, Basarov, etc., to combine Marxist policies with more modern philosophical attitudes — the doctrines of Mach, Avenarius, etc. — first by trying to prove that they contradict the views of Marx and Engels. These views appear as authoritative. How can one be a Marxist and contradict the text of the masters? But it would be unjust to overlook that Lenin accepts the authority of Marx and Engels just because they have, as he believes, uncovered the truth. "From the beginning to the end Marx and Engels were party men in philosophy; they knew how to discover deviations from materialism and concessions to idealism and fideism." For Lenin there is an absolute truth, expressed by Marx and Engels. Therefore it is not justifiable to oppose them. Those who are against them or, what is worse, by pretending to be Marxists reinterpret them, deviate from this truth. The partisan (*partiinyi*) character of Marxism is not the expression of individual preferences, subjectivism, but true objectivism, the recognition of the truly objective world and its laws of movement and structure. On the contrary the thinking of the bourgeois is wrong, for it sees only partial aspects of the world which it erroneously enlarges to the whole; therefore the Marxian dialectical materialism is able to understand it — and to uncover the sources of its errors and its character as serving the bourgeoisie, the superstition of the fantastic religious world, etc., as fetishistic character. Those "Marxists" who try to adapt "Marxism" to new philosophies simply capitulate to the bourgeois and superstitious priest-ridden society and its interests. Philosophy is seen by Lenin not as a system of theoretical knowledge, but as a force determined by and shaping social political development. But this pragmatism is combined with an unshakable, naïve belief that absolute truth, identical with the knowledge of the world which is matter and determined by the movements of matter, is fully accessible to man. The *Ding an sich* will become more and more knowable, says Lenin, accepting fully Engels' statement about the progress of human knowledge. Most energetically Lenin opposes all kinds of skepticism, agnosticism, and idealism, which undermine the objectivity and knowability of the world, making them dependent upon the knowing subject.

III

The views of Marx and Engels on the bourgeois limitations which make the bourgeois unable to understand his own world and the movements of history leading to the future have determined Lenin's thought though in a somewhat simplified and streamlined way. It is characteristic that at least in his *Materialism and Empiriocriticism* Lenin seems to be more influenced by the writings of the older Engels than by the Hegelian elements of Marxism. In a similar way the Soviet practice and theory emphasizing the *partiinost'* (party or partisan character) of all knowledge simplifies and streamlines Lenin. In his book Lenin had limited the party character of knowledge to general statements about social movements and to philosophy. He recognized explicitly that men, committing the greatest errors in philosophy, could produce excellent work in disciplines in which they were specialized. Lenin stated:

We cannot trust what concerns philosophy to any of those professors who are able to produce most valuable works in the special fields of chemistry, history, physics. Why? For the same reason for which we cannot put our trust in one word of a professor of political economy, who is able to produce most valuable research in the field of factual specialized investigations, if he talks about the general theory of political economy. For the latter is a party-science (*partiinaia nauka*) in the present society.

The errors of science in the bourgeois society consist in their service to the bourgeois society. The bourgeois scholars — even when competent in their field — act as flunkies of the capitalists.

But the situation manifestly changes when, with the October Revolution, the Party — the group which has the right, true philosophy and knows about the aims of society and its development — comes to power. The wrong world outlook, in whose service science and knowledge stood, is no longer dominant. The true, useful results of science and research can be retained; they can even be perfected by the destruction of their connection with bourgeois-capitalist prejudices. They are no longer destined to be utilized as parts of an ideology, reflecting and often unconsciously justifying the bourgeois-capitalist world. The practice serving the building of the truly human socialist world helps and favors the flourishing and progress of theory and science. On the other hand, theory and science can now find their true application — for there is no longer a split between theory and practice. The Soviet political system, overcoming the imperfect world of the past and working to realize the perfect world of the future, determines also all theoretical thinking and scientific research. Therefore there can be no toleration of a science which is opposed or only "neutral" to the system existing in the Soviet Union. The political power is not limited to a particular realm; it is an instrument of a transformation of the whole society and the whole nature of man — his hitherto multilated nature is now being developed to its purity and fullness. The Soviet government is the expression and instrument of a party, *the* Party which has the true practice and also the true theory — knowing the laws and developments determining this practice. Therefore the Party and its instrument, the Soviet government — which claim to carry out the real will of the class, the proletariat, destined to bring about the end of history, the perfect classless society — have the right and the duty to correct, direct, and orientate all scientific work. Thought without or against the Party, the bearer of the truth, must be wrong — it corresponds to social conditions of the past, before the victory of socialism was inaugurated with the rise of the Soviet government today. Such non- or anti-Party thought today has a negative, reactionary character, serving a defeated order whose surviving representatives try to stop progress. Science has to serve the work of building the new society; its general character has been anticipated in the Marxian philosophy and doctrine, but its details have to be worked out in the various steps and measures of daily and historical practice.

Therefore science and knowledge must not only correspond to the general Marxian theory which alone is true — of course, in the interpretation given to it by Lenin and his successors — but they must move also according to the directives given by the Party, the institution based upon and authoritatively interpreting this true doctrine. All knowledge has to serve the Party and its government, shaping men and society.

IV

What does the required *partiinost'* mean under the Soviet system? This question can only be answered if one remembers the system of identifications upon which the Soviet regime is built. First truth and science are identified with the Marxian philosophy, as interpreted by Lenin-Stalin — all philosophical schools have to be classified and judged according to the basic Marxian-Leninist distinction between a materialism accepting the existence of a reality independent of the human mind and an idealism identified with the more or less radical denial of such a reality; the right philosophy corresponds to a right practice, which helps to accelerate and bring about the necessary and, at the same time, ethical transformation of society. This right theory expressing itself in right practice is realized by the Party, the Communist Party. Therefore the Party determines what is the right practice and the true theory; science and reason can be as little incompatible with the doctrine of the Party and its interpretation as the practice of the Party can be unjust or unwise. Therefore *partiinost'* is not a subjectivism, but agreement with the objective truth, and coöperation with the work of the Party for the coming perfect world. In his *Materialism and Empiriocriticism* Lenin had energetically opposed all agnosticism, skepticism and relativism. For Lenin it was self-evident that the human mind was able to reach the objective true realities, and that in human history a constant process of coming closer and closer to the truth was taking place. The Marxist doctrine, as interpreted by him, was in his eyes the decisive help to make new discoveries in the realm of truth, of transforming the unknown into something known and understood. Outside Marxism and its authoritative representative as well as interpreter, the Party, there could be no truth — there could only be erroneous attitudes, which took parts, particular aspects, for the whole and in practice represented not human universal knowledge, but only the ideologies of particular interests.

Therefore the regime of the Party, the Soviet regime, is not only a regime which ought to determine some realms of life — political institutions, social policies, relations with other powers — but it ought to determine the whole of human life and existence. There can be no free intellectual or cultural activities independent from the power of the regime. If non-Marxist demands are accepted, the acceptance is only a provisional matter, until the development of the society has matured enough to make all heritages of the past superfluous.

What are the practical consequences of these views going back to the Marxist creed as interpreted by Lenin? The ruling Party rules not only over limited realms, but over the total existence and development of man and his society. The *partiinost'* in science and knowledge is the expression of objective truth and the right practice, corresponding to the existing conditions and their requirements for advancement toward a deeper penetration of truth and realization of the individual human and the necessary end of history and development of mankind.

Only *partiinost'* sees and *reveals* the various wrong bourgeois ideologies. *Partiinost'* consists, of course, in being in agreement with the Party, its doctrine and its orders. If the Party — that is, its leadership — condemns as wrong an interpretation or application of the Marxist doctrine, this condemnation must be accepted. That is illustrated by the case of such schools and doctrines as those of the historian Pokrovskii and the philologist Marr. Their claims that their theories were based on Marxist views were rejected by the Party. It did not help them that for years they had successfully destroyed their opponents in the name of Marxism — for only the Party decides what is true Marxism. The Party particularly decides what aspects of the truth must be emphasized at a particular moment. Pokrovskii was condemned for his abstract schematism and neglect of facts — later those historians who neglected the theory and emphasized facts too much were severely criticized. The claim to have the true doctrine and to be the authority for its application results in bringing about the limitless power of the Party. What does not correspond to the policies of the Party can be condemned either as open hostility to the truth — in the case of "bourgeois," non-Marxists — or as treacherous deviations and falsifications — in the case of those who claim to be Marxists and Communists.

V

This scheme determines the policies of the Soviet government on the so-called theoretical and cultural fronts. The power of the openly non-Marxist scholars and their ideas must be broken; the institutions dominated by them are suppressed or transformed, their neutrality is not tolerated in the long run; everything and everybody must positively serve Soviet policies, not only silently tolerate them or cautiously avoid an active opposition. Then, after smashing the non- and anti-Marxist forces in science, all science and all cultural intellectual activities must be put into the service of the Soviet policies and their plans. After the Soviet government accepted the view that Lysenko's theories corresponded to a practice most useful for their aims in agriculture, these theories had to be accepted by all scientists and those who continued to reject them were condemned, silenced, and eliminated. The historians had to become patriotic and to emphasize the peculiar character and mission of the Russian developments after the Soviet government had turned toward emphasizing Soviet patriotism and the particular merits of the Russian people.

Partiinost' does not consist in a set of fixed rules, from which one ought not deviate, or a stock of principles. True, some basic slogans are always quoted such as dialectical materialism, anti-idealism, rejection of a religious outlook, mechanicism; others are added in particular epochs as emphasis upon love for the motherland and rejection of cosmopolitanism. But these slogan-principles are so general and ambiguous that they permit interpretation and application according to the changing situations and policies. A classic example of this flexibility was given by those decisions of Party authorities which condemned the originally accepted satirical treatment of Russia's Christianization and, on the contrary, proclaimed that this Christianization corresponded to a cultural progress.

The *partiinost'* which originally seemed to be based on the belief that there was an all-embracing true doctrine represented and developed by the Party moves in the direction of a decisionism. That means: What the Party, that is, the Party leadership, decides to be true, must be true and accepted as such, and what the Party, that is, the Party leadership, decides to be wrong and therefore condemns must be regarded as wrong and condemned. But the pretense of knowing the absolute truth, based on the right scientific knowledge, remains. It must remain because the Party does not pretend to be based on a revelation of some sort, but to correspond to reason and science, which it alone correctly expresses and directs. The reason and science of the Party are not static-fixed, but dynamic-evolutionary. The Party knows not only the final end of mankind, but the various stages through which mankind passes until it reaches the perfect form, the complete manifestation, and knows what practice is the right and required one at each moment. Therefore, the Party is always the greatest unerring educator in all situations. It takes into account existing backwardness and immaturity — realizing that an open, direct atheist propaganda would be wrong, for the social roots of religion have not yet disappeared and one cannot abolish the belief in God by decree. The Party is ready to go a step backward if its leaders realize that one has been overzealous and too optimistic — for instance, planning in art can be relaxed for a time because it has stifled creative initiative. This initiative can be emphasized — as a proof of what can be achieved in a society dominated by the Party. For the Party can do everything; in the name of the required *partiinost'* artists and scholars had to become servants of all-embracing controlling machines, engineers, carrying out the orders of the Party bosses, the managers. In the name of the Party the controls can be restricted for the artists and scholars are now educated enough to advance without visible direct guidance in the right direction. Upon order from the Party, the Party mouthpiece, Ehrenburg, proclaims new policies of freedom quite opposite to the previous policies of direction and control inaugurated by Zhdanov. But the changes are not changes of the Party; they prove only that it is always right, understands any situation and adapts successfully to it. True *partiinost'* consists in the enthusiastic acceptance and realization of the Party line. The doctrine shrinks to the claim that the changing decisions and policies of the Party always correspond to the general line of Marxism-Leninism. The doctrine has justified the subjection of all intellectual and cultural activities and life to the domination of the Party masters. They decide how this doctrine is interpreted and applied. What matters is not a specific conduct — though the slogan-principles remain the same, constituting likewise the basis of the Soviet tradition. What matters is the possibility of interpretation and application concerning the requirements of maintaining and expanding the power of the Party. Changes of emphasis in policies in both the practice and the theory can be easily justified and covered up with the help of the appeal to the unerring authority of the Party. First the seizure of power in Russia is mastered in the name of the world revolution — the regime of the October Revolution can only last if it is a signal, a preparatory step for revolutions in other more mature, technically more advanced countries. Then the fact that the Soviet regime lasts, although the expected revolutions in the West do not come, results in the development of a Soviet patriotism. The Soviet Union and its existence become more and more the end — its role as a means for a universal development becomes of secondary importance. In the same way, the proletarian dictatorship, the Soviet state, loses more and more its character as a transition, perhaps, even a short-lived one, to the classless society which no longer needs the state, the instrument of coercion. The Utopian-anarchic elements of the doctrine are not abandoned, their realization is only more and more postponed. The reality of the present is determined by the power needs of the Party using the Soviet state as its instrument. And these needs are also realized by cultural and intellectual life. In the name of *partiinost'* this life has to serve the Party politics; it has to help to realize the five-year plans, to unmask all those who are declared by the Party to be its enemies, to praise the Party leadership, to be for stricter controls or relaxation according to Party orders. What is incompatible with *partiinost'* is free, independent thought and research. For it is just its essence that everything has to be in accordance with the Party. In a thesis which he developed while fighting the "pseudo-Marxists" who denied his dialectical materialism, Lenin asked them: Do you dare to claim that your philosophy is a Bolshevik Party philosophy? It was for him self-evident that the Party must be able to determine the true philosophy, the theory which alone would also guarantee and make possible the right practice — that practice corresponding to the true human nature and in line with the necessary development of history and society. When Lenin wrote his thesis, he was a powerless writer; the *partiinost'* in Soviet cultural policies takes his claims seriously, realizes them by backing them up with the power at its disposal.

Darwinism and the Russian Orthodox Church

GEORGE L. KLINE

I

In the course of the nineteenth century the intellectual elite of Russian society experienced the successive impact of a series of philosophic and scientific doctrines from the West.[1] The most dramatic — and, indeed, traumatic — of these waves was doubtless that of Hegel (following upon a milder influence of Fichte and Schelling) which broke in the mid-1830's. Somewhat later, beginning in the 1850's, Hegel's absolute idealism was supplanted by the positivism of Comte, Spencer, and Mill. And soon thereafter the new theory of biological evolution set forth in Darwin's *Origin of Species* (1859) burst upon Russian intellectual circles. Like the above-mentioned philosophies, which were received not as academic or technical theories but as total world views — indeed, vessels of consolation or instruments of salvation — Darwinism was viewed by the positivistically and materialistically inclined radical intelligentsia as a support for their "realism" (that is, anti-idealism and antiromanticism) and their "nihilism" (antitraditionalism). Beginning in the 1860's, Darwinism was vigorously, and sometimes stridently, popularized by such critics as Chernyshevskii and Pisarev, and by such scientists as Sechenov, Timiriazev, Pavlov, and Mechnikov.

Some measure of Darwin's influence is indicated by the rapidity with which all of his major works were translated into Russian. *The Origin of Species* (1859) appeared in Russian in 1864 (2nd edition, 1865); *The Descent of Man* appeared in Russian translation by Sechenov in 1871, the same year as the English original (2nd edition, 1874); *Variation of Animals and Plants under Domestication* (1868), *The Expression of the Emotions in Animals* (1872), and the *Voyage of the Beagle* (1839) were translated in the early 1870's. By 1896 at least three volumes of Darwin's works, including his autobiography, had appeared in Russian; between 1907 and 1909

[1] Grateful acknowledgment is made to Professor Sewall Wright, Department of Zoölogy, the University of Chicago, for generous and expert guidance on technical points of biological theory. Professor Wright is not, of course, responsible for any theoretical inexactnesses or oversimplifications which may appear in the following discussion.

his complete works were reissued in eight volumes, under the editorship of the plant physiologist K. A. Timiriazev, whom we shall encounter below.[2]

The general attitude of Russian intellectuals toward Darwinism during the 1860's was eloquently summed up a half-century later by S. S. Glagol'ev. In Moscow and St. Petersburg, he wrote, one hardly dared mention Darwin's name without doffing one's cap: "To express doubts as to Darwin's scientific competence on any of the questions investigated by him was to defy truth itself. Darwin was proclaimed the most competent, objective, and genius-like of investigators."[3] And again: "There was a time when no one in Russia was permitted to open his mouth to object to the 'eternal truths' enunciated by Darwin."[4]

I have been speaking of Russian "intellectuals" as though they formed a single, more or less homogeneous, group, united in their acceptance of Darwinism. Actually this is not true without qualification, even in the case of the radical intelligentsia, the *raznochintsy;* and it scarcely applies at all to the Churched intellectuals and their sympathizers. Furthermore, as Weidlé has recently reminded us, during the 1860's and 1870's the gap between the radical secular intelligentsia and other Russian intellectuals was virtually unbridgeable.[5] No priest, no professor in a theological academy, however learned or "intelligent," was admitted into association with the secular intelligentsia (assuming he sought such admission), even to the extent of being permitted to publish in radical or liberal journals.

Significantly, on the controversial issue of Darwinism there was one area of agreement (although it is likely that neither side was clearly aware of this agreement) between secular and religious intellectuals. Furthermore, there was little if any such agreement among analogous contending factions in the West during this period. In Russia, what was regarded as Darwin's virtually exclusive emphasis upon struggle for existence as a factor in biological evolution drew sharp criticism, first from secular intellectuals, then, somewhat later, and independently, from representatives of the Church. The relevant views of Prince Peter Kropotkin, the anarcho-socialist, are well known. His *Mutual Aid, a Factor in Evolution* was first published in English in serial form during the 1890's, and appeared as a book in 1902.[6] Since Kropotkin's works are readily accessible, I shall not pause to discuss them, but I should like to mention a little-known anticipation of these views by

[2] A. F. Wallace, Darwin's competitor, and independent discoverer of the theory of natural selection, was also well represented. His *Natural Selection* (1870) appeared in Russian translation in 1878, his *Darwinism* (1889), in 1898.

[3] *Bogoslovskii vestnik,* III (1912), 651.

[4] *Ibid.* II (1911), 434.

[5] Cf. Wladimir Weidlé, *Russia Absent and Present* (New York, 1952), pp. 66–67.

[6] Kropotkin's critique, directed chiefly at T. H. Huxley's formulation of Darwinism, has been continued and expanded by such recent investigators and theorists as W. C. Allee, *Cooperation among Animals* (2nd ed., New York, 1951) and M. R. Ashley-Montague, *Darwin, Competition and Cooperation* (New York, 1952).

N. D. Nozhin in the 1860's, and a similar critique by N. G. Chernyshevskii in the 1880's.[7]

Nozhin (1841–1866) was a brilliant young biologist, whose death at the age of twenty-five was a great loss to Russian science. Mikhailovskii, who knew him well, called him a "genius" and spoke with highest praise of his personal qualities and scientific abilities.[8] Nozhin's critique of Darwin's doctrine of struggle for existence is, to my knowledge, the first to appear in Russia and perhaps in the West. "Darwin fails to see," he wrote in 1866, "that the struggle for existence is disadvantageous for development, that in itself it can produce only pathological phenomena." The experimental work of Lieberkuhn, Haeckel, and Trembley, he adds, indicates that "identical organisms do not engage with one another in a struggle for existence, but, on the contrary, strive to combine together, so to speak, to unify their homogeneous forces, their interests; and in this process we find . . . coöperation . . ."[9]

In 1888 Chernyshevskii published in *Russkaia mysl'*, the journal which carried Timiriazev's (pro-Darwinian) side of the Strakhov-Timiriazev polemic, an article entitled "The Origin of the Theory of the Beneficence of Struggle for Life." It was essentially an expansion of Nozhin's point, although Chernyshevskii does not refer to Nozhin, and there is no evidence that he was familiar with the latter's much earlier and very brief statement. The only substantial addition is an analysis of Darwin's personal and political motives and those of his intellectual sources, especially Malthus — whose *Essay on Population*, according to Chernyshevskii, was an "antireformist" Tory pamphlet. Chernyshevskii asserts that "the theory of the beneficence of struggle for life contradicts all the facts of every branch of science in which it is applied . . . [as well as] the meaning of all the rational lifeworks of man . . ."[10] If struggle for existence and natural selection actually prevailed in nature, he insists, there could be no evolutionary progress. Nothing higher than single-celled organisms would have developed, and even these, if they developed at all, would forthwith degenerate into amorphous bits of protoplasm. This appears to be a reformulation of Nozhin's assertion that "the struggle for existence . . . can produce only pathological phenomena."

According to Darwin, Chernyshevskii continues,

. . . the cause for the improvement and perfection of organizations, the source of the progress of organic life, is struggle for life, i.e., hunger and the ills produced by it; and the way in which perfected organizations are produced is through natural selection, i.e., suffering and death. . . . The result of the struggle for

[7] N. K. Mikhailovskii elaborated Nozhin's critique during the 1870's, but he added nothing new in principle.

[8] Cf. Mikhailovskii, *Sochineniia* (St. Petersburg, 1896–97), IV, 276.

[9] "Nasha nauka i uchënyie," *Knizhnii vestnik*, no. 7 (1866), pp. 173f.

[10] *Polnoe sobranie sochinenii* (St. Petersburg, 1905–1906), X (1906), Part II, 16.

life is a degrading of the organization; . . . natural selection is . . . a degrading force . . .[11]

This, he concludes bitterly, is a theory worthy of Torquemada.

Here, as elsewhere, Chernyshevskii overstates his criticism;[12] but I think that we must recognize a certain force in his argument (and those of Nozhin, Mikhailovskii, and Kropotkin) vis-à-vis the Darwinian theory of the 1860's and 1880's, or, indeed, at any time before de Vries' formulation of mutation theory (first put forward in 1900). That is, Darwin offered no explanation of the *source*, and only an obscure and inadequate account of the *nature*, of the variations upon which natural selection operates. This gap in Darwinian theory was later filled by mutation theory.

Thus far I have cited representatives of the secular intelligentsia. That their criticism of Darwin on this specific point was shared by at least some of the ecclesiastical intelligentsia, and by certain lay figures sympathetic to the Church, is indicated by the publication, in 1892, in the journal of the Kharkov Theological Seminary, of Glubokovskii's article "On the Question of Darwinism." [13] This was devoted largely to an exposition of a public lecture by Professor I. Skvortsov, defending the thesis that struggle for existence is a secondary factor in biological evolution. If it were the exclusive agency, life would not advance beyond the simplest forms. Coöperation, mutual support, symbiosis — both organic and ecological —are the primary factors.[14] Reformulating the point made by Nozhin, Chernyshevskii, and Kropotkin, in a theological metaphor, Glubokovskii charges Darwin with holding that "the world not only lies in evil, but stands, is built upon evil, and not upon good . . ." And he concludes, referring to Skvortsov: "For the first time in scientific literature a fully authoritative voice has been raised against the theory of the prevalence in the world of an evil principle — and this on the basis of the very facts to which Darwin appealed." [15] This claim for priority, though misplaced, is doubtless sincere. Probably Glubokovskii knew nothing of Nozhin; perhaps — with some justice — he considered the voices of Mikhailovskii and Chernyshevskii as less than "authoritative." And Kropotkin's views, at this time, had scarcely been expressed in print — and then only in French- and English-language publications, politically subversive in character, which Glubokovskii is not likely to have encountered.

---

[11] *Ibid.*, pp. 43–46. Kropotkin, in 1889, reformulated this position, with an important qualification: intraspecific struggle (i.e., that between members of the same species) is retrograde; only interspecific struggle (that between different species) — or the struggle of a species with the natural environment — can lead to evolutionary progress (*La morale anarchiste* [Paris, 1889], p. 35).

[12] Chernyshevskii signed his article "Staryi transformist," and it seems clear that his own position was essentially the "transformisme" of Lamarck. In one place he speaks of the latter's *Philosophie zoölogique* as "a work of genius" (ref. 10, p. 22).

[13] M. Glubokovskii, "K voprosu o darvinizme," *Vera i razum*, I (1892), 60–65.

[14] *Ibid.*, p. 62.

[15] *Ibid.*, pp. 60, 65.

One other preliminary remark. I would warn against the assumption that critiques of Darwinism, formulated by spokesmen for the Church, were scientifically justified, or even respectable, only when, as in the above case, they happened to agree with those of the radical intelligentsia or of the professional biologists who sided with the latter. The facts of the matter are more complex.

1. With respect to the doctrine of the inheritance of acquired characteristics, which was halfheartedly and somewhat inconclusively accepted by Darwin himself: Chernyshevskii, Pisarev, Lavrov, Mikhailovskii, Kareev, Kropotkin, and, among botanists, Timiriazev and Michurin, accepted this doctrine, whereas Glagol'ev, the chief ecclesiastical critic of Darwinism, was highly skeptical of it.

2. With respect to Mendel's discovery of the mechanism of heredity: Mendel's work was greeted with enthusiasm by Glagol'ev and with skeptical suspicion by Timiriazev — as late as 1911. Timiriazev was harshly critical of Bateson's high judgment of Mendel's "discovery," which, he asserted, applied only to a special case, and was wholly inapplicable (!) to the most interesting case of all — that of human heredity. Timiriazev denied that Mendel had discovered the "laws of heredity" and upbraided Bateson for asserting that the new science of "genetics" was anything more than a branch of physiology.[16] "Biologists," he added, "vainly proclaim Mendel's modest observations as works of genius simply because their author is a monk . . ."[17] In the light of these remarks it is not hard to see why Lysenko and his followers found Timiriazev such a congenial ally in their attacks upon Mendelianism.

3. Glagol'ev was one of the first Russians to recognize the significance of de Vries' theory of mutations. (He encountered one of de Vries' early papers [1900] during a trip to Paris in 1901.) I have not found clear evidence that Russian Darwinians rejected mutation theory, but Glagol'ev, who is usually very accurate, reports that as late as 1907 mutation theory had received very little notice in Russia. And he noted in 1913 that de Vries' works still had not been translated into Russian.[18] (In contrast, English translations of de Vries' two major works appeared in 1905 and 1909–10.)

4. Glagol'ev, between 1893 and 1917 — at a time when most Darwinists, both Russian and Western, were discussing man's antiquity in terms of several million years — formulated and defended a drastically shorter chronology. Perhaps this was just a lucky guess (and there were doubtless theological motives for the shortened chronology), but the fact remains that in 1893 Glagol'ev suggested that man, as man, probably appeared "toward the end of the glacial epoch." If we interpret this, as seems reasonable, to mean

---

[16] "Sezon nauchnykh s"ezdov," *Vestnik Evropy* (November 1911), p. 367.

[17] *Ibid.,* p. 368.

[18] "Mendelizm," *Bogoslovskii vestnik,* III (1913), 504*n.*

"during the last interglacial period" — about 50,000 years ago, by current estimates — we find that Glagol'ev anticipated by more than half a century the most recent estimates of man's antiquity, revised sharply downward on the basis of fluorine and radio-carbon dating.[19]

II

Naturally enough, Russian intellectual resistance to Darwinism centered at the four theological academies[20] which were active in the late nineteenth century at Moscow, Kiev, Kazan, and St. Petersburg. All of these academies published scholarly journals, although not all of the journals were equally devoted to theoretical discussion of scientific and philosophic — as opposed to strictly theological, historical, or homiletic — questions. In fact, it was the Moscow Academy and, to a lesser extent, the Kharkov Seminary which furnished the great bulk of the theoretical materials.

Moscow Theological Academy, although it was founded in 1814, shortly after the defeat of Napoleon, did not set up a learned journal until 1860. The original journal, called *Pravoslavnoe obozrenie* (Orthodox Review) ceased publication in 1891 and was succeeded the following year by *Bogoslovskii vestnik* (Theological Messenger), which continued publication until 1918, when it was suspended by the Soviet authorities. During the fifty-eight years of their publication, these two journals offered their readers a broad and varied fare, including philosophical and scientific discussions, translations of Western works in philosophy and science, and reviews of books both secular and religious, as well as more strictly theological and ecclesiastical materials. Unfortunately, there seems to have been almost no communication between those who wrote for, or read, these journals and those who wrote for, and read, organs of the secular intelligentsia, whether radical or liberal.

Theoretical materials also appeared, though not so copiously, and over a shorter period of time, in *Vera i razum* (Faith and Reason), organ of the Kharkov Theological Seminary. *Vera i razum* was not established until 1884, and after 1906 (when its previously separate "philosophical" and "ecclesiastical" sections were fused) it printed substantially less theoretical material. It ceased publication altogether in 1917.

---

[19] See K. P. Oakley, "Dating Human Fossil Remains," *Anthropology Today* (Chicago, 1953), pp. 143–157; S. L. Washburn, "The New Physical Anthropology," *Transactions of the N. Y. Academy of Sciences,* XIII (1951), 298–304. For a clear nontechnical account of these developments — and for an excellent introduction to evolutionary theory generally — the reader is referred to Ruth Moore's *Man, Time and Fossils* (New York, 1953). I would merely add the warning that Miss Moore's book, like all works dealing with anthropological paleontology published in recent decades, will have to be revised in those passages which deal with "Piltdown man," established in November 1953 as a deliberate hoax, and cf no paleontological significance whatever.

[20] The theological *academies,* which offered courses at the university level, should not be confused with the more numerous theological *seminaries,* which offered courses at the "middle school" level.

The publications of the other academies[21] contained almost no theoretical material, and thus were not involved in the controversies over Darwinism.

It will be convenient for our further exposition to divide the history of relations between Darwinism and the Russian Orthodox Church into three periods: (1) a preliminary phase: from the first publication of Darwin's *Origin of Species* (1859) to the establishment of *Vera i razum* (1884); (2) a "lay" phase, during which persons sympathetic to the Church, who were neither members of the ecclesiastical hierarchy nor officially connected with the academies offered the chief criticisms: this extends from the publication of Danilevsky's monumental critique of Darwinism (1885) to the appearance of Chicherin's chief critical works (1892); (3) a "Church" phase, during which Glagol'ev and a few others published careful technical critiques of various aspects of Darwinian evolutionary theory: this extends from 1893, when Glagol'ev published his first work on this subject, to 1917, which marked the effective termination of such criticism in Russia.

III

The "preliminary" phase may be dealt with in a few words. It is remarkable chiefly for its *lack* of anti-Darwinian statements on the part of representatives of the Church, since this period (extending to 1884) was marked in the West by many violent clashes, in print and on the public platform (between T. H. Huxley and Bishop Wilberforce, for example). To be sure, during this period only one Russian theological journal, *Pravoslavnoe obozrenie,* was printing theoretical articles. In any case, its editors apparently did not regard Darwinism as a threat to faith or morals, or else had not yet decided how to meet this threat, for only two articles were published during this entire twenty-four-year period which touched upon the question of Darwinism. These appeared in 1873[22] and 1877.

The first, by G. Malevanskii, bears the title: "On Man's Spiritual Nature: versus Materialism and Darwinism." [23] It is a wholly derivative work, based — as the author himself acknowledges — upon certain sections of C. E. Baumstark's *Christliche Apologetik auf anthropologischer Grundlage,* Vol. I, Frankfurt am Main, 1872.

The second, by the philosopher-theologian V. D. Kudriavtsev-Platonov (1828–1891) is entitled "The Teleological Idea and Materialism." [24] It was directed primarily against such materialists and positivists as Büchner and

---

[21] They include: *Pravoslavnyi sobesednik* (Kazan, 1855–1917); *Trudy* (Kiev, 1860–1917); *Tserkovnyi vestnik* (St. Petersburg, 1875–1915).

[22] It may, or may not, be significant that 1873 also saw the appearance in Russia of an abridged edition of Darwin's *Origin of Species.*

[23] *Pravoslavnoe obozrenie,* I (1873), 537–568, 723–769.

[24] *Ibid.,* I (1877), 11–52, 496–529; III (1877), 52–85.

Littré. Ironically, Kudriavtsev mentions Darwin's views as lending support to defenders of teleology in their dispute with the mechanistic materialists.[25]

The first detailed and systematic critique of Darwinism to be put forward by a representative of the Russian Orthodox Church trained in the biological sciences did not appear until 1893; its author was S. S. Glagol'ev. But, before turning to Glagol'ev's work, we must consider the second, or "lay," phase of the controversy, which involved such names as Danilevsky, Strakhov, Timiriazev, Rozanov, and Chicherin. All of these men — except, of course, Timiriazev who was defending Darwin — were ideologically close to, though not "official" spokesmen for, the Church.

IV

N. Ia. Danilevsky (1822–1885), who is best known for his passionate and controversial *Russia and Europe* (1869), also produced the longest and most detailed critique of Darwinism ever to appear in Russian. It runs to twelve hundred pages, and would have been even longer if Danilevsky had lived to complete it.[26] Though it contained, and aroused, almost as much passion and controversy as its more celebrated predecessor, this book is a serious, though largely derivative and "compilative," critique of Darwinism. One would have expected it to draw considerable comment, even if hostile, from the secular press. Instead, Danilevsky's book received the "treatment of silence." In the first two years after its publication no radical or liberal journal noticed it; the only "review" to appear in a secular journal was that of N. P. Semënov — a childhood friend of Danilevsky's, to whom *Darvinizm* was dedicated — in the conservative *Russkii vestnik*.[27] This was not in fact a review, but an appreciation of Danilevsky as man and thinker (with quotations from Bestuzhev-Riumin's extremely warm and laudatory "obituary" notice), together with an expression of Semënov's "sincere and heartfelt wish" that young Russian scientists should approach Danilevsky's study in-

---

[25] Earlier, in the first issue of the new journal, Kudriavtsev had published an article entitled "The Original Appearance of the Human Race on the Earth" (*Pravoslavnoe obozrenie*, I [1860], 173–203, 326–362), which one might expect to refer to Darwin. In fact, the only Darwin mentioned is Dr. Erasmus Darwin, Charles's grandfather! The article is directed against certain materialists, empiricists, and positivists; Lamarck is mentioned only in passing.

[26] *Darvinizm: kriticheskoe issledovanie*, I, Parts I & II (St. Petersburg, 1885). Only one chapter of Vol. II was completed; it was published by Strakhov in *Russkii vestnik* (May and June 1887) and appeared as a book in 1889, with an index and a long introduction by Strakhov. Vol. I discussed Darwin's *Origin of Species* and *Variation of Animals and Plants under Domestication;* Vol. II was to have treated *The Descent of Man.* Danilevsky, like Darwin, spent nearly twenty years in preparing his magnum opus for publication. For details of Danilevsky's life and work the interested reader is referred to Robert E. MacMaster's careful study, "Danilevskii: Scientist and Panslavist," a Harvard University dissertation (1952), which has been announced for book publication. The extent and nature of my (minor) disagreement with MacMaster will become apparent below.

[27] December 1886, pp. 783–788.

dependently and without prejudice. The important thing, he concluded, is not that any particular favorite theory should triumph, but that the truth about an "incomparably important question" should be brought to light.[28] According to Semënov, Danilevsky's study was superior to the existing foreign works. Wigand's *Darwinismus* (3 vols., 1874–1877), the only serious contender, was not so well organized, nor did it refute Darwinism "internally," as Danilevsky did.

From the beginning, Danilevsky's work was taken seriously by ecclesiastical circles. *Vera i razum* published a review by I. A. Chistovich, author of a history of St. Petersburg Theological Academy.[29] Chistovich was apparently untrained in biology; in any case, he offers only general criticisms (such as that Darwinism is based upon "chance," that it is a form of "crude materialism") and some remarks about the incompatibility of Darwin's "deistic" notion of God, as creator of simple organic forms capable of evolution to the level of man, with "many religious convictions." Chistovich notes the influence upon Danilevsky of K. E. von Baer, Cuvier, Agassiz, and Quatrefages. He concludes that Danilevsky's careful and competent critique — which refutes Darwin both empirically and philosophically — is most welcome; it has "removed the brilliant shell in which Darwinism was enclosed and shown its rotten and venomous core . . ."[30]

A somewhat more serious evaluation was offered in the following year by P. Ia. Svetlov (Moscow).[31] Svetlov concurs in the high opinion of Danilevsky's work expressed by Semënov and Chistovich; indeed, he calls it outstanding among studies of Darwinism, both in Russia and Europe.[32] Baer, Agassiz, and Quatrefages, he notes, wrote only "apropos" of Darwinism. And even Wigand, whose treatment is exhaustive, is too technical for the general reader, and is deficient in certain respects. Danilevsky's work also has the virtue of including Darwin's important *Variation of Animals and Plants under Domestication* as well as the more widely criticized *Origin of Species* and *Descent of Man*. Svetlov goes on to repeat the charge made by Chistovich (and, of course, developed at great length by Danilevsky himself) that Darwinism rests upon "chance" — since the variations upon which natural selection operates are completely random with respect to frequency, degree, and direction. It is a mistake, he insists, to call Darwinism a "theory of evolution"; it is wholly unlike the theory of the growth or evolution of an individual organism from embryo to adult. Instead of lawlike growth, Svetlov charges, Darwin offers us an "accumulation of small random variations, which result from external, not internal, causes . . ."[33] This charge, in fact,

[28] *Ibid.*, p. 788.
[29] *Vera i razum*, I (1886), 131–136.
[30] *Ibid.*, p. 136.
[31] "K voprosu o darvinizme," *Pravoslavnoe obozrenie*, I (1887), 498–530.
[32] *Ibid.*, p. 499.
[33] *Ibid.*, p. 516.

is formulated in a misleading way, since Darwin himself was not clear or consistent about the "cause" of variation, and never definitely decided whether it was "external" or "internal" to the organism, or in what sense. This question was not satisfactorily settled until de Vries developed mutation theory; and the question of what *causes* gene mutations has not yet been answered. For the geneticist, they are still "random" — "internal lightning" that cannot be predicted either as to time or mode of occurrence.

Svetlov also objected that, since there are many more lethal, deleterious, and neutral variations than beneficial ones, the species will run a very considerable risk of destruction, and there will be "a very low probability of its improvement by random gains. Thus the increase of these chances with the increase of time is fictive." [34] The flaw in this argument, of course, is that even a vanishingly small probability is not equal to *zero* probability, that is, impossibility. Even if, on the average, only *one* in every million variations (mutations) is beneficial — as modern evolutionary theory admits — sufficient material will be provided for natural selection to work on.

But Svetlov's (and Danilevsky's) criticism of the extremely small, indeed imperceptible, variations posited by Darwin is essentially sound. Only definite perceptible leaps (mutations), reinforced by widespread genetic recombination, could have resulted in the procession of multifarious species — from single-celled organisms to the higher vertebrates and mammals, including man — which has in fact occurred within the time-span geologically available (on the order of magnitude of two billion years).

These three were the only reviews, strictly speaking, which Danilevsky's book received. Doubtless this deliberate silence resulted in part from the prejudgment of the book which radical and liberal intellectuals had formed on the basis of Danilevsky's earlier work. And many readers were doubtless repelled by Danilevsky's religious, ethical, and aesthetic indictment of Darwinism — which is expressed with great passion and force at the very end of the book.[35] In 1887 Danilevsky's friend and collaborator, N. N. Strakhov (1828–1896), apparently decided that further silence was intolerable, that anything, even the most hostile and destructive criticism, would be preferable to blank neglect. In any case, he published in *Russkii vestnik* a long and deliberately provocative article, almost grotesquely overstating the merits of Danilevsky's book. Its title was "A Thorough Refutation of Darwinism." [36] K. A. Timiriazev (1843–1920), Professor of Botany at Moscow University and author of a popular work on Darwin,[37] could hold back no longer. Sup-

---

[34] *Ibid.*, p. 523.

[35] It is also possible that Danilevsky's death, coming, as it did, just after the publication of Vol. I, Part I and before that of Vol. I, Part II, may have led some reviewers to refrain from printing their sharply critical notices. Timiriazev reports that this was true in his own case.

[36] "Polnoe oproverzhenie darvinizma," *Russkii vestnik* (1887). Reprinted in Strakhov's *Bor'ba s zapadom*, Vol. II.

[37] *Charl's Darvin i ego uchenie* (Moscow, 1883, 3rd ed., 1894).

pressing his "dislike for polemic" — especially of the *ad hominem* and un-scientific kind practiced by Strakhov — he rolled up his sleeves and delivered a stinging public lecture under the title, "Has Darwinism Been Refuted?" The lecture was published in expanded form in *Russkaia mysl'*.[38]

Timiriazev began by comparing Danilevsky most unfavorably with such "scientific" Western critics as Romanes, Weissmann, and Nägeli. The latter, he asserted, attack specific parts of the theory; Danilevsky rejoices in its total destruction. For Timiriazev, Danilevsky is a mere "compiler," a dilet-tante; his arguments are "sophistries." Later he went so far as to declare that the whole logical structure of Danilevsky's book rested upon "two or three miserable sophisms." [39] All of Danilevsky's arguments, according to Timi-riazev, are old, borrowed, shopworn, and — of course — long since fully answered! The silence which greeted this "thousand-page pamphlet," he concludes sourly, was well deserved.

The polemic, now launched in earnest, continued for two years, searing the pages of *Russkii vestnik* and *Russkaia mysl'*, and generating much heat but little, if any, light. Timiriazev accused Strakhov of misquoting and dis-torting; of being irrelevant and anti-Western (the last charge, of course, was essentially just). Strakhov returned most of the charges, *mutatis mutandis*. It must be admitted that, if Strakhov was often digressive and always prolix, Timiriazev was often evasive and sometimes disingenuous. He tended to answer a respectable objection by saying (a) that it had been made nine years earlier by a Western critic and (b) that Darwin, or one of Darwin's followers, had answered it. In many cases he gave no indication of what the answer might be.

On only one point did Danilevsky, Strakhov, and Timiriazev concur: all agreed that Darwin's theory of heredity ("pangenesis") was, as Timiriazev put it, "unscientific at its base and sterile in its results." [40] But Timiriazev quickly added that this was virtually the only mistake Darwin had ever made!

This polemic cannot be considered further here,[41] but I should like briefly to record my bewilderment at MacMaster's judgment of it. "Much of this argument," he writes, "bears a striking resemblance to the present-day 'argument' between the Western geneticists and the Soviet followers of Lysenko. Timiriazev is now, incidentally, one of the historical heroes of the Lysenkoists — and Danilevsky is one of their bêtes noires." [42] But are not

[38] "Oprovergnut li darvinizm?" *Russkaia mysl'* (May 1887), pp. 145–180; (June 1887), pp. 1–14.

[39] *Russkaia mysl'* (May 1889), p. 18.

[40] *Ibid.*, p. 38.

[41] In addition to the articles cited, we note the following. Strakhov, "Vsegdashniaia oshibka darvinista," *Russkii vestnik* (1887); "Suzhdenie A. S. Famintsyna o 'Dar-vinizme' N. Ia. Danilevskogo," *Russkii vestnik* (1889); "Spor iz-za knig N. Ia. Danilev-skogo," *Russkii vestnik* (1889). Timiriazev, "Bessil'naia zloba antidarvinizma," *Russkaia mysl'* (May 1889), pp. 17–52; (June 1889), pp. 65–82; (July 1889), pp. 58–78.

[42] Ref. 26, pp. 249–250.

the *differences* even more striking? The chief point at issue in the Lysenko controversy was the inheritance of acquired characteristics. Lysenko asserted, and his opponents denied, such inheritance; whereas in the Strakhov-Timiriazev polemic *both* parties to the argument *accepted* this doctrine. A second main point at issue in the Lysenko controversy concerned the role of chance in biological phenomena generally and in evolutionary development in particular. Lysenko declared that "chance is alien to science," and repudiated the notion of *random* variations (mutations) as basic to the evolutionary process. In the Strakhov-Timiriazev polemic, the positions were exactly reversed. Timiriazev defended the role of chance; Strakhov (and Danilevsky) denied, or attempted to minimize it. The only "striking resemblance" that I can see is in the *ad hominem*, abusive, and ill-mannered character of the two polemics. But surely these qualities could be found equally well in a thousand polemical exchanges, new and old, Russian and Western!

It was not until 1889 that Danilevsky's book received a fair and dispassionate appraisal. The review in question was published in the moderate-liberal journal *Vestnik Evropy*, and was written by A. S. Famintsyn (1835–1918), a reputable botanist, who had previously written in defense of Darwinism.[43]

Famintsyn's review article, a model of restraint and cool-headed objectivity, contrasts sharply with the intemperate outbursts of Strakhov, Timiriazev, and Danilevsky himself. Famintsyn deplores the harshness and occasional haughtiness of Danilevsky's critique, and challenges Danilevsky's assumption that the whole scientific world had blindly accepted Darwinism, noting that he himself, though essentially a Darwinian, departs from Darwin on many important points. Famintsyn is also disturbed by Danilevsky's crusading tone, his view that Darwinism is not only theoretically false but also dangerous, immoral, unaesthetic, antireligious. Famintsyn asserts — citing Darwin as well as Wigand and K. E. von Baer for support — that Darwinian theory is compatible with religious conviction. (Strakhov later took violent issue with this "compromising" attitude.) Baer's attitude is worth noting since Danilevsky who, as Baer's pupil and admirer, took much from him (including a large part of his general criticism of Darwinism), differed sharply on this point. Baer had written: "Even if it should turn out that higher animal forms come from lower forms, this should not affect our religious convictions; we should simply try to harmonize these convictions with the newly discovered facts."[44]

---

[43] It was Famintsyn's review ("N. Ia. Danilevskii i darvinizm," *Vestnik Evropy*, XXIV, no. 2 [February 1889], 616–643), written by a "respectable" scientist who thought Danilevsky (and Strakhov) worthy of mention in the same breath with Timiriazev, that drove the latter to break his long silence and answer Strakhov's second article. Cf. Timiriazev, *Russkaia mysl'* (May 1889), p. 20.

[44] *Studien aus dem Gebiete der Naturwissenschaften* (St. Petersburg, 1876), II, 273. Glagol'ev reports that Rachinskii, the Russian translator of Darwin's *Origin of Species*,

But what of the *scientific* value of Danilevsky's strictures on Darwinism? Famintsyn asserts (and this judgment strikes me as essentially sound) that almost none of his objections, including those which are most important, is original with Danilevsky, but that Danilevsky has only elaborated them in greater detail, adding certain new examples. Furthermore, Famintsyn notes, Danilevsky often fails to make clear to the reader which criticisms are his own and which are borrowed. For example, his arguments for the fixity of species are taken from Cuvier and Agassiz; those related to the plasticity of domesticated plants and animals are expansions of arguments clearly formulated a decade earlier by Wigand and Quatrefages. Danilevsky's own contribution (data on the distribution and cultivation of various kinds of plants, for example), while scientifically interesting, is of limited relevance to his critique of Darwinism.[45]

Famintsyn considers Chapter 6 (Part I) the most important part of Danilevsky's book, and adds that it is "worthy of serious attention."[46] I would concur. In fact, Danilevsky's mention of the results of crossing and sudden sharp variations — as opposed to the accumulation of small, barely perceptible variations, which Darwin posited — as giving rise to new varieties of plants may be viewed as a significant, though undeveloped, anticipation of de Vries' mutation theory (which was not formulated until nearly two decades later).[47] It is only fair to add, however, that Danilevsky found this idea in Baer.

In Chapter 7 Danilevsky notes that struggle for existence is a conservative rather than progressive factor in evolution (Nozhin!). The arguments in Chapters 8 through 11 (a critique of the principle of natural selection), Famintsyn correctly points out, are drawn chiefly from Wigand and Nägeli.

Famintsyn concludes: "I consider Danilevsky's book useful for zoölogists and botanists; all of the objections which have been raised against Darwin are collected in it, and it is strewn with interesting factual material, for which science will remain grateful to Danilevsky."[48] Scientists, he adds, will not be led astray by Danilevsky's lyrical effusions or his outbursts of righteous indignation. But Famintsyn adds a final qualification: Danilevsky, though he is both "honest and talented," sometimes misinterprets Darwin's views, and he consistently ascribes to them an almost diabolically destructive

---

planned to publish a work "harmonizing" Darwinism and Christian faith in the Synod's official *Tserkovnye vedomosti,* but that Pobedonostsev refused to print it (*Bogoslovskii vestnik,* I [1909], 477).

[45] Apparently this view was shared by the Russian Academy of Sciences, which considered Danilevsky's book for a prize, but refused to award the prize on the ground that the book was essentially a compilation of Western criticisms, merely developed, systematized, and supported by new examples. See N. O. Lossky, *History of Russian Philosophy* (New York, 1951), p. 72.

[46] Ref. 43, p. 641.

[47] Danilevsky, ref. 26, Part I, p. 423; cf. also Part II, p. 509.

[48] Ref. 43, p. 643.

and corrupting power. The spread of such an extreme attitude toward Darwinism, Famintsyn adds, "seems to me extremely . . . undesirable, and harmful, especially in Russian society, which is as yet relatively insensitive and unperceptive in scientific matters." [49]

I shall briefly consider two other "lay" critics of Darwinism before turning to the "ecclesiastical" critics.

In 1889, V. V. Rozanov (1856–1919), reviewing Danilevsky's posthumous (and unfinished) second volume, touched briefly and deftly upon the sore point of classical Darwinian theory. Darwinism, he notes, though it makes a pretense of being "a theory of the *origin* of organic forms . . . in fact speaks only of their *preservation;* or more precisely, of the nonpreservation of those forms which, by their disappearance, leave the forms which we observe." [50] Darwin, Rozanov continues, regards the variations as already given; but it is precisely the *cause* of these variations which a theory of the *origin* of species should attempt to explain. Natural — or, for that matter, artificial — selection, he asserts, "does not create any new characteristic in an organism . . ." [51] After a few critical remarks on the allegedly disproportionate role of chance in Darwinian theory and a long digression on causal versus teleological explanation, Rozanov states the Lamarckian conviction (already formulated by Baer and Danilevsky) that "internal purposiveness moves and directs the organic world, in each of its parts and as a whole." Like Baer, he appeals to embryological morphogenesis as a prime example of such purposive or teleological development. [52]

In a later article Rozanov made an attempt to explain Darwin's theory in terms of his biography, temperament, etc. [53] This article makes fascinating reading, if only for its imaginativeness and ingenuity, but I shall pass it by as not strictly relevant to our theme.

Less imaginative, and more abusive, was the critique published by B. N. Chicherin (1828–1903) in 1892. (Chicherin says it was originally written in 1883.) [54] In view of the widespread acceptance of the inheritance of acquired characteristics by Russian critics of Darwin — Glagol'ev being an isolated exception — it is worth noting that Chicherin calls this hypothesis "groundless." [55] He notes that Darwin himself admits ignorance of the cause of variations, and adds that Darwin's assumption that variations are continuous and gradual doesn't help: if the cause of variations exists, it can

---

[49] *Ibid.*

[50] "Vopros o proiskhozhdenii organizmov" (1889) reprinted in *Priroda i istoriia* (St. Petersburg, 1900), p. 3.

[51] *Ibid.*

[52] *Ibid.*, p. 24.

[53] "Teoriia Charl'sa Darvina, ob"iasniaemaia iz lichnosti eë avtora," in *Priroda i istoriia*, pp. 25–37.

[54] "Opyt klassifikatsii zhivotnykh" printed as an appendix to *Polozhitel'naia filosofiia i edinstvo nauki* (Moscow, 1892).

[55] *Ibid.*, p. 179.

operate either gradually or by leaps, if it doesn't exist, then no posited gradualness or continuity will help.[56] And he adds, coming close to de Vries' later famous phrase ("Natural selection creates nothing; it only sifts"): "Natural selection itself produces nothing, but merely stabilizes what is produced by other forces." [57] For Chicherin (as for Rozanov and Danilevsky), variations are not to be conceived as random with respect to the needs of the organism. Chicherin, in fact, anticipates Bergson, insisting upon the existence and efficacy of an inner, purposive "life force" as the cause of all variations, whether large or small, gradual or sudden. This antimechanistic and teleological position, of course, is rejected by contemporary geneticists — with the lone exception of the Lysenkoists.

v

S. S. Glagol'ev, Professor of Christian Apologetics at Moscow Theological Academy, was both the most prolific and the most technically competent of the "ecclesiastical" critics of Darwinism. Born into the family of a priest in Tula *Guberniia* in 1865, he was graduated from Moscow Theological Academy and then studied science at Moscow University. After two years of teaching at the Vologda Theological Seminary, he accepted a Chair at the Moscow Theological Academy. His publications extend from 1889 to 1917 (after which date I have been unable to find any trace of him), and include, in addition to works on Darwinism and related biological subjects, articles on geology, astronomy, logic, methodology of science, philosophy, and theology. He even wrote a study of religion in Japan and Korea. And he was one of the many churchmen of the time to break a critical lance against Leo Tolstoy's ethical and religious doctrines.

Glagol'ev's Master's thesis was a careful and detailed study of a subject close to Darwinism: "The Origin and Original Condition of the Human Race." [58] One of his first publications on Darwinism was a highly critical review of a third-rate imitation of Danilevsky by a certain I. A. Chemen.[59] Glagol'ev called it an uninformed and silly book, and charged the author with misunderstanding Darwinism and being an all-around ignoramus in zoölogy, geology, astronomy, and theology. Chemen's intention was doubtless good, but he corrupted his good end by using improper means. Glagol'ev agrees with Chemen that Darwin's theory of man's animal origin is "ground-

---

[56] *Ibid.*, appendix, p. 10.

[57] *Ibid.*, p. 22.

[58] *O proiskhozhdenii i pervobytnom sostoianii roda chelovecheskogo* (Moscow, 1894). This "thesis" was more than 500 pages long! A detailed account of Glagol'ev's defense of the thesis was published in *Bogoslovskii vestnik*, III (1894), 290–302. Parts of this work were originally published in *Chteniia v obshchestve liubitelei dukhovnogo prosveshcheniia*, nos. 1, 2, 4, 6, 10–12 (1893) and no. 3 (1894).

[59] *Darvinizm. Nauchnoe issledovanie teorii Darvina o proiskhozhdenii cheloveka* (Odessa, 1892) — also over 500 pages! Glagol'ev's review appeared in *Bogoslovskii vestnik*, III (1893), 478–490.

less"; but he adds that Chemen's "refutations" of Darwinism are no better grounded.[60]

In 1896 Glagol'ev added some further anti-Darwinian criticisms to those rendered familiar by Danilevsky, et al. To begin with, he denied the Darwinian assertion that animals which are physically more like man are also psychically more like man. The beaver, he suggests, is a conspicuous counterexample.

Second, it has been clearly established, according to Glagol'ev, that certain animals regularly go to fixed spots to die. For example, Argentine guanacos — relatives of the llama — when they sense the imminent approach of death, migrate to the southern tip of Patagonia, seeking out a particular river valley. Glagol'ev suggests that this (presumably instinctive) behavior cannot be explained by natural selection: such acts could have no *survival* value, since, in any case, they immediately precede the death of the individual in question.[61]

In 1911, Glagol'ev made a point very close to that formulated earlier by Nozhin and Chernyshevskii: that the Darwinian ideal of the "perfectly adapted organism" lies not ahead but behind, in the trematode (parasitic flatworm) or the foraminifers (tiny marine creatures whose shells make up white chalk). On Darwin's hypothesis of "survival of the fittest" (the formulation, of course, is Spencer's), where "fittest" means "best adapted to a given environment," there is no reason why such primordial, simple, well-adapted organisms should have begun to evolve, to become complex, unstable, "less well adapted." I think we must admit that Glagol'ev's critique, as applied to Darwin's original theory, unmodified by mutation theory or Mendelian genetics, is essentially sound.[62]

In 1896, and again in 1909, Glagol'ev thoroughly discussed Dubois' discovery of fossil fragments of "Java man" (*pithecanthropus erectus*), reaching a negative conclusion concerning the relevance of this bit of paleontological "evidence" to Darwinian theory. Such a conclusion was substantially justified at that time; but, of course, subsequent fossil discoveries, especially the recent ones in South Africa, have drastically changed the picture.[63] Glagol'ev insisted that such paleontological evidence is persuasive only if one accepts two controversial assumptions: that structural similarity reflects phylogenetic relatedness, and that "ontogeny recapitulates

[60] *Ibid.*, p. 482.

[61] Review of the Russian edition of Hudson, *A Naturalist in La Plata* (St. Petersburg, 1896) in *Bogoslovskii vestnik* (September 1896), pp. 387–401. Glagol'ev, in another work, reformulates Danilevsky's and Rozanov's questions: What causes variations? How are they fixed in the offspring? How are they transmitted? And he adds that classical Darwinism has not answered any of these questions satisfactorily. (*Bogoslovskii vestnik*, II [1911], 436.)

[62] "Vzgliad Vasmanna na proiskhozhdenii cheloveka," *Bogoslovskii vestnik*, III (1911), 250–251.

[63] See Moore, ref. 19, chs. xiii–xv.

phylogeny." In fact, he says, only a few, not all, lower animal forms are represented in embryological development, and the similarity is only a very general one.[64]

In 1907, in an article called "Botany and Darwinism," Glagol'ev reported, and deplored, the fact that de Vries' mutation theory had been so little noticed in Russia,[65] since "de Vries had indicated a new point of view with respect to the organic world . . . which has philosophic as well as biological significance." [66] He does not, of course, fail to mention that de Vries himself considered his results a refutation of classical Darwinism.

In 1911, Glagol'ev offered the readers of *Bogoslovskii vestnik* a careful and conscientious exposition of Weissmann's *Die moderne Biologie und die Entwickelungstheorie* (3rd ed., 1906), but found himself unable to accept the German Jesuit's "modernist" compromise with Darwinism: namely, that man's body may be of animal origin, but the human soul was supernaturally introduced into this body at some definite point in the evolutionary process. Glagol'ev feels that this "obscure" doctrine raises grave theological difficulties, and he considers it less satisfactory than either pure Darwinism or pure Scripture.[67]

Glagol'ev notes in this article that the "conflict between science and religion" is nothing new; there has always been such a conflict. But when science and religion conflict only three solutions are possible; one may: reject the scientific theory, reject the religious doctrine, or show that the two are actually compatible. The fourth alternative urged by some writers — conjoint "independent" assertion of contradictory doctrines — is not to be allowed.[68]

One of Glagol'ev's most important contributions to the theoretical discussion of Darwinism in Russia was his long, careful, and sympathetic paper on Mendelianism, which included a competent exposition of Mendel's work, drawing heavily upon such Western accounts of Mendelianism as those of Morgan (*Experimental Zoölogy*), Doncaster, Punnett, and Strassburger.[69] All of these, incidentally, appeared in Russian translation between 1909 and 1913.

Glagol'ev, in this paper, summed up the conclusive objections against Darwin's naïve and fanciful theory of heredity ("pangenesis" based upon "cell gemmules"), especially those raised by Nägeli. Darwin himself called his theory a "provisional hypothesis" (1868); and, as we have seen, even such a loyal Darwinian as Timiriazev was forced to admit that it was

[64] "Vzgliad Vasmanna . . . ," pp. 233–235.
[65] In the body of this article Glagol'ev gives a complete translation of de Vries' latest paper (1906).
[66] "Botanika i darvinizm," *Vera i razum*, no. 1 (1907), p. 49.
[67] "Vzgliad Vasmanna . . . ," *Bogoslovskii vestnik*, II (1911), 253.
[68] *Ibid.*, p. 246.
[69] *Bogoslovskii vestnik*, III (1913), 250–285, 476–505, 725–737.

unscientific and sterile. Needless to say, "pangenesis" has long since been abandoned by professional biologists. Glagol'ev also offers apt criticism of the alternatives to Darwin's theory of heredity put forward by Brooks, Haeckel, Weissmann, Nägeli, Kölliker, and Romanes. After careful analysis, he rejects all of them in favor of Mendelianism:

> Mendel's experiments . . . furnish the best critique of the theories expounded above. The statistical laws established by Mendel are wholly incompatible with the metaphysical speculations of these . . . doctrines . . . The monk Mendel with his experiments and formulae satisfied the rigorous definition of the father of positive philosophy, Comte: *savoir, c'est prévoir* — to know is to predict.[70]

Glagol'ev concluded that Mendelianism not only discloses extreme complexity in a mechanism which Darwin assumed to be simple, but also contradicts two of Darwin's fundamental assumptions: first, that variability is continuous, that there are no leaps in nature. (*"Natura non facit saltum,"* the axiom basic to Darwin's view, is today, according to Glagol'ev, as much a "Baconian idol" as nature's alleged *"horror vacui"* was a few centuries ago.) Secondly, all variations (including acquired characteristics) may be inherited. For Mendel, he correctly notes, "nature, in the course of many generations, may elaborate a [genotypic] factor, which is not expressed externally [phenotypically], but which subsequently and abruptly, in a certain combination of gametes, becomes dominant and produces a new species." [71] Glagol'ev rightly emphasizes that de Vries' mutation theory forms an indispensable complement to Mendelian genetics, and that together they constitute a radical revision, indeed a repudiation, of classical Darwinism. This last is an overstatement, even for 1913; and the reason for the overstatement is doubtless a theological one. In one place, for example, Glagol'ev wrote that "the Darwinian world view" had passed into history, partly under the pressure of the Mendelian critique. We may hope, he added, that the further development of Mendelianism will bring about a greater harmony between positive knowledge and Christian faith — showing for example that, as a result of the abruptness of variation, the formation of different races might have occurred within the limits set by scriptural chronology, broadly interpreted.[72] Later, Glagol'ev asserted that biblical chronology should not be interpreted too rigidly: "Chronology," he wrote in 1916, "has nothing to do with religion." And he rebuked those "who for the sake of [chronology] are ready to charge one with heresy . . . In the question of chronology full freedom of opinion should be permitted." [73]

Glagol'ev's article on Mendelianism is basically sound, and represents

---

[70] *Ibid.*, pp. 284–285.
[71] *Ibid.*, p. 502.
[72] *Ibid.*, pp. 504–505, 737.
[73] "Proshloe cheloveka," *Vera i razum*, no. 8–9 (1916), pp. 922–923.

a contribution to the popularization of Mendelianism that ranks with the best of its time in Russia. In fact, considering the things that Timiriazev and Michurin were saying about Mendelianism during this same period, it is to be regretted that Glagol'ev's article did not reach a wider public.

The anti-Darwinian writings of Rumiantsev,[74] Kirilovich,[75] and Voinov[76] add little to what we find in Glagol'ev. The first is a derivative work based on Danilevsky, Quatrefages, and Glagol'ev's own early work (1893–1894). The second relies heavily on E. von Hartmann, and to a lesser extent on Teichmüller and Spencer. The third is a compilation of arguments put forth by Baer, Wigand, and other German writers. The same applies, so far as one can judge from the reviews — mainly Glagol'ev's — to three anti-Darwinian monographs published in 1907, 1912, and 1916 by A. A. Tikhomirov, Professor of Zoölogy at the University of Moscow.

The zoölogist P. N. Kapterev, in an article on Neo-Lamarckianism, raised, but did not develop, the point that Darwin and his followers had neglected phenomena of regeneration, some of which offer difficulties for Darwinian theory; he also expanded, with apt examples, Spencer's objection that individuals, not abstract characteristics, or sets of such characteristics, are the units of "selection" and survival. Then, turning to "natural selection," he put de Vries' objection in graphic terms: "Natural selection has turned out to be not a creative factor in evolution, but only a blind executioner of the laggard and the sick in the army of organisms; everything that is created, is created independently of it; its work is not life, but death."[77] And Kapterev himself agreed with the Neo-Lamarckians to the extent of ascribing this creative power to the organism as a whole.

VI

Thus far I have been dealing with criticism of Darwinism as a biological theory. I should now like to turn briefly to certain criticisms of "social Darwinism" and "Darwinian morality" on the part of representatives of the Russian Orthodox Church.

Religious and secular-minded Russians found themselves on the same side, to a large extent, in criticizing Western "social Darwinists" — especially Spencer. The most important of the secular critiques were those of Lavrov, Mikhailovskii, and — to a lesser degree — Chernyshevskii. The

---

[74] "Darvinizm (Kriticheskoe issledovanie)," *Vera i razum*, II (1895), 1–31, 135–170, 291–302, 488–504; II (1896), 25–45, 90–110, 139–160, 240–268.

[75] "'Darvinizm' pred sudom filosofa Gartmana," *Vera i razum*, 1902, pp. 176–202, 223–244.

[76] "Nauchnye gipotezy darvinizma," *Vera i razum*, III (1911), 229–256.

[77] "Teleologiia neolamarkistov," *Bogoslovskii vestnik*, I (1914), 101. One Russian philosopher-theologian aptly noted that "natural *selection*" was a misnomer; Darwin should have called it "natural *rejection*" (M. M. Tareev, *Vera i razum* [1909], p. 83).

chief theological critiques were those of Govorov,[78] Levitskii,[79] Seleznev,[80] and Tikhomirov.[81]

On the other hand, the attempt to construct a "Darwinian ethics," which was generally welcomed by secular thinkers as an alternative to supernaturalism which could "account for" the phenomena of moral obligation and conscience, was roundly repudiated by religious writers.

Bagehot in England, developing hints set forth in Darwin's *Descent of Man,* asserted that it is not merely the animal strength and cunning of the individual that leads to survival in the struggle for existence; the unit of struggle, and hence of survival, is the social group. Thus, coöperative behavior patterns and social instincts have high survival value. (*Physics and Politics,* 1872.) A similar position was tentatively taken up by Bakunin, Nozhin, and Lavrov in the 1860's and 1870's, and elaborated by Kautsky and Kropotkin beginning in the 1880's.

The relevant criticisms of this Darwinian grounding of ethics were made by Glagol'ev in 1893, and expanded by Popov and Gorodenskii in 1897 and 1903.[82] Glagol'ev makes a preliminary distinction between "useful" and "useless" individuals. He then puts his objections formally: consider two societies, A and B, each containing N useful members and M useless (sick, crippled) members. Assume, for the sake of simplicity, that the strength (P) of all useful members is the same. Now assume that in society A each member has an instinctive feeling of love (in Kautskian-Kropotkinian terms: "solidarity, sympathy, mutual aid") toward all the other members of the society. Assume that in society B this instinctive feeling has been modified in such a way that it extends only to those members who are (at least potentially) useful to the society, and does not include the crippled and weak. It is clear, Glagol'ev concludes, that society B's available energy, $P \times N$, can be wholly applied to furthering the prosperity and cohesion of the society. But part of the available energy of society A will be expended in maintaining the useless members: hence the net available energy will be $(P \times N) - X$. Thus society B will be better adapted for intergroup struggle, that is, will have a higher probability of surviving in the struggle for existence.

Consequently, according to Glagol'ev, "Darwinian moralists" who main-

---

[78] "Evoliutsionnaia teoriia v primenenii k nauke o nravstvennosti," *Vera i razum,* I (1889), 131–153, 186–216.

[79] "Darvinizm i nravstvennii vopros," *Bogoslovskii vestnik,* III (1898), 241–280.

[80] "Osnovy morali evoliutsionizma," *Vera i razum* (1894), pp. 463–504, 97–118, 135–155, 247–266.

[81] "Nauchnoe i filosofskoe znachenie evoliutsionnoi teorii," *Vera i razum* (1899), pp. 245–258. In 1905 Russian translations of critiques of social Darwinism by Fouillée and Frommel were published in *Vera i razum* and *Bogoslovskii vestnik,* respectively.

[82] See I. V. Popov, *Estestvennyi nravstvennyi zakon,* Sergiev Posad (1897); Nikolai Gorodenskii, *Nravstvennoe soznanie chelovechestva,* Tr.-Serg. Lavra (1903).

tain that sympathy, mutual aid, even Christian love and charity, follow from Darwinian principles, are grossly mistaken:

From the Darwinian point of view, the animal species or genus whose individual members combine maximum intellectual development with an instinct impelling them to love, and further the interests of, those of their associates who are or may be useful to the species, is the one which is best adapted in the struggle for existence. Individuals who love equally those who are useful and those who are not, evidently would be at a disadvantage in furthering the well-being of their species . . . A sense of compassion toward useless or even harmful individuals is an impractical feeling, and [according to Darwinian morality] mankind should re-educate itself so that this feeling would disappear.[83]

Needless to say, Glagol'ev considers this last an immoral and unchristian suggestion. And, of course, a Darwinian moralist like Kropotkin would agree. But neither Kropotkin nor Kautsky nor any of their followers ever faced the powerful theoretical objection here raised by Glagol'ev.

VII

In the light of the foregoing it is evident, I think, that the resistance to Darwinism on the part of the Russian Orthodox Church was of a comparatively dispassionate and "rational" kind, and that most, though not all, of the criticisms directed at Darwinian theory were scientifically justified, or at least intellectually respectable, in their historical setting. The contrast would be sharper if this chapter in Russian intellectual history were compared to disputes of the same period in Western Europe and the United States (such a comparison, unfortunately, is precluded by the limits of this paper). There was no "Scopes trial" in Russia; and I have found no evidence of attempts to restrict or suppress the teaching of Darwinism in the public schools or secular universities.[84] Furthermore, the most impassioned and "nonrational" criticisms of Darwinism came not from official representatives of the Church, but from devout laymen like Danilevsky and Strakhov whose opposition to Darwinism was interwoven, not only with their religious views, but, perhaps more importantly and directly, with their Russian nationalism and anti-Westernism.

The question naturally arises: What was the reason for this relatively rational and dispassionate attitude toward the Darwinian "threat to morals and religion" in Russia? I can only suggest a partial and tentative answer: namely, that in the West the most obdurate and least rational opposition to

---

[83] "Darvinizm i pravo," *Russkoe obozrenie,* no. 3 (1893), p. 491. This article is a review of S. Novicow, "La Théorie de Darwin et la justice," *Revue Scientifique* (1893).

[84] The contrast between the policy of the Russian Orthodox Church toward Darwinism and that of the Communist Party of the Soviet Union toward "Mendel-Morganite" genetics (after August 1948) will be evident to the reader of Professor Dobzhansky's paper.

Darwinism came from the "fundamentalist" Protestant sects (for example, in the "Scopes trial" at Dayton, Tennessee, in 1925), and that in Russia — for various reasons which cannot be explored here — "fundamentalist" sects, in the period under discussion (1859–1917), played a relatively negligible role. Furthermore, it is historically the case that on certain questions — in particular those concerning philosophic and, to a lesser extent, scientific beliefs — the Russian Orthodox Church permits its members considerable individual freedom.

Whatever the full *explanation* may be, the historical *fact* remains. It is my hope that the present modest exploration of this fact may serve to throw new light on a neglected aspect of Russian cultural and intellectual history.

The Crisis of Soviet Biology

THEODOSIUS DOBZHANSKY

Even though it has been suggested that the genius of Russian culture lies mainly in fine arts and in belles-lettres, Russian science has reached the forefront of the world scientific movement. Despite a late start, Russia produced the imposing figure of Lomonosov as early as the eighteenth century. By the second half of the nineteenth century, Russian science definitely outgrew its apprenticeship to Western European, and particularly to German, science, and by the early twentieth century shook off whatever provincialism it may have had. The Soviet government has consistently claimed, from the earliest days of its existence to the present, that science is entitled to, and is in fact receiving, most generous support from the state. More than that: the government and the Communist Party have maintained that their policies are strictly "scientific," and, accordingly, that science and scientists are most instrumental in the formulation and execution of these policies.

Some of the pronouncements of the Soviet authorities concerning the importance of science have an odd resemblance to the ancient theories of church-state relationships. The Divine Charisma is replaced in the Soviet Union by a sanction of scientific truth.[1] This doctrine has brought several consequences. Perhaps the least important one has been that the Soviet leaders, and particularly Lenin and Stalin, are constantly hailed not only as great politicians, but also as scientific geniuses. Much more important is that scientific research, both in applied and in basic sciences, has been encouraged as never before, and the dissemination of scientific education has reached to some extent all levels of Soviet society. The growth of the numbers of scientific, educational, and research institutions, and of the numbers of persons employed in scientific activities, has been most impressive. Even though the quality has not always kept up with quantity, the accomplishments of Russian science during the Soviet period can justly be claimed to represent one of the positive and lasting achievements of the regime.

However, the exalted position of science in the Soviet scheme of things

---

[1] It should, of course, be kept in mind that the English usage of the word "science" is more restrictive (natural science) than the Russian usage, which includes social sciences, history, philosophy, and, in pre-Soviet days, theology.

brings with it difficulties which are greater than those which science encounters anywhere else. It cannot be gainsaid that science performs increasingly important functions in all modern industrial civilizations. This being the case, it is inevitable that every modern society will by some means endeavor to control the development of science and of its uses. The problem is what forms this control will take and by what means it will be exercised. The Soviet policy in this respect has been stated many times, but never more clearly and explicitly than by G. F. Aleksandrov, one of the most authoritative members of the Academy of Sciences of the U.S.S.R.[2] According to Aleksandrov,

> Since Communism is being built on the basis of the highest achievements of all modern sciences of society and of nature, the Communist Party and the Soviet state take effective measures to insure complete freedom of the development of science, to keep open the road to everything progressive, and to discard and destroy all antiquated opinions and theories.

But who is to decide which opinions and theories are true and which are useless and false? Aleksandrov is quite explicit about this:

> The entire experience of building socialism and Communism in the U.S.S.R. shows that the force which directs, organizes, and inspires the development of Soviet science and culture is the Communist Party, its wise and farseeing leader comrade Stalin, and its commanding general staff, the Central Committee . . . The historic experience of the development of our country shows that science can consistently serve the liberation of the working masses from economic and spiritual slavery when it becomes permeated by Marxist-Leninist philosophy . . . The followers of progressive opinions and trends in science, supported by the Communist Party and by public opinion, gain the leading posts in science, direct its development, help to overcome errors and defects in the activities of various scientists and the wrong opinions which arise in isolated individuals among the Soviet intelligentsia under the influence of bourgeois ideologies.

How the application of the above policy has influenced the functioning of Russian science is a matter of the now already fairly long and developing record. The interest of the Russian situation is enhanced by the fact that any relationship that may be established between science and the state should be regarded as experimental. The forms which this relationship should take have not been perfected by experience, since the issue is a relatively new one. The fate of biology in the U.S.S.R. can be considered the result of one large-scale experiment.

*   *   *

The crisis of biology in the U.S.S.R. arose at first in one discipline — in genetics. Perhaps because this discipline occupies a pivotal position in biology, the infection spread rapidly to other branches — theory of evolution, agronomy, and ecology. In recent years it hit all biological sciences except

[2] G. F. Aleksandrov, "Borba mnenii i svoboda kritiki — zakon razvitia peredovoi nauki," *Priroda* (June 1952), pp. 3–12.

the purely descriptive studies of animal and plant taxonomy and morphology.

In 1930, an agronomist, T. D. Lysenko (1898 —), claimed the discovery of vernalization, a method whereby seeds of winter wheat may be sown in spring. Vernalization under laboratory conditions had been known for decades, but Lysenko claimed that his particular treatment made the use of vernalization profitable in agricultural practice — a contention never confirmed by agronomists outside of the U.S.S.R. Nevertheless, the Soviet press hailed vernalization as a discovery of tremendous importance, and Lysenko himself published seventy-seven journal and newspaper articles about it in four years, 1931–1935.[3] Whatever may be said about the practical usefulness of vernalization, it obviously changes only the behavior of the plants of the generation to which it is applied. Lysenko alleged that it changed also the heredity, the breed itself. At first nobody took him seriously. But in 1934, Lysenko made an alliance with I. I. Prezent, a Party propagandist turned theoretical biologist, and an effective though unscrupulous polemist. The Lysenko-Prezent axis evidently won recognition by the Party as leading the "progressive" trend in biology.

In 1935 Lysenko and Prezent struck. They urged that genetics was a bourgeois corruption of Darwinism, and that unadulterated Darwinism was available in the works of the native genius — Michurin; that genetics led to idealism, mysticism, and even to religion, while the materialist biology could be found in the writings of Timiriazev; and that while genetics produced no improved breeds of agricultural plants and animals, they could produce them very rapidly — by vernalization and similar methods. On December 19–27, 1936, the first dramatic public discussion of the sins of genetics was held in Moscow.[4] N. I. Vavilov (1887–1942), the leader of Russian genetics and the target of most determined attacks, attempted to defend himself, and so did other geneticists. But the stenographic records of this meeting show clearly that the issue was prejudged by the government against them, and that they knew it.

Lysenko and Prezent, together with more and more numerous bandwagon followers, now pursued the attack not only by means of a great stream of propaganda (in 1936–1940 Lysenko published 131 newspaper and magazine articles), but also by occupying all important administrative and academic posts related to plant and animal breeding and to agricultural education. Vavilov was dismissed from the directorship of the All-Union Institute of Plant Industry which he created, and was replaced by Lysenko. He and other Russian geneticists were prevented from attending the International Congress of Genetics which met in Edinburgh in August of 1939 and which wanted to elect Vavilov its president. But on October 7–14, 1939, another public trial of genetics was staged in Moscow.[5] Vavilov still tried to defend

[3] Bibliography, in T. D. Lysenko, *Agrobiologiia* (2nd ed., Moscow, 1952).

[4] O. M. Targulian, ed., *Spornye voprosy genetiki i selektsii* (Moscow, 1937).

[5] "Soveshchanie po genetike i selektsii, "*Pod znamenem Marksizma*, no. 11 (1939).

himself, but his spirit had been broken, and his speech, constantly interrupted by hecklers from the floor, was definitely weak. Some other geneticists
made pathetic attempts to show that genetics was compatible with Michurin,
Timiriazev, and Lysenko, only to be told that their attempts deceived
nobody. Lysenko clearly carried the day. In early August of 1940 Vavilov
was arrested; his subsequent fate is not known with certainty, except that
he died in Magadan, in northern Siberia, some time in 1942. His name
became unmentionable in the U.S.S.R., so much so that it is absent in the
lists of either living or dead members of the Academy of Sciences of the
U.S.S.R., published since his disgrace. Several other geneticists also vanished
without trace. Among them should be named G. D. Karpechenko, G. A.
Levitskii, I. I. Kerkis and more recently N. V. Timofeev-Ressovskii, N. P.
Dubinin, and some less well-known figures.

Despite these sinister happenings, during and after the war genetics
teaching and research continued in some of the universities and scientific
institutes which Lysenko's hand did not reach until then. The end came
when the last and most widely publicized discussion of genetics took place
between July 31 and August 7, 1948, in Moscow.[6] This gathering has been
referred to by Soviet writers as "the historic session of the Lenin Agricultural
Academy which has established a complete supremacy in our country of the
Michurin doctrine as the sole correct line in biological science." Indeed,
Lysenko made there the historic pronouncement that "the Central Committee
of the Party examined my report and approved it." This was enough to end
all opposition. Genetics in the U.S.S.R. ceased to exist on August 7, 1948.
Since then not a single work dealing with fundamental genetics has been
published. Almost five years later, Lysenko added an interesting detail:

> Comrade Stalin has shown the ways to develop the theory of Michurinist
> materialist biology . . . He has personally edited the draft of the report on the
> "Situation in Biological Science," explained to me in detail the corrections which
> he had made, and gave directions concerning the presentation of some parts of
> the report.[7]

Some foreign commentators have interpreted this sentence as meaning
that Stalin was the real author of Lysenko's "theories," and that Lysenko
now wishes to disavow them. This interpretation is, of course, gratuitous.
But what Lysenko's statement does mean is that the late dictator was a
geneticist by avocation — a fact hinted at earlier by Lysenko and others
but now explicitly set down on the record.

*   *   *

The startling fact about the "progressive Michurinist dialectical biology"
which the rulers of the Soviet state have seen fit to establish as the official

---

[6] *The Situation in Biological Science* (Moscow, 1949).
[7] T. D. Lysenko, *Pravda* (March 8, 1953).

creed, is that it lacks any novelty. The most incredible thing in Lysenko's incredible career is that neither he nor any of his followers, willing or unwilling, have so far had a single new or original idea, right or wrong. All they have offered is a return to the theories and opinions which were current in biology in the past and which were rejected because they were shown to be invalid. Like the king's new dress in Andersen's tale, "the new biology" simply does not exist.

Lysenko denounces the gene and chromosome theories as "metaphysical, reactionary, pseudo-scientific Mendelism-Weismannism-Morganism." All these epithets are applied because geneticists allegedly assume the existence of a hereditary substance which is isolated from and impervious to the influences of environment. Needless to say, no geneticist assumes anything of the sort, although Prezent has displayed real ability in unearthing and quoting awkward and injudicious statements, especially of the early geneticists. Even before 1900 every biologist knew that the chromosomes and the genes which they contain reproduce themselves in the intervals between successive cell divisions. The genes build their copies from nongenic materials, ultimately from food which the organism gets from its environment. The nucleoproteins of which the genes and chromosomes are composed can easily be changed by many kinds of physical and chemical agents. The relative stability of the genes in development and evolution is really a remarkably dynamic one: the genes interact with the environment to produce their own copies. To be sure, the cyclic process of self-reproduction can easily be interfered with by environmental influences, but it is a demonstrable fact that the changed genes usually do not reproduce at all. It is hard to tell whether Lysenko is really ignorant of all this. Ascribing opinions which they never held to his adversaries is his favorite polemical technique, and one which he uses with great skill.[8]

Up to about 1940, the Lysenkoists claimed to be Darwinists, whose mission it was to cleanse Darwinism of corruption by capitalist biologists. Now, modern genetics has led to the formulation of a theory of evolution based on experimental findings. This theory is obviously not identical with Darwin's, for the good reason that many new and important facts have been discovered during almost a century since the publication of the *Origin of Species,* but it is clearly derived from the Darwinian prototype. Its basic postulate is that organic diversity arises as a response to the diversity of environments which exist on earth. Lysenko's argument against this theory is that it denies all influence of environment in evolution.

Having swept away the modern theories of genetics and evolution, the Lysenkoists had nothing better to propose than a return to the views of the Russian pioneer Darwinist, K. A. Timiriazev. Timiriazev was, no doubt, an eminent physiologist as well as an excellent writer on evolution and general

[8] T. D. Lysenko, *Heredity and its Variability* (New York, 1946).

biology. About 1890, when he was at the height of his powers, his biological outlook was up to date, and his writings could be used as a guide and an inspiration. But biological science has not stood still. Taking Timiriazev, or for that matter Darwin, as infallible authorities means a setback to the stage of scientific development passed half a century ago.

However, since 1940, Timiriazev and Darwin have been steadily losing prestige to the even more antiquated views of Michurin and Lamarck. Michurin (1855–1935), who has now been built up to be a popular hero and a scientific genius, was a practical breeder who did have remarkable success in creating varieties of fruit trees adapted to Russian climates and soils. But as a biologist he was an amateur, like his American counterpart and contemporary, Burbank. Like every breeder before and after them, Michurin and Burbank used the methods of hybridization and selection. An understanding of the basic nature of these methods has become possible only recently, from the vantage point of modern genetics. In the absence of such understanding, Burbank, and especially Michurin, had great faith in some spurious additional "methods," such as mentors, vegetative hybridization, destabilization of heredity, etc. The best that can be said about these "methods" is that good breeding work can be done in spite of their use.

Now, these spurious "methods" have become the very core of "progressive" Michurinism. Anybody familiar with modern biology simply cannot take these "methods" and the beliefs associated with them seriously. All of them were current among biologists and breeders in the nineteenth century, and all of them were invalidated by experimental tests made from Darwin's time on. It is impossible to tell from the writings of Michurinists whether or not they are aware of this. All they have to offer is a return to the biology of a century ago.

*   *   *

In 1936, Lysenko and Prezent repudiated any connection with Lamarckism.[9] Gradually Lysenko discarded this pretense, and declared that evolution was "unthinkable" without the acceptance of the Lamarckian principle of the inheritance of acquired characters. Not stopping at this, Lysenko has proposed a theory to explain how this inheritance takes place. This theory,[10] duly applauded by his followers as the work of a genius, assumes that the sex cells are compounded of particles produced by all parts of the body. If the body is changed by environmental influences, it produces changed "particles," which enter the sex cells and give rise to a changed body in the next generation. No doubt, an interesting theory; but any competent biologist cannot fail to recognize in it Darwin's so-called "provisional hypothesis

[9] Targulian, *Spornye voprosy*, p. 57.
[10] Lysenko, *Heredity and its Variability*.

of pangenesis," which was shown to be invalid in the nineteenth century, soon after it was first suggested. Recently, Russian readers were, however, reminded about Darwin's pangenesis by Nuzhdin, who camouflaged with fulsome praise the implicit accusation of Lysenko of ignorance or plagiarism. It may be noted in this connection that Nuzhdin is the only Russian geneticist who became an active Lysenkoist after having done very competent work in modern genetics.[11]

In 1945, Michurinism was further enriched by a discovery which comes the closest to being an original idea not known to biological historians. This is Lysenko's denial of the existence of competition between individuals of the same species in nature. Darwin regarded such competition as the source of evolution by natural selection, and acknowledged that the writings of Malthus suggested this idea to him. Now, anything connected with Malthus is taboo in the U.S.S.R., and the discovery of the Malthusian taint in Darwin led not only to the latter's expulsion from the Soviet pantheon, but even to a posthumous reprimand to Timiriazev, who was, after all, an unashamed Darwinist. Another comic situation resulted from this. While Darwin was in official favor, all the universities in the U.S.S.R. established courses called "Darwinism"; the change in the biological Party line necessitated that these courses be devoted chiefly to showing that Darwin was, after all, just another benighted Mendelist-Morganist.

But to come back to Lysenko's denial of intraspecific competition. The whole problem is obviously spurious, and the master simply became entangled in his own words. It is known at present that natural selection tends, in general, to limit the intensity of competition even between species, and within a species coöperation of nonspecific individuals is more favorable for evolution than noncoöperation. But individuals of a species may be said to "compete" for food and space even though they do not actively harm one another, just as competition in an oratorical contest does not require that the contestants denounce each other, and participants in a beauty contest need not scratch each other's faces.[12]

*   *   *

Final repudiation of Darwinism came in 1950, when Lysenko discovered that Darwin's theory was "metaphysical at its base" and a "flat evolutionism." The "flatness" consists, it would appear, in the recognition of the fact that evolutionary changes in nature are usually slow, and that biological species are end products of a usually fairly gradual process of divergence.[13]

Being used to faster tempos, the Michurinists resolved to speed things up. In 1948, Karapetian made the "discovery" that hard wheat, *Triticum*

[11] N. I. Nuzhdin, "Darvin i Michurinskaia biologiia," *Priroda* (May 1952).
[12] Lysenko, "Estestvennyi otbor i vnutrividovaia konkurentsiia," *Agrobiologiia.*
[13] Lysenko, "Novoe v nauke o biologicheskom vide," *ibid.*

durum, planted under unfavorable conditions, produced some seeds of a different species, the soft wheat, *Triticum vulgare.* A year later, Iakubziner found that wheat also produced seeds of rye, which belongs to a different botanical genus, *Secale.* Since then, the most wonderful biological upheavals have been taking place before the unstartled eyes of Michurinists. Different species of wheat change into rye, rye changes into different wheats, millet (*Panicum miliaceum*) changes into cockspur, *Panicum crus galli, Panicum glaucum,* and even into bristle grass, *Setaria viridis.* The common cabbage, *Brassica oleracea,* turns into rape, *Brassica napus.* The crowning achievements, so far, are the finding by Karapetian that hornbeam (*Carpinus*) mutates into hazelnut (*Corillus*), and by Avotin-Pavlov that a pine tree gave birth to a fir.[14]

One might almost think that these claims were practical jokes, but Lysenko has expressed regret that all the evidence against the "flat evolutionism" had come so far from the plant kingdom only, and has predicted that similar discoveries would soon be forthcoming from the animal kingdom as well. So we may presently hear that a house cat produced a lion cub, and that a bird of paradise was hatched from a hen's egg, or vice versa. The Michurinists are now satisfied that all evolution takes place by means of such transformations. This represents a relapse of more than a century, to the pre-Darwinian era, when St. Hilaire speculated that organisms may undergo sudden changes, resembling monstrosities. Or is it more correct to regard this a relapse into the fairy tale stage, where animals turn into men and vice versa? In any case, it is not possible to treat this nonsense as scientific theory.

*   *   *

Starting with genetics and evolution, Michurinism has now engulfed all of biology in the U.S.S.R. Only strictly descriptive work remains relatively safe, provided that the investigator or teacher refrains from approving discoveries made by bourgeois scientists and from mentioning the work of certain especially obnoxious persons. This writer must admit having experienced acute nostalgia on finding that the collector's name had inadvertently been omitted in the description of a new species of insect which he found many years previously in a remote corner of Turkestan.

The most recent triumph of Michurinism took place in histology and microscopic anatomy. O. B. Lepeshinskaia has long contended that the cell theory, which for a century was considered a part of elementary biological knowledge, is completely wrong. Madame Lepeshinskaia thinks that full-fledged cells, with nuclei and chromosomes, arise from undifferen-

[14] S. K. Karapetian, "Porozhdenie leshchiny grabom," *Agrobiologiia* (1952); K. I. Avotin-Pavlov, "Porozhdenie eli sosnoi," *ibid.;* L. V. Mikhailova, "Porozhdenie rapsa kochannoi kapustoi," *ibid.;* P. K. Kuzmin, "Porozhdenie shchetinnikov i proso kurinogo posevnym prosom," *ibid.*

tiated "living substance," like egg yolk and wound debris. For years she was making little headway in persuading her colleagues that her contentions were valid, until Lysenko appreciated the full significance of her discoveries. One of Lysenko's students has promptly confirmed Lepeshinskaia's findings on plant cells:[15] undifferentiated protoplasm gives rise to "prokaryons" (meaning, apparently, nuclei in the process of formation from non-nuclear materials), and the latter become real nuclei, with a full complement of chromosomes characteristic of the species.

In contrast to Lysenko, who habitually announces his major discoveries in speeches and newspaper articles, Lepeshinskaia and her students have published their evidence in full, with numerous microphotographic illustrations.[16] Examination of this evidence shows most convincingly that cells do not arise from noncellular matter. But Michurinists hail the work of Lepeshinskaia as the opening of a new era in biology as well as in medicine. Is it not clear that these discoveries explain the origin of cancer?

Lysenko came forward with a theory of his own, which subsumes Michurin and Lepeshinskaia in one grand synthesis.[17] All cells arise from mysterious "granules" contained in the protoplasm. Often these granules play unexpected tricks, such as suddenly transforming into granules of quite different species. Here, then, is the explanation of the transmutations of wheat into rye, of rye into wheat, of pine into fir, etc. Is this at last an original idea of Lysenko, however fantastic it may sound? Or is this only a disguised version of spontaneous generation, which was disproved by Spallanzani in the eighteenth century and finally disposed of by Pasteur in the nineteenth? The Michurinists have evidently "progressed" back to the prescientific stage.

*   *   *

The utter vacuity of "Michurinist" biology is hard for a nonbiologist to comprehend and to believe. Is it possible that there may be, after all, some real scientific issues behind all this sound and fury? Why were genetics and evolution theories the first to be subjected to the attack, and was there anything on the Russian scientific and cultural scene which favored Lysenko?

Indeed, the roots of the situation go back almost a century, to the intellectual climate in Russia at the time of the publication of Darwin's *Origin of Species,* and to the tragic misjudgments made by that otherwise illustrious personality — K. A. Timiriazev. The fifties and sixties of the last century were the time of unprecedented intellectual ferment in Russia, immortalized in Turgenev's *Fathers and Sons.* The liberal wing of the nation,

---

[15] A. M. Siniukhin, "K voprosu ob ontogenese rastitel'nykh kletok," *ibid.*

[16] O. B. Lepeshinskaia, *Proiskhozhdenie kletok iz zhivogo veshchestva i rol' zhivogo veshchestva v organizme* (Moscow, 1950).

[17] Lysenko, "O rabotakh deistvitel'nogo chlena Akademii Meditsinskikh Nauk SSSR O. B. Lepeshinskoi," *Agrobiologiia.*

and especially the younger generation, had resolutely embraced materialist philosophy, expounded with messianic zeal and burning conviction by such writers as Chernyshevskii, Dobroliubov, and Pisarev. These writers presented their views as necessary conclusions from positive achievements of natural science, the study of which they urged on their readers as the source of all wisdom and a safe guide in problems of conscience and morality. Pisarev, though not a biologist by training, was particularly insistent that it was biology which furnished the foundation for the new and incontrovertible faith. The writings of these apostles of materialist science in Russia were "must" reading for every forward-looking liberal in Russia up to the time of the Revolution. That the founders of the Soviet government were nurtured on them is evident from the numerous references in the writings of Lenin and others.

The appearance of Darwin's *Origin of Species* was hailed in Russia not merely as an attainment of science, but a new revelation which establishes the materialist faith ever more securely. It was especially the reception of the evolution theory in Russia that gave rise to Dostoyevsky's angry remark, to the effect that what others regard as plausible speculation becomes indisputable dogma in Russia. It appears that S. S. Kutorga was the first to lecture about Darwin's theory to the students of the University of Moscow in 1860, and that among his listeners was K. A. Timiriazev, then a seventeen-year-old freshman.[18] In 1861, Kutorga published the first Russian account of the new theory, and, in 1864, Timiriazev wrote a series of brilliant essays on Darwinism, which, in 1865, appeared in book form, and later went through a series of editions, the latest of which came out under Lysenko sponsorship. Also in 1864, Darwin's theory was proclaimed by D. I. Pisarev to be a part of the new gospel. A Russian translation of Darwin's work appeared in 1864, and a second edition was required a year later.

An account of the struggle for Darwinism in Russia would be out of place here, but it must be emphasized that the controversy acquired the character not of a scientific but of a philosophical and political dispute. This can be illustrated by the following statement of the antievolutionist Danilevsky:

It is clear how vitally important not only for zoölogists and botanists, but for any moderately intelligent person is the issue whether Darwin is or is not right. It is so important that I am firmly convinced that no equally important problem exists either in any other field of knowledge or in any realm of practical life. Indeed, this is the problem of "to be or not to be" in the strictest and broadest sense . . . The question at issue in Darwinism is immeasurably more important than all material goods, than the life of any one of us personally and than the lives of all posterity collectively.[19]

[18] G. V. Platonov, *Mirovozzrenie K. A. Timiriazeva* (2nd ed., Moscow, 1952).
[19] Quoted in Platonov, *ibid.*, pp. 113–114.

It was not so much Darwin's way of looking at certain biological facts that was espoused by some and negated by others; it was rather an essential part, or even the keystone, of the materialist creed and of the liberal and Leftist political views that was at issue. Such overtones were, of course, present in the controversies about evolution also in countries other than Russia,[20] but in Russia they became the gist of the matter.

Timiriazev (1843–1920) soon became the principal Russian exponent and defender of Darwinism. His importance in the intellectual history of Russia is analogous to, but greater than, that of T. H. Huxley in England or of E. Haeckel in Germany, for he was not only a leading scientist but also a political figure, and finally a hero. His monument now stands on one of the important squares in Moscow. His international reputation rested on his experimental studies on chlorophyll and on plant nutrition, but in Russia his fame as investigator was far exceeded by his prestige as a brilliant lecturer, the author of fine popular books on general biology, and a courageous defender of liberal causes.

Timiriazev's sharpest battle was with Danilevsky and Strakhov, who in 1885–1887 attempted to invalidate the theory of evolution with all its philosophical corollaries. Timiriazev counterattacked by vehement polemical articles and public lectures. His recently published marginal notes on Danilevsky's book show that his feelings in this matter were violent.[21] Although Danilevsky's arguments, many of which paralleled those of Samuel Butler, were expressed with much brilliance and force, he was no match for Timiriazev either as a scientist or as a polemist.

*   *   *

The rediscovery in 1900 of Mendel's laws, and the rapid development of the new science of genetics in the years that followed this rediscovery, happened to coincide with a crisis in the history of evolutionism. By that time most competent scientists were fully satisfied that evolution was a historical fact, in the sense that the organisms existing on our time level have arisen from very different ancestors who lived in the geological past. No understanding of the mechanisms which bring about evolutionary changes was, however, reached. Darwin's natural selection was accepted by most biologists as a plausible theory, but the origin of the hereditary variability with which it was supposed to operate was just as obscure as it was in Darwin's own time (which Darwin himself frankly admitted). For some decades (very roughly, 1890–1930) evolutionary theories and hypotheses that were published seemed merely to reflect individual preferences of their authors, but failed to discover any convincing new evidences.

[20] See, for example, Stow Persons, ed., *Evolutionary Thought in America* (New Haven, 1950).
[21] Platonov, *Mirovozzrenie,* pp. 115–118.

It is precisely this situation that the discoveries being made in genetics were destined to rectify. But the synthesis of genetics and evolutionism was still remote in 1900 — it did not begin until about 1930, did not take shape until the forties, and is far from complete now. The pioneer geneticists were busily accumulating facts, and some of them did not perceive at once the bearing of these facts on evolution. In particular, Bateson, who was the leader of genetics in its early years, tried to be scrupulously open-minded with respect to evolutionary problems. Although his own interest in genetics arose from his previous evolutionary studies, some of his writings took an agnostic position concerning evolution. There can be no doubt at present that Bateson was leaning too far backwards in this attitude.

Timiriazev was deeply disturbed by these developments, in which he saw the apparition of a new campaign against Darwinism. In 1913, the septuagenarian Timiriazev thundered against genetics: "The clerical reaction against Darwinism has found in Bateson a faithful servant. Mendelism is only a small incident on this background . . . of the struggle between science and the clerical obscurantism which feels again powerful." [22] Timiriazev carried on his war of vituperation against genetics unrelentingly during the closing years of his long life. There can be no doubt that his prestige and authority have created a distrust of genetics, particularly among the liberal and radical groups of Russian intelligentsia. It was rumored among Russian geneticists during the thirties that it was Timiriazev, who, not long before his death, urged on Lenin that it was Michurin, not Mendel or Bateson, who had discovered the most important laws of heredity. This story is most doubtful; at any rate, the published correspondence between Timiriazev and Lenin contains no mention of Michurin.

When the storm of the Revolution had passed, genetics was however not suppressed but, on the contrary, stimulated to grow. Three major schools soon took shape; that of N. I. Vavilov (who received part of his training under Bateson!), that of I. A. Filipchenko in Leningrad, and of N. K. Koitsov in Moscow. Vavilov's group was by far the largest. A man of inexhaustible energy and enthusiasm and a master of organization, he was selected by Lenin to develop scientific plant breeding work in the U.S.S.R. This herculean task Vavilov fulfilled in a remarkably short time: having inherited only a vestigial bureau of the old Ministry of Agriculture, he transformed it within less than ten years into a federation of research institutes and experiment stations scattered over the whole vast territory of the U.S.S.R., employing thousands of scientific and technical personnel, including such internationally known men and women as G. D. Karpechenko, G. A. Levitskii, E. I. Barulina, V. E. Pisarev, K. A. Flaksberger, and many others. Koltsov's school included S. S. Chetverikov, A. S. Serebrovskii, N. P.

[22] Cited from Platonov, *ibid.*, p. 128.

Dubinin, S. Gershenson, and others. Filipchenko's group included I. I. Kerkis, T. K. Lepin, A. A. Prokofieva-Belgovskaia, and others.

These men and women, and their numerous colleagues, working often under very harsh conditions, built Russian genetics to a position where it was regarded as one of the leading schools in world biology. In the twenties and the early thirties, the volumes of international biological periodicals rarely failed to include a research paper by a worker from the U.S.S.R. Since before the Revolution only a beginning of genetics research existed in Russia, the Soviet government had a right to claim credit for the remarkable development of genetics after the Revolution, and for a time this government did claim it. Moreover, the broadly conceived agricultural breeding work directed by Vavilov's Institute was developing on a vast scale. Whatever parts of it were not destroyed by Lysenko bore fruits which helped to swell Lysenko's fame as a breeder.

But pride goeth before a fall. Clouds started to gather already during the twenties. Anatole Lunacharskii, the redoubtable Commissar of Education, remembered that genetics was a product of bourgeois mentality. There occurred the dramatic incident of the invitation to the Lamarckist Kammerer to take refuge from persecutions by his capitalist and clerical enemies in his native Austria by becoming a director of a research institute in Moscow. When Kammerer committed suicide, his fate was the subject of a movie film, in which the villain of the piece resembles none other than Gregor Mendel (who died, of course, long before Kammerer began his experiments).[23]

Some geneticists, among them Koltsov, Filipchenko, and especially Serebrovskii (the last-named having been seemingly in the best of graces in the Party), organized a eugenic movement in Russia. Some of their pronouncements were drafted so carelessly that they bore resemblance to the kind of race and class eugenics which was soon to blossom out in Nazi Germany. Serebrovskii had some grand ideas of eugenical measures involving mass artificial insemination of women by the sperm of great men. This was just too much, and poor Serebrovskii was pitilessly lampooned in verse on the pages of *Pravda* by the then poet laureate Demian Bednyi. The deadly serious aspect of these slips was that it began to look to Party leaders as if Timiriazev was right after all in denouncing genetics as a vehicle of reaction.

In retrospect it is clear that about 1930 a decision was reached by some high Party authorities that genetics, and biology as a whole, should be cleaned of potential subversives. The question evidently was only who should do the cleaning, and the finger of fate did not at once touch Lysenko. On March 14–24, 1931, a series of meetings of the Society of Marxist Biologists took place at the Communist Academy in Moscow. The published proceed-

[23] R. Goldschmidt, "Research and Politics," *Science*, CIX (1949).

ings of these meetings[24] show that what took place was a dress rehearsal of the grandiose congresses later staged by Lysenko to try and condemn genetics. However, the name of the future leader of "progressive biology" was not even mentioned in 1931; his role being played by B. P. Tokin, who was later stripped of all influence by Lysenko. The geneticists, Serebrovskii, Koltsov, and the brothers B. Zavadovskii and M. Zavadovskii were made to recant their sins, without however being subjected to the degree of humiliation which became customary later. But the leader, Tokin, showed what now seems sweet reasonableness in view of what was to follow. Although he spoke of "a considerable group of biologists, and especially of geneticists, who proved prisoners of bourgeois ideas," nevertheless he admitted that:

. . . genetics is one of the biological disciplines which can and must play a great role in the hands of the proletariat. Within a brief period genetics has become firmly founded; during the last decade, it has caused a revolution in many biological problems, a revolution which is not yet completed. It has shed some light on certain processes of individual development. Genetics has helped to unmask the metaphysics of Lamarckism. But since a correct statement and application of genetics can be very important in socialist construction and especially in plant and animal breeding, since genetics is the branch of biology directly concerned in evolutionary problems, and since genetics is being used by bourgeois scientists for reactionary interpretation of eugenical and race issues, the attacks of the class enemies are especially strong in genetics . . .

Clearly, Mr. Tokin and the Communist Philistines who took part in this meeting were ready to reform genetics to conform to the will of the Party. But they were sufficiently familiar with elementary biology not to urge replacement of genetics by Michurinism. Although Michurin was at that time being showered with signs of official esteem, and his quaint notions concerning biology were becoming known among Russian geneticists and breeders, neither he nor his views were mentioned during the discussion. What, then, happened to bring on the Lysenko scourge five years later?

*   *   *

The spectacle of governments and nations adopting foolish and even suicidal policies has not been a rarity in our time. Nevertheless, the destruction of biology in the U.S.S.R. probably sets a world record. It seems incredible that any government would so deliberately substitute quackery for the scientific direction of its agriculture, on which the food supply of its people ultimately depends. Some foreign observers have tried to read hidden motives into this irrational behavior. The most popular guess has been that biological science had to be done away with because it contradicts the assumption of the equality of men on which Communist ideology is allegedly built. This guess is wrong on several counts. The doctrine of equality is

[24] *Protiv mekhanisticheskogo materializma i menshevistvuiushchego idealizma v biologii,* 104 pages (Moscow, 1931).

ethical, not biological; men need not be biologically alike to be equal before the law and before God. Although the assumption of equality is basic for democracy, as its inclusion in the American Declaration of Independence shows, recognition of biological variability among men contradicts neither the democratic nor the Communist world view. Finally, it is a fact that some biologists in and out of the U.S.S.R. are adherents of Communism without subscribing to the Michurinist folly.

Just as groundless is the surmise that biology was sacrificed to Lysenko because of the latter's alleged usefulness to agriculture. In reality, Lysenko has caused great and enduring harm to Soviet agriculture, the magnitude of which future statisticians may estimate. He destroyed or stultified the efforts of a whole generation of plant and animal breeders, and caused another generation to be brought up on old wives' tales instead of on scientific knowledge.

This is not to deny that, being a master of propaganda, Lysenko may well have been useful as a bureaucrat in the Ministry of Agriculture. He has repeatedly claimed sensational achievements, beginning with the vernalization of wheat, and ending with a variety of wheat which yields almost ten times as much as standard varieties. All that can be said about these claims is that they invariably fail to be substantiated when tested by bourgeois agronomists, who, after all, would not refuse any methods which would increase the yield of their crops. Again, Lysenko has taken the credit for much breeding work done by Russian agronomists with the aid of genetic methods. One cannot read without smiling the publications of one agronomist who recants his error of having first ascribed his success to genetics instead of to Michurinism, and of another who claims to have successfully used in his work the methods of hybridization and selection which, he writes, were invented by Michurin and Lysenko.[25]

The causes of the downfall of Soviet biology lie outside biology or agriculture. They have been stated by Academician Aleksandrov as follows:

The historical experience of the Soviet fatherland shows that science serves the interests of the people only when it becomes permeated with progressive ideas of the Communist Party, and when scientists grasp the real future of science and of mankind, which is their harmonious fusion in socialism and Communism.

and further:

Constructive discussion in Soviet science does not mean equality in rights for scientists who are partisans of Communism and who are struggling against it. Comrade Stalin teaches us that Soviet society needs only that kind of criticism and self-criticism which advances things, and which assists the building of Communism.[26]

[25] I. Vasilchenko, *I. V. Michurin* (Moscow-Leningrad, 1950).
[26] G. F. Aleksandrov, *Priroda* (June, 1952), p. 11.

Since the early thirties it has become the policy of the Party to create in the U.S.S.R. science answering to the above specifications. And also in the late thirties it was decided to stimulate in the Russian people a national pride and xenophobia, although traditionally they were singularly free of these passions. For these purposes Lysenko has been a willing and efficient tool. This is not to say that competent scientists did not show devotion to their country and to Communism. Vavilov, who suffered martyrdom for his opposition to Lysenko, was certainly a great patriot, one who faithfully served the Soviet government for the sake of what he believed to be the best interests of his country. But Vavilov knew well that the validity of scientific knowledge is independent of the nationality, and for that matter of the political beliefs, of the discoverer. Lysenko and his followers are free of such scruples; they owe allegiance to the Party and to it alone. Vavilov could not be forced to damn Morgan because he was an American and to accept Michurin's quaint notions because he was a Russian. To the Michurinists this is the obvious thing to do.

The lengths reached by nationalism in Soviet science are almost unbelievable. Some twenty years ago it became unpatriotic for Soviet scientists to publish any of their works in international scientific periodicals. Then, the periodicals published in the U.S.S.R. lost the articles printed in foreign languages. Next, the summaries, tables of contents, and even the names of the periodicals themselves were printed only in Russian. Finally the point was reached when most authors considered it prudent to avoid references to foreign works. The result was that the periodicals became totally useless to anybody who is not at home in the Russian language. This may be flattering to national pride, but certainly is not conducive to appreciation of the attainments of Russian scientists by colleagues throughout the world. The Michurinists have, to be sure, suffered no loss of prestige on account of this isolation, but other scientists certainly have.

Complete collections of works of Timiriazev, Michurin, Mechnikov, Pavlov, and some lesser Russian biologists of the past have been published in large popular editions. This is a boon to a historian of science, since some of these men were real leaders of science in their day, and their original publications are hard to get. Yet it does not seem to occur to the present masters of Russian science that a biologist who has not yet gone beyond Timiriazev and Pavlov is an anachronism.

*   *   *

There has been no shortage of informed people in the U.S.S.R. who realize clearly that the "discoveries" of Lysenko, Lepeshinskaia, and their followers are a travesty of science. Furthermore, not a few of these informed people have had the courage to say so publicly, although they knew that by so doing they were risking their livelihood, if not their lives. This is evident to even a casual reader of the proceedings of the genetics "discussions" which took place in Moscow in 1939 and 1948 (see notes 5 and 6). As stated above, Nuzhdin proved to be the only person who became a Lysenkoist after having done valuable, though not outstanding, research in genetics. Little is known of the fate of the others, numbering somewhere between fifty and one hundred, except that they no longer publish works in their specialty. Those whose names still appear in print have switched to "safe" topics in descriptive biology and natural history.

For about four years, between 1948 and 1952, no opposition to Lysenko was permitted to appear in print. Then a botanical periodical addressed to a specialized audience suddenly published two critical articles by Professors Turbin and Ivanov. The learned critics found:

> Of late, the opinions of T. D. Lysenko are not subject to criticism of his colleagues, although without criticism, as pointed out by our teacher I. V. Stalin, science cannot progress. This is a fault of all scientists working in the field of biology.[27]

But the arguments which Turbin and Ivanov have adduced against Lysenko's disproof of the "flat evolution" are mostly quotations from the following biological authorities: Malenkov, Stalin, Engels, Marx, Lenin, Michurin, and Timiriazev. The strongest argument is that Lysenko's views do not agree in every particular with those of Michurin, and even resemble those of Morgan and other Mendelists-Weismannists! It does not seem to occur to these critics to inquire whether Lysenko's views agree with facts, regardless of whether they agree with Michurin. Lysenko's followers have reacted promptly and violently. The venerable Lepeshinskaia herself accused Turbin and Ivanov of dishonesty.[28] Dvoriankin[29] found that the editors of the botanical periodical publishing criticisms of Lysenko are guilty of the crime of *"de facto* restoration of the two conflicting tendencies which existed in biological science prior to the August session" (the genetics "discussion" in August 1948). Dmitriev[30] is still more outspoken, and appeals to the Council of the Academy of Sciences to restrain the editors of the botanical periodical from discussing Lysenko's dicta, since Lysenko's views are completely demonstrated!

A new wind, however, is blowing in the Moscow biological world in 1953 and 1954. The last two issues of the *Botanicheskii zhurnal* for 1953,[31] con-

[27] N. V. Turbin, "Darvinism i novoe uchenie o vide," *Botanicheskii zhurnal* (1952), XXXVII, 798; see also *ibid.,* N. D. Ivanov, "O novom uchenii T. D. Lysenko o vide."

[28] O. B. Lepeshinskaia, "Nedobrokachestvennaia kritika N. V. Turbina i N. D. Ivanova raboty T. D. Lysenko o vide," *Botanicheskii zhurnal* (1953), XXXVIII, 386–388.

[29] F. A. Dvoriankin, "O vnutrividovykh i mezhvidovykh vzaimootnosheniakh sredi rastenii," *Zemledelie,* no. 1 (1953), pp. 87–92.

[30] V. S. Dmitriev, "O nekotorykh neobychnykh diskussiakh," *Selektsia i Semenovodstvo,* no. 2 (1953), pp. 49–68.

[31] *Botanicheskii zhurnal,* XXXVIII, nos. 5 and 6 (September–October and November–December 1953).

tain eleven articles criticizing Lysenko. To be sure, their fire is concentrated on just one aspect of Michurinism — the alleged sudden transformations of a plant into a quite different plant. Some startling facts are revealed here. Thus, Baranov[32] quotes Lysenko's address delivered on February 6, 1953, advancing a novel interpretation of the biology of a well-known bird, namely the cuckoo. It would seem that the cuckoo produces no eggs of its own, and cuckoo birds arise through the same process which allegedly transforms wheat into rye or pine into fir! But the transformation of the hornbeam into hazelnut previously claimed by Lysenko's student Karapetian (see note 14) did not fare so well. Karapetian's evidence proved to be a simple fake.[33]

*　　*　　*

When, at the beginning of his career, those in power decided to support Lysenko, they assuredly did not realize the magnitude of the blunder they were making. After all, there were others, just as willing to become faithful instruments of the Party's will, who would not have made a laughingstock of themselves and of Soviet science, and, more important, would not have so completely ruined agricultural research and training. But there was a real and urgent need to improve agriculture, which Lysenko promised to do more rapidly and efficiently than scientists burdened with moral scruples.

Lysenko posed as a scientific pioneer whose progress was being obstructed by stubborn conservatives. The Party authorities who chose Lysenko felt sure that they were acting rationally. Most likely they congratulated themselves on being hard-boiled realists. But, by a species of dialectics of ideas, their vaunted rationality turned into its opposite — utmost irrationality. A dictatorial power cannot, however, easily admit its blunders. Having glorified Lysenkoism as one of its most splendid attainments, it has become too deeply committed to the latter. And the Lysenkoist coterie is even more deeply committed to the power which has made their existence possible: free criticism would destroy their influence overnight! Russian science and agriculture are the sufferers. If any one deliberately had aimed to cripple and demolish them, he could not have pursued a more treacherous course than that of these pseudo scientists.

[32] P. A. Baranov, "O vidoobrazovanii," *Botanicheskii zhurnal* (1953), XXXVIII.
[33] A. A. Rukhkian, "Ob opisannom S. K. Karapetianom sluchae porozhdenia leshchiny grabom," *ibid*.

Dialectic and Logic Since the War

HERBERT MARCUSE

Nothing is perhaps more revealing for the basic trends of Soviet Marxism than its treatment of dialectic.[1] The dialectical logic is the cornerstone of Marxian theory: it guides the analysis of the prerevolutionary as well as of the revolutionary development, and this analysis in turn is supposed to guide the strategy in both periods. Any fundamental "revision" of the dialectical logic that goes beyond the Marxist application of dialectic to a new historical situation would indicate not only a "deviation" from Marxian theory (which is only of dogmatic interest), but also a theoretical justification for a new strategy. Interpreters of Stalinism have therefore correctly drawn attention to events in this sphere. They have concluded that Soviet Marxism has toned down and arrested the dialectic in the interest of the ideological justification and protection of a regime which must appear as regressive and to be surpassed by the dialectical development. Chief support for this conclusion is seen in the Soviet Marxist reformulation of the concept of dialectical contradictions (following the disappearance from the dialectical vocabulary of the "negation of the negation") and of the relation between base and superstructure, and in the reintroduction of formal logic.

The first and most fundamental of these apparent revisions predates the Second World War. Antagonistic and nonantagonistic contradictions are already distinguished in the representative articles of the *Bol'shaia sovetskaia entsiklopediia* (Great Soviet Encyclopedia) on Historical Materialism[2] and on the Law of the Unity and Conflict of Contradictions.[3] The distinction becomes central in Zhdanov's ideological offensive in the Aleksandrov controversy (June 1947)[4] and has since remained a decisive feature of Soviet Marxist dialectic. In Stalin's last article, the doctrine of nonantagonistic contradictions is made the theoretical foundation of the "transition to Com-

---

[1] This paper is part of a larger study on Soviet Marxism, written under a grant by the Russian Institute, Columbia University.

[2] Vol. XXIX (1935).

[3] Vol. XLVII (1940).

[4] *Bol'shevik*, no. 16 (1947); *Voprosy filosofii*, no. 1 (1947).

munism." [5] The two other events in the development of Soviet Marxist dialectics belong altogether to the postwar period and are closely connected in substance. The official statement of the relation between base and super-structure is given in the context of Stalin's "Marksizm i voprosy iazykozna-niia" (Marxism and Linguistic Problems), 1950; the reintroduction of formal logic in the schools was decreed in 1944, but the broad discussion begins only in 1948 and culminates in 1950–51. [6]

The attempt to evaluate the significance of these developments requires brief consideration of the function of dialectic within the system of Soviet Marxism as a whole. By themselves, they reveal neither their philosophical nor their political implications — they do not even appear as "revisions"; we shall see that each of the three reformulations could pass as a perfectly legitimate and "orthodox" inference from the Hegelian as well as Marxian dialectic. But while not a single one of the basic dialectical concepts has been revised or rejected in Soviet Marxism, the function of dialectic itself has been significantly changed: it has been transformed from a mode of critical thought designed to guide Marxist practice into a fixed universal system no longer inherently connected with the actual practice. This trans-formation itself is part of the reorientation of Marxism in terms of the development of capitalist society since about the turn of the century. Pres-ently we shall try to indicate some of the factors which altered the relation between Marxism and the reality which Marxism was designed to change.

The historical ground for the transformation of Marxism was provided by the transition from the free capitalism of the nineteenth century (the liberalistic period) to the "organized capitalism" of the twentieth century. The tremendous growth in productivity led to a considerable rise in the standard of living in the advanced industrial countries — a rise in which organized labor participated. Consequently, the class position of the Marxian proletariat changed: a large part of the laboring classes acquired a vested interest in the society whose "absolute negation" they were supposed to represent. To the Marxist theoreticians, the trend toward class coöperation, the growth of trade-unionism and social democracy appeared not only as a false strategy but as a threat to the basic Marxian conception of socialist theory and practice. In his struggle against revisionism and economism, Lenin answered this threat with a decisive reorientation. His theory of Bolshevism amounted to acknowledging that the revolutionary forces had to be re-created and organized outside and even against the "immediate interest" of the proletariat whose class consciousness had been arrested by the system in which they functioned. The Bolshevik doctrine of the pre-dominant role of the Party leadership as the revolutionary vanguard grew

---

[5] "Economic Problems of Socialism in the U.S.S.R.," in *Current Digest of the Soviet Press*, Special Supplement (1952).

[6] Summary of the discussion in *Voprosy filosofii*, no. 6 (1951).

out of the new conditions of Western society (the conditions of "imperialism" and "monopoly capitalism") rather than out of the personality or psychology of the Russian Marxists. The increasing power of advanced capitalism, the coördination of Western social democracy with this society, Leninism, and the idea of "breaking the capitalist chain at its weakest link" are parts and stages of one and the same historical trend. But although the Leninist reorientation foreshadows the development of "socialism in one country," that is to say, *outside* the centers of advanced industrial civilization, and thus implies a basic modification of Marxism, Lenin did not follow up his strategic reorientation. He remained "orthodox." In line with Marxist orthodoxy, he first regarded the Bolshevik Revolution as preliminary to the revolution in one of the advanced capitalist countries, namely, Germany. The Leninist policy during the first years of the Bolshevik dictatorship was tentative in the sense that it relied to a great extent on the working of the revolutionary dialectic *within* the capitalist world. "Socialism in one country" became definitive only after the failure of the Central European revolutions had become definitive, that is to say, after 1921. The building of socialism on a backward and (for a long time to come) isolated base found no theoretical guidance in Marxian theory. Lenin, and also Stalin, never abandoned the notion that "socialism in one country" could be ultimately victorious only through the triumph of socialism in the advanced industrial society of the West. In this respect, Stalinism remained as orthodox as Leninism.

Then, however, the growth of the Soviet state into a strong national and international power led to a unification and integration of the Western world which made the expectation of an indigenous collapse of capitalism appear more unrealistic than ever before. This "uneven development toward socialism" inside and outside the Soviet Union generated the rift between theory and practice which is characteristic of Soviet Marxism. The goal remained the same, but the ways and means for attaining it had become very different. As a result of the historical changes in the international arena, the historical carrier of the revolutionary dialectic was no longer the industrial proletariat in the advanced industrial countries but the Soviet state. Its development was to be interpreted in terms of a socialist rather than capitalist dialectic, of nonantagonistic rather than antagonistic contradictions. And outside the Soviet orbit, there was still the dialectic of capitalism. During the Stalinist period, the interrelation between the two remained almost taboo. Only recently, there are indications that, in line with a general reorientation of Soviet policy, the problem of dialectic is redefined. In order to understand the implications of this development, a restatement of the original function of the Marxian dialectic will be necessary.

Marx elaborated his dialectic as a conceptual tool for comprehending an inherently antagonistic society. The dissolution of the fixed and stable

notions of philosophy, political economy, and sociology into their contradictory components was to "reflect" the actual structure and movement of
this society: the dialectic was to reproduce in theory what happened in the
reality. To reproduce it adequately, in order to provide the true theory of
this society, the traditional categories had to be redefined since they concealed rather than revealed what happened. The theory of society had to
be elaborated in its own terms. But the dialectical relation between the
structure of thought and that of reality is not merely that of reflection
and correspondence. If Hegel consistently transgresses the clearly established
distinction between thought and its object, if he talks of "contradictions"
(a "logical" term) in the reality, of the "movement" of concepts, of quantity
"turning" into quality, he indeed stipulates a specific identity between
thought and its object — he assimilates one with the other. But it may be
assumed that the wisdom of his critics, who note that Hegel confuses two
essentially different realms, was not beyond the reaches of his intelligence
and awareness. According to Hegel, the traditional distinction between
notion and reality is "abstract" and falsifies and prejudices the real relation.
Thought and its object have a common denominator, which, itself "real,"
constitutes the substance of thought as well as its object. This common
denominator, this structure common to thought and object is the structure
of Being as a process comprising Man and Nature, Idea and Reality. The
process of Thought, if true, that is to say, if it "comprehends" the reality,
if it is the Notion (*Begriff*) of its object, *is* the process in which the object
constitutes itself, becomes what it is, develops itself. As such this process
appears in three different realms of Being: in Nature, in History proper, and
in "pure" Thought (Logic). They are essentially different stages of "realization," essentially different realities. Hegel's Logic, far from obliterating
these differences, is their very elaboration. But their common structure and
common Telos (Reason — the realization of the free Subject) establishes
for Hegel the supremacy of the Notion, the reality of the Logos. The (true)
thought process is in a strict sense an "objective" process. Thus, when Hegel
speaks of one notion turning into another he says that the notion, thought
through, reveals contents which at first seem alien and even opposed to
this notion; thinking only reproduces the movement of the objective reality
of which the notion is an essential part. What happens in the thought
process is not that one notion is replaced by another one more adequate to
the reality, but that the same notion unfolds its original content — a dynamic which is that of the reality comprehended in the notion. The reality
has (or rather is) its own Logos and thus its own Logic. This is not just
a manner of speech. Since the Greeks first defined the essence of Being as
Logos, the idea of the logical essence of reality (and of the reality of logic)
has dominated Western thought; the Hegelian dialectic is only its last
great development.

The Marxian "subversion" of Hegel's dialectic remains committed to this idea. The driving forces behind the social process are, not certain conflicts and antagonisms, but *contradictions* because they constitute the very Logos of the social system from which they arise and which they define. According to Marx, (the Logos of) capitalist society speaks against itself: its economy functions normally only through periodic crises; growing productivity of labor sustains scarcity and toil, increasing wealth perpetuates poverty; progress is dehumanization. Specifically, as Marx claims to show in *Capital,* it is the free wage contract and the just exchange of equivalents which generate exploitation and inequality; it is the realization of freedom, equality, and justice which turns them into their opposite.[7]

The rationality of the system is self-contradictory: the very laws which govern the system lead to its destruction. These laws originate in the basic societal relations which men enter in reproducing their life: with this materialistic foundation, the Logos is conceived as a concrete *historical* structure, and the logical dynamic as a concrete *historical* dynamic.

This brief restatement of some of the basic concepts of dialectic may serve to illustrate the hypostatization it underwent in Soviet Marxism. Here, dialectic is identified with the method and "theory of knowledge" of Marxism, and the latter with the only true scientific "world outlook" of the Communist Party.[8] Marxian theory may perhaps be called a "world outlook," but as such it claims to validate the abstract-philosophical generalities by their concrete historical content. To be sure, dialectical materialism can be presented as a series of general assumptions, categories, and conclusions — but the general scheme immediately cancels itself, for its categories come to life only in their dialectical use. Consequently, in trying to present dialectic "as such," Soviet Marxists can do nothing but abstract from the concrete dialectical analysis of the "classics" certain principles, to illustrate them, and to confront them with "undialectical" thought. The principles are those enumerated in Stalin's "Dialectical and Historical Materialism" which, in turn, are only a paraphrase of Engels' propositions in his *Dialectics of Nature.*[9] In terms of Hegel's and Marx's dialectic, they are neither true nor false — they are empty shells. Hegel could develop the principles of dialectic in the medium of universality, as a Science of Logic, because to him the structure and movement of Being was that of Thought and attained its Truth in the Absolute Idea; Marxian theory, however, which rejects Hegel's interpretation of Being in terms of the Idea, can no longer unfold the dialectic as logic: its medium is now the historical reality, and its universality is that of history.

The problem whether or not the Marxian dialectic is applicable to Nature

[7] *Capital,* Vol. I, ch. iv.

[8] See the report on the results of the discussion of the problem of logic in *Voprosy filosofii,* no. 6 (1951).

[9] For the "omission" of the "negation of the negation," see below, p. 355.

must here at least be mentioned because the emphasis on the dialectic of Nature is a distinguishing feature of Soviet Marxism — in contrast to Marx and even to Lenin. If the Marxian dialectic is in its conceptual structure a dialectic of the *historical* reality, then it includes Nature insofar as the latter is itself part of the historical reality (in the *Stoffwechsel* between man and Nature, the domination and exploitation of Nature, Nature as ideology, etc.). But precisely insofar as Nature is investigated in *abstraction* from these historical relations, in the natural sciences, by that very token it seems to lie outside the realm of dialectic. It is no accident that in Engels' *Dialectics of Nature* the dialectical concepts appear as mere analogies, figurative and superimposed upon the content — strikingly empty or commonplace compared with the exact concreteness of the dialectical concepts in the economic and socio-historical writings. And it is the *Dialectics of Nature* which has become the incessantly quoted authentic source for dialectic in Soviet Marxism. Inevitably so, for if "dialectic reigns everywhere," [10] if dialectical materialism is a "scientific world outlook," then the dialectical concepts must first and foremost be validated in the most scientific of all sciences — that of Nature. The consequence is a dehistorization of history.

The Soviet Marxist hypostatization of dialectic into a universal scientific world outlook entails the division of Marxian theory into dialectical and historical materialism, the latter being the "extension" and "application" of the former to the "study of society and its history." [11] The division would be meaningless to Marx, for whom dialectical materialism was throughout historical materialism. In Soviet Marxism, historical materialism becomes one particular branch of the general scientific and philosophical system of Marxism which — codified into an ideology and interpreted by the officials of the Party — justifies policy and practice.

The significance of this transformation for the Soviet state is so obvious that some important implications are generally overlooked. The dimension of History which, in Marxian theory, is the determining and validating dimension of dialectic, is, in Soviet Marxism, a special field in which suprahistorical laws assert themselves. The latter, arranged into a universal system of propositions, become the ultimately determining forces in History as well as Nature. The dialectical process thus interpreted is no longer in a strict sense a historical process — rather is History reified into a second Nature. Soviet developments thereby obtain the dignity of the objective natural laws by which they are allegedly governed and which, if correctly understood and taken into consciousness, will eventually right all wrongs and lead to final victory over the opposing forces. If there is anything which strikingly distinguishes Soviet Marxism from previous Marxian theory, it is — apart from

---

[10] K. S. Bakradze, "On the Relation Between Logic and Dialectic," *Voprosy filosofii,* no. 2 (1950).

[11] Stalin, "Dialectical and Historical Materialism," *History of the Communist Party of the Soviet Union: Short Course* (New York, 1939), p. 105.

the codification of Marxian theory into an ideology — the interpretation of socio-historical processes in terms of objective determinism. For example, in Rozental's *Marksistskii dialekticheskii metod* (Marxist Dialectical Method), the capitalistic development, the transition to socialism, and the subsequent development of Soviet society through its various phases are presented as the unfolding of a system of objective forces that could not have unfolded otherwise. Stalin's emphasis on the superstructure as a "powerful active force" which helps the base to assume its adequate form[12] does not contradict this trend. Not only is the activity of the superstructure itself derived from the base, but two years later Stalin insists that the "laws of political economy under socialism are objective laws . . . which proceed irrespective of our will," and that the state can "rely" on them and utilize them consciously and according to plan, but not abolish or even change them.[13] To be sure, strong and constant emphasis is placed on the guiding role of the state and of the Communist Party and its leadership, which holds the monopoly of interpreting and formulating the dialectical laws, and on the patriotic heroism of the Soviet people, but their action and success are made possible only by their understanding of and obedience to the laws of dialectic. At a first glance, this seems to be "orthodox Marx." Marx and Engels maintained throughout that the historical process is governed by objective laws, operating with the inexorable force of the laws of nature. However, as objective laws, they remain *historical* laws, laws of history; they express the dialectical relation between man and nature, freedom and necessity. The objectivity of these laws preserves the "subjective factor": they contain the Subject as conscious agent — not merely as the obedient servant and executor of the laws, but as the medium through whose actions and thoughts alone the historical laws become laws. Marx's statement that "man himself is the basis of his material as well as of any other production" [14] is more than an incidental remark; it proclaims indeed the first principle of the materialistic interpretation of history, which begins to take shape in formulations like these:

> Man has only to learn to know himself, to measure all existential conditions against himself, to judge them according to his own essence, to organize his world in a truly humane manner, in conformity with the demands of his nature — and he will have solved the riddle of our time . . . We see in history, not the revelation of God, but of man, and of man only . . .[15]

Nor are these formulations characteristic only for the early period in the development of Marx and Engels.[16] If, after 1848, and especially in *Capital,*

[12] "Marksizm i voprosy iazykoznaniia."

[13] "Economic Problems . . . ," ref. 5, p. 2.

[14] Marx, *Theorien über den Mehrwert,* ed. Kautsky (Stuttgart, 1910), I, 388.

[15] Engels, "Die Lage Englands, 1844," *Marx/Engels Gesamtausgabe,* ed. Marx-Engels Institute (Moscow, 1930), II, Part I, 427–428.

[16] For a discussion of this problem, see Leonard Krieger, "Marx and Engels as Historians," *Journal of History of Ideas,* XIV, no. 3 (June 1953), 396ff.

the subjective factor seems to be completely absorbed by the determining objective factors, this shift in emphasis and weight is caused by the concentration of Marxian theory on the "critique of the political economy" of capitalism. It is one of the main propositions of this critique that the economic laws of capitalism assert themselves "behind the back" of the individuals. The blind supremacy of the objective factors, the victimization of the Subject appears to Marx as the result of "man's enslavement under the means of his labor." But the reëstablishment of the Subject remains the aim.

In contrast, Soviet Marxism subjugates the subjective to the objective factors in a manner which transforms the dialectical into a mechanistic process. Characteristic is the interpretation of the relation between necessity and freedom: it is the key problem in the Hegelian as well as Marxian dialectic, and we have seen that it is also a key problem in the idea of socialism itself. Soviet Marxism defines freedom as "recognized necessity." [17] The formula follows Engels' restatement of Hegel's definition according to which freedom is "insight into necessity." [18] But for Hegel, freedom is not merely "insight" into necessity, but comprehended (*begriffene*) necessity. As such, necessity is realized *and cancelled* (*aufgehoben*) in freedom. Mere "insight" can never change necessity into freedom; Hegel's "comprehended" necessity is "not merely the freedom of abstract negation, but rather concrete and positive freedom" — only thus is it the "truth" of necessity. The transition from necessity to freedom is that into a fundamentally different dimension of Being, and Hegel calls it the "hardest" of all dialectical transitions.[19]

Soviet Marxism minimizes this transition and assimilates freedom to necessity — in ideology as well as in reality. This assimilation is expressed in the Soviet Marxist interpretation of dialectical change, that is, of the socio-historical development from one stage to another. The interpretation itself adheres to the inherited theoretical conception. The Marxian dialectic stipulates that the contradictions which determine the structure and course of a social system change with a change of the system. Soviet Marxism correlates "antagonistic contradictions" ("conflicts") to class societies, and "nonantagonistic contradictions" to classless and socialist societies. The former are irreconcilable and can be "resolved" only through explosion; the latter are susceptible to gradual solution through "scientific" social and political control.[20] But in both cases the contradictions tend toward a qualitative change of the social system — only on the basis of a classless society is the turn from quantity to quality "nonexplosive."

[17] For example, M. D. Kammeri, in *Voprosy filosofii*, no. 6 (1952).
[18] *Anti-Dühring*, Part I, ch. xi.
[19] *Encyclopedie* . . . , Vol. I, pars. 158–159. *Science of Logic*, Book I, sec. iii, ch. iii, C.
[20] See in addition to the references above, M. M. Rozental', *Marksistskii dialekticheskii metod* (Moscow, 1951), pp. 283ff.; S. P. Dudel, "K voprosu o edinstve i bor'be protivopolozhnosti kak vnutrennem soderzhanii protsessa razvitiia," *Voprosy dialekticheskogo materializma* (Moscow, 1951), pp. 73ff.

The elimination of "explosions" from the dialectical development is inherent in the Marxian conception itself. According to Marx, the "catastrophic" character of the transition from quantity to quality belongs to the realm of blindly operating, uncontrolled socio-economic forces; with the establishment of socialism, these forces come under the rational control of society as a whole, which self-consciously regulates its struggle with nature and with its own contradictions. Moreover, the change in the mode of transition from one stage to another is already stipulated in Hegel's system: once the level of free and self-conscious rationality has been reached ("Being-in-and-for-itself"), such rationality also governs the further transitions at this level. Similarly, Marx applied the notion of the "negation of the negation" specifically to the capitalist development. It is the "capitalist production" which, with the necessity of a "law of nature," engenders its own negation: socialism is this "negation of the negation." [21] Soviet Marxism claims that the Bolshevik Revolution has created a qualitatively new base — the base for socialism. Consequently, Stalin drops the "law of the negation of the negation" from his table of dialectical laws. Moreover, according to Soviet Marxism, the socialist base renders possible, within the framework of the central plan, a constant and conscious adjustment of production relations to the growth of the productive forces. Even the basic contradiction becomes amenable to control. The treatment of the dialectic merely reflects these fundamental propositions. The Soviet Marxist "revision" is "orthodox." Since Soviet Marxists maintain that Soviet society is a socialist society, they consistently invest it with the corresponding dialectical characteristics. What is involved is not a revision of dialectic, but the claim of socialism for a nonsocialist society. Dialectic itself, in the transmitted orthodox form, is used for substantiating this claim.

All this seems to confirm that the Soviet Marxist treatment of dialectic just serves to protect and justify the established regime by eliminating or minimizing all those elements of the Marxian dialectic which would indicate a continuation of the socio-historical development beyond this regime — toward a qualitatively different future. In other words, Soviet Marxism would represent the "arresting" of dialectic in the interest of the prevailing state of affairs — the ideology would follow the arresting of socialism in reality. However, the situation is more complicated. Neither the Soviet ideology nor its application are immune to the objective historical dynamic which the regime claims as its supreme law and basis. Even the most centralized and totalitarian plan remains subject to this dynamic, which, to a great extent, operates outside the reaches of the planning powers. It appears that the international development after the Second World War, especially the internal stability and the intercontinental integration of the Western world, drives the Soviet Union toward a general reorientation which calls for inten-

[21] *Capital*, Vol. I, ch. xxiv.

sified efforts to solve the "internal contradictions" in order to break the stale-mate in the field of the "external contradictions." [22] In Soviet Marxist lan-guage, the internal contradictions derive from the still persisting lag of the production relations behind the productive forces,[23] and the gradual correc-tion of this lag is to be undertaken by measures for preparing the "transition to Communism." This trend would also lead to changes in the "superstruc-ture." In line with the assimilation of the ideology to the reality, the trend would not only be noticeable but perhaps even anticipated in the ideology. Recent developments in the Soviet Marxist treatment of dialectic seem to corroborate this assumption. It appears that ideological preparations are being made for increasing the flexibility of the regime — ideological prepara-tions which would parallel a new adjustment of production relations and consumption standards to the growing productive capacity, and a correspond-ing adjustment of international strategy.

This trend seems to be reflected precisely in that Soviet Marxist position which appears as a defense against the application of dialectical logic to the present state of affairs — namely, the reinstatement of Formal Logic. The recent discussion of the relation between Formal and Dialectical Logic was linked throughout with Stalin's "Marxism and Linguistic Problems." There Stalin had pointed out that it is "un-Marxist" and incorrect to talk of the "class conditioning" of language and to envisage a specifically "socialist language." He had maintained that language "differs in principle" from a "superstructure" in that it does not change with the basis but outlives this or that basis: it is created by and "serves," not certain classes, but society as a whole over the course of centuries. By the same token, Soviet Marxism now holds, it is incorrect to treat Formal Logic as "class conditioned" and to envisage a specific "Soviet Logic" corresponding to the new basis of Soviet society.[24] The report on the results of the discussion on Logic sums up: "the logical forms and laws of thought are no superstructure over and above the basis . . ." "Formal Logic is the science of the elementary laws and form of correct thinking." "There are no two Formal Logics: an old, metaphysical, and a new, dialectical Logic . . . There is only one Formal Logic, which is universally valid . . ." [25] Dialectical Logic does not deny, cancel, or contra-dict the validity of Formal Logic; the former belongs to a different dimen-sion of knowledge and is related to the latter like higher to elementary mathematics.

We are not concerned here with the course and conclusions of the discus-

---

[22] I have tried to develop this thesis in my study on Soviet Marxism. For the distinc-tion between internal and external contradictions, see Stalin's *K itogam rabot XIV konferentsii RKP(b). Doklad aktivu moskovskoi organizatsii RKP(b), 9 maia 1925 g.* (Moscow, 1933).

[23] Stalin, "Economic Problems . . . ," ref. 5, p. 14.

[24] V. I. Cherkesov, in *Voprosy filosofii*, no. 2 (1950).

[25] *Voprosy filosofii*, no. 6 (1951).

sion.[26] Significantly, the changing trend announces itself in a return to Marxian orthodoxy after the Leftist "Marrist deviations." In terms of Marxian theory, neither language nor logic as such belong to the superstructure: they rather belong to the preconditions of the basic societal relationships themselves: as instruments of communication and knowledge, they are indispensable for establishing and sustaining these relationships. Only certain manifestations of language and thought are superstructure, for example, in art, philosophy, religion. Following the Marxian conception, the Soviet discussion distinguished between Logic itself and the *sciences* of Logic: as a specific interpretation of Logic, some of the latter must be classified as ideological.[27] But neither the Hegelian nor the Marxian dialectic denied the validity of Formal Logic: they rather preserved and validated its truth by unfolding its content in the dialectical conception which reveals the necessary abstractness of "common" as well as "scientific" sense.

Compared with this tradition of dialectic, "Marrist" linguistics and logic must indeed appear as a gross "Leftist deviation," as an "infantile disease" of Communism in its age of immaturity.[28] It seems to be an ideological by-product of the first phase of the Stalinist construction of socialism in one country. The violent struggle to overcome the technological and industrial backwardness of the country, imposed by terror upon a largely passive and even hostile population, found its ideological compensation in the various doctrines of the uniqueness and superiority of Soviet man, deriving from his "possession" of Marxism as the only true and progressive "world outlook." But Marxian theory is in its very substance international: within its framework, nationalism is progressive only as a stage in the historical process — a stage which, according to Marx and Engels, had already been surpassed by the advanced Western World; Soviet Marxism never succeeded in reconciling the contradiction between its own nationalism and Marxian internationalism either in its strategy or in its ideology, as is demonstrated by the painful distinctions between "bourgeois cosmopolitanism" and genuine internationalism, between chauvinism and "Soviet patriotism." Moreover, the emphasis on a special Soviet mentality, logic, linguistics, etc. was bound to impair the appeal to the international solidarity in the ultimate revolutionary objective which neither the doctrine of socialism nor of Communism in one country could altogether discard. The "Marrist" theories may have fulfilled a useful function in the "magical" utilization of Marxian theory, but with the technological and industrial progress of Soviet society, with the growing political and strategic power of the Soviet state, they came into conflict with the more fundamental objectives. As Soviet policy began to be oriented to the

[26] They are summarized in *Voprosy filosofii, ibid.,* and in Gustav Wetter, *Der Dialektische Materialismus* (Vienna, 1952), pp. 544ff.

[27] I. I. Osmakov, in *Voprosy filosofii,* no. 3 (1950).

[28] We are here concerned only with the Stalinist evaluation of Marr's doctrine—not with this doctrine itself.

transition to Communism, the Marrist doctrines had to give way to more "communist," more universal and internationalist conceptions. Far from signifying the "arrest" of dialectic in the interest of the stabilization of the attained level of development, the recent reiteration of the common human function and content of language and logic seems to be designed to bring the ideology in line with the drive toward the "next higher stage" of the development, that is (in Soviet terms), the second phase of socialism, or (in more realistic terms) the intensified effort to improve living conditions in the Soviet Union and to stabilize the international situation.

Part IV

Review

GEROID TANQUARY ROBINSON

". . . not to laugh at the actions of men, nor yet to deplore or detest them, but simply to understand them." — Spinoza.

I

The theme of rationality and nonrationality is perhaps the most impalpable and diffuse of all the themes proposed for consideration in this book.[1] We are not dealing with one specific category of ideas, as determined by their content, but rather with one very important measure of the pitch and quality, the level and tone, of Russian thought in general, first *before* and then *after* the Revolution of 1917. The scale of measurement here proposed, for so wide and miscellaneous an application, is the scale of *rationality*. And what result may one hope to derive from the broad application of this very rough scale?

To put it very boldly, my own theses are: first, that in terms of rationality Russian thought was rather poorly developed before the Revolution; second, that the level of rationality prevailing in Soviet thought is likewise low; and, third, that the cause of today's low level is to be found *in part* in the underdevelopment of rationality in the years and even the centuries that stretch back through the prerevolutionary history of Russia. Stated in another form, the suggestion is that in terms of the development of systematic thinking, prerevolutionary Russia was intellectually somewhat immature, and that this condition *helps* to explain both the immaturity of the Bolshevik ideology and its success in winning a certain following in the Soviet Union.

Currently there is a great deal of talk about the prospects of Communist revolution in "advanced countries" and in "backward countries." These dis-

---

[1] This review refers to the five papers prepared for this session in the form in which they were circulated in advance of the conference. Because of subsequent revisions of these papers, the present review may not now be applicable to them at every point.

I am much indebted to Michael J. Petchkovsky for his assistance in the collection of materials for this paper.

cussions usually place the emphasis on economic, social, and political conditions, but if a backward intellectuality is also favorable to the rise of Soviet Communism, it is high time that we took some account of this circumstance in our attempts to assess the future.

It is my expectation that the three broad theses outlined above, respecting the general level of Russian intellectuality before and since the Revolution, will turn out to be highly provocative of both thought and feeling — even *too* provocative of the latter, I am afraid. But whether the discussion can lead us to any agreed conclusion is doubtful indeed.

The theme of rationality and nonrationality interpenetrates every other theme of this book, and touches every category of ideas already discussed herein, or still to be discussed, plus many other groups of ideas. In the present and past of Russia, materials for the papers of this section are heaped up in limitless profusion. It would of course be impossible to examine all the pertinent evidence here. The five set papers and the present brief review can bring together only a minute fraction of the relevant data, and must still leave us astronomically short of a coverage of the field. Is this undertaking, then, a piece of folly that should never have been attempted? Since the preliminary conference fifteen months ago, when I suggested the theme for this section, there have been times when I felt that this is so.

These qualms have not been due in any sense to the qualities of the papers that were prepared for this section, since each of these papers certainly makes an original contribution of value within its special field. What was and is in doubt is the possibility of establishing here, even tentatively, any kind of general conclusions respecting the level of rationality in Russia before the Revolution, the level since, and the relation or lack of relation between these earlier and later levels. A lifetime of research could hardly lay a really adequate foundation for such conclusions. It would be well to keep this grim fact in mind, as we proceed.

II

The history of Western Europe has been characterized by perennial intellectual ferment, rising and falling in intensity but almost never lapsing into inertia. Rarely in the West has either an institution of power, or a system of thought, been so secure in its position that it was free from intellectual challenge and therefore from the necessity for intellectual self-defense. When a conflict of arms arose, it was very often at the same time a conflict of ideas. In the West, some of the great formative conflicts of ideas plus force, or of ideas alone, were those of the Middle Ages between mysticism and scholastic learning in the Church, between Empire and Papacy, and between monarchy and nobility; later between clerical and secular thought in the Renaissance; between Catholicism and Protestantism in the Reformation; between national monarchy and the Church; between traditionalism and rationalism in the Enlightenment; between science and religion in the later age; and in various times and places between minorities with power and possessions and larger groups that demanded a share of one or both. It is worth emphasizing again that these Western conflicts involved on both sides an outpouring of intellectual activity which contributed richly to the growth in the West of systematic thought and intellectual maturity. This general thesis is damaged, but hardly destroyed, by the short-lived success of Fascism, and especially of Nazism — a system so irrational and so atypical of the later centuries of Western history.

Many of the historic conflicts of the West had a kind of physical parallel in Russian history, but only to a far more limited extent did they have an intellectual parallel there. This is broadly true of the relations of both the Russian Orthodox Church and the Russian autocracy with their enemies. In the course of the long conflict of the Russian monarchy with the great nobles, its rather secondary difficulties with the Church, and its great and finally disastrous struggles with various popular forces of revolt, the builders and defenders of the tsar's power never elaborated in its support a broad and systematic theory of autocracy. Ivan the Terrible vigorously asserted the principle of monarchy by divine right, but Peter the Great was little concerned with theory. Catherine II was so dissatisfied with any theoretical formulations that she could discover in Russia that she borrowed heavily from the West — and then repudiated her borrowings when the French Revolution showed where Western theories might lead. Alexander I also borrowed from the West, and then largely rejected what he had learned; and after that, the tsars were not even active borrowers, much less creative theorists.

Among the later theoreticians of autocracy, the most widely known is undoubtedly Konstantin Pobedonostsev, Over-Procurator of the Most Holy Synod from 1880 to 1905. His shortcomings as a systematic thinker have been made sufficiently clear in the paper presented by Professor Byrnes.

A contemporary of Pobedonostsev, B. N. Chicherin, has sometimes been called the father of Russian political science. In an extensive work, *Course in Political Science,* published in three large volumes in Moscow in the 1890's, he occasionally mentions a Western authority in this field, but rarely if ever cites any Russian author. In this work he presents a very brief but very intelligent analysis of the advantages and disadvantages of absolute monarchy.[2] On balance, his account is adverse to contemporary absolutism; but in this work (probably in deference to the Russian censorship) he himself does not draw a final balance, either favorable or unfavorable. However he does this with a will in another book, *Russia on the Eve of the Twentieth Century,* which he published abroad in 1900, under the pseudonym, "Russian

[2] B. N. Chicherin, *Kurs gosudarstvennoi nauki,* 3 vols. (Moscow, 1894–98), III, Book II, 126–134.

Patriot." Here he says that in Russia absolutism has outlived its earlier usefulness, and should certainly be replaced by limited monarchy;[3] the present policy, he says, will "lead inevitably to the intellectual and moral decline of society, and then to some sort of catastrophe . . ."[4] For those who would like to believe that the autocracy of the tsars had the support of a substantial body of systematic theory, there is little comfort to be found in the writings of the father of Russian political science.

Perhaps the most prolific of the late theoreticians of autocracy was L. A. Tikhomirov. He at least knew something at firsthand about the enemies of autocracy, since he was first numbered among them, and served for a time as a member of the executive committee of the terrorist "People's Will." Thereafter he became a collaborator of Katkov and other reactionaries, and from that time forward he was a very ardent supporter of all that he had once attacked.[5]

In his major four-part work, *The Monarchic State Principle*, published in 1905, Tikhomirov speaks of ". . . our inadequate success, for a period of two hundred years, in the achievement of political consciousness . . ." "In this period," he says, "it was in the field of political creativeness that Russia accomplished least of all . . . Russia discovered herself in the field of art — music, painting . . . But in the field of intellectual consciousness, up to this moment [1905] all our work is still concerned with the first rudiments."[6] Speaking still of the entire period since Peter, he says,

. . . the development of the monarchical principle was at a low ebb. As before, it was supported among us by the voice of instinct, but it was not clarified by reason. Thus among all the branches of scientific achievement, with us it was public law that, for the entire new period [since Peter] remained the least developed, the most imitative, the most permeated with simple copies of European ideas.[7]

". . . the monarchical idea was elucidated chiefly by publicists in conflict with their opponents, and not through strict scientific analysis."[8] ". . . our [science of] public law has done scarcely anything for the development of our monarchist consciousness . . ."[9]

All this was set down by an ardent defender of the Russian autocracy, in a long treatise that reviewed at some length the works that Katkov, I. S. Aksakov, Kireev, Leont'ev and various others had written in support of the emperor's power. With all this before him, Tikhomirov could still say in

---

[3] B. N. Chicherin, *Rossiia nakanune 20-go stoletiia* (3rd ed., Berlin, 1901), pp. 147–149. Editions 1–4 were published in Berlin, 1900–1901.

[4] *Ibid.*, p. 144.

[5] T. G. Masaryk, *Spirit of Russia*, 2 vols. (New York, 1919), II, 228.

[6] L. A. Tikhomirov, *Monarkhicheskaia gosudarstvennost'*, 4 vols. (Moscow, 1905), III, 118–119.

[7] *Ibid.*, p. 121.

[8] *Ibid.*, p. 124.

[9] *Ibid.*, p. 153.

1905 that in Russia the monarchical idea had not been subjected to "strict scientific analysis," and had not been "clarified by reason."

In 1913, eight years after the publication of Tikhomirov's major work, there appeared in Russia a volume of more than nine hundred pages called *The Power of the All-Russian Emperor*. The author was P. E. Kazanskii, again a strong partisan of the autocracy, and Dean of the Juridical Faculty at the University of New Russia (Odessa). This book makes a very thorough examination of Russian law within its field, and also reviews systematically the body of Russian writings in support of the autocratic system. Professor Kazanskii's conclusion is that in excellent studies of specific questions, "many *strong* foundations have already been laid for the determination of the essence" of the imperial power. "The next step is," he says, "to construct the theory of the Russian autocracy"[10] — a task which his book did not undertake to perform. The next step — and this was 1913!

Thus in the last prewar year of the tsardom, Kazanskii concludes, as Tikhomirov had done shortly before him, that at this late day a systematic theory of autocracy had not yet been developed in Russia. This was nearly one thousand years after the first major contacts of the Russians with the Byzantine autocracy, about three hundred and fifty years after the famous correspondence of Ivan the Terrible with Prince Kurbskii, three hundred years after the coronation of the first Romanov tsar — and only four years before the fall of the last one.

Tikhomirov and Kazanskii knew very well what had been written on their subject; they were not hostile to autocratic theory, but devoted contributors to it; if they had any bias, it was toward an overvaluation of the work of their fellow supporters of the tsar. Thus there seems to be no good reason to question their judgment or to dissent from their astonishing verdict.

It is too much to say that where general theory was concerned, the autocracy was a kind of gargantuan body without a mind — but the figure has some point, none the less.

III

In the intellectual history of Russian autocracy and Russian Orthodoxy, there are certain similarities. In the West, the relations between Popes and emperors, Church and state, involved on the side of the Church as well as of the state, a great outpouring of intellectual activity, from the Middle Ages onward. In Russia, the corresponding relations produced a far more limited intellectual harvest. In the West many men died but many ideas were born in the conflicts between Catholics and Protestants, while in Russia the relations between the Orthodox Church and the various schismatic and sectarian groups were far less bloody, but also far less productive in intellectual terms.

From first to last, the Russian Church placed more emphasis on mysti-

---

[10] P. E. Kazanskii, *Vlast' vserossiiskago imperatora* (Odessa, 1913), p. 39.

cism, and less on intellectualism, than either the Catholics or the major Protestant communions of the West. This is strikingly illustrated in the characteristics of the saints who lived in the West, and of those canonized in Russia. There is no thought of suggesting here that most Western saints were not only holy men but men of learning; yet a significant number of them had scholarly attainments. Among these may be listed St. Cyprian, St. Hilary, St. Ambrose, St. Jerome, St. Augustine, St. Gregory I, St. Anselm, St. Dominic, St. Bonaventure, and, of course, the greatest of all — "the Angelic Doctor," St. Thomas Aquinas.[11]

In the Russian Church, says Fedotov in *Saints of Old Russia,*

there was great respect for spiritual enlightenment on the part both of the saints and of their biographers. But only a few [saints] attained erudition — for example, Avramii Smolenskii, Stefan Permskii, Dionisii Troitskii; and still more rarely do we see among the Russian saints genuinely spiritual authors; actually we can name only two altogether: Iosif and Nil.[12]

The Russian Church inherited its store of doctrine from the writings of the Fathers of the Church and the decisions of the Ecumenical Councils, and thereafter it preserved this inheritance largely unchanged.[13] Father Florovsky says in his history of Russian theology that

after the fall of Byzantium, only the West occupied itself with theology. Theology is in its essence a catholic task [here he of course uses the word "catholic" in the sense of "universal"], but in the end it results only in schism; this is a basic paradox of the history of Christian culture. The West theologizes while the East remains quiet — or still worse, without thought, and after delay, repeats the Western movements. Even down to the present time [1937], the Orthodox theologian is, in his constructive work, too dependent upon the West. Specifically he receives his primary sources from Western hands, reads the Fathers and the works of the Church Councils in Western editions, and learns in a Western school the method and technique of dealing with the collected materials.[14]

From this and many other sources, one derives a strong impression that among the Orthodox clergy the life of the mind did not flourish with great vigor. Quite deliberately the Orthodox Church placed an overwhelming emphasis elsewhere — upon mystical religion.

In view of this history and tradition, it was hardly to be expected that the Russian Orthodox clergy in general would be deeply disturbed by the scien-

---

[11] Alban Butler, *Lives of the Fathers, Martyrs and other Principal Saints,* 3 vols. (London, 1926). Some of the figures mentioned in the present text are discussed in F. P. Cassidy, *Molders of the Medieval Mind* (St. Louis, 1944), pp. 99–158.

[12] G. P. Fedotov, *Sviatye drevnei Rusi (X–XVII st.)* (Paris, 1931), p. 249. Cf. E. Behr-Sigel, *Prière et sainteté dans l'église russe* (Paris, 1950), pp. 15–18, 128, 730 note 5, *et passim;* Ivan Kologrivov, *Essai sur la sainteté en Russie* (Bruges, 1953), pp. 442, 444–445, but see also p. 293.

[13] Paul Miliukov, *Outlines of Russian Culture,* 3 vols. in 1 (Philadelphia, 1948), I, 132–133.

[14] Georgii Florovskii, *Puti russkago bogosloviia* (Paris, 1937), p. 515.

tific discoveries of the nineteenth and twentieth centuries which caused such a profound upheaval of thought and feeling among both Catholic and Protestant clergy of the West.

In his paper Dr. Kline has made a fresh contribution to Western knowledge of the intellectual history of the Russian Church by surveying the articles on Darwinism which appeared in certain Russian theological journals between 1859, the date of publication of the *Origin of Species,* and the Revolution of 1917, and by showing that most of the criticisms in these articles were "scientifically justified, or at least intellectually respectable." Dr. Kline examined five major theological journals, and the total number of articles listed in his bibliography is twenty-two (some being in several parts). He believes that the Russian Church resisted Darwinism, and that its resistance was of a "comparatively dispassionate and 'rational' kind." In terms of their *quality,* the articles he cites do indeed appear to point in this direction.

On the other hand, the evidence before us will perhaps permit a very different conclusion. After the appearance of the *Origin of Species,* the Russians had to wait fourteen years for the publication of the first of these articles, and only four of the listed articles appeared during the first twenty-two years after the publication of Darwin's book. On a subject that produced a profound upheaval in the Western churches, these five leading ecclesiastical journals of Russia published, in the course of more than half a century, only some twenty-two articles of consequence, five of them by foreign authors, and none from the hand of members of the Russian priesthood.[15] It is not surprising, then, that among the Western developments that affected Russian theology, Father Florovsky's history nowhere mentions the new scientific discoveries of Darwin and his successors.[16] In all this, there is a suggestion that the response of the Russian clergy to Darwinism was long delayed; that they were not stirred to any major activity, rational or nonrational, by the issues that had been raised; and that their attention was in fact very largely occupied with other matters. A situation of this kind could have developed quite naturally out of the history and traditions of a mystical Church that had not customarily given great emphasis to problems of the mind.

In the nineteenth century, by far the most influential religious thinkers of Russia were not clerics but laymen. The Slavophile Aleksei Khomiakov (1804–60) is sometimes spoken of as "the father of lay theology in Russia." [17] Outstanding among the lay religious thinkers who came after him were Konstantin Leont'ev (1831–1891), who became a monk toward the end of his life; Vladimir Solov'ëv (1853–1900), about whom more will be said

---

[15] P. A. Svetlov, the author of one of these articles, published in 1887, entered the Orthodox priesthood at some subsequent date.

[16] See, for example, Florovskii, ref. 14, p. 512, where various other Western influences are mentioned.

[17] Miliukov, ref. 13, I, 141.

in a moment; Fëdor Dostoyevsky, Lev Tolstoy, and Nikolai Berdiaev (1874–1948). In the judgment of Khomiakov, one of the greatest weaknesses of the West was its intellectualism, its rationalism — not only among its agnostics, but within the Western churches both Catholic and Protestant. In emphasizing this distinction between Russia and the West, Khomiakov was speaking not only for himself but for many who came after him. Among the Russian lay prophets who have just been mentioned, there are many differences, but among the traits that they all have in common is a distrust of intellectuality. I shall try later to show that this is true even of Solov'ëv, especially in his final maturity. Tolstoy called for "Simplicity! Simplicity!" and went out to plow the fields with the peasants. Khomiakov and other lay theologians of Russia said that rationality played a smaller role in the Russian Church than in the churches of the West; and, when they said this, they were not pleading guilty to a fault but *speaking proudly of a cherished virtue.*

Clearly this was not fully representative of the attitude of Vladimir Solov'ëv in the period of his greatest productivity. His first work concluded with a statement of the need for "a universal synthesis of science, philosophy, and religion" which would restore "the complete inner unity of the intellectual world." [18]

Solov'ëv (1853–1900) is often called "the first Russian philosopher";[19] more guardedly he is described as "the first to create an original Russian system of philosophy," [20] or as the first "to mold . . . into an integrated system" the philosophical ideas that had already found expression in Russia.[21] But whichever of these descriptions may be the most accurate, it is in some way deeply characteristic of the course of Russian history that no such philosopher was born in that country until the middle of the nineteenth century. It is hardly necessary to labor just here any point of chronological comparison with the West.

The only other point that requires emphasis here is that in the working of Solov'ëv's mind, faith was of primary importance, and reason decidedly secondary. Father Florovsky's paper clearly indicates that this was so. In the words of Solov'ëv, both philosophy and science must devote themselves completely "to the attainment of the supreme and universal end of knowledge, which is *defined by theology.*" To the achievement of this universal synthesis in the service of religion, Solov'ëv devoted most of his life.[22]

In the fertility of his thought, Solov'ëv was a kind of volcanic genius, but when one samples his writings, without any pretense to exhaustive study,

---

[18] Quoted in V. V. Zenkovsky, *History of Russian Philosophy,* 2 vols. (New York, 1953), II, 487.

[19] See, for example, Masaryk, ref. 5, II, 224, quoting Lopatin.

[20] N. O. Lossky, *History of Russian Philosophy* (New York, 1951), p. 133.

[21] Zenkovsky, ref. 18, II, 469–472.

[22] *Ibid.,* II, 487, 489, 529.

areas are found that seem almost as chaotic as the deposit of a volcanic eruption. This is scarcely surprising, in view of experiences that recurred repeatedly to Solov'ëv throughout his life: He said that he regarded dreams as "a window, as it were, into the other world";[23] in waking moments, he sometimes sensed happenings at a distance;[24] in his later years Satan appeared before him repeatedly in various forms;[25] while in his youth he saw bright visions of Sophia, the Eternal Feminine, the World Soul.[26] The mystical concept of Sophia persists, in changing forms, throughout his life, and is perhaps the most baffling of all the major elements of his thought;[27] "he now speaks of Sophia as of a being eternally perfect and invariably obeying God's will, now as of the World Soul temporarily falling away from God and then reuniting with Him in the slow process of creating the 'absolute organism.' "[28] Sophia is the Wisdom of God, the Eternal Feminine, the Mother of God, the Humanity of Christ, the Soul of the World, the Church as the Bride of Christ.[29] Sophia is, Solov'ëv says, "both one and all," occupying "a mediating position between the plurality of living entities and the unconditional unity of Deity."[30]

In terms of some of the things that were omitted, as well as some that were included, Solov'ëv's work revealed certain shortcomings in rationality. He devoted his life to an attempt to synthesize science, philosophy, and religion, but a cursory examination of the ten volumes of his collected writings has brought to light only four brief references to Charles Darwin,[31] that particular scientist who had done most, during Solov'ëv's lifetime, to make his synthesis difficult. Still another thinker of the period was developing a far greater potential menace to the religious synthesis, but apparently Solov'ëv never once mentioned his name; this particular absentee is Karl Marx.

Great as was Solov'ëv's contribution to the history of Russian thought, the later years of his life found his own spirit still torn by that conflict which he had so long sought to heal for the help of mankind — the conflict between science and religion, between reason and faith, between critical rationalism and traditional mysticism.[32] Toward the end of his life "he experienced the reality and force of evil with special torment"; the devil appeared before him in different shapes, and in his final book he presented "the last act of the historical tragedy" of the race. Here in his "Tale of Anti-Christ," an evil

---

[23] Quoted in Lossky, ref. 20, p. 91.

[24] *Ibid.*

[25] *Ibid.*, pp. 91–92; Masaryk, ref. 5, II, 264.

[26] Lossky, ref. 20, pp. 83–84, 91.

[27] Zenkovsky, ref. 18, II, 478–480, 483.

[28] Lossky, ref. 20, p. 131.

[29] Masaryk, ref. 5, II, 246; Lossky, ref. 20, p. 83; Zenkovsky, ref. 18, II, 504, 509; P. P. Zouboff, *Vladimir Solovyev's Lectures on Godmanhood* (New York, 1944), p. 74.

[30] Quoted in Zenkovsky, ref. 18, II, 505.

[31] Vladimir Solov'ëv, *Sochineniia*, 10 vols. (St. Petersburg, Obshchestvennaia Pol'za, 1901–1903), III, 263–264; VII, 43, 44–47, 52.

[32] Masaryk, ref. 5, II, 282–285.

genius builds an earthly Utopia that is accepted by most of mankind, while the few men who remain faithful turn their backs upon the world and retire into the desert to await the second coming of the true Christ.[33] As Father Florovsky says, one should not expect to find philosophical precision in such a parable; yet in this withdrawal of the faithful from the world, one may see a representation of the final abandonment by Solov'ëv himself of his attempt to produce a synthesis of earth and heaven — his own final abandonment to antichrist of everything but mystical religion itself. With this surrender, the distinctive work of his life was at an end, and shortly after that he died — at the age of forty-seven. Someone has said that only a really great spirit can come to its end in a great tragedy.

In the period of his broadest attempts at synthesis, his greatest rationality, Solov'ëv had been deeply involved with the Roman Catholic Church, and Catholics claim that he renounced his own Church for theirs. The Orthodox maintain that he had merely acted on "the conviction that the Eastern and Western Churches, despite the outward breech, had not severed their mystical bond." If it is true that toward the end he was less the rationalist and more the mystic than ever before, there is a special appropriateness in the fact that in his last hours he made his confession and received the Sacraments of the Eastern, not the Western, Church.[34]

This was the Church whose reaction toward Darwinism Dr. Kline has studied. It was entirely appropriate that in doing this he should have drawn a comparison between the Russian Church and the "fundamentalists" of the West. But having done this much, one should surely do more. The West had its fundamentalist crusaders against science, but it also had other groups, both Catholic and Protestant, who have turned out by now to be far more influential. These were the priests, pastors, and laymen who labored arduously for decades in an attempt to produce some such synthesis of science and religion as Solov'ëv tried to achieve, and then abandoned, in Russia. There are many in the West who think that this attempt has there met with some success; but whether it has succeeded or failed is not to be argued here. The point is that these particular Western churchmen, generations of them, neither made a wholesale attack upon science, nor turned away from its problems toward another world. They made no apology for the intellectuality of the Western churches, but attempted instead to master the new situation intellectually (as well as spiritually); in making this effort, they helped in a major way to deepen and broaden the area of rational thinking in the Western lands.[35]

[33] Zenkovsky, ref. 18, II, 477, 526; Lossky, ref. 20, p. 84.
[34] Lossky, ref. 20, pp. 84–86; Zenkovsky, ref. 18, II, 477, 526.
[35] See, for example, on the Roman Catholic Church: E. Wasmann, "Evolution: Attitude of Catholics toward the Theory," *Catholic Encyclopaedia* (New York, 1941), V, 654; J. J. Walsh, *Catholic Churchmen in Science*, 1st series, 2nd ed., 1910, 2nd series, 1909, 3rd series, 1917. On the Anglican Church: Charles Gore, ed., *Lux Mundi*, 1889;

There are some who would say that only a deep mysticism can provide the final answer to the Communists. But others may hold that in going as far as it did in renouncing the world, the Russian Church may in some fashion have renounced it to Lenin.

IV

In an attempt to examine one specific characteristic of Russian thought before the Revolution — that is, its level of rationality — this review has considered, thus far, some of the thinking that gave support to two major Russian institutions, the autocracy and the Church. It now remains to give brief attention to those movements of Russian thought, much better known abroad, which were hostile both to Orthodoxy and to autocracy.

If it is argued that much of the radical Russian thinking of prerevolutionary days was not done by Russians in Russia but by Russians abroad, the answer is that most of the Russian *émigrés* of that period were well formed in the Russian setting before they went into exile; that they very often wrote for publication in Russia, or for publication abroad and illegal export to Russia; that they hoped to return to Russia; and that in the meantime their personal contacts were largely with Russians, and their thoughts were largely on Russia. In the less-censored or uncensored atmosphere abroad, they were still spiritually in Muscovy and their writings reveal those very characteristics that mark the parallel writings produced in Russia at the time. In those little *émigré* islands in the sea of Western Europe, the Russian police and the Russian censors were absent, but the Russian tradition was present always, and the character of the work produced there offered striking testimony to the power of that tradition.

It is hardly necessary to emphasize here the contrast in both attitude and achievement between the prerevolutionary emigration and the emigration that came after.

Omitting all discussion of developments before the middle of the nineteenth century, and beginning arbitrarily with the 1860's, one may distinguish three major trends of Russian nonmonarchist and nonclerical thought: the liberal, the *narodnik* (or peasantist), and the Marxist.

The liberal trend will not be treated here — for two reasons. First, whatever effect, under other circumstances, the liberal movement might eventually have had on the general character of Russian thought, the events of 1917, and particularly the elections to the Constitutional Assembly, seemed to show that liberalism was not by that time well rooted in Russia. Second, if the theses that have here been suggested respecting rationality are sound with reference to certain other major schools of Russian thought, this will

---

S. C. Carpenter, *Church and People, 1789–1889* (New York, 1933); and especially P. N. Waggett, "The Influence of Darwin upon Religious Thought," *Evolution in Modern Thought* (New York, Modern Library, n.d.), pp. 223–245.

perhaps suffice to establish for these theses a rough and general validity that will serve the purposes of this review.

However, the *narodnik* trend cannot be omitted from this discussion, for these or any other reasons. In the elections of 1917, the *narodnik* Party of Socialist Revolutionaries demonstrated that it had a following that was very numerous (though it was surely for the most part ill informed). A more compelling reason for discussing the *narodniki* here is that before the Revolution they were involved far more deeply than any other group in direct polemics with the Russian Marxists, and therefore had a specific and long-continuing opportunity, as critics, to raise the level of rationality in the Marxist thinking which they criticized.

Under these circumstances, the problem of the level of rationality in *narodnik* thought is one of first-class importance. It goes without saying that this level was affected by the general ideological climate in which *narodnichestvo* developed; but more specifically, the development of *narodnik* thinking was affected by two limitations, one deliberately self-imposed, the other quite unrecognized by the *narodniki* themselves.

The self-denying factor appeared most clearly in the "Going-to-the-People" — the movement that took *narodnik* intellectuals to the village, not so much to teach and lead the peasants, as to learn from them. This veneration for the wisdom of the peasantry runs throughout the *narodnik* movement from end to end, and without any doubt it imposed a greater self-limitation on the rational processes of the *narodnik* leaders than is involved in the Western democratic procedure of formulating policies at the center, and then putting them to the test of a popular vote.

The other limitation on the rationality of *narodnichestvo* is not so easily identified and demonstrated, and there may be some who will deny its presence. The matter may be put very briefly by saying that by and large the *narodnik* writings seem usually to reveal a great and persuasive warmth of heart, but at the same time a certain lack of intellectual firmness and maturity.

Chernyshevskii seems to fall, in the main, within the *narodnik* line of descent; yet his work reveals unresolved conflicts that have led the *narodniki* and the Marxists to quarrel interminably over the relics of this revolutionary saint. At times one finds him talking of laws of historical development that would require any given society to attain a full maturity of capitalism, before it could pass to socialism. At other times he says that men could have averted the capitalist stage in Western Europe and America, and can still do so in Russia if only they have the knowledge, the virtue, and the will to take free and conscious control of their own history. The second of these positions seems to be supported by the prevailing mood of Chernyshevskii's work, but the obscurities and contradictions remain. He wanted to be an economist and a philosopher of history, but he had no great success as a systematic thinker. Yet in spite of this shortcoming he still became one of the chief contributors to *narodnik* thought.

The most influential *narodnik* of the twentieth century was Victor Chernov. As both the active leader and the chief theoretician of the Socialist Revolutionaries in this period, he was, in his own camp, the opposite number to Lenin among the Bolsheviks. Yet his theoretical work is often obscure and almost always derivative, and his acceptance by the last *narodnik* group as their principal contemporary theoretician supplies a kind of index of the intellectual status of their movement in the later prerevolutionary years.

There are, of course, many fields of thought to which no attention has been given here. For example, authoritative judgments might be quoted respecting the notable achievements of Russians in mathematics and in the physical sciences. However, if this were done it would be necessary also to introduce judgments respecting the corresponding achievements of the West in these same fields. It seems unlikely that this double extension of evidence would reverse the balance and vitiate the rough and tentative comparison that has already been drawn here between prerevolutionary Russia and the West.

v

It is suggested in this paper that in terms of rationality Russian thought was somewhat underdeveloped before the Revolution. If this is true, then Russia did not provide, specifically, an intellectual climate favorable to the development and maintenance of a high level of rationality in Bolshevik thinking. The Russia of the later prerevolutionary years furnished neither competitive stimulus nor corrective criticism of a quality fully conducive to that end. For example, a few hours with the theoretical writings of Lenin's chief *narodnik* opponent, Victor Chernov, will convince anyone that he was hardly the critic to enforce upon Lenin a high standard of clarity and consistency.

In the planning stage of this section it was hoped that the names of Marx and Engels could be omitted from our proceedings, and that in the field of Marxist thought this section could concentrate on certain aspects of Lenin's thinking before the Revolution, and on certain aspects of Soviet-Communist thought since the Second World War. However, in the paper of Dr. Gurian, and especially in that of Dr. Marcuse, a good deal of time is devoted to pre-Leninist Marxism; hence it seems that we ought now to follow these papers into that obscure ideological forest.

One of the handicaps encountered in studying the writings of Marx, Engels, Lenin, and Stalin is the extreme difficulty of sampling. In any coherent and rational pattern of thought, the parts are, of course, consistent one with another; yet on many major questions it is possible to quote each member of the Marxist pantheon in opposition to himself. For example, it is rarely possible to say simply that on any given point of consequence, at a given time, Lenin thought so-and-so; on the point in question, major variants or outright contradictions can very often be quoted from Lenin himself. Usually the very best that one may hope for, in this general field, is to determine where the *major emphasis* lies — and often it is impossible to do even this beyond dispute. If students of the Communist classics contradict one another, it is very often because the authors of the classics contradict themselves. It is not difficult to see the bearing of all this on our problem of the level of rationality in Soviet-Communist thought.

Dr. Gurian's paper offers useful insights into the relations between "Party-ism" (*partiinost'*) and knowledge, and between theory and practice, in the works of Marx, in the prerevolutionary writings of Lenin, and in Soviet-Communist theory since the Revolution. In all this, Dr. Gurian quite properly gives major emphasis to the role, not of the proletariat as a class, or even of the limited Party as a whole, but of a still smaller and much more powerful group — the *leaders* of the Party. On the other hand, Dr. Gurian's paper perhaps somewhat exaggerates the difference between the ideological position of Lenin before the Revolution and the pattern of Soviet-Communist thinking in subsequent years. Again, his paper does not attempt any specific assessment of the degree of rationality revealed in the theories that it examines.

If I understand Dr. Marcuse correctly, he believes that the pre-Soviet Marxist philosophy did not provide a universal world-outlook fully embracing both man and nature; for Marx, he says, "dialectical materialism was throughout historical materialism." It is of course true that Marx occupied himself very largely with the data and philosophy of history, in the broadest sense of that term. Yet Engels discussed problems of science with Marx for many years, and wrote all or most of his *Dialectics of Nature* during Marx's lifetime.[36] Another book, the *Anti-Dühring*, a major work applying dialectical materialism broadly to both man and nature, was published in 1878, five years before the death of Marx. Engels was of course the principal author of this work, but Marx wrote one of the chapters in the section on Political Economy, and in the preface to the second edition (1885), Engels said:

. . . inasmuch as the genesis and development of the mode of outlook expounded in this book were due in far greater measure to Marx, and in only a very small degree to myself, it was of course self-understood between us that this exposition of mine should not be issued without his knowledge. I read the whole manuscript to him before it was printed . . . we had always been accustomed to help each other out in special subjects . . . Marx and I were pretty well the only people to rescue conscious dialectics from German idealistic philosophy and apply it in the materialist conception of nature and history.[37]

[36] Friedrich Engels, *Dialectics of Nature* (New York, 1940), preface, pp. viii–ix.
[37] Friedrich Engels, *Herr Eugen Dühring's Revolution in Science* (New York, 1939), pp. 15, 17. This book is commonly spoken of as Engels' *Anti-Dühring*.

On the evidence quoted, as well as for reasons of logic, it is difficult to believe that Marx failed to include in his materialist philosophy the material universe within which history is unfolded. If one speaks not only of Marx but also of his fellow "Marxist" Engels, the case is of course indubitable.

However, if Dr. Marcuse wishes to say simply that Bolshevik theoreticians have in general given more emphasis to the dialectics of *nature* than did any significant earlier group of Marxists elsewhere, he is almost certainly correct. This change on the part of the Russians is in harmony with another much more complex shift of emphasis that the Bolsheviks have developed in the area of a problem long dear to philosophers — the problem of necessity and freedom, determinism and indeterminism.

The thought of Marx and Engels is dominated by a system of determinism, for nature and for history. Through the inexorable operation of class conflict, the successive stages of history follow one upon another: primitive-communal, slave, feudal, capitalist, socialist. For the rise and fall of the capitalist stage in each society, the chain of "inexorabilities" is set out in considerable detail: in a given society, capitalism will attain a full development before its end; in so doing, it will turn the masses of the population into proletarians, and subject them to formative experience in large-scale enterprise; out of their proletarian experience (their hardships, and their labor discipline), the proletarian masses will develop the class-conscious will and ability to destroy their masters and, in the course of a transitional period, to build a socialist society. When socialism is achieved, freedom and abundance for all will be achieved with it; Marx and Engels say, ". . . we shall have an association in which the free development of each is the condition for the free development of all." [38] That is, at a particular time and with respect to a particular fraction of the cosmos, the universal dialectic of contradiction and conflict will be tamed; still ruling elsewhere as before, the dialectic will *be ruled* here by society as a whole; determinism, still flourishing beyond the socialist frontiers, will here have abolished itself permanently. To some, this of course seems a promise of a miracle — and far from congruent with Marx's general scheme of things.

Such, in briefest outline, is the dominant system of Marx and Engels, though noncongruent ideas of indeterminism sometimes intrude into their discussions of the presocialist stages of history.

Dr. Marcuse thinks that, in the main, Soviet-Communist theory has followed a course consistent with Marx; in spite of some persistence of ideas about "objective determinism" that are not effectively coördinated with the main trend of Soviet thought, the increasing concern of most Soviet ideologists is, Dr. Marcuse believes, to emphasize that the contradictions of their "socialist" society are "nonantagonistic" in character and "are susceptible to gradual solution through 'scientific' social and political control"; and

[38] Karl Marx and Friedrich Engels, *Communist Manifesto* (New York, 1948), p. 31.

there are signs, Dr. Marcuse says, that they are preparing the way ideologically for a "nonexplosive" transition to "the second phase of socialism," or Communism proper.

If this means that in recent ideological developments in the Soviet Union, there is some half-convincing promise of that socialist freedom for all which was promised (unconvincingly) by Marx and Engels, I am bound to say that I do not see important evidence of this development. I believe the general trend of Bolshevik thought has run for a long time in the opposite direction, toward more and more authoritarianism, and I see no good reason to expect a change in this trend.

Dr. Marcuse mentions, without much stress, two points that seem to me to be of *outstanding* importance: he says that the indeterminacy supposedly characteristic of a socialist society is claimed by Soviet ideologists for a Soviet society that is not actually socialist, and he also says that "strong and constant emphasis is placed on the guiding role of the state and of the Communist Party and its leadership, which holds the monopoly of interpreting and formulating the dialectical laws . . ."

These two statements do not represent, I believe, a recent innovation in Bolshevik thinking. Rather, they represent the results of a change of emphasis that was initiated long before the Revolution by Lenin — the most important departure of Bolshevism from classical Marxism, and one of the most important ideological developments known to history. *This was the shift of revolutionary emphasis from the deterministic thought and action of the proletariat to the free thought and action of the leadership.*

There is evidence that about the beginning of the century Lenin began to be tormented by two ideas: first, if the masses in backward Russia must pass *through* capitalism *to* socialism, then Russia would have to wait a very long time for the revolution; second (and this was much more serious), perhaps mass proletarian experience would not in itself produce the desired revolution — in Russia or anywhere else; certainly it had not yet done so, even in the most advanced countries of the West where proletarian experience was most widespread.

In this situation, was Lenin to give up the deterministic theory, or was he to give up the revolution? On the level of theory, he never made a really clear-cut decision. He went on making statements about the inevitability of the revolution, but with greater emphasis he began to assert another conflicting theory of history; and he never brought these two theories into one coherent pattern. He began to deny the creation by proletarian experience of the attitude that had been declared to be the indispensable prerequisite of class revolution. For example, he said that to accept passively the limits of proletarian spontaneity *"is tantamount to the abandonment of socialism"* (the italics are Lenin's).[39] And again, "Social Democracy . . . does not

[39] V. I. Lenin, *What Is to Be Done?*, first pub. 1902, *Selected Works*, 12 vols. (New York, 1943), II, 63.

soothe itself by arguments about . . . concrete conditions fatalistically impelling the labor movement onto the path of revolution." [40] He thought that the proletarians might accept *either* socialist leadership *or* bourgeois leadership; if left to themselves, they would turn to the latter.[41] If this all-important choice stood open, what had happened to determinism? What had happened to the inexorable laws of social development? What had happened to the inevitability of the revolution?

What Lenin really tried to do, in the long run, was to preserve the system of determinism, where he thought it would serve the cause of the revolution, and to replace determinism with voluntarism, where he believed that *that* would serve the revolution. Eventually he elaborated at considerable length a *deterministic* theory of the *self-destruction* of capitalism. But more and more he emphasized a *voluntarist* theory of the *self-initiation* and *self-construction* of socialism. In Leninist thought, the deterministic aspect of the revolutionary movement was much reduced, and the area of free decision much expanded, *long before* the Russian Revolution itself took place; but in Lenin's scheme of things it was the revolutionary leaders, and not the revolutionary masses, who were to take up the function of decision-making *before* the revolution, and it is the leaders who have continued to exercise this function ever since.

It is of supreme importance for both theory and practice that Lenin's shift of emphasis from determinism to indeterminism, and from proletariat to elite, was initiated *long before* the Russian Revolution. More than anything else, this gave the Bolsheviks the audacity to seize power in backward Russia in 1917 (as the more deterministic Mensheviks would never have dreamed of trying to do); and it nerved the Bolsheviks to fight for the retention of power after they had seized it, and to launch a program of "building socialism" from the top down in their largely peasant country. The Leninist emphasis in the prerevolutionary period was the ideological ancestor of the concept of "socialism in one [backward] country" and of the five-year plans. As this Leninist emphasis matured in the experience of the Russian Revolution, it supplied the Soviet Communists with a revolutionary ideology and a revolutionary technique that could be exported to almost any country with some hope of success, especially if the export could be offered on the long arm of Soviet military force. In advanced, industrialized, democratic countries, the Bolshevik methods of dictatorship and conspiracy could be applied within the very proletariat that had once been counted on to generate the revolution spontaneously. In a backward nonindustrial country, the Communist leaders could hope to exploit any sort of local discontent in order to establish their dictatorship, and could then proceed from above with the dictated construction of socialism in an area that had scarcely yet heard of capitalism.

[40] *Ibid.,* p. 114.
[41] *Ibid.,* pp. 61, 62, 64, 112.

Inasmuch as the Bolsheviks had breached the determinist system in their own country, in order to make there a revolution that was in Marxist terms startlingly premature, they were in a particularly good position to urge other backward societies to do the same. Both in its birth and in its long-term development toward socialism, the revolution, and particularly the "premature" revolution, would require (in Russia and elsewhere) highly expert surgery and after-care — always to be provided, of course, by the Communist dictators.

VI

The Soviet Communists maintain constantly in full view, and in high-speed operation, a vast display of the trappings and processes of rational thinking. Yet sometimes one is tempted to say that in their handling of this or that problem of the highest order, there is no rationality whatever behind all this external show. In this or that instance, is there really evidence of a search for truth, or only of an arbitrary process of decision by ukase?

It is highly significant that such a thought can arise abroad — and not infrequently. However, it is irrational and dangerous on our own part to emphasize too strongly the nonrational aspects of Bolshevik thinking. It has to be remembered that, if the Soviet leaders did not maintain some substantial contact with reality, they would have destroyed themselves long ago. But just what kind of contact they do maintain continues to be one of the world's most baffling problems.

This problem in one of its most acute forms is posed very lucidly and forcefully in Professor Dobzhansky's paper. In some sense the Bolshevik leaders were acting in harmony with the general long-term trend of Bolshevik ideology when they suppressed genetics, and adopted and promoted Lysenkoism. For half a century, Bolshevik ideology has been emphasizing increasingly the rolling back of the frontiers of determinism, and the corresponding expansion of the frontiers of control by Communist leadership. Science has been moving into the captured territory, but of course under the tightening command of the dictators. The Lysenkoite policy *promised* to give the dictatorship a firmer control over the scientists working in a very important field, as well as a rapid improvement in the output of agriculture and animal husbandry (with all the added power that that would imply). Also, it may not be too fanciful to imagine that Stalin, who was accustomed to give orders in so many other spheres, may have been attracted in a special way by a promise of increasing his personal command over the very processes of life itself.

Professor Dobzhansky shows that the scientific fallaciousness of Lysenkoism is well established. But are we sure that the system has caused a considerable economic loss in the Soviet Union? If Lysenkoism has really intensified the already serious difficulties in the tightest major sector of the Soviet economy, then no argument available to us appears to offer an adequate explanation, in terms of Bolshevik thinking, of their long support of Lysenko's system. Their behavior in this matter is the kind of thing that causes some people to ask — probably much too hopefully — whether Bolshevik irrationality cannot go to the lengths of self-destruction.

The design of Bolshevik thought is certainly not now in the finished state of the central prototype that was left behind by Marx and Engels. These two constructed for themselves a mansion of determinism — which, however, they flanked incongruously with a detached outhouse of free will. In Bolshevik thought the reversal of the central emphasis, from determinism to indeterminism, is plain enough; the outhouse has become the mansion.

But Bolshevik ideas on freedom (for the leadership) are by no means so systematic as was Marx's thinking on necessity; such fateful words as "inevitable" turn up in the most unlikely places; and the basic contradiction in Communist philosophy — the contradiction between determinism and indeterminism, necessity and freedom — is not only unresolved but in the main unrecognized. In Soviet Communism there is an inherited strain of bad thinking that could hardly be so strong today if the intellectual atmosphere of Russia had been more rational when the Old Bolsheviks were young.

In the fashion of their own murky illogic, the Communist rulers rule. As the self-chosen representatives of science, they dictate to the scientists; as the self-chosen representatives of proletarianism, they dictate to the proletariat; as the self-chosen representatives of "Party-ism," they even dictate to the Party. This is the land where theory and practice, philosophy and power, are united — the land of the perfect union of the Communist Church and the Communist State in the Communist Dictatorship.

This review opened with the statement of three theses: first, that in terms of rationality Russian thought was rather poorly developed before the Revolution; second, that the level of rationality prevailing in Soviet-Communist thought is likewise low; and third, that the cause of today's low level is to be found *in part* in the underdevelopment of rationality in prerevolutionary Russia. These theses have an all-too-positive ring, but they are to be regarded, nevertheless, as only preliminary and suggestive. The emphasis throughout this tentative review has been on a certain apparent degree of continuity between past and present. But the problem of rationality and non-rationality in Russian and Soviet thought is so broad, so amorphous, and at the same time so novel that no one would be bold enough to claim that here and now an accurate balance can be struck between continuity and change.

PART V
LITERATURE, STATE, AND SOCIETY

Social and Aesthetic Values in Russian Nineteenth-Century Literary Criticism (Belinskii, Chernyshevskii, Dobroliubov, Pisarev)

RENÉ WELLEK

I

Russian literary criticism has a special appeal for the student of criticism outside as well as inside Russia and independent of the light it may throw on Russian literature itself. More sharply than anywhere else in the West, Russian criticism has elaborated three clearly defined positions. One seeks the essence of literature in its philosophical ideas, a point of view which has found its fullest statement in the writings of a number of critics concerned mostly with the interpretation of Dostoyevsky. The names of Rozanov, Merezhkovskii, Shestov, Viacheslav Ivanov, and Berdiaev come to mind. Obviously, this attitude grew out of the Russian symbolist movement; and ultimately Vladimir Solov'ëv and Dostoyevsky himself are its inspirers. The second position, taken with radical consistency, is that of Formalism, upheld by a whole school of brilliant students of literature (Eikhenbaum, Shklovskii, Tomashevskii, Tynianov, Victor Vinogradov, Zhirmunskii, etc.) who began to write around 1913, and managed to flourish and survive the rigors of the Revolution until they were suppressed in the late twenties. The Formalists can look to the great nineteenth-century comparatist, Alexander Veselovskii, and to the linguist Potebnia as their forerunners in Russia. The third position, the sociological view of literature, has, in its Marxist version, become the official Soviet creed and is thus today felt as peculiarly representative of Russian criticism. As our general topic is "Continuity and Change in Russian and Soviet Thought," we shall commit the glaring injustice of ignoring both the philosophical and formalist movements that sprang up in Russia before the Revolution and shall focus on the ancestors of Marxist criticism, or rather on the critics who today in Russia are glorified and studied as the precursors of Marxist criticism: Belinskii, whose writings date from 1834 to 1847, Chernyshevskii, Dobroliubov, and Pisarev whose critical activities extend from about 1853 to 1868. We shall thus get nowhere near

the Revolution of 1917 and shall leave about fifty years (1868–1918) completely untouched. We shall ignore the many critics, even of the early period
under discussion, who do not fit into this pedigree of sociological criticism:
for example, Apollon Grigor'ev, who seems to me in many ways a more
distinguished critic than some we shall discuss in detail.

Space is limited and we must concentrate on one question: the relation
of social and aesthetic values as conceived of by the four critics selected.
Still, we cannot discuss the question in complete isolation; one must see it as
part of a conception of literature, of the course of history, of the task of criticism.

II

Belinskii, on questions of theory, must be considered as a follower of
German romantic criticism, of the whole body of aesthetic thought elaborated
by Herder, Goethe, Schiller, the Schlegels, Schelling, and Hegel. One cannot,
however, make Belinskii an adherent of any single one of these authors. He
was never a Hegelian, in a strict sense, in aesthetics, as he does not share
Hegel's view of the imminent demise of art and has no sympathy for his
nostalgic exaltation of the Greeks and of Greek sculpture as the highest
summit of art. One cannot distinguish neat periods in Belinskii's critical
thought: there was no definitely Fichtean, Schellingian, Hegelian, or Feuerbachian period in his criticism. From the beginning of his writing, starting
with the "Literary Reveries" (1834) to the last annual survey of Russian
literature, that of 1847, Belinskii uses the same categories, concepts, and
procedures, the same basic theoretical idiom, whatever his shifting philosophical opinions or whatever his political convictions. Only in the last five
years of his life can one discern a definite change. And even this change
occurs in the same tradition and runs exactly parallel to the change which
the followers of German speculative thought went through both in Germany
and in other countries. Belinskii's evolution is, in this respect, roughly similar
to that of Arnold Ruge, De Sanctis, Carlyle, or even Taine, who all absorbed
the German conceptions and later modified them in favor of what they considered a closer approach to empirical reality, to facts, to science, to national
and social needs of the time. I cannot see on what grounds Belinskii, at least
in his critical thought, can be described as a "materialist" or even "realist"
in the sense in which the French began to use this term as a literary slogan
after 1857.

Belinskii begins his career by proclaiming literature to be the "expression
of the national spirit, the symbol of the inner life of a nation, the physiognomy of a nation." [1] This is, of course, a concept imported from Germany;
Friedrich Schlegel's *History of Ancient and Modern Literature,* owned and
annotated by Belinskii in Russian translation, opens with a similar declara-

---

[1] *Sobranie sochinenii,* ed. F. M. Golovenchenko (Moscow, 1948), I, 16, 22–23.

tion.[2] The point of Belinskii's "Literary Reveries" is, however, a negative one: the Russians hitherto do not have a literature which truly expresses the national spirit. Belinskii severely criticizes the aristocratic "artificial" literature of the eighteenth century and also refuses to recognize Russian folk literature as truly expressive of a national spirit. He felt strongly its involvement in a serf civilization from which he wanted Russia to emerge into the light of freedom. Thus he argues against two things: the bookish derivative literature of the eighteenth century, and the popular folklore and local color nationalism of the Russian romanticists. His own ideal of literature, from the very beginning of his writings, is suggested by the terms national, genuine, natural, real. But what is meant by "naturalness" and "reality"? Surely not anything, at least in these early writings, which even remotely resembles later nineteenth-century realism. By "real" poetry, Belinskii means Shakespeare and Scott. Shakespeare, he says, "reconciled poetry with real life," and Scott, "the second Shakespeare, achieved the union with life." [3] Truth and reality mean essential truth, inner reality, the truth of imagination. Belinskii sets no limits to the poet's themes and devices: he admires Shakespeare's *Tempest,* is in raptures over the dream in Gogol's "Nevskii Prospect," and praises Gogol's "Old World Landowners" for "not being copied from reality, but achieved by feeling in the moment of poetic discovery." [4] Belinskii exalts the "objective" poet, Shakespeare or Goethe, who reproduces and mirrors the universe in its totality, whose method of creation is "visionary, even somnambulistic." [5] About 1840, Belinskii reached the stage of complete identification with the German theories. "The contents of art," he asserts, "are not the problems of the day, but those of the ages, not the interests of a country, but of the world, not the fate of parties, but of mankind." [6] Art, one hears, should serve society. "If you like, it does so by expressing its self-knowledge, but it exists for itself, has an aim in itself." [7] Art serves society by serving itself. Art purifies reality.[8] Reality, often dark and ugly, is illuminated and harmonized in the poet's vision. Naturalism is expressly disparaged. "One can naturally describe a drinking party, an execution, the death of a drunkard who fell into a cesspool, but such descriptions lack a rational idea and aim." [9] Only "rational reality" exists for the artist: he transforms ordinary reality by his ideals. Poetry, Belinskii declaims rapturously, is the quintessence of life, the poet is the organ of universal life, lives in everything, becomes everything. It is ludicrous to ask him to serve current needs. He does not imitate nature but rather competes with her. Art

[2] *Literaturnoe nasledstvo* (1948), LV, 512–513.

[3] *Sobranie sochinenii,* I, 107–108.

[4] *Ibid.,* pp. 135, 141–142.

[5] *Ibid.,* pp. 107, 111, 127, 129.

[6] *Ibid.,* p. 431.

[7] *Ibid.,* pp. 430–431.

[8] *Ibid.,* pp. 437, 641.

[9] *Ibid.,* pp. 631, 643.

is higher than nature.[10] One could hardly wish for a more complete repertory of German romantic phrases with a definite touch of Schelling at a time when Belinskii is supposed to have been in his Hegelian period.

But in this same article, the one on Lermontov's *Poems* (1841), Belinskii begins to expound views which proved ultimately destructive of this position. He declares what would have been acceptable as such to any of these Germans: "The greater the poet, the more he belongs to the community in which he was born, the closer is the development, tendency, and character of his talent tied up with the historical evolution of society." [11] But this evolution is now conceived as a progress toward reflection and subjectivity. The assumption is made (though never argued) that the progress of society and literature must be toward reflection and subjectivity, contemporaneity and immediate relevance. Belinskii recants his earlier praise of Goethe, deploring now his lack of historical and social pathos, his satisfied acceptance of reality.[12] Subjectivity and contemporaneity are now accepted, at least as a historical necessity. Somewhat tortuously, all these arguments are put forward to justify Lermontov's poetry of despair and revolt.

Shortly afterwards, in 1842, Belinskii still tried to reconcile the objective idealism of the Germans with the historical relativism, the belief in contemporaneousness and progress, which he began to hold side by side. Art is concerned with the eternal truths of existence, while subject to the process of historical evolution. In criticism there is first an aesthetic judgment which decides whether a work of art is worthy of the attention of historical investigation. Belinskii sees no conflict between historical and aesthetic criticism: each requires the other, and cannot exist without the other. Neither does he see any conflict between aesthetic and social demands on a writer. He declares somewhat blandly, that it is easy to reconcile art with service to the community. The poet must be a citizen, a child of his society and age; he must adopt its interests, fuse his desires with those of his society.[13] The serious conflicts between society and art of the following hundred years are not even seen as a possibility.

In 1843, however, Belinskii embraced the *mystique* of time and progress completely. He still agrees that the aim of criticism is to distinguish between the temporal and the eternal, the historical and the artistic, but he now assigns this task neither to the critic nor to aesthetics, but to the "historical movement of society itself." [14] This view is used to buttress the main conclusion of his long series of articles on Pushkin: Pushkin belongs to a bygone and superseded stage of Russian literature and society while Lermontov satis-

---

[10] *Ibid.*, pp. 643–644, 649.
[11] *Ibid.*, p. 653.
[12] *Ibid.*, p. 670.
[13] *Ibid.*, II, 357, 361, 363.
[14] *Ibid.*, III, 174.

fies a new and superior time.[15] The assumption has become that of an automatic fateful progress, a higher and higher rising of the wave of the future. Even critical opinion can form itself only by time and from time. Responsibility for art is shifted to society. The materials ready-made for the poet's use by society have become the determinant of his work. Rather naïvely, Belinskii declaims about the happy Greeks who saw beautiful men in the streets at every step and the Italians of the Middle Ages, who had Madonna-like women as models for their paintings. Pushkin, he analogizes, "appeared in a time when it was for the first time possible to have poetry in Russia." [16] This type of pronouncement may seem merely a comfortable hindsight, an irrefutable but meaningless assertion that things could not have been different. But it also implies not only a trust in the stream of history, but a praise of Russian life and its awakening toward freedom.

The last two annual surveys of Russian literature, those for 1846 and 1847, formulate Belinskii's final position most memorably. He now has come to emphasize standards of naturalistic lifelikeness. He definitely rejects the fantastic as an artistic device when he criticizes Dostoyevsky's "The Double." "It can have its place only in lunatic asylums, not in literature. It is the business of doctors and not of poets." [17] Belinskii even goes so far as to demand the "closest possible resemblance of the persons described to their models in real life." [18] Gogol is praised for concentrating his attention on the crowd, the mass, the ordinary people.[19] The inundation of literature by peasant types is defended: literature, he now argues, "facilitated the appearance in society of this movement (in favor of the serfs) rather than merely reflected it. Literature anticipated it rather than merely succeeded in keeping abreast of it." [20] Belinskii seems to give up his former view of literature as a reflection of society which it can never transcend or outstrip. He seems to assign it a role of leadership, even of anticipatory divination. The strength of modern art, he finds, is "in nobly undertaking to serve the interests of society." [21] Again and again Belinskii asserts his confidence in progress: "one can only go forward, never back." [22]

We can understand how these last pronouncements have largely determined the image of Belinskii in the eyes of posterity. Soviet criticism and the whole tradition of radical thought since Chernyshevskii find here the earliest local justification of their general point of view. But the image is a grossly simplified one. It ignores the bulk of Belinskii's earlier writings and it ignores

[15] *Ibid.*, p. 178.
[16] *Ibid.*, p. 337.
[17] *Ibid.*, p. 674.
[18] *Ibid.*, p. 783.
[19] *Ibid.*, p. 781.
[20] *Ibid.*, pp. 788–789.
[21] *Ibid.*, p. 797.
[22] *Ibid.*, pp. 677, 767.

the many reservations even in these last two articles. Belinskii did not become simply the propounder of a realistic art which is to serve a specific social and didactic purpose. In his attack on the doctrine of art for art's sake, Belinskii recognizes that "art must be first art and only afterwards can it be the expression of the spirit and drift of the society of a given age." [23]

He rejects what seems to him both bad extremes: art for art's sake and didacticism. He argues that pure art is a dreamy abstraction which has never existed anywhere. "To deny art the right of serving public interests means debasing it, not raising it, for that would mean depriving it of its most vital force, that is, the Idea, and would make it an object of sybaritic pleasure, a plaything of lazy idlers." [24] Belinskii, one sees, does not attack the autonomy of art as understood by Kant and Schiller, who would never have doubted its great role in world history and would never have thought of it as sensual pleasure. What Belinskii is arguing against is rather a purely ornamental hedonistic view of art. He disapproved also of didacticism. It is cold, dry, and dead. "With whatever beautiful ideas a poem is filled and however much it deals with contemporary problems, if it has no poetry in it, it can neither contain beautiful ideas nor any problems." [25] Even in the very last article, Belinskii emphasizes the difference between art and science or philosophy. The poet speaks in images and pictures, shows things and does not prove them. Belinskii by no means thinks of "naturalism" merely in terms of accuracy and even of insight into social realities. He sees that, in a work of art, "reality must have passed through imagination," that imagination must create "something whole, complete, unified, and self-contained." [26] We must always keep in mind the fact that Belinskii precedes the victory of nineteenth-century realism and naturalism. What he is arguing against is pseudoclassicism, still a force in Russia, and romanticism, which Belinskii thinks of as conservative medievalism and folklore worship, or as fantastic and gruesome claptrap. Within the fold of "realism" he includes writers as diverse in their procedures and techniques as Shakespeare, Scott, Cooper, George Sand, and Dickens abroad. In Russia the "natural" school means Gogol and any writer who seems to Belinskii to have created something substantial, "real," natural. He praises the rather humble beginnings of local-color realism, in sketches of Petersburg and peasant stories, and is interested in novels which raise and debate social questions. But he does not lose his critical sense. Thus Herzen's *Who Is to Blame?*, a book which appealed to his ideology very strongly, is still said not to be a work of art, not a real novel but rather a document.[27] One usually hears of Belinskii's

[23] *Ibid.*, p. 791.
[24] *Ibid.*, p. 797.
[25] *Ibid.*, p. 789.
[26] *Ibid.*, p. 790.
[27] *Ibid.*, p. 809.

rejection of Pushkin's fairy tales and Dostoyevsky's "The Double" as instances of his prejudice against nonrealistic art, but one should remember that he also praised *The Bronze Horseman, The Stone Guest,* and even *Rusalka,* almost unreservedly, and that his objections to "The Double" are not merely those of realism. He criticized "The Double," not unreasonably after all, for Dostoyevsky's inability to master the overflow of his great powers, to define and limit the artistic development of his conception.[28]

Belinskii, we must conclude, was a critic steeped in the views of the German theorists and firm in his hold on their central doctrine: art is concrete, sensuous knowledge; a work of art is an organic whole; the artist is the unconscious creator of a world of imagination on the analogy of nature. Art is the expression of a nation and age, is "characteristic" of that nation and age and should be so. In the last years of his life, however, Belinskii experienced a change: it was undoubtedly caused by his turn toward political radicalism; it may have had something to do with a religious crisis. It is closely parallel to the development of many of his contemporaries, especially the Young Hegelians. With them, just as with Belinskii, the "spirit" of Hegel lost its meaning as a force penetrating into the mysteries of the universe. It was replaced by the "spirit of the time," by the idea that man's mind is merely an expression of social and historical reality. Arnold Ruge, for example, proclaimed the power of time to be the absolute master of history. Similarly, Belinskii proclaimed reality his God and embraced a *mystique* of time, a blind trust in progress. In his last stage, Belinskii advocated "naturalism" in the sense of a description of Russian social conditions by realistic techniques and with a social purpose which would help in organizing public opinion hostile to the regime. But he did not lose his generally firm hold on the nature of art nor his fervent devotion to the cause of Russian literature. However much we may disagree with many of his particular judgments today — his low ranking of Russian folklore, his underestimation of Russian eighteenth-century literature, his disparagement of the remarkable poets around Pushkin, his excessive praise for contemporary celebrities like George Sand, James Fenimore Cooper, and Béranger — we must admire Belinskii's great achievement in defining the status of Pushkin, Gogol, and Lermontov, and in welcoming the early promise of Dostoyevsky, Turgenev, Goncharov, and Nekrasov. In spite of the necessity, for reasons of censorship, of making criticism the vehicle for much general discussion on politics, society and morals, in spite of the prevailing conditions of magazine writing which encouraged a tendency to diffuse description, repetition, digression, incessant polemics, and rhetorical overemphasis, Belinskii must be admired as a genuine critic who kept up aesthetic standards rigorously and firmly to the last. Belinskii, almost singlehanded, established the position of literary criticism as a public force in Russia.

[28] *Ibid.,* pp. 673–674.

Belinskii had one very important historical function: he transmitted the ideas of German idealism to the tradition of Russian criticism. He was the authority for the critics of the fifties and sixties though they tried to ignore or minimize the idealistic elements in their master. Later Marxist criticism could appeal to Belinskii: in him, certainly, they found the view of literature as evolving automatically with society, the *mystique* of time, which came to them also from Marx and Engels, since all three have their common source in Hegel. The Marxists could also find an advocacy of realism in the last stage of Belinskii's writings, which, though far removed from their own conceptions, was sufficiently social in its emphasis to allow its assimilation. Belinskii thus set a mark on Russian criticism which even today has not been completely obliterated.

III

The continuity between Belinskii and the critics of the fifties and sixties — Chernyshevskii, Dobroliubov, and Pisarev — is obvious. Still, they differ sharply from their master, however sincerely they may have thought that they were only developing the ideas and conceptions of his last stage. The intellectual atmosphere had changed greatly: Belinskii had grown in the shadow of German idealism and had never abandoned its basic doctrines on art and history. Chernyshevskii, Dobroliubov, and Pisarev had no understanding of the German romantic views. Their philosophy precluded this: it is frequently called Feuerbachian and considered identical with that of the latest stage of Belinskii. But I cannot see any evidence that these writers adopted the specific doctrines of Feuerbach, a highly sentimental fervid theologian, imbued with Hegel's way of thinking. They must rather be described as materialistic monists, most deeply influenced by popularizers of the scientific outlook, such as Vogt, Moleschott, and Büchner, and by the English Utilitarians.

Of the three, Chernyshevskii, however eminent in other respects, must be ranked lowest as a literary critic. Chernyshevskii, even when speaking of literature, is preoccupied with immediate politics. He does not even believe in the social role of art. He argues at length that "not by books or periodicals or newspapers is the spirit of a nation awakened — but only by events." [29] Rather, literature induces a peaceful and reasonable disposition in the mind aroused by events. It cannot incite new demands and promote new tendencies. Though this might seem to be said with tongue in cheek for the benefit of the censor, we must conclude from Chernyshevskii's other writings that he actually thought of literature as a mere surrogate, ersatz for life, a passive mirror of society.

Chernyshevskii's theoretical views are most fully stated in his dissertation *The Aesthetic Relations of Art to Reality* (1855). Art, he argues, is an

[29] *Polnoe sobranie sochinenii*, ed. V. Iu. Kirpotin *et al.* (Moscow, 1939–1951), IV, 765.

inferior reproduction of reality. Its only function is that of spreading knowledge about reality, to remind us of it or to inform those who have not experienced it. The purely aesthetic is dismissed as mere sensual pleasure, trivial at its best, reprehensible at its worst. Beauty is simply life; thus almost all young women are beautiful. Sculpture is quite useless: any number of persons walking the streets of Petersburg are more beautiful than the most beautiful statue. Painting is even more inferior to reality; poetry, as it appeals to the imagination, is still worse off. Words are always general and hence pale and feeble. The poet's invention should not be overrated: most poets write their autobiographies. Nor is plot invention anything to boast of: any French or English crime gazette contains more gripping and more intricate real-life stories than any writer can devise. Why then is art valued at all, asks Chernyshevskii, and he can answer only that man values what he has made himself, out of vanity, or because art satisfies his propensity to daydreaming, his innate sentimentality, or simply because art reinforces our memory. A portrait reminds us of an absent friend, a picture reminds us of the sea. Imagination is weak: we need such reminders. Basically art does no more than any reasonable discussion of a subject. Art is, at most, a "handbook" for those beginning to study life.[30] In Chernyshevskii aesthetics has reached its nadir: or rather it has been asked to commit suicide.

Chernyshevskii, like Belinskii, attacks art for art's sake, "pure art." But he does not deal with German theories of the autonomy of art or even with the flaming proclamations of the French. Chernyshevskii can think of pure art as nothing but drinking songs and erotic conversations:[31] art, I would say, not for art's sake, but for the sake of wine and sex. It is thus easy for him to argue that this Epicureanism lacks a vital link with the rational needs of the modern age, an age devoted to the struggle for the betterment of human life. In contradiction to his usual skepticism as to the social effect of art, Chernyshevskii says, that "poetry is life, action, struggle, passion" and that literature cannot help serving the tendencies of an age.[32] In practice, he admired and recommended the social writers of his time: George Sand, Béranger, Heine, Dickens, Thackeray, Gogol, Tolstoy. While he recognized and praised Pushkin's historical role, he tried to minimize his significance. He considered him as lacking in "deep meaning, clearly discerned and coherent ideas." [33]

But most of Chernyshevskii's writings are not literary criticism: the famous article on Turgenev's *Asya*, "The Russian at a Rendez-vous" (1858), is an attack on liberalism disguised as a review. This melancholy story of an abortive love is used as an allegory of Russian willessness, as a peg to hang

---

[30] *Izbrannye sochineniia* (Moscow-Leningrad, 1950), pp. 422, 437, 438, 440, 441, 443, 449.

[31] *Ibid.*, p. 677.

[32] *Ibid.*, p. 678.

[33] *Polnoe sobranie*, II, 475.

on a warning to the bourgeoisie to heed the needs of the time. The general attitude is set forth in an often quoted passage: "Goodbye erotic questions! A reader of our time, occupied with problems of administrative and judiciary institutions, of financial reforms, of the emancipation of the serfs, does not care for them."[34] The reader is Chernyshevskii, and the public for which he spoke. They rejected art as sensual pleasure or wanted to use it as an instrument for propaganda.

But it would be a mistake to deny to Chernyshevskii all literary sensitivity and ability in analysis. His discussion of the second volume of Gogol's *Dead Souls* shows some literary discernment in pointing out the passages and scenes where Gogol preserves the continuity with the first volume and keeps up its standard of imaginative writing.[35] Granted the limits imposed by Chernyshevskii's incomprehension of the religious and conservative outlook on life, his view of Gogol's political evolution is surprisingly sympathetic. He certainly recognized that one cannot speak of a betrayal of the liberal cause by Gogol, as his later views were prepared and anticipated from the first.[36]

Chernyshevskii speculated even on prosodic questions arguing that dactylic and anapaestic feet are natural to Russian in order to defend folk rhythms and colloquial verse which Nekrasov cultivated at that time. The standard, as always, is naturalness: verse which is nearer to prose is better verse. Though we may doubt his assumption, four unfinished papers show serious study of technical matters.[37]

The review of Tolstoy's *Childhood* and *Boyhood*, together with the *Sevastopol Stories* (1856), is Chernyshevskii's best piece of literary criticism. Tolstoy is praised as a psychologist who describes the "psychic process, its forms, its laws, its dialectics accurately." Chernyshevskii quotes a passage describing the feelings of a soldier waiting for the fall of a shell and calls it "interior monologue," using the term apparently for the first time in a literary context.[38] He then compares Tolstoy's art with that of the painter who catches the sparkling reflection of light on quickly bouncing waves, or the flicker of a ray of light on rustling leaves. Something similar, it seems to him, is achieved by Tolstoy in describing the mysterious movement of the life of the soul. Chernyshevskii points out what has been elaborated since:

[34] *Izbrannye sochineniia*, p. 743.
[35] *Ibid.*, p. 515n.
[36] *Polnoe sobranie*, IV, 641.
[37] See Vasilii Gippius, "Chernyshevskii stikhoved," in *N. G. Chernyshevskii* (Saratov, 1926), and "Neizdannaia stat'ia Chernyshevskogo" in *ibid.* (1928).
[38] *Izbrannye sochineniia*, p. 706. The question of the term "interior monologue" is baffling. It seems improbable that Chernyshevskii could have invented it as he uses it casually without emphasis. Still, the only earlier use, in a most unlikely place, Alexandre Dumas' *Trente ans après* (1845), has no literary implication and seems only a chance collocation of two words. Cf. Gleb Struve, *Monologue intérieur*, in *PMLA*, LXIX (1954), 1101–1111.

Tolstoy's technique has affinity with impressionism. But it is typical of Chernyshevskii and his audience that after praising Tolstoy's moral purity, Chernyshevskii suddenly turns to an embarrassed defense of Tolstoy's theme of childhood. *Childhood*, he says, at great length, is about a child and not about issues such as war and social reform, but it is still worth reading.[39]

Dobroliubov was as little interested in art as his master, though he wrote much more exclusively on belles-lettres. But he applied more consistently, more systematically and consciously the point of view indicated by Chernyshevskii. Dobroliubov never tires of repeating the view expounded by Chernyshevskii, that literature is only a mirror of life, which reflects, but cannot change, reality. Literature did not raise the question of the emancipation of the serfs: rather it was raised by life and then literature brought about a "calm discussion, a cold-blooded survey of all the aspects of the problem."[40] Ostrovskii's plays make us see the realm of darkness among the Russian merchant class. But the cure must be found by life itself: "literature only reproduces life, it never portrays what does not exist in reality."[41] Dostoyevsky shows us the insulted and the injured, but he has no remedy to offer: he needs supplement and commentary,[42] presumably of a kind Dobroliubov was anxious to supply.

But at times, Dobroliubov modifies his thesis about art as the mere passive mirror of society. Literature helps to clarify existing tendencies in society. It may be useful in "quickening and giving greater fulness to the conscious work of society."[43] It is an "auxiliary force, the importance of which lies in propaganda, and the merit of which is determined by what it propagates and how it propagates it." Dobroliubov even recognizes that artists became the historical leaders of mankind who symbolize, like Shakespeare, an entire phase of human development.[44] Thus Dobroliubov runs the gamut from complete pessimism to messianic hopes: from the view that literature is a passive mirror of society to the view that it incites to direct action. He is caught in a net of conflicting views: his theoretical conviction that literature is mere words which cannot affect reality, his doctrinaire determinism, and the practical impossibility of the resignation implied, the need to demand from literature a discussion of what he considered new and progressive ideas in the hope that they might, in the end, prevail.

Surveying the history of Russian literature,[45] Dobroliubov displays the same hesitation: on the one hand the development of literature is said to

---

[39] *Izbrannye sochineniia*, pp. 709ff.

[40] N. A. Dobroliubov, *Izbrannye sochineniia*, ed. A. Lavretskii (Moscow-Leningrad, 1947), p. 27.

[41] *Ibid.*, p. 166.

[42] *Ibid.*, pp. 333, 350.

[43] *Pervoe polnoe sobranie sochinenii*, ed. M. K. Lemke (Petersburg, 1911), IV, 233.

[44] *Izbrannye sochineniia*, p. 292.

[45] In an early essay "O stepeni uchastiia narodnosti v razvitii russkoi literatury" (1858), *Izbrannye sochineniia*, pp. 23–53.

reflect the changes of society passively and inertly; on the other, it seems
to him shameful that literature has not expressed what he considers the real
needs of the nation. Dobroliubov wants an all-national literature, above
classes, parties, and cliques, but recognizes that Russian literature has hitherto appealed only to a small reading public. He wavers in his hopes for
the future between a romantic conception of nationality as something
uniquely Russian, and a literature written for the peasant masses, representing them and comprehensible to them.[46] But Dobroliubov merely raises the
question of popular art: in his criticism he is rather occupied with one
problem, the truth to life of the novels and plays he discusses. Dobroliubov
made a real contribution to the theory of the social study of literature. He
apparently for the first time thought clearly of "social types" as revealing an
author's world view, independently of or even contrary to his conscious
intentions. The attitude of a writer must be sought for in the living images
he creates. "In these images the poet may, imperceptibly even to himself,
grasp and express an inner meaning long before his mind can define it. It is
precisely the function of criticism to explain the meaning hidden in these
images." [47] The conscious intention of an author remains a secondary question. This method of studying social types or heroes, with its dismissal of
what today is called "The Intentional Fallacy," seems a valuable technique:
it distinguishes between an overt and a latent meaning of a work of art
somewhat as, in different philosophical contexts Engels, Freud, Pareto, or
Mannheim distinguish them. Social types such as the gentleman or the
intellectual had begun to attract consideration in French literary criticism.
George Sand defended the idealized workmen in her social novels; they
should incite a desire to resemble them in intelligent and good workmen.[48]
The German romantic critics had discussed the great mythic types of
humanity: Hamlet, Faust, Don Quixote. The Schlegels had dismissed conscious intention as a criterion of value. But these motifs had not yet coalesced as they did in Dobroliubov.

Unfortunately, Dobroliubov was unable to keep steadily to his central
insight. In practice he succumbed to simple didacticism and even to crude
allegorizing to serve his polemical purposes. Oblomov, in a famous article,
is declared a "key to the riddle of many manifestations of Russian life."
"Oblomovka is our motherland: a large portion of Oblomov is within every
one of us." [49] Dobroliubov sees the continuity between Oblomov and the
type of "superfluous man" depicted in Onegin and Pechorin, yet he wanted
to dismiss these two fictional heroes as belonging to a dead past. "They have
lost their significance, they have ceased to mislead us with their enigmatic

[46] *Ibid.*, p. 28.
[47] *Ibid.*, p. 130, cf. pp. 104, 136–137.
[48] See 1851 Preface to *Le Compagnon du Tour de France.*
[49] *Izbrannye sochineniia*, pp. 79, 92.

mystery." [50] But instead of trying to analyze Oblomov, Dobroliubov dismisses him as a "disgusting nonentity," [51] holding him up as a kind of warning example, a bogyman, an allegory of Russian indolence and backwardness. He has lost sight of the book and the figure.

Similarly, Dobroliubov analyzes the plays of Ostrovskii, using them to document tyranny, oppression, ignorance, superstition, and downtrodden resignation. Only the heroine of Ostrovskii's *Storm*, Katerina, seems to him the "representative of a great national idea," a "reflection of a new movement of national life." He glorifies her suicide in the Volga as "the height to which our national life is rising in its development." He sees it as "a challenge to the power of tyranny." [52] But if my own reading of the play is anywhere near the text, Katerina must rather be considered a pitiful figure, dominated by dark instinct, who rushes into an adulterous adventure, trembles before the wrath of God, shudders at a thunderstorm and pictures of hell-fire, and finds refuge, from her sense of sin and guilt, in the waters of the Volga. The atmosphere of the play is that of a fairy tale. The evil mother-in-law, the stupid husband, the lover at the gate, the watchmaker who tries to discover the secret of perpetual motion, the gossipy pilgrim-woman, the half-mad lady shouting: "All of you will burn in unquenchable fire!" give the play a tone of weird unreality. But to make Katerina, an adultress and a suicide, a superstitious ignorant woman pursued and crushed by a sense of doom, into a symbol of revolt, seems the very height of what could be called "loss of contact" with the text. Anything must serve the cause and if it does not, it must be made over to fit it. Similarly, Turgenev's *On the Eve* is merely used as a pretext to call for a Russian Insarov. An ominous "the day will come" concludes the piece.[53] Only in Dobroliubov's last essay on Dostoyevsky's *Insulted and Injured* can one discern some progress of sensibility. He suddenly recognizes the role of imagination. An artist is not a "photographic plate." "He supplements the isolated moment with his artistic feeling. He creates a whole, finds a vital link, fuses and transforms the diverse aspects of living reality." The poet's work is "something that must be so, and cannot be otherwise." [54] Though Dobroliubov is puzzled by Dostoyevsky's novel and denies even that it is art, the power of Dostoyevsky's imagination had its effect. But unfortunately, Dobroliubov died in the year of this article (1861), aged not yet twenty-six.

Dmitri Pisarev (1840–1868) first rose to prominence as a rival to Dobroliubov. He established his reputation by contradicting and refuting Dobroliubov's views on Goncharov and Ostrovskii. But this rivalry should

[50] *Ibid.*, p. 92.
[51] *Ibid.*, p. 93.
[52] *Ibid.*, pp. 315–316, 321.
[53] *Ibid.*, pp. 241–242.
[54] *Ibid.*, p. 328.

not obscure the fact that Pisarev was also a pupil of Chernyshevskii and of the later Belinskii and that on matters of literary theory and general philosophical outlook there is little difference between Pisarev and his elders. Pisarev in the Soviet Union today is not so highly valued or so widely studied and reprinted as Chernyshevskii and Dobroliubov, mainly because he is suspected of radical individualism and even anarchism. Even Masaryk compared him with Stirner and Nietzsche.[55] But there seems little justice in all this: Pisarev, after four years in prison, became skeptical of the imminence of revolution. He put all his hopes into the dissemination of rational and scientific ideas, into the slow creation of a materialistic intelligentsia. He feared an omnipotent state. But in his writings there is hardly any trace of romantic individualism. He is, like Chernyshevskii and Dobroliubov, a rigid naturalistic monist. He is, even more completely, cut off from the romantic past. Pisarev, for example, ridicules the whole idea of unconscious creation. A poet is an artisan, like a tailor who cuts his cloth, adds to it, snips a bit off, changes this or that.[56] Form and content are divorced. What interests him is only what a writer did for social awareness, not his merits as an artist. On aesthetic matters, Pisarev pushes the ideas of Chernyshevskii to even greater polemical extremes. His notorious paper "The Destruction of Aesthetics" (1865) is an enthusiastic endorsement of Chernyshevskii's dissertation. If beauty is life, he says, then "every healthy and normal person is beautiful," and aesthetics, to Pisarev's apparent satisfaction, dissolves into physiology and hygiene.[57] The "destruction of aesthetics" with Pisarev widens into a destruction of art itself. The arts of music, painting, and sculpture are dismissed as having no possible social use. Verse is completely outmoded. Poetry is a dying art and we should rejoice at it.[58] What remains is the novel and the drama with a social purpose. Even these are considered temporary expedients, makeshift instruments of propaganda, of no intrinsic value. Some of Pisarev's attacks on aesthetics and art were rhetorical flourishes, polemical extravagances, *boutades* designed to shock the reader. But, I think, Pisarev was at bottom quite serious: he belongs to the long line of thinkers which begins with Plato and goes to the English Utilitarians and men such as Proudhon, who wanted to banish the poets from the republic. Pisarev was concerned with the economy of society and of the Russian intelligentsia in particular. He felt that young men should be warned off the arts; science and the spread of science is the one thing needful, at least in Russia. Pisarev's slogan "realism" has no primary aesthetic connotation at all. It means simply analysis, criticism, intellectual progress.[59]

[55] *Rusko a Evropa* (Prague, 1921), II, 112–114.
[56] *Sochineniia. Polnoe sobranie*, ed. F. Pavlenkov (4th ed., Petersburg, 1904–1907), V, 77.
[57] *Ibid.*, IV, 502.
[58] *Ibid.*, III, 269.
[59] *Ibid.*, IV, 61.

Literature, or rather the art of the novel, is, at most, admitted as a means of communicating and disseminating such ideas. It helps in forming public opinion. But if Pisarev grants that Nekrasov may continue to write verse, and that Turgenev and even Chernyshevskii may write novels,[60] he makes only a temporary concession to the weaknesses of human nature. Pisarev sees art consistently as a past form of human endeavor which has been vanquished or should be vanquished shortly by science.

These grossly utilitarian theories augur ill for the value of Pisarev's practical criticism. But strangely enough, he has genuine critical insights and a considerable power of analysis. He is a far more lively writer than either the dry Chernyshevskii or the stodgy Dobroliubov. He has even wit and polemical brilliance and he can give evocative descriptions which are quite beyond the reach of his elders. One must, however, make large allowances: the famous attack on Pushkin is often simply silly and brutal. The conclusion that Pushkin reveals his "inner vacuity, his spiritual poverty, and intellectual impotence," that he was, at most, "a great stylist," [61] does not differ very much from what had been said by Dobroliubov and by Chernyshevskii. But Pisarev says it so bluntly and harshly that the modicum of polemical truth becomes a falsehood.

Pisarev is at his best when he tries to define the "new man," the new hero. He hailed Bazarov as the representative of the new man and analyzed him penetratingly and sympathetically.[62] He saw that Turgenev's attitude toward his hero is what we today would call "ambivalent." Turgenev does not fully sympathize with any one of his figures: he is not content with either fathers or children. He does not share Bazarov's ruthless negations, but he respects them.[63] In Bazarov, Pisarev discovered himself and his generation. His criticism was a genuine act of self-knowledge: a justification of a method which treats a fictional figure as a symbol quite apart from the overt intentions of the author.

There is nothing as good in Pisarev's other writings: his identification with Chernyshevskii's point of view was too complete to make him see the grave shortcomings of *What Is to Be Done?* [64] His review of *Crime and Punishment* serves too narrowly a practical purpose to be just to the complexities of the book. Pisarev announces that he will ignore the point of view of the author and discuss only the manifestations of social life depicted in the novel. The method is the same as he had used on Bazarov. Pisarev assumes that the author, if he is a good writer, reflects life accurately, and that his mere theories are irrelevant: intentions do not count.[65] He has suc-

[60] *Ibid.,* III, 269.
[61] *Ibid.,* V, 55, 85.
[62] In the essay "Bazarov" (1862), and in part of the essay "The Realists" (1865).
[63] *Sochineniia,* II, 396–398.
[64] Article "The Thinking Proletarian," originally called "A New Type" (1865), in "Supplement," *Sochineniia,* VII, 53–102.
[65] *Sochineniia,* VI, 343.

ceeded well with Bazarov, but he fails with Raskolnikov. He does not see that Dostoyevsky does not merely impose his ideology upon his figure (he does little of that) but actually presents a drama of ideas in the actions and persons of the novel itself. Pisarev, knowing that Dostoyevsky wants to show up the "new men," adopts the strategy of proving that Raskolnikov's crime was entirely due to poverty. "The root of his illness was not in his brain but in his pocket." [66] His views have nothing in common with those of the new men who would never endorse his romantic belief in the superman. Pisarev simply distorts the book because he ignores half of Raskolnikov's motivation, the theory of utility, and almost all that follows after the crime. Pisarev's review of *War and Peace* (1868) is even a worse failure: it is merely used as a pretext to attack the old aristocracy by describing two minor characters, Boris Drubetskoi and Nikolai Rostov, in satirical terms.[67] When Pisarev committed suicide by drowning, he was, as he confessed in a letter to Turgenev, quite alone.[68]

IV

Looking back to these three critics we should recognize that they were not primarily interested in literature at all. They were revolutionaries, and literature was only a weapon in the battle. They did not see that man is confronted with questions which surpass those of his own age: that the insight art provides into the full meaning of existence does not necessarily grow out of his immediate social preoccupations. As critics they constantly lose sight of the text, confuse life and fiction, treat figures in novels as if they were men or women in the street, or allegorize a fictional character, make it evaporate to represent some generalization such as the decadent aristocrat, the desire for freedom, the new man. They constantly succumb to two not unrelated fallacies: naturalism and intellectualism. They have lost hold on the concrete universal, the fusion of the particular and general in every work of art, which Belinskii had understood. Content and form are divorced with them: the unity of the work of art is broken up, imagination is reduced to a mere combinatory power. Art, in short, is denied as a value in itself. It is distributed between the despised sensual pleasure of form and a purely intellectual or hortatory content. Art is, at bottom, superfluous. Given the premises, Pisarev spoke only the truth, like any *enfant terrible*.

But this tendency, destructive of the very nature of art and literary criticism, should not make us ignore the real contribution of the three critics to a social study of literature. Their analysis of social types was something important, also methodologically. Besides, one must recognize that Russia at

---

[66] *Ibid.*, 352.
[67] *Ibid.*, VI, 479ff.
[68] Convincing circumstantial evidence of suicide in Armand Coquart, *D. Pisarev* (Paris, 1946), pp. 38off. The letter to Turgenev (May 8, 1867), in *Raduga. Almanakh Pushkinskogo Doma* (1922).

that time was actually producing a social novel, that poetry then was derivative, and the drama rather a reflex of the novel. Our critics helped to define and describe the nature of the social novel, the obligation of the writer toward social truth, his insight, conscious or unconscious, into the structure and typical characters of his society. It seems a pity that they did so in narrow local terms, shackled by their gross utilitarianism. The noise of the battle deafened them.

Social and Aesthetic Criteria
in Soviet Russian Criticism

VICTOR ERLICH

The aim of this paper is to examine the role which social and aesthetic considerations have played in Russian literary criticism in the last thirty-five years. The terms "social" and "aesthetic" do not seem to require definition; yet a semantic caveat may be in order. For reasons which will become, I hope, increasingly clear in the course of the argument, the word "aesthetic" will be used throughout this paper in what might be called its minimum or residual sense. It will connote not so much preoccupation with beauty, with formal excellence, as the emphasis on the unique character of imaginative writing, recognition that literary art has qualities which cannot be reduced to, or deduced from, other modes of human endeavor. Conversely, the "social" approach as discussed here will in its more extreme variant tend toward crude utilitarianism, viewing literature as a product or a tool rather than an entity in its own right. Clearly what is at stake in this juxtaposition is the problem of the relative autonomy of literature, of the degree to which it can be discussed and evaluated in its own terms.

It is no exaggeration to say that this query has been at the heart of all significant critical controversy in the Soviet Union. To do justice to the matter would mean to write a full-scale history of Soviet criticism. All we can do here is to outline briefly the principal stages of the tension between the two critical emphases and to indicate some of its salient symptoms.

Our discussion will be not only schematic, but somewhat lopsided as well. The first decade of the Soviet era will be given more space than the subsequent twenty-five years. This unequal distribution of emphasis, while in part a matter of strong personal bias, is justified if not necessitated by a crucial difference of intellectual climate between the two phases of our narrative. The 1920's were in many crucial respects a sequel to that intellectual and aesthetic ferment which Russia had witnessed at the beginning of the century. The October Revolution frustrated some of those impulses and gave some others a different slant. But for a while cultural continuity remained unbroken. As long as the official doctrine had not degenerated into a rigid dogma, as long as some measure of free speech still prevailed, a search for new methods of artistic expression as well as bona fide discussion of critical principles was still possible. The tug-of-war between the "aesthetic" and the "social" approach could still assert itself in the form of a free-swinging debate, where the contenders would be now the "Formalists" versus the "sociologists," then the "Right-Wing" Marxist-Leninists versus the "Left-Wing" Marxist-Leninists.

By 1930 genuine methodological controversy had virtually ceased. Literary theorizing becomes increasingly a matter of intellectual shadowboxing, of timid exegesis on insipid or ambiguous official pronouncements. As we shall attempt to show, the tension between political and aesthetic criteria was to persist somehow, albeit in a muffled, distorted form. It will now find expression not in an open clash between well-defined critical positions, but in embarrassing contradictions within the official credo, in unwitting confusion or deliberate doubletalk.

I

To one who judges all Soviet criticism by the drab uniformity of the last two decades, it may seem almost inconceivable that the first attempt ever made in Russia to attack the problems of literary craft in a systematic fashion should have been launched in the first years of the October Revolution. And yet this is precisely the time when the Russian Formalist movement got under way.

The term "Formalism" has been of late bandied about so recklessly in the Soviet Union that one is likely to forget its initial meaning. What can be legitimately referred to as "Russian Formalism" is a school in Russian literary scholarship which originated in 1915–16 and was championed by unorthodox young philologists and students of literature such as B. Eikhenbaum, R. Jakobson, V. Shklovskii, and Iu. Tynianov. The Formalists viewed literature as a distinct field of human endeavor, as a verbal art rather than a reflection of society or a battleground of ideas. They were more interested in the actual works of literature than in their alleged roots or effects. Intent upon disengaging literary studies from contiguous disciplines, such as psychology, sociology, or cultural history, the Formalist theoreticians were quick to focus on "distinguishing features" of literature, on the artistic devices peculiar to imaginative writing. "The subject of literary scholarship," said Jakobson in an early study, "is not literature in its totality, but literariness, i.e., that which makes of a given work a work of literature." [1]

In their quest for the differentia of literary endeavor, the Formalists tried to steer clear of traditional answers and pat solutions. They had little use for such notions as "intuition," "imagination," or "genius," locating the peculiarly literary in the poet rather than in the poem. The situs of "literari-

[1] Roman Iakobson, *Noveishaia russkaia poeziia* (Prague, 1921), p. 11.

ness" was to be sought not in the author's or the reader's psyche, but in the work itself, more specifically, in the techniques whereby the creative writer reshapes his subject matter — reality — and manipulates his medium — language.

According to the Formalists, imaginative literature is a unique mode of discourse, characterized by the "emphasis on the medium" [2] or "perceptibility of the mode of expression." [3] In literary art, especially in poetry, it was argued, language is not simply a vehicle of communication. From a mere tag, a proxy for an object, the word becomes here an object in its own right, an autonomous source of pleasure as multiple devices at the poet's disposal — rhythm, meter, euphony, imagery — converge upon the verbal sign to reveal its complex texture. Artistic prose, conceded the Formalists, lacks the tight organization of language which is so typical of verse. But the difference here is not one of kind but one of degree. Narrative fiction has its own intricate patterns of tensions and balances, of parallels and contrasts. The events or "motifs" which constitute the basic story stuff are not simply related; they are organized for maximum aesthetic effect.

These basic assumptions were tested in acute studies of rhythm, style, and composition as well as in forays into literary history and practical criticism. The Formalist approach to literature was a drastic departure from that concern with "social significance" and "message" which dominated so much nineteenth-century Russian literary criticism. Consequently, the Formalist research in the Golden Age of Russian literature resulted in significant shifts of historic perspective, in drastic reëxaminations. Gogol's famous story, "The Overcoat," hailed by Belinskii as a deeply moving plea for the "little man," became under the hands of B. Eikhenbaum primarily an intricate piece of grotesque stylization. Pushkin, viewed this time at the level of style and genre rather than that of *Weltanschauung,* appeared as a magnificent culmination of Russian classicism. And the moral crisis of the young Tolstoy was reinterpreted in largely "aesthetic" or literary terms as a struggle for a new style, as a challenge to the romantic clichés grown stale.

The Formalist responses to the contemporary scene testified to the same single-minded concern with craftsmanship. In dealing with the current literary production the Formalist critics favored novelty, "inventiveness," aesthetic sophistication. They praised the linguistic experiments of the Futurist poets, the grotesque whimsy of Kaverin's fiction. In visual arts they encouraged such trends as Cubism or Constructivism.

Youthful exuberance as well as the shrill tenor of early Soviet critical controversy impelled the Formalists to overstate their case. In their early studies Shklovskii and Jakobson played down the links between literature

---

[2] *Ibid.,* p. 10.
[3] N. I. Efimov, "Formalizm v russkom literaturovedenii," *Nauchnye izvestiia Smolenskogo Gosudarstvennogo Universiteta,* V (1929), Part III, 70.

and society and questioned the relevance of any "extra-aesthetic" considerations. In so doing they provided easy targets for their Marxist-Leninist opponents who were becoming increasingly concerned over what one of them called the "triumphant upsurge" of the Formalist school.[4]

Formalism was soon to be labeled a "vegetable out of season,"[5] a stubborn relic of the past. Now it must be admitted that for a relic it was doing amazingly well. Throughout the years of the Civil War and the NEP the movement was making considerable headway in academic scholarship as well as in the critical reviews. Perhaps the Formalist methodology was after all more akin to the *Zeitgeist* than the Soviet-Marxist stalwarts were ready to admit. The rigorously scientific approach to poetic language found in Jakobson, Tynianov, Eikhenbaum, suited the empiricist frame of mind of the younger linguists and literary historians. The hard-boiled preoccupation with literary technology, with the "laws of literary production,"[6] was well attuned to the temper of the age which with Lenin defined socialism as "Soviet system plus electrification."

Be that as it may, the Soviet Marxist literary theorists could ill afford to ignore the Formalist school. This dynamic heresy presented the only serious challenge to the supremacy of historical materialism in the Soviet literary studies.

It goes without saying that the Marxist's opposition to the Formalist movement was not solely a matter of a struggle for power in Russian literary criticism. Many basic tenets of Formalism were, or seemed to be, in flagrant contradiction to the Marxian interpretation of literature. The ultra-Formalist tendency to divorce art from social life was bound to provoke a vehement reaction on the part of critics, bent, in the words of late G. Plekhanov, on establishing the "sociological equivalent" of the literary phenomenon. The playing down of ideological considerations was obviously anathema to theorists who viewed literature as a weapon in the class struggle, as a potent means of "organizing the social psyche."[7]

By the mid-twenties a full-dress offensive against Formalism got under way: it was spearheaded by no lesser figures than L. Trotsky, N. Bukharin, and A. Lunacharskii.

While the bulk of Marxist-Leninist critics took exception to the Formalist doctrine, their lines cf attack varied considerably. The attitudes toward Formalism, expressed during the debate of 1924–25, ranged all the way from wholesale rejection to attempts at assimilating the Formalist insights. Indeed one gets the impression that the Formalist challenge served here as a catalytic agent. It compelled the leading Marxist critics to take a stand on

[4] See U. Fokht, "Problematika sovremennoi marksistskoi literatury," *Pechat' i revoliutsiia*, no. 2 (1927), p. 78.
[5] A. V. Lunacharskii, "Formalizm v iskusstvovedenii," *ibid.*, V (1924), 25.
[6] O. M. Brik, "T. n. formalnyi metod," *Lef*, no. 1 (1925).
[7] See V. Friche, *Sotsiologiia iskusstva* (Moscow, 1929), p. 13.

some fundamental problems of literary theory and to reveal in so doing deep cleavages within their ranks.

Trotsky's attitude towards Formalism was sharply critical but not altogether hostile. The brilliant Communist chieftain had a field day puncturing holes in the more extravagant Formalist statements. He charged, with his usual polemical gusto, into Shklovskii's "immature and arrogant" raids on sociological criticism.[8] At the same time Trotsky admitted grudgingly that "a certain part of the research done by the Formalists is useful."[9] In another passage he wrote: "The methods of Formalism if confined within legitimate limits may help to clarify the artistic and psychological peculiarities of literary form."[10] Trotsky was reluctant to credit analyses of style or rhythm with a more than "subsidiary and preparatory character." Treated as an auxiliary device, he argued, Formalism is a legitimate, indeed a rewarding critical procedure. Erected into a full-fledged theory of literature, it becomes inadequate, in fact dangerous. The implicit Formalist philosophy revolves around the cult of the Word; it smacks of Neo-Kantianism, worse still — of St. John.[11]

The monopoly of dialectical materialism as the only legitimate world view and philosophy of history was thus emphatically upheld. "Marxism alone," said Trotsky, "can answer the crucial question why and how a given tendency in art has originated in the given period of history."[12] In the realm of causal explanation the dialectician has no equals. But this in itself, conceded Trotsky, does not make him capable of sound aesthetic judgment. Marxism cannot yield any criteria for evaluating artistic phenomena.

While the cruder practitioners of Marxist criticism saw in literature merely a medium for "registering social phenomena,"[13] Trotsky was aware that artistic creation was "a deflection, a transformation of reality, in accordance with the *peculiar laws of art*" (italics mine).[14] "A work of art," he said elsewhere, "should in the first place be judged by its own law, the law of art."[15] Since Marxists qua Marxists are in no position to identify these laws, they cannot completely disregard whatever assistance they can get from the ideologically alien Formalist writings.

A similar position was taken by another Communist leader who, on several occasions, was called upon to formulate the Party policy on literature — N. Bukharin.[16] He too saw considerable merit in the Formalist

[8] Lev Trotsky, *Literatura i revoliutsiia* (Moscow, 1924). English translation: Leo Trotsky, *Literature and Revolution* (New York, 1925).

[9] *Literatura i revoliutsiia*, p. 163.

[10] *Ibid.*, p. 164.

[11] *Ibid.*, p. 183.

[12] *Ibid.*, p. 178.

[13] V. Friche, *Ocherki*, quoted by Il'ia Gruzdev, *Utilitarnost' i samotsel'* (Petrograd, 1923), p. 45.

[14] *Literatura i revoliutsiia*, p. 175.

[15] *Ibid.*, p. 178.

[16] Nikolai Bukharin, "O formalnom metode v iskusstve," *Krasnaia nov'*, III (1925).

explorations of poetic art even while he went beyond Trotsky in minimizing, not to say misrepresenting, the scope of the Formalist concern. If one is to believe Bukharin, all that the Formalists were trying to do was to compile a "catalog" of individual poetic devices. This "analytical job," declared Bukharin, "is wholly acceptable as long as you treat it as a spadework preliminary to future critical synthesis"; but it is no substitute for such a synthesis.[17]

Once again the task of providing the larger view was reserved for the Marxist. But if, according to Bukharin, an inventory of literary techniques is no substitute for a broader sociological framework, neither does the latter offer a solution to specific literary problems.

Bukharin was to elaborate this point nearly a decade later, at the First All-Union Congress of Soviet Writers in Moscow. In his judicious report on "Poetry, Poetics and Problems of Poetry in the U.S.S.R.," Bukharin made the distinction between "extreme Formalism which tears out of social context," and "formal analysis which is highly useful and now, when one of our chief tasks is to master the technique, absolutely indispensable."[18] In this respect, added Bukharin, "we may learn something even from the Formalists, who dealt systematically with these problems, while Marxist literary scholars blithely ignored them."[19]

Trotsky and Bukharin were very broad minded indeed by comparison with the Marxist-Leninist stalwarts who in 1924 took up cudgels against Formalism in the influential literary magazine, *Press and Revolution*. The tenor of this attack was unqualified rejection. P. Kogan did not have any use whatever for the Formalist "spadework."[20] This prolific literary historian and critic, whose brand of Marxian dialectics sounded at times like a refurbished version of Pisarev's social utilitarianism, prided himself on never having had "time for the study of literary form."[21] Small wonder he saw in the Formalist's concern with literary craft simply a symptom of distasteful "aesthetic gourmandise."[22]

Equally vehement was the reaction of A. Lunacharskii,[23] the first Soviet Commissar of Education, an influential critic and publicist. He spoke grimly of "Formalist escapism," and diagnosed the enemy as "the last refuge of the unreconstructed intelligentsia looking furtively toward bourgeois Europe."[24]

This harshness of tone may sound a bit surprising in one who enjoyed the reputation of a relatively enlightened cultural politician. Now it seems that Lunacharskii's unmitigated hostility towards the Formalists was not

[17] *Ibid.*
[18] *Problems of Soviet Literature* (New York, 1935), p. 207.
[19] *Ibid.*
[20] P. S. Kogan, "O formalnom metode," *Pechat' i revoliutsiia*, V (1924).
[21] *Idem, Literatura etikh let* (Leningrad, 1924).
[22] "O formalnom metode," *Pechat' i revoliutsiia*, V (1924), 22.
[23] "Formalizm v iskusstvovedenii," *ibid.*, V (1924).
[24] *Ibid.*, p. 25.

merely a matter of Bolshevik orthodoxy. The position from which he attacked "Formalism in the study of art" was a curious combination of Marxist
dialectics and Tolstoyan philosophy of art. Together with some other Soviet
Marxists, for example Bogdanov or Lelevich, who viewed art as an affective
rather than cognitive mode of activity, Lunacharskii stated his plea for
ideological art in terms closely reminiscent of Tolstoy's "infection theory."
"Real art," he wrote, "is always ideological. By 'ideological' I mean one
stemming from an intense experience which drives the artist toward spiritual expansion, toward rule over souls." [25]

Proclaiming emotional intensity and spontaneity as ultimate tests of
greatness in art, Lunacharskii termed the Formalist preoccupation with the
artifice a sign of intellectual and moral aridity. He spoke with indignation
about Eikhenbaum's "soulless" analysis of Gogol's "The Overcoat," accus-
ing the Formalist critic of turning a heart-rending tale into a mere stylistic
exercise.[26]

While Kogan and Lunacharskii were thus labeling Formalism an alien
limb in the Soviet body politic, at the opposite pole of the Marxist spectrum
an attempt was under way to incorporate the Formalist procedures into a
flexibly conceived scheme of Marxian criticism. A. Tseitlin[27] spoke out
boldly against "hasty monistic raids" on literature by sociologists who were
apparently impatient with literary values, against the tendency to reduce
literary scholarship to a mere subdivision of social history.

To be sure, argued Tseitlin, the study of literature must take due cog-
nizance of social factors. The critic's analytical efforts must culminate in an
act of synthesis, placing the phenomenon under consideration within a
recognizable social context. Unfortunately, however, at the present stage of
Russian literary studies, such a synthesis is not yet feasible. "There is no
point," said Tseitlin, "in discussing the sociological implications of literary
facts, as long as the facts themselves are not established." "Before one sets
out to interpret an object of analysis," he continued, "one ought to delimit
its area, to find out what it is . . . explanation must be preceded by
description." [28] Hence the importance and the timeliness of the Formalist
contribution. By focusing on the close analysis of the text, on systematic
description of literary facts, Formalism was breaking ground for the truly
scientific study of Russian literature. The Formalists, declared Tseitlin, were
the "engineer battalions of Russian literary historians." [29]

A call for a peaceful coexistence, indeed harmonious collaboration, between Marxism and Formalism, was also sounded by M. Levidov.[30] "One does

---

[25] *Ibid.*
[26] See above, pp. 401–402.
[27] A. Tseitlin, "Marksisty i formalnyi metod," *Lef*, III (1923).
[28] *Ibid.*, p. 125.
[29] *Ibid.*, p. 131.
[30] Cf. *Proletariat i literatura* (Leningrad, 1925).

not need," he wrote, "to quote Engels in order to know that each superstructure, having once emerged from its class basis, becomes subject to immanent laws of its own, *acquiring, so to say, internal autonomy*" (italics mine).[31] It is to the credit of the Formalist school, continued the critic, that it has embarked upon systematic examination of these structural properties. "Only the joint effort of the Formalist and the sociologist," he concluded, "can produce a Marxist study of literature worthy of the name." [32]

This plea for reconciliation fell on deaf ears. The Formalists who in 1924–25 bravely stood their ground showed little enthusiasm for conceptual schemes so "extraneous" to literature as historical materialism.[33] The large bulk of Marxists would agree with U. Fokht who, in summing up the Formalist-Marxist controversy of the mid-twenties,[34] insisted on the basic incompatibility of the two schools of thought.

Yet, while rejecting the Formalist methodology, Fokht was much less sanguine than Kogan about the results heretofore achieved by Marxist criticism. The Formalist challenge, he argued, can be met not by dodging the questions it raises, but by solving them more successfully. This, warned Fokht, Marxist literary scholarship is still incapable of doing. "It lacks a well worked out system of literary concepts; it does not have its own poetics." [35]

Fokht was not alone in calling for a "sociological poetics," that is, a typology of poetic forms and devices evolved within the framework of historical materialism. Indeed it can be said that this precarious slogan, clearly a by-product of the "Formalist" controversy, marked a watershed between two basic strands in the Soviet-Marxist criticism of the 1920's — the purely genetic and the quasi-structural one.

"Geneticists" were quite content with probing the social derivation of the literary work or the class allegiance of the writer, with translating the "literary fact" back into the language of sociology and economics. The structure-minded Marxists sought to combine sociological synthesis with intrinsic analysis. They felt with Tseitlin that in order to be able to explain a phenomenon one ought first to describe it, to find out what it was.[36]

To more rigid exponents of Marxism-Leninism, this latter question seemed

---

[31] *Ibid.*, pp. 166–167.

[32] *Ibid.*, p. 166.

[33] Cf. B. Eikhenbaum, "Vokrug voprosa o formalistakh," *Pechat' i revoliutsiia,* V (1924).

[34] U. Fokht, "Problematika sovremennoi marksistskoi literatury," *Pechat' i revoliutsiia,* II (1927).

[35] *Ibid.*, p. 91.

[36] That this tug of war between "geneticism" and "structuralism" rending the early twentieth-century European scholarship could assert itself in Soviet Russia, muffled but not superseded by inevitable Marxian rhetoric, is testimony to the basic continuity between Soviet culture of the 1920's and its immediate antecedents as well as the current Occidental developments.

irrelevant, if not illicit. Where causal explanation was seen as the only legitimate frame of reference, the problems of the nature and function of literary creation were overshadowed, indeed submerged, by the overriding concern with the "underlying" social forces. Thus, V. Pereverzev maintained that the "value of a device cannot be understood without a genetic explanation. One cannot answer the question 'what for' without answering the question 'why.' " [37] V. Pertsov put it even more drastically: "I cannot visualize a Marxist raising the question 'how is this work of literature constructed?' without this question being immediately superseded by another question: 'why is this work of literature constructed this way and not another?' " [38] Having thus completely dissolved the "what" and the "how" of critical analysis in the "why," Pertsov went on to reject the very concept of "Marxist poetics" as a contradiction in terms.

Clearly what was challenged here was Levidov's "internal autonomy" of literature or, in Trotsky's phrase, "the peculiar laws of art." Stripped of irrelevant verbiage, the crucial question or questions which confronted the Marxian literary theorists in the twenties could be stated thus: is literature a mere by-product of social strife, just another weapon in the class struggle, however potent and strategic, or does it have exigencies of its own which cannot be derived either from its "class roots" or from its social import? Is the nature of a literary work totally determined by the writer's class allegiance and is consequently the value of this work to be assessed solely or primarily in terms of a "class-determined" conscious ideology? Or, to put this a little differently, should the aesthetic judgment be a corollary of the political verdict?

It will be noted that the last question was left untouched by most of the Marxist pronouncements cited above. The methodological debate precipitated by the rise of Formalism had to do with analytical procedures rather than with criteria of evaluation. It is scarcely surprising that the latter should have been contested even more fiercely than the former. The relative status of aesthetic and social considerations became a matter of strategic importance, whenever the Soviet critic was called upon to pass a judgment on the desirability of a given type of imaginative writing.

The "Left-Wing" position in this controversy, despite a thick overlay of Marxist lingo, had more in common with Pisarev or late Tolstoy than it did with G. Plekhanov or, for that matter, with F. Engels. To the men of the 1860's literature was primarily a handmaiden of progressive journalism. To Vardin, Averbakh, or Lelevich, the spokesmen of the doctrinaire literary faction, "On Guard," art was a weapon in the class struggle. In the 1925

---

[37] F. Pereverzev, *Tvorchestvo Gogolia* (Leningrad, 1926), p. 10. In this otherwise valuable study Pereverzev insisted on deducing all the characteristics of Gogol's literary art from the fact that Gogol was a small landowner.

[38] V. Pertsov, "K voprosu ob edinoi marksistskoi nauke o literature," *Literaturnaia gazeta* (April 14, 1930).

resolution of the group we read: "Imaginative literature is one of the last areas in which an implacable class war is taking place between the proletariat and the bourgeoisie for hegemony over intermediate groups." [39] More generally, art was to be defined as an "instrument of emotional infection, a means of organizing the reader's psyche in conformity with the interests of the given class." [40]

An inevitable consequence of such a view was a plea for an unqualified Party support to "proletarian," — orthodox — writers, and for the virtual ban on the independent if vaguely sympathetic "fellow travelers" (*poputchiki*). If, as Lelevich maintained, a writer always fulfills the unwritten "social command" — that of infecting his audience with the emotions of his class — the "petty-bourgeois" intruders could not be tolerated: they were liable to poison the trusting Soviet reader with alien emotional bacilli.

The pigheaded orthodoxy of the "On Guardites" was challenged by Trotsky in his few ventures into literary politics. A still more sustained attack on the "proletarians" was launched by one of the most gifted and broad-minded of the Soviet Marxist critics, A. Voronskii.

A dedicated Communist, Voronskii was not averse to the idea of enlisting the vast emotional potential of imaginative literature in the service of the October Revolution. But he was too astute a student of literature to measure it by Party yardsticks. Like Trotsky, he knew that one must not "approach the problems of art as one approaches those of politics," that art "possesses its own devices and methods and its own laws of development." [41]

To Voronskii art was not primarily a matter of mobilizing or manipulating emotions. It was a form of cognition, a largely intuitive, nonrational mode of apprehending reality.[42]

Voronskii's aesthetics, not unlike that of his opponents, harks back to Tolstoy. But, where Lelevich as well as Lunacharskii show affinity for Tolstoy's crudely didactic pamphlet *What Is Art?* Voronskii's key formula is an echo from *Anna Karenina*. It is from the painter Mikhailov, a secondary character of the novel, that Voronskii borrows his description of a creative act as "removing the veils" from the actual, thus reaching beyond the often misleading surface of things into their very essence.

Of course, argued Voronskii, the way in which the artist perceives reality, or, to put it differently, the degree to which he is likely to achieve the insight into things as they really are, is strongly affected by his class allegiance. But this connection is not a point-to-point correspondence. A great

[39] Quoted in Edward J. Brown, *The Proletarian Episode in Russian Literature, 1928–1932* (New York, 1953), p. 29.

[40] *Proletariat i literatura*, p. 85.

[41] Cf. *K voprosu o politike RKP(b) v khudozhestvennoi literature* (Moscow, 1924), pp. 14–21 *passim*.

[42] Cf. A. Voronskii, "Iskusstvo kak poznanie zhizni i sovremennost'," *Krasnaia nov'*, no. 5 (15) (August 1923).

writer is apt to transcend the limitations of his milieu. Guided by his intuition and bolstered by his creative integrity, he often cannot help but see and embody in his work certain truths which run counter to his own conscious bias and which are damaging to the interests of his class. Indeed this ability to rise above one's environment is the earmark of truly great art.

The recognition of the "supraclass" elements found in any genuine work of art determined Voronskii's attitude toward contemporary writers as well as toward the literary "heritage." This assumption was invoked in support of the thesis that a non-Party writer of talent and integrity can be not only aesthetically but also ideologically more worthwhile than a mediocre "proletarian," since the former can provide a more accurate insight into the social situation and thus a better guide to political action. Likewise a great artist's capacity to reach beyond his class was cited to explain the staying power of "feudal" and "bourgeois" masterpieces.

A form-conscious modern critic is not likely to find Voronskii's view of literature either novel or especially rewarding. The notion of art as "thinking in images," as a sensuous mode of knowing, is at least as old as German romanticism. In Voronskii's practical criticism formal considerations are largely overshadowed by problems of psycho-ideological content, by discussions of the writer's intuitive world view. Nor should Voronskii's broadmindedness be overestimated. He tolerated, indeed, encouraged, the independent writers such as Fedin, Leonov, and Pil'niak, who sympathized with the October Revolution but steered clear of a total political commitment. Yet he showed little tolerance for the militant nonconformism of E. Zamiatin, one of the most brilliant prose writers of the period.

Clearly, broad-mindedness is a relative notion. Viewed against the background of his era, Voronskii's critical achievement inspires respect not only because of the accuracy of some of his judgments, but, more importantly, because of his steadfast refusal to sacrifice literary criteria, to disregard the uniqueness of the artistic creation, which apparently he could sense better than he could define. Whatever the shortcomings of Voronskii's aesthetics, his insistence on the role of the "subconscious" and the intuitive in the creative process provided a refreshing contrast to the bleak rationalism of so much Marxist-Leninist literary theorizing. Whatever the rigors of Voronskii's ideological commitment, it did not quite succeed in dulling his sense of literary values, in dampening his genuine delight in creativity. He knew and said in no uncertain terms that Esenin, a nostalgic and wayward peasant poet, was "unfortunately, immeasurably more gifted than Bezymenskii," a shrill Communist versifier.[43] Small wonder Voronskii's was one of the first heads to roll in the grim process of streamlining Soviet criticism. "Voronskiism" became one of the chief terms of abuse, when the doctrinaires and the zealots whom he had fought so valiantly gained the upper hand in Soviet letters.

[43] Cf. *Proletariat i literatura*, p. 139.

II

Toward the end of the twenties the methodological debate was rudely called to a halt. Formalism, declared to be "false because it was reactionary, and reactionary because it was false," [44] was driven from the scene. The last-minute attempts on the part of the Formalist spokesmen to combine formal analysis with a sociological approach were of no avail. The time for such experimentation was long past as Marxist-Leninist criticism was being whipped into uniformity. Voronskii's aesthetics, accused of such deadly sins as "Bergsonian idealism," was bitterly condemned. Pereverzev's peculiar brand of social determinism was rejected as "crude sociologism," a label not altogether inaccurate, but singularly inappropriate when coming from people who were no less "crude" and less imaginative than their target. Soviet criticism was inexorably moving toward a single aesthetic credo of "Socialist Realism."

The dismal story of the increasing regimentation of Soviet literature in its basic outline is familiar enough and need not be retold here. True, one facet of the picture has recently appeared in a somewhat different perspective. A detailed inquiry into the Russian literary life during the First Five-Year Plan has cast a new light on the role of L. Averbakh's ultra-orthodox faction, so-called RAPP (Russian Association of Proletarian Writers), hitherto regarded as the villain in the piece.

In his study, *The Proletarian Episode in Russian Literature*, Edward J. Brown marshals substantial evidence in support of the thesis that at some point the RAPP leadership developed too much concern with literary values to serve as an effective instrument of the Party tutelage over literature. Having obtained the coveted supremacy in Soviet criticism, argues E. J. Brown, the "proletarians" eventually evolved a theory of art which claimed for the writer more autonomy than the regime, turning Soviet literature into a handmaiden of "socialist construction," was willing to countenance. It would seem thus that when in 1932 RAPP was abruptly disbanded to the accompaniment of vituperation about "sectarianism" and "ideological sabotage," its *real* crime was not excessive utilitarianism but excessive intransigence.

One may add that what was at stake here was not only the degree of political interference with literature, but the mode of control as well. From this standpoint, as Ernest J. Simmons has pointed out,[45] the shift from RAPP to a single Union of Soviet Writers responsible to and supervised by the Central Committee, apparently meant the substitution of direct Party

[44] M. Gel'fand, "Deklaratsiia tsaria Midasa ili chto sluchilos' s Viktorom Shklovskim?" *Pechat' i revoliutsiia*, II (1930).
[45] Ernest J. Simmons, "Soviet Literature and Controls," *Through the Glass of Soviet Literature* (New York, 1953), p. 11.

controls for the dictatorship of a zealous, yet increasingly erratic, literary coterie.

For a while, the new "line," adopted in 1932 and solidified in 1934, was, or seemed to be, an improvement over the preceding period, a partial vindication of aesthetic values. Some of the statements made at the First All-Union Congress of Soviet Writers in 1934 sounded very promising indeed. In his speech, already quoted, Bukharin spoke of the "mastering of the literary technique" as the most urgent task of the Soviet writer. He rebuked gently but firmly the shrillness and slogan-mongering of much Bolshevik poetry. Poetic "paraphrases of newspaper articles," he argued, are no longer enough. What is needed is a richer, more sophisticated poetic fare which would do justice to the "growing complexity, the heightened tone, the changed dimensions of our social life." [46]

This was an implicit admission that the "literary shock-brigade" tactics had been a dismal failure. The thematic monotony and crudeness of the *agitprop* literature — the psychological aridity of "production novels," the thin rhetoric of industrial poetry — must have given pause to many a Party leader. Hence, perhaps, the strident call for better artistic quality, for emphasis on human beings rather than on industrial paraphernalia. Hence, too, a measure of tolerance for (or should one say, lip service to?) psychological complexity in the novel and lyrical self-expression in poetry.

Whatever the rationale behind this apparent liberalism, it seems to have encouraged some manifestations of artistic integrity in creative writing and of sensitivity in criticism. In his collectivization novel, *Virgin Soil Upturned,* M. Sholokhov gave proof of considerable objectivity as well as capacity for vivid, well-individualized character drawing. Likewise, the best essays of V. Goffenshefer, I. Kashkin, and Iu. Iuzovskii were testimony to perceptiveness and aesthetic sophistication which makes one feel that the Formalists had not labored in vain.

This is of course only one part of the story. If Sholokhov's artistic honesty can be said to reflect "Socialist Realism" at its best,[47] it may be pointed out that this very quality made the writer suspect in the eyes of some official critics. Sholokhov's refusal to provide his Cossack epic, *The Silent Don,* with a conventional "happy ending" and turn duly the hero Gregor Melekhov into a Communist convert, displeased many a Party stalwart. Shortly afterwards the Soviet reviewers were waxing rhapsodic over A. Tolstoy's slick and dishonest Civil War novel, *Bread.* That this thinly disguised piece of Stalinist apologetics could have been hailed as a triumph of "Socialist Realism," calls into question the validity and the true meaning of the crucial term of official Soviet aesthetics.

---

[46] *Problems of Soviet Literature,* p. 220.

[47] Even this can be doubted, since *Virgin Soil Upturned* had been conceived and in a large part executed prior to the "Reform" of 1932.

The amount of attention which over the last twenty years has been lavished on the defining of "Socialist Realism" is so overwhelming as to discourage analysis. Equally, if not more forbidding, is the intellectual quality of these exegeses. Where discussion of fundamentals is supplanted by sterile terminological quibbling, or worse still by a transparent manipulation of slogans to fit the needs of a shifting Party line, the "definitions" tend to degenerate into double talk. One often gets the impression that "Socialist Realism" has become simply an honorific label, a convenient name for any aesthetic phenomenon which at the moment the Party considers acceptable or desirable. A recent attempt at definition made by A. Belik frankly equates "Socialist Realism" with "Party spirit" (*partiinost'*) or "Party-minded attitude toward socialist realities." [48] True, A. Belik's statement immediately drew fire from official quarters. But I am inclined to agree with G. Struve that what infuriated the *Pravda* publicist was not Belik's "crudeness" but his unnecessary candor.

Is then "Party spirit," meaning political expediency, the last word and the guiding principle of Soviet criticism? It has certainly been of late the most important single criterion and, in periods such as *Zhdanovshchina*, a decisive one. It is scarcely necessary to add that the obtrusive guidance of "the Party and the government" in matters of form as well as those of content has been conducive to a type of literature which is hardly worthy of aesthetic analysis.

Yet the picture is somewhat more complex than this. Genuine aesthetic criticism has become impossible. Consistent champions of literary values both within the Marxist camp and outside of it have been silenced if not liquidated. But the aesthetic considerations keep getting in through the back door. Nor could it be otherwise. No literature which wants to be effective, be it at a purely pragmatic, propaganda level, can afford to do away with qualities which make it appealing to the reader, to disregard what Trotsky had called the "peculiar laws of art." Moreover, some recognition of these laws is implicit in the Marx-Engels heritage to which the champions of *partiinost'* are ostensibly committed.

In the mid-thirties, when the canon of "Socialist Realism" was being established, the philosophy of art of Marx and Engels was often invoked with a due show of reverence. Actually "philosophy of art" is much too grand a term for a number of casual observations scattered across the writings of the founders of historical materialism. They had neither the time nor the urge to evolve a full-scale theory of art or, for that matter, to do much original thinking about aesthetic problems. But as men of culture and sensitivity they were undoubtedly interested in literature, and in responding to it

---

[48] A. Belik, "O nekotorykh oshibkakh v literaturovedenii," *Oktiabr'*, no. 2 (1950), pp. 150–164, quoted in G. Struve, *Soviet Russian Literature 1917–1950* (Norman, 1951), p. 369.

showed often sound if somewhat conventional judgment and a good sense
of literary values.

Like many of their contemporaries, Marx and Engels had a distinct bias
in favor of "realistic" literature. They refused to measure art by narrowly
ideological yardsticks, knowing that the writer's intuition often outstrips his
politics. While emphasizing the social relevance of literature, they discour-
aged preaching and overexplicit "messages." Art, felt Marx and Engels, is a
sphere of sensuous immediacy rather than of general propositions. In line
with this, the authors of the *Communist Manifesto* praised the Royalist
Balzac, in fact, found his portrayal of contemporary French society more
instructive than many sociological treatises. In the realm of drama they
favored emphatically Shakespeare over Schiller. By this they meant that an
imaginative grip on the actual, vivid, and many-sided portrayal of life, credi-
ble and thoroughly individualized characters, will serve the playwright better
than abstract rhetoric and mere noble sentiments.[49]

"Vividness," "concreteness," "accurate portrayal of life in all its complexity and many-sidedness" — all become part and parcel of the Soviet post-
1932 canon. Balzac's realism has been since, up to a point, a test case and a
model for the Soviet novelist.

"Up to a point," because "Socialist Realism" is presumably a realism
with a difference. The masters of the nineteenth-century novel, it was argued,
were critical realists; whatever their conscious ideology, they could not help
but reveal in their works the shortcomings and vices of their decaying society
or their reactionary class. But as "bourgeois" artists, they were in no position to find the positive way out of the impasse and thus were increasingly
driven towards pessimism and despair. Not so with "Socialist Realism," part
and parcel of a new, sprawling society; it is affirmative, optimistic, it says
"yea" to "the supreme joy of living on the earth." [50]

But, to follow the official rhetoric one step further, there is another still
more important difference between the traditional brand of realism and its
new "socialist" species. As Zhdanov proclaimed in 1934,[51] Soviet literature
cannot be content with merely "reflecting" or "truthfully portraying" reality; it must be *"instrumental in the ideological remolding of the toiling people in the spirit of socialism"* (italics mine). Has not Stalin called the
writers the "engineers of the human soul"? The duality of Zhdanov's formula
— "truthful portraying" plus "ideological remolding" — reflects, to use a
dialectical term, an internal contradiction of Soviet literary theory. As soon
as we translate "ideological remolding of the toiling people" *et al.* into "Party
spirit," the precarious character of the definition becomes obvious. It is diffi-

---

[49] For a recent "orthodox" discussion of Marx's and Engels' views on literature, see
Georg Lukacs, "Asthetische Schriften von Marx und Engels," *Sinn und Form*, no. 1
(1953), pp. 5–34.
  [50] *Problems of Soviet Literature*, p. 65.
    [51] *Ibid.*, p. 21.

cult enough to conceive how conscious promotion of any set of political objectives could be reconciled with a "vivid and many-sided portrayal of life." But such a coexistence becomes utter impossibility when the objectives which are to be promoted are those of a totalitarian regime whose propaganda apparatus conjures up a fictitious image of the world [52] and which has a vested interest in, and a physical capacity for, suppressing information about "whole vast tracts of Soviet reality." [53] The "complexity" urged on Marxist writers by Engels would provide too stark a contrast to the ritualistic simplicity of the official catechism permitting of two colors only — the purest white and the unrelieved black.

Were the matter to be tackled at the level of nomenclature, the internal contradiction within the official aesthetic doctrine could be construed as a "tension" in the concept of "Socialist Realism" between the modifier "Socialist" (read: Stalinist) and the noun "Realism." The latter calls for the portrayal of "life as it really is"; the former points toward "life as it ought to be," or as it supposedly is, according to the extravagant claims of Party propaganda.

Czeslaw Milosz recently observed that in the Iron Curtain countries "Socialist Realism" had become a mode of evading the actual by means of explaining it away.[54] As a thin conceptual scheme is being superimposed upon a complex and often "embarrassing" body of experience, those segments of reality which do not fit the scheme are brushed off as mere irrelevancies or "relics of the past."

The recent Soviet criticism has sought to bridge the gap between realism and idealization, between obtrusive "appearances" and often intangible "essentials" by means of manipulating the notion of the "typical" for all it is worth. This emphasis has its ultimate source in Engels' often quoted definition of realism as "accurate portrayal of typical characters under typical circumstances." [55]

However, Engels' dictum admits of differing interpretations. Where "typical" means "representative," the claims of "life as it really is" remain as obtrusive as ever. Fortunately the present-day Soviet critic has a more convenient and a more recent text to fall back on. In his speech before the Nineteenth Party Congress, that new expert on Marxian aesthetics, Georgii Malenkov, argued thus: "In the Marxist-Leninist understanding, the typical by no means signifies some sort of statistical average. Typicalness corresponds to the essence of the given social-historical phenomenon; it is not simply the most widespread, frequently occurring and ordinary phenomenon." As if the import of these remarks were not sufficiently clear, Malenkov

---

[52] Cf. Hannah Arendt, *Origins of Totalitarianism* (New York, 1951).

[53] Struve, *Soviet Russian Literature*, p. 371.

[54] Czeslaw Milosz, *The Captive Mind* (New York, 1953).

[55] Quoted in G. Lukacs, *Sinn und Form*, no. 1 (1953).

added significantly: "The typical is the basic sphere of the manifestation of Party spirit [*partiinost'*] in realistic art. The problem of typicalness is always a political problem." [56]

So it is indeed. What at each given moment is dramatized as "typical" depends not on the actual social relevance of the phenomenon in question, but on its status in the official view of reality. Whenever necessary, "dialectics," or more exactly, "double think," is called upon to explain away the rule as nontypical and to claim typicalness, that is, a higher order of reality for the exception.

It is scarcely possible to exaggerate the precariousness of the situation which today confronts the Soviet writer. Not only is he told in so many words what to say and how to say it. Worse still, he is caught between two mutually exclusive sets of requirements. He is urged to report accurately and fully on what he sees, but he knows from his own — or his confrere's — bitter experience that he had better not act upon this request. He is stalemated between the Scylla of nonconformism and the Charybdis of schematism. The actual is too explosive for comfort, the "typical" too lifeless for dramatic interest, too far removed from the writer's or reader's experience for credibility.

Of course, some themes have been a little safer than others. A number of novelists, at the risk of being accused of escapism, have chosen to salvage a degree of creative integrity by plunging into the past (for example, K. Fedin's memoir *Gorkii Among Us* or his retrospective novel, *First Joys*). There have been those who have bypassed "contemporary Soviet realities" in time or in space in order to avoid some of the obvious pitfalls of "typicalness." Some Soviet readers are likely, one assumes, to take at its face value A. Tolstoy's garbled account of the Civil War or the lurid picture of Anglo-American "warmongers" in the recent novel of N. Shpanov's *The Conspirators*. Or are they? One wonders especially whether the Soviet reading public has been sufficiently conditioned to the hate-America campaign in order to be able to swallow Shpanov's ludicrous panorama of U. S. politics where John Foster Dulles spends most of his time being (literally!) knocked about by his boss, a singularly ill-mannered tycoon, and where a sinister group of big businessmen assembled in 1942 acclaims the still obscure Senator Fruman as the man of the hour.

But by and large the "contemporary Soviet realities" have a way of catching up with the Soviet novelist, poet, and playwright. This is especially true of the latter; in drama timeliness is a strategic asset. A recent controversy, if one can call it that, has pointed up in a somewhat pathetic fashion the predicament of the present-day Soviet playwright and of his tutor, the drama critic. I'm referring to the turmoil around the notion of "conflictless-

[56] *Pravda*, October 6, 1952 (quoted in Simmons, *Through the Glass of Soviet Literature*, p. 25).

ness" (*bezkonfliktnost'*). This awkward term was coined about two years ago in an equally awkward attempt to evolve a new theory of drama, allegedly more congruent with the Soviet conditions than the traditional one.[57]

In the past, so the argument ran, the drama had centered around a conflict which was basically of an ideological or class nature. Now since Soviet society had done away with classes, such a conflict became by definition an anachronism. In the Soviet Union injustice and poverty have been banned; brutal social strife typical of the capitalist system has been replaced by coöperation — a joint effort directed toward the common goal. Thus the only kind of rivalry or tension which can legitimately find its way into Soviet drama is "socialist competition" in which Soviet men and women joyously outbid each other in civic zeal.

It should be admitted that the concept of "conflictlessness" did not fare too well. The idyllic view of Soviet life underlying it was so palpably ludicrous as to destroy any claim to plausibility. Moreover, the elimination of conflict from the dramatic plot would strike at the very core of drama as an art form, would rob this genre of its aesthetic *raison d'être,* and consequently of its propaganda value.[58]

A recent article by N. Abakin, "In Quest of a Conflict," [59] is worth quoting in this connection. Having acknowledged briefly the total failure of the *bezkonfliktnost'* theory, Abakin proceeds to rebuke the bulk of postwar Soviet drama for the spuriousness of the conflicts it portrays. One misses in these plays, he complains, the "turbulent seething of life, interesting characters, vivid portrayal of what the Soviet people actually live by." The classics of Russian literature, Abakin reminisces wistfully, had succeeded in showing life in "all its complexity." The contemporary dramatic fare suffers from "schematism, bleak clichés . . . and poverty of design." No proliferation of technical detail, warns Abakin, can serve as a substitute for interaction between live human beings.

Every Soviet writer worthy of the name would wholeheartedly agree. But what can he do? When, in his novel, *The Young Guard,* A. Fadeev portrayed with a degree of candor the confusion which had prevailed in official quarters during the first months of the Nazi-Soviet war, he was slapped hard for having failed to emphasize the constructive role of the Party leadership.

---

[57] See especially *Voprosy filosofii,* no. 5 (1952).

[58] An additional weakness of the "conflictlessness" theory, from the official viewpoint, lay in its implicit denial of "bourgeois survivals," the reactionary residues which are part and parcel of Soviet demonology. Totalitarianism cannot do without strategically selected scapegoats. The negative characters in Soviet fiction and drama have been, to be sure, a double-edged weapon. But they have often performed a "constructive" function akin to that of "self-criticism" of *Pravda* or *Izvestiia* local correspondents. Properly channeled "gripes" tend to siphon off some popular discontent and to alert the Party to the malfunctioning of certain parts of the system without challenging the validity of the system as such.

[59] N. Abakin, "V poiskakh konflikta," *Novyi mir,* no. 5 (1953).

Fadeev took the hint and hastened to include in the revised version of his book what should have occurred rather than what had actually occurred. When Iuri German embarked upon a psychological novel about a somewhat neurotic officer of the Soviet Medical Corps, he was taken to task for having selected such a "nontypical" hero and sternly reminded that there is no such thing as a neurotic in the Soviet Union.

Thus, the dilemma remains to plague the Soviet critic and literary theorist. The tension between "social" criteria — more exactly, crude political expediency — and residual aesthetic requirements was driven underground but not resolved. This tension reflects the paradox of a regime which calls stridently for a "great literature" — because the Marxist tradition it feeds upon involves respect for cultural values and because bad literature would be worthless even as a vehicle of propaganda — while doing everything within its power to prevent the emergence of such a literature. The totalitarian tutelage over the writer hacks away at the qualities which make literature worthy of man's interest and devotion — bewildering complexity of psychological insight, wayward spontaneity of artistic vision, imaginative use of the medium.

Lately there has been some speculation as to the possibility of changes in Russia's aesthetic climate. In fact, even before Stalin's death, faltering attempts had been made to apply his "epoch-making" statement on linguistics to literature and art and to question the dogma about the "superstructural" character of the arts. (It is safe to assume that, especially among the older generation of Soviet literary scholars, there are still those who are only too eager to utilize any loophole in order to claim for literature a degree of autonomy vis-à-vis the economic process.) More recently, there have been reports of the sensational pronouncements by Khachaturian and Il'ia Ehrenburg which raised the problem of creative freedom with a candor we had not witnessed for a long time.

Are the "peculiar laws of art" again coming into their own? Is a new NEP in literature in the offing? One wonders.

The composer may yet regain some freedom of action. After all it was not until the last years of the Stalin rule that music was subjected to outright Party dictation. But in literature the Malenkov era is likely to prove as destructive of aesthetic values as was the Stalin regime. Certainly, no one can expect the revival of Formalism with its frankly hedonistic delight in sheer verbal play. But will the Party dare to act consistently upon its own, "realistic" aesthetics? Perhaps a measure of skepticism is in order. As long as the fallen idols of the Politburo are consigned to the Orwellian "memory hole," Engels' call for a literature that would portray life "in its all-embracing totality" will have little chance of being heeded.

Freedom and Repression in Prerevolutionary

Russian Literature

LEON STILMAN

Preliminary censorship, initiated by the Catholic Church, became a general practice in European countries in the course of the sixteenth century. England was first to abandon this system in 1694; Sweden followed suit in 1766, and Denmark a few years later. In most countries of the European continent, however, preliminary censorship survived until the middle of the nineteenth century.

In Russia, the printed word became a matter of governmental concern only in the eighteenth century when various restrictive measures were taken with regard both to printing and to the importation of printed matter. After some experimenting in liberalism, Catherine II instituted preliminary censorship in 1796.

A detailed statute was enacted under Alexander I, in 1804. The new law was submitted to the Emperor for his approval with the following comment: "These regulations do in no sense infringe upon the freedom of thought and of writing; they merely institute appropriate measures against the abuse of this freedom." [1]

The principal purpose of censorship, as the new law defined it, was "to provide society with books and writings furthering true enlightenment of minds and improvement of morals, and to suppress books and writings antagonistic to this purpose" (Article 2). The business of censorship was entrusted to the universities (in St. Petersburg, where no university yet existed, there was to be formed a committee of "learned persons residing in the capital"). Consequently, university professors and other "learned persons" were to decide whether a book would, if published, contribute to enlightenment and to the improvement of morals. The censors were instructed to exercise "reasonable tolerance, refraining from any biased interpretation" (Article 21), and Article 22 used this boldly liberal language:

[1] See Law of July 9, 1804, in *Sbornik postanovlenii i rasporiazhenii po tsenzure* (St. Petersburg, 1862), pp. 81–95.

Modest and reasonable search for every kind of truth pertaining to religion, humanity, civil condition, legislation, state government, or any particular branch of administration is not only exempt from even the most tolerant censorship, but it is to enjoy a complete freedom of printing, which furthers the advancement of enlightenment.

The benevolent, the almost idyllically liberal law of 1804 remained on the statute books for over twenty years. But after a decade or so it was hardly more than a memento of that period which Pushkin called "of Alexander's days the beautiful beginning." He referred to those days with melancholy in a poem he wrote in 1822, during his Kishinev exile. In this poem, "A Message to the Censor," Pushkin recognized the need for censorship in Russia ("What is necessary in London would be premature in Moscow"); but while he sang the praise of the ideal censor, a "friend of the writer," he stigmatized the capricious tyranny of the cowardly ignoramuses for whom "satire was libelous lampoon, poetry was debauchery, and the voice of truth rebellion." "Are you not ashamed," he asked the censor, "that thanks to you no books are yet to be seen in Holy Russia?" Bigotry and obscurantism were rampant when Pushkin wrote these lines; the rather ugly end of Alexander's days was approaching. The statute of 1804 was not repealed, but it was superseded by a great number of arbitrary interferences of a reactionary and suspicious administration.

New legislation was enacted during the first years of the reign of Nicholas I. The Statute of 1826,[2] which came to be known as the "Iron Code," was fathered by Minister of Education A. Shishkov. Shishkov was a retired admiral who believed in discipline and in the "purity of the Russian language," which, he felt, had been corrupted by too many foreign borrowings. The admiral's purism is reflected in the following paragraph of the Code:

Works and manuscripts in our native tongue in which the norms and the purity of the Russian language are clearly violated, or which abound in grammatical mistakes, are not approved for publication before the necessary corrections have been made by the authors or the translators. (Article 154.)

Aside from Shishkov's special sensitivities in matters of language, the Code was essentially a protective barrier against any attack "not only deliberate and criminal, but even unintentional, against Religion, the Throne, Established Authority, the Law, and the Morality and Honor of the Nation and of individuals" (Article 3). The general purpose of censorship, as defined in Article 1, was to impart to published works in the realms of literature, the sciences, and the arts, "a tendency useful, or at least harmless, with respect to the welfare of the country." Literature and the arts, consequently, were not necessarily expected to perform a positively useful task: the government of Nicholas I did not object to "harmless" literary and artistic pursuits.

The tendency to direct opinion is reflected in Article 6 of the Code, insti-

---

[2] *Ibid.*, pp. 125–196.

tuting a Supreme Committee on Censorship, to be composed of three cabinet ministers; the inclusion of the Minister of Foreign Affairs was deemed necessary because one of the concerns of the censorship was "to direct public opinion in accordance with the present political circumstances and the views of the government." It was, therefore, in matters of foreign policy that opinion was to receive positive guidance. But restrictions were also established in this sphere; it was forbidden to publish "anything disrespectful or offensive for countries maintaining friendly relations with Russia, and in particular the Holy Alliance . . ." (Article 170). In this connection one may recall that Gogol's "The Diary of a Madman" ended, in the original version, with this question: "And do you know that the King of France has a bump right under his nose?" This was found objectionable, although Nicholas I showed little friendship toward Louis-Philippe, all but a subversive in his judgment. The resourceful author then volunteered to place the bump under the nose of the Bey of Algiers, and the story was passed; the friendship of this potentate, apparently, was not claimed by the Russian government.

If opinion was "directed" in matters of foreign policy, it is not that it was free from tutelage in domestic affairs. Rather, in domestic matters, there was no need for guidance because no opinion was expected to be expressed at all. The Code forbade "any writing not only rebellious against the government and the established authorities, but merely tending to weaken the respect to which they are entitled" (Article 166). The censor was to be vigilant lest "anything steal in capable of weakening the feelings of devotion, loyalty, and voluntary submission to the decisions of the supreme power and to the laws of the land" (Article 167).

The following paragraph formulated a basic principle maintained throughout the reign of Nicholas I:

It is prohibited to publish any considerations by private individuals relative to reform in any part of government administration, or to any changes in the rights and privileges granted by the Monarch to the different estates and classes of the Empire, if such considerations have not yet received the approval of the government. (Article 169.)

Contrary to the 1804 statute, an ambiguous passage was now to be stricken out if one of the two possible interpretations appeared objectionable. This actually barred any text into which an imaginative censor could read either criticism of any agent of authority or any suggestion of improvement; criticism obviously tends to weaken respect, and the government expressly monopolized the right to consider reforms (a right which, incidentally, it showed little inclination to exercise).

A truly remarkable feature of Shishkov's Code was that under it the censor's visa did not exonerate an author from responsibility; the author could be prosecuted if his work, published with the censor's consent, were later to be found harmful by the government. This extraordinary piece of legislation was motivated as follows:

> For far more guilty is he who, being free to dedicate himself entirely to his writing, meditates in the quiet of his study something harmful to public safety and morality, than the censor who examined the work, together with a number of others, in the performance of his duty. (Article 213.)

The monstrosity produced by Shishkov in 1826 was replaced two years later by milder and more reasonable legislation sponsored by the new Minister of Education, Prince Lieven.[3] Among the more important rules set forth in the new statute were the following:

> Censorship is to direct special attention to the spirit of a book under consideration, to the manifest purpose and intention of the author; and it shall base its judgment on the manifest meaning of the text without indulging in arbitrary interpretation . . . (Article 6.)
> Censorship has no right to decide whether the opinions and judgments of an author are justified or lack foundation, as long as they are not contrary to the general rules governing censorship; it may not pass judgment on whether the work considered is useful or useless, as long as it is not harmful; and it ought not to correct the style or to take notice of the author's faults from a literary viewpoint . . . (Article 15.)

The last lines were clearly a rebuke to the admiral, and the text as a whole indicates definitely that the government did not intend to make any positive demands on literature.

The relatively liberal tendency embodied in this statute was soon reversed. Censorship was once more tightened and repression increased after 1830, under the impact of the revolutionary wave in Western Europe and of the Polish uprising.

The government reverted to a policy of silence; this policy had been criticized earlier by the father of the Russian "commercial" press, the able and utterly cynical Faddei Bulgarin, in a lengthy memorandum which was read by the Emperor only a few days before Shishkov's statute received his sanction. Bulgarin wrote:

> Since opinion cannot be destroyed, it would be far better if the government took upon itself the task of guiding and directing it by means of the press . . . Complete silence gives rise to distrust and suggests weakness; unrestrained publicity generates wilfullness; but publicity inspired by the government itself reconciles both sides and is beneficial to both. Having shaped opinion, it is very easy to direct it as one's own undertaking of which one knows all the hidden springs.

Elsewhere in his memorandum Bulgarin complained:

> . . . instead of forbidding writing *against* the government, the censorship forbids writing *about* the government, even in its favor. Any article in which the words

---

[3] *Ibid.*, pp. 311–396.

government, minister, governor, and director appear is forbidden in advance, regardless of what it contains.[4]

This was true not only in 1826, but in later years as well. In 1849 Bulgarin himself was severely reprimanded for an article in which he commended the institution of State Control, created by Speranskii, and especially for referring to a former state comptroller, "the late Baron B. B. Kampenhausen," as "a man of extraordinary intelligence, diligence, and integrity." The official document commented:

> This kind of depiction of what was formerly, opposed, as it were, in disparaging contrast to a later and to the present state of things, and equally the opinion so strongly worded on the usefulness of government measures, were regarded by His Majesty the Emperor as highly improper.[5]

For many years Bulgarin's *Northern Bee* was the only private newspaper in Russia, and the only private periodical authorized to publish political news. In 1831 an attempt to break Bulgarin's monopoly was made by Pushkin. The application he sent to General Benckendorf on this occasion is a document of considerable interest; it reads in part:

> If his Majesty the Emperor were pleased to use my pen, I should endeavor to carry out His will accurately and zealously, serving Him to the best of my abilities . . . In Russia, periodical publications do not represent different political parties (for we do not have any), and it is not necessary for the government to have an official journal of its own; yet public opinion is in need of being guided. With joy I would undertake the editing of a *political* and *literary* journal, that is, of one which would publish political and foreign news. Around it I would group writers of talent and in this way would bring closer to the government men who are capable of rendering service and who still shy away, in the mistaken belief that the government is hostile to enlightenment.[6]

Pushkin's offer — which was not accepted — must be considered against the background of the situation prevalent in those years. Obviously no overt opposition was then possible. For liberal nobles like Pushkin, for the survivors of the disaster of December 1825, the choice was one between complete exclusion from public life and some sort of a rapprochement with the government, some attempt to bridge the chasm between the government and the educated nobility which was willing to serve both the Emperor and the country well and loyally. This was Utopian; the Russian monarchy rarely accepted coöperation; it was tragically consistent in rejecting offers of loyal and enlightened service.

In 1832, an indictment against the press in general and the Moscow journals in particular was presented to the Emperor by the Vice-Minister (later Minister) of Education, S. S. Uvarov; this remarkable document read in part:

---

[4] Mikhail Lemke, *Ocherki po istorii russkoi tsenzury i zhurnalistiki XIX stoletiia* (St. Petersburg, 1904), p. 380.

[5] *Ibid.*, p. 216.

[6] A. S. Pushkin, *Polnoe sobranie sochinenii* (Moscow-Leningrad, 1949), X, 637–638.

When I assumed my duties, I believed that once restrained from their rash impulses to concern themselves with affairs of state, the journalists could be given complete freedom to discourse about literary matters, despite their vulgar name-calling, their careless style, their complete lack of taste and of decency; but after further consideration I saw that the influence of the journalists upon the public, and especially upon university students, was not harmless, even in its literary aspects; corruption of taste brings about corruption of morality . . . The inexperienced reader wanders in the dark and little by little becomes accustomed to the language of the gutter and the rudeness of antagonists equally unworthy of respect . . . Considering the present circumstances and the state of the public mind, it is necessary to restrain the latter by increasing the number of "dikes" wherever possible.[7]

Even before Uvarov's report, the censorship suppressed Baron Delvig's *Literary Gazette* for a reference to the revolutionary events in France. In 1832 the same fate befell Ivan Kireevskii's *European,* suppressed as a result of an extraordinary feat of reading between the lines of his article on nineteenth-century literature; the official report stated:

Although the author asserts that he is speaking not of politics but of literature . . . a little attention suffices to see that he means something quite different: by "enlightenment" he means "freedom"; "intellectual activities" signify "revolution," and the "expertly-found mean" is nothing other than "constitution." [8]

Kireevskii's prose was at times nebulous, and years later an article he wrote was suppressed with this comment: "It is not known what Kireevskii means by 'totality of being,' but clearly there is here something subversive." In 1834 Nikolai Polevoi's *Moscow Telegraph* was suppressed for an unfavorable review of a bombastically patriotic play by Kukol'nik, which had been well received in high quarters in St. Petersburg, something Polevoi learned too late to stop the distribution of the issue. The year 1836 saw the end of Nadezhdin's *Telescope,* which was suppressed for publishing Chaadaev's "Philosophical Letter." While many journals were suppressed, the government showed an increasing reluctance to grant permission to publish new ones. Pushkin was permitted to publish his *Contemporary* after many difficulties, only a year before his death. But when, in 1844, Granovskii applied for permission to publish a journal, Nicholas I wrote on his petition: "Enough of them as it is."

Whatever the severity of the repression in those years, the worst was yet to come. The new climax was provoked by the revolutionary movement which swept Western Europe in 1848. Nicholas I wrathfully raised his sword against the criminals who were assaulting various thrones abroad, and started a wild hunt after subversion at home.

[7] Lemke, ref. 4, p. 188.
[8] Nikolai Engelgardt, *Ocherk istorii russkoi tsenzury v sviazi s razvitiem pechati* (St. Petersburg, 1904), p. 112.

In February 1848 a special secret committee was appointed to investigate both the press and the censorship. On April 2 it was made permanent and was placed under the chairmanship of a reactionary bureaucrat, D. P. Buturlin. The "April 2 Committee," as it came to be known, was given unlimited powers and used them to terrorize journalists and censors alike, the latter being often placed under arrest for lack of vigilance.

Remarkable for his vigilance was General Dubbelt, the commandant of the gendarmes, as may be seen from his communication to the Minister of Education to the effect that:

> . . . in recent times there has been formed in Moscow a society of Slavophiles; that the goal of these men consists in imparting a new direction to Russian letters by avoiding the imitation of Western writers and by choosing original, native subjects for their writing; that although a secret surveillance over the members of this society has hitherto failed to reveal anything positively harmful, but since, coming under the influence of ill-intentioned persons, this society might easily assume a harmful tendency, and since the members of the said society are for the most part authors . . . it has been His Majesty the Emperor's pleasure to order that writings in the Slavophile spirit submitted to the censors be treated by them with especially strict attention.[9]

As for Buturlin and his committee, their antics eclipsed completely the earlier feats of Russian censorship. One episode will be here related, for it gave Nicholas I an opportunity to formulate some basic principles of his philosophy of government.

Early in 1849, Buturlin, a consistent advocate of strong measures, came forth with a proposal for closing all universities and institutions of higher learning in Russia. Rumors of this plan spread in society causing considerable alarm. In March 1849, the *Contemporary* published an unsigned article alluding to rumors of what was euphemistically referred to as a forthcoming "reform" of the universities; it commented, in substance, that the passion for reforms was a disease afflicting the godless and lawless West, but unknown in Russia; no reform of the universities was necessary, the article asserted, for they performed a great service as they were in educating noble youths for faithful service to their beloved monarch.

A few days later, Minister of Education Uvarov, still nominally responsible for the censorship, was advised by Buturlin that the Emperor wished to know how the article could have been passed; the main objections were stated by Buturlin as follows:

> This act of submitting a government matter to the judgment of the public, this appeal to public opinion, constitutes a development which is as novel as it is intolerable in our system. If similar articles are passed, no measure contemplated by the government, were it in some way to become known to the public, will

⁹ Evgenii Solov'ëv, *Ocherki iz istorii russkoi literatury XIX veka* (St. Petersburg, 1907), p. 107.

escape criticism in the form of objections to alleged expressions of private opinion, and then the journals would arrogate to themselves the function of judges in
matters of government.[10]

The irony of the situation was that Uvarov had not only personally passed
the article, but had actually inspired it; it was written by one of his immediate subordinates. In a lengthy report to the Emperor, the minister attempted
a defense of the article. The monarch's resolution read:

I find the article passed for publication in the *Contemporary* improper, for it
is inconsistent with the dignity of the government and with that order of things
which fortunately we have, whether to praise or to blame our government institutions in reply to empty rumors. One is to obey and to keep his reasonings to
himself.[11]

When another reference to the universities was made in the press, Nicholas personally forbade "all articles for and against the universities." Defeated
in his conflict with Buturlin, Uvarov, the "builder of dikes," resigned a few
months later.

The policy of Nicholas' reign in matters of the press may be described as
one of total silencing of public opinion, of a total exclusion of society from
the consideration of all public matters. Public affairs were an exclusive pre-
rogative of the government. No support, coöperation, or approval were
sought. Criticism was not tolerated, and even favorable comment was often
judged improper interference; to criticize was criminal, to approve was ir-
reverent. From the sacrosanct person of the monarch emanated orders.
Through the channels of the bureaucracy they were conveyed to the citizenry; they were to be obeyed in silence.

A difficult and annoying problem for the regime was that of literature,
of belles-lettres. The printed word, unless it was used for official business,
generally tended to disturb Nicholas' bureaucrats. It was so difficult to guard
the forbidden area of government affairs from intrusions of authors or literary
critics, were it only by allusion or innuendo. Minister Uvarov is reported to
have once remarked wistfully and, one would assume, humorously, that if
only literature ceased to exist in Russia altogether, he might at last sleep
in peace. Literature, however, did not cease to exist. There was actually a
certain ambivalence in the attitude of the regime toward literature. Together with the hostility toward culture, some vestiges of the tradition of
Enlightened Absolutism were still present in Nicholas' days. Some semblance
of culture needed to be preserved be it only as an adornment of the state,
and a poet or an artist, it was felt, might be entitled to some protection, perhaps even to some respect.

Of course, the works produced had to be "harmless," and the limits of
the "harmless" were defined narrowly and capriciously. It is, nevertheless,

[10] Lemke, ref. 4, p. 228.
[11] *Ibid.*, p. 233.

highly important that in principle harmless pursuits were permitted and that literature was not required to perform any particular task or to render any positive service. The idea of harnessing literature to specific tasks was of a much later origin.

The achievements of Russian literature under the regime of Nicholas I were truly remarkable. Griboedov, Pushkin, Lermontov, and Gogol wrote during his reign, and died before it came to its end. Goncharov, Turgenev, Nekrasov, Dostoyevsky, and Tolstoy published their early works during the period of censorship "terrorism" inaugurated in 1848. True, Griboedov did not live to see a public performance of his famous comedy, and Pushkin's *Bronze Horseman* or Lermontov's *Demon,* to mention only these major works, could not be published in their lifetime; true, Pushkin, Lermontov, Dostoyevsky and so many others had known the rigors of the police state. Yet a national literature, vigorous and often brilliant, was born and had grown rapidly, despite the distrust, the harassment and the persecutions.

In the earlier years of the century, literature often reached its small audience without the help of the printing press. Pushkin mentions, in his "Message to the Censor," as examples of works circulated in manuscript copies without the censor's visa, the amiable pornography of Barkov, the writings of "the foe of slavery" Radishchev, finally his own condemned poems. Even works approved by the censorship often carried some message, couched in "Aesopian language" or otherwise disguised; for censors are never quite vigilant enough, nor are the gendarmes always sufficiently diligent to catch up with the elusive inventiveness of the human mind. In the game of blind-man's buff between the authorities and society, it often happened that the "innocent" were grabbed while the "guilty" escaped.

Nicholas' regime did not achieve its purposes because one cannot maintain a vacuum. A far more effective policy is to pump ideology into people's minds, but again this was a later invention; and the method can be effective only with the help of modern techniques of communication and diffusion of ideas (or of their various substitutes). But Nicholas I demanded silence in matters of public interest, not active conformism. In this silence, every word, spoken or printed, had a great resonance. It is this silence precisely that explains the tremendous resonance of Belinskii's often nebulous, often self-contradicting, but always impassionate writings; they were important primarily as a powerful assertion of the intellect, free by its very nature. Thus literary criticism, and rather helpless philosophizing apropos of literature, expanded in volume and in importance in the vacuum which the government sought to maintain. Similarly any reference, in narrative fiction or in drama, to reality, to "things as they really are," was amplified in the people's minds, arousing them to social criticism and to social consciousness.

No doubt, Nicholas I and his regime succeeded in retarding the development of Russian society, if not in arresting this development; and when the reign ended and the regime collapsed in a military, administrative, and economic bankruptcy, Russian society as a whole was not immediately ready to assume an active role in public affairs. An effective liberal leadership, however, was provided by members of the upper classes; and it is significant that among the advisers of Alexander II, at least in the early years of his reign, were men with past Decembrist connections, like Lanskoi or Rostovtsev.

In sharp contrast with the practices and the whole philosophy of government of Nicholas I, at least a part of Russian society was allowed, even invited, to express opinion on the crucial problem of the emancipation and to participate in its solution.

As the "dikes" built under Nicholas crumbled and broke down, the silencing of opinion by means of the censorship was strongly condemned by men who certainly did not belong to the radical wing of Russian society. In 1856 the following statement was made by Prince P. Viazemskii, then Vice-Minister of Education, and member of the Central Administration of Censorship:

> All the manifold, suspicious, and all too cleverly planned restrictions of the censorship do not serve the purpose of changing the trends of opinion or its sympathies. On the contrary, they merely irritate the minds and draw away from the government those people whose talents could render important services.[12]

This is closely reminiscent of the words written by Pushkin, Viazemskii's close friend, a quarter of a century earlier. Another representative of the elite may be quoted: Fëdor Tiutchev, a career diplomat and a great poet, who was made head of the Foreign Censorship in 1857; in a memorandum presented on that occasion to the Minister of Foreign Affairs, Prince Gorchakov, he wrote:

> Absolute and prolonged restriction and oppression cannot be imposed upon minds without causing substantial harm to the social organism as a whole . . . In the long run authority itself cannot escape the consequences of a similar regime. A desert, an immense intellectual void, is created around the sphere where it resides, and the governing authority, finding outside of itself no control, no indication, no fulcrum of any kind, is finally troubled and falters under its own weight, even before it succumbs under the fatality of circumstances.[13]

The *Russian Messenger,* newly founded by Katkov, a cautious liberal in those days, asserted in 1858 that "the easiest way to kill a belief in people's minds and to undermine its moral force is to place it under official tutelage." [14]

In 1859, in the first issue of his *Sail,* the Slavophile Ivan Aksakov eloquently demanded the right to express opinion straightforwardly, without ruse and paraphrase. "Would it not be an advantage for the government," he

[12] K. K. Arsen'ev, *Zakonodatel'stvo o pechati* (St. Petersburg, 1903), p. 13.
[13] Engelgardt, ref. 8, p. 232.
[14] Arsen'ev, ref. 12, p. 14.

asked, "if it knew the honest opinion of every one and his attitude toward it?" And the conservative Pogodin, in an open letter to the Minister of Education published in the same issue, demanded trial by the courts for offenses committed through the printed word, declaring himself ready to suffer any punishment as long as it was imposed by law. The government's response to these eloquent appeals was the suppression of the publication.[15]

Freedom was not yet in sight. Of all the great reforms, that of the press was the last to materialize; it came only in 1865, ten years after Alexander II ascended the throne, four years after the emancipation. In the meantime the government wavered, frequently changing and redefining its attitude. It was, however, becoming increasingly apparent to the government that restrictive censorship was not an effective way of handling opinion in a period of far-reaching reforms and of deep social changes. The government turned to the idea of an active guidance of the press, functioning along the lines of the French *Bureau de la Presse*. A committee was set up in January 1859. A. V. Nikitenko, a university professor and a censor of great experience and liberal views, was invited to sit on it and to act as intermediary between this government agency and the press. After only a few months, the committee had to admit its complete failure: the press was unanimous in resisting the government's attempts to guide or use it as a vehicle for influencing public opinion. Another plan, growing out of the first, materialized two years later, thanks to the efforts of Nikitenko and to the support he received from the new Minister of the Interior, P. A. Valuev. This was the creation, or rather the resurrection, of a government organ, the *Northern Post*, which had been defunct since 1819. This official publication never succeeded in its mission, which Valuev defined in a secret circular as that of "counteracting the Russian press." [16]

These various undertakings were reflected in a remarkable "Plan for the Establishment of Uniformity of Thought in Russia," drafted by Kozma Prutkov (in 1859, according to the editors; it was published in 1863); introducing his plan, Prutkov pointed out the "harmfulness of divergency of opinion" and proceeded to state:

. . . every Russian nobleman is possessed of the desire not to err; but in order to satisfy this desire it is necessary to have material with which to form opinion. But where is this material? The only material can be the opinion of the authorities; otherwise there is no assurance that the opinion is correct.

Further he very convincingly sets forth the idea that a private citizen cannot possibly judge the plans of the government, for they appear to him as disconnected fragments, and only history reveals them in their grandiose unity. But, asks Prutkov, "how is the subject to know the government's opinion as long as history has not stepped forward?" And to know it is of great

[15] *Ibid.*, pp. 13–14.
[16] Lemke, ref. 4, p. 368.

importance: "Many are those who have been judged subversive solely because they were ignorant as to what opinion would best please the higher authorities." The conclusion is that the need, "particularly in our vast country, to establish a uniform point of view with respect to all social requirements and government measures" can be best satisfied only by an official periodical; thanks to such a periodical:

> . . . the baneful inclination of the human mind to discuss everything occurring in the earthly sphere would be bridled and directed toward serving exclusively the indicated goals and views. One *dominating* opinion would be established on all issues and questions. It would even be possible to counteract the growing tendency to raise "questions" on matters of social and political life, for where do they lead? A true patriot should be an enemy of all so-called "questions"!

While the experiments in directing opinion, so brilliantly satirized by Kozma Prutkov, were carried on, the discussion continued between opposing factions within the administration on a new legislation on the press. A compromise was finally reached; it was embodied in the "temporary" law of April 6, 1865, a halfway concession to the demands of society. The essential feature of this law was that it abolished preliminary censorship (a) for original works in book form of not less than ten folios (twenty folios for translated works), and (b) for periodicals then in existence, published in St. Petersburg and in Moscow. Provincial periodicals, consequently, and new publications remained subject to preliminary censorship, unless exempted by the Minister of the Interior. Censorship was also maintained for pamphlets and brochures (of less than ten folios) which, the government feared, could spread dangerous ideas among the lower and broader strata of the population.

These limited freedoms being granted, it was thought necessary to set up safeguards against possible abuses. The liberal faction in the administration, with the Minister of Education Golovnin, advocated trial by the courts for offenses specifically defined by law. The reactionaries, however, led by Valuev, succeeded in writing into the new law a text whereby the Minister of the Interior was given authority to suspend a publication after two "warnings," and even to suppress it under certain conditions — a system largely modeled after the one introduced in France by the decree of Napoleon III of February 17, 1852.

With all its limitations, the 1865 law was an event of great significance: it made it possible for the first time in Russia to publish books and periodicals which did not bear the odious visa of the censor. For the first time manuscripts could go to the press without being exposed to mutilation by a government official.

Soon, however, the government began to reconsider the new statute, especially with regard to books. In the few attempts that were made to bring books for trial before the courts, the government met with little success. It was consequently decided to strengthen the power of the executive. In 1872, the executive was given the authority not only to seize books if their dissemination was found to constitute an immediate danger (this authority was vested in the Minister of the Interior), but also to suppress them by decision of the Council of Ministers, without trial by court.

These measures formed the framework of a legislation which, with a number of minor revisions, ruled the press in Russia up to the revolution of 1905.

This regime was certainly not a liberal one. It may be said, however, that, beginning with the reign of Alexander II, censorship and other government interferences ceased to be a major factor in the development of Russian literature. Among the books suppressed under the law of 1872, original works of fiction were relatively few, and hardly any of them were works of lasting significance. The main victims were works, for the most part translated, in the fields of the social and political sciences and of the natural sciences, either dangerous on political grounds or, in the case of the last mentioned category, anti-religious. The government acted in a rather haphazard and ineffectual manner. To quote one example, the translation of the first volume of *Das Kapital* was made available to the reading public only a few years after the suppression of a translation of Hobbes' *Leviathan.*[17]

Another development pertaining to the relations between literature, the government, and society in Russia may be briefly considered at this point. After the end of the reign of Nicholas I, Russian literature saw, if not freedom, then at least a relaxation of governmental controls and restrictions; at that very time it found itself exposed to very strong societal pressures and demands. During the decade from 1855 to 1865, a trend in literary criticism was particularly vocal which sought to force literature into a total and militant participation in the struggle for social and political issues. Literature offered, however, a vigorous resistance to these demands.

The separation between literature and militant journalism was climaxed in the conflict which opposed the literary contributors of the *Contemporary* to its critics. This conflict certainly had deeper causes than the noble birth of the contributors or their personal idiosyncrasies. The basic issue was that, according to Chernyshevskii's materialist aesthetics, art was but a substitute for reality. Turgenev, among others, saw the implications of this thesis, which he called "nonsensical," [18] even if he continued to defend Chernyshevskii, and also Belinskii, as he did in his correspondence with Tolstoy, for several years after the publication of Chernyshevskii's dissertation.

The refusal of the major Russian writers to follow the radical critics who insisted that literature be committed to the struggle for social justice, does not mean that these writers chose the alternative of a deliberately anti-social

[17] A list of books suppressed by the Russian government, brought up to 1902, is given under "Tsenzurnyia vzyskaniia," in *Entsiklopedicheskii slovar'* (St. Petersburg, 1903), XXXVIII, 1ff.

[18] See letter of July 25, 1855 to V. P. Botkin, in *Sobranie sochinenii* (Moscow, 1949), XI, 130.

isolation in subjectivism or in contemplative aestheticism. It does mean that they felt the need to assert their freedom from externally imposed commitments, their freedom of "engagement" or of "disengagement" in current issues at their own choice and on their own terms. The great Russian novel developed upon these premises during the second half of the nineteenth century. This is not to say that earlier, during the reign of Nicholas I, Russian literature had been predominantly topical or tendentious; this it was not and could not be. But the interpretation of this literature by the radical critics — notably that of Gogol by Chernyshevskii — sounded so convincing that even an outspoken opponent of Chernyshevskii, the critic Druzhinin, did not actually question Chernyshevskii's understanding of Gogol, but instead undertook to revive the tradition of Pushkin, who in his belief provided an aesthetic antithesis to Gogol's "social realism."

To be sure, the tendentious novel did exist; it even prospered, especially in the later sixties and in the seventies, when both the liberal and the reactionary camps produced fiction in which this or that creed was extolled and its enemies were confounded and destroyed.

To be sure, with his solid education in civic and didactic and moralistic — and later philosophic — criticism, the Russian reader showed a persistent tendency to turn to literature, whether for guidance in matters of immediate concern, or for enlightenment on the vaster problems of the destinies of his country or of human destiny in general. The Russian reader had been told, and firmly believed, that "the poet thought in images," and in one famous instance, it was not a critic like Belinskii or Dobroliubov, but a great novelist, Dostoyevsky, who revealed to the Russian audience all the profundity of the poet's "thought" embodied in the "images" of a Tatiana or an Aleko.

Nevertheless, the great masters of the Russian novel creatively asserted the autonomy and the integrity of their art, despite their critics and their readers, and in some instances it might be added, even despite themselves. From a different viewpoint the government too came to admit, by gradual steps, the essential difference between the writer of fiction and the publicist. The period of reforms inaugurated direct and overt expression of opinion, within limits, naturally, and at times very narrow ones. The period of reforms did not bring freedom as it is known in democratic countries; the next battle for freedom was fought, and a new if still indecisive victory was won, forty years after the first uncensored publication appeared in Russia. The Manifesto of October 17, 1905 proclaimed the freedom of the press; it was followed by the Regulations on the Press of November 24 of the same year into which the government had written a few limitations of no great importance.

But much earlier, soon after 1855, freedom had become, in Russia, an active force; the press, not yet commercialized, or only partly commercialized, had a significance and a prestige enhanced by the very fact that its survival was under constant menace. Russian society was an ideologically open society, with various trends of opinion represented and often opposed in more or less violent clashes. There were periods of retreat, of weariness and stagnation. But, as a whole, freedom of the word made considerable advances during the second half of the nineteenth century, and after the 1905 Revolution very little if anything remained of the former restrictions. The final triumph of the progressive forces in March 1917 was short-lived. They were swept away in the chaos of a military disaster inherited from the old regime and in social and economic disintegration.

This defeat, however, does not permit us to erase Russian liberalism from the pages of history, for it was a widely accepted ideology and an active political force. As all historical events, the defeat of the liberal cause in Russia was the resultant of many conflicting forces. And even if a nation has a "character," or a collective will, mind, or soul — this will or this mind is as often distorted or defeated as it is expressed in actual historical events.

Nor is it certain that the elusive and mysterious principles of national character or behavior found adequate expression in the oracles delivered by the various native authorities in Russian destiny: the Chaadaevs, the Leont'evs, or the Dostoyevskys. It is no doubt only natural to search for some constants or invariables which would make the behavior of a people intelligible and perhaps to some extent even predictable. But objective study of facts does not seem to reveal any such constant or ultimate principle. It reveals a picture of diversity, of conflicting trends and forces, favored or hampered by circumstance.

One may note in conclusion, however, that the problem of individual freedom holds a very large place in the works of the great Russian writers of the nineteenth century (even if it may not be necessarily stated in political or constitutional terms); that the great Russian writers jealously preserved their autonomy and their integrity against attempts to commit them to causes, progressive or otherwise; and that Russian society refused to be guided or indoctrinated by the government.

Those who exercise controls over present-day Russian literature — choosing for it, and imposing upon it, ideology, thematic material and even form — often invoke the authority of Chernyshevskii and of the other "revolutionary democrats" of the 1860's. Chernyshevskii did assign a subsidiary, an auxiliary role to literature and the arts in the fight he was waging. But Chernyshevskii was a dissenter; even if his views were narrow, he sought to mobilize the forces of the intellect against the forces of the police state. It would be futile to surmise what attitude he would have taken toward nonconformists and dissenters had he achieved power: the meditations of Dostoyevsky's Shigalëv are not necessarily a prediction of "things that came."

But be that as it may, the rather crude utilitarianism of Chernyshevskii ceased to be a dominant, or even an important trend long before the Revolution. The present condition of Russian literature can hardly be seen as a stage in a continuous development; rather, it is the result of a sharp break with a vigorous and productive tradition of liberalism and of respect for the independence of the creative writer.

Main Premises of the Communist Party
in the Theory of Soviet Literary Controls

ROBERT M. HANKIN

There is no "theory of literary controls" known under that title in Soviet parlance. Nevertheless, such a theory exists. It is compounded of various ingredients, of which two are the most important. The first of them is the experience accumulated by the Party in observing and guiding literary developments from the Revolution of 1917 to the year 1932, from which we date the exercise of this theory of controls. The second is a complex of critical assumptions in Leninist philosophy, as interpreted in the Stalin era. The second of these constituents is, in our view, the weightier. Yet it cannot be isolated mechanically from the first. For the history of the early period informs us how, and in what measure, certain nascent "proletarian" hypotheses concerning the role of literature in Soviet society, which in retrospect now seem to be fundamental Leninist assumptions, were momentarily arrested in their development, only to be incorporated subsequently in a monolithic credo. We shall ascertain from this amorphous phase, the period of the New Economic Policy, what it was the Party was rejecting when it repudiated the counsel of its more catholic adherents and adopted the platform of 1932. And we shall endeavor to probe the rationale of the theory of controls in its ultimate appearance.

The great majority of the Russian intelligentsia shrank from the cataclysm of 1917. The new literary mandates imposed by the Revolution were deemed by most of the writers to be crippling and intolerable. The literati found themselves defenseless, and wholly dependent on the whims of a monopolistic patron whose concerns were exasperatingly political. As the society from which these artists had sprung collapsed, so also did their literary organizations, leaving each writer to face the turbulent events alone. Politically inimical to the new regime, isolated in and by the new community, while faced with hopeless living conditions, the writers emigrated in considerable numbers. Of those who stayed behind, the majority remained silent. They were sustained in their boycott by their confused perception of the events which they were witnessing, and by the dislocation of literary

publishing. Piously they clung to the belief that the dictatorship of the proletariat had not long to endure.

Among the writers who did choose to support the revolutionary effort,
the Futurists were most conspicuous. They crowded noisily into the literary
void, candidly embracing the Revolution and what were — in their opinion
— its cultural aspirations. Rashly repudiating the literary heritage of the
classics as a link with the odious past, they defined the task of art as the
creation of entirely new forms inspired by industrialization. On the strength
of their belief that theirs was a unique spiritual affinity with the proletariat,
they demanded the prerogatives of literary hegemony. However, except for
the friendly reception accorded the best of the Futurists, Maiakovskii, the
proletariat which they idolized failed to appreciate, much less comprehend,
their antics. On the other hand their disdain for the past, deriving as it so
often did from ignorance, held but little appeal for intellectuals of more substantial mold. Aggressive tactics swelled the hosts of their ill-wishers. Their
claim to speak in the name of the Party was declined. The stock of talent
and organizational skill at their disposal proved inadequate to the task of
revolutionizing culture. The star of Futurism faded fast.[1]

The Futurists competed for attention with the Proletcult (Proletarian
Cultural and Educational Organization) which similarly aspired to monopo-
lize cultural development. Unlike the Futurists, however, the Proletcult im-
prudently championed the independence of cultural activities from Party
controls. Mistrustful of heresy which might find nurture in such soil, and
mindful of his long-standing suspicion of the Proletcult's most distinguished
theorist, Bogdanov, Lenin moved abruptly against the movement; at his
insistence the Proletcult was subordinated to the Commissariat of Enlightenment. From this early skirmish a permanent principle of Party controls
emerged: the State would countenance no form of cultural autonomy.

The role which the Proletcult leaders arrogated to their movement seemed
to them consistent with their definition — prophetic in retrospect — of the
function of art in the proletarian dictatorship. For Bogdanov, art was an
expression of class consciousness and "a means of uniting and rallying class
forces." [2] It was his contention that all previous definitions, from whatever
source, had slighted this activating function. He held, furthermore, that the
artist's psyche was the captive of his class; hence the art of the bourgeoisie
necessarily reflected and imparted an alien ideology, unsuitable for directing
proletarian consciousness. What the proletariat needed was an original art,
and this he proposed to produce in a network of studios and laboratories
under the auspices of a cultural Gosplan. As we shall see shortly, Lenin was

---

[1] V. Polonskii, "Literaturnoe dvizhenie oktiabr'skogo desiatiletiia," *Pechat' i revoliutsiia*, no. 7 (1927), pp. 21–23. (Reactions of the intelligentsia to 1917 Revolution; rise
and fall of Futurism.)

[2] *Ibid.*, p. 34.

out of sympathy with this program for laboratory culture, considering it to be blind to the real needs of the cultural revolution.

Before the Proletcult had passed from the scene, it had succeeded in enlisting an impressive following among politically conscious youth, factory workers included. It had articulated many of the crucial issues which were to face proletarian culture, provoked an intensely partisan interest in literary matters and, in the process, given rise to a fundamental rift among writers. Discord within Proletcult ranks led in 1920 to the establishment of the proletarian Smithy Group, from which, through the continuing process of doctrinal ramification, the October Group issued shortly thereafter. It was the platform of this organization, and of its most influential publication, the magazine *On Guard,* which represented the "artistic banner of proletarian literature"[3] in the early twenties, claiming to speak for the only ideologically qualified, consistently "proletarian" writers on the scene. The October movement constituted a vitriolic and concerted bid for proletarian hegemony in literature. But if any sort of hegemony did reside with one or another warring faction, such hegemony lay with the writers known as Fellow Travelers. This group has been described as comprising those "writers who reflected the ideology of the Soviet petty bourgeois intelligentsia, and were characterized by marked political indecision, but who nonetheless sought to collaborate with the proletariat."[4] Their activities, commencing in 1921, betokened the renascence of literature after the chaos of the Civil War. In a short time the Fellow Travelers and their partisans found themselves engaged in mortal combat with the proletarian Left which demanded unconditional surrender to the October platform. The dispute extended to the highest echelons of the Party, and in the ensuing atmosphere "Party men scorned each other as though they were class enemies."[5]

The proletarian Left held the Fellow Travelers to be a source of contamination of the body politic. Art, for the Left, was a weapon of class struggle, effective because it held the power of emotional infection:

> The reader tends to *yield* to the influence of the artistic image, and *only when* his own class nature becomes indignant over this influence does he *begin* to resist. The degree of resistance depends exclusively on the steadfastness, consistency, and wholeness of the reader's class identification.[6]

Only that literature was permissible, in their view, which infected the reader with "emotions appropriate to the ideology and psychology of the proletariat as a class,"[7] and organized the consciousness of the reader — the proletarian

[3] "Kuznitsa," *Literaturnaia entsiklopediia,* V (1931), 705.

[4] "Poputchiki," *Literaturnaia entsiklopediia,* IX (1935), 142.

[5] Polonskii, *Pechat' i revoliutsiia,* no. 7 (1927), p. 62.

[6] G. Lelevich, "Snova o nashikh literaturnykh raznoglasiiakh," *Pechat' i revoliutsiia,* no. 8 (1925), p. 86.

[7] A. Lezhnëv, review of "Voprosy literatury i dramaturgii. Disput v Malom teatre pod predsedatel'stvom A. V. Lunacharskogo, 26 maia 1924 g.," *Pechat' i revoliutsiia,* no. 2 (1925), p. 257.

reader in the first instance — toward the ultimate goal of Communism. As the Left saw them, the Fellow Travelers fell hopelessly short of qualifying on this score. To mold proletarian consciousness in the fashion desired, literature had to contain a true picture of life, and truthfulness in art, said the Left, was a concomitant of the artist's class origins. Only those writers were equal to the assignment, in the dictatorship of the proletariat, who viewed the Revolution "through the eyes of the proletariat," that is, the proletarian vanguard, in short, through the eyes of the Party. Such writers must necessarily be primarily of proletarian extraction. To acknowledge any other source of literature would be to foster the revival of bourgeois thinking. Fellow Travelers, by virtue of their equivocal class orientation, could fulfill only one useful function, which was the "ideological disarmament" of the bourgeoisie.[8] It was altogether inconsistent — so ran the conclusion of the Left argument — that the dictatorship of the proletariat in the state should be accompanied by the domination of a nonproletarian ideology in literature. The Party must pronounce officially in favor of proletarian hegemony, matching the seizure of power in the state with a proletarian seizure of power in art.

The Left intimated, however, that the Fellow Travelers did not stand condemned beyond reprieve, and might aspire to salvation. Time would be needed for reclamation, a process which must induce first the reconciliation and ultimately the synthesis of the writer's *Weltanschauung* with his artistic inspiration. The breach between the writer's convictions and his creative muse could be sealed organically only if he acquiesced to monolithic conformity. Lelevich, one of the most vociferous of the Left spokesmen, prescribed a specific therapeutic regimen: instead of surrendering to his artistic instincts on the assumption that the appropriate revolutionary message would spontaneously follow, the writer must reverse the process. He must first set for himself a missionary goal, and then, by dint of scrupulous effort to give his message artistic implementation, must strive to rechannelize his artistic psyche. From this art would surely follow. *But if one were to assume,* said Lelevich, *that in the end consistent and revolutionary ideology should prove incompatible with art, for a genuine revolutionary Marxist there could be only one decision: "Down with artistic mastery!"* (Italics mine.)[9] However, Lelevich denied that art was, in fact, incompatible with revolutionary ideology.

The opponents of the Left in the Party disdained the call for the unconditional surrender of the Fellow Travelers. In prescribing conformity, said Trotsky, the Left was displaying abysmal ignorance of the nature of art, a specialized sphere of human activity with its own laws of development, in

---

[8] Polonskii, *Pechat' i revoliutsiia,* no. 7 (1927), p. 60.
[9] G. Lelevich, "V. V. Vorovskii i ocherednye problemy marksistskoi literaturnoi kritiki," *Pechat' i revoliutsiia,* no. 3 (1925), p. 80.

which a vital role was played by the subconscious. To deflect the subconscious was a lengthy, complex, and delicate undertaking, frequently attended by fatal spiritual crisis. Conformity under the present circumstances was unimaginable.[10] In Polonskii's opinion, Lelevich was mechanically superimposing on art techniques which he — Lelevich — had put to creditable use as an historian, but which, when applied to literature, embodied an ultimatum to writers to repudiate their own personalities. For his part, Lunacharskii had declared in 1920: "It goes without saying that the state has no intention of forcibly imposing revolutionary ideas and tastes upon artists. Such coercive pressure can result only in the falsification of revolutionary art, for the first quality of true art is the artist's sincerity." [11] There was fundamental concurrence in this camp, therefore, that the coercive policy advocated by the Left would be destructive of artistic integrity, and hence of art. (This should not be taken to imply, however, that they questioned either the Party's general supervision of literary development, or the exercise of censorship in detecting and prohibiting "counterrevolutionary" manifestations in art.)

Many other Left propositions were rejected. Voronskii challenged the premise that proletarian writers had a monopoly on objective truth. Class origin, he believed, did not necessarily predetermine subjective distortion of reality. Any class had need of objective knowledge, and confidently entrusted this function to its writers. The valid cognitive elements in bourgeois literature might, in his opinion, be of considerable use to the proletariat.[12] Lunacharskii demurred from the idea that bourgeois art might contaminate the proletariat since, for him, faith in one's own class constituted effective immunization. Besides, he declared, under present conditions the proletarian impact on the bourgeoisie was more potent than the reverse.[13] Voronskii, considering the function of art, insisted that the exclusive utilitarianism of the Left had produced a misdefinition of art. He declared art to be primarily cognition, and decried the view that it deliberately aspired to evoke "good feelings" in the reader. Others — Polonskii, Lunacharskii, Bukharin, etc. — entertained more eclectic opinions in this regard, and proffered a diversity of definitions, which in some instances embraced the utilitarian premise of the Left as one of several valid functions of art.

To these attempts at combining definitions of art Lelevich retorted by casting doubt upon their methodology. The relative correctness of formulas

[10] L. Trotskii, "O Khudozhestvennoi literature i politike R.K.P. (Rech' na soveshchanii pri Ts.K. R.K.P. o literature, 10 maia 1924 g.)," *Pechat' i revoliutsiia*, no. 3 (1924), pp. iii–xiv.

[11] A. V. Lunacharskii, "Revoliutsiia i iskusstvo," *Stat'i ob iskusstve* (Moscow-Leningrad, 1941), p. 492. Reprinted from *Kommunisticheskoe prosveshchenie*, no. 1 (1920).

[12] "Voronskii, Aleksandr Konstantinovich," *Literaturnaia entsiklopediia*," II (1930), 314–315.

[13] Polonskii, *Pechat' i revoliutsiia*, no. 7 (1927), p. 68.

other than his own was, according to him, beyond dispute. Art was unquestionably a means of cognition, an ideology, a reflection of social mores, a device of class self-recognition, etc., besides being a weapon of class struggle. However, it was incumbent upon a revolutionary Marxist to select the *one* criterion "most essential from the standpoint of social specificity." [14] This, he said, was how Lenin approached similar questions in other domains. It would be hard to overstate the importance of Lelevich's line of reasoning for the Stalin era which followed.

In 1925 the Party published a formal pronouncement on the issues which had aroused such intense partisanship in the two preceding years. By Soviet standards of a later day the resolution was a middle-of-the-road solution. It promised, on the one hand, that the Left dream of one day reigning supreme in literature as in all other domains should come true, but on the other hand disclaimed the Left bid for prompt accession to authority, on the ground that hegemony had not yet been earned. The Left was called to task for its arrogance, and admonished to handle the Fellow Travelers tactfully so as to win over the more amenable of them to closer coöperation with the Communists. Though referring to the need for writers to develop a style comprehensible to a mass public, the Party championed a free competition of literary styles.[15]

This resolution ushered in a brief period of tranquillity in literature. For the moment the threat of monolithic coercion had been turned back and the abusive, fulminating tone of the Left castigated. In the list of Party statements on literature, the resolution is distinguished for its moderate tone. The Party's unwillingness to heed the importunities of the Left amounted almost to nonintervention. The factors which help to clarify this reluctance to act more decisively are significant, since only when it is contrasted with the earlier period is the subsequent Stalinist era seen in proper relief.

For one thing, the nature of the reading public precluded any broader commitment to the Left. The mass public which we have come to regard as a permanent feature of Soviet life did not exist at this time; hence concern over literary contamination had little basis in fact. Statistics on the dissemination of printed matter among workers and peasants seemed impressive, but were deceiving. The really important facts are to be discerned in the high cost of books in relation to low peasant-worker purchasing power, the insufficiency of libraries and their slow progress in attracting a mass membership. Serious literature, moreover, was beyond the comprehension of the reader scarce emerged from illiteracy.[16] Of the prerevolutionary literary public, little remained. The intelligentsia had emigrated on a large scale.

[14] G. Lelevich, "Snova o raznoglasiiakh," *Pechat' i revoliutsiia*, no. 8 (1925), p. 84.

[15] "O politike partii v oblasti khudozhestvennoi literatury. Resoliutsiia Ts.K. R.K.P. (b) ot 18 iiunia 1925 g.," *Sovremennaia literatura* (Moscow, 1939), pp. 7–10.

[16] A. Kurs, "Zabytaia direktiva," *Pechat' i revoliutsiia*, no. 4 (1926), p. 101.

Among those who remained, mortality had been high in the first years of the Revolution, and the impoverishment of the survivors made a book the rarest of luxuries. The only elements possessed of the wherewithal to indulge in literature were to be found among the new bourgeoisie of the NEP. And their tastes ruled. Proletarian writers found themselves at a hopeless disadvantage when it became apparent that the fare which they served the neobourgeois reader was unpalatable. Blatant didacticism, the minute dissecting of everyday phenomena, the reader's awareness that literature was telling less than the whole truth, above all the disappearance of interesting plots from their works, explain their failure with the public. Their works had to be sold by the pound to dispose of them. What the reader craved above all in literature was excitement, and the State Publishing House sought to gratify this passion by contracting for innumerable translations from contemporary Western literature. In 1926, 50 per cent of its output consisted of such translations; the same proportion was scheduled for the following year.[17] In short, the NEP literary market would have paralyzed a more aggressive Party policy.

Frustrated by the market, most writers were destitute. A multitude of youthful authors had sprung up. Aspiring to a permanent career in literature, they severed their connections with factory or field with the first gestures of encouragement. "Only a few — they can be counted on the fingers — lead a tolerable existence." [18] Writers appeared to be worse off than they had been before the "commanding heights" rested securely in proletarian hands. Independent publishing before the Revolution had featured multiple opportunities to win the sympathetic attention of a publisher. Where one might turn a work down, another often welcomed it. During the NEP, though private publishing existed, it could not compete on equal terms with the government-supported press. A single ideological patron held sway; editors were for the most part merely his administrative agents. While inhibited ideologically in the range within which they could indulge their literary preferences, these editors — if they wished to remain solvent — had at the same time to satisfy the demands of the NEP reading public. The gap between the writer and the mass which the Revolution had, in theory, sealed, remained after all. Dislodged from solid footing in society by the vagaries of this market many writers — Fellow Travelers and proletarians alike — sought solace in bohemianism. Suicides were not uncommon. More and more the writer was coming to view his endless struggle on the market as a war on organized society.[19]

The 1925 resolution is symptomatic of another development inevitably attendant upon Lenin's decision to usher in the NEP: disharmony in Party

[17] "Khronika. V. literaturno-khudozhestvennom otdele Gosudarstvennogo izdatel'stva," *Pechat' i revoliutsiia*, no. 1 (1927), p. 229.

[18] V. Polonskii, "Zametki zhurnalista," *Pechat' i revoliutsiia*, no. 7 (1926), p. 86.

[19] Kurs, "Zabytaia direktiva," *Pechat' i revoliutsiia*, no. 4 (1926), p. 198.

ranks. The supreme bid for power of the Stalinist Center, and the triumph of Stalinist antideterminism lay ahead. Meanwhile a struggle was under way in all spheres of Soviet ideology between the mechanistic determinists and the activists in the Party.[20] This struggle seems to be in evidence in the Party Resolution of 1925. The document is said to have been written in its final form by Bukharin,[21] and one is tempted to see in it elements of the theory of "equilibrium" associated with Bukharin's name at a somewhat later date. It is true that in the resolution the Party took great pains to explain that it was collaborating with the bourgeoisie only with a view to forcing it out, and was seeking to create conditions for the Fellow Travelers to accept the state's ideology as soon as possible. Furthermore, it reiterated its intention to retain control over literary development and held out the hope that sooner or later dialectical materialism would win the day in literature. Yet these are passive formulations, when contrasted with subsequent Party opinions. The mere fact that the document recognized the artistic inadequacy of Left literary production and advocated victory through artistic competition comes perilously close, on Soviet soil, to admission that the immanent nature of literary evolution made forceful Party intervention in this sphere undesirable. Significant by its absence from the 1925 resolution is a definition of literature as a tool in directing consciousness.

With the end of the NEP the Party line on literature changed. In December 1927 Trotsky and his faction were expelled from the Party. In April 1929 the Sixteenth Party Conference approved the "optimal" variant of the First Five-Year Plan and called for a cultural revolution to accompany and facilitate economic changes. It was in December 1929 that Stalin attacked the theories of "equilibrium" and "spontaneous development" as un-Marxist and demanded a fresh theoretical approach to keep pace with changes under way in the economy.[22] An era was drawing to a close and literature was at once affected.

The end of Trotsky's power in the state, Voronskii's expulsion from the Party in 1927, Polonskii's fall from grace, and Lunacharskii's capitulation to the new day symptomized the death of a cause. In several speeches in 1928, Party officials were no longer hesitant in demanding that literature be subordinated to socialist construction. Two decrees on the press which appeared in 1928 — the first on children's literature, the other called "On Servicing the Mass Reader with Books" — defined literature as "a tool in the organization of the masses," summoned writers to all-out war on "bourgeois influences," expressed positive preference for Communist writers in

---

[20] Raymond A. Bauer, *The New Man in Soviet Psychology* (Cambridge, Mass., 1952). See pp. 13–33 for an excellent presentation of the details of this struggle.

[21] V. Polonskii, "Na puti k edinomu literaturnomu frontu," *Pechat' i revoliutsiia*, no. 1 (1927), p. 74.

[22] I. Stalin, "K voprosam agrarnoi politiki v SSSR. Rech' na konferentsii agrarnikov-marksistov 27 dekabria 1929 g.," *Voprosy leninizma* (11th ed., 1935), pp. 299–304.

accomplishing the literary plan, and catalogued the writers' ideological goals for the Plan period: "Communist education," "inculcation of militant Bolshevist traditions," "cultivation of class irreconcilability," "raising of the cultural level," "propaganda of Leninism and struggle against its distortion . . ." [23] Thus were obliterated the last traces of passivism from the Party's direction of literature.

It was only natural that the Party should turn to its favorite sons, the proletarian writers, for support in executing the new line. Was it not now adopting much of the early Left program? But the Party's hopes were misplaced. Too faithfully had the proletarian literary leaders heeded the admonition of their ideological mentors to suppress arrogance and learn from the Fellow Travelers what they had to teach. In the intervening three years the leaders of the Russian Association of Proletarian Writers (RAPP) had developed a sober respect for intrinsic literary values and a new insight into the creative process. In the next few years relations between the Party and the RAPP are a record of the RAPP leaders' tenacious defense of the bastions of literary individuality. Their purpose was to prevent literature from being administered as a mere channel of communications between the Party and the mass. After 1930 friction developed between the two centers at an accelerated pace. The Party complained that RAPP was tardy in its response to literary assignments; in reality this was a thrust at the RAPP leaders for maintaining that blatantly agitational literature was a violation of art. The Party wished to have done with RAPP-Tolstoyan psychological realism, alleging that it yielded an "objectivist" portrait of the class enemy, and was insufficiently denunciatory. The Party reprimanded RAPP for abusing its initially favored position to encroach on Party publishing prerogatives. Zealous and vituperative defense by the RAPP leaders of their now strangely conservative platform elicited the charge that they were suppressing opposition and resorting to abusive tactics. By reviving their earlier onslaught on Fellow Travelers, the RAPP leaders collided head-on with Stalin's command that specialists be handled with consideration in all fields at the current stage. RAPP recalcitrance on this issue was doubly irritating to the Party when it became apparent that the Fellow Travelers were proving both coöperative and effective in implementing the line.[24]

From the RAPP episode the Party drew a conclusion significant for the future of Soviet literary controls. In its dealings with RAPP, it had sought to command the obedience of a cultural organization which seemingly had every reason to be closely attuned to the requirements of the day. The experience demonstrated, however, that a dual loyalty could spring from a

[23] A. I. Nazarov, *Ocherki istorii sovetskogo knigoizdatel'stva* (Moscow, 1952), pp. 155–157.

[24] I should like to express my indebtedness to Edward J. Brown, author of *The Proletarian Episode in Russian Literature, 1928–1932* (New York, 1953) for his fresh insight into the relations between the Party and RAPP.

literary organization resting on an independently developed platform. Clearly, there was no way of guaranteeing that such a platform would coincide with Party desiderata. Dual loyalty was something which the Party had not the slightest intention of countenancing. Lenin, scenting in his day a similar threat to the unmitigated authority of the Party, had been quick to nip in the bud the Proletcult's bid for autonomy. This analogy with the Proletcult may help to explain the unceremonious gesture with which RAPP was wiped off the slate by the Party decree in 1932. The framework of RAPP might, of course, have been preserved. The title could easily have been altered, the directing staff replaced. The total extinction of RAPP is symbolic. A new organization would signify in literature the complete rupture with the past which the Plan itself envisaged in the economic and social order. The new Union of Soviet Writers would start ideologically "pure" in its adjustment to Stalin's designs. The epoch of "proletarian" literature would yield to the "socialist," thereby according recognition to the Fellow Travelers for their newly manifested spirit of coöperation. Monolithic direction of literature would be more feasible if everything — the structure of the new organization, its platform — seemed brand new and if the accessory purpose of literature was formalized beyond suspicion of doubt in the Charter of the Writers' Union.

In the twenties it was pretty generally conceded that the principles of Marxist literary criticism, such as they were, had in the main been the contribution of Plekhanov. Plekhanov was more than a literary critic; he was a Marxist philosopher as well and, in that capacity, he also enjoyed tremendous prestige. In 1931 Stalin administered the *coup de grâce* to the authority of Plekhanov in the Soviet Union, evidently considering this to be an essential step in effecting the new approach in theory on which he insisted. The regnant philosophical cadres were summarily dismissed and branded "Menshevizing idealists," a term intended to describe Plekhanov's philosophical adherents. Lenin's ideas — in their Stalinist interpretation — became codified orthodoxy. "Bolshevist *partiinost'*," "militancy," "irreconcilability" — these were the new battle cries. The newly installed philosophers lost no time in turning upon RAPP with an encyclical which is the dogma of Stalinism in literature:

> The contemplative attitude, objectivism, the failure to understand the *partiinost'* of science, philosophy and literature, characteristic of the whole world-view of Menshevism, were reflected in all questions resolved by Plekhanov, and were also reflected in his esthetic views. The decisive condition for the current development of literary science is the task of mastering and working out Lenin's theoretical testament in this field . . . We have in Lenin a colossal theoretical wealth which must now be mastered . . . and applied to literary science. Lenin's works on philosophy, his teaching on *partiinost'* of science . . . his works on problems of culture and the cultural revolution provide such material as will raise literary science to a new level. The struggle for Leninism in literary science and proletarian litera-

ture is a most important immediate task, and it must be made the cornerstone of our proletarian literary movement.[25]

By contrast with Plekhanov, Lenin's comments bearing directly on literary questions are tangential. It was his general philosophical premises, particularly his ideas on *partiinost'*, which were emphasized, and applied to literature as to any other "superstructural" category. Nevertheless, Lenin's comments on various aspects of cultural problems provided a pattern of guiding lines which were elevated to the status of binding Party directives.

Lenin's views on the role of the past in the new society, and on the popular nature of Soviet art, can be ascertained with reasonable certainty. Before the Revolution, his opponents had insisted that it would be a fatal error to attempt socialism in a land completely lacking in the prerequisite dissemination of culture. Lenin proceeded, nonetheless, with his Revolution. He remained, however, painfully cognizant of Russian cultural backwardness and feared it might prove to be Bolshevism's Achilles' heel. After coming to power, therefore, he reversed his attitude to bourgeois culture. Before the Revolution he had abused the bourgeois order as "civilized barbarism"; after 1917 he argued for the enlightenment which the bourgeois order must be made to contribute to the new order. Although he spoke of the need to refashion this legacy and adapt it to current demands, he was explicit in contending that proletarian culture must be an extension of all antecedent cultural developments. It was from this premise that he censured the efforts of the Proletcult, upbraiding them for placing the cart before the horse. Their experiments on the creation of new values appeared to him to bypass and divert attention from the real and crying need, which was to raise the level of the most elementary culture, a task in which the "old" culture — bourgeois science, technology, and art — must play the major role. In the First Five-Year Plan the consuming importance of the cultural revolution emerged into the foreground. Every variety of specialized knowledge and skill was in desperate demand, and an unprecedented role had been assigned to the participation of the masses. For its general cultural strategy the Stalin regime drew upon Lenin's exhortation to the educated upper stratum to sacrifice personal artistic preferences on the altar of revolutionary priority. Since Stalin's triumph this principle — *narodnost'* — formulated by Lenin in his talk with Klara Tsetkin, has been taken for gospel:

It is not our opinion of art which is important. It is not what art gives to several hundreds, even several thousands, of a total population numbering millions, which is important. Art belongs to the people. Its deepest roots must lie in the very thick of the broadest masses of the people. It must unite the feelings, thoughts and will of these masses, elevate them. It must rouse artists among them

[25] M. Mitin, "Ocherednye zadachi na filosofskom fronte v sviazi s itogami filosofskoi diskussii," *Pod znamenem marksizma*, no. 3 (March 1931), p. 19. Quoted from E. Brown, "The Russian Association of Proletarian Writers (1928–1932)," doctoral dissertation (Columbia University, 1950), pp. 334–335.

and develop them. Should we serve sweet, delicate biscuits to a small minority while the worker and peasant masses need black bread? I mean this, naturally, not only in the literal sense, but figuratively as well. We must have the workers and peasants constantly in mind. For their sake we must learn to administer, to keep accounts. This refers also to the field of art and culture.[26]

For Lenin, moreover, the restriction of the province of art for which he was here calling constituted no violation of his personal artistic sensibilities. Lenin was a man of conservative tastes in literature and art. To dispense with artistic novelty and experimentation caused scarcely a ripple of concern in him: ". . . I make bold to call myself a 'barbarian.' I fail to see in the works of expressionism, futurism, cubism and other 'ism's' the highest manifestations of artistic genius. I do not understand them. I experience no joy from them." [27] He denied that contemporary art was superior and decried "cultists" as hypocrites displaying "unconscious deference to Western artistic fashion." [28] The relentless animosity of Stalin's regime to formal experimentation derives much of its orthodox justification from these two Leninist theses: the obligatory *narodnost'* of art and the banishment of innovation for its own sake.

From the vantage point of the Stalinist epoch, Lenin's most significant pronouncement on artistic policy is embodied in his 1905 article "Party Organization and Party Literature." This article has been cited since 1932 as the fundamental law of the land for literature. In the twenties, however, the document was held to be either of such extraliterary significance, or of such exclusive pertinence to the time of its writing, that it is not even mentioned in a catalogue of Lenin's important statements on cultural problems compiled by Polonskii in 1927.[29] In 1932 we are informed by Lunacharskii that "the motive for writing this article was the wish to organize the Party's *political literature,* its *publicism,* its *scientific publications,* . . ." (italics mine). Lunacharskii volunteers the opinion, however, that the principles of the 1905 article applied equally well at the time to belles-lettres, and that, as of 1932, the article contained "administrative instructions" for Party literary policy.[30] Though there may be some reason to doubt that Lenin himself intended the directives contained in this article to apply to imaginative literature, they were so applied under Stalinism. In 1946 Zhdanov asserted that the 1905 article was the source of "all the foundations on which the development of our Soviet literature rests." [31]

[26] Klara Tsetkin, "Vospominaniia o Lenine," *Lenin o kulture i iskusstve* (Moscow-Leningrad, 1941), p. 138.
[27] *Ibid.*, p. 137.
[28] *Ibid.*
[29] Polonskii, "Literaturnoe dvizhenie," *Pechat' i revoliutsiia,* no. 7 (1927), p. 18.
[30] A. V. Lunacharskii, "Lenin i literaturovedenie," *Literaturnaia entsiklopediia,* VI (1932), 257–259.
[31] A. A. Zhdanov, "Doklad o zhurnalakh *Zvezda* i *Leningrad,*" *Sovetskaia kniga,* nos. 8–9 (1946), p. 20.

It is in this article that Lenin demands of literature that it identify itself with Party policy by accepting *partiinost'*, the concept which is at the very heart of Soviet literary controls. Lenin's definition of *partiinost'* is contained in the following:

> . . . for the socialist proletariat literature cannot be an instrument of gain for persons or groups; it cannot altogether be an individual matter, independent of the whole proletarian cause. Down with non-Party writers! Down with literary supermen! Literature must become *part* of the general cause of the proletariat, the "wheel and the screw" of a single great Social Democratic mechanism, set in motion by the entire politically conscious vanguard of the whole working class. Literature must become a component part of the organized, planned, united Social Democratic Party work.[32]

When these lines were written the Party had just emerged from a position of illegality. It faced the prospect of attracting to its standards heterogeneous elements which, out of a diffuse opposition to the tsarist regime, might briefly fraternize with the Bolsheviks, but could not conceivably accept the fundamental philosophy of the movement. Lenin agreed to accept such traveling companions on one condition: they must obey the Party line. ("Writers must without fail join Party organizations!")[33] This demand, Lenin declared in the article, did not constitute a violation of free speech and press. It served notice that the Party reserved the privilege of purging its ranks of elements it considered undesirable. Under conditions obtaining in 1905, a writer rejected by the Party might affiliate with some other group. Lenin's injunction to writers to join Party organizations was automatically realized in 1932, when the monopolistic Union of Soviet Writers was established with a Communist fraction. But the accessory condition, under which the writer retained *potential* freedom of movement after joining a Party organization, ceased to be meaningful after 1932. Once expelled from the writers' organization, the writer is not at liberty to join some other literary organization. There is only one. The choice before him — provided the grounds for his purging do not result in even more oppressive measures against him — is hardly a choice: either to mend his ways in the hope that the writers' organization can be prevailed upon to readmit him to membership, or resign himself to permanent separation from a literary career.

We have suggested that Lenin's personal views on the writer's role in society are of less moment than the actual use to which his words — regardless of the context in which they may have been uttered — were put. But the temptation is strong to speculate on the potential in the man himself for concurrence with the interpretation placed upon his literal statements. One remark made to Klara Tsetkin in the conversation already alluded to contains a hint of a possible wavering in him, perhaps reflecting conflict

[32] V. I. Lenin, "Partiinaiia organizatsiia i partiinaia literatura," *Sovremennaia literatura* (Moscow, 1939), p. 4.
[33] *Ibid.*, pp. 4–5.

between whatever there may have been in him of the Western-style emancipator, and his dominant traits conditioned primarily by the native revolutionary tradition. He is quoted as saying:

> In a society based on private property the artist produces goods for the market, he needs customers. Our Revolution has released artists from the oppression of these extremely prosaic conditions. The Soviet state now defends them and places orders with them. Each artist, every one who feels he is an artist, has the right to create freely, according to his own ideal, dependent upon nothing whatsoever.[34]

One might almost derive from this the startling conclusion that in Lenin's opinion the writer's sole responsibility after the Revolution was to himself! As though catching himself up, however, Lenin at once added: "But, of course, we are Communists. We must not stand by idly and permit chaos to develop where it will. We must direct this process in a wholly planned fashion and determine the results." [35] On other occasions his remarks clearly indicate that the latter half of the statement above more correctly reflected his views. The strictures which he vented in the course of his feud with the Proletcult seem quite closely akin to ideas prevailing after 1932:

> In the Soviet Workers-Peasants Republic the entire organization of enlightenment, both in the sphere of political enlightenment in general and in the sphere of art in particular, must be permeated with the spirit of the proletariat's class struggle for the successful accomplishment of the purposes of its dictatorship.[36]

As a canny tactician who veered repeatedly in plotting the Party's course, he would not, presumably, have hesitated to apply *partiinost'* to creative writers, and in its sternest variant, if he felt the situation warranted the restraint. Nothing would have been allowed to temper his militancy if, in his view, circumstances made the imposition of a tight harness on artists important for the survival of the Revolution. Moral scruples against the invasion of sacred areas of human personality could not have deterred him since for Lenin morality was synonymous with the interests of the proletarian class struggle.[37]

Oddly enough, however, in Leninist philosophy freedom and *partiinost'* are easily reconciled. Indeed, the contention is often voiced that these terms are virtually synonymous, that "the *partiinost'* of Soviet literature guarantees the genuine freedom of the artist." [38] The devious thinking by which this conclusion is reached intrigues with its insight into the labyrinth of the Bolshevist mind. Lenin characterized Party-line literature as "free" because it would be motivated by "the idea of socialism and sympathy for the

---

[34] Tsetkin, *Lenin o kulture i iskusstve*, p. 137.
[35] *Ibid.*
[36] V. I. Lenin, "O proletarskoi kulture," *Lenin o kulture i iskusstve*, p. 37.
[37] F. V. Konstantinov, ed., *Istoricheskii materializm* (Moscow, 1951), p. 573.
[38] "Literatura i iskusstvo," *Bol'shaia sovetskaia entsiklopediia*, supplementary volume (Moscow, 1947), p. 1472.

workers," because it would serve the masses and enrich Party theory with experience.[39] In his thinking, however, this was a conclusion which presumed acceptance of his theory of cognition and the definition of the Party as the proletarian vanguard. The first premise of Leninism is that a real, material, world exists independent of our senses. Matter is seen to be in constant, interrelated motion, propelled by the struggle of opposites. This world, furthermore, is declared to be knowable through sensory perception and consciousness; to consciousness is attributed the capacity to reflect objective reality. A satisfactory theory, however, more fully reflects reality than the consciousness of any individual, and the distinction of being the only scientific theory of reality Lenin reserves for Marxism, which, in his opinion, by virtue of unique and consistent materialism had alone attained a valid understanding of how the laws of nature and history operated. Applied to social phenomena, the Marxian dialectic is presumed capable of pointing out from the welter of antagonistic forces in play at a given phase of history the specific social class whose aims and activities coincide with the unfolding of historical progress. This vision, once imparted to the Marxist, obliges him — in Lenin's version of Marxism — to side unreservedly with this class, the proletariat. *Volitional identification with the proletarian cause is the first essential of* "partiinost'." Continuing this line of reasoning, if the Leninist defines the reverse of freedom as man's enslavement to historical laws owing to inadequate comprehension of their operation, then freedom is viewed not as exemption from those laws (this is contemptuously rejected as the very essence of idealism in philosophy), but (quoting Engels) as "cognition of those laws and the opportunity to use them in planned fashion for specific goals." [40] Freedom is "necessity comprehended." Having once comprehended necessity the individual — again, in the Leninist version of Marxism — is obliged to act in such a way as to contribute to the remaking of human society. Thus, *the second essential of* "partiinost'" *is the call to action in conformity with the operation of historical laws.* Not action on one's own initiative, however. The right to initiate the design for refashioning society resides exclusively in the Party, called the elite of the class, the "organized vanguard of the proletariat." On the strength of the superior indoctrination and tempering which it claims, the Party exercises an unchallenged monopoly not only in the sphere of action, but also in the right to interpret Marxism at every conjuncture. A concomitant, therefore, of the obligation to act imposed by *partiinost'* is that *such action must be under Party direction.* Thus, *partiinost'* emerges as the ubiquitous assumption of the Bolshevik, be he kolkhoz chairman, minister of heavy industry, or writer.

In the Stalin era this general concept of *partiinost'* was supplemented, in the case of literature, with a more specialized formula. This was Socialist

[39] Lenin, *Sovremennaia literatura*, p. 6.
[40] "Svoboda," *Bol'shaia sovetskaia entsiklopediia*, L (1944), 510.

Realism, at once an aesthetic formulation and a specific theory of controls for literature. The doctrine is said to have been defined by Stalin personally, in a conversation with writers in 1932:

> Socialist Realism, being the basic method of Soviet artistic literature and literary criticism, demands of the artist a truthful, historically specific depiction of reality in its revolutionary development. Moreover, truthfulness and historical specificity in the depiction of reality must be combined with the task of ideologically remaking and educating the toilers in the spirit of socialism.[41]

The definition contains an obvious rephrasing of Lenin's conception of matter propelled by the struggle of opposites. When applied to literature, the obligation to view matter "in its revolutionary development" is supposed to direct the writer's attention to seeds of the future visible in the present, since, through the predictable efficacy of planning, what may be scarcely apparent today will, if such is the Party's intention, predominate tomorrow. This process of detection and depiction constitutes the cognitive function assigned to literature. The latter part of the definition treats the activating function of literature, the role to which Stalin added emphasis when he referred to writers as "engineers of human souls." [42]

How is the Soviet writer expected to exercise this capacity to "engineer" souls? The Party, as we have seen, interprets its historical function to be the guidance of the proletariat toward the accomplishment of historical necessity. Since the shift in theory which occurred during the First Five-Year Plan, the Stalinists have been violent in condemning notions of spontaneous development, which preclude the necessity of feasibility of human intervention in the "inexorable" movement of society to socialism. They have elevated conscious human motivation to a position of prominence, regarding the Party's success or failure in leadership as dependent upon its ability to achieve the maximum unity of will among the masses. Hence the avowed purpose of propaganda and agitation has been to infuse, mobilize, and channelize conscious motivation, if possible, on a total scale. Within this scheme the writer is assigned two fundamental tasks in his "engineering" capacity. First he is required to toil without surcease over the alignment of his own mental processes. The imposing proportions of indoctrinational activities among the literati are geared to facilitate the closest possible identification of the writer's views with those of the Party. Having tended to his personal ideological "purity" — an unending procedure effected under relentless pressure from the Party and its "fraction" in literature — the writer's next assignment is to enlist his craft in the Party's service as a transmission belt. He must communicate in persuasive imagery the emotions

---

[41] L. Timofeev and N. Vengrov, *Kratkii slovar' literaturovedcheskikh terminov* (Moscow, 1952), p. 121.
[42] "Rech' sekretaria TsK VKP(b) tov. A. A. Zhdanova na I vsesoiuznom s"ezde sovetskikh pisatelei," *Sovremennaia literatura*, p. 15.

and ideas which the Party wishes to inculcate in the masses. He has become the Party's creature:

> To indicate where to direct artistic forces, artistic attention, artistic talent — that is the natural conclusion from all our understanding of socialist construction. We know very well that we have the right to intervene in the course of culture, starting with mechanization in our country, with electrification as part of it, and ending with the direction of the most delicate forms of art.[43]

These are the words of Lunacharskii, the same Lunacharskii whose defense of literature's unique prerogatives ten years earlier had played such an effective part in repulsing the Left assault. As the situation appeared to him in 1933, the only question then remaining was *where* — not whether — to direct literature.

Except for the inevitable aberration of the war years, 1941–1945, the literary scene in the U.S.S.R. exhibits a consistent trend toward tighter controls. Before the war a number of developments revealed a pattern of crescent intolerance of heterodoxy: the revision of attitudes to Russian history with the aim of inculcating militant patriotism, the purge trials and the resultant fear craze in the Party, the massive consolidation of the regime and its ideology in 1935–1937, the mounting fury of broadsides against bourgeois culture which accompanied the rising threat of war, etc. The conclusion of the Second World War was succeeded by a brief interlude of liberal relaxation. Several writers, of proved fidelity to the regime, made so bold as to caution against administrative interference in artistic creation, denying that it was feasible to "organize" great art. But the Zhdanov Report in 1946 and the Party decrees on the arts which accompanied it, banished the hope that *partiinost'* might be so interpreted after the war as to allow a fair margin for creative individuality. Zhdanov's speech is a disquisition on Party literary controls at their most constraining phase. It surveys and reëmphasizes, point by point, the cardinal premises on controls which we have been considering: the frank subordination of literature to the state, compulsory homage to *narodnost'*, — above all, *partiinost'*, the *principle* from which all the rest are derived. No document has so rigidly repudiated exceptionalism in the treatment of art.

The ascending curve of astringency appears to coincide roughly with the course of the postwar Plan. The "philosophers" rode roughshod over the arts, prescribing areas of interest, selecting themes and heroes, dictating precise viewpoints, dotting *i*'s and crossing *t*'s, carrying the latent assumptions of "Party Organization and Party Literature" to a new height of absolute realization. It seems plausible to assume that this policy rested on a knowing sacrifice of inspiration, quality, truth to some other consideration

---

[43] A. V. Lunacharskii, "O roli proletarskogo gosudarstva v razvitii sotsialisticheskoi kultury," *Stat'i ob iskusstve*, p. 461. Reprinted from *Pod znamenem marksizma*, no. 6 (1933).

deemed to command priority. If one such overriding consideration does exist, it is the morale of the population, the conscious identification of the mass with the success of the Plan. In the postwar period, reconstruction needs made this identification a matter of the greatest urgency. The majority of the well-indoctrinated Party members had perished in the war, leaving the "vanguard" decimated at a moment when the new challenges to the efficacy of its leadership appeared to be of unprecedented gravity. The Party responded with a massive campaign of propaganda and agitation to condition the new membership for the efficient exercise of its functions, and to organize the activities of the masses in conformity with the new line. Since the Party exerts absolute control over all media of communication, it was in a position to supervise the exposition of the new line, in such fashion as to guarantee that the line remained one and immutable regardless of the media employed to convey it. Lest literature offer sanctuary to a citizenry at all times the target of a barrage of exhortation, scrupulous care was taken to assure that its tone and content faithfully reflected the same ideas and feelings as the radio, newspapers, political journals, etc. Literature must be held to its oath of fealty to the Plan.

Partiinost', it will be recalled, binds the writer to see life through the Party's eyes. What matters, therefore, in appraising the constraints which prevail in literature is precisely *how* the Party may elect to see life, and *what* it may choose to see. Preoccupied with postwar reconstruction of heavy industry and agriculture, the Party wore blinkers and imposed on every last one of its followers the obligation to do the same. Nothing was to be allowed, it was clear, to divert it or them from the straight and narrow course leading to the completion of economic plans. As a series of recent statements by Soviet writers themselves so dismally confirm, literature fared badly in the process. It would be foolhardy to predict that the premise of the policy of monolithic controls, which takes its inception from 1932, will undergo serious reëxamination. That policy rests on *partiinost'*. Were Bolshevism to relinquish *partiinost'*, it would cease to be Bolshevism. It may confidently be assumed that the extent to which the writer's creative individuality continues to be constrained will depend, as it has for so long now, on the insistence with which the Party employs literature as an auxiliary device in achieving extraliterary goals.

Part V

Review

ERNEST J. SIMMONS

I

The history of the Russian people is faithfully reflected in their literature. Down through the centuries the developing realities of social existence as they affected landowner and merchant, peasant and proletarian found brilliant and often poignant expression in the vast wealth of fiction, drama, poetry, and literary criticism. Critics and writers in tsarist Russia, often hindered by governmental censorship, were the conscience of a nation. In Belinskii's words:

> Our culture is the direct action of our literature on the mentality and mores of society. Our literature created the mores of our society . . . laid the foundation for the inner rapprochement of social classes, formed a kind of public opinion, and produced something in the nature of a special class in society . . . consisting of persons from all classes, brought together by culture, which in our land is concentrated exclusively in the love of literature.[1]

In the revolutionary upheaval of 1917, literary traditions possessed a greater survival value than nineteenth-century currents of social, political, and economic thought. At the outset continuity was more in evidence than change, though the latter did not lack vociferous champions immediately after October. To be sure, very few men of letters, like the poet Briusov, accepted the new regime. Many established writers fled the country, and the few who remained kept silent, boycotting the "usurpers of power." Literature came almost to a standstill in the period of War Communism, for publication was extremely difficult and writers, while confronted with various ideological, moral, and artistic problems, were largely absorbed in keeping alive under the stress of their desperate material plight.

When it became possible for literature to function again, writers were caught up in the tremendous release of energy brought about by the Revolution, but at this point prerevolutionary literary trends manifested an unusual

[1] *Sochineniia V. Belinskogo* (Moscow, 1889–1895), XII, 237–238.

vitality and exercised a significant influence on those who began to create Soviet literature. In fact, one may doubt whether the Revolution seriously disrupted Russian literary tradition. A changing society and Communist Party ideological demands enforced important changes in literature, but they have been changes within the framework of a continuity of Russian literary tradition. And these changes appear to become less significant as the Revolution grows more conservative.

In no field of intellectual endeavor in the Soviet Union has there been more prolonged and inconclusive controversy than in literary theory. From time to time deviations and revisions have occurred in political, social, and economic theory, but the Party, whether it inherited or created these controversies, has always been able to settle them to its own satisfaction within a Marxian frame of reference in these fields. The non-Marxian inheritance in such subjects had been rejected at the outset and was useful solely to be stigmatized all over again as the cause of a "deviation." In literary controversy, however, there can be no conclusive appeal to Marxian doctrine. The literary theorizing of Marx and Engels is a thing of shreds and patches, out of which Plekhanov tried to make a whole cloth of Marxian aesthetics. But Soviet critics reject Plekhanov, and neither Lenin nor Stalin, no more than Marx or Engels, had either the interest or competence to develop a Marxian theory of aesthetics. Nor have the voluminous writings of Soviet literary critics over the last thirty-seven years resulted in an officially accepted body of doctrine which could be called a "Marxian aesthetic," as the plaints of various thinkers in recent issues of *Voprosi filosofii* would testify.[2] Literary controversies have been settled by Party dictation, Central Committee resolutions, official articles in *Pravda,* or by a speech of Zhdanov. This lack of an official Marxian aesthetic has no doubt had much to do with the tenacity of surviving elements of prerevolutionary mentality in literary theory and in belles-lettres in the Soviet Union.

The extraordinary renaissance in the arts in Russia, which took place in the decade before 1917, carried over into the early 1920's when activity in this sphere could be resumed, and finally exhausted itself at the end of the 1920's when the First Five-Year Plan got under way, although traces of its influence continued until the first half of the 1930's. That is, such prerevolutionary schools of literature and criticism as Symbolism, Imagism, Acmeism, Futurism, and Formalism had their adherents after 1917, often the same devotees that had helped to develop these movements in the decade before the Revolution. The scope of Mr. Wellek's paper did not permit a consideration of these prerevolutionary movements, but Mr. Victor Erlich concentrates on one of them in the early period — Formalism — because of its highly significant contribution to critical theory, and perhaps also because, whatever its roots in the past, it pursued a peculiarly Soviet develop-

---

[2] See, for example, *Voprosi filosofii,* nos. 1 and 2 (1951).

ment, even attempting to coquette with Marxism, until its liquidation at the end of the 1920's. (Thereafter, Formalism was resurrected only as a general term of abuse, aimed at criticism or literature deviating from the official line, or for that matter, at Donbas miners for failure to fulfill their quota of coal.)

The concentration on Formalism, however, gives an inadequate picture of the vigorous experimentation in non-Marxian critical theorizing and literary production in the early years of the Revolution. A spirit of revolt against all accepted conventions and canons of taste was behind this ferment, but a close examination of the values professed leads us once again to that prerevolutionary cultural renaissance of the decade before 1917, with its emphasis upon sheer aesthetic refinement at the expense of the ethical and the spiritual. Prerevolutionary Symbolism, Futurism, Imagism, and Acmeism not only continued but inspired further literary groupings, each with its own critical manifesto — the Bio-Cosmists, Formlibrists, Emotionalists, Expressionists, Luminists, Classicists, Neo-Classicists, Constructivists, and the Nothingists (*Nichevoki*). In fact, the search for new forms and potentialities in art was carried on largely by people who had nothing in common with Bolshevism.

It was a literary revolt, but not in a proletarian sense. Only the Futurists, who opposed the literature of the past, made a determined effort to hitch their wagon to the proletarian star, but they were soon dropped by the wayside. Yet it was a period of unusual freedom of expression. When the printing of belles-lettres became possible again, these writers got a hearing, if not always in the government press, then in the private press that operated in the early years of the New Economic Policy. And critical controversy raged on all the literary fronts. The critic Polonskii tells how, between 1920 and 1923, in the famous House of the Press in Moscow, more or less the official headquarters of writers,

. . . old and new literature, proletarian or bourgeois, the central questions of Marxist literary study, literature and psychoanalysis, the new theater and new music, the intelligentsia and Communism, the style of revolutionary and the style of bourgeois art . . . all were judged within the walls of the House of the Press.[3]

There was change, of course, as well as continuity in the development of social and aesthetic criteria in Soviet literary criticism over these early years of the Revolution. And the change, as Mr. Erlich suggests, consists of the "social approach" of the Soviet Marxian literary theorists. But once again, his concentration on the opposition of Marxian critics to Formalism, while quite representative of such opposition in this early period, hardly brings out the complexities and ambiguities of the total situation or the nuances of change.

[3] V. Polonskii, *Ocherki literaturnogo dvizheniia revoliutsionnoi epokhi* (2nd ed., Moscow, 1929), p. 36.

In a revolution dedicated to establishing a new socialist order of society according to the doctrine of Marx, it was a natural assumption that the ideology of literature in the superstructure would change in relation to the economic base. Of course, this was a very remote expectation in 1917. However radical the leaders of the Revolution were about the need of political, social, and economic change, they were quite conservative in affairs of the arts. And for that matter, so were Marx and Engels who preferred the classical beauty of the art of slave-owning Greece or the Shakespearian plays of feudal England to the works of the progressive writers of their own day. Lenin had no pretensions to a knowledge of literature and was not particularly well read in it. He had a few favorites among the great Russian authors of the nineteenth century, and he shied away from innovation in literature with as much determination as he approved of it in political, social, and economic thought. Bukharin, Trotsky, Kamenev, and Lunacharskii were more interested in literature and evinced a certain sympathy for progressive trends in it, but their rather extensive literary culture had been formed by their admiration for the great works of the Russian and Western past.

In general, the leaders of the Revolution had little time for the problems of literature in those frantic early years after 1917. One gathers the impression that they would have preferred to let these problems solve themselves. They appeared to feel — as Mr. Hankin points out in the case of Lenin[4] — that if a proletarian culture were to be developed, it would be based on the rich inheritance of bourgeois culture, which at best would have to be adapted to the current new demands. The masses must first be taught to read, and then they must have easy access to the great works of the past of which they had been deprived. And soon the regime took steps to publish such works in large quantities at cheap prices.[5] In short, the first vision of literature for the masses on the part of the leaders amounted not to change, but to continuity with the past.

Further, a well-defined sentiment of freedom of literary creation existed among the revolutionary leaders in these early years. This was no doubt a legacy of nineteenth-century democratic Russian Marxism. There was no disposition to tolerate counterrevolutionary literature or any overt challenge to the Party's authority in the ultimate control of cultural matters. But this authority of the Party was sparingly used in the early years, and apparently not only out of a sense of the insecurity of its own power, but because its leaders tended to believe in literary freedom of expression. In fact, the whole literary climate up to 1928 was one of unusual freedom, in which various literary groups, some of them with little sympathy for the regime,

[4] Robert M. Hankin, "Main Premises of the Communist Party in the Theory of Soviet Literary Controls," pp. 443–446.

[5] By a decree of the Central Committee of the Party on December 29, 1917, a State Publishing House was to be set up, and one of its major purposes was to provide cheap editions of the Russian classics.

competed with each other for leadership in a policy deliberately sanctioned by the Party. And many works were published which were highly critical of the government.

However, the conservatism and inattention of the Party leaders in literature were not shared by scores of writers, young and old, who thronged the stage shortly after 1917. It was a time of revolution and on all sides the cry went up for a revolution in literature. The violent controversies that ensued have been traced by both Mr. Erlich and Mr. Hankin in their papers. However, the relation of the central theme of continuity in literary tradition to these competing groups has not been emphasized.

In these early years there were three broad currents of literary opinion and activity, each of which responded to the revolutionary demand for change in terms of its own independent approach to literature. They were made up of various and often deviating factions and groupings, and the fierce struggle among them for preëminence was motivated almost as much by selfish and material aims as by aesthetic and political factors, although these latter played a prominent part.

At one extreme was the proletarian movement in literature, initially headed by the Proletcult organization, dedicated to the class struggle in literature and to the conviction that an original art must be developed which would reflect proletarian consciousness. This represented change with a vengeance. But the Proletcult brashly advocated a literature that would be entirely free from governmental or Party direction, and thus it quickly fell afoul of Lenin. Yet even before its fall, young writers from its ranks, in such newly formed organizations as the Octobrists and On Guardists, struck out to achieve proletarian hegemony in literature, only now an hegemony identified entirely with the Party.

In their efforts to dignify their approach by developing a new theory of literature, the proletarian critics at first succeeded in presenting little more than a composite of Left-Wing sloganeering, seasoned with a dash of Marxian clichés. As time went on, however, these efforts became more extensive and refined until under the leadership of RAPP (Russian Association of Proletarian Writers) in 1928–32, a theory of literature was advanced which had substance and direction. When closely examined, however, this theory, in its essentials, represents a reversion to type — to some of the commonplaces of nineteenth-century literary criticism naturalized in a Soviet environment. For under the sunshade of "dialectical materialism" were gathered such wanderers from the past as "psychologism," the "living man," and the Tolstoyan "tearing the veils from life." [6] In fact, Leo Tolstoy had become a kind of literary hero for some of these RAPP proletarian critics. Such allegiances must have been disturbing to the Party, and though RAPP professed to be

[6] For an excellent discussion of the RAPP critical theory, see Edward J. Brown, *The Proletarian Episode in Russian Literature, 1928–1932* (New York, 1953).

a mouthpiece of the Party in matters literary, it was dissolved in 1932. But the proletarian current in Soviet literature and criticism continued under the guise of Socialist Realism, and in its future course the break with the nineteenth-century past was emphasized, especially in the retention of its initial criterion, *partiinost'* (that is, after the demise of the Proletcult), which has grown in significance over the passing years as Party controls became more and more strict until today it is the dominating factor in Soviet literature.

In short, it is this proletarian current which, after many vicissitudes and with the transformation of "proletarian" art into "socialist" art, that has persisted, ideologically, down to the present day. But its creative efforts in the early years reflected very little that was either new or artistic. The writers of the Futurist movement, essentially bourgeois in origin, which for a time attached itself to the Left-Wing proletarian current, were more successful in their works in breaking with the literary traditions of the past.

At the other extreme from the proletarian current in Soviet literature in the early years was that of the Fellow Travelers. In general, they were in sympathy with the October Revolution, but they demanded the right to interpret it in literature and criticism as they saw fit. This current has been described or mentioned by both Mr. Erlich and Mr. Hankin, but once again its connections with the literary traditions of the past need to be underscored.

Whether they were young or old writers, the literary roots of the Fellow Travelers went deep into the past. Both the critics among them (many of the Formalists could correctly be described as "Fellow Travelers") and the creative writers, such as those belonging to the group known as the Serapion Brothers, found their major inspiration among the literary scholars and great authors of the past. However progressive were some of the ideas of the Formalist critics, they often applied them in studies of the works of nineteenth-century authors. And the novels and short stories of such Fellow Travelers as Leonov, Pil'niak, Fedin, Zoshchenko, and Kataev reflect the patent influence of Gogol, Dostoyevsky, Tolstoy, and Chekhov. (It should be realized, of course, that so-called "proletarian" or "Communist" writers did not escape this kind of influence, for example, the influence of Gorkii and Tolstoy on Fadeev and of Tolstoy on Sholokhov.)

The Fellow Travelers wished to say a new word in literature and criticism in the spirit of the times, but they wished it to be their own, not dictated by the government or the Party. Their writings often had the flavor of the great nineteenth-century classics though little of their profound art. And in the treatment of the themes of some of their novels, so often concerned with a struggle between the old and the new, one can sometimes detect a nostalgia for a way of life that was to return no more.

For the first fifteen years of the Revolution the Fellow Travelers perhaps did most to form the new literary taste of the Soviet reading public. They were able to do it so successfully not only because most of the literary talent was on their side, but also because they created in a spirit familiar to millions of readers brought up on the Russian classics of the nineteenth century. Here was the "new wine in old bottles" which that conservative in literature, Lenin, who preferred Pushkin to Maiakovskii, might have approved. Indeed, important Party leaders, such as Bukharin, Lunacharskii, and Trotsky, did favor the works of the Fellow Travelers over those of the opposing militantly Communist proletarian writers. And the historic resolution of the Party on literature, in 1925, granted the Fellow Travelers protection from the fierce onslaughts of the proletarian faction. However, the struggle between these two currents went on relentlessly and ended with the final victory of the Left-Wing in literature in 1932, when another Party resolution declared that there were no longer any Fellow Travelers in literature, that they had become converts to the ideals of the new regime and to the new credo of Socialist Realism in literature.

Thus ended the most fruitful development in Soviet literature, and one that promised a real measure of continuity with the literary traditions of the past. Such an ending was inevitable once Stalin's absolute control over the Party became assured. Literature, like every other endeavor in the Soviet Union, had to submit to controls. Whatever their sympathies with the aims of the Revolution, the position of the Fellow Travelers on creative freedom was inconsistent with totalitarian ideological controls. Theirs was the familiar tragedy in the Soviet Union of men who gave their support to the Revolution but were unable to become the intellectual and creative slaves of a Party.

The third current in these early years may properly be described as the "Marxian approach to literature." It occupies a position between the proletarian current and the Fellow Traveler current, and its many adherents, representing a variety of shades within the Marxian spectrum, accepted and rejected aspects of both the other approaches. Of course this was essentially a development in critical theory, although the Marxian critical position advanced by Voronskii found its reflection in creative writing in the works of authors belonging to the Pereval group, whose major efforts were directed toward bridging the gap between past and present in literature.

Within the brief scope at his disposal, Mr. Erlich has summarized very well the social and aesthetic criteria underlying the varied and often conflicting views of these Marxian literary critics. The wide divergencies reflected the lack of a formal aesthetic system in the writings of Marx and Engels. Prerevolutionary echoes of the aesthetic theorizing of Tolstoy, Pisarev, and Plekhanov mingle with purely *ad hoc* criteria of evaluation that could be expressed in terms of the class struggle and dialectical and historical materialism. Most of these critics were Communists and some of them, like

Lunacharskii, Voronskii, Pereverzev, and Polonskii, were men of wide culture in the literature and theory of the past. Yet lacking the certitude of ignorance, they were unable to achieve among themselves the dogma of Party design. Basically, they saw their problems as a dichotomy: Did literature have any value in itself, or did it have only a political value? Was it a by-product of the class struggle or an expression of man's eternal urge to embody human aspirations in beautiful and enduring form? Imaginative critics, like Voronskii and Pereverzev, tried to reconcile the dichotomy by setting up values that would serve both Marx and literature as an end in itself. But this was old-fashioned. In a few years the official Marxian literary critics would decide that the sole value of literature was a political one.

II

We have observed that the shadow of the past had fallen across developments in literature and critical theory in the early years of the Revolution. Unusual freedom of discussion prevailed among adherents of the three broad approaches to literature which have been described. In responding to the demands of the Revolution, a sharp division of opinion may be discerned: those who felt the demands would best be served by building on the foundation of the past a literature that would answer the needs of the present; and those who insisted that writers and critics must turn their backs utterly upon the past and develop an entirely new revolutionary and proletarian literature.

In all this controversy the Party tended to remain aloof; it interceded only when its authority was directly defied, as in the case of the Proletcult in 1920, or when the public bitterness of the struggle called for arbitration, as on the occasion of the name-calling between the On Guardists and the Fellow Travelers in 1924–25. And as we have seen, the leadership of the Party at this time, without repudiating the Left-Wing proletarian movement, favored the notion that a revolutionary literature should be built on the best of the heritage of the past. In fact, the Party "line" throughout all this controversy was to approve the competition of the various literary groups and to refuse to give any one of them the stamp of Party authority.

As Mr. Hankin has indicated, this whole situation of relative freedom of discussion and creation in literature came to an end at the beginning of the First Five-Year Plan (1928–29). Lenin had died, Trotsky was exiled, and Stalin was in the saddle of power. A new Party line was laid down, and in keeping with it the "socialist command" in literature was introduced. The Party had come to the full realization of the propaganda value of literature and of its consequent importance as a weapon in securing its own power and aims.

The Central Committee's resolution on literature in 1932, at the end of the First Five-Year Plan, signalized the Party's wholesale appropriation of literature as an important instrument to be used in the furtherance of its policies. For not only was the leading writers' organization, RAPP, dissolved on that occasion, but all the other competing literary groups obligingly liquidated themselves upon a hint from the Party, which had decreed the establishment of a single Union of Soviet Writers for the whole of the U.S.S.R. This amounted pretty much to complete control, for it may be conjectured that the Party fractions in all the chapters of the Union of Soviet Writers would take their orders from above and enforce them upon the members. Further, a uniform approach to literature, Socialist Realism, was required of all members who joined the Union. In short, the three broad and conflicting literary currents of the 1920's had been forced into the single stream of Socialist Realism, the direction and rate of flow of which were rigidly controlled by the Party.

The subsequent development of literary criticism and the theory of controls that regulated it and the production of belles-lettres have been well treated by Mr. Erlich and Mr. Hankin. In these respects it would appear that all continuity with the literary traditions of the past had been broken as the Party now demanded that literature and criticism must serve the political and social needs of the state as determined by the Communist Party. Though much literary criticism was written in the 1930's and after the war, it amounted largely to adorning the whirling dervish of Socialist Realism in the dress and ornament of Marxian verbiage. Whatever twists and turns were made to accommodate fluctuations in the Party line, as time went on one single constant began to emerge as more and more important in all this criticism — *partiinost'*. The Party spirit in literature, in its latest formulation, became the *sine qua non* in every novel, play, or poem.

Though Mr. Erlich's final summary of social and aesthetic criteria in Soviet criticism does represent them as peculiarly Soviet, these criteria do suggest certain points of comparison with the social and aesthetic values of the nineteenth-century materialist critics, whom Mr. Wellek treats in his paper. By the middle of the 1930's, the materialist critics, especially Belinskii, Chernyshevskii, and Dobroliubov, had come into particular favor in the Soviet Union. Editions of their works have multiplied, an extensive and entirely eulogistic literature has grown up about them, and Marx, Engels, and Lenin are frequently cited in their praise. Not a little dialectical shuffling is indulged in by Soviet apologists in explaining away the idealistic conception of history, the corrosive element of anthropologism in the understanding of materialism, and excessive fondness for Utopian socialism in one or the other of the materialist critics. But since the war it has been found necessary to warp them gently into the new dry dock of Soviet anti-Westernism for extensive ideological rehabilitation. This process has had its difficulties since for generations Russian intellectual history has acclaimed the materialist critics as outstanding Westernizers. The metamorphosis has been accomplished, however, by the "discovery" that the main struggle in the

1840's and 1850's in Russia was not really between Westernizers and Slavophiles, but between a landlord-bourgeois camp and incipient revolutionary democracy, to which latter group the materialist critics are now said to have belonged.[7] In any event, the materialist critics are now hailed as the democratic revolutionary predecessors of Russian Marxism in political and social thought, and, in their critical realism in literature, as the forerunners of Soviet literary criticism today.

It is the official emphasis upon cultural nationalism which enables the Soviets in all good conscience to regard the materialist critics as precursors of their own approach to literature. As Mr. Wellek points out, the materialist critics were revolutionaries who looked upon literature as a weapon in their revolt, which led them to deny that art has any value in itself. The Soviets have carried this utilitarian position to its logical extreme — the essential value of literature is that of a tool or weapon or an instrument in the service of the Party. There were differences, to be sure, in the views of Belinskii, Chernyshevskii, and Dobroliubov on the purpose of literature, but in general they all agreed that it should play an active role in the transformation of society, a conviction that Soviet critics accept. Chernyshevskii and, to a certain extent, Dobroliubov may be considered exceptions in this respect, but Soviet scholars, with some justification, insist on the point. Chernyshevskii's novel, *What Is to Be Done?*, is an example of literature that preaches the need to transform life. On the other hand, Belinskii, though arguing at the end of his career that literature must take the lead in society and strive to change it for the better, yet never ceased to insist, unlike Chernyshevskii, Dobroliubov, and Soviet critics today, that no social purpose in literature could ever compensate for a lack of true artistic merit.

Another line of continuity between the past and the present may be observed in the conception of the hero, a subject fully treated by Mr. Mathewson in another paper in this book, but it may be permitted to mention it here briefly in connection with the materialist critics. They revolted against the dominant type of the superfluous hero in Russian nineteenth-century literature and demanded characters who, by their sense of social significance and forthright action, would attempt to change society for the better. And in a real sense Rakhmetov in Chernyshevskii's *What Is to Be Done?*, who renounces all the conventional pleasures of life in order to devote himself to the triumph of the Revolution, is an active answer to the passive superfluous hero. Though he became the ideal of revolutionary youth in Russia for years, and is recalled by Soviet critics with affection, no more boring, dull, flat, two-dimensional, unreal hero has ever been created in serious fiction since Richardson's Sir Charles Grandison, who, Taine said, deserved to be stuffed and mounted in a museum as a curiosity. The Soviet positive hero is cast in the image of Rakhmetov. He is likewise an active

[7] See *Istoriia SSSR*, ed. M. V. Nechkina (2nd ed., Moscow, 1949).

person, bent on changing life, and of late, especially in his postwar appearances, he has no more living personality or psychological depth than Rakhmetov. Chernyshevskii in his novel, with his eye fixed on the goal of a future socialist existence, portrayed life as it should be. And the Soviet author, straining towards a vision of Communism, also describes life as it should be or even must be, but always in terms of an idealized picture of the reality of Soviet life today.

There is, of course, an abiding fallacy in this particular claim of continuity which is unwittingly suggested in a Soviet writer's critical comment on Dobroliubov, one that might also be applied to Belinskii and Chernyshevskii: "Dobroliubov did not reach a correct understanding of partisanship in literature, but he clearly saw that in the society of his day, 'even poetry has been constantly affected by the spirit of parties and classes.' "[8] True, the materialist critics had no Communist Party to belong to, nor had they acquired a Marxian understanding of the class struggle. On the other hand, they were contending, not only against art for art's sake and the aesthetics of liberal writers, but also against a reactionary regime that tolerated a surprising amount of freedom of expression in belles-lettres and literary criticism. If Dobroliubov were living in the Soviet Union, he would be relieved of the necessity of struggle against a regime; he would find no opposing camps of literary criticism; and he would not be troubled by the nice matter of conflict in the selection of subjects to write about. He would have a full understanding of "partisanship." *Partiinost'* would simplify all his problems of literary criticism. In this sense change and not continuity needs to be emphasized in any comparison of the literary theories of the materialist critics and Soviet literary criticism.

III

These conjectures lead naturally to a consideration of what has frequently been accepted as a major element of continuity between the past and present — governmental control of literary expression in the time of the tsars and in the Soviet Union. Mr. Stilman has treated the factors behind such controls in the prerevolutionary period, and Mr. Hankin in the period after 1917. When the findings of these studies are juxtaposed, however, the pattern reveals more change than continuity in both the theory and practice of literary controls.

In the light of the mutual acceptance of literary censorship by both regimes, one might be persuaded that development rather than change more accurately describes the relationship. But the facts as brought out by Mr. Stilman and Mr. Hankin would refute this contention. As Mr. Stilman ably shows, literary controls developed from a point of rigid application in the

[8] M. Yovchuk, "Introduction," *N. A. Dobrolyubov, Selected Philosophical Essays* (Moscow, 1948), p. xlviii.

time of Nicholas I to virtual nonexistence after 1905, whereas Mr. Hankin's paper reveals that the Soviet regime began with very considerable freedom of literary expression which has ended today in monolithic controls. The reasons for this striking change are to be sought in the different theories of power and the aspiration of the ruling polity of the government of the tsars in its long period of development as contrasted with the theory of power and aspirations of the leaders of the Soviet regime.

In general, the tsars regarded belles-lettres as a harmless pursuit provided the writer did not concern himself with the affairs of state. At its very worst, under the "iron code" of censorship of Nicholas I, as Mr. Stilman has pointed out, society could have no opinion on public affairs. An author was expected to obey the government and to keep his reasoning to himself. If the writer differed, he had only the privilege of keeping silent, a kind of freedom not graciously accorded Soviet writers who are at odds with the scheme of things. Yet in spite of these restrictions, a magnificent literary development took place during the lifetime of this reactionary regime, because within certain limits writers had considerable freedom in the selection of themes and in expression. By the 1860's, Mr. Stilman indicates, censorship in Russian literature had ceased to be a major factor, and, toward the end of the century, literature enjoyed almost complete freedom. In fact, so strong had become the sentiment against any form of interference that many of the liberal writers in the second half of the nineteenth century deeply resented even the efforts of the radical critics, such as Chernyshevskii and Dobroliubov, to commit literature to the struggle for social justice.

It is true that writers were often persecuted and kept under surveillance by the government of the old regime and for periods were subjected to devastating preliminary censorship, and many literary magazines were suspended for real or fancied affronts to the government. Yet once preliminary censorship was abolished, writers courageously risked legal prosecution by criticizing in their publications the actions of the government and by condemning its interference with the freedom of the press. On the whole, the government of the tsars, with minor exceptions, was not interested in directing the course of literature, in imposing its will or its philosophy of rule on writers, save to the extent of refusing them the right to criticize the actions of the government, a form of censorship that has sometimes reared its ugly head in the more democratic governments of the West. On one occasion, when the tsar's government did attempt to direct public opinion, it was answered, as Mr. Stilman explained, by the publication of Kuzma Prutkov's delightfully satiric "Plan for the Establishment of Uniformity of Thought in Russia." Declaring the "harmfulness of divergency of opinion," Prutkov asserts that, after all, it is necessary to obtain material with which to form opinion. "But where is this material?" he disarmingly asks. "The only material can be the opinion of the authorities; otherwise there is no assurance that the opinion is correct." [9]

This satire was published in 1863, but the "Plan for the Establishment of Uniformity of Thought in Russia" would have infinitely more point in the Soviet Union today. Such an observation suggests the positive element of change between even the most repressive period of literary censorship in the time of the tsars and the situation in this respect that exists in the Soviet Union. For the Soviet government not only exercises widespread preliminary censorship, but also directs the total ideology of literature, its content and form, what subjects may be written about and how they should be treated. This intent was no doubt implicit in the Communist Party's theory of power from the very beginning; its application wavered in the early years of the Revolution, but by 1932 it had become explicit. Mr. Hankin establishes its explicitness in a quotation drawn from one of the early waverers, the Commissar of Enlightenment, Luncharskii, in 1933:

> To indicate where to direct artistic forces, artistic attention, artistic talent — that is the natural conclusion from all our understanding of socialist construction. We know very well that we have the right to intervene in the course of culture . . . ending with the direction of the most delicate forms of art.[10]

Clearly what is aimed at is literally the establishment of uniformity of thought in the medium of literature, which the Party regards as one of its principal instruments in the education and propagandizing of the people of the Soviet Union.

Mr. Stilman, in his paper, quotes the *Russian Messenger* of 1858 to the effect that "the easiest way to kill a belief in people's minds and to undermine its moral force is to place it under official tutelage." [11] The devices and efficacy of Soviet propaganda, however, were unknown to the old regime, which tended to discourage education among the masses on the theory that their ignorance would prove a bulwark to authoritarian rule, whereas the Soviets promote widespread education in the conviction that if the state directs it and firmly controls its content, the people will remain enthusiastic supporters of the power that suppresses them.

There is no sure way of ascertaining the truth of the quotation from the *Russian Messenger* with reference to the vast outpouring of controlled Soviet literature. No doubt much of it has the desired propaganda effect on readers entirely conditioned by the mores and education of Soviet life and denied any possibility of an objective comparison of their experiences with those of people outside the Soviet Union. The persistence of the theme of

---

[9] Quoted by Leon Stilman in "Freedom and Repression in Prerevolutionary Russian Literature," p. 427.

[10] Quoted by Hankin, ref. 4, p. 449.

[11] Quoted by Stilman, ref. 9, p. 426.

"bourgeois survivals" in the content of so much of this literature, after thirty-seven years of Party-directed efforts to eliminate them, suggests something less than a propagandistic success. An interview and questionnaire study by the present author on literary controls among a sizable sample of Soviet displaced persons, most of them former writers, involved answers to questions on the faithfulness to Soviet reality in fiction and plays and the degree of its acceptance by readers. The results were not conclusive in all respects, but a familiar answer was that Soviet readers reject the positive heroes and heroines in novels and plays as unreal and regard the so-called negative characters, those who oppose the official scheme of things, as true to Soviet reality.

IV

There is some further evidence of the rejection of controlled belles-lettres by Soviet readers which in turn has a direct bearing on one phase of literary continuity between the past and the present that did not fall within the scope of the papers in this section. This has to do with the apparent preference of readers for the great Russian classics of the nineteenth century over the novels, drama, and poetry written by Soviet authors. The existence of such a preference and the means of satisfying it could be a matter of some consequence in counteracting the official ideology of the Communist Party, and it may help in part to explain the persistent survival of "bourgeois elements."

In the early years of the Soviet regime there was some official hesitancy about the wisdom of providing for popular consumption the works of many writers of the past, despite a Party conviction, as already indicated, that the masses had a right to their great artistic heritage of which they had been deprived. For a time even Pushkin was regarded with suspicion because of his noble lineage and political beliefs. By the early 1930's, however, the deliberate Russian nationalism line of the Party hardened. The Communists set out to represent themselves as the continuators and consummators of all that was great and glorious in the Russian historical past.

In this process the publication and distribution of the Russian classics won official approval. The works of most authors of consequence in the nineteenth century have been published in the Soviet Union. Endless literary and scholarly studies are devoted to them, and selections of the writings of the greatest are regularly studied in the schools. The supernationalism of the war and postwar period has served to intensify this trend. In addition, efforts were made to purify these nineteenth-century authors of any taint of Western influence, and continuity was emphasized in studies that attempted to prove that Soviet writers were carrying on the literary traditions of these great figures of the past. Thus it was "discovered" that the revolutionary verse of the famous Soviet poet Maiakovskii stems directly from the verse of Pushkin.

In all this activity, of course, some care is taken to isolate Soviet readers from the politically undesirable elements of these prerevolutionary writers by a process of selection from their works in popular editions. And many of the studies of both writers and works are designed to render them suitable as forerunners of Soviet culture, no matter how much distortion of fact this may involve. Yet the point is worth emphasizing that for some years now millions and millions of copies of the novels, short stories, plays, poems, and critical and polemical writings of the most famous authors of nineteenth-century Russia have been available to Soviet readers.

The official position today is that Soviet literature, while continuing the best traditions of the Russian cultural past, is really the highest form of literature ever achieved, and that by virtue of its artistic appeal, content, and ideology it is preferred by Soviet readers to any other literature. If this were so, then we would have to conclude that the kind of "planned continuity" effected by Soviet authorities in making available to readers all this Russian literature of the prerevolutionary past has been successful, that extensive conditioning by propaganda has made them immune to the artistic beauties, emotional appeal, and way of life described in one of the truly great literatures of the world. If the contrary were true, then we would be able to conclude that a real continuity with the past exists, and that the old literature has triumphed over the new.

To establish this preference of the old literature over the new with utter conclusiveness is extremely difficult, but an important contribution to its validation has been made in the excellent little study of a Soviet refugee, Mr. George Denicke, executed under the direction of the Coordinator of Psychological Intelligence, Department of State.[12] Mr. Denicke attempts to establish his point by the evidence of publishing statistics. He is able to show that the editions of popular Soviet authors are less than those of the great Russian writers of the past, of whom 170,000,000 copies had been published up to 1947, and this trend has been increasing since the war. Pushkin, he claims, is the most popular author in the Soviet Union, though Leo Tolstoy must be running him a close second if we may judge from a still more recent Soviet estimate. I could add to Mr. Denicke's figures — 55,548,000 copies of Tolstoy's works have been published since 1917. From various statistics Mr. Denicke constructs a list of the ten most-read authors of 1951 and compares it with a similar list for 1947 by way of showing that Soviet authors are losing out in the popularity contest. Only four Soviet

---

[12] George Denicke, "Links with the Past in Soviet Society," External Research Staff, Office of Intelligence Research, Series 3, no. 84 (Washington, D.C.: Dept. of State, March 21, 1952).

authors appear in the 1951 list, and these at the bottom (they include Gorkii, not entirely a Soviet author). The list runs: Pushkin, Leo Tolstoy, Turgenev, Chekhov, Gogol, Goncharov, Gorkii, Ostrovskii, Sholokhov, and Aleksei Tolstoy, in that order.

Mr. Denicke also examines the preference of theatergoers, a study which takes on added significance in the light of the decree of March 4, 1948, which halted all direct or indirect subventions to the theaters. That is, with the elimination of the practice of the distribution of free tickets by factory committees, attendance at theaters now bears a realistic relation to the kind and quality of the plays performed. By statistical and other evidence, Mr. Denicke is able to prove quite conclusively, what has been tacitly implied or frankly admitted in the press recently, that theatergoers almost ostentatiously prefer Russian prerevolutionary or foreign plays to contemporary Soviet plays.[13] For some time now the plays of the great nineteenth-century Russian dramatist Ostrovskii have been the most popular in the Soviet Union. Generalizing on the themes and their treatment in the most frequently performed plays of Ostrovskii, as well as on other evidence, Mr. Denicke comes to the conclusion, despite all official propaganda to the contrary, that the Soviet public prefers drama and literature which conveys the message that everyone has the right to be happy in his own way and which expresses "a compassion for men and especially for women who are victims of a will imposed on them by somebody else." [14] Such a message, which runs through so many of the Russian classics of the past, is of course alien to Communist ideology and to the whole spirit of contemporary Soviet literature.

Some support for Mr. Denicke's conclusion may be found in the study of one of my own students, Mr. Maurice Friedberg, "Literary Habits and Tastes of Former Soviet Citizens." [15] For this purpose Mr. Friedberg analyzed the reading habits in the full-life interviews of 329 Soviet non-returners, material drawn from the valuable interview project of the Harvard

[13] In this connection it should be pointed out that foreign literature of the past, as well as foreign plays, is enormously popular in the Soviet Union. According to official figures, between 1918 and 1951, 210,000,000 copies of the various works of English, American, German, French, and other foreign authors have been published in the Soviet Union. Some of the most popular authors are Shakespeare, Mark Twain, Jack London, Balzac, Hugo, and Heine (see Zinaida Gagarina, "Kultura i mir," *Literaturnaia gazeta* [December 13, 1951]). Though this eagerness on the part of Soviet citizens to read foreign literature may be motivated by a desire to escape from the drab reality of their daily existence, it may also bear a relation to the popularity of the Russian classics. That is, both foreign and Russian classics seem to be preferred over contemporary Soviet literature, and both types of reading suggest a deep interest in life other than that in the Soviet Union.

[14] Denicke, ref. 12, p. 40.

[15] Maurice Friedberg, "Literary Habits and Tastes of Former Soviet Citizens" (Russian Research Center, manuscript, 1953. An analysis of the interviews with former Soviet citizens conducted by the Russian Research Center of Harvard University in Munich and New York, in 1950–51).

Research Center. The findings are necessarily inconclusive since these interviews placed no special emphasis upon the reading habits and preferences of the respondents. The information is incidental rather than directed. Yet Mr. Friedberg was able to obtain a surprising amount of evidence from the interviews which provides a pattern of reading habits from which certain conclusions, however tentative and qualified, may be drawn.

The answers of the respondents concerning their interest in Soviet literature were not very indicative, but those concerning interest in the literature of the past were numerous and positive and enabled Mr. Friedberg to conclude that "the pre-revolutionary Russian classics and foreign authors in translation enjoyed tremendous popularity . . ." [16] In all, twenty-five Russian authors of the past were mentioned as having been read by these respondents. Pushkin was the most popular, followed by Leo Tolstoy, Lermontov, and Dostoyevsky in that order. It may be illuminating to quote a few comments from these interviews which Mr. Friedberg has included in his study.

A thirty-nine-year-old construction worker answers: "Classics are better than Soviet authors; there is no comparison." [17]

A sports instructor of twenty-nine remarked: "I was interested in the question: Why do we live and for what do we live? I came to the conclusion that there must be something higher and not understandable for human thought. Then the works of certain writers taught me to think about this subject, like Dostoyevsky and [Leo] Tolstoy." [18]

The answer of a thirty-seven-year-old schoolteacher is particularly interesting: "I think that the greatest influence on my religious formation was Dostoyevsky's *Brothers Karamazov*. I read the novel four times and all the time I found in it something new and refreshing . . . Due to the powerful voice of Dostoyevsky my faith became very strong." [19]

"Many times," writes Mr. Friedberg on the basis of these interviews, "we feel a tendency to idealize the freedom enjoyed by the writer in tsarist Russia." [20] As a young Soviet teacher put it: "The classics were true because they wrote freely." [21] Or, as a Soviet mechanic declares: "Dostoyevsky is better than any Soviet novelist because he was free to write whatever he wanted." [22]

The significance of all this evidence on Soviet interest in prerevolutionary Russian literature is summed up by Mr. Denicke:

First of all it demonstrates beyond any doubt that Russian classical literature does not appear to the Soviet people as something strange and incomprehensible

[16] *Ibid.*, p. 154.
[17] *Ibid.*, p. 85.
[18] *Ibid.*, p. 86.
[19] *Ibid.*
[20] *Ibid.*, p. 89.
[21] *Ibid.*
[22] *Ibid.*

. . . it is meaningful and pregnant with important consequences because it reveals the existence of a continuity which, *a priori*, could be doubted because of changes which took place after the Revolution . . . To be sure, for many people reading a pre-revolutionary novel or seeing a non-Soviet play has been also a welcome opportunity to escape for a while from Soviet reality. But the character of the works evidently enjoying the most widespread and consistent preference of the Soviet public proves that the popularity of these works is based primarily on their emotional appeal, on the spell of what may be called their psychological and moral climate . . . The evidence certainly confirms that "survivals of bourgeois ideology" are not an invention of Soviet propaganda and that they are much more widespread than the propaganda is prepared to admit.[23]

It is more than likely that much of the spirit behind the present unusual revolt over the abysmal failure of severely regimented postwar literature derives from this now widely prevalent sense of continuity with the literary traditions of the past. In fact, the revolt, in part, may well be considered a striking example of the struggle between the dynamics of continuity and change. Various factors have entered into this revolt, and the Party, no doubt, has had a hand in the making of it. And from one point of view the revolt may be regarded as a literary manifestation of the several domestic changes on behalf of the people that have taken place since Stalin's death, although widespread demands for a change in literature have been accumulating over the last three years.

However this may be, much of the focus, in this demand for a change, is centered on a comparison between Soviet literature and prerevolutionary Russian literature. The regime could not educate a generation in the wonderful literary culture of the past and expect them to act as ignoramuses in judging the perpetrations of Soviet literature since the war. It could not expose them to the frank thought of the materialist critics and to the style, artistic realism, the humor and pathos of life, the struggle against the tyranny of man and ideas, the freedom of the spirit, and the human embodiment of virtue and sin, doubt, and suffering in exquisite characterizations in the great poetry and fiction of such writers as Pushkin, Gogol, Dostoyevsky, Turgenev, Tolstoy, and Chekhov and expect them to accept uncritically the inane situations, uniform plots, stereotyped characters, controlled ideology, forced optimism, and official dullness of much postwar Soviet literature.

It is little wonder that a good deal of the sharp criticism against Soviet literature in recent months takes as its point of departure a comparison with prerevolutionary literature. The justification for Ehrenburg's now celebrated article in this cause was the letter of a young engineer, who asked: "How do you explain the fact that our literature is feeble and colorless as compared with our life? . . . Can one compare our Soviet society with tsarist Russia? Yet the classical writers were better." [24] And throughout all the long answer

---

[23] Denicke, ref. 12, pp. 37–39.
[24] Il'ia Erenburg, "O rabote pisatelia," *Znamia*, no. 10 (1953), p. 160.

to this question in the article, Ehrenburg brings out again and again the superiority of the great writers of the Russian past, the appreciation of their works among Soviet readers, and the necessity of using them as models in creative art. In the recent protests of Ehrenburg, Khatchaturian, Shostakovich, Pomerantsev, and others, one hears an echo of the struggle for artistic freedom in the works of the materialist critics;[25] one hears the strident voice of Belinskii's ". . . art must first be art and only afterwards can it be the expression of the spirit and drift of the society of a given age."[26]

One cannot leave this particular phase of continuity without suggesting a final possibility. So much of the best Russian literature of the nineteenth century, now so popular with vast masses of Soviet readers, was inspired by and often reflected libertarian principles utterly foreign to Soviet ideology. One may well wonder to what extent Soviet citizens are affected by such principles in their favorite reading matter and how successfully the official propaganda counteracts this dangerous influence.

[25] See A. Khachaturian, *Sovetskaia muzyka,* no. 11 (1951), pp. 7–13; D. Shostakovich, *Sovetskaia muzyka,* no. 1 (1954), pp. 40–42; V. Pomerantsev, "Ob iskrennosti v literature," *Novyi mir,* no. 12 (1953).

[26] Quoted by René Wellek, "Social and Aesthetic Values in Russian Nineteenth-Century Literary Criticism," p. 386.

PART VI
RUSSIA AND THE COMMUNITY OF NATIONS
(MESSIANIC VIEWS AND THEORY OF
ACTION)

Herzen and Bakunin on Individual Liberty

ISAIAH BERLIN

"Human life is a great social duty" [said Louis Blanc], "man must constantly sacrifice himself for society."

"Why?," I asked suddenly.

"How do you mean 'why?' — but surely the whole purpose and mission of man is the well-being of society."

"But it will never be attained if everyone makes sacrifices and nobody enjoys himself."

"You are playing with words."

"The muddle-headedness of a barbarian," I replied, laughing.

Alexander Herzen, Past and Reflections, ch. lii.

Since the age of thirteen I have served one idea, marched under one banner — war against all imposed authority — against every kind of deprivation of freedom, in the name of the absolute independence of the individual. I should like to go on with my little guerilla war — like a real Cossack — *auf eigene Faust* — as the Germans say.

Alexander Herzen, Letter to Mazzini.

I

Of all the Russian revolutionary writers of the nineteenth century, Herzen and Bakunin remain the most arresting. They were divided by many differences both of doctrine and of temperament, but they were at one in placing the ideal of individual liberty at the center of their thought and action. Both dedicated their lives to rebellion against every form of oppression, social and political, public and private, open and concealed; but the very multiplicity of their gifts has tended to obscure the relative value of their ideas on this crucial topic.

Bakunin was a gifted journalist, whereas Herzen was a writer of genius, whose autobiography remains one of the great masterpieces of Russian prose. As a publicist he had no equal in his century. He possessed a singular combination of fiery imagination, capacity for meticulous observation, moral passion and intellectual gaiety, with a talent for writing in a manner at once pungent and distinguished, ironical and incandescent, brilliantly entertaining and at times rising to great nobility of feeling and expression. What Mazzini did for the Italians, Herzen did for his countrymen: he created, almost singlehanded, the tradition and the "ideology" of systematic revolutionary agitation and thereby founded the revolutionary movement in Russia. Bakunin's literary endowment was more limited, but he exercised a personal fascination unequalled even in that heroic age of popular tribunes, and left behind him a tradition of political conspiracy which has played a major part in the great upheavals of our own century. Yet these very achievements, which have earned the two friends and companions in arms their claim to immortality, serve to conceal their respective importance as political and social thinkers. For whereas Bakunin, for all his marvelous eloquence, his lucid, clever, vigorous, at times devastating, critical power, seldom says anything which is precise, or profound, or authentic — in any sense personally "lived through" — Herzen, despite his brilliance, his careless spontaneity, his notorious "pyrotechnics," expresses bold and original ideas, and is a political (and consequently a moral) thinker of the first importance. To classify his views with those of Bakunin as forms of semi-anarchistic "populism," or with those of Proudhon or Rodbertus or Chernyshevskii as yet another variant of early socialism with an agrarian bias, is to leave out his most arresting contribution to political theory. This injustice deserves to be remedied. Herzen's basic political ideas are unique not merely by Russian, but by European standards. Russia is not so rich in first-rate thinkers that she can afford to ignore one of the three moral preachers of genius born upon her soil.

II

Alexander Herzen grew up in a world dominated by French and German historical romanticism. The failure of the great French Revolution had discredited the optimistic naturalism of the eighteenth century as deeply as the Russian Revolution of our own day weakened the prestige of Victorian liberalism. The central notion of eighteenth-century enlightenment was the belief that the principal causes of human misery, injustice, and oppression lay in men's ignorance and folly. Accurate knowledge of the laws governing the physical world, once and for all discovered and formulated by the divine Newton, would enable men in due course to dominate nature; by understanding and adjusting themselves to the unalterable causal laws of nature they would live as well and as happily as it is possible to live in the world as it is; at any rate, they would avoid the pains and disharmonies due to vain and ignorant efforts to oppose or circumvent such laws. Some thought that the world as explained by Newton was what it was *de facto*, for no discoverable reason — an ultimate, unexplained reality. Others believed they could discover a rational plan — a "natural" or divine Providence, governed by an ultimate purpose for which all creation strove; so that man, by submitting to it, was not bowing to blind necessity, but consciously recognizing the part which he played in a coherent, intelligible, and thereby justified process.

But whether the Newtonian scheme was taken as a mere description or as a theodicy, it was the ideal paradigm of all explanation; it remained for the genius of Locke to point a way whereby the moral and spiritual worlds could at last also be set in order and explained by the application of the selfsame principles. If the natural sciences enabled men to shape the material world to their desire, the moral sciences would enable him so to regulate his conduct as to avoid forever discord between beliefs and facts, and so end all evil, stupidity and frustration. If philosophers (that is, scientists), both natural and moral, were put in charge of the world, instead of kings, noblemen, priests, and their dupes and factotums, universal happiness could in principle be achieved.

The consequences of the French Revolution broke the spell of these ideas. Among the doctrines which sought to explain what it was that must have gone wrong, German romanticism, both in its subjective-mystical and its nationalist forms, and in particular the Hegelian movement, acquired a dominant position. This is not the place to examine it in detail; suffice it to say that it retained the dogma that the world obeyed intelligible laws; that progress was possible, according to some inevitable plan, and identical with the development of "spiritual" forces; that experts could discover these laws and teach understanding of them to others. For the followers of Hegel the gravest blunder that had been made by the French materialists lay in supposing that these laws were mechanical, that the universe was composed of isolable bits and pieces, of molecules, or atoms, or cells, and that everything could be explained and predicted in terms of the movement of bodies in space. Men were not mere collocations of bits of matter; they were souls or spirits obeying unique and intricate laws of their own. Nor were human societies mere collocations of individuals, they too possessed inner structures analogous to the psychical organization of individual souls, and pursued goals of which the individuals who composed them, might, in varying degrees, be unconscious. Knowledge was, indeed, liberating. Only people who knew why everything was as it was, and acted as it did, and why it was irrational for it to be or do anything else, could themselves be wholly rational: that is, would coöperate with the universe willingly, and not try to beat their heads in vain against the unyielding "logic of the facts." The only goals which were attainable were those embedded in the pattern of historical development; these alone were rational because the pattern was rational; human failure was a symptom of irrationality, of misunderstanding of what the times demanded, of what the next stage of the progress of reason must be; and values — the good and the bad, the just and the unjust, the beautiful and the ugly — were what a rational being would strive for at a specific stage of its growth as part of the rational pattern. To deplore the inevitable because it was cruel or unjust, to complain of what must be, was to reject rational answers to the problems of what to do, how to live. To oppose the stream was to commit suicide, which was mere madness. According to this view, the good, the noble, the just, the strong, the inevitable, the rational, were "ultimately" one; conflict between them was ruled out, logically, a priori. Concerning the nature of the pattern there might be differences; Herder saw it in the development of the cultures of different tribes and races; Hegel in the development of the national state. Saint-Simon saw a broader pattern of a single western civilization, and distinguished in it the dominant role of technological evolution and the conflicts of economically conditioned classes, and within these the crucial influence of exceptional individuals — of men of moral, intellectual, or artistic genius. Mazzini and Michelet saw it in terms of the inner spirit of each people seeking to assert the principles of their common humanity, each in its own fashion, against individual oppression or blind nature. Marx conceived it in terms of the history of the struggle of classes created and determined by growth of the forces of material production. Politico-religious thinkers in Germany and France saw it as *historia sacra,* the progress of fallen man struggling toward union with God — the final theocracy — the submission of secular forces to the reign of God on earth.

There were many variants of these central doctrines, some Hegelian, some mystical, some going back to eighteenth-century naturalism; furious battles were fought, heresies attacked, recalcitrants crushed. What they all had in common was the belief, firstly, that the universe obeys laws and displays a pattern, whether intelligible to reason, or empirically discoverable, or mystically revealed; secondly, that men are elements in wholes larger and stronger than themselves, so that the behavior of individuals can be explained in terms of such wholes, and not *vice versa;* thirdly, that answers to the questions of what should be done are deducible from knowledge of the goals of the objective process of history in which men are willy-nilly involved, and must be identical for all those who truly know — for all rational beings; fourthly, that nothing can be vicious or cruel or stupid or ugly that is a means to the fulfillment of the objectively given cosmic purpose, cannot, at least, be so "ultimately," or "in the last analysis" (however it might look on the face of it), and conversely, that everything that opposes the great purpose, is so. Opinions might vary as to whether such goals were inevitable — and progress therefore automatic; or whether, on the contrary, men were free to choose to realize them or to abandon them (to their own inevitable doom). But all were agreed that objective ends of universal validity could be found, and that they were the sole proper ends of all social, political, and personal activity; for otherwise the world could not be regarded as a "cosmos" with real laws and "objective" demands; all beliefs, all values, might turn out merely relative, merely subjective, the plaything of whims and accidents, unjustified and unjustifiable, which was unthinkable.

Against this great despotic vision, the intellectual glory of the age, revealed, worshipped, and embellished with countless images and flowers by the metaphysical genius of Germany, and acclaimed by the profoundest and most admired thinkers of France, Italy, and Russia, Herzen rebelled violently. He rejected its foundations and denounced its conclusions, not merely because it seemed to him (as it had to his friend Belinskii) morally revolting; but also because he thought it intellectually specious and aesthetically tawdry, and an attempt to force nature into a strait jacket of the poverty-stricken imagination of German philistines and pedants. In *Letters from France and Italy, From the Other Shore, Letters to an Old Comrade*, in *Open Letters* to Michelet, Linton, Mazzini, and, of course, throughout *Past and Reflections*, he enunciated his own ethical and philosophical beliefs. Of these, the most important were: that nature obeys no plan, that history follows no libretto; that no single key, no formula can, in principle, solve the problems of individuals or societies; that general solutions are not solutions, universal ends are never real ends, that every age has its own texture and its own questions, that short cuts and generalizations are no substitute for experience; that liberty — of actual individuals, in specific times and places — is an absolute value; that a minimum area of free action is a moral necessity for all men, not to be suppressed in the name of abstractions or general principles so freely bandied by the great thinkers of this or any age, such as eternal salvation, or history, or humanity, or progress, still less, the state or the Church or the proletariat — great names invoked to justify acts of detestable cruelty and despotism, magic formulas designed to stifle the voices of human feeling and conscience. This liberal attitude had an affinity with the thin but not yet dead tradition of Western libertarianism, of which elements persisted even in Germany — in Kant, in Wilhelm von Humboldt, in the early works of Schiller and of Fichte — surviving in France and French Switzerland among the Idéologues and in the views of Benjamin Constant, Tocqueville, and Sismondi; and remained a hardy growth in England among the utilitarian radicals.

Like the early liberals of Western Europe, Herzen delighted in independence, variety, the free play of individual temperament. He desired the richest possible development of personal characteristics, valued spontaneity, directness, distinction, pride, passion, sincerity, the style and color of free individuals; he detested conformism, cowardice, submission to the tyranny of brute force or pressure of opinion, arbitrary violence, and anxious submissiveness; he hated the worship of power, blind reverence for the past, for institutions, for mysteries or myths; the humiliation of the weak by the strong, sectarianism, philistinism, the resentment and envy of majorities, the brutal arrogance of minorities. He desired social justice, economic efficiency, political stability, but these must always remain secondary to the need for protecting human dignity, the upholding of civilized values, the protection of individuals from aggression, the preservation of sensibility and genius from individual or institutional bullying. Any society which, for whatever reason, failed to prevent such invasions of liberty, and opened the door to the possibility of insult by one side, and groveling by the other, he condemned outright and rejected with all its works — all the social or economic advantages which it might, quite genuinely, offer. He rejected it with the same moral fury as that with which Ivan Karamazov spurned the promise of eternal happiness bought at the cost of the torture of one innocent child; but the arguments which Herzen employed in defense of his position, and the description of the enemy whom he picked out for pillory and destruction, were set forth in language which both in tone and substance had little in common with either the theological or the liberal eloquence of his age.

As an acute and prophetic observer of his times he is comparable, perhaps, to Marx and Tocqueville; as a moralist he is more interesting and original than either.

III

Man, it is commonly asserted, desires liberty. Moreover, human beings are said to have rights, in virtue of which they claim a certain degree of freedom of action. These formulas taken by themselves strike Herzen as hollow. They must be given some concrete meaning, but even then — if they are taken as hypotheses about what people actually believe, they are untrue; not borne out by history; for the masses have seldom desired freedom:

> The masses want to stay the hand which impudently snatches from them the bread which they have earned . . . They are indifferent to individual freedom, liberty of speech; the masses love authority. They are still blinded by the arrogant glitter of power, they are offended by those who stand alone. By equality they understand equality of oppression . . . they want a social government to rule for their benefit, and not, like the present one, against it. But to govern themselves doesn't enter their heads.[1]

On this topic there has been altogether too much "romanticism for the heart" and "idealism for the mind"[2] — too much craving for verbal magic, too much desire to substitute words for things. With the result that bloody struggles have been fought and many innocent human beings slaughtered and the most horrible crimes condoned in the name of empty abstractions:

> There is no nation in the world which has shed so much blood . . . for freedom as the French, and there is no people which understands it less, seeks to realize it less, in the streets, in the courts, in their homes . . . The French are the most abstract and religious people in the world; the fanaticism of ideas with them goes hand in hand with lack of respect for persons, with contempt for their neighbors, the French turn everything into an idol, and then woe to him who does not bow the knee to the idol of the day. Frenchmen fight like heroes for

---

[1] *S togo berega,* in A. I. Gertsen, *Izbrannye filosofskie proizvedeniia* (Moscow, 1946), II, III.

[2] *Ibid.,* p. 20.

freedom and without a thought drag you to jail if you don't agree with their opinions . . . The despotic *salus populi* and the bloody and inquisitorial *pereat mundus et fiat justitia* are engraved equally in the consciousness of royalists and democrats . . . read George Sand, Pierre Leroux, Louis Blanc, Michelet . . . you will meet everywhere Christianity and romanticism adapted to our own morality; everywhere dualism, abstraction, abstract duty, enforced virtues and official and rhetorical morality without any relation to real life.[3]

Ultimately, Herzen goes on to say, this is heartless frivolity, the sacrifice of human beings to mere words which inflame the passions, and which, upon being pressed for their meaning, turn out to refer to nothing, a kind of political *gaminerie* which "excited and fascinated Europe," but also plunged it into inhuman and unnecessary slaughter. "Dualism" is for Herzen a confusion of words with facts, the construction of theories employing abstract terms which are not founded in discovered real needs, of political programs deduced from abstract principles unrelated to real situations. These formulas grow into terrible weapons in the hands of fanatical doctrinaires who seek to bind them upon human beings, if need be, by violent vivisection, for the sake of some absolute ideal, for which the sanction lies in some uncriticized and uncriticizable vision — metaphysical, religious, aesthetic, at any rate, unconcerned with the actual needs of actual persons, in the name of which the revolutionary leaders kill and torture with a quiet conscience, because they know that this and this alone is — must be — the solution to all social and political and personal ills. And he develops this thesis along lines made familiar to us by Tocqueville and other critics of democracy, by pointing out that the masses detest talent, wish everyone to think as they do, and are bitterly suspicious of independence of thought and conduct:

> The submission of the individual to society — to the people — to humanity — to the idea — is a continuation of human sacrifice, the crucifixion of the innocent for the guilty . . . The individual who is the true, real monad of society, has always been sacrificed to some social concept, some collective noun, some banner or other. What the purpose of the sacrifice was was never so much as asked.[4]

Since these abstractions — history, progress, the safety of the people, social equality — have all been cruel altars upon which innocents have been offered up without a qualm, they are deserving of notice. Herzen examines them in turn.

If history has an inexorable direction, a rational structure, and a purpose (perhaps a beneficial one), we must adjust ourselves to it or perish. But what is this rational purpose? Herzen cannot discern it:

There is no sense in history, only one, universal chronic madness. It seems unnecessary to cite examples, there are millions of them. Open any history you like

---

[3] "Pis'mo desiatoe," *Pis'ma iz Frantsii i Italii*, in A. I. Gertsen, *Polnoe sobranie sochinenii i pisem*, ed. M. K. Lemke, 22 vols. (Petrograd, 1919–1925) — hereafted cited as *Sochineniia* — VI, 96.

[4] *S togo berega*, ref. 1, p. 112.

and what is striking is that instead of real interests everything is governed by imaginary interests, fantasies. Look at the kind of causes in which blood is shed, in which people bear extreme sufferings; look at what is praised and what is blamed, and you will be convinced of a truth which at first seems sad — of a truth which on second thoughts is full of comfort, that all this is the result of a deranged intellect. Wherever you look in the ancient world, you will find madness almost as widespread as it is in our own. Here is Curtius throwing himself into a pit to save the city. There a father is sacrificing his daughter to obtain a fair wind, and he has found an old idiot to slaughter the poor girl for him, and this lunatic has not been locked up, has not been taken to a madhouse, but has been recognized as the high priest. Here the King of Persia orders the sea to be flogged, and understands the absurdity of his act as little as his enemies the Athenians, who wanted to cure the intellect and the understanding of human beings with hemlock. What frightful fever was it that made the emperors persecute Christianity? And after the Christians were torn and tortured by wild beasts, they themselves, in their turn, began to persecute and torture one another more furiously than they themselves had been persecuted. How many innocent Germans and Frenchmen perished just so, for no reason at all, while their demented judges thought they were merely doing their duty, and slept peacefully not many steps from the place where the heretics were being roasted to death . . .[5]

"History is the autobiography of a madman." [6] This might have been written with equal bitterness by Voltaire and by Tolstoy. The purpose of history? We do not make history and are not responsible for it. If history is a tale told by an idiot, it is certainly criminal to justify the oppression and cruelty, the imposition of one's arbitrary will upon many thousands of human beings, in the name of hollow abstractions — "the demands" of "history" or of "historical destiny," of "national security," of "the logic of the facts." *Salus populi suprema lex* and *ruat coelum, fiat justitia* — have about them a strong smell of burnt bodies, blood, inquisition, torture, and generally of 'the triumph of order.' " [7] Abstractions, apart from their evil consequences, are a mere attempt to evade facts which do not fit into our preconceived schema.

A man looks at something freely only when he does not bend it to his theory, and does not himself bend before it; reverence before it, not free but enforced, limits a man, narrows his freedom; something in talking of which one is not allowed to smile without blasphemy . . . is a fetish, a man is crushed by it, he is frightened of confounding it with ordinary life . . .[8]

It becomes an icon, an object of blind, uncomprehending worship, and so a mystery justifying excessive crimes. And in the same vein:

[5] Doktor Krupov, in *Sochineniia*, ref. 3, V, 104.
[6] *Ibid.*, p. 105.
[7] *S togo berega*, ref. 1, p. 125.
[8] *Pis'ma iz Frantsii i Italii, Sochineniia*, ref. 3, VI, 20. See also the remarkable analysis of the universal desire to evade intellectual responsibility by the creation of idols and the transgression of the Second Commandment in "New Variations on Old Themes" (*Sochineniia*, V, 18–26), which originally appeared in *Sovremennik*.

The world will not know liberty until all that is religious, political, is transformed into something simple and human, is made susceptible to criticism and denial . . . logic when it comes of age detests canonized truths . . . she thinks nothing sacrosanct . . . if the republic arrogates to itself the same rights as the monarchy, it will despise it as much, nay, more . . . it is not enough to despise the crown — one must not be filled with awe before the Phrygian Cap . . . it is not enough not to consider *lèse majesté* a crime: one must look on *salus populi* as being one.[9]

And he adds that patriotism — to sacrifice oneself for one's country — is doubtless noble; but it is better still if one's country survives as well as oneself. So much for "history." "Human beings will be cured of [such] idealism as they have been of other historical diseases — chivalry, Catholicism, Protestantism . . ."[10]

Then there are those who speak of "progress," and are prepared to sacrifice the present to the future, to make men suffer today in order that their remote descendants might be happy; and condone brutal crimes and the degradation of human beings, because these are the indispensable means toward some guaranteed future felicity. Against this attitude — shared equally by reactionary Hegelians and revolutionary Communists, speculative utilitarians and ultramontane zealots, and indeed all who justify repellent means in the name of noble, but distant, ends — Herzen reserves his most violent contempt and ridicule. To it he devotes the best pages of *From the Other Shore* — his political *profession de foi,* written as a lament for the broken illusions of 1848.

If progress is the goal, for whom are we working? Who is this Moloch who, as the toilers approach him, instead of rewarding them, draws back; and as a consolation to the exhausted and doomed multitudes, shouting *"morituri salutant,"* can only give the mocking answer that after their death all will be beautiful on earth. Do you truly wish to condemn the human beings alive today to the sad role of caryatids supporting a floor for others some day to dance on . . . or of wretched galley slaves who, up to their knees in mud, drag a barge . . . with the humble words "progress in the future" upon its flag? . . . a goal which is infinitely remote is no goal, only . . . a deception; a goal must be closer — at the very least the laborer's wage, or pleasure in work performed. Each epoch, each generation, each life has had, has, its own fullness; and en route new demands grow, new experiences, new methods . . .[11]

The end of each generation is itself. Not only does Nature never make one generation the means for the attainment of some future goal, but she doesn't concern herself with the future at all; like Cleopatra, she is ready to dissolve the pearl in wine for a moment's pleasure.[12]

If humanity marched straight towards some result, there would be no history, only logic . . . human beings possess reason which develops, which doesn't exist in nature, nor outside nature . . . one has to arrange life with it as best one can,

[9] *S togo berega,* ref. 1, p. 41.
[10] *Ibid.,* p. 31.
[11] *Ibid.,* p. 30. See also ref. 8.
[12] *Ibid.,* p. 31.

because there is no libretto. If history followed a set libretto it would lose all interest, become unnecessary, boring, ludicrous . . . great men would be so many heroes strutting on a stage . . . history is all improvisation, all will, all extempore — there are no frontiers, no itineraries. Predicaments occur; sacred discontent; the fire of life; and the endless challenge to the fighters to try their strength, to go where they will, where there is a road; and where there is none, genius will blast a path.[13]

Herzen goes on to say that processes in history or nature may repeat themselves for millions of years; or stop suddenly; the tail of a comet may touch our planet and extinguish all life upon it; and this would be the finale of history. But nothing follows from this, it carries no moral with it. There is no guarantee that things will happen in one way rather than another. The death of a single human being is no less absurd and unintelligible than the death of the entire human race; it is a mystery that we accept, and with which there is no need to frighten children.

In nature, as in the souls of men, there slumber endless possibilities and forces — in suitable conditions they develop — and develop furiously; they may fill the world, or fall by the roadside, take a new direction, stop, collapse . . . Nature is perfectly indifferent to what happens.[14]

But [you may then ask] "what are all these efforts for?" The life of peoples becomes a pointless game . . . Men build something with pebbles and grass and sand — only to see it all collapse again; and human creatures crawl out from underneath the ruins, and again start clearing spaces and build huts of moss and planks and broken capitals, and after centuries of endless labor it all collapses once more. Not in vain did Shakespeare say that history is a tedious tale told by an idiot . . .

I reply that "You are like those very sensitive people who shed a tear whenever they recollect that 'man is born but to die.' To look at the end and not at the action itself is the greatest of errors. Of what use is this bright magnificent bloom to the plant, this intoxicating scent which will pass away? None at all. But nature is not so miserly, and does not disdain what is transient, what lives only in the present. At every point she achieves all that she can achieve. She goes to extreme limits . . . until she reaches the outer frontier of all possible development — death — which cools her ardor, and checks the excess of her poetic fancy, her unbridled creative passion . . . Who will find fault with nature because flowers bloom in the morning and die at night, because she has not given the rose or the lily the hardness of flint? And we want this miserable, pedestrian principle to be applied to the world of history . . . Life has no obligation to realize the fantasies and ideals of civilization . . . life loves novelty."

"History is an improvisation, she seldom repeats herself . . . she uses every accident, simultaneously knocks at a thousand gates which may open, who knows? . . ."

"Baltic ones perhaps — and then Russia will pour over Europe?"

"Possibly . . ."

Human beings have an instinctive passion to preserve anything that they like: man is born — and therefore wishes to live forever; he falls in love: he wishes

[13] *Ibid.*, p. 32.
[14] *Ibid.*

to love and be loved forever as in the first moment of avowal . . . but life . . . gives no guarantees, does not insure existence or pleasure, does not answer for their continuance . . . Every historical moment is full and beautiful, self-contained in its own fashion, and every year has its spring and summer, winter and autumn, storms and fair weather. Every period is new and fresh, filled with its own hopes, carrying within itself its own joys and sorrows; the present belongs to it. But human beings are not content with this: they want to own the future too.[15]

What is the purpose of the song that the singer sings? If you look beyond your pleasure in it for something else, for some other goal, the moment will come when the singer has stopped singing, and then you will have only memories and regrets, you will feel remorse because instead of listening you were waiting for something else . . . You are confused by categories not adapted to catch the flow of life . . . Think: this goal for which you seek — is it a program, an order? Who conceived it — to whom was it assigned? Is it something inevitable? Or not? If it is, are we mere puppets? . . . Are we morally free beings, or wheels in a machine? I prefer to think of life, and therefore of history, as goals attained, not as means to something else.[16]

Is the whole purpose of the child to grow up simply because it does grow up? No, its purpose is to play, to enjoy itself, to be a child; if we follow out the other line of reasoning, the purpose of all life will be death.[17]

The purpose of the singer is the song. And the purpose of life is to live it. Everything passes, but what passes may reward the pilgrim for his sufferings. Goethe has told us that there is no insurance, no security, man must be content with the present; but he is not; he rejects beauty and fulfillment because he must own the future too. This is Herzen's answer to all those who like Mazzini or Kossuth, or the socialists or the communists, called for supreme sacrifices and sufferings for the sake of civilization, or equality, or justice, or humanity, if not in the present, then in the future. But this is "idealism," metaphysical "dualism," secular eschatology. The purpose of life is itself, the purpose of the struggle for liberty is the liberty here, today, of living individuals, each with his own individual ends for the sake of which they move and fight and suffer, ends which are sacred to them; to crush their freedom, stop their pursuits, to ruin their ends for the sake of some ineffable felicity of the future, is blind, because that future is always too uncertain, and vicious, because it outrages the only moral values we know, tramples on real human lives and needs, and in the name of what? Of freedom, happiness, justice — fanatical generalizations, mystical sounds, abstractions. Why is personal liberty worth pursuing? Only for what it is in itself, because it is what it is, not because the majority desires freedom. Men in general do not seek freedom, despite Rousseau's celebrated exclamation that they are born free; that, remarks Herzen (echoing Joseph de Maistre) is as if you were to say "Fish were born to fly, yet everywhere they swim." [18] Ichthyo-

[15] *Ibid.,* pp. 26–28.
[16] *Ibid.,* p. 29.
[17] *Ibid.,* pp. 83–84.
[18] *Ibid.,* p. 85.

phils may seek to prove that fish are "by nature" made to fly; but they are not. And most people do not like liberators; they would rather continue in the ancient ruts, and bear the ancient yokes, than take the immense risks of building a new life. They prefer (Herzen repeats again and again) even the hideous cost of the present, muttering that modern life is at any rate better than feudalism and barbarism. "The people" do not desire liberty, only civilized individuals do; for the desire for freedom is bound up with civilization. The value of freedom, like that of civilization or education — none of which is "natural" or obtainable without great effort — consists in the fact that without it the individual personality cannot realize all its potentialities — cannot live, act, enjoy, create in the illimitable fashions which every moment of history affords, and which differ in unfathomable ways from every other moment of history, and are wholly incommensurable with them. "Man wants to be neither a passive gravedigger of the past, nor the unconscious midwife of the future." [19] He wants to live in his own day. His morality cannot be derived from the laws of history (which do not exist) nor from the objective goals of human progress (there are none such — they change with changing circumstances and persons). Moral ends are what people want for their own sake. "The truly free man creates his own morality."

This denunciation of general moral rules — without a trace of Byronic or Nietzschean hyperbole — is a doctrine not heard often in the nineteenth century; indeed in its full extent, not until well into our own. It hits both right and left: against the romantic historians, against Hegel, and to some degree against Kant; against utilitarians and against supermen; against Tolstoy, and against the religion of art, against "scientific" ethics, and all the churches; it is empirical and naturalistic, recognizes absolute values as well as change, and is overawed neither by evolution nor socialism. And it is original to an arresting degree.

If existing political parties are to be condemned, it is not, Herzen declares, because they do not satisfy the wishes of the majority, for the majority, in any case, prefer slavery to freedom, and the liberation of those who inwardly still remain slaves always leads to barbarism and anarchy. "To dismantle the Bastille stone by stone will not of itself make free men out of the prisoners." [20] "The fatal error [of the French radicals in 1848] was to have tried to free others before they were themselves liberated . . . They wanted, without altering the walls of the prison, to give it a new function — as if the plan of a jail could be useful for a life of freedom." [21] Economic justice is certainly not enough: and this is ignored, to their own doom, by the socialist "sects." As for democracy it can well be "a razor" with which an immature people — like France with its universal suffrage in 1848 —

[19] Letter to his son Alexander, "On the Freedom of Will," *Sochineniia,* ref. 3, XXI, 4.
[20] *S togo berega,* ref. 1, p. 25.
[21] *Ibid.,* p. 43.

nearly cut its own throat;[22] to try to remedy this by a dictatorship ("Petro-grandism") leads to even more violent suppression. Gracchus Babeuf, who was disappointed by the results of the French Revolution, proclaimed the religion of equality — "the equality of the gallows."[23] As for the Commu-nists of our own day what is it they offer us? The "forced labor camps" of Cabet? The "Egyptian slave labors" of Louis Blanc? The neatly laid out little phalansteries of Fourier, in which a free man cannot breathe — in which "one side of life is permanently repressed for the benefit of others"?[24] Communism is merely a leveling movement, the despotism of frenzied mobs, of Committees of Public Safety invoking the security of the people — always a monstrous slogan, as vile as the enemy they seek to overthrow. Barbarism is abominable whichever side it comes from: "Who will finish us off, put an end to it all? The senile barbarism of the scepter or the wild barbarism of Communism? A blood-stained saber or the red flag?"[25] It is true that lib-erals are feeble, unrealistic, and cowardly, and have no understanding of the needs of the poor and the weak, of the new proletarian class which is rising; it is true that the conservatives have shown themselves brutal, stupid, mean, and despotic — although let it be remembered that priests and landowners are usually closer to the masses and understand their needs better than liberal intellectuals, even if their own intentions are less benevolent or honest. It is true that Slavophiles are mere escapists, "defenders of an empty throne," "condoning a bad present in the name of an imaginary past." These men follow brutal and selfish instincts, or empty formulas. But the unbridled democracy of the present is no better, and can suppress men and their liber-ties even more brutally than the odious and sordid government of Napoleon III.

What do the masses care for "us"? "The masses can hurl in the teeth of the European ruling class, 'we were hungry and you gave us chatter, we were naked and you sent us beyond our frontiers to kill other hungry and naked men.' "[26] Parliamentary government in England is certainly no an-swer, for it, in common with other so-called democratic institutions ("traps called oases of liberty") "merely defend the rights of property, exile men in the interests of public safety, and keep under arms men who are ready, with-out asking why, to fire instantly as soon as ordered." Little do naïve demo-crats know what it is that they believe in, and what the consequences will be. "Why is belief in God and the Kingdom of Heaven silly, whereas belief in earthly utopias is not silly?"[27] As for the consequences, one day there

---

[22] *K staromu tovarishchu,* in Gertsen, *Izbrannye filosofskie proizvedeniia,* ref. 1, II, 292.

[23] *Ibid.*

[24] *Ibid.*

[25] "Pis'mo chetyrnadtsatoe," *Pis'ma iz Frantsii i Italii, Sochineniia,* ref. 3, VI, 126.

[26] *Kolokol,* no. 131 (1862).

[27] *S togo berega,* ref. 1, p. 94.

really will be democracy on earth, the rule of the masses. Then indeed something will occur.

> The whole of Europe will leave its normal courses and will be drowned in a general cataclysm . . . Cities taken by storm and looted will fall into poverty, education will decline, factories will come to a stop, villages will be emptied, the countryside will remain without hands to work it, as after the Thirty Years' War. Exhausted and starving peoples will submit to everything, and military discipline will take the place of law and of every kind of orderly administration. Then the victors will begin to fight for their loot. Civilization, industry, terrified, will flee to England and America, taking with them from the general ruin, some their money, others their scientific knowledge or their unfinished work. Europe will become a Bohemia after the Hussites, and then, on the brink of suffering and disaster, a new war will break out, home grown, internal, the revenge of the have-nots against the haves . . . Communism will swarm across the world in a violent tempest, dreadful, bloody, unjust, swift; in thunder and lightning, amid the fire of the burning palaces, upon the ruin of factories and public buildings the New Commandments will be enunciated . . . the New Symbols of the Faith. They will be connected in a thousand fashions with the historic ways of life . . . but the basic tone will be set by socialism. The institutions and structure of our own time and civilization will perish . . . will, as Proudhon politely puts it, be liquidated. You regret the death of civilization? I, too, I am sorry. But the masses will not regret it, the masses to whom it gave nothing but tears, want, ignorance and humiliation.[28]

It is prophecies of this type by the founding fathers of the New Order that cause embarrassment to contemporary Soviet critics and hagiographers. They are usually dealt with by omission.

Heine and Burckhardt too had seen nightmarish visions, and spoke of the demons called into being by the injustices and the "contradictions" of the new world, which promised not Utopia but ruin. Like them, Herzen harbors no illusions:

> Do you not perceive these new Christians, these countries on the march, new barbarians marching to destroy? Like lava they are stirring heavily beneath the surface of the earth; when the hour strikes, Herculaneum and Pompeii will be wiped out, the good and the bad, the just and the unjust will perish equally. This will be not a judgment, not a vengeance, but a cataclysm, a total revolution. This lava, these barbarians, this new world, these Nazarenes who are coming to put an end to the impotent and decrepit — they are closer than you think. For it is they, none other, who are dying of cold and of hunger, it is they whose muttering you hear from the garrets and the cellars, while you and I in our rooms on the first floor are chatting about socialism "over pastry and champagne." [29]

Herzen is more consistently "dialectical" than the "scientific" socialists who swept away the "utopias" of their rivals, only to succumb to millennial fantasies of their own. To set by the side of the classless idyl of Engels in the Communist Manifesto let us ch ose these lines by Herzen:

[28] "Pis'mo chetyrnadtsatoe," ref. 25, p. 131.
[29] *Ibid.*

Socialism will develop in all its phases until it reaches its own extremes and absurdities. Then there will again burst forth from the titanic breast of the revolting minority a cry of denial. Once more a mortal battle will be joined in which socialism will occupy the place of today's conservatism, and will be defeated by the coming revolution as yet invisible to us.[30]

The historical process has no "culmination." Human beings have invented this notion only because they cannot face the possibility of an endless conflict.

Such passages as these have their analogues in savage prophecies by Hegel and by Marx, who also predicted the doom of the bourgeoisie, and death and lava and a new civilization. But, whereas there is in both Hegel and Marx an unmistakable note of sardonic, gloating joy in the very thought of vast, destructive powers unchained, and the coming holocaust of all the innocents and the fools and the contemptible philistines, so little aware of their terrible fate, Herzen is free from this prostration before the mere spectacle of triumphant power and violence, from contempt for weakness as such, and from the romantic pessimism which is at the heart of the nihilism and Fascism that was to come; for he thinks the cataclysm neither inevitable nor glorious. He despises these liberals who begin revolutions and then try to extinguish their consequences, who "at the same time undermine the old order and cling to it, light the fuse and try to stop the explosion," who are frightened "by the emergence of that mythical creature, their 'little brother,' the worker, the proletarian who demands his rights, who does not realize that while he has nothing to lose, the intellectual may lose everything." It is the liberals who betrayed the revolution in 1848 in Paris, in Rome, in Vienna, not only by taking flight and helping the defeated reactionaries to regain power and stamp out liberty, but by first running away, then pleading that the "historical forces" were too strong to resist. If one has no answer to a problem, it is more honest to admit this, and to formulate the problem clearly, than first to obscure it, commit acts of weakness and betrayal, and then plead as an excuse that history was too much for one. True, the ideals of 1848 were themselves empty enough; at least they looked so to Herzen in 1869: "not one constructive, organic idea . . . economic blunders which lead not indirectly, like political ones, but directly and deeply, to ruin, stagnation, a hungry death."[31] Economic blunders plus "the arithmetical pantheism of universal suffrage, and superstitious faith in republics" is his summary of the ideals of 1848. Nevertheless, the liberals did not fight even for their own foolish program. And in any case liberty was not to be gained by such means. The claims of our time are clear enough, they are social more than economic; for mere economic change, as advocated by socialists, unaccompanied by a deeper transformation, will not suffice to abolish

[30] *Ibid.*, p. 99.
[31] *K staromu tovarishchu*, ref. 22, p. 285.

. . . civilized cannibalism, monarchy and religion, courts and governments, moral beliefs and habits. The institutions of private life must be changed too. The problem is clear enough: it is to understand fully the sacred rights of the individual and yet not to destroy, not to pulverize society into atoms. The past has failed to perform this most difficult of social tasks.[32]

Science will not solve it, *pace* Saint-Simon, nor will preaching against the horrors of unbridled competition, nor advocacy of the abolition of poverty, if all they do is to dissolve individuals into a single, monolithic, oppressive community — Gracchus Babeuf's "equality of the gallows." [33]

History is not determined. Life, fortunately, has no libretto, improvisation is always possible, "nothing makes it necessary for the future to fulfill the program" [34] prepared by the metaphysicians. "Socialism is neither impossible nor inevitable" and it is the business of the believers in liberty to prevent it from degenerating either into *bourgeois* philistinism or communist slavery. "Life is neither good nor bad," men are what they make themselves. "Without social sense they become orangutans, without egotism, tame monkeys," [35] but there are not inexorable forces to compel them to be either. Our ends are not made for us, but by us;[36] hence to justify trampling on liberty today by the promise of freedom tomorrow, because it is "objectively" guaranteed, is to make use of a cruel and wicked delusion as a pretext for iniquitous action. "If only people wanted, instead of saving the world, to save themselves — instead of liberating humanity, to liberate themselves, they would do much for the salvation of the world and the liberation of man." [37]

Herzen goes on to say that man is of course dependent on his environment and his time — physiologically, educationally, biologically, as well as at more conscious levels; and he concedes that men reflect their own time and are affected by the circumstances of their lives. But the possibility of opposition to the social medium, and protest against it is nevertheless just as real; whether it is effective or not; whether it takes a social or an individual form.[38] Belief in determinism is merely an alibi for weakness. There will always be those fatalists who will say "the choice of the road to follow is not in the individual's power. Events do not depend on persons, but persons on events: we only seem to control our direction, but actually sail wherever the wave takes us." [39] But this is not true.

Our paths are not unalterable at all. On the contrary, they change with circumstances, with understanding, with personal energy . . . the individual is made

[32] *S togo berega,* ref. 1, p. 23.
[33] *Sochineniia,* ref. 3, XXI, 436.
[34] *Ibid.,* V, 407 and 454.
[35] *Ibid.,* V, 482.
[36] *Ibid.*
[37] *Ibid.,* pp. 472–473.
[38] *Izbrannye filosofskie proizvedeniia,* ref. 1, II, 107.
[39] *K staromu tovarishchu,* ref. 22, p. 206.

by events, but events are also made by individuals and bear their stamp upon them — there is perpetual interaction. Passive tools of forces independent of us — that is not something that we can be; to be the blind instrument of fate — the scourge, the executioner of God, one needs naïve faith, the simplicity of ignorance, wild fanaticism, a pure, uncontaminated, childlike quality of thought.[40]

To pretend that we are like this today would be a lie. Leaders arise, like Bismarck (or Marx) who claim to guide their nation or their class to the inevitable triumph reserved for them by destiny, whose chosen instruments they feel themselves to be; in the name of their sacred historic mission they ruin, torture, enslave. But they remain brutal impostors.

What thinking persons will forgive Attila, the Committee of Public Safety, even Peter, they will not forgive us; we have heard no voice calling to us from on high to fulfill a destiny; no voice from the nether regions to point a path to us. For us, there is only one voice, one power, *the power of reason and understanding*. In rejecting them we become the unfrocked priests of science, renegades to civilization.[41]

IV

If this is a condemnation of Bismarck or Marx, it is directed more obviously and expressly at Bakunin and the Russian Jacobins, at Karakozov's pistol and Chernyshevskii's "axe," sanctified by the new young revolutionaries; at the terrorist propaganda of Zaichnevskii or of Serno-Solovievich, and the culminating horror of Nechaev's activity and the final perversions of revolutionary doctrine, which went far beyond its Western origins, and treated honor, compassion, and the scruples of civilization as so many personal affronts. From this it is not far to Plekhanov's celebrated formula of 1903, "the safety of the revolution is the supreme law," which sanctioned the suspension of civil liberties; and so to the April Theses, and the treatment of "inviolability of the person" as a luxury to be dispensed with in difficult moments.

The chasm between Herzen and Bakunin is not bridgeable. And the half-hearted attempts by Soviet historians, if not to slur over the differences, at any rate to represent them as necessary and successive stages in the evolution of a single process — necessary both logically and historically (because history and the development of ideas obey "logical" laws) are melancholy failures. The views of those who, like Herzen (or Mill) place personal liberty in the center of their social and political doctrine, to whom it is the holy of holies the surrender of which makes all other activities, whether of defense or attack, valueless;[42] and, as opposed to them, of those for whom such

---

[40] *Ibid.*

[41] *Ibid.*

[42] "However low . . . governments sank," Herzen once remarked about the West in contrast to Russia, "Spinoza was not sentenced to transportation, nor Lessing to be flogged or conscripted" (*Sochineniia*, ref. 3, V, 388). The twentieth century has destroyed the force of this comparison.

liberty is only a desirable by-product of the social transformation which is the sole end of their activity, or else a transient stage of development made inevitable by history — these two attitudes are opposed, and no reconciliation or compromise between them is conceivable; for the Phrygian Cap comes between them. For Herzen the issue of personal liberty overshadows even such crucial questions as centralism against free federation; revolution from above versus revolution from below; political versus economic activity; peasants versus city workers; collaboration with other parties versus refusal to transact and the cry for "political purity" and independence; belief in the unavoidability of capitalist development verus the possibility of circumnavigating it; and all the other great issues which divided the liberal and revolutionary parties in Russia until the Revolution. For those who stand "in awe of the Phrygian Cap" *salus populi* is a final criterion before which all other considerations must yield. For Herzen it remains "a criminal" principle, the greatest tyranny of all; to accept it is to sacrifice the freedom of individuals to some huge abstraction — some monstrosity invented by metaphysics or religion, to escape from the real, earthly issues, to be guilty of "dualism," that is, to divorce the principles of action from empirical facts, and deduce them from some other set of "facts" provided by some special mode of vision; to take a path which in the end always leads to "cannibalism" — the slaughter of men and women today for the sake of "future happiness." [43] "The Letters to an Old Comrade" are aimed, above all, at this fatal fallacy. Herzen rightly held Bakunin guilty of it, and behind the ardent phrases, the lion-hearted courage, the broad Russian nature, the gaiety, the charm and the imagination of his friend — to whom he remained personally devoted to the end — he discerned a cynical indifference to the fate of individual human beings, a childish enthusiasm for playing with human lives for the sake of social experiment, a lust for revolution for revolution's sake, which went ill with his professed horror before the spectacle of arbitrary violence or the humiliation of innocent persons. He detected a certain genuine inhumanity in Bakunin (of which Belinskii and Turgenev were not unaware), a hatred of slavery, oppression, hypocrisy, poverty, in the abstract, without actual revulsion against their manifestations in concrete instances — a genuine Hegelianism of outlook — the feeling that it is useless to blame the instruments of history, when one can rise to a loftier height and survey the structure of history herself. Bakunin hated tsardom, but displayed too little specific loathing of Nicholas; he would never have given sixpences to little boys in Twickenham to cry, on the day of the Emperor's death, "Zarnicoll is dead!" or feel the emancipation of the peasants as a personal happiness. The fate of individuals did not greatly concern him; his units were too vague and too large; "First destroy, and then we shall see." Temperament, vision, generosity, courage, revolutionary fire, elemental force of nature, these Bakunin had to over-

[43] *Ibid.*, p. 478.

flowing. The rights and liberties of individuals play no great part in his apocalyptic vision.

Herzen's position on this issue is clear, and did not alter throughout his life. No distant ends, no appeals to overriding principles or abstract nouns can justify the suppression of liberty, or fraud, violence, and tyranny. Once the conduct of life in accordance with the moral principles that we actually live by, in the situation as we know it to be, and not as it might, or could, or should be, is abandoned, the path is open to the abolition of individual freedom and of all the values of humane culture. With genuine horror and disgust Herzen saw and denounced the militant, boorish anti-humanism of the younger generation of Russian revolutionaries — fearless but brutal, full of savage indignation, but hostile to civilization and liberty, a generation of Calibans — "the syphilis of the revolutionary passions" of Herzen's own generation. They paid him back by a campaign of systematic denigration as a "soft" aristocratic dilettante, a feeble liberal trimmer, a traitor to the revolution, a superfluous survival of an obsolete past. He responded with a bitter and accurate vignette of the "new men": "The new generation will say to the old: 'you were hypocrites, we are cynics; you spoke like moralists, we shall speak like scoundrels; you were civil to your superiors, rude to your inferiors; we shall be rude to all; you bowed without feeling respect, we shall push and jostle and make no apologies.' "[44]

It is a singular irony of history that Herzen, who wanted individual liberty more than happiness, or efficiency, or justice, who denounced organized planning, economic centralization, governmental authority, because it might curtail the individual's capacity for the free play of fantasy, for unlimited depth and variety of personal life within a wide, rich, "open" social milieu, who hated the Germans (and in particular the "Russian Germans and German Russians") of St. Petersburg because their slavery was not (as in Russia or Italy) "arithmetical," that is, reluctant submission to the numerically superior forces of reaction, but "algebraical," that is, part of their "inner formula" — the essence of their very being,[45] that Herzen, in virtue of a casual phrase patronizingly dropped by Lenin, should today find himself in the holy of holies of the Soviet Pantheon, placed there by a government the genesis of which he understood better and feared more deeply than Dostoyevsky, and whose words and acts are a continuous insult to all that he believed and was.

Doubtless, despite all his appeals to concreteness, and his denunciation of abstract principles, Herzen was himself, at times, Utopian enough. He feared mobs, he disliked bureaucracy and organization, and yet he believed in the possibility of establishing the rule of justice and happiness, not merely for

[44] *Byloe i dumy*, Part VI, ch. xii, in *Sochineniia*, ref. 3, XIV, 420.
[45] *Du développement des idées révolutionnaires en Russie*, in *Sochineniia*, ref. 3, VI, 202, 677–678. Arnold Ruge was outraged by this and protested vehemently in his notice of the essay on its original appearance.

the few, but for the many, if not in the Western world, at any rate in Russia; and that, largely out of patriotism: in virtue of the Russian national character which had proved itself so gloriously by surviving Byzantine stagnation, and the Tartar yoke and the German truncheon, its own officials, and through it all preserving the inner soul of the people intact. He idealized Russian peasants, the village communes, free *artel's;* similarly he believed in the natural goodness and moral nobility of the workers of Paris, in the Roman populace, and despite the increasingly frequent notes of "sadness, skepticism and irony — the three strings of the Russian lyre," [46] he grew neither cynical nor skeptical. Russian populism owes more to his ungrounded optimism than to any other single source of its inspiration.

Yet compared to Bakunin's doctrines, Herzen's views are a model of dry realism. Bakunin and Herzen had much in common: they shared an acute antipathy to Marxism and its founders, they saw no gain in the replacement of one class of despotism by another, they did not believe in the virtues of proletarians as such. But Herzen does at least face genuine political problems, such as the incompatibility of unlimited personal liberty with either social equality, or the minimum of social organization and authority; the need to sail precariously between the Scylla of individualist "atomization," and the Charybdis of collectivist oppression; the sad disparity and conflict between many, equally noble human ideals; the nonexistence of "objective," eternal, universal moral and political standards, to justify either coercion or resistance to it; the mirage of distant ends, and the impossibility of doing wholly without them. In contrast to this, Bakunin, whether in his various Hegelian phases, or his anarchist period, gaily dismisses such problems, and sails off into the happy realm of revolutionary phraseology with the gusto and the irresponsible delight in words which characterized his adolescent and essentially frivolous outlook.

V

Bakunin, as his enemies and followers will equally testify, dedicated his entire life to the struggle for liberty. He fought for it in action and in words. More than any other individual in Europe he stood for ceaseless rebellion against every form of constituted authority, for ceaseless protest in the name of the insulted and oppressed of every nation and class. His power of cogent and lucid destructive argument is extraordinary, and has not, even today, obtained proper recognition. His arguments against theological and metaphysical notions, his attacks upon the whole of Western Christian tradition — social, political, and moral — his onslaughts upon tyranny, whether of states or classes, or of special groups in authority — priests, soldiers, bureaucrats, democratic representatives, bankers, revolutionary elites — are set forth in language which is still a model of eloquent polemical prose. With

[46] "Russkii narod i sotsializm. Pis'mo k Zh. Mishle," *Sochineniia,* ref. 3, VI, 453.

much talent and wonderful high spirits he carried on the militant tradition of the violent radicals among the eighteenth-century *philosophes*. He shared their buoyancy but also their weaknesses, and his positive doctrines, as so often theirs, turn out to be mere strings of ringing commonplaces, linked together by vague emotional relevance or rhetorical afflatus rather than a coherent structure of genuine ideas. His affirmative doctrines are even thinner than theirs. Thus as his positive contribution to the problem of defining freedom, he offers: "Tous pour chacun et chacun pour tous."[47] This schoolboy jingle, with its echo of *The Three Musketeers*, and the bright colors of historical romance, is more characteristic of Bakunin, with his irrepressible frivolity, his love of fantasy, and his lack of scruple in action and in the use of words, than the picture of the dedicated liberator painted by his followers and worshiped from afar by many a young revolutionary sent to Siberia or to death by the power of his unbridled eloquence. In the finest and most uncritical manner of the eighteenth century, without examining (despite his Hegelian upbringing and his notorious dialectical skill) whether they are compatible (or what they signify), Bakunin lumps all the virtues together into one vast undifferentiated amalgam: justice, humanity, goodness, freedom, equality ("the liberty of each for the equality of all" is another of his empty incantations), science, reason, good sense, hatred of privilege and of monopoly, hatred of oppression and exploitation, of stupidity and poverty, of weakness, inequality, injustice, snobbery — all these are represented as somehow forming one single, lucid, concrete ideal, for which the means would be only too ready to hand if only men were not too blind or too wicked to make use of them. Liberty will reign in "a new heaven and a new earth, a new enchanting world in which all the dissonances will flow into one harmonious whole — the democratic and universal church of human freedom."[48] Once launched upon the waves of this type of mid-nineteenth-century radical patter, one knows only too well what to expect. To paraphrase another passage, I am not free if you, too, are not free; my liberty must be "reflected" in the freedom of others — the individualist is wrong who thinks that the frontier of my liberty is your liberty — liberties are complementary — are indispensable to each other — not competitive.[49] The "political and juridical" concept of liberty is part and parcel of that "criminal" use of words which equates society and the detested State. It deprives men of liberty for it sets the individual against society; upon this the "thoroughly vicious" theory of the social contract — by which men have to give up some portion of their original, "natural" liberty in order to associate in harmony — is

[47] "Lettre à la Commission du journal *l'Égalité*," *Oeuvres Complètes*, ed. J. Guillaume, V (Paris, 1911), 15.

[48] Quoted by A. Ruge in his memoirs of Bakunin, in *Neue Freie Presse* (April-May 1876).

[49] *Trois Conférences: faites aux ouvriers du Val de Saint-Imier*, in *Oeuvres Complètes*, ref. 47, V, 321–322.

founded. But this is a fallacy for it is only in society that men become both human and free — only "collective and social labor liberates us from nature" and without such liberation "no moral or intellectual liberty" is possible.[50] Liberty cannot occur in solitude, but is a form of reciprocity. I am free and human only so far as others are such. My freedom is limitless because that of others is also such; our liberties mirror one another — so long as there is one slave, I am not free, not human, have no dignity and no rights. Liberty is not a physical or a social condition but a mental one: it consists of universal reciprocal recognition of the individual's liberties: slavery is a state of mind and the slaveowner is as much a slave as his chattels.[51] The glib Hegelian claptrap of this kind with which the works of Bakunin abound has not even the alleged merits of Hegelianism, for it contrives to reproduce many of the worst confusions of eighteenth-century thought, including that whereby the comparatively clear, if negative, concept of personal liberty as a condition in which a man is not coerced by others into doing what he does not wish to do, is confounded with the Utopian and perhaps unintelligible notion of being free from laws in a different sense of "law" — from the necessities of nature or even of social coexistence. And from this it is inferred that since to ask for freedom from Nature is absurd, since I am what I am as part of her, therefore, because my relationships with other human beings are part of "Nature," it is equally senseless to ask for freedom from them — what one should seek is a "freedom" which consists in a "harmonious solidarity" with them.

Bakunin rebelled against Hegel and professed to hate Christianity; but his language is a conventional amalgam of both. The assumption that all virtues are compatible, nay, mutually entailed by one another, that the liberty of one man can never clash with that of another if both are rational (for then they cannot desire conflicting ends), that unlimited liberty is not only compatible with unlimited equality but inconceivable without it; reluctance to attempt a serious analysis of either the notions of liberty or of equality; the belief that it is only avoidable human folly and wickedness which is responsible for preventing the natural goodness and wisdom of man from making a paradise upon earth almost instantaneously, or at least as soon as the tyrannical State, with its vicious and idiotic legal system, is destroyed root and branch — all these naïve fallacies, intelligible enough in the eighteenth century, but endlessly criticized in Bakunin's own sophisticated century, form the substance of his sermons *urbi et orbi;* and in particular of his fiery allocutions to the fascinated watchmakers of Chaux des Fonds and the Valley of Saint-Imier.

Bakunin's thought is almost always simple, shallow, and clear; the lan-

---

[50] *Knuto-Germanskaia Imperia i sotsialnaia revoliutsiia,* 2nd ed., in Mikhail Bakunin, *Izbrannye sochineniia,* II (Petersburg-Moscow, 1922), 235–239.
[51] *Ibid.*

guage is passionate, direct, and imprecise, riding from climax to climax of rhetorical violence, sometimes expository, more often hortatory or polemical, usually ironical, sometimes sparkling, always gay, always entertaining, always readable, seldom related to facts of experience, never original or serious or specific. Liberty — the word — occurs ceaselessly. Sometimes Bakunin speaks of it in exalted semireligious terms, and declares that the instinct to mutiny — defiance — is one of the three basic "moments" in the development of humanity, denounces God and pays homage to Satan, the first rebel, the true friend of freedom. In such "Acherontic" moods, in words which resemble the opening of a revolutionary marching song, he declares that the only true revolutionary element in Russia (or anywhere else) is the doughty (*likhoi*) world of brigands and desperadoes, who having nothing to lose, will destroy the old world — after which the new will arise spontaneously like the phoenix from the ashes.[52] He puts his hopes in the sons of the ruined gentry, in all those who drown their sorrows and indignation in violent outbreaks against their cramping milieu. Like Weitling, he calls upon the dregs of the underworld, and, in particular, the disgruntled peasants, the Pugachëvs and Razins, to rise like modern Samsons and bring down the temple of iniquity. At other times, more innocently, he calls merely for a revolt against all fathers and all schoolmasters: children must be free to choose their own careers; we want "neither demigods nor slaves," but an equal society, above all not differentiated by university education which creates intellectual superiority, and leads to more painful inequalities than even aristocracy or plutocracy. Sometimes he speaks of the necessity for an "iron dictatorship" during the transitional period between the vicious society of today with its "knuto-German" army and police, and the stateless society of tomorrow confined by no restraints. Other times he says that all dictatorships tend inevitably to perpetuate themselves, and that the dictatorship of the proletariat is yet one more detestable despotism of one class over another. He cries that all "imposed" laws, being man-made, must be thrown off at once; but allows that "social" laws which are "natural" and not "artificial" will have to be obeyed — as if these latter are fixed and immutable and beyond human control. Few of the optimistic confusions of the eighteenth-century rationalists fail to make an appearance somewhere in his works. After proclaiming the right — the duty — to mutiny, and the urgent necessity for the violent overthrow of the state, he happily proclaims his belief in absolute historical and sociological determinism, and approvingly quotes the words of the Belgian statistician Quetelet: "Society prepares crimes, individuals merely execute them." Belief in free will is irrational, for "with Hegel" he believes that "Logic herself entails natural necessity." Our

---

[52] "Soedinimsia s likhim razboinchiim mirom, etim istinnym i edinstvennym revoliutsionerom v Rossii." See the penultimate prayer of the *Catechism of the Revolutionary*.

human, as well as natural environment, shapes us entirely: yet we must fight for "the completest possible development of all the natural faculties of every individual and . . . his independence (not of natural or social laws) but of all the laws imposed by other human wills whether collective or isolated." [53] That is Bakunin's final, most sophisticated definition of liberty, and the meaning of this phrase is for anybody to seek. All that clearly emerges is that Bakunin is opposed to the imposition of any restraints upon anyone at any time under any conditions. Moreover he believes, like Holbach or Godwin, that once the artificial restraints imposed upon mankind by blind tradition, or folly, or "interested vice," are lifted, all will automatically be set right, and justice, virtue, happiness, pleasure, and freedom will immediately commence their united sway on earth. The search for something more solid in Bakunin's utterances is unrewarding.[54] He used words principally not for descriptive but for inflammatory purposes, and was a great master of his medium; even today his words have not lost their power to stir.

Like Herzen he disliked the new ruling class, the "Figaros in power," "Figaro-bankers" and "Figaro-ministers" whose livery could not be shed because it had become part of their skins. He liked free men and unbroken personalities. He detested spiritual slavery more than any other quality. And like Herzen he looked on the Germans as irredeemably servile and said so with insulting repetitiveness:

> When an Englishman or an American says "I am an Englishman," "I am an American," they are saying "I am a free man"; when a German says "I am a German" he is saying "I am a slave, but my Emperor is stronger than all the other emperors, and the German soldier who is strangling me, will strangle you all"; every people has tastes of its own — the Germans are obsessed by the big stick of the State.[55]

Bakunin recognized oppression when he saw it; he genuinely disliked every form of authority and order, and he knew an authoritarian when he met one whether he was Tsar Nicholas and Bismarck, or Marx and Lassalle ("triply authoritarian as Germans, Hegelians and Jews"). But he is not a serious thinker; he is neither a moralist nor a psychologist; what is to be looked for in him is not social theory or political doctrine, but an outlook and a temperament. There are no coherent ideas to be extracted from his writings of any period, only fire and imagination, violence and poetry, and an ungovernable desire for strong sensations, for life at a high tension, for the disintegration of all that is peaceful, secluded, tidy, orderly, small scale, philistine, established, moderate, part of the monotonous prose of daily life. His attitude and his teaching were profoundly frivolous, and, on the whole, he knew this

---

[53] *Oeuvres Complètes,* ref. 49.

[54] Herzen, in a letter to Turgenev written in 1862 justly called it *"fatras bakuninskoi demagogii." Sochineniia,* ref. 3, XV, 549.

[55] *Gosudarstvo i anarkhizm,* trans. Cherkezov (Moscow, 1922), p. 248.

well, and laughed good-naturedly whenever he was exposed.[56] He wanted to set on fire as much as possible as swiftly as possible; the thought of any kind of chaos, violence, upheaval, he found boundlessly exhilarating. When in his famous *Confession* he said that what he hated most was a quiet life, that what he longed for most ardently was always something — anything — fantastic, unheard of adventures, perpetual movement, action, battle, that he suffocated in peaceful conditions, he summed up the content as well as the quality of his writings.

VI

Despite their prima-facie similarities — their common hatred of the Russian regime, their belief in the Russian peasant, their theoretical federalism and Proudhonian socialism, their hatred of bourgeois society and contempt for middle-class virtues, their antiliberalism and their militant atheism, their personal devotion, and the similarity of their social origin, tastes, and education — the differences of the two friends are deep and wide. Herzen (although this has been seldom recognized even by his greatest admirers) is an original thinker, independent, honest, and unexpectedly profound. At a time when general nostrums, vast systems, and simple solutions were in the air, preached by the disciples of Hegel, of Feuerbach, of Fourier, of Christian and neo-Christian social mystics, when utilitarians and neomedievalists, romantic pessimists and nihilists, peddlers of "scientific" ethics and "evolutionary" politics, and every brand of communist and anarchist offered short term remedies and long term utopias — social, economic, theosophical, metaphysical, Herzen retained his incorruptible sense of reality. He realized that general and abstract terms like "liberty" or "equality," unless they were translated into specific terms applicable to actual situations, were likely, at best, merely to stir the poetical imagination and inspire men with generous sentiments, at worst to justify stupidities or crimes. He saw — and in his day it was a discovery of genius — that there was something absurd in the very asking of such general questions as "What is the meaning of life?" or "What accounts for the fact that things in general happen as they do?" or "What is *the* goal or *the* pattern or *the* direction of history?" He realized that such questions made sense only if they were made specific, and that the answers depended on the specific ends of specific human beings in specific situations. To ask always for "ultimate" purposes was not to know what a purpose is; to ask for the ultimate goal of the singer in singing was to be interested in something other than songs or music. For a man acted as he did, each for the sake of his own personal ends (however much, and however rightly, he might believe it to be connected or identical, with those of others) which were sacred

---

[56] "By nature I am not a charlatan," he said in his letter to the tsar, "but circumstances (for which, in point of fact, I was myself responsible) sometimes made me a charlatan against my will." See *Materialy dlia biografii M. Bakunina*, ed. Viacheslav Polonskii, 3 vols. (Moscow, 1923), I, 159–160.

to him, ends for the sake of which he was prepared to live and to die. It is for this reason that Herzen so seriously and passionately believed in the independence and freedom of individuals; and understood what he believed in, and reacted so painfully against the adulteration or obfuscation of the issues by metaphysical or theological patter and democratic rhetoric. In his view all that is ultimately valuable are the particular purposes of particular persons; and to trample on these is always a crime because there is, and can be, no principle or value higher than the ends of the individual, and therefore no principle in the name of which one could be permitted to do violence or degrade or destroy individuals — the sole authors of all principles and all values. Unless a minimum area is guaranteed to all men within which they can act as they wish, the only principles and values left will be those guaranteed by theological or metaphysical or scientific systems claiming to know the final truth about man's place in the universe, and of his functions and goals therein. And these claims Herzen regarded as fraudulent, one and all. It is this particular species of nonmetaphysical, empirical, "eudaemonistic" individualism that makes Herzen the sworn enemy of all systems, and of all claims to suppress liberties in their name, whether in the name of utilitarian considerations or authoritarian principles, of mystically revealed ends, or of reverence before irresistible power, or "the logic of the facts," or any other similar reason.

What can Bakunin offer that is remotely comparable? Bakunin with his gusto and his logic and his eloquence, his desire and capacity to undermine and burn and shiver to pieces, now disarmingly childlike, at other times, pathological and inhuman; with his odd combination of analytical acuteness and unbridled exhibitionism; carrying with him, with superb unconcern, the multicolored heritage of the eighteenth century without troubling to consider whether some among his ideas contradicted others — the "dialectic" would look after that — or how many of them had become obsolete, discredited, or had been absurd from the beginning — Bakunin, the official friend of absolute liberty, has not bequeathed a single idea worth considering for its own sake; there is not a fresh thought, not even an authentic emotion, only amusing diatribes, high spirits, malicious vignettes, and a memorable epigram or two. A historical figure remains — the "Russian Bear," as he liked to describe himself, morally careless, intellectually irresponsible, a man who, in his love for humanity in the abstract, was prepared, like Robespierre, to wade through seas of blood; and thereby constitutes a link in the tradition of cynical terrorism and unconcern for individual human beings, the practice of which is the main contribution of our own century, thus far, to political thought. And this aspect of Bakunin, the Stavrogin concealed inside Rudin, the fascist streak, the methods of Attila, "Petrograndism," sinister qualities so remote from the lovable "Russian Bear" — *die Grosse Lise* — was detected not merely by Dostoyevsky, who exaggerated and caricatured it, but by Herzen himself, who drew up a formidable indictment against it in the *Letters to an Old Comrade*, perhaps the most instructive, prophetic, sober, and moving essays on the prospects of human freedom written in the nineteenth century.

Dostoyevsky and Danilevsky: Nationalist Messianism

HANS KOHN

Herzen and Bakunin belonged to the same generation; they were born in 1812 and 1814 respectively. The great event which inspired their boyhood was the Decembrist uprising; the axis of their life was formed by the Revolution of 1848. Their common concern was the liberation of the individual personality, in Europe and in Russia, two worlds which were equally near to their hearts and which they tried to harmonize in a common effort of freedom. Each lived the greater part of his mature existence in Europe. Fëdor Mikhailovich Dostoyevsky and Nikolai Yakovlevich Danilevsky belonged to the following generation. They were a decade younger; Dostoyevsky was born in 1821 and Danilevsky in 1822.[1] The decisive period through which they lived was between the Crimean War and the Congress of Berlin, the conflict between Russia's imperial ambitions and European resistance, the two decades during which the nationalist movements in Italy, Germany, and the Balkans found their initial fulfillment thanks to the combination of a semimystical nationalist ideology and a semi-Machiavellian political strategy. In this general atmosphere, Dostoyevsky and Danilevsky were less concerned with individual liberty than with Russian national power and destiny. They boundlessly loved and admired Russia, but harbored no such feelings toward Europe. During the years which Dostoyevsky lived in Europe, his letters were a continuous outcry of utter indignation and misery. The two decisive events for them in the Russia of their time were the emancipation of the serfs in 1861 and the Polish uprising in 1863. The one filled them with immeasurable pride and hope, the other was a dire warning of the evil West's intentions.

Though the violent Revolution of 1848 had failed in Europe and the freeing of the slaves in democratic America had been achieved only at a terrific cost of blood and devastation — was a social revolution not consummated peacefully in Russia, thanks to the blessings of autocracy and

---

[1] See on Dostoyevsky my *Prophets and Peoples* (New York, 1946), pp. 131–160, 198–206, and on Danilevsky my *Pan-Slavism, Its History and Ideology* (Notre Dame, 1953), pp. 152–166, 302–304. In *Prophets and Peoples*, p. 201, I remarked that unfortunately no English translation of Dostoyevsky's *Dnevnik pisatel'ia* existed. Now it exists, *The Diary of a Writer*, trans. Boris Brasol, 2 vols. (New York, 1949) — hereafter cited as *Diary*.

the greater morality of the Russian people? The emancipation of the serfs in Russia proved the civic primacy of the Russian people and of their governmental system; it promised social harmony and avoidance of the revolutionary chaos and civil wars which were the fate of Europe and America. The West's understandable envy and hostility became manifest in 1863 when official France, Britain, and Austria, and general public opinion everywhere outside Russia, sympathized with the Poles. Few Russians indeed took a stand opposed to Russian imperialism; among them Bakunin and Herzen unequivocally defended the right of the Poles and Ukrainians to independence. Other Russian liberals like M. N. Katkov turned, as a result of the Polish uprising, to a fervent Russian nationalism. "Russia," he wrote in 1867, "needs a unitarian state and a strong Russian national idea. We shall create such a national idea on the basis of a common language and a common faith for all the inhabitants [of the Russian empire] and on the basis of the Slav *mir*. Whatever opposes us, will be overthrown by us." [2] Dostoyevsky and Danilevsky became the most famous exponents of this Russian national idea. In nineteenth-century Europe no other nationalism approached the messianic fervor, the *Sendungsbewusstsein*, the expectation of a decisive apocalyptic struggle against the alien world, expressed by Dostoyevsky and Danilevsky. Even in the Russia of their time they represented a minority. Only seventy years later, though Dostoyevsky was the least popular Russian classic and Danilevsky was not reprinted in Stalin's Russia, the Russian nationalist messianism which flourished in the later years of Stalin's regime showed surprising similarities to the views put forward so decisively by the two nineteenth-century Russian spokesmen.[3]

Nationalist messianism in the nineteenth century was in no way an exclusively Russian phenomenon. There were overtones of it in Johann Gottlieb Fichte's praise of the German *Urvolk*, in Michelet's glorification of France, and above all in Mazzini's expectation of the Third Rome.[4] But by 1860 this mood had almost completely vanished in Europe. Cavour and

[2] Th. G. Masaryk, *Russland und Europa. Studien über die geistigen Strömungen in Russland* (Jena, 1913), II, 198.

[3] "The curious fact is that if one substituted communism for [Dostoyevsky's] conception of the mission of the Orthodox faith, and world revolution for his notion of a Pan-Slavic war against Europe, the identity of his whole position with that of modern Soviet Russia would be striking" (Ernest J. Simmons, *Dostoevski, the Making of a Novelist* [New York, 1940], pp. 327-328). "Danilewski gibt darin eine klare und freimütige Darstellung der sich aus seiner allgemeinen Kulturtypenlehre für die russische Aussen- und (in geringerem Grade) Innenpolitik ergebenden allgemeinen Grundsätze und konkreten Postulate, die eine auffallende Verwandtschaft mit der gegenwärtigen aussenpolitischen Praxis der Sowjetunion zeigen" (Alexander von Schelting, *Russland und Europa im russischen Geschichtsdenken* [Berne, 1948], p. 392).

[4] Compare also Vincento Gioberti: "In the Italian Nationality are founded the interests of religion and the civil and universal hopes of mankind. Italy is the chosen people, the typical people, the creative people, the Israel of the modern age" (*Prophets and Peoples*, p. 183). See also Guido de Ruggiero, *The History of European Liberalism* (London, 1927), pp. 298f.

Bismarck were as alien to all *Schwarmgeisterei* as were the representative political and imaginative writers of later nineteenth-century Europe. In Dostoyevsky and Danilevsky, nationalist messianism found its strongest expression anywhere in the nineteenth century; similarly Stalin's nationalist messianism went further and was presented in a more extreme and authoritative form than any other nationalism in the middle of the twentieth century. Danilevsky's nationalism — in his nationalist messianism the emphasis was on nationalism — was stated in his *Russia and Europe, an Inquiry into the Cultural and Political Relations of the Slav and the Germano-Latin Worlds,* which first appeared in 1869 in the monthly *Zaria,* before being published two years later in book form. Dostoyevsky, who was then abroad and who had known Danilevsky as a fellow-member of the socialist Petrashevskii circle in St. Petersburg twenty years before, wrote an enthusiastic letter to *Zaria*'s editor, his friend, N. N. Strakhov:

> Danilevsky's article . . . will assuredly be for many a day the "household companion" of every Russian . . . The article is so in harmony with my own views and convictions that here and there I stand amazed at the identity of our conclusions; as long as two years ago, I began to jot down certain of my reflections, for I had proposed to write an article with a very similar title, and with the same tendency and the same conclusion. How great was my joy and amazement when I beheld this plan, which I had hoped to carry out in the future, already carried out, and that . . . with such knowledge as I, with the best will in the world, could never have brought to the task.[5]

In fact, Dostoyevsky was then expressing his messianism — in his nationalist messianism the emphasis was on messianism — in the two great novels *The Idiot* (1868) and *The Possessed* (1871–1872); later, from 1873 to 1880, he expanded and applied his ideas to the intellectual and political problems of contemporary Russia in many articles of *The Diary of a Writer.* In the above-quoted letter to Strakhov he mentioned the one great difference between him and Danilevsky, a difference of emphasis. Danilevsky thought primarily in historico-political terms and tried to approach the subject in a scientific spirit; for Dostoyevsky the core of the problem, and of all problems, was Russia's own Christ. Like Tolstoy, Dostoyevsky was fundamentally a religious anarchist and a God-seeker; but whereas Tolstoy was a humanitarian optimist who believed in a rationalist and universal Christ, Dostoyevsky was a Christian pessimist who proclaimed a Russian God and the world's salvation through Him.

Nationalist messianism has grown out of a twofold root: the one in Israel and its all-pervasive consciousness of being a chosen people, the other in the world-vision of Augustian Rome. In the Christian Roman Empire the two branches met. The religious element deepened national political hopes into

---

[5] Letter from Florence, March 18 (30), 1869, in *Letters of Fyodor Michailovitch Dostoevsky to His Family and Friends,* tr. Ethel Colburn Mayne (New York, n.d.), pp. 165f — hereafter cited as *Letters.*

the belief that their fulfillment was a preordained action of divine justice and that the struggles for their realization must be carried on as God's commands: the nation, the chosen vehicle of God's designs, sees in its political triumph the march of God in history.[6] It thus transcends the limits of a historical or social concept and becomes a holy body sanctified by God; nationalism is no longer a political loyalty but a religious duty, burdened with responsibility toward God and the redemption of mankind. In all these conceptions nationalist pride, often cloaked in humility and grounded in real or imaginary sufferings and offenses, claims to serve the cause of universal peace and justice. Narrow tribalism and lofty ideals, dominion and compassion are often inextricably mixed.

To Dostoyevsky and to Danilevsky Russia appeared as a new Israel. Israel was the religious people *kat exochen*. "The religious aspect of their life and activity was so exalted and so perfect," Danilevsky wrote in the last chapter of his book, "that this people is justly called: the people chosen by God." With the coming of Christ, the Christians became the true Israel; Danilevsky and Dostoyevsky had no doubt that the Russians were the truly Christian people, in the succession of the Orthodox Church, and thereby the new Israel, or, after the Hebrews and Byzantium, the Third Israel. "From an objective, factual viewpoint, the Russians and the majority of the Slavs became," Danilevsky wrote, "with the Greeks, chief guardians of the living traditions of religious truth — Orthodoxy — and in this way the continuators of the high calling, which was the destiny of Israel and of Byzantium, to be the chosen people." Russian nationalists were convinced that not only by historical succession but by the very character of the Russian people, with its deep humility and its willing suffering, it was the true Servant of God, the bearer of the fulfillment of history, a fulfillment visualized as coming about in an apocalyptic struggle between the forces of Light and the forces of Darkness.

Neither Dostoyevsky nor Danilevsky had the slightest doubt what the forces of Darkness were: middle-class Western society, with its spirit of greed embodied in capitalism and its violent internal dissensions expressed in the multiparty system and in racial and class strife. They, especially Danilevsky, did not deny a certain greatness to modern Western civilization, as Karl Marx likewise had recognized the progressive achievements of bourgeois society. But through its social injustices and the alienation of man from his true humanity, the West, in spite of its apparent strength and proud achievements, was doomed to go down in the inevitable struggle with the new Israel — Russia in the case of Dostoyevsky and Danilevsky, the proletariat in the case of Marx, Russia and the proletariat in the case of Stalin. The God of History was on the side of righteousness.

---

[6] See chapter on messianism in my *Revolutions and Dictatorships* (3rd ed., Cambridge, Mass., 1943), pp. 11–37.

Russia, however, was not only the new or Third Israel but also the new and Third Rome. From the fourth to the sixteenth century the thought of the Christian world acknowledged the Roman mission of world leadership; the question which divided it was that of Rome's succession. In the twelfth century Bishop Otto of Freising wrote his *Chronica sive historia de duabus civitatibus* to prove how the imperial power was transferred from the Romans to the Franks or Germans: "Quomodo ad Francos, qui occidentem inhabitant, translatum fuerit." The German humanists not only accepted the theory of the *translatio imperii* — Ulrich von Hutten addressed Maximilian as successor "Augusti, aemule Trajani, dominator orbis, rector humani generis" — they and the writers of the Reformation added the point that the Germans had not only conquered Rome but were entitled to it by their moral superiority. Following Tacitus, they contrasted Roman depravity and German piety. Such a contrast was even more emphasized by the Russians, only that with them Roman depravity included the Germans and true piety was reserved for the Russian people. To the Orthodox Greeks, Papal Rome and the Western Empire were usurpers who had inherited the spirit of pagan Rome; the unparalleled horrors perpetrated by the Western crusaders in the conquest of Constantinople, the Second Rome and the true Christian Rome, bore witness to this spirit. When Constantinople was conquered for the second time — by the Turks instead of by the West — Moscow, which meanwhile had grown by God's guidance into a seat of power, became the Third Rome, the successor of Byzantium and the guardian of the true faith. This *translatio imperii* to the Russians burdened them with a twofold task: the opposition to, and ultimate salvation of, the West and the reconquest of Constantinople. For Dostoyevsky and Danilevsky these two tasks fused into one, the reconquest of Constantinople, for the true faith became the key to the defeat and conversion of the West. It presupposed a total and undeviating devotion of the Russians to their national idea; the rejection of all spiritual servility before the West; and the growing material power of Russia. The inevitable war was no war for conquest or power; it would usher in a new era for mankind. Dostoyevsky and Danilevsky were convinced that the new Russian civilization which would emerge from this victory would be a panhuman civilization, the fulfillment of all historical trends, the first all-rounded universal civilization. "Russia," Dostoyevsky wrote in his *Diary* for January 1877:

. . . in conjunction with Slavdom, and at its head, will utter to the whole world the greatest word ever heard, and that word will precisely be a covenant of universal human fellowship, and no longer in the spirit of personal egoism by means of which at present men and nations unnaturally, because of the struggle for existence, unite with each other in their civilization, . . . digging ditches for each other and spreading about each other lies, blasphemy and calumnies . . . The Russian national idea, in the last analysis, is but the universal fellowship of men.[7]

[7] *Diary*, p. 578.

Thus the Third Rome and the Third Israel are at one in the preparation of the advent of the messianic order. To Dostoyevsky and Danilevsky the 1870's seemed the age of conflict immediately preceding the fulfillment; to Stalin perhaps the 1940's held a similar promise. They overrated the dynamic force of the Russian *Sendungsbewusstsein,* they underestimated the strength of the West.

Of the three men, only Danilevsky was a systematic thinker, who tried to clothe his diagnosis of the present and his wishful expectations about the future with the scientific respectability of a theory of history of his own. To that end he adapted or invented a doctrine according to which history passes through a cycle of independent civilizations, or historico-cultural types, of which "Europe" was the latest but not the last one. Europeans liked to think of their civilization as the final and therefore universally valid stage of human development, the mature fruit and radiant crown of all history. The Russians had accepted this evaluation and willingly put themselves into a position of inferiority. In reality Europe was, like all preceding civilizations, only a passing stage in the march of history and by the nineteenth century it was in full decay without acknowledging it even to itself. Europe nevertheless felt that its end was fast approaching and that another historico-cultural type was to replace it: Russia was the bearer of the new civilization. For that reason Europe hated Russia and pretended to despise it. The heir of Europe's world position was envied and feared; not out of premeditation but instinctively Europe always united against Russia, whenever the latter tried to grow in strength.

For the realization of her world-historical mission Russia had to turn away from imitating Europe and to concentrate on the development of her own spiritual resources. But Russia alone was not strong enough for the task. She needed a broader basis to gain the feeling of security and destiny. She had to gather around her all the lands inhabited by kindred Slavs. "For every Slav — Russian, Czech, Serb, Croat, Slovene, Slovak, Bulgar (I wish to add also Pole) — after God and His Holy Church, the idea of Slavdom must be the highest idea, higher than any earthly good, for none of these is attainable to him without its existence, without an intellectually, nationally, and politically independent Slavdom; on the other hand, all these blessings will be the inescapable consequence of its independence and originality (*samobytnost'*)." [8] Only if Russia succeeded in expanding her hold over all the Slavs, could she bring the original Slav civilization to fruition. A Pan-Slav union was the indispensable condition for the flowering of the new historico-cultural type and thereby for the fulfillment of history. In 1869 Danilevsky anticipated the composition and frontiers of the Pan-Slav union which the disintegration of the Austro-Hungarian empire made possible and which Stalin almost realized in 1945. It was to consist of eight parts:

[8] *Zaria,* no. 3 (1869), p. 38.

The Russian Empire in its frontiers of 1869, including Poland and with the addition of Austrian Galicia and northern Bukovina and of Hungarian Carpatho-Ukraine;

The Kingdom of Bohemia, Moravia, and Slovakia (Czechoslovakia);

The Kingdom of the Serbs, Croats, and Slovenes (Yugoslavia) which would also include Montenegro, Bosnia-Herzegovina, and northern Albania from Turkey, the Voivodina, and the Banat from Hungary, Dalmatia, Istria, Carnola, two-thirds of Carinthia, and one-fifth of Styria from Austria;

The Kingdom of Bulgaria with the greater part of Macedonia;

The Kingdom of Rumania with half of Austrian Bukovina and of Hungarian Transylvania;

The Kingdom of Hungary shorn of the territories ceded to Russia, Bohemia, Serbia, and Rumania;

The Kingdom of Greece with Thessaly, Epirus, southwest Macedonia, Crete, Rhodes, Cyprus and the Anatolian coast of the Aegean Sea;

Constantinople and its environment.[9]

Danilevsky did not wish to annex Constantinople to Russia but to establish it as a city common to the whole Orthodox and Slav world. Like Stalin's Russia eighty years later, Danilevsky's Russia was in his interpretation neither imperialist nor aggressive. Her function in international relations was diametrically opposed to that of the West, in spite of the misinterpretations of her intentions and actions by her enemies. The European powers, in order to grow in strength, had to subject or to enslave other peoples and to numb their cultural growth; Russia on the contrary had to liberate other peoples and to help them to realize their destiny. "In this divine and perhaps unique coincidence of moral motives and obligations with political advantage and necessity, we must see a guarantee for the fulfillment of Russia's great task. Otherwise our world will be only a miserable chain of accidents and not the reflection of supreme reason, right and goodness." But not only history was on the side of Russia and the Slavs; it was supported by their superior number and moral force. "It is as impossible to fight the historical course of events as it is impossible to fight superior violence. From these general considerations we gain the certitude that the Russian and Slav sacred cause, which is in truth the universal and panhuman cause, cannot be lost." Danilevsky sounded no less confident than Stalin's spokesmen were.

In order to fulfill her historical mission the Slav world had to be strong, united, and above all freed from subservience to European mentality. The continuous politico-cultural struggle with Europe (which is called today "cold war") would separate the Slavs from Europe and unite them more closely with Russia. But to heal the deep wounds inflicted by the imitation of Europe and to restore the purity of the Slav historico-cultural type, a real war was needed which would inaugurate "a series of events the like of

[9] *Ibid.,* no. 9 (1869), p. 21. It is part of ch. xiv, which is entitled "Tsargrad," the Russian name for Constantinople.

which the world has not seen since the fall of the western Roman Empire."
The outcome of the war could be in no doubt, for the West lacked the
burning devotion of the Slav world to the one all-absorbing cause. "We
must have the firm faith that our goal is sublime and sacred, that only that
which leads to it should concern us, that we promote every good cause —
humanity, freedom, civilization, etc. — only if we serve our goal and in no
other way." For that purpose the Russian leaders had to understand the
immutable laws of historical development as shown by Danilevsky:

> Only a false concept of the general development of the relationship of the na-
> tional to the panhuman, a concept incompatible with the real principles of the
> systematization of scientific natural phenomena as well as with so called progress,
> could lead to the confusion of European civilization with universal civilization.
> Only such a concept could lead to such a pernicious delusion as Westernism
> which . . . assigns to us and our brothers the pitiful insignificant role of imitators
> of the West. Such a delusion deprives us of the hope for any cultural significance,
> i.e., for a great historical future. I attempted to develop this theoretical approach
> and to supplement it with indications about the main differences between the Slav
> and the Germano-Roman cultural-historical types and about the fatal consequences
> of this Westernization or Europeanization, and how far it is the origin of the
> disease from which Russia's social body suffers, a disease which is the source of
> all our social ills. Only the healthy force of historical events can remedy this
> disease and can raise the spirit of our society, suffering precisely from spiritual
> decay and abasement. The cure is possible and probable because luckily the dis-
> ease has so far penetrated only the surface of the social structure. We can see
> such an event, or rather a whole series of events, endowed with a healthy dynam-
> ism, in the latest phase of the struggle known as the Eastern Question, which . . .
> shortly must stamp its imprint upon an entire historical period. The importance
> of this inevitably approaching struggle forces us to try to understand the objec-
> tions raised against the only decision useful to the Slav world — the full political
> liberation of all the Slav peoples and the formation of a Pan-Slav union under
> Russia's leadership — and the guarantee of our success in this struggle.[10]

All preceding great historico-cultural types have never realized the fullness of civilized existence, which embraces four different aspects, in which
the creative abilities of a type can unfold: religion; humanities and science;
political order; and social-economic organization. In antiquity Israel had
excelled in the first of those aspects, Greece in the second, Rome in the
third. Modern Europe developed the second and third of the four aspects
to new heights. But only the coming Slav historico-cultural type will realize
the total human civilization, as soon as it will have achieved complete independence and thereby "eradicated the cancer of imitativeness and the servile
attitude toward the West, which through some unfavorable circumstances
has eaten its way into the Slav body and soul." Because the Slavs were, at
the time when Danilevsky wrote, not yet spiritually and politically independent, they had not yet had the opportunity of showing their full measure

[10] From the beginning of the seventeenth and last chapter of Danilevsky's book
(*Rossiia i Evropa* [1869]).

in the humanities and science.[11] He has no difficulty in proving the exceptional religious gifts of the Slav type. More ingenious are his arguments for the unique qualifications of the Slavs to create a true political order; they anticipate some of the recent Soviet arguments:

Russia does not have colonial possessions, like Rome or England. The Russian state from early Muscovite times on is Russia herself, gradually, irresistibly spreading on all sides, settling neighboring non-settled lands, and assimilating into herself . . . foreign populations. This basic character of Russian expansion was misunderstood by the distortion of the original Russian point of view through Europeanization, the origin of every evil in Russia . . . Is the Russian people capable of freedom? . . . There hardly ever existed and exists a people as capable of enduring such a large share of freedom as the Russians and being less inclined to abuse it, due to its ability and habit to obey, its respect and trust in the authority, its lack of love for power and its loathing of interference in matters where it does not consider itself competent. If we look into the reasons of all political troubles, we shall find their root not in the striving for freedom but precisely in love for power and in the vain cravings of people to interfere in affairs that are beyond their comprehension . . . This nature of the Russian people is the true reason why Russia is really the only state which never had (and in all probability never will have) a political revolution, i.e., a revolution having as its aim the limitation of the power of the ruler.

But Russia is above all called upon to realize the perfect social-economic organization, which Europe with its contradiction between political democracy and economic feudalism was unable to achieve:

Russia is the only large state which has solid ground under its feet, in which there are no landless masses and in which, consequently, the social edifice does not rest on the misery and insecurity of the majority of the citizens; in Russia alone there cannot and does not exist any contradiction between political and economic ideals . . . On this health of Russia's social-economic organization we found our hope for the great social-economic significance of the Slav historico-cultural type. It has been able for the first time to create a just and normal system of human activities, which embraces not only human relations in the moral and political sphere, but also man's mastery of nature, which is a method of satisfying human needs and requirements. Thus it establishes not only a formal equality in the relations between citizens, but a real and concrete one.

In his scientific approach Danilevsky stressed frequently that the new Slav type, following the European type in the course of history, would not be the last word of history. But at the end of his work he is overcome by the messianic finality of his vision:

The main stream of universal history starts from two sources on the banks of the ancient Nile. From there the one, celestial and divine, has reached by way of Jerusalem and Constantinople, in perfect purity, Kiev and Moscow; the other, terrestrial and human, divided itself again into two rivers, that of culture and

[11] Against all historical evidence, Danilevsky insists on the nationalist contention that great cultural creations presuppose national independence and power. Italy during the Renaissance, German classicism from 1760 to 1830, the Polish emigré literature in the 1830's, and Jewish intellectual life in the Diaspora contradict Danilevsky's assumption.

that of politics, and flowed through Athens, Alexandria and Rome into Europe, sometimes desiccated, then again enriched with new and ever fuller waters. On Russian soil a new and fourth river originates, a social-economic system which satisfies the masses in a just way. These four rivers will unite on the wide plains of Slavdom into a mighty sea.[12]

Dostoyevsky had not the scientific hesitations of Danilevsky. To him as to Shatov in *The Possessed*, the Russians were the only God-bearing people on earth, "destined to regenerate and save the world in the name of a new God, and to whom are given the keys of life and of the new world." [13] Shatov continued:

If a great people does not believe that the truth is only to be found in itself alone (in itself alone and in it exclusively); if it does not believe that it alone is fit and destined to raise up and save all the rest by its truth, it would at once sink into being ethnographical material, and not a great people . . . But there is only one truth, and therefore only a single one out of the nations can have the true God, even though other nations may have great Gods of their own.

A few years later Dostoyevsky, in his *Diary*, reiterated this:

Every great people believes, and must believe if it intends to live long, that in it alone resides the salvation of the world; that it lives in order to stand at the head of the nations, to affiliate and unite all of them, and to lead them in a concordant choir toward the final goal preordained for them.[14]

The law of history which Dostoyevsky here formulated has as little general validity as another "law" which he proclaimed: "There is a political law, even a law of nature, according to which one of two strong and close neighbors, whatever their friendship may be, wishes to destroy the other and sooner or later will realize that wish." Dostoyevsky was not the only one who generalized his own theory and desires into general maxims. Dostoyevsky, as apparently the Stalinists today, could not conceive that other great nations were not driven by the same dynamic messianism which he believed characteristic of the Russians. That explains his conviction of the inevitability of the fast approaching decisive struggle between Russia and the West, which on the part of Russia was not a war but a crusade for a holy cause. In January 1877 he started his *Diary* by asking: "In point of fact, what awaits the world not only in the last quarter of the century but even . . . perhaps, this year? . . . apparently the time has come for something sempiternal, millenarian, for that which has been moulding itself in the world ever since the beginning of its civilization . . . [With the rise of the Russian or Slav idea] we have something universal and final, which,

---

[12] These are the final words of Danilevsky's seventeenth chapter, from which the two preceding quotations also are taken. See my *The Mind of Modern Russia* (New Brunswick, 1955), ch. x.

[13] *The Possessed*, tr. Constance Garnett, Modern Library ed., VII, Part II, ch. i, 250–256.

[14] *Diary* (January 1877), p. 575.

though by no means solving *all* human destinies, brings with it the beginning of the end of the whole former history of European mankind . . ." In the May issue of the *Diary* he foresaw for Europe a gigantic, elemental, and dreadful catastrophe and congratulated himself that Russia had separated herself from Europe and thus had become more than ever independent of the fatal problems besetting decrepit Europe. Never was Russia more powerful than at present, Dostoyevsky jubilated, and that at a time when the great world problems could no longer be settled by "appeasing diplomatic means."

Dostoyevsky's *Diary* is one of the most illuminating sources for an understanding of him and of Russian anti-Westernism. In a letter to Vsevolod Sergeevich Solov'ëv, Vladimir's brother, Dostoyevsky emphasized the importance of the June 1876 issue of the *Diary:*

> I have never yet permitted myself to follow my profoundest convictions to their ultimate consequences in my public writing — had never said my *very last word* . . . So I decided that I *would* for once say the last word on one of my convictions — that of Russia's part and destiny among the nations — and I proclaimed that my various anticipations would not only be fulfilled in the immediate future, but were already partly realized . . . One may set up any pardox one likes, and so long as one doesn't carry it to its ultimate conclusion, everyone will think it most subtle . . . But once blurt out the last word, and quite frankly declare: "This is the Messiah!" why, nobody will believe in you anymore — for it was so silly of you to push your idea to its ultimate conclusion.[15]

Dostoyevsky's paradox consisted in his classifying the most ardent Russian Westernizers, the advocates of radical reforms, as fervent champions of Russia and of the Russian spirit, to which European culture had always been hateful. Did they not join the extreme Left in Europe, the very group which rejected Western modern society and civilization and which was most critical of all the manifestations of European culture alien to the Russian soul? Was there not hope that once the misunderstanding was dispelled these Westernizers would discover themselves full-blooded Russians? Will they not join the Slavophiles in believing in Russia's disinterested leadership toward the brotherhood of men, a union founded upon the principles of common service to mankind?

In the *Diary* Dostoyevsky returned again and again to his fundamental conviction that Europe was unalterably hostile to Russia and unable to understand her true intentions. Though Russia stands, in Dostoyevsky's opinion, for peace and love, his writings on her behalf are so full of detestation and invective that in their shrillness they recall the discrepancy between Stalin's gospel of peace and its wording of hatred. Two forces in Europe arouse Dostoyevsky's special animosity: money — plutocracy, big business, the stock exchange, the Jews — and the Catholic Church. He was deeply convinced that these two forces conspired against Russia. It is difficult to

[15] Letter from Bad Ems in July 1876, *Letters*, pp. 215f.

say which he abhorred more, but the "Roman conspiracy" appeared to him more dangerous. Many passages of the *Diary* read like restatements of Prince Myshkin's famous outburst against the Catholic Church which he called not only an unchristian religion but worse than atheism.[16] The Russian intelligentsia, Prince Myshkin and Dostoyevsky maintained, having lost its root in the Russian people and idea, embraced atheism, the product of Catholic Europe, and by turning it into a new absolute religion proved thereby their truly Russian character. But let them discover the true humanity on the basis of the Russian idea, the Russian God and Savior, Prince Myshkin went on, and the world will be astonished and incredulous at the sight of Russia as a powerful, wise and benign giant, "for Europe expects from us only the sword and violence, because it judges us after its own image and cannot imagine us without barbarism."

Against the corruption of man by the powers (or the lust for power) of money and of the Catholic Church, Dostoyevsky put his hope of salvation in the true faith of the Russian people and its national messianic vocation:

> Isn't there in Orthodoxy alone both the truth and the salvation of the Russian people, and — in the forthcoming centuries — of mankind as a whole? Hasn't there been preserved in Orthodoxy alone, in all its purity, the Divine image of Christ? And, perhaps, the most momentous preordained destiny of the Russian people, within the destinies of mankind at large, consists in the preservation in their midst of the Divine image of Christ, in all its purity, and, when the time comes, in the revelation of this image to the world which has lost its way! [17]

Thus Dostoyevsky wrote in 1873. Four years later it was no longer Orthodoxy as such but the Russian national genius which was the hope of the world, or perhaps that inextricable fusion of the Russian national genius with the true universal faith which also characterizes the later stage of Stalinism:

> . . . our great Russia, at the head of the united Slavs, will utter to the world, to the whole of European mankind and to civilization, her new, sane and as yet unheard-of word. That word will be uttered for the good and genuine unification of mankind as a whole in a new, brotherly, universal union whose inception is derived from the Slavic genius, pre-eminently from the spirit of the great Russian people who have suffered so long, who during so many centuries have been doomed to silence, but who have always possessed great powers for clarifying and settling many bitter and fatal misunderstandings of Western European civilization.[18]

Europe, Dostoyevsky believed, did not fear so much Russian imperialism as the very fact that Russia brought salvation. For the Russian eagle:

---

[16] It is interesting that Dostoyevsky regards socialism and materialism as a product of Catholicism, while some Catholic thinkers believe socialism and materialism to be the result of anti-Catholic trends.

[17] *Diary*, p. 63.

[18] *Ibid.*, p. 780.

. . . seeks no conquest or acquisition, no expansion of his borders, but the liberation of the oppressed and the downtrodden, giving them new life for their benefit and that of mankind . . . It is this that Europe refuses to believe . . . Europe fears not so much the possible growth of Russia's strength as she fears the fact that Russia is capable of undertaking such a task . . . To undertake something not for one's direct benefit seems to Europe so unusual . . . that Russia's act is naturally regarded by Europe not only as the barbarity of "a backward, bestial and unenlightened nation" capable of *vileness and stupidity,* of embarking in our age upon something on the order of the crusades of the dark ages, but even as the most immoral fact fraught with danger to Europe and supposedly threatening her great civilization.[19]

The wars of Dostoyevsky's Russia, like those of the Soviet Union, were not wars of conquest but wars for the liberation of the oppressed. Such wars are sacred, they fulfill the command of History. In September 1877 Dostoyevsky felt the inescapable fate knocking at the door. Dying papal Catholicism was preparing to fight the last battle for its existence against the whole world, and France was its instrument. The Russo-Turkish war, then waged for the solution of the Eastern Question, would inevitably be converted into an all-European war, which would end with the victory of the East. Though much precious human blood would be shed, Dostoyevsky comforted himself with the thought that this blood would save Europe from a ten times greater loss of blood should the war be postponed. Above all, the war would solve so many problems and would establish such new and progressive relationships between men and between nations, that one should not fear too much the last convulsions of Europe on the very eve of her great regeneration through Russia's victory.

Dostoyevsky relied not only upon the guardianship of the true faith for his claim of Russia's messianic leadership, but he adduced certain historical character traits of the people which qualified them for their sublime task. In 1873, apropos of a showing of Russian paintings to be sent to an international exhibition in Vienna, he maintained that the Europeans were incapable of understanding Russia while the Russians understand everything European and alien perfectly well, a theme to which he returned in the famous address on Pushkin which he delivered at the meeting of the Society of Lovers of Russian Literature on June 8, 1880. Russians had an intuitive understanding of everything human (or at least, as Dostoyevsky emphasized, of everything European and Aryan) and thus could rise to the height of universal man. In this disinterested service to Europe, Slavophiles and Westernizers could find common ground, for in uttering Russia's ultimate word of universal harmony, they would reconcile all the discords and con-

---

[19] *Ibid.,* p. 781. An article like "The Very Last Word of Civilization," which Dostoyevsky wrote in July 1876 (*ibid.,* pp. 376–378) could have appeared with minor changes in any Stalinist paper after 1945, if Stalinist scribes had the power of Dostoyevsky's pen. The same is true of his "The Metternichs and the Don Quixotes," which he wrote in February 1877 (*ibid.,* p. 607).

troversies rending Europe and as genuine Russians embrace all in their brotherly love. Like the Stalinists, Dostoyevsky extolled Pushkin as the purest incarnation of Russian genius and as the miraculous, unique and most complete reincarnation of the spirit of all foreign nations, thereby surpassing even the greatest poets of all other civilizations.

In addition to their panhuman national character, Dostoyevsky maintained that the Russians were the people most capable of real liberty, of firm unity and of social justice. In the last month of his life, in the very last piece published by him, he returned again to the virtues of Russian autocracy and Russian "socialism," to the fundamental difference between the West with its need of legal safeguards and formal constitutions and the freedom of the chosen people:

> Civil liberty may be established in Russia on an integral scale, more complete than anywhere in the world, whether in Europe or even in North America. It will be based not upon a written sheet of paper, but upon the children's affection of the people for the Tsar as their father, since children may be permitted many a thing which is inconceivable in the case of contractual nations; they may be entrusted with much that has nowhere been encountered, since children will not betray their father, and, being children, will lovingly accept from him any correction of their errors.[20]

Such a complete liberty under the loving care of a great father and teacher of his peoples was claimed for Russia by Stalinist writers who knew at the same time how limited the liberties were in actual life which the constitutional countries of the West enjoyed. That was due, in the imaginary Russia of Dostoyevsky and of the Stalinist writers, to the unbreakable monolithic unity of the Russian people. Europe was threatened, Dostoyevsky wrote in 1877, by the unrest of the oppressed and suffering classes. She was altogether dependent upon the stock exchanges of her bourgeoisie and purchased the momentary tranquillity of her proletarians with the last resources of her governments. In Russia similar weaknesses could be observed, but only because she showed herself subservient to European ideas; once she will have returned to her original nature, all the millions of European gold and of the European armies cannot prevail against her. After his address on Pushkin, in a lengthy and violent reply to a liberal critic of his, Professor A. D. Gradovskii, who argued that Europe was far ahead of Russia in social justice and reforms, he exclaimed: "Why, Europe is on the eve of a general and dreadful collapse . . . Well, our social and civic ideals are better, more solid and even . . . more liberal than your European ideals! Yes, they are more liberal because they emanate directly from our people's organism, and are not a slavish impersonal transplantation from the West." [21] For all these reasons Russia was "stronger than the rest," Dostoyevsky wrote in April

[20] *Diary,* p. 1033.
[21] *Ibid.,* pp. 1003–1004.

1877, and yet in spite of her ever growing strength she will not, as the Europeans expect, draw the sword against them. "Not only shall we not seize and take away anything from them, but the fact itself that we shall greatly strengthen ourselves — through the alliance of love and brotherhood, and not usurpation and violence — will finally enable us not to draw the sword, but on the contrary in the tranquillity of our might, to reveal an example of sincere peace, international fellowship and disinterestedness." [22] In view of this ultimate goal, Russia's wars could not be judged with the same yardsticks as other wars; they were "the first step toward the realization of perpetual peace, of *real* international fellowship and *true* human welfare."

In all his mature years, while adhering firmly to these principles and ultimate end, Dostoyevsky showed a surprising flexibility in his "foreign policy." In April 1876 he was convinced that "the future of Europe belongs to Russia," and in November 1877 it was an axiom with him that "Constantinople must be *ours,* conquered by *us,* Russians, from the Turks and remain ours forever." On the conquest of Constantinople depended then the future of Russia, for it would give her the opportunity "of fostering the brotherhood of the peoples and of ardent motherly service to them as to dear children." [23] Apparently, to Dostoyevsky, Russia was to become the motherland of all truly progressive mankind. The need to conquer Constantinople was not an outcome of modern power politics. Dostoyevsky stressed repeatedly that it was a fundamental Russian idea, going back to the time of the rising Moscow tsardom and that to leave it without solution "would be equivalent to smashing Russia into pieces."

Yet only three years later, on the last pages of his *Diary,* he came to the conclusion that at the present time nobody would consider it common sense that Constantinople must be ours, save in some remote unknown future. His restless mind had discovered new and greater spheres of conquest. He hoped to see Russia's domination established over all Asia. Russia was as much Asiatic as European, he maintained, "our hopes lie perhaps more in Asia than in Europe: in our future Asia will be our salvation." In Asia the Russians would not appear as imitators but as civilizers. Yet Dostoyevsky thought of Russia's Asiatic mission as a means to the end which was always before his mind, Russia's messianic role in the world. Russia should for the time being turn away from Europe, as she should have done in 1812, after having driven Napoleon from her territory. If she then had divided the world with Napoleon, leaving to him the West and conquering the East, then Napoleon's dynasty would have been overthrown in the quarrels of Europe, but the Orient would have remained Russian, "and we would at present have controlled the oceans and could have opposed

[22] *Ibid.,* p. 667.
[23] *Ibid.,* p. 906.

England at sea as well as on land." [24] Dostoyevsky visualized Asia becoming Russia's America, where the Russians would produce immense wealth and, with the help of science, exploit the resources and build mighty industries and thus acquire a new sense of power, dignity, and creative joy. This new Russia in Asia would regenerate old Russia and make her masses understand her destiny. With the productive power and the population of her Asiatic empire, Russia would become materially and morally strong enough to fulfill her world mission. Meanwhile the European countries, freed from the specter of Russian aggressive desires, would start to quarrel among themselves, and, as soon as their discord came to a crash, Russia would find an opportunity to solve the Eastern Question and to seize Constantinople. In the meantime Dostoyevsky advised patience and noninterference in Western affairs.

A Western reader of Dostoyevsky's *Diary* today will not only admire the depth of his convictions and the flight of his imagination, he will be comforted by the thought that — to conclude from Dostoyevsky's own violent vilifications of the Russian liberals and Westernizers — his opponents must have been very numerous and that probably the majority of the Russian educated classes of his day were truly European in their thought and aspirations. Nor was such abuse and hatred of Western middle-class civilization confined to Russian writers. Danilevsky's *Russia and Europe* found its counterpart in Oswald Spengler's *Untergang des Abendlandes;* Dostoyevsky's *Diary* was matched by Thomas Mann's *Betrachtungen eines Unpolitischen.* Dostoyevsky wrote in a period of comparative liberty, when liberals could still freely object to national self-glorification and when Vladimir Solov'ëv could regard the idealization of the Russian people and Russia's isolation from the West as a misfortune for the nation and the greatest obstacle for its progress. Today in Russia all such objections have been silenced. Are we allowed to conclude from the violent vilifications of servility before the West, of cosmopolitanism and objectivity in the Stalinist press, that today too nationalist messianism does not hold undisputed sway over the Russian mind and perhaps represents only a minority opinion? In any case, there is one fundamental difference between Dostoyevsky's age and the concluding years of Stalin's Russia: then nationalist messianism was voiced by individuals and small groups, among whom was a spiritual giant and man of genius, who claimed to speak on behalf of the silent Russian people; under Stalin nationalist messianism was authoritatively proclaimed by the men in power who, though they seemed to descend from the "possessed" whom Dostoyevsky abhorred, were the illegitimate heirs of some of Dostoyevsky's most cherished and characteristic visions.

[24] He proposed a similar partition of the world with Germany in November 1877. See *Prophets and Peoples*, p. 153. Such a division became possible in 1940; it foundered then on Russia's insistence on the control of Constantinople. See also *Prophets and Peoples*, p. 204.

The Messianic Concept in the Third International, 1935–1939

KERMIT E. McKENZIE

I

In the history of the Communist International, the period opened by its Seventh Congress in 1935 and closed by the outbreak of the Second World War stands as one of the most noteworthy phases of the Communist-led world revolutionary movement. Achievements were registered in theory and in practice alike. In terms of the latter, it is well known that Communist parties of several countries temporarily enjoyed a very considerable growth in membership, often accompanied by a disproportionate increase in political influence. In the realm of theory, a more meaningful development was the presentation of a complex messianism which sought not only to justify the immediate practical activity of the Communist parties, but also to preserve unaltered the ultimate goals of the Comintern. This paper seeks to present and analyze the content of this modified messianic concept as it emanated from the Comintern leadership during that period.[1]

Stated in simplest terms, the reformulation which was given the messianic idea in the late thirties resulted in an extension of the concept of the Comintern's mission beyond the traditional definition and in the elaboration of appropriately enabling strategical and tactical concepts. Perhaps the most important thing about the reformulation is that it not only was valid from 1935 through 1939 but also holds true in a broad sense for the present day. Indeed, the years of Comintern and post-Comintern history which follow 1935 constitute a phase clearly distinguishable from the first fifteen years of the Comintern — from 1917 to 1934. In other words, the late thirties

---

[1] Chief sources for the period are *VII Congress of the Communist International: Abridged Stenographic Report of the Proceedings* (Moscow, 1939) — hereafter cited as *VII Congress;* the periodicals, *Kommunisticheskii Internatsional,* official organ of the Comintern Executive Committee, and *International Press Correspondence,* which became *World News and Views* with the July 2, 1938 issue; the two collections of several important works of Georgi Dimitrov, Secretary-General of the Comintern from 1935 to 1943: *The United Front* (New York, 1938) and *Selected Speeches and Articles* (London, 1951).

laid the major ideological foundations of an era having an inner unity that demarcates it from the pre-1935 period of the Third International.

What were the essential elements embraced within the messianic concept prior to 1935? In what fashion was the messianic concept broadened during 1935–1939? The answers to these questions serve to define the basic principles of the new era. It may safely be said that the traditional messianic concept involved a revolutionary reconstruction of society by the Communist-led working class, during which the bourgeois state would be smashed and its social and economic structure transformed, all to the end of building a new society along the lines of Lenin's, and later Stalin's, interpretation of the principles of Marxism. However, during the late thirties, the messianic idea was elaborated in such a fashion that it also included, given certain conditions, the salvation of "bourgeois" democracy and "bourgeois" culture in the form of a somewhat socialized democracy — the "democracy of a new type," neither purely bourgeois nor completely socialist. The promise of an improved version of bourgeois democracy was offered in mass propaganda to broad categories of the population — the proletariat, the peasantry, and much of the middle class. The impermanence of this "new democracy" was fully explained in Communist theory, but seldom mentioned in mass propaganda except in vague terms. Correspondingly, talk of revolution and proletarian democracy was deëmphasized in propaganda.

The Comintern presented itself as the stalwart defender of bourgeois democratic achievements, as the advocate of moderate change, and as the champion of the interests of many classes. Thus its leadership became more palatable to many who had formerly looked askance. To Communists analyzing the course of world affairs, the enlargement of their mission was frankly regarded as an expedient measure. For the Comintern, the mission of world revolution and world Communism remained as real as ever.

To understand the international Communist movement during the late thirties it is necessary to have in mind the essential elements of the Comintern's appreciation of current history. Underlying the thinking of Moscow and the Comintern in 1935 was the threat of German aggression and the growth of fascism and fascist tendencies in other countries. War against the Soviet Union must have appeared as a grave possibility. The course of events seemed about to confirm what theory had predicted earlier. According to Comintern periodization of history since the First World War, a "third period" of postwar development had begun by 1928. It was defined as a period of "intense development of the contradictions of world capitalism," which would give rise to a new round of wars and revolutions.[2] A first

---

[2] "Theses and Resolutions of the VI World Congress of the Communist International," *International Press Correspondence* (November 23, 1938) — hereafter cited as *Inprecor* — p. 1567. This periodization is indicated in *History of the Communist Party of the Soviet Union (Bolsheviks): Short Course* (New York, 1939), pp. 270–271, and in other Soviet literature.

period of "extremely acute crisis of the capitalist system, and of direct revolutionary action on the part of the proletariat," had ended in 1923, and had been followed by a second period of "gradual and partial stabilization of the capitalist system," during which the proletariat was restricted to "defensive battles" and the possibility of a seizure of power seemed relatively remote.[3]

In the absence of evidence to the contrary, the idea of a third postwar period appears to have been considered by the Communists as valid for the remainder of the Comintern's existence, or until May 1943. It is a matter of record that the congress meeting in 1935 considered its most important task to be the discovery of the best means "to secure victory in the second round of revolutions and wars."[4] In Communist thinking, the subsequent developments in Spain and China, to mention only a few, coupled with the Second World War, constituted sufficient proof of the accuracy of its earlier analysis.

The anticipated economic crisis of the third period (which opportunely occurred and doubtless strengthened the confidence of the Comintern), was expected to result in attempts to solve the crisis by substituting fascism for bourgeois democracy and by preparing and conducting wars for a fresh repartition of colonial empires. From 1928 through 1933, the official Comintern viewpoint dictated that fascism and imperialist war should be answered by proletarian revolution and civil war. "The Communist parties must with full decisiveness set before the masses the task of a revolutionary way out of the crisis of capitalism."[5] Thus declared the Thirteenth Plenum of the Executive Committee of the Comintern in December 1933. Otto Kuusinen's report on fascism and the war danger sanctioned the slogan of "revolutionary civil war" as appropriate if war should break out.[6]

A much revised solution was elaborated in 1935. The term "fascist," loosely applied in former years to bourgeois governments in general, was now given a restricted and more precise meaning. Fascism, defined as the "power of finance capital," was carefully distinguished from traditional bourgeois rule. "The accession to power of fascism is not an *ordinary succession* of one bourgeois government by another, but a substitution of one state form of class domination of the bourgeoisie — bourgeois democracy — by another form — open terrorist dictatorship."[7] This concept of two separate forms of bourgeois rule was sharpened by Dimitrov's charge that the "fascist counterrevolution" was attacking bourgeois democracy in order to

[3] *Ibid.*, p. 1568.
[4] "Nakanune VII Kongressa Kommunisticheskogo Internatsionala," *Kommunisticheskii Internatsional* (July 1, 1935) — hereafter cited as *KI* — p. 3. An unsigned editorial indicates that the official viewpoint of the Executive Committee of the Communist International is being expressed.
[5] *XIII Plenum IKKI: stenograficheskii otchët* (Moscow, 1934), p. 594.
[6] *Ibid.*, p. 18.
[7] Dimitrov, *The United Front*, pp. 11-12.

establish "the most barbaric regime of exploitation and suppression of the toiling masses." [8] Dimitrov's reconstruction of the whole problem is fundamental to an understanding of the period under survey: the choice to be made by the "toiling masses" was "not between proletarian dictatorship and bourgeois democracy, but between bourgeois democracy and fascism." [9]

Justification of the new mission followed several themes. In terms of the internal situation within the capitalist countries, it was frequently argued that the weakness of the Communist parties and their followings dictated a solution to fascism other than by way of a proletarian revolution. Even before the new line was enunciated, the judgment of one of the most authoritative Comintern leaders, Dmitrii Manuil'skii, was that "In the overwhelming majority of capitalist countries the Communists have not yet won over the majority of the working class." [10] In similar vein, the Seventh Congress freely admitted that only a minority of the working class had accepted the Communist outlook. Maurice Thorez declared bluntly that the proletarian revolution could not be the immediate goal of the present struggle.[11] The admitted failure up to that time to capture a mass basis was utilized to justify the temporary postponement of proletarian revolution.[12] In such a negative fashion the longstanding weakness of the Communist parties was exploited as evidence of the rationality of a more modest policy.

Lenin's comments on the relative merits of democracy in the presocialist era were mustered in support of the new orientation. Karl Radek, pointing to Lenin's appreciation of the progressive features of bourgeois democracy, wrote: "We must keep these words of Lenin's clearly before us, if we do not wish to fall into the mistake of a summary, antihistorical denial of bourgeois democracy." [13] Another writer acknowledged Lenin's criticism of the "restricted character" of bourgeois democracy, but pointed out that Lenin regarded bourgeois political liberty as a useful "weapon for struggle" against exploitation and poverty.[14]

Accompanying the revision of the pattern of domestic tactics in capitalist countries was a similar reappraisal of the threat of a new imperialist war. As late as the Seventeenth Congress of the Communist Party of the Soviet

---

[8] *Ibid.*, p. 110.

[9] *Ibid.* One year later, at the Ninth Convention of the American Communist Party, Earl Browder announced that "the direct issue of the 1936 elections is not socialism or capitalism, but rather democracy or fascism" (*The People's Front* [New York, 1938], p. 32).

[10] From his report to the Seventeenth Congress of the Soviet Communist Party (January-February 1934) on behalf of the Soviet delegation in the ECCI (*Socialism Victorious* [Moscow-Leningrad, n.d.], p. 319).

[11] *VII Congress*, p. 217.

[12] On the point that world revolution as the ultimate goal was not abandoned, see K. E. McKenzie, "The Soviet Union, the Comintern and World Revolution: 1935," *Political Science Quarterly*, LXV (June 1950), 214-237.

[13] *Inprecor* (August 15, 1936), p. 1006.

[14] *Ibid.* (January 23, 1937), p. 62.

Union in 1934, Manuil'skii's report in the traditional vein defined all capitalist countries as predatory and imperialistic. "Imperialist war," he declared, "is the order of the day for all capitalist governments of the world." [15] In particular, England was credited with "the leading role in the preparations for war against the U.S.S.R." [16] Nor does Stalin's report to the same Congress preview the later temporary division by the Comintern of the capitalist world into "nonaggressive" states and "aggressive" states.[17]

Such a division was made by Dimitrov at the Seventh Congress of the Comintern and remained generally characteristic of Comintern thinking until late fall of 1939. Dimitrov sought, moreover, to distinguish the current international scene from the situation in 1914:

. . . the world at that time was divided into two military-imperialist coalitions which were equally striving to establish their world hegemony and which had equally prepared and provoked the imperialist war. At that time there were neither countries where the proletariat had conquered, nor countries with a fascist dictatorship.[18]

The world picture in 1935–1939 included not only *aggressive* fascist states (Germany, Italy, and Japan), but also a proletarian state (U.S.S.R.) and a number of *nonaggressive* capitalist states (Britain, France, the United States, and small countries fearful of losing their independence), which for the moment were interested in the maintenance of peace. Only after the outbreak of war between Germany and the Western Powers in September 1939 was this picture revised by Dimitrov, although it is anticipated earlier in 1939 by increasing reference to the "reactionary ruling circles" of Britain and France.[19]

In the light of this appraisal of the situation in the capitalist world in 1935, the Comintern defined its tasks as the defense of peace and democracy, of the U.S.S.R. and the international working class, against the onslaught of fascism and imperialist war.

The messianic theme was explicitly and frequently utilized by Dimitrov at the Seventh Congress in 1935, when it became his duty to outline what he termed the *"new tactical orientation for the Communist International."* [20] Dimitrov spoke of "the most important, the greatest class of modern society

[15] *Socialism Victorious*, p. 303.

[16] *Ibid.*, p. 305.

[17] For this report, see Vol. XIII of Stalin's *Sochineniia* (Moscow, 1951), especially pp. 282–306. English translations are given in his *Problems of Leninism* (Moscow, 1940), pp. 470–539, and in *Socialism Victorious*, pp. 1–93.

[18] *Inprecor* (May 16, 1936), p. 613.

[19] "In its character and essence the present war is, on the part of both warring sides, an *imperialist, unjust* war, despite the fraudulent slogans being employed by the ruling classes of the warring capitalist states . . ." *World News and Views* (November 11, 1939), p. 1079.

[20] Dimitrov, *The United Front*, p. 136.

— the working class, to whose destiny it falls to free mankind from the sufferings of the capitalist system . . ." This class, having partially realized its mission in one-sixth of the world where it "has already cast off the yoke of capitalism and constitutes the ruling class," was confronted with great obstacles in the middle thirties — the immediate challenge of fascism and imperialist war, against which above all else the Comintern had to devise a suitable policy.

The mission to save the world from fascism did not entail, for the time being, the method of revolutionary overthrow of capitalism, but rather the defense of bourgeois democracy. In the capitalist countries, Dimitrov explained, "we defend and shall continue to defend every inch of bourgeois-democratic liberties, which are being attacked by fascism and bourgeois reaction, because the interests of the class struggle of the proletariat so dictate." [21] Rejecting any "cut-and-dried approach to the question of defense of bourgeois democracy," [22] Dimitrov made clear that changing conditions required a change in Comintern attitude. It had been perfectly valid for the German Communist Party to fight against the Weimar Republic in the twenties, when it represented counterrevolution, but the Party had erred in 1932 when, with the rise of fascism, it continued its tactics unchanged.[23] Moreover, Dimitrov denied that the Comintern, in proposing joint action by all working class parties against fascism, intended to proclaim the dictatorship of the proletariat. "We make no such proposal now," he declared.[24] Immediate tasks dictated otherwise.

II

It is in the selection of adequate forms for the implementation of the messianic concept that the Seventh Congress developed several concepts, which, still utilized today, served then to introduce a new era of Comintern phraseology. The terminological revolution was revealed in the new phrases, "people's front," "government of people's front," and "democracy of a new type." One well-worn concept, the "united front," was refashioned.

The term "popular front" apparently does not exist in Comintern literature before 1934, while the term "united front" can be traced back to 1921 and the Third Congress of the Comintern.[25] At that time the failure of the European revolutionary movement to meet Communist expectations produced a retreat to the more limited goal of winning mass working-class

[21] *Ibid.*, p. 111.

[22] *Ibid.*, p. 34.

[23] *Ibid.*, pp. 110–111.

[24] *VII Congress*, p. 126.

[25] On the origin of the united front, see especially Franz Borkenau, *European Communism* (New York, 1953), pp. 50–68; E. H. Carr, *The Bolshevik Revolution, 1917–1923* (New York, 1953), III, 383–425.

support, chiefly at the expense of those Social Democratic parties which had been accused since 1919 of splitting the labor movement. The tactics of the united front, operating strictly within a proletarian framework, called for joint action between working-class parties for the achievement of specific short-range aims. The application of the united front tactic "from above" was to be based on an agreement between the Communist Party and the Social Democratic leadership, while the united front "from below" was an attempt to win the rank-and-file of social democracy away from its leaders. In anticipation of the Seventh Congress, a shift was made in 1934 to the united front "from above," reversing the form preferred since the Sixth Congress of the Comintern in 1928.[26]

The popular or people's front was given its first clear exposition by Dimitrov at the Seventh Congress. It transcended a purely working-class arrangement and sought to compose an alliance with peasant, petty-bourgeois, and bourgeois parties for immediate aims of a specific nature. The people's front presupposed the existence of the proletarian united front which it resembled in structure. It was composed of an extragovernmental hierarchy of popularly elected committees from the local to the national level. Inevitably, the original Russian soviets come to mind. Regardless of the varieties of political alignments and group interests that might be represented, these committees were dedicated to the support of mutually agreeable aims, usually embodied in a written program to which the several party leaderships had formally subscribed.

The later history of the people's front can be briefly sketched. In November 1939, with a new turn in Comintern policy, the slogan of the "popular front" was reinterpreted to mean necessarily a people's front "from below," and the leaders of the democratic and Social Democratic parties were condemned as "traitors." [27] Only after the Nazi invasion of the Soviet Union was the people's front resumed in its original form, that is, "from above." During the struggle against Hitler, the people's or national fronts reappeared, later to become transformed in Eastern Europe into new types of governments, the "people's democracies."

Satisfactory evidence is not available with respect to the role of certain personalities in the Comintern's decision to adopt the people's front policy. The attitudes of Stalin, Dimitrov, and Manuil'skii have not been fully clarified. Dimitrov's name was necessarily linked with the new "line" in his capacity as Secretary-General of the Comintern. There is considerable difference of opinion among authors, including ex-Communists, concerning the power position of Dimitrov and Manuil'skii in the Comintern and their

[26] See the "Theses of the VI World Congress," *Inprecor* (November 23, 1928), p. 1573.

[27] *World News and Views* (November 11, 1939), p. 1082.

relation to Stalin.[28] Whether Manuil'skii was fully sympathetic to the new line has been answered variously.[29]

Attempts were made, however, to place the people's front on a Leninist and Stalinist foundation. An editorial in the *Communist International* could do little more than indicate a parallel in Lenin's concern for a united movement in the struggle against tsarist autocracy. "For the realization of this task Lenin united all toilers, all democratic forces, able to fight for the victory of the bourgeois-democratic revolution." [30] Another writer cited Lenin's approval of Communist agreement and compromises with other working-class parties and petty-bourgeois parties, if such tactics raised, rather than lowered, the political consciousness of the worker and his capacity for revolutionary struggle.[31] Manuil'skii pieced together the essentials of the people's front from various elements emphasized in Stalin's writings: the utilization of the slightest opportunity to secure a mass ally, the need of the masses for political experience, and the importance of the middle strata of society.[32]

The concept of a government of the people's front proved to be one of the most fruitful ideas advanced in this period. Dimitrov provided an initial exposition of the general conditions under which it was possible to form a government of the people's front. In effect, he appreciated that there might arise a political situation sufficiently unstable to be exploited by the Communists but not to the point of a direct seizure of power by armed uprising. He postulated an intermediate situation between that relative stability which would permit no opportunity for an effective challenge to bourgeois rule and an unstable situation fully vulnerable to revolution.

His "half-way house" abandoned Communist exclusiveness in relation to other parties and to prerevolutionary governments. His conceptual scheme permitted a tapping of hitherto untouched mass support and opened at once new approaches to power that had been entirely lacking in preceding years.

[28] Ruth Fischer obviously does not regard Dimitrov as a mere puppet and remarks that he "shared the leading place in the Comintern with Dimitri Manuilsky" (*Stalin and German Communism* [Cambridge, Mass., 1948], p. 309). The anonymous authors of *Pattern for World Revolution* (Chicago and New York, 1947), using the pseudonym "Ypsilon," state that the "intelligent Bulgarian" Dimitrov became "Stalin's new man" and the "dictator of the Comintern," to whom Manuil'skii "adjusted" quickly (p. 252). Eudocio Ravines, *The Yenan Way* (New York, 1951), states that Manuil'skii "dominated the Comintern even after the presidency passed to Dimitrov" (p. 315).

[29] Borkenau, *European Communism*, pp. 143–144, claims that Manuil'skii was interested in a more elastic line than that which prevailed from 1928 to 1934. On the other hand, Ravines, *The Yenan Way*, pp. 115–116, suggests considerable reluctance by Manuil'skii to accept the people's front as a policy suitable for all countries.

[30] "Vernost' leninizmu — zalog dal'neishikh pobed," *KI* (January 1938), p. 10.

[31] F. Dengel, "Kommunisticheskii Internatsional i bor'ba za edinstvo rabochego klassa," *KI* (May 1939), p. 27.

[32] D. Manuil'skii, "Stalin i mirovoe kommunisticheskoe dvizhenie," *KI* (April 1939), p. 64.

Formerly the question had been whether or not a revolutionary situation existed. Bound by traditional concepts of "objective" and "subjective" conditions with which to estimate a political situation, the Communists more often than not found themselves in a situation that was by definition "non-revolutionary." Their activity was confined to struggle for the daily interests of the working class and to propaganda about ultimate aims. The reception of their claims to leadership was severely restricted by their exclusiveness and extreme radicalism. The postulation of an intermediate situation now permitted temporary activity *through* a prerevolutionary governmental structure and not *outside* it, on behalf of several social groups and not for one alone, before the final move was made toward a Communist seizure of power. This gradualistic approach performed the function of pushing the distasteful specter of street barricades into a more remote future.

The prerequisites for a people's front government which seemed most important to Dimitrov were three: first, the bourgeois state apparatus must be "disorganized and paralyzed" to such an extent that the bourgeoisie cannot prevent such a people's front government; second, popular feeling must be in a state of "vehement revolt *against fascism and reaction*" though not ready for an armed uprising against capitalism; third, the leftward movement in the ranks of the parties participating in the united front must be sufficiently vigorous so that a "considerable proportion" demand *"ruthless measures against the fascists and other reactionaries,"* and are willing to work with the Communists and against the anti-Communist wing within their own parties.[33] That such prerequisites are vague does not cancel the fact that a new channel for Communist activity had been opened. These preconditions might possibly develop in any capitalist country involved in political crisis. Such a crisis, for Dimitrov, appears to mean simply the threat of fascist dictatorship at home or fascist aggression from another country.[34]

Specific limitations were placed by the Communists on the capacity of the people's front government to achieve ultimate aims. *"Final salvation* this government *cannot bring,"* Dimitrov warned. It could not overthrow the class rule of the exploiters, though it was designed to limit its worse features. It could not insure against fascist counterrevolution. "Consequently," the Secretary-General emphasized, "it is necessary to prepare for the socialist revolution! Soviet power and *only* Soviet power can bring salvation!"[35] Such exhortations demonstrate that within the dualistic messianism of the late thirties the "salvation" promised to non-Communists hardly had a permanent character in the eyes of members of the Third International.

[33] Dimitrov, *The United Front*, p. 71.

[34] *Ibid.*, p. 178.

[35] *Ibid.*, p. 76. "Soviet power" does not seem to mean here the power of the Soviet Union, but rather a domestic dictatorship of the proletariat in Soviet form.

The people's front was obviously not a government to be formed after the proletarian revolution but on the eve of and before the victory of revolution.[36] The people's front government would, therefore, constitute a transitional form, following Lenin's idea, to the proletarian revolution.[37] However, it was not regarded as indispensable or inevitable, but rather as strongly probable.[38] Where fascist dictatorship existed, the united front government would be created as the result of the overthrow of fascism. It does not appear from Dimitrov's analysis that he excluded the possibility that a dictatorship of the proletariat might directly replace the fascist dictatorship, but later Communist statements seem to rule this out. In countries where the so-called bourgeois-democratic revolution was still uncompleted, Dimitrov suggested that the people's front government might become a "democratic dictatorship of the proletariat and the peasantry."[39] In the event that a number of important bourgeois reforms had not yet been achieved, the people's front government would effect such reforms.

As a *sine qua non,* the people's front government must allow full freedom to the Communist Party and other organizations of the working class.[40] The government, which might not necessarily include Communists, was promised the support of the Communist Party if it implemented the "antifascist" program upon which the parties of the people's front had agreed. In this connection, the hierarchy of united front and people's front committees was to be used as an extraparliamentary vehicle for mass activity and Communist propaganda, agitation, and pressure. The importance of such committees in Communist eyes would, of course, depend on whether and to what extent Communists held posts in the national government.

It is interesting to observe that Dimitrov in 1937 considered it necessary to caution the members of the Third International against allowing the new tactics to mislead them into a relaxation of their revolutionary principles. He warned:

> When carrying out the policy of the People's Front against fascism and war
> . . . the Communists do not lose sight of the historic need for the revolutionary
> overthrow of capitalism which has outlived its day and for the achievement of

[36] *Ibid.,* p. 70.

[37] *Ibid.,* p. 75. Lenin, according to Dimitrov, referred only to transitional forms to proletarian revolution and rejected the idea of peaceful transitions to socialism.

[38] *Ibid.,* p. 107.

[39] *Ibid.,* p. 108. Conceivably, Dimitrov may have believed also that even in an advanced capitalist country a lengthy rule of fascism could cause a "completed" bourgeois-democratic revolution to revert to an "uncompleted" condition through the abolition of democratic gains and thus require a "democratic dictatorship of the proletariat and peasantry." For Lenin's invention of this term, see Bertram D. Wolfe, *Three Who Made a Revolution* (New York, 1948), pp. 291–298. There is a clear consistency in the Comintern's view that a people's front government and not a proletarian dictatorship should succeed fascism.

[40] Dimitrov, *The United Front,* p. 70.

socialism which brings emancipation to the working class and the whole of mankind.[41]

Citing the position of the Seventh Congress on the duty of Communists to criticize their allies within the people's front, Dimitrov warned that joint action with the socialist parties rendered even more necessary the "serious and well-founded criticism of reformism, of social-democracy as the ideology and practice of class collaboration . . ." He regarded as mistaken the view that the existence of a people's front freed the Communists from the need to conduct a struggle for the basic principles of the working-class movement.[42]

The term "new democracy" was applied to the society which would result from and, at the same time, would nourish the government of the people's front. The application of the tactics of the people's front assumed a variety of forms, depending on the economic and political structure of the country and upon its foreign policy, especially with reference to the existing attitude of the Soviet Union to world problems.[43] The numerous programs of economic and political reform, proposed by Communists as minimum demands for a people's front, suggest some features of the "democracy of a new type" which was to emerge. This term, apparently not used by Dimitrov himself, came into increasing usage as a label for what was considered by the Comintern in the late thirties to be its most urgent short-term mission — the salvation and improvement of bourgeois democracy. The "new democracy" thus was to occupy temporarily a middle position between bourgeois and Soviet democracy.

Yet this concept — perhaps the most important theoretical contribution of the Comintern in this period — should not be interpreted as a static but rather as a dynamic stage in the advance toward other aims. Its duration was never precisely defined, but its function was frequently made clear. According to Maurice Thorez, the government of the people's front would be a government for the purpose of leading the masses to the dictatorship of the proletariat, to the Soviet Republic.[44] The "new democracy" was repeatedly characterized, in rather vague terminology, as one in which "fascism" and the "economic basis of fascism" would be destroyed and never allowed to reappear. The definition of fascism as the "terrorist rule of finance

---

[41] *Inprecor* (May 8, 1937), p. 468. This important May Day article, "Unity of the International Proletariat Is the Supreme Demand of the Present Moment," was printed also in *KI* (May 1937), and in Soviet newspapers on May Day.

[42] *Inprecor* (May 8, 1937), pp. 467–468.

[43] The history of the Popular Front in France and Spain is given in Borkenau, *European Communism*, pp. 115–229. See also Hugh Seton-Watson, *From Lenin to Malenkov* (New York, 1953), pp. 176–191. For the developments in Spain, see also Max Beloff, *The Foreign Policy of Soviet Russia, 1929–1941* (Oxford, 1949), II, ch. ii; Gerald Brenan, *The Spanish Labyrinth* (Cambridge, Eng., 1943), chs. xiii and xiv.

[44] M. Thorez, "K s"ezdu kompartii Frantsii," *KI* (January 10, 1936), p. 34.

capital" suggests the direction of the purging of bourgeois democracy to be undertaken by the people's front government.

In the German Party, for example, there was much discussion of the form of government which should succeed the Nazi state. An article in the *Communist International* described the desired regime as a democratic republic, but a republic that would materially differ from the weak Weimar Republic which fell under the blows of fascism.[45] The munitions magnates and the Junker landlords would no longer rule. The basis of their economic power would be destroyed. The German Communist Party promised not to isolate itself from the people's front after the overthrow of Hitler, and pledged its support for the new democratic regime in its struggle with reactionary elements. Walter Ulbricht summarized his Party's position:

> In the future democratic republic, a republic of a new, higher type, the people will enjoy overwhelming influence: the privileges of big capital will be destroyed and the roots of fascism will be torn out. *The working class, advancing the slogan of a democratic republic, comes forth as the standard-bearer, as the advance fighter, for the cause of uniting the people for the overthrow of the Hitlerite dictatorship.*[46]

Germany was thrown back a hundred years by the Nazi liquidation of democratic institutions, Ulbricht wrote, and therefore on the present-day agenda stood once more a number of tasks of a democratic character.[47] Wilhelm Pieck indicated in a later article that it would be self-deception "to think that the majority of the German working class, the middle classes, and the peasantry are already prepared to fight for Soviet power." In such conditions, could the new type of democracy create a socialist Germany? Pieck answered in the negative, affirming that it would be completely misleading to conceive of a socialist Germany "without a proletarian revolution and without Soviet power."[48]

The specific economic reforms which are outlined in the various programs of the people's front suggest a "welfare state" pattern, with limited nationalization of the economy. In the financial sphere, the programs usually called for tax reforms at the expense of the wealthy and cheap credit for the peasantry and petty bourgeoisie. Labor reforms included an eight-hour day, a minimum wage, and social insurance where these did not exist. Nationalization was often limited to the armaments industry, as in the case of Great Britain.[49] In an economically backward country such as Greece, the platform of a "democratic people's government" proposed the end of dependence

---

[45] W. Florin, "Bor'ba protiv fashizma — eto bor'ba za mir," *KI* (July 1936), p. 18.
[46] W. Ulbricht, "Novye zadachi kompartii Germanii," *KI* (April 1937), p. 26.
[47] *Ibid.*, p. 24.
[48] W. Pieck, "O narodnom fronte v Germanii," *KI* (October 1937), p. 33.
[49] James Campbell, "Bor'ba za narodnyi front v Velikobritanni," *KI* (June 6, 1938), p. 52.

upon foreign capital.[50] The distribution of land to poor and landless peasantry was a common element in the program for agrarian states, such as Spain and the Latin American republics. José Diaz, the leader of the Spanish Communist Party, encouraged the formation of collective farms, but cautioned against full-scale, forced collectivization.[51]

The continuity of the policies and practices of the Communist-led world revolutionary movement since 1935 emphasizes that the basic attitudes embraced within the complex messianism of the late thirties remain operative today. It has been customary to trace the origin of the theory of the people's democracy of today only as far back as the later period of the Second World War, when new governments were installed in the vacuum created in Eastern Europe by Hitler's departing puppets. However, the original theory of the people's democracy was quite similar to that of the "democracy of a new type" of 1935–1939, with the major exception that the people's democracy, unlike the people's front government, performed a peaceful transition to socialism. Beginning late in 1947, a reconsideration of the theory resulted in an equating of the people's democracy with the dictatorship of the proletariat, though in a non-Soviet form.[52] Dimitrov became the first major Communist figure to proclaim the new definition on the occasion of the Fifth Congress of the Bulgarian Workers' Party in December 1948.[53] No attempt was made by Dimitrov to link the theory to the prewar people's front era of the Comintern; it is rare that Soviet theorists have done so.[54] But William Z. Foster has acknowledged the heritage in an important article, and has supported as still "fundamentally correct" the tactics of the Seventh Congress.[55] It is of interest that the Program of the Yugoslav Communist Party, adopted in 1948, does place the origin of the present-day national or people's front "in the struggle against foreign aggressors and domestic traitors . . ."[56] It appears safe to state that the origin of the idea of "people's

---

[50] N. Zakhariadis, "Bor'ba i uspekhi narodnogo fronta v Gretsii," *KI* (March 25, 1936), p. 75.

[51] José Diaz, "Za organizatsiiu bor'by i pobedy," *KI* (March 1937), p. 70.

[52] See especially the articles by Professor H. Gordon Skilling, " 'People's Democracy' in Soviet Theory, I, II," *Soviet Studies*, III (July 1951), 16–33; (October 1951), 131–149. See also Ruth A. Rosa, "The Soviet Theory of People's Democracy," *World Politics*, I (July 1949), 489–510.

[53] "In accordance with the principles of Marxist-Leninism, the Soviet system and the people's democratic system are two forms of one and the same power . . . They are two forms of the proletarian dictatorship" (*Politicheskii otchët Ts. K. BRP(c)* [Sofia, 1948], p. 130). An English translation of the report is in Dimitrov, *Selected Speeches and Articles*.

[54] H. Gordon Skilling, "People's Democracy, the Proletarian Dictatorship and the Czechoslovak Path to Socialism," *American Slavic and East European Review*, X (April 1951), 106.

[55] William Z. Foster, "People's Front and People's Democracy," *Political Affairs*, XXIX (June 1950), 19.

[56] *Program i status komunistichke partije Jugoslavije usvojeni na V Kongresu KPJ* (n.p., 1951), p. 62.

democracy" must be traced to the speculation within the Comintern in the years before the Second World War.

III

The features of the messianic concept, as it has emerged thus far in the description of the background of the third period, its tasks, and the techniques developed for the solution of those tasks, are the characteristic features of a secular, political messianism. "Instead of a next world, there is an earthly future," writes Jules Monnerot in his excellent study.[57] The ingredients of the messianism of the Comintern are clear: one truly creative social group (the proletariat), a general will expressed through an elite (the Communists), the harmony of interests between leader and led, the monopoly of truth (dialectical and historical materialism), the evil (capitalist society) from which salvation will bring deliverance.[58]

As Professor J. L. Talmon indicates, secular messianism replaces empirical thinking "with reasoning by definition, based on a priori collective concepts which must be accepted whatever the evidence of the senses . . ."[59] So it was in the Comintern. By Communist definition, an identity of interests existed for the time being between the Soviet Union, the working class, and the cause of peace. One could not oppose the U.S.S.R. without being an enemy of the latter. Dimitrov is quite specific on this point:

> In the present situation there is not, nor can there be any other more certain criterion than one's attitude toward the Soviet Union in determining who is the friend and who is the enemy of the cause of the working class and socialism, of determining who is a supporter and who an opponent of democracy and peace.[60]

The exalted position accorded the Soviet Union in the struggle "for democracy and peace" merely reëmphasized in another fashion its hegemony in Comintern mythology as the locus of the partially realized mission of the proletariat. Stalin himself held an unchallenged position as the fourth great teacher of dialectical materialism, following Marx, Engels, and Lenin.

The universality of the struggle at hand is another theme in messianic schemes. Defense of peace and resistance to fascism were considered to be as valid in Asia and Latin America as in Europe. Resistance against the fascists in Spain was the "common cause of advanced and progressive mankind" and helped at the same moment to aid Czechoslovakia against fascist Germany and to bolster China against imperialist Japan.[61]

An inevitable accompaniment of the messianic outlook is a bisection of

[57] Jules Monnerot, *Sociology and Psychology of Communism* (Boston, 1953), p. 156.

[58] Compare especially the recent study of Professor J. L. Talmon, *The Rise of Totalitarian Democracy* (Boston, 1952). Part III, "The Babouvist Crystallization," is penetrating and rewarding.

[59] *Ibid.*, p. 253.

[60] *Inprecor* (November 13, 1937), p. 1179.

[61] Dimitrov, "Ko vtoroi godovshchine geroicheskoi bor'by ispanskogo naroda," *KI* (July 1938), p. 21.

the world into two hostile camps and the impossibility of a middle or neutral position. Such was the case in the 1930's. Even the neutrality of the Scandinavian states was attacked as, in effect, hostility to the cause of democracy and peace.[62] A denial of the necessity of the people's front was equated with the encouragement of war; but whoever stood with the people's front stood, by definition, on the side of peace.

It should not be overlooked that member sections of the Comintern, encouraged by the blessing given to "national forms of the proletarian class struggle," [63] took up the messianic idea in terms of their national heritages. A resolution of the German Communist Party spoke of the "historical mission" of the German working class in the struggle to preserve peace and to secure the future of Germany.[64] Frequently the proletariat was replaced as the instrument of salvation by a larger entity, the nation. One writer spoke of the need for France to return to "its old traditions and remain true to its great past" and to its "historical mission of liberator." [65] An entire section of Thorez's speech at the Ninth Congress of the French Party in December 1937 was devoted to "the mission of France in the world." [66] Bourgeois tradition was freely exploited. The "principles of 1789" were appealed to in French Communist literature and throughout Europe. Earl Browder spoke of the American Party as "destined to carry on and complete the work begun by Tom Paine, George Washington, Thomas Jefferson, and Abraham Lincoln," and admitted that the American revolutionary heritage had long been neglected by the Party.[67]

Comintern messianism, it may be stated in conclusion, was presented on two levels during the late 1930's. On one level, the ultimate goals were maintained intact for the elite, that is, the Communist parties of the world. But on another level, the Comintern offered salvation from imperialist war and fascism, and extended the hand of fellowship to broad categories of the population for the satisfaction of common interests. In doing so, Dimitrov and the Comintern spokesmen elaborated new and fruitful techniques for the exercise of influence and control over non-Party allies.

Throughout the period from 1935 through 1939, the continuing validity of the mission of the Communist-led proletariat to transform society by revolutionary action was upheld. World revolution and the violent overthrow of capitalism were not regarded as immediate tasks; but in the struggle against fascism the proletariat was expected to achieve unity and experience, prerequisites for the fulfillment of its historical mission.

[62] R. Magnus, "Protiv lzheneitraliteta v skandinavskikh stranakh," *KI* (September 1938), p. 64. Even Lord Palmerston's views on the vulnerable nature of the neutrality of small states were cited (*World News and Views* [August 6, 1938], p. 890).
[63] Dimitrov, *The United Front*, p. 80.
[64] *World News and Views* (July 2, 1938), p. 789.
[65] *Inprecor* (December 31, 1937), pp. 1397–1398.
[66] *Inprecor* (January 8, 1938), p. 17. For the speech, see Maurice Thorez, *Une Politique de grandeur française* (Paris, 1945), pp. 114–203.
[67] Browder, *The People's Front*, p. 235.

Great Russian Messianism
in Postwar Soviet Ideology

FREDERICK C. BARGHOORN

There is an important and complex, though partly "synthetic," messianic theme in Soviet ideology. Soviet Russian messianism is part of the offensive-defensive symbol system by which the Kremlin seeks to justify and legitimize its rule. The Kremlin seeks to expand its power and ultimately to achieve universal dominion. It fears the world which it wishes to reorganize and it also fears the peoples which it already rules. Moscow seeks the support of the peoples of the world in its struggle to subvert and destroy the "ruling classes" of the non-Soviet world. It holds out to mankind the vision and prophecy of the earthly paradise, the harmonious society without coercion and inequality. This is the Utopian aspect of Soviet Russia's message to the world. It pivots around the concept of world proletarian struggle against the class enemy for the ultimate purpose of building the new order and creating the new, Soviet man.

Thus the Kremlin's missionary activities, its expansionist policies, and their supporting ideological instruments rest upon at least a formal foundation of Marxist-Leninist universalism. This point must be stressed at the outset, for otherwise we might fall into the serious error of regarding contemporary Soviet Russian messianism as simply a modern version of nineteenth-century Pan-Slavism, or of Dostoyevsky's doctrines that the Russians were "panhuman" and that to be fully human one must be Russian.[1] As one authority puts it, the ideas of old Russia were parochial, "despite occasional traces of messianic doctrine."[2] In contrast, the Kremlin today has a plan not only for ruling the world, but for transforming it in its own image. To support this unique program, it has developed the doctrine of the uniqueness, superiority, and universal applicability of the Soviet way of life.[3]

[1] On Dostoyevsky as an epitomy of nineteenth-century Russian nationalism and messianism, see Hans Kohn, *Prophets and Peoples* (New York, 1946), ch. v.

[2] Philip E. Mosely, "Aspects of Russian Expansion," *The American Slavic and East European Review*, VII, no. 3 (October 1948), 213.

[3] I am aware that some students, including distinguished Russian scholars, stress more than I do the continuity between pre-Soviet and Soviet ideology. Outstanding

But if Soviet Russian messianism is Communist imperialism in Russian guise, in what does its "Great Russian" character consist? I think the answer is that the Kremlin in the postwar period more than ever before has realized that the success of its program of world expansion, and also its ability to maintain its power at home, depend upon securing the maximum possible support from the Great Russian people. This is the continuation of a policy implicit in Lenin, and rendered explicit and systematic by Stalin as far back as the early 1920's. Lenin, in the most important of all his writings, *What Is to Be Done?*, laid considerable stress upon the uniqueness of the mission of the Russian proletariat in the world revolutionary movement. Stalin built his own thesis of Russian leadership in world Communism upon this and other statements of Lenin, although at the cost of considerable distortion. But having captured the Russian base of world Communism, the Bolsheviks were in turn bound to be at least to some degree influenced by the Russian mentality and traditions out of which they had sprung and which survived in the population they controlled.[4] The basis of this whole system is contained in that portion of Stalin's basic work, *Problems of Leninism,* which deals with the "historical roots of Leninism," and which emphasizes that the immediate task of the Russian proletariat is the most revolutionary of any proletariat and builds on this dictum of Lenin the conclusion that the center of the world revolutionary movement has moved to Russia. It should also be emphasized that Stalin in reaching this conclusion added forcefully that the Russian Communists could not limit their work to "the narrow national framework of the Russian revolution."[5] This is not the place to develop the Lenin-Stalin concept of the mission of the Great Russian people as instruments of the Communist world revolution, but I think it is important to realize how basic this doctrine is to present-day Soviet political thought. In analyzing Soviet thought at any given time we must always take into account the carry-over of the "classics" of Marxism-Leninism-Stalinism. The continued relevance of this system of thought to current Soviet ideology and policy was brought out forcefully by the publication, on July 26, 1953, of a brief history of the Bolshevik Party which prominently featured the basic propositions of Lenin and of Stalin's interpretation of Lenin which we

among such scholars was the late G. P. Fedotov. See his brilliant collection of essays, *Novy Grad* (New York: Chekhov Publishing House, 1952). But Fedotov, Berdiaev and others who emphasized this continuity also recognized the differences between Russian nationalism and Soviet Communism, and the much more insistent and ambitious claims of the latter.

[4] It is significant that in 1938 when Stalin was preparing the way for adoption of the supremely authoritative *History of the Communist Party of the Soviet Union,* he caused to be published a series of booklets entitled *K izucheniyu istorii VKP (b),* containing selections from Lenin and Stalin emphasizing the role of the Russian, "most revolutionary proletariat in the world."

[5] *Ibid.,* I, 20. This and connected statements are of course available in all editions of Stalin's *Problems of Leninism.*

have been discussing, although without in some important cases attribution of key passages to their author, Stalin.

Soviet Russian messianism interprets and utilizes some elements of the pre-Soviet and Soviet Russian culture. It rejects, suppresses, and if possible destroys everything in the Russian culture pattern that it does not consider useful. A recent writer has pointed out that the "Russian mannerisms" of the Soviet regime represent "more nearly the long run infiltration of an occupation regime by the area and society it rules" than they reflect the aspirations of the Russian people.[6] Perhaps equally important is the skill of the Soviet regime in the use of ideas calculated to evoke a favorable response among the Russian people. Russian words and gestures may have different meanings to different Russians.

I have indicated some of the factors in the synthesis of Russian, Marxist, Leninist, and Soviet factors which have shaped the messianic theme in Soviet ideology. Geography, demography, and demagogy certainly bulk large in this synthesis. Like everything totalitarian, it has an artificial, synthetic character. But it would be a mistake to underestimate the power of this doctrine, or to fail to see that it has real, organic connections with the Russian and Soviet past, and with powerful social and psychological forces in present-day Soviet society. Since this paper deals primarily with the content of Soviet Russian messianism, I shall discuss these background factors here only briefly. Those which I should like to discuss here might be called, respectively, the historical-cultural, the political-institutional, and the social-psychological factors. What was said earlier about the "parochial" character of prerevolutionary Russian ideology applied primarily to the official ideology. If one can speak of an official creed of pre-Soviet Russian imperialism, it was "reactionary," but probably not more expansionist or messianic than that of any other great power of its time. But as I have also indicated, the same cannot be said of some of the main streams of "unofficial" prerevolutionary Russian thought. Many of the more extremist Russian thinkers, both conservative and radical, were highly messianic. At the risk of great oversimplification, one can say that Russian extremist and maximalist thought tended to assign to Russia both a negative and a positive world mission. The negative mission was to assist in bringing about the destruction of the "decadent," bourgeois Western "capitalist" order. The positive mission was even more vague, but it stressed such elements as were suggested by the statement of Belinskii, made in 1840 and often quoted in Soviet publications, to the effect that in a hundred years he expected to see Russia standing at the head of the civilized world. It should be emphasized of course that by no means all of nineteenth-century radical and messianic thought was in Russia anti-Western. The radicals, in particular, who have always been revered in Soviet Russia as "forerunners of Marx," were opposed to the

---

[6] W. W. Rostow, *The Dynamics of Soviet Society* (New York, 1953), ch. vii, p. 134.

"bourgeois" aspects of Western civilization, but of course they took as their model and inspiration Western European and American radicalism. However, it might be said that some of the messianic elements in Bolshevik thought are derived from a kind of "rebounding Westernism." Since the West failed to follow the teachings of its own prophets and seers, the Russians fell heir to them. Some such thought as this is suggested by Lenin's fury at the "treason" of the Western European Social Democrats during the First World War, as well as by other elements in Lenin and subsequent Soviet thought.[7] We cannot pursue this fascinating but rather tenuous link between Soviet Russian messianism and the heritage of Russian radical thought further here, but it should be recalled that study of, and appropriate comment on, the works of Belinskii, Chernyshevskii, Pisarev, Dobroliubov, and other representatives of what is now called "Russian classical philosophy" plays a very important role in Soviet higher education.

Current Soviet thought distorts the heritage of nineteenth-century Russian radicalism, exaggerating the nationalist, antiforeign, and messianic elements. This may be partly the result of further development of, or coming into existence of, new and aggravated forms of political, social and psychological conditions which in the prerevolutionary period gave rise to less extreme manifestations of similar phenomena. The similarity between pre- and post-revolutionary Russia is probably least in the political, particularly the international political field. However, it may not be entirely fruitless to look for parallels even here. There is a similarity in geopolitical terms between nineteenth-century Russia and the Soviet Union of 1953. A much stronger Russian colossus faces a much weaker and less technically superior Western Europe, but one backed by the transatlantic giant. These facts, together with the "bi-polarity" which followed the Second World War, have intensified the formerly weak "encirclement" psychology of the Russian elite. This psychology of a regime facing threats abroad and at home creates a mental climate favorable to messianic doctrines. Internal social-psychological and cultural similarities between prerevolutionary and Soviet Russia also exist, and doubtless are related to the messianic components in Soviet Russian ideology. Social distance between the elite and the peasant and worker masses is considerable and, in the opinion of most objective Western students of Soviet society, is gradually increasing.[8] There is certainly no such cultural gulf between elite and masses in Soviet Russia as existed in prerevolutionary Russia, divided, as Lenin put it, into "two nations." However, I found in my own four years in the Soviet Union that there was a very real cultural

---

[7] For interesting links between nineteenth-century Russian radical thought and Soviet thought, see Richard Hare, *Pioneers of Russian Social Thought* (New York, 1951); and on the essentially Western character of the Russian pre-Marxist revolutionary movement, Franco Venturi, *Il populismo russo* (Turin, 1952).

[8] See, for example, Barrington Moore, Jr., *Soviet Politics: The Dilemma of Power* (Cambridge, Mass., 1950).

and psychological distance between the "simple" people and the "educated" people. Soviet Russians have, I think, a far greater aversion than Americans to manual labor. The European ideal of membership in the intelligentsia, or at least of achieving "white collar" status, is stronger in Soviet Russia than it is in the "capitalist" United States. Inequality, social distance, hierarchical subordination and regimentation, and the terrors of the police state all stand, of course, in glaring contrast with the promises for the future contained in such works as Lenin's *The State and the Revolution,* still an integral part of Soviet doctrinal and political education material. It is this contrast between ideals and realities which may impel the regime to offer to the Soviet people chauvinistic substitutes for the constantly postponed but still formally professed goals of the official ideology.[9]

The sociological concept of ethnocentrism may assist us in understanding Soviet, and pre-Soviet, Russian messianism. William Graham Sumner in his classic *Folkways* set forth the view that each social group, and in particular each state, regarded itself as the leader of civilization, the best, the freest, and the wisest, and all others as inferior. Sumner, and following him, most modern social scientists, considered that all nations were equally messianic and equally intolerant. Sumner's appraisal should serve as a warning against attributing such characteristics to others, without examining ourselves. In this connection, it is interesting to note the recent warning by Professor Merle Curti contained in his question "May, perhaps, a future historian conclude that the dominant faith of our time is the religion of nationalism — the American way?" [10] I think that in the America of today the words of Sumner and Curti should have a sobering effect. But at the same time I think that one could somewhat modify the doctrine of ethnocentrism and express the opinion, or at least the hope, that Western ideology is less ethnocentric than post-revolutionary Russian ideology. The phenomenon of ethnocentrism, and its associated attitudes of hostility toward others and an arrogant sense of mission for one's "own" group, have in large part developed from a combination of cultural isolation and unfavorable experiences in contact with representatives of a foreign culture. If this is true, and I believe it is, then I think one can say that nineteenth-century Russian culture, with the exception of a small cosmopolitan component, was more provincial than that of Western Europe or America. It might also follow that since isolation has increased and contact with Western culture, though in some ways favorable, has been in large part symbolized by the invasion and devastation connected with the Second World War, Soviet ethnocentrism and its accompanying messianic attitudes represent something more intense and virulent than

[9] Alexander von Schelting, in *Russland und Europa* (Bern, 1948), Part V, offers some interesting but, in part at least, tenuous comparisons between the pre-Soviet radical Russian intelligentsia and its ideology, and their Soviet counterparts.

[10] Merle Curti, "Human Nature in American Thought," *Political Science Quarterly,* LXVIII, no. 4 (December 1953), 492–510. Quotation on p. 507.

their counterpart in pre-Soviet Russia. Increased isolation, fresh memories of frightful suffering, and the internal hostilities and aggression engendered by normal functioning of the Soviet social system would all seem to furnish an environment favorable to messianic sentiments and moods. I do not mean to suggest that these factors make it certain that the Kremlin can fully exploit these attitudes for its own purposes. But their existence, of which there can be no doubt, helps us to understand how such attitudes can develop and should heighten our awareness of the possibility that Soviet messianism, particularly its Great Russian component, may well be not only a part of the system of synthetic identities by which the Kremlin seeks to enlist the support of the Soviet intellectuals and masses, but also an "independent" force, which would continue to exist even if the Soviet regime were to collapse. I think it is important to entertain at least the possibility that Soviet Russian messianism has vitality as a "real" and "independent" psychological factor, while at the same time keeping ever in mind its demagogic and manipulative aspects. Let us now turn to an examination of the content of the Great Russian "message" to the world in the postwar period.

The Russian theme in Soviet ideology is part of and is inextricably intertwined with the larger "Soviet" message which promises salvation to mankind, sets forth the strategy by which believers throughout the world may assist Moscow in saving the world, and incidentally install these followers in power over their fellow citizens in their respective countries, and issues a constant stream of directives, exhortations and promises to agents, fellow-travelers and others. This is a special, new kind of messianism. It combines the policy of a great totalitarian state with the aspirations of an international political sect and is ideologically unified by Marxist philosophy of history. This is a potent combination, but it is one that contains its own "contradictions." Will it be possible to combine indefinitely the parochial and universalist elements? Similar questions might be raised about the clash within this system of its "scientific" and its mystical-Utopian aspects. Without attempting to deal with these questions here, it is well to point out that Moscow has apparently always been aware of the problems they pose. It has achieved considerable success in presenting its centrally determined but universally applicable policy in terms of local cultural patterns, in the symbology and idiom of the particular audience addressed at a given time.[11]

The reader is doubtless familiar with the main lines of Soviet doctrine, as it has been set forth in Soviet propaganda since 1945, although surprisingly little analytical or even descriptive work has been done on this material.[12] Perhaps we should refresh the reader's memory with a few brief

[11] For a discussion of some of the problems of "diffusion" of a world revolutionary pattern, see H. D. Lasswell, particularly in *World Politics and Personal Insecurity* (New York, 1935), and other studies edited or directed by him.

[12] See F. C. Barghoorn, *The Soviet Image of the United States* (New York, 1950), Ithiel de Sola Pool, *Symbols of Democracy* (Stanford, 1952), and *Symbols of Internationalism* (Stanford, 1951 and 1952).

remarks regarding the content of Soviet communications to the Soviet and non-Soviet world. It is my impression, based on a careful reading of *Pravda* since about January 1, 1943 and a less careful reading of other newspapers and magazines, such as *Bolshevik* (title changed to *Kommunist* after the Nineteenth Party Congress of October 1952) that the main general ideological symbols of Soviet propaganda, applicable both to the "home" and "foreign" audiences, are "peace, democracy and socialism." During the "Fatherland War" Soviet propaganda deëmphasized these most universal of its symbols and pivoted around the struggles between the "freedom-loving peoples," headed by the Soviet Fatherland, and the Hitlerites and their "accomplices." But both in the war and in the postwar periods, Soviet propaganda maintained what Raymond Aron refers to as the "Manichaean" dichotomy between the "socialist" and the "capitalist" forces struggling to control the destinies of mankind.[13] Pool found that Soviet editorials were four or five times as rich in "ideological symbols" as *The New York Times* or the London *Times*. He also found that a decrease of the practice of democracy in the U.S.S.R. was accompanied by the increasing use of the word "democracy" in Soviet editorials.[14] It is true that, as Pool has pointed out, Soviet propaganda is unusually rich in general ideological symbols. At the same time, we must also bear in mind that "practical" themes predominate even in the Soviet press. In a recent check of *Pravda* editorials for the month of September 1953, I found only two of the thirty editorials for that month that I would consider primarily "ideological." I would estimate that two or three or perhaps four "ideological" editorials are published each month. Special occasions, such as November 6 or May 1, elicit an unusual concentration of ideological material, set forth in such a fashion as to proclaim that certain principles have already been realized in the Soviet Union, and will and should be realized eventually throughout the entire world. Let us look at a recent example. *Pravda* for December 5, 1953 devoted its normal, single front page editorial to the theme "Socialism and Democracy Are Invincible." The editorial marked the seventeenth anniversary of Soviet "Constitution Day." Formerly, the Constitution of December 5, 1936, was referred to as the "Stalin Constitution," but this year it was simply referred to as the "Constitution of the U.S.S.R.," its provisions, according to the editorial, confirming the statement of the "Great Lenin" to the effect that Soviet power was a million times more democratic than the most democratic bourgeois republics. As might be expected, the editorial celebrated the domestic policies and achievements of the Soviet Union, supported "unanimously" by the "peoples of the U.S.S.R.," and its foreign policy which it said "corresponds to the aspirations and interests of all peoples, and is the only just, democratic policy."

[13] Raymond Aron, "La Russie après Staline," *Preuves*, XXXII (October 1953), 5–13. See especially p. 12.

[14] Pool, *Symbols of Democracy*, pp. 11–13.

The most important "international" theme of Soviet propaganda, presented in the "Manichaean" spirit noted by Aron, is the peace theme. Formal Soviet ideology proclaims insistently that the world can enjoy peace, as well as welfare, only if socialism is adopted everywhere. And only the leadership of the Soviet Union has the formula by which the socialism which will bring peace and welfare can be achieved. This "messianic" or "imperialistic" Soviet attitude toward peace finds expression in Soviet establishment, sponsorship and manipulation of the World Peace Council. As has often been noted by political commentators, one can substitute the word "revolution" or perhaps "world Soviet authority" for "peace" and one can find in the frequent Soviet editorials, pamphlets, and books propagandizing the activities of the World Peace Council, an expression of the Soviet program for the world and of Communist messianic fervor.[15]

There is no doubt that the Soviet universal ideological symbols referred to above quantitatively overshadow the Russian theme in Soviet ideology, whether one is looking for its "messianic" or other aspects. It is rather rare to find a *Pravda* front page editorial such as that of September 9, 1953, entitled "The Glory of Russian Literature," although the Soviet press certainly takes more than full advantage of opportunities to publish special feature articles on the anniversaries of births or deaths of Pushkin, Glinka, Chernyshevskii, and other great figures of the Russian past.[16]

But the Russian theme is probably far more important than its quantitative manifestations would indicate. It has a "covert" quality. One can speak of it as submerged, subterranean, "erupting" from time to time into the "overt" expression of the normal flow of Soviet communications. This "covert-overt" relationship may perhaps be illustrated by the physical traits of "positive" figures in the cartoons in the important Soviet satirical publication, *Krokodil* (Crocodile). My impression is that ideal or "heroic" or even "normal" figures of the Soviet worker or executive or scientist are shown as possessing the features of typical "Great Russians," with high cheekbones, blue eyes, blonde hair, and stocky figures.[17] In this connection, it may also be interesting to recall that during the "anticosmopolitan" campaign early in 1949, "negative" types of the "capitalist," etc. were sometimes presented as having Semitic features. These remarks are presented in a very tentative spirit. The research which would be necessary to establish, or even to indicate strongly, that a "master race" conception plays a part in Soviet Russian nationalism and messianism has not been done. Still, and remember-

[15] See, for example, "The Voice of the Peoples in Defense of Peace," *Pravda* (editorial), December 1, 1953.

[16] A kind of "model" for the expression of Soviet Russian national cultural pride was set by Stalin's list of Russian military, literary, cultural, and ideological figures in his speech of November 6, 1941. Stalin's list and accompanying remarks have been embellished upon thousands of times subsequently in the Soviet press.

[17] I am indebted to Mr. Paul W. Friedrich for calling this phenomenon to my attention. It might open up interesting possibilities for research.

ing that we are again in a realm of speculation, future research might possibly find a connection between the covert Soviet Russian self-image and the officially sponsored doctrine of "Lysenkoism" which proclaims that acquired characteristics can be inherited. Perhaps the idea that the "Soviet man" is superior to, and has the right to "teach" the rest of mankind, because he has lived under a Soviet system, exists side by side in the minds of at least some Soviet Russians with an older conception of the superiority of Russians and their culture to the rest of mankind? [18] Of course, there is a logical conflict between supporting Moscow's "world mission" on a Russian cultural and on a Soviet, environmentally determined foundation.[19] Also, I think that postwar Soviet emphasis upon the "Soviet man" has a strongly "anti-Russian" significance. The Soviet leaders were worried by some of the implications of the postwar revival of Russian national feeling, which they wanted to channel strictly into what to them seemed appropriate lines of development. But if we keep in mind the distinction between "covert" and "overt" elements in Soviet thought, it may not be completely incorrect to consider that both the Russian self-image, culturally inherited, and the Kremlin's official doctrine that socialism has produced a new, superior type of human being may be part of the same general xenophobic nationalistic and messianic pattern. The Russian and Soviet elements in this pattern stand in an uneasy relationship to one another. At times they will be for all practical purposes the same thing. But at other times they may clash. Theirs is the relationship and the antagonism of the traditional, the emotional, the unique and personal and lyrical on the one hand, with the rational, purposive and scientific elements in Soviet ideology.

The Russian element in Soviet Russian messianism is the emotional addition which the rulers realized must be added to coldly rational Marxist-Leninist-Stalinist ideology. But it is also a body of culturally determined attitudes common, in greater or lesser degree, to elite and masses, and, I think also, to the Russian and non-Russian peoples of the Soviet Union. The latter point is of course extremely complex and debatable, and I do not intend to discuss it here. In times of grave crisis, the Russian and Soviet components of Soviet Russian ideology achieve their closest harmony. This explains the greater measure of freedom granted to Soviet Russian and non-Russian intellectuals

[18] See the provocative article by Edward N. Megay, "Lysenkoism and the Classless Society," *Journal of Politics*, XV, no. 2 (May 1953), 211–230. Megay argues that the Central Committee's approval of Lysenko's doctrines in August 1948 "challenged" the Soviet regime to do something "here and now" to realize Communism. Megay's implication, as well as statements of a more explicit character in Ivan Kurganov, "Natsionalnaia problema v Rossii" in *Novy Zhurnal*, XXV, 264–289, is that there is a Soviet "master race" concept.

[19] It should also be borne in mind that, as Raymond Bauer brings out in his *The New Man in Soviet Psychology* (Cambridge, Mass., 1952), Soviet psychological theory rejects any simple theory of the determination of personality by environment, and insists upon its own special kind of "responsibility" and what one might call "planned free will."

during the war. Both the primarily Marxist-Communist-Soviet and the primarily Russian sectors of the population, if one may thus divide the Soviet population, respond in the same way, I think, to foreign threats. Probably they also respond in rather similar fashion to real or fancied foreign "insults." Soviet national pride has a "touchy" quality. In this, it certainly is in some ways a continuation of prerevolutionary Russian attitudes. There is a kind of "persecution complex" quality in many Soviet political utterances, which I think find an echo in wide circles of the Soviet population. These, I think, also represent something of a continuation of prerevolutionary Russian attitudes. And such attitudes are the stuff of which a compensatory messianism is composed.

In the remainder of this paper I propose to discuss some features of the Russian messianic theme in Soviet ideology which I consider to be interesting and important for our understanding and dealing with the Soviet regime and the Soviet people as a whole. These themes are as follows: "Russia's military services to humanity"; secondly, what one might call the "internal mission" of the Russian people; thirdly, the "world significance" of Russian culture and especially language. One might refer to the glorification of Russian arms by the Soviet press and in Soviet scholarship as a "retroactive sense of mission." Obviously, the military glories which are celebrated in the Soviet propaganda media are matters of history. This point is of more than merely formal importance. We must remember that the Soviets exert a strict self-censorship on any overtly bellicose utterances. They cannot therefore consistently suggest that Russian and Soviet military glory may be expected to flourish again in the future. Such a conclusion can at best only be implied, and Soviet utterances concentrate on celebrating past military achievements. In this, there is of course a sharp contrast between the shrewdness and wisdom of Soviet tactics and the flamboyant and bellicose predictions and threats which have been indulged in by military and political leaders of other extremist nationalistic regimes in the past.[20]

This retroactive Russian military messianism of which we are speaking has been perhaps most eloquently embodied in the numerous brilliant books and articles by the late Eugene Tarle, one of the leading historians and public figures of the U.S.S.R. However, not only Tarle, but full regiments of historians and journalists, military men and political figures, including of course Stalin himself, contributed to its development. The Soviet position is that Russia saved the world, or at least Europe and Asia, from German

---

[20] It should, however, be remembered that pacifism has no place in Soviet ideology and that the possibility of future conflict involving the Soviet Union is implied in many key statements of Lenin and Stalin. Moreover, the Soviet press abounds in thinly veiled warnings of the future spread of Communism by violence. For example, warning in the *Pravda* editorial for June 24, 1953, at the height of the Soviet-sponsored "world campaign for negotiation," that the use of force against "any national-liberation movement" could lead to "a new hearth (*ochag*) of war."

fascist enslavement. Even in 1945, only slight credit was given to the Anglo-American contribution to victory in the Second World War. As early as April 3, 1945, Professor Tarle delivered a lecture in Moscow in which he credited the English and Americans with little more contribution to the war against Hitler than good will.[21] He did, however, pay tribute to President Roosevelt and to Lady Churchill, who was visiting Moscow at the time. Extending Russia's role into the past, Tarle set forth a pattern which he himself had helped to create in his well-known book published shortly before the war, *Napoleon's Invasion of Russia*. Russia had saved Europe also in the days of Napoleon. Tarle also credited Russia with having played the major role in the defeat of Germany in the First World War.

This pattern, which first took shape in the Soviet Union in preparation for the war against the Nazis, has apparently become a long-term feature of Soviet ideology. The theme of Russia's services to civilized mankind is of course extended far back beyond the Napoleonic era. It is interesting that the old Russian belief that Russia saved Europe from enslavement by the Mongols is a part of current Soviet doctrine.[22] The 1950 edition of the standard Soviet medieval history textbook, which is the only authorized book for the entire country, makes the following statement: "In their cultural level the Mongols stood much lower than the Russians. Their power was maintained by force alone. The Russian people deeply hated the fierce conquerors and gradually gathered strength in order to throw off the terrible yoke. At the cost of tremendous suffering and constant struggle with the merciless conquerors, the Russian people shielded Western Europe from the horrors of the Mongol yoke." [23] It is extremely interesting and significant, incidentally, to note that the 1946 edition of the same work declared that the "heroic struggle of the Russians and *Ukrainian* (italics mine) peoples" saved Europe from suffering at the hands of the Mongols.[24]

The claim that Russia has "saved" Europe by shedding its blood in so many "wars of liberation" is no doubt in part a propaganda device. But it is more than that. It certainly reflects the deep feelings of many Russians. It also corresponds, at least in part, and with regard for the historical context, to historical truth. Wars for national survival have bulked unusually large in Russian history. These wars, and the historical memories engendered by them, have played perhaps a bigger part than any other factor in developing Russian nationalism and Great Russian messianism. It is no accident that the Soviet regime called the war against Hitler the "Great Fatherland War,"

[21] Based on notes taken at the lecture.
[22] The famous Russian historian Kliuchevskii concluded ch. i, Vol. I of his *Kurs russkoi istorii*, 5 vols. (Moscow, 1937) with a comparison of the much more unfavorable factors, including a constant struggle with the steppe nomads, facing ancient Russians and in comparison with which the peoples of Western Europe were in a relatively advantageous situation.
[23] E. A. Kosminskii, *Istoriia srednikh vekov* (Moscow, 1950), p. 99.
[24] *Ibid.* (Moscow, 1946), p. 108.

after the model of the national struggle against Napoleon. And just as the "War of 1812" called forth much of the nationalistic and messianic mood of early nineteenth-century Russia, similar sentiments were engendered by the Second World War. The Kremlin attempted to appropriate credit for Russian military achievements, and to turn to its own use the feeling of pride engendered by Russian achievements and courage. However, if one searches the Soviet press carefully, one can find here and there reflections of a more "popular" and less official conception of Russian and Soviet patriotism. In *Bolshevik*, No. 3–4, for February 1944, the writer Nikolai Tikhonov, during the war one of the most popular Soviet poets, although demoted in the 1946 "cultural purge," wrote: "National pride, hitherto buried in the hearts of the Soviet people, burst forth in a bright flame before the threat of enslavement and in the face of deadly danger." [25]

One result of the resurgence of the sentiment referred to by Tikhonov was that Russian writers, and even Party propagandists, searched the Russian past and also the life of Lenin for evidences of Russian national pride. For example, the propagandist M. Mitin, in an article in the July 1, 1943 *Red Star* on "Lenin and Stalin on Soviet Patriotism," quoted Gorkii on Lenin's Russian pride. On Capri, when Lenin and Gorkii were living together in exile, Lenin is reported to have said that Russians work "more cleverly" than the native fishermen, and when Gorkii demurred, Lenin reproached him for forgetting Russia. In 1946, a Soviet scholar, G. Samarin, published a very interesting study entitled *The Patriotic Theme in the Choral Art of the Russian People*. The publication of this book, as well as the profusion of folk songs and Soviet patriotic war songs, incidentally furnishes interesting confirmation of the theory set forth by Robert Michels in his *Der Patriotismus* about the importance of popular songs in nationalism.[26] Samarin's work traced the theme of the defense of the Motherland back to the earliest Russian literature. A typical statement was Samarin's reference to the "age-long and glorious struggle, which our forefathers carried on, defending the independence of their Motherland, the Russian land." [27] He went back into the Russian *byliny*, or sagas, searching for the vivid imagery in which descriptions of Russian warriors and their heroism were expressed.

The theme that we have just touched upon is inexhaustible. But we must turn from it now to that of the Russian "internal mission," the "gathering of the lands." A comparison of the statements referred to in the 1946 and 1950 edition of the Soviet required medieval history text sheds some light on postwar treatment of the role of the Russian people in creating the "multi-

---

[25] P. 27.
[26] (Muenchen and Leipzig, 1929). The whole final section of the book, pp. 181–248, is devoted to the "Sociology of National Songs."
[27] *Patrioticheskaia tema v pesennëm tvorchestve russkogo naroda* (Frunze, 1946), p. 6.

national Soviet state."[28] Increasingly, the tendency has been to revert to the prerevolutionary concept of "the peoples of Russia," although of course the official Soviet terminology is "peoples of the Soviet Union." This is not the place to attempt to deal with the whole question of the relationship between Russians and non-Russians in the Soviet system. What we do wish to emphasize is that in the war and postwar periods, particularly the latter, the "elder brother" role of the Russians has been stressed.[29]

The theme of the services of the Russian people to the other peoples of the Soviet Union represents a sort of Soviet version of the nineteenth-century British idea of the "white man's burden." To modern Western ears it certainly sounds very "reactionary." It is the height of irony that a regime which claims to be the "leader of progressive mankind" should now be engaging in this type of propaganda. Like the other themes discussed in this section, the concept that Russian colonization means liberation had its origin before the Second World War. One of the demands made upon Soviet historians in a series of decrees which began to appear as far back as 1934 was that more attention should be paid to the positive aspects of the bringing into the Russian state of non-Russian peoples. Klaus Mehnert coined the provocative expression "world revolution through world history" to describe this view, according to which peoples benefited by incorporation into the Russian or Soviet Russian state.[30]

I should like here to bring out only one aspect of this part of the Great Russian messianic theme. This is the way in which non-Russians are represented in the Soviet publications as expressing gratitude for the leadership and help extended to them by the Russians. At the Nineteenth Congress of the Communist Party of the Soviet Union, in October 1952, speaker after speaker representing Party organizations of the non-Russian political units of the U.S.S.R. eloquently paid tribute to the Russians. These tributes were accompanied by scathing criticism of non-Russian artists and scholars for allegedly hindering the publication of creative and scholarly works on the "progressiveness, the beneficence of the adherence of the non-Russian peoples to Russia," as M. D. Bagirov, at that time head of the Azerbaizhanian Party

[28] It should be noted that part of the nationalist revival which began in the 1930's consisted in emphasis upon the role of the Great Russians in building the "Russian multinational state."

[29] Since 1951, an extensive literature has developed on the nationality problem in the Soviet Union, setting forth the social and cultural tensions of which the new "elder brother" line is a reflection. See, for example, much of the material in *Soviet Imperialism*, ed. Waldemar Gurian (Notre Dame, 1953); Walter Kolarz, *Russia and Her Colonies* (New York, 1952); and Olaf Caroe, *Soviet Empire* (London, 1953).

[30] See his *Weltrevolution durch Weltgeschichte* (Kitzingen-Main, 1950). An English translation has been published recently under the title *Stalin versus Marx*. For an exhaustive treatment of the development of Soviet historiography, including some interesting comment on the theme discussed above, see Georg von Rauch in *Europa-Archiv*, V (July-December 1950).

organization, put it. Bagirov's friend and colleague of many years, Lavrentii Beria, was at particular pains to emphasize the role of the Russians and the bonds of gratitude and friendship binding his own Georgian and other non-Russian peoples to the Great Russian people. For a few months after Stalin's death, it appeared that the trend toward exalting the leading role of the Great Russians was being reversed. For example, in June 1953 the Communist Party of the Ukraine received, in the person of Kirichenko, its first Ukrainian head. But since Beria's arrest, it seems likely that the Russification trend, of which emphasis on the "elder brother" role of the Russians is a reflection, has been resumed, although perhaps more slowly. Without getting too much involved in extraneous detail, it may be interesting to note that most of the high police officials executed in December 1953, together with Beria, were Georgians. This clean up of the Caucasian element which had played such a prominent role in the Soviet security organs since 1938 may be symbolic of the ending of the privileged positions held by the Georgians in the Soviet Union under Stalin, at least in this vital section of the administration.

Since the preceding paragraph was written, an important new twist of the Party line has developed regarding the Ukrainians. One of the greatest propaganda efforts of all history was developed in the fall of 1953 and the winter and spring of 1954 on the theme of the 300th anniversary of the "reunion" (*vossoedinenie*) of Ukraine and Russia. In some ways this campaign represents a sop to the Ukrainians and reflects anxiety about their attitude toward Moscow. The demonstrative gesture of Russia "giving" the Crimea to Ukraine fits in with this pattern. This may well be an effort also to involve the Ukrainians in complicity with the Great Russians against the Turco-Tatar peoples, within and outside the U.S.S.R.

But at the same time careful reading of the propaganda accompanying this campaign indicates that it represents a softer, more tactful, and more subtle version of Moscow's centralizing and assimilationist policy vis-à-vis Ukraine. Incidentally and ironically, the "reunion" concept is an unacknowledged borrowing from "reactionary" nineteenth-century Russian historians, who formerly were denounced in standard Soviet encyclopedias and textbooks.

The Turkic peoples of the Soviet Union have never held a privileged position, and have, together with the Ukrainians, been the main objects of the Russification aspects of Soviet cultural policy. For this reason, it is not surprising that there is much evidence in the Soviet press of discontent among these peoples, and a corresponding effort to force them to express their gratitude to the Great Russians. For illustration of this trend I shall confine myself to two items. *Izvestiia* for February 16, 1947 published a typical item entitled "Glory to the Russian People!" The author was M. Aibek, an Uzbek, and President of the Union of Soviet Writers of the

Uzbek Republic. Aibek declared that election day caused millions of people of the "Soviet East" to turn their thoughts in gratitude to the great and mighty Russian people. With the aid of the Russian people, the Uzbek people, like other peoples of the East, had established their socialist economy and social system. During the war, the Russian people had developed the industry of Uzbekistan. The two peoples were working together fraternally.

A more interesting item perhaps was the poem contributed to *Komsomolskaia Pravda* for November 15, 1952, by Hafur Guliam entitled "To the Great Russian People." In words of deep humility the poet addresses his Russian brother. He pays tribute to the Russian for leading him toward Communism. He refers to his own people as the "younger brother Uzbek." The Uzbek is grateful to the Russian for inventing the airplane and for bringing the gift of literacy. And so on.

Permitting or perhaps forcing representatives of the non-Russian peoples to express gratitude to the Great Russians thinly veils the imperialist assimilationist aspects of Soviet nationality policy. These are of interest and concern not only to the non-Russian peoples of the Soviet Union, but to all the peoples of the world, particularly to the peoples of Asia, whom the Soviet rulers are so ardently wooing. If Russian culture and a policy made in Moscow were and are beneficial to the Uzbeks and the Latvians, for example, would not Moscow consider them very good for peoples of India, or for that matter, for those of France, Canada, or the United States? [31]

We come now to the theme of the "world significance" of Russian culture and language. This is of course an almost inexhaustible theme. I shall touch upon four of its aspects. One of these is the assertion of the moral and cultural superiority of the people of Soviet Russia to those of the "bourgeois" world. We should not underestimate the significance of this assertion for all the peoples of the world. I have no doubt that in the mind of at least some of the Soviet leaders it constitutes justification for the unlimited extension of Soviet power, and for the "reëducation" of non-Soviet humanity. This assertion was made most emphatically and systematically by the late Andrei Zhdanov in his famous speech to the Writers of Leningrad in August 1946. The key passage reads as follows:

Is it up to us, representatives of advanced Soviet culture, and Soviet patriots to assume an attitude of subservience to bourgeois culture or to act as if we were students? Of course, our literature which reflects an order higher than any bourgeois-democratic system and a culture many times more advanced than bourgeois culture has the right to teach others a new general human morality. Where

[31] Lack of space makes it impossible for me to deal here with the question of the sovietization and accompanying Russification of the Eastern European captive states, or of China. On Russification in Eastern Europe see the publications of the National Committee for a Free Europe, such as its magazine, *News from Behind the Iron Curtain*. It should be noted that Moscow is more tactful in its dealings with China. Only two peoples, the Russians and the Chinese, are consistently and frequently referred to in the Soviet press as "Great."

will you find such a people and such a country as ours? Where will you find such splendid people, who displayed their qualities in the Great Fatherland War, qualities which they also display every day in work and in approaching the peaceful development and reëstablishment of their economy and culture? Every day our people rises higher and higher. Today we are not that which we were yesterday, and tomorrow we will not be what we are today. We today are not the Russians that we were before 1917 and our *Rus'* [archaic word for Russia] already is not that of yesterday and our character also is not the same. We have changed and grown together with those very great transformations which have radically changed the physiognomy of our country.[32]

There is no reason to doubt that the attitude expressed by Zhdanov in supervising the postwar "cultural purge" remains that from which important segments of the policy-making Soviet elite view the Western world. This is an attitude which may win some support from among the Soviet intelligentsia in general. It appeals to the deep-rooted persecution and inferiority feelings which have roots in the Russian past and which have probably been intensified by the isolation and sense of insecurity, and by the knowledge of foreign hostility, assiduously played upon by the Soviet propaganda machine. An appeal to these sentiments was made by the same Zhdanov in his speech of November 6, 1946, a few months after the August speech. Zhdanov here said:

Recently there have appeared so many "researches" on the theme of the character of Soviet people in general, on the national character of the Russians in particular, and in connection with all this many articles do not spare efforts to depict Soviet people in the most unpleasant light. Read and you will be surprised how quickly Russian people have changed. When our blood was flowing on the battlefields, they were thrilled by our bravery, our courage, our high moral qualities and our unlimited patriotism. And now when we, in coöperation with other peoples, wish to realize our equal right to participation in international affairs, they begin to pour torrents of abuse and slander upon us.[33]

Zhdanov set a line which has been followed since 1946. This line presents the Soviet system as the model for humanity and the Russian people as the leaders of mankind in the difficult but inevitably victorious struggle for Communism. An interesting development of recent years is the idea that the Russians hold world leadership in science and technology. It will be recalled that Stalin in his famous preëlection speech of February 9, 1946, called upon Soviet scientists to "overtake and surpass" the scientists of the "capitalist" world. Since 1949, Soviet propaganda has maintained that this goal has been achieved. The connection with atomic energy is obvious. From time to time the Soviet press publishes items depicting the Russians as the teachers of the

[32] *Doklad t. Zhdanova o zhurnalakh "Zvezda" i "Leningrad"* (Moscow, 1946), pp. 35–36. This work is available in several English translations. With perhaps unconscious humor, the British Communist Publishing House, Lawrence & Wishart, published a collection of Zhdanov's pronouncements under the title *A. A. Zhdanov on Literature, Music and Philosophy* in 1947.

[33] *Bolshevik*, no. 21 (November 1946), p. 11.

technological arts to other peoples. An excellent example was the article by the well-known Soviet writer, Aleksei Surkov, in *Pravda* for May 1, 1953, entitled "An Indissoluble Brotherhood." The article asserts that a steady stream of foreign guests and friends visit Moscow to learn "from the people who have constructed socialism, and to acquire their precious experience of the establishment of a new world." Because of the leadership of the Communist Party and also because of the "inborn talent" of the Soviet people, the Soviet Union has become the mightiest industrial power of the world. Surkov waxes especially eloquent in describing the instructor's role of the Russians. "The great new dams and factories of Germany, Eastern Europe, etc. are being built with Soviet machines. Wherever you look, you see 'wise and strong machines' built by our engineers."

The treatment of Russian social thought in current Soviet ideology must inevitably be retrospective. Thus far at least only indirect criticism has been voiced of any of the ideas of Marx and Engels. In 1948 the philosopher G. F. Aleksandrov was criticized for allegedly failing to emphasize the enormous and radical break with the past represented by the ideas of Marx and Engels. However, the Russians are presented as a kind of "chosen people," the first to see the light of Marxism. As I have indicated in this paper, this doctrine is still firmly on a Leninist-Stalinist foundation. Actually, the Soviet interpretation of Russian intellectual history goes as far as it is possible, without abandoning Marxism, to turn Marx into a sort of "honorary Russian." By emphasizing that it was only the Russian proletariat, and their leader Lenin, who understood and appreciated Marx, Soviet thought strengthens the concept of the right of the Russian people to take into their hands direction of the destiny of humanity. This line of thought is summed up in the expression, frequently used in the Soviet press, "Leninism, the highest achievement of world culture," which is the modern version of Stalin's 1926 description of Leninism as the "supreme achievement of Russian culture."

Messianic fervor and purposeful calculation are combined in current Soviet linguistic policy.[34] Like so much in mature Soviet Communism, this combination has some of its roots in Lenin. Soviet sources frequently quote statements by Lenin expressing pride in the Russian language, such as in his 1914 essay, "On the National Pride of the Great Russians." They refrain, however, from quoting Lenin's bitter condemnations of Russian chauvinism, his acknowledgments of the cultural superiority of the Western working class, or his biting criticisms of Russian "Asiaticism."

[34] I have dealt with some political implications of this policy in my article "Stalinism and the Russian Cultural Heritage," *Review of Politics* (April 1952), pp. 178–203. Subsequently I benefited by reading Professor Jindric Kucera's excellent doctoral dissertation on Soviet linguistic policy, which is on deposit in the Harvard University Library.

The Pushkin anniversary celebration of 1937 marked the beginnings of what became even before Hitler's attack on Russia a rather flamboyant campaign of cultural and linguistic self-praise. In 1941, for example, the State Publishing House for Light Industry published a fascinating volume entitled *The Language of a Newspaper*. This work runs the gamut of famous statements about the greatness and virtues of Russians, from Lomonosov through Turgenev and Pushkin to Marx and Lenin.

During and after the Second World War Great Russian linguistic messianism reached a crescendo. By 1949 the theoretician T. P. Lomtev could write: "The Russian language is the instrument of the most advanced socialist culture, the most advanced science, and it is the language of peace and progress."[35] In 1949 Stalin's 1929 article, "The National Problem and Leninism," was published in the eleventh volume of his *Sochineniia*, and of course in 1950 Stalin laid down a system of policy on language, state, and nation in his *On Marxism in Linguistics*. Stalin not only frees language from dependence on the changing social "base" by removing it from the "superstructure" of ideas and institutions, but he dubs Russian a "victorious" language that has always absorbed languages with which it has come into conflict. Stalin sees Russian as one of the "zonal" languages which will serve as instruments of communication for a long time after the "final victory of socialism on a world scale." Russian is also to play an important part in the development of the "world language" of the far distant future Communist world.[36]

Thus we have a design for a Russian Communist world and a system of justifications for establishing such a world, governed from Moscow. To be sure, this messianic doctrine is "self-liquidating," since it also maintains that eventually all forms of state will disappear. But that is in the far distant future, a future which by official Soviet interpretation is being constantly pushed farther forward. Thus we are dealing with a potent and menacing force. However, I should not like to close on a note of pessimism. As I have suggested from time to time in this article, Soviet Russian messianism is "defensive" as well as offensive. It represents in large part attitudes of a people that has been subjected to excessive strain and suffering. To the extent that the world can move toward stability, and the Russians and other peoples of the Soviet Union toward prosperity, their messianic fervor may decline. Moreover, as I have also tried to indicate, official Soviet Russian messianism is by no means a perfect reflection of the attitudes of the Soviet people or of the Russian intelligentsia. On the contrary, the very propaganda

---

[35] *Voprosy filosofii*, no. 2 (1949), p. 138.

[36] For a valuable interpretation of the political import of Stalin's linguistic concepts, see George A. Morgan, "The Motivation of Soviet Policy Toward the Non-Soviet World," in *The Threat of Soviet Imperialism* (Baltimore, 1954), pp. 33–35.

in which it is contained severely criticizes the Soviet intelligentsia for "kow-towing" to the West. For these and other reasons we may regard the messianic theme in Soviet propaganda as worthy of the closest scrutiny but not as cause for despair or justification for adopting similarly intolerant attitudes ourselves. It is a challenge to communication.[37]

[37] The author wishes to thank Yale University for making available to him funds and assistance which made possible the research on which this paper is based. This paper is part of a study of Soviet Russian nationalism on which the author is at present engaged.

Part VI

Review

PHILIP E. MOSELY

Messianism, as a political and intellectual phenomenon, is not something unique to Russian thought nor has it been a dominant phenomenon in most periods of Russian history. Other peoples, other eras, have felt the impact of strong currents of messianic thought and feeling. There has, in fact, usually been something tentative and groping in the quality of pre-Soviet Russian messianic sentiment. Three of the four preceding papers have thrown new light on the content of this concept in critical periods of Russian and Soviet thought and action. Isaiah Berlin, with his delightful unpredictability, has chosen to write on "Herzen and Bakunin on Personal Freedom"; but with richness of insight he has illuminated by indirection some of the factors which entered into the complex currents of messianism.

Since these studies represent an initiation rather than the completion of an investigation into an elusive and powerful type of spiritual and intellectual experience, it might be helpful to suggest a number of criteria which may be useful in classifying various types of thought commonly lumped together under the rubric of "messianism." For economy of effort, "messianism" can be defined as "the striving to attain a stage of collective perfection, harmony, and unity." If the ultimate stage envisaged is one of tranquillity and harmony, surely the process of its attainment is filled with strife and contradiction.

What is the embodiment of a prospective messianic stage? What is the nature of the leadership which defines the goal and announces its completion? Is it an individual messiah, as in a number of the world's religions, or is it a ruling minority, as in Plato's philosopher-ruled republic? Or is it an harmonious and conflictless whole, in which shared strivings predominate over conflicts between groups or among individuals?

What is the process by which the messianic stage is to be achieved? Is it through a single catalysmic transformation, as envisaged in eschatological religions, or in Alexander Blok's poetic acceptance of the Russian revolution, "The Twelve"? Is it a goal which can be reached only through many steps and stages, and, if so, can the steps be outlined in a foreordained sequence to be defined and traversed by conscious will?

What are the assumed sources of messianic sentiment? Does it arise from an exaltation, a collective ferment, generated in a society which confronts new problems in an era of rapid change, problems which cannot be managed or solved by appeals to established social habits or to existing institutions? Is it due to offended national pride, and does it serve as a compensation for the felt backwardness or weakness of a nation and its culture?

What is the emotional impact of any given messianic concept? Does it dominate the thought and action of a single leader or of a ruling elite, or is it widely felt throughout the society in groups capable of taking action? Is it felt constantly, as a directing force, or is it only a latent force whose impact is reserved to occasions of national crisis or national exaltation? Is the outward expression of a messianic concept optional among members of the society, or is it enforced through the educational and other controlling or action-provoking channels used for the inculcation of ideas?

Finally, where a messianic upsurge is found to exist, is it directed inward, toward perfecting the society, toward removing felt injustices and rebuilding the social structure, or is its urge directed outward, toward imposing its system of values and its institutions upon other peoples through example or through force?

These suggested criteria for coming to grips with the analysis of messianism are doubtless far from complete or exhaustive, and each student of messianism will need to define his own set of criteria. The suggestions for classification set forth above are probably more useful in analyzing this aspect of Russian and Soviet social thought than in studying comparable phenomena which have made their appearance in other parts of the world in various epochs.

The reputation of Alexander Herzen as an original thinker has suffered in the eyes of later generations because he never reduced his own aspirations and insights to a single disciplined whole. Frequently he can be quoted on several sides of the same issue. However, if we look, as Isaiah Berlin has done, to his life and to his underlying system of values, it is possible to encompass the messianic strain in his thought. The source of Herzen's messianism lay in his unique sensitivity to the appalling range of unresolved problems which, heaped together, were concealed behind the iron mask of the Russian autocracy, and in Herzen's profound realization that their solution demanded many drastic changes in people's minds as well as in the structure of Russian society. While he seems at times to have believed that Russia could and perhaps would solve the problem of social justice before the industrialized West, he never believed for a moment that Russia had already solved these problems. The final goal was suggested rather than defined by Herzen, and he did not attempt systematically to outline the steps by which the goal could be reached.

While Herzen felt that an enlightened and philanthropic ruler could provide the most expeditious means for change, basically he placed his hope in the development and spread of enlightenment. In his view, educated people possessed of good will and of a sense of responsibility for society as a whole were the most important factor in moving toward a better society. He assumed that advance toward the goal would come through a broadening down of enlightenment from a small elite to the entire people, and that the ultimate and desired stage of collective social harmony would be achieved gradually and along paths which could not be outlined rigidly in advance. Most important of all, Herzen's messianic feelings were directed toward the inward improvement of people and of society. While his impatience with the West, which seemed to him to be wasting its opportunities for fruitful change, led him occasionally to impatient assertions that Russia might show other peoples the right path, the basic drive in Herzen's messianism was inward, toward the perfection of human relations within Russian society.

Bakunin's messianic concept was in complete contrast to that of Alexander Herzen. For him, the messianic stage lay only a few years ahead and could be achieved perhaps in his own lifetime. The goal was a simple one. The destruction of all political, social, and spiritual oppressions would open the way for the natural goodness of men to recreate society in a new and messianic stage. While Bakunin found it unnecessary to define the immediately attainable stage of perfection, he devoted great effort of thought and action to the means, the techniques, by which existing authorities would be destroyed. He was fascinated by the mirage of an "organized revolution." For him, the guide to the messianic future must be the "profesional revolutionaries" spontaneously cast up by the wrath of the people. This dedicated minority could not be a collective dictator, for it was only the conscious expressor of the underlying aspirations of the entire society. Even less did he picture it as a minority which would set up its rule over the great bulk of the people once the stage of "creative destruction" had been completed. While Bakunin expected the example of a successful revolution to be contagious, he assumed that it would expand through imitation, not through military power, which, in his eyes, was the ultimate embodiment of the tyrannical power which he wished to see destroyed.

For Danilevsky, the messianic stage already existed in Russia, or, at least, it would exist there as soon as the ruling authorities adopted his program. Basically, Danilevsky wished to meet the problems of change by reënforcing the existing order of autocracy and social conservatism and enlisting the entire society behind his own emotional and pseudoscientific enthusiasm. The embodiment of messianism, in his view, was an all-powerful and traditional ruler, supported and guided by the entire society in fulfillment of the messianic goal. The steps by which the goal was to be achieved required the preservation of the existing system within Russia, the advancing assimilation of all non-Russian peoples to the dominant Russian nation, and the establishment of a great Slavic federation under the autocratic Russian ruler. A further step, clearly suggested but not outlined, was domination over all Europe, or at least over all continental Europe, to be exercised by the Slavo-Russian empire. Danilevsky was completely clear that these steps required the use of force, and thus outward expansion became the main goal of his messianic program.

For Dostoyevsky, as for Danilevsky, messianic feeling arose in large part from a patriotic rejection of the assumption of the unchanging backwardness of Russia, of its inferiority to the West. For him, the messiah was present in the Russian people and its spiritual experiences, and its only necessary guide was the divine-right autocracy, provided it was inspired by the same aspirations as those which moved its people. Dostoyevsky did not ignore the problem of bringing about spiritual change and establishing a missing spiritual harmony within Russian society, but at moments of crisis, as during the Russo-Turkish war, he tended to accept the full range of virtues described as present in the Russian people and therefore to direct his messianic urge outward, to exact from "Europe" the recognition of Russia's superior virtues and power. Dostoyevsky, unlike Danilevsky, was often quite aware that no people, and especially perhaps the Russian people, had achieved the necessary inner purity and coherence; in him the messianic urge was directed equally toward inward perfection and external expansion.

Turning to the papers by Mr. McKenzie and Professor Barghoorn, it is clear that the traditional and fitful Russian "messianism" has undergone a profound change under the impact of Bolshevik ambitions. Both in the late 1930's and in the period since 1945, Soviet official thinking has assumed that the messianic stage has already been achieved within the Soviet Union. In 1935 the Soviet leaders might still have been willing to admit that their system had not yet achieved the stage of harmony and unity postulated by messianism. Since 1945, however, there has been an increasing insistence not only that the Soviet program is the only viable guide to a perfect future but that the existing Soviet system is already "perfect"; any minor blemishes on it are attributed solely to "remnants of capitalist ideology" within Russia or to the intrigues of foreign enemies. Unlike pre-Soviet thinkers except Danilevsky, Soviet officialdom asserts that the messianic stage is "here and now." The gap between messianic vauntings and the everyday realities of Soviet life has been illuminated vividly by the reactions of large numbers of Soviet people to the German invasion of 1941, and by the willingness of many hundreds of thousands of Soviet subjects to seek an unknown future in the West in preference to returning to the life familiar to them in the Soviet Union. Perhaps a part of the youth, many of the officer and official class, and other people who achieve or hope to achieve their personal and professional goals within the Soviet system, actually attribute some reality to the messianic claim in Soviet thinking. For the large majority of Soviet subjects this claim seems to be a hollow one. A gap yawns between official claims and ordinary reality.

For the Soviet leadership, there can be but one infallible guide to the attainment of the messianic stage of history, namely, the Communist Party of the Soviet Union. In this respect, the Bolshevik claim to exclusive wisdom and leadership shows a wavering and indirect line of descent from Bakunin's concept of the decisive role of a self-chosen caste of professional revolutionaries, and from Danilevsky's concept of an all-powerful ruling group confident of its exclusive right to foresee and mold the future of mankind.

The steps required for the outward expansion of the messianic society are set forth in the recommendations of the Third International, as outlined by Mr. McKenzie, and in Soviet postwar foreign policy, as summarized by Professor Barghoorn. The steps required, according to the 1935 definition, demanded a substantial adjustment of Soviet actions to the existing balance of political and military forces within the international setting and within individual countries. The program of 1935 called for applying the techniques of the "popular front," and the "people's democracy," as transitional stages to the status of the obedient satellite, ever mindful of the single source of messianic wisdom as well as of ultimate control — the Soviet leadership.

In the post-1945 period, success has led to an even greater simplification of the means and stages required. Proximity to the Soviet Union, preponderance of Soviet military power, the "cold *Putsch*" imposed from above or from without, are the basic elements in a crude and impatient rewriting of the concept of Bolshevik messianism. Of "spontaneous" revolutionary movements abroad, which still were reflected faintly in the Comintern resolutions of 1935, there is no trace left. "Spontaneity," which now means "unpredictable" and "uncontrolled," is a force to be distrusted, and even feared.

Whether "Soviet" has become more "Russian," or whether "Russian" messianism has been reshaped into a "Soviet" tool of action, requires extensive and closer analysis. Insofar as the Soviet version of messianism has become more "Russian" in insisting on Russian cultural superiority, on the widespread adoption of the Russian language, and on the outright transplanting of Soviet-Russian institutions, it may tend over a period of time to limit its capacity for expansion. Today, however, "messianism" as a form of discontent with the existing order and of the search for a better order of collective perfection, harmony, and unity seems to work more effectively abroad for Soviet goals, especially in the underdeveloped areas with their accumulation of unsolved problems, than it does within the Soviet Union, where its claims can be tested in day-to-day experience.

INDEX